Jesus as a Figure in History

Second Edition

Jesus as a Figure in History

*How Modern Historians
View the Man from Galilee*

Second Edition

MARK ALLAN POWELL

WJK WESTMINSTER
JOHN KNOX PRESS
LOUISVILLE · KENTUCKY

© 1998, 2013 Mark Allan Powell
First edition published 1998.

Second edition
Published by Westminster John Knox Press
Louisville, Kentucky

13 14 15 16 17 18 19 20 21 22—10 9 8 7 6 5 4 3 2 1

Book design by Sharon Adams
Cover design by Dilu Nicholas
Cover illustration: Jesus_02 © perefu at istockphoto.com

Library of Congress Cataloging-in-Publication Data
Powell, Mark Allan, 1953–
Jesus as a figure in history : how modern historians view the man from galilee / Mark Allan Powell. — 2nd ed.
    p. cm.
Includes bibliographical references and indexes.
ISBN 978-0-664-23447-8 (alk. paper)
1. Jesus Christ—Historicity. 2. Jesus Christ—Person and offices. I. Title.
BT303.2.P68 2013
232.9'08—dc23

                                    2012039439

Most Westminster John Knox Press books are available at special
quantity discounts when purchased in bulk by corporations,
organizations, and special-interest groups. For more information,
please e-mail SpecialSales@wjkbooks.com.

for Brandon Paul Curtis

Regardless of what anyone may personally think or believe about him, Jesus of Nazareth has been the dominant figure in the history of Western culture for almost twenty centuries. If it were possible, with some sort of super-magnet, to pull up out of that history every scrap of metal bearing at least a trace of his name, how much would be left?

—Jaroslav Pelikan
Jesus through the Centuries:
His Place in the History of Culture

Contents

Preface to the Second Edition

My background is in journalism. I have been a New Testament professor for twenty-five years, but I suppose that I will always be a newspaper reporter at heart. It was in that spirit that I accepted the invitation to write the first edition of this book.

I approached the topic as a journalist, researching a current movement in academic studies, interviewing the major figures, and writing it all up in as descriptive and ideologically neutral a tone as possible. When I finished a section, I would send it to the scholar whose work was being discussed and solicit his or her feedback. After receiving the feedback, I would revise the chapter in question repeatedly until it met with the approval of the scholar whose work was under analysis. I heard back from everyone except E. P. Sanders. Thus, I did everything I could to ensure accuracy and fairness in my reporting. Contrary to popular opinion, I believe that is what most journalists do most of the time, at least when they are not under deadline.

I also tried not to have too many opinions—and this was fairly easy, because, although my level of *interest* in the topic was extraordinarily high, my level of *investment* was not. As a Christian, my faith in Christ does not depend on historical reconstruction for legitimation. And as a biblical scholar, most of my own professional work has involved the development and use of literary critical methods (narrative criticism, reader-response) for which questions of historicity tend to be irrelevant. Accordingly, it did not really matter to me personally or professionally which of the historical scholars were doing Jesus research right and which might be doing it wrong. I just found all of these scholars to be interesting and engaging people, and I found their work (except for some of the fine points on method) to be intrinsically fascinating.

The book did very well. It had little competition aside from a couple of survey volumes written by major players (Borg, Witherington) whose level of personal investment was high and who therefore evaluated everyone's contributions by measuring them against the gold standard of their own work (nothing wrong with that—those books are excellent resources for their intended audiences). Since then, a few other surveys have appeared—the best, I think, is David B. Gowler's *What Are They Saying about the Historical Jesus?* (Paulist, 2007). But after my book came out and I imagined I was finished with historical Jesus studies—I'd moved on to research a book on Christian rock music—a strange invitation came to me from out of the blue. I was asked to become Chair of the Historical Jesus Section of the Society of Biblical Literature. This is the most important professional organization in America (and possibly in the world) for scholarship on the topic. The previous three chairs had been John Dominic Crossan, Marcus J. Borg, and N. T. Wright (three of the most important Jesus scholars of our day). To add Mark Allan Powell as the fourth name to *that* list did not seem right. "I'm *not* a historical Jesus scholar," I protested, like Moses before the bush. "But you know the field," Wright said. "And you're fair to everyone . . . and people seem to like you." Whether or not that last point was correct (more so *then* than now, I suspect), it did the trick. I am a sucker for flattery.

I took on a position I probably didn't deserve to hold and did my best to live into it. I determined that this would now be the focal point of my professional life, and for the past decade, I have read everything I could find on the historical Jesus. I chaired all those meetings (aided by a revolving steering committee), deciding who should give papers—and on what topic—and who should respond to those papers or reply to the respondents. I became one of the founding editors of the *Journal for the Study of the Historical Jesus*. I even made a few minor contributions to the field myself. And, now, I am happy to present a second edition of the book that started it all, written by someone who is no longer an outsider. On the one hand, that means this edition is a lot better informed than the first edition was. On the other hand, it means that I now have a lot more opinions than I used to; that said, I went back into journalist mode to produce this book, and I'm not sure that you will be able to tell what those opinions are. It is not that I try to feign neutrality; rather, I simply focus on *description* rather than on argument or advocacy. I describe views (whether or not I agree with those views) and then I describe criticisms of the views (whether or not I agree with those criticisms).

In any case, I definitely still know the field, I hope that I am still fair to everyone, and it would be really nice if people would still like me.

This edition of the book is over 50 percent longer than the last one, and about 33 percent of the material is completely new (which means there were a few, though not many, cuts). Nevertheless, the basic structure of the book (the outline of the chapters) remains the same. The centerpiece comprises chapter 3, which describes the work of several scholars who offer what I call snapshot images of particular aspects of who Jesus was, and chapters 4 through 9, which describe the work of scholars who have tried to produce comprehensive portraits or biographies of Jesus, taking into account everything we can possibly know about him. I have added more scholars to the "snapshots" chapter, but the "big six" scholars in the other chapters remain the same: in my appraisal of the scene, fifteen years after the publication of the first edition, these scholars remain the most deserving of our primary attention. These are the people whose work defines almost all discussion of the historical Jesus, especially in the United States.

It bothers me that all of the scholars discussed in these six focal chapters are male—and all but N. T. Wright are North Americans. Maybe Paula Fredriksen or Gerd Theissen should have received the full chapter treatment. But for better or for worse, Crossan, Borg, Sanders, Meier, and Wright continue to be the names most cited in seminar papers, journal articles, dissertations, and the like—almost everybody else builds on their work or argues with it. And all but Sanders have continued to produce new works on Jesus since the first edition of this book appeared, requiring significant updates to their respective chapters.

But that's only five names—the sixth "scholar" to get a full chapter is the corporate entity known as the Jesus Seminar. They are not really around anymore, and their influence as such may have faded. Still, the legacy of the Jesus Seminar remains strong; many individual members of the group remain active in the guild; and, let's face it, of all the people discussed in this book, they are probably the most *interesting*. So grant a journalist that much: we can't leave out the Jesus Seminar; at the very least, they provide an antidote to some of the boring stuff on method.

And that leads me to share a Jesus Seminar-related anecdote.

In the late 1990s, Robert W. Funk was invited to speak at a meeting of the Ohio Academy of Religion. The controversial founder of the Jesus Seminar was slated to give a very academic and fairly noncontroversial address on some topic of historical interest, but his mere presence in the heartland was noticed by the general populace, and the building where he was to lecture was surrounded by protestors with picket signs. Persons with bullhorns informed Funk, as he approached the building, that he was possessed by a demon and that he was going to hell. Indeed, threats of violence had been called in, necessitating police protection and armed bodyguards—a first for any plenary session of the OAR. The lecture was delayed because a man who claimed God had told him to prevent Funk from speaking stood up in the hall and began a filibuster of loud Scripture recitation until he was placed under arrest and physically removed.

I had been chosen to introduce Funk that night. When I finally got the chance to do so, appraising the situation, I began by saying, "Robert Funk is a man who gets people stirred up over things that matter." I remember now that he liked that—it is a given that people will get stirred up; better they get stirred up over *things that matter* than over things that don't.

But I said earlier that I approached the first edition of this book as a journalist who found the topic intriguing but for whom the results did not much matter, personally or professionally. I am hung now by my own words: these things *do* matter. The historical study of Jesus touches on topics of fundamental importance to religion and to society, topics with profound implications for theology and piety as well as for politics, philosophy, and the very self-image of Western civilization.

When I wrote the first edition of this book, I think that people were more easily stirred up over these issues than they are now. I'm not sure whether that is entirely good or only partly so. But historical Jesus scholars, their detractors, and even third-party observers should all recognize that these *are* things that matter.

Introduction

He comes as yet unknown into a hamlet of Lower Galilee. He is watched by the cold, hard eyes of peasants living long enough at subsistence level to know exactly where the line is drawn between poverty and destitution. He looks like a beggar, yet his eyes lack the proper cringe, his voice the proper whine, his walk the proper shuffle. He speaks about the rule of God, and they listen as much from curiosity as anything else. They know all about rule and power, about kingdom and empire, but they know it in terms of tax and debt, malnutrition and sickness, agrarian oppression and demonic possession. What, they really want to know, can this kingdom of God do for a lame child, a blind parent, a demented soul screaming its tortured isolation among the graves that mark the edges of the village? Jesus walks with them to the tombs, and, in the silence after the exorcism, the villagers listen once more, but now with curiosity giving way to cupidity, fear, and embarrassment. He is invited, as honor demands, to the home of the village leader. He goes, instead, to stay in the home of a dispossessed woman. Not quite proper, to be sure, but it would be unwise to censure an exorcist, to criticize a magician.

—John Dominic Crossan[1]

On a spring morning in about the year 30 CE, three men were executed by the Roman authorities in Judea. Two were "brigands" . . . the third was executed as another type of political criminal. He had not robbed, pillaged, murdered, or even stored arms. He was convicted, however, of having claimed to be "king of the Jews"—a political title. Those who looked on . . . doubtless thought that . . . the world would little note what happened that spring morning. . . . It turned out, of course, that the third man, Jesus of Nazareth, would become one of the most important figures in human history.

—E. P. Sanders[2]

1

Wake up Sunday morning and travel about your town. No matter where it is in America, you will find churches—congregations of all different sizes and structures, historic denominations and recent innovations, major "name brands" and generic community fellowships, sects, cults, and anonymous gatherings of people who haven't yet figured out what sort of organization, if any, they want to employ. You will find people meeting in towering cathedrals and in rented-out storefronts, in spacious auditoriums and in ranch-style sanctuaries. You will see vestments and paraments, stained glass and video screens, expensive commissioned artwork and tacky homemade banners. And the people are as diverse as their furnishings. Look around long enough and you will see every sort of person in America: Democrats and Republicans, liberals and conservatives, men and women, old and young, rich and poor, executives, laborers, citizens, refugees, illegal aliens, the educated, the illiterate, the aged, the infirm, gays, lesbians, Asian Americans, African Americans, Hispanic Americans, Native Americans, and so forth.

The most amazing thing about this is that all of these people have gotten out of bed and gathered with others on Sunday morning because of one person—a Jewish man who was born on the other side of the world over two thousand years ago.

Listen! You will hear congregations singing: "Jesus shall reign where'er the sun . . ."; "What a friend we have in Jesus..."; "All hail the power of Jesus' name . . ."

You will hear groups reciting a creed:

> We believe in one Lord, Jesus Christ
> the only Son of God,
> eternally begotten of the Father,
> God from God, Light from Light
> true God from true God,
> begotten not made,
> of one Being with the Father.

You will hear an evangelist exhorting individuals to accept Jesus as their personal Lord and Savior, inviting them to ask him into their hearts to cleanse them from sin. You will hear inspired worshipers claiming that Jesus has spoken to them this very morning and given them a word of direction for others who are present. You will hear a priest intoning Latin or Greek and promising those who have gathered that they are about to eat the flesh of Jesus and consume his blood.

If you are not one of these people—if you are not a Christian—all of this may seem bizarre. Even if you are a Christian, *some* of this may seem bizarre, for you probably have some ideas about which groups of Christians have got this Jesus stuff right and which have got it wrong.

What could we say about Jesus that almost everyone would agree is right? What could we possibly say that all the different types of Christians and even the non-Christians would accept? That he lived and died? Anything else?

Studying Jesus as a figure in history is different from studying him as the object of religious devotion or faith. That much is clear, but just *how* is it different? Many may think that religion should be concerned with *beliefs* about Jesus, and history with *facts* concerning him. For example, if I say, "Jesus died by crucifixion," that is a historical fact, but if I say, "Jesus died for our sins," that is a religious belief. We would expect for good history to confine itself to the facts. Historians should do history, and theology should be left to the theologians.

If only it were that simple! The line between facts and beliefs is not always as clear as in the example just cited. In a sense, nothing can ever be proven absolutely to have happened. History, especially ancient history, deals with degrees of plausibility. Some matters do come to be regarded as facts after careful analysis of evidence, but the standards by which this evidence is evaluated are grounded in beliefs. Honest historians readily admit to the role that ideology plays in their discipline. At the very least, they approach their task with ideas about what is intrinsically likely or unlikely and about what constitutes good evidence. Such ideas are inevitably debatable.

With regard to Jesus, the task of defining what constitutes a historical approach can be especially difficult. For one thing, most scholars who study Jesus are likely to have personal investment in the outcome of their work. In itself, this problem is not unique, since historians do not usually study people they care nothing about. Still, with Jesus, the level of investment tends to be especially pronounced. Paul Hollenbach admits that he pursues the Jesus of history "in order to overthrow, not simply correct, the mistake called Christianity."[3] Frederick Gaiser maintains that he undertakes such historical investigation as an act of faith in "the incarnational God who took the risk of making himself the object of historical study."[4] What do we make of such biases? Some may think Hollenbach and Gaiser are likely to be bad historians because they are so blatantly prejudiced. Others may think they could be good historians because they are aware of their prejudices and state them outright. In any case, the mere fact that they *have* biases does not invalidate their research. If they uncover significant points about Jesus, they deserve to have these considered (and tested) by the academic guild of their peers as surely as do scholars who do not pursue their work with an admitted agenda.

Jesus studies can also be complicated by the exceptional character of the incidents reported. Various sources (biblical and otherwise) claim that Jesus was known for doing extraordinary things—working miracles, knowing the thoughts of others, predicting the future, and so on. Historians are accustomed to dismissing such reports. Some sources attribute miracles to Julius Caesar, for instance, but no reputable modern biography would claim that the Roman emperor possessed supernatural powers. Rather, historians realize that such legends often accrue around figures of renown and that such accounts may have been received more readily at a time when superstition held more sway than science. But the connection of Jesus to events that would be considered exceptional (if not impossible) is hardly peripheral. Many would claim that apart from some such events (for instance, his resurrection from the dead), he would not be remembered at all. So what is the historian to do? To claim that something happened that historical science regards as impossible seems by definition to be bad history. But to dismiss a claim that something ordinarily impossible happened by saying, "It could not have happened because it is impossible," is clearly an exercise in circular reasoning. As we shall see, the historians discussed in this book deal with this philosophical problem differently.

So the distinction between historical and theological studies of Jesus is neither absolute nor clear. Apart from these problems, however, at least two points of agreement can be stated.

First, studying Jesus as a figure in history means studying the person who lived on this earth in the early decades of what we now call the first century (because of him, in fact). It does not involve studying the heavenly or spiritual figure whom Christians worship, or the entity who Christians say dwells in the midst of their assemblies or lives in their individual hearts. It does not involve studying the Second Person of the Holy Trinity, whom Christians claim has been present since before the creation of the cosmos and, indeed, was responsible for its creation. Theology connects all of these figures with Jesus, but historical science does not.

Over a century ago, a scholar named Martin Kähler made a distinction between "the Jesus of history" and "the Christ of faith."[5] The former is the subject of historical study; the latter, of theological reflection and religious devotion. The distinction proved both useful and problematic. Most Christians would reject the notion that the Jesus who now sits at the right hand of God to hear their prayers is a different person than the Jesus who lived and worked in Galilee. Recently, Marcus Borg has tried to offer a more neutral distinction: historians study the "pre-Easter Jesus" while Christians not only revere this person but also worship and claim to experience the reality of a "post-Easter Jesus."[6] Christians may believe the post-Easter Jesus is the same person as the historical figure if they wish, but historians do not have to believe in this post-Easter figure to study the man who lived before Easter.

Christians who find this distinction unsettling may take comfort in recognizing that it is made in the New Testament by Jesus himself. In the Gospel of Matthew, Jesus (before Easter) tells his disciples, "You will not always have me [with you]" (Matt. 26:11). Then, a few days later (after Easter), he tells those same disciples, "I am with you always" (Matt. 28:20). This is not a contradiction; the point is simply that Jesus will be present with his followers after Easter in a different way than he was before Easter. To use Borg's terminology, Matthew 26:11 refers to the pre-Easter Jesus (who the disciple will not always have with them); Matthew 28:20 refers to the post-Easter Jesus (who, according to this Gospel, will always be with the disciples).

Second, studying Jesus as a figure in history means treating all of the ancient sources regarding him as historical documents rather than as privileged or inspired literature. Historians may, of course, believe that the writings about Jesus in the Bible are Holy Scripture, but, *as historians,* they cannot simply assert that claim to justify what they say about him. No historian can get away with saying, "I think this should be regarded as a historical fact because the Bible says this and I believe everything the Bible says is true." Such a statement might be regarded as good theology in some camps, but in no quarter would it be regarded as good history. Those who study Jesus as a figure in history are not trying to summarize what the Bible says about Jesus (which would be a relatively simple task). They are trying to sift through that material, as well as other, nonbiblical materials, to find content that can be judged reliable from the perspective of modern historical science.

Christians need to keep this point in mind when evaluating historical treatments of Jesus. There may be a subconscious tendency to evaluate positively anything a historian asserts that accords with biblical content and negatively anything that contradicts it. To take an example, when historian John Meier says that Jesus baptized people,[7] we should not think that he erroneously derived this from John 3:22 without paying attention to the correction offered in John 4:1–2. Meier knows these verses (as well as John 3:26). He bases his claim that Jesus baptized people on his critical decision as a historian that John 4:1–2 does not seek to correct a misunderstanding but to refute a correct understanding (that Jesus was in fact baptizing). Those who understand Meier's position may think that he is wrong; they might decide that his historical judgment is flawed and that a different conclusion makes better sense. Still, that would be quite different from saying Meier is wrong because he doubts the accuracy of a statement in the Bible. In the latter instance, the argument cannot be pursued on historical grounds. Unless we recognize these ground rules, arguments can quickly become silly as the dialogue partners discover (or, worse, fail to discover) that they are speaking different languages.

These two points are only exemplary of the sort of concerns that emerge when scholars decide to study Jesus as a figure in history. Other issues will come to the fore as we proceed. For now, I suggest that readers consider a question that sometimes helps to bring some of these points into focus: What should be taught about Jesus in the public schools? In the United States, it is considered inappropriate if not illegal for a public school teacher to instruct students in matters of religious faith. Most Americans, including Christians, would consider a public school teacher out of line if he or she spoke of Jesus as a living reality today (e.g., telling students, "Jesus loves you and he will answer your prayers") or affirmed the authority of the Bible as a divinely inspired source for learning about Jesus. Most would probably also think it inappropriate for a teacher to tell public school children that Jesus was miraculously born to a virgin or that he rose from the dead. It might be appropriate for a teacher to say that the Bible reports these things about Jesus or that Christians believe these things about him, but it would be crossing a line to state that such things actually happened. But what are "the facts" about Jesus? What is there about Jesus that *all* children—be they Christian, Jewish, Muslim, Buddhist, or atheist—ought to know?

By almost any account, Jesus is one of the most significant persons ever to have lived. Recognizing this, the public schools have not ignored him completely.

Figure 1 presents everything that one widely used high school textbook has to say about Jesus. Supposedly, all of this information is based on solid historical research, apart from presuppositions of faith. Although many contemporary historians would actually dispute a number of matters reported here (e.g., that Jesus was born in Bethlehem), almost all modern historians would also regard the information presented in this text as skimpy. Fear of controversy, perhaps, assures Jesus of receiving less attention in the curriculum than his influence on world history would commend. Ironically, public school students in countries where the presence of Christianity is minimal often learn more about Jesus than do students in the United States.

We can make two further observations about the information presented in figure 1: On the one hand, nothing is asserted here that would necessarily prove the legitimacy of the Christian faith; on the other hand, nothing is asserted that would expose it as fraudulent. As we will see, the historians discussed in this book go beyond the observations offered in these schoolbooks in ways that defy both of these points. Sometimes, those who study Jesus as a figure in history do offer assertions that, if valid, would either confirm or challenge tenets of faith. If beliefs affect how one determines facts, then facts may also affect what one determines to believe.

The historical study of Jesus has progressed for more than two centuries now, and significant results have started to come in. Toward the end of the twentieth century, they began *pouring* in, and the last twenty-five years of scholarship have witnessed an avalanche of published tomes on Jesus written by a variety of historical scholars. Sometimes the results of these studies are sensationalized in media reports; more often, they remain hidden in academic literature not accessible to the general reader. In any case, it seems appropriate now to provide a simple, sober, and sincere report of this quest in its current stage. We should not expect unanimity, but we will discover broad areas of agreement. We will also see, in sharp focus, what remain the "hot topics" for discussion and dialogue, the questions on which even the most reputable historians do not agree.

Chapter 1 will offer a brief tour of the discipline up to the present, focusing on some of the key players and the contributions they have made to defining the questions that must now be addressed. Those who want to skip this and jump right into the main part of the book can probably do so without severe penalty, but the chapter does provide a good context for understanding how we got to where we are.

Chapter 2 describes principles and procedures that are widely accepted by those who do this sort of work. In particular, we will identify the key sources for studying Jesus (not just the Bible) and list the criteria that scholars use in making historical judgments on particular matters. Unless you are familiar with this material already, this chapter is probably a prerequisite for making sense of the rest of the book.

Chapter 3 presents what I call "snapshots," brief descriptions of images that scholars have suggested may apply to Jesus. Some of these are controversial;

Figure 1. Section on Jesus in a Public School Textbook

Although the exact date is uncertain, historians believe that sometime around 6 to 4 B.C., a Jew named Jesus was born in Bethlehem in Judea. Jesus was raised in the village of Nazareth in northern Palestine. He was baptized by a prophet known as John the Baptist. As a young man, he took up the trade of carpentry.

At the age of thirty, Jesus began his public ministry. For the next three years, he preached, taught, did good works, and reportedly performed miracles. His teachings contained many ideas from Jewish religion, such as monotheism, or belief in only one God, and the principles of the Ten Commandments. Jesus emphasized God's personal relationship to each human being. He stressed the importance of people's love for God, their neighbors, their enemies, and even themselves. He also taught that God would end wickedness in the world and would establish an eternal kingdom after death for people who sincerely repented of their sins.

Historical records of the time mention very little about Jesus. The main source of information about his teachings is the Gospels, the first four books of the New Testament of the Bible. Some of the Gospels are thought to have been written by one or more of Jesus' disciples or pupils. These 12 men later came to be called apostles.

As Jesus preached from town to town, his fame grew. He attracted large crowds and many people were touched by his message. Because Jesus ignored wealth and status, his message had special appeal to the poor. "Blessed are the meek, for they shall inherit the earth," he said. His words, as related in the Gospels, were simple and direct.

Jesus' growing popularity concerned both Roman and Jewish leaders. When he visited Jerusalem about A.D. 29, enthusiastic crowds greeted him as the Messiah or king—the one whom the Bible had said would come to rescue the Jews. The chief priests of the Jews, however, denied that Jesus was the Messiah. They said his teachings were blasphemy, or contempt for God. The Roman governor Pontius Pilate accused Jesus of defying the authority of Rome. Pilate arrested Jesus and sentenced him to be crucified, or nailed to a large wooden cross to die.

After Jesus' death, his body was placed in a tomb. According to the Gospels, three days later his body was gone and a living Jesus began appearing to his followers. The Gospels go on to say that then he ascended into heaven. The apostles were more convinced than ever that Jesus was the Messiah. It was from this belief that Jesus came to be referred to as Jesus Christ. *Christos* is a Greek word meaning "messiah" or "savior." The name *Christianity* was derived from "Christ."

—Roger B. Beck, Linda Black, Larry S. Krieger, Philip C. Naylor, and Dahia Ibo Shabaka, *World History, Grades 9–12: Patterns of Interaction* (McDougal Little/Houghton Mifflin, 2007), 168–69.

some are pretty traditional. In no case does one image or snapshot offer a full picture of Jesus. Rather, they offer proposals regarding certain aspects of who Jesus was, or suggestions of how he appeared to some people some of the time. I suspect that many readers will find the material in this chapter quite fascinating.

Chapters 4 through 9 offer in-depth descriptions of six highly influential studies of Jesus, all of which were produced in the last twenty-five years. In each of these cases, the scholar or group of scholars has attempted to produce a more-or-less comprehensive biography of Jesus—not just a "snapshot" image of one particular feature or aspect. These six chapters may be read in any order, depending on interest. In each case, I present (1) an overview of the method or approach used by the particular scholar or team of scholars, (2) a summary of the results that have been obtained (a portrait of who Jesus was according to this view), and (3) a summary of the criticisms of this work that have been offered by other historians.

Finally, chapter 10 offers some summary, cross-referencing topics on which scholars agree and disagree.

The appendixes—new to this edition—deal with matters of interest that are somewhat tangential to mainstream historical Jesus research. We take up, in turn, the work of scholars who (1) claim Jesus never existed, (2) seek to defend the historicity of biblical reports, or (3) try to develop a psychological profile for Jesus.

I strive to offer unbiased reports throughout, yet I do not wish to feign objectivity, to pretend that I myself am somehow free of that element of personal investment that affects those I describe. I think, therefore, that I must now state what I believe.[8] I shall intrude so blatantly in this manner only once now, and then, again, at the very end. I will try very hard to keep my prejudices in check the rest of the time.

I now have a strong professional interest in what I call the "Jesus of history" but, as a Christian, I trust my life and destiny to what I call "the Jesus of story," that is, the Jesus who is revealed in the gospel story disclosed in the Bible, proclaimed by the church, and received (accepted or rejected) by the world. By identifying Jesus with a story, I do not mean to indicate that I regard him as no more than a fictional character in literature. I think I would have to be a bigger fool than I am to trust my life or destiny to a cipher. No, I mean that for me the identity and significance of Jesus is inextricably caught up with a story, and that the Jesus of this story is given meaning and content by the effect and impact that his story has on its audience. Every reaction to Jesus, positive or negative, may become part of the story of Jesus—a story I personally regard as ultimately trustworthy, transformative, and true.

The distinction between what I call the "Jesus of story" and the "Jesus of history" is not chronological, as are Kähler's and Borg's distinctions. The story of Jesus begins before anything that can reasonably be identified as historical and continues long after everything that can be identified as historical. The Jesus of story is the larger entity of which the Jesus of history is but a part. History *is* a part of the story, so understanding Jesus as a figure in history remains significant to anyone who wants to believe the story and trust the Jesus it reveals. Still, for me, trusting the Jesus of this story means more than knowing history: it also involves being attentive to the witness of the Spirit, to the testimonies of saints, sinners, martyrs, and heretics, and to my own life experience.

The story is grounded in history, but, for me, the authenticity (or "truth") of the story does not ultimately depend on the historicity of every aspect or detail. If one asks *how much* of the story—or *which aspects* of the story—must be historically accurate (or even historically verifiable) for the story to remain trustworthy and true, . . . I have no good answer. That would be a *theological* question or even a *spiritual* question; it is something that I think about from time to time, but I have never been able to answer. I am sure that there is a line somewhere, a point at which if I became convinced the story lacked historical viability I would have to regard it as a falsehood, as a story to be rejected—or, at least, as a tale to be valued only for its charm, values, and symbolism. I am not certain where that line might be, but, in my most honest pursuit of the historical Jesus thus far, I can say that I have never come close to crossing it.

I hope this book proves as useful and important as its subject matter warrants. If you appreciate it, you will want to join me in thanking Trinity Lutheran Seminary for providing a community that encourages and facilitates such contributions on the part of its faculty; Westminster John Knox Press (with editor Marianne Blickenstaff) for helping me to develop the manuscript, improve it, and bring it to publication; and Melissa, David, Michael, Brandon, and Jillian—my lively, loving family—for filling my life with the joy that, I hope, pervades everything I do.

Chapter 1

Historians Discover Jesus

He comes to us as one unknown.

—Albert Schweitzer (1906)[1]

I do indeed think that we can now know almost nothing concerning the life and personality of Jesus.

—Rudolf Bultmann (1926)[2]

No one is any longer in the position to write a life of Jesus.

—Günther Bornkamm (1956)[3]

We can know quite a lot about Jesus; not enough to write a modern-style biography, including the colour of the subject's hair, and what he liked for breakfast, but quite a lot.

—N. T. Wright (1996)[4]

Historians search for Jesus for a variety of reasons. Some may be intellectually curious or intrigued by the challenge. Some hope to facilitate dialogue between religious communities and secular society. Some may wish to substantiate the Christian faith while others may want to discredit it. Many, no doubt, just want to submit their faith to honest scrutiny in the belief that only then can it be confessed with integrity. For whatever reason, the historian's quest for Jesus has been proceeding for over two centuries now. Although this book is primarily concerned with the flood of Jesus scholarship produced in the last twenty-five years (or so), we should begin with a survey of what has come before.

GOSPEL HARMONIES

For centuries, Jesus was not studied as a historical figure in the modern sense. Non-Christian scholars took little or no interest in him, and Christian scholars simply regarded the biblical accounts as straightforward historical records of his life. One problem, however, was noted early on: The Bible presents four different records of Jesus' life, and those four accounts do not always seem to agree on what they report concerning him. Thus, for many centuries, creating a historical biography of Jesus was basically a matter of harmonizing the four Gospel narratives. This was actually done for the first time less than a hundred years after the Gospels themselves were written. A Mesopotamian Christian named Tatian wove the four Gospel accounts together into one continuous narrative, which he called the Diatessaron ("four-in-one"). The work was translated into several languages and was widely used for three hundred years. The Syriac version appears to have replaced the four individual Gospels in the Bibles of some churches.

We can only imagine what sort of decisions Tatian and others like him had to make as they sought to harmonize the Gospels. First would be the simple question of chronology: even if we grant that Jesus did all of the things reported in all of the Gospels, we will still have to ask in what order he did these things. Creating one story from four accounts forces the scholar to place some events ahead of others. In addition, we would have to ask about repetition. All four Gospels contain stories of Jesus turning over tables in the Jerusalem temple (Matt. 21:12–17; Mark 11:15–19; Luke 19:45–48; John 2:13–17). Do we assume that these are four reports of the same event? In the first three Gospels, the account comes near the end of the story, but in John it comes near the beginning. Did Jesus turn over tables in the temple twice? Some thirteen hundred years later, Martin Luther, confronted with precisely the same problem, would write, "The Gospels follow no order in recording the acts and miracles of Jesus, and the matter is not, after all, of much importance. If a difficulty arises in regard to the Holy Scripture and we cannot solve it, we must just let it alone."[5]

There also would be the question of contradiction. In Matthew 8:5–13, a centurion comes to Jesus in Capernaum and asks that Jesus heal his servant, while in Luke 7:1–10, the same centurion sends Jewish elders to ask Jesus to heal his servant. The words attributed to the centurion (Matt. 8:8–9) or to his friends (Luke 7:6–8) are almost identical. How are these two accounts to be harmonized? It seems unlikely that they are reports of two different events, that Jesus healed this poor man from a distance twice, saying the same things both times (once to the centurion's representatives and once to the centurion himself). The latter view has actually been tried[6] and is still sometimes asserted by fundamentalists,[7] but for the most part has been found wanting. But if the two stories report the same event, should a Gospel harmony such as Tatian's have the centurion go to Jesus in person, send a delegation, or both? Some scholars, notably John Calvin, despaired of producing a continuous narrative like the *Diatessaron* and simply presented similar stories from different Gospels side by side in parallel columns.[8]

In producing Gospel harmonies, scholars were already asking historical questions about Jesus, but they did so within a context of faith, not skepticism.[9] But this approach would be challenged by the Enlightenment, the European movement that exalted the use of reason as the best means for discovering truth. The Enlightenment emphasized the orderliness of nature and so encouraged disciplined scholarship that adhered to well-defined methods for testing and verifying hypotheses. It furthered the acquisition of knowledge and the development of critical thinking. Though initially a philosophical movement (featuring such luminaries as Descartes, Locke, Rousseau, and Voltaire), the new orientation led to tremendous advances in science and mathematics. Eventually, its effects were felt on politics and on religion. One legacy of the Enlightenment for Western thought was a lasting distrust of assertions that cannot be verified. The distinction between religious faith and superstition came to be regarded as simply a matter of perspective.[10]

"LIVES" OF JESUS

During the period following the Enlightenment, scholars embarked on what came to be known as "the quest for the historical Jesus." They went beyond the production of Gospel harmonies to write biographies, called Lives of Jesus. A Life of Jesus might draw heavily upon harmonization of the Gospel accounts, but it differed from such accounts in at least three ways. It would (1) typically impose some grand scheme or hypothesis upon the material that allowed everything to be interpreted in accord with a consistent paradigm (for example, "Jesus was a social reformer" or "Jesus was a religious mystic"); (2) exclude material in the Gospels that did not fit with this paradigm, submitting the biblical record to the author's critical judgment of what seemed most likely to be correct; and (3) include reflection about Jesus not derived from the Gospels, attempting to fill in gaps in the biblical record with the author's own projections concerning Jesus' motivations, goals, or self-understanding.

Hundreds of these Lives of Jesus were produced, mainly during the nineteenth century. Below is a sampling of some of the most influential.

Hermann Samuel Reimarus (1694–1768). Reimarus was a respected professor of Oriental languages at the University of Hamburg and his works on Jesus were not published until after his death. Apparently, he feared retribution for his controversial views during his lifetime. In any case, fragments of a large unpublished manuscript were printed between 1774 and 1778, and these mark what many consider to be the beginning of the quest for the historical Jesus.[11] Reimarus maintained that Jesus (the actual historical person, not the theological figure created by the church) was an unsuccessful political claimant who thought it was his destiny to be established by God as king of the restored people of Israel. Reimarus interpreted all the passages in the New Testament where Jesus speaks of "the kingdom of God" or "the kingdom of heaven" as references to a new political reality about to be established on earth. Thus, Reimarus said, Jesus believed he was the Messiah (or "Christ"), but he meant this in a worldly sense. He thought that God was going to deliver the people of Israel from bondage to the Romans and create a new and powerful kingdom on earth where Jesus himself would rule as king. This is why he was executed, charged with the crime of claiming to be the King of the Jews (Matt. 27:37). This is also why, when he died, he cried out, "My God, my God, why have you forsaken me?" (Matt. 27:46). He realized in his last moments that God had failed him, that his hopes had been misplaced. His disciples, however, were unable to accept this outcome. Not wanting to return to their mundane lives in Galilee, they stole his body from its tomb, claimed he had been raised from the dead (see Matt. 28:11–15), and made up a new story about how Jesus had died willingly as an atonement for sins. The message of the kingdom was spiritualized, and the teaching of the failed religious fanatic was transformed into a religion promising salvation after death to those who joined an organization led by his followers. Thus, "the new system of a suffering spiritual savior, which no one had ever known or thought before, was invented only because the first hopes had failed."[12] Reimarus's work seemed to be obviously agenda-driven, attacking a religion he had come to despise. Still, it raised questions and issues that had not been examined previously, and the audacity of his claims demanded engagement on historical grounds. Thus, Albert Schweitzer, who completely disagreed with the main thesis, nevertheless hailed Reimarus's publication as "one of the greatest events in the history of criticism." As a side note, he also called it "a masterpiece of general literature," reflecting on the passion with which Reimarus spewed his venom against Christian religion: "It is as though the fires of a volcano were painting lurid pictures upon dark clouds. Seldom has there been a hate so eloquent, a scorn so lofty."[13]

Heinrich Eberhard Gottlob Paulus (1761–1851). Paulus was a veteran rationalist who would become best known for offering naturalistic explanations for miracle stories reported in the Gospels. As professor of theology at the University of Heidelberg, he published a two-volume work on the life of Jesus in 1828.[14] In essence, it was a Gospel harmony with explanatory notes. Paulus accepted the miracle stories as reports of historical events, but he reasoned that a primitive knowledge of the laws of nature led people in biblical times to regard as supernatural occurrences what the advancement of knowledge has rendered understandable. For example, Jesus may have appeared to walk on water when he strode along the shore in a mist and he may have received credit for stilling a storm when the weather coincidentally improved after he awoke from sleep on a boat trip. Jesus healed people by improving their psychological disposition or, sometimes, by applying medicines mixed with mud (John 9:6) or saliva (Mark 8:23). Likewise, his disciples were provided with medicinal oil to use for curing certain ailments (Mark 6:13). The story of the feeding of the five thousand recalls a time when Jesus and his disciples generously shared their own provisions with those who had none, inspiring others in the crowd to do the same until everyone was satisfied. Paulus's book evoked a good deal of opposition at the time of its appearance, but its ideas continued (and still continue) to resurface, especially in writings of those who do not otherwise know what to do with the miracles.

David Friedrich Strauss (1808–1874). Strauss appealed to modern understandings of mythology to steer a middle course between naive acceptance of Gospel stories and the sort of simplistic explanations for these stories offered by Paulus. In 1835, Strauss published *The Life of Jesus Critically Examined,* a two-volume work over fourteen hundred pages in length.[15] He called for unbiased historical research to be done on the Gospels, establishing an orientation for scholarship that is still followed by many today. He discerned, for instance, that the stories in the first three Gospels are less developed than those in John which, accordingly, is the least valuable book for historical reconstruction. Still, Strauss regarded most of the stories in all the Gospels as myths, developed often on the pattern of Old Testament prototypes. The point of such tales is not to record a historical occurrence as it happened but, rather, to interpret an event in light of religious ideas. For example, the story of Jesus' baptism includes references to the Spirit descending as a dove on Jesus and a voice speaking from heaven. These things did not actually happen in the strict historical sense, but they interpret the significance of something that did occur. Jesus really was baptized by John, and his sense of mission was somehow related to what he experienced on that occasion. Strauss's view of the Gospels as "history interpreted through myth" evinced a growing recognition on the part of scholars that these books describe "the Jesus of history" from a perspective that regards him as "the Christ of faith," a perspective that (supposedly) unbiased historians cannot endorse. Nevertheless, in its own day Strauss's work was highly controversial, and the publication of this influential book caused him to lose his position at the University of Zurich.

Ernst Renan (1823–1892). Renan combined critical scholarship with novelistic aesthetic appeal to create what was probably the most widely read Life of Jesus in his day.[16] Published in 1863, the book broke with rationalism in its attempt to discern the emotional impact of the Jesus tradition and to trace the reasons for this to the passions, individuality, and spontaneity of Jesus himself. Regarding the Gospels as "legendary biographies," Renan sought to uncover the personality that inspired the legends while also displaying his own penchant for poetic, even sentimental, description. For example, since Jesus is said to have ridden into Jerusalem on a mule (in modern translations, an ass or a donkey), Renan imagines that he typically traveled about the countryside seated on "that favorite riding-animal of the East, which is so docile and sure-footed and whose great dark eyes, shaded with long lashes, are full of gentleness."[17] Renan also attempted to fit the Gospel materials into an overall chronology for the life of Jesus. He described the initial years as "a Galilean springtide,"[18] a sunny period in which Jesus was an amiable carpenter who rode his gentle mule from town to town sharing a "sweet theology of love" that he had discerned through observation of nature.[19] Eventually, however, Jesus visited the capital city of Jerusalem, where his winsome message met with opposition from the rabbis. This led him to develop an increasingly revolutionary stance with a harsher tone, to despair of earthly ambitions, and at last to invite persecution and martyrdom. Renan's book was a bestseller, but it did not receive universal acclaim. Its imaginative reworking of biblical materials invoked the wrath of traditional Christians (Renan suggested the raising of Lazarus was a "staged miracle," a deliberate hoax designed to win acclaim for Jesus), while its sentimental features brought scorn from other historical Jesus scholars.[20] Like Strauss, Renan was fired from his university professorship, in this case from a position at the College de France that he had held for less than a year.

What lessons are to be learned from these Lives of Jesus, aside from the observation that such scholarship can be deleterious to one's career? While Reimarus's writings were overtly hostile to Christianity, the other three authors all viewed themselves as Christian theologians who sought to discover or salvage something in the biblical tradition that could be recognized as universally true. All four were skeptical of the miracle stories, displaying a reluctance to accept anything that deals with the supernatural as a straightforward historical account. All questioned the accuracy of the Gospels at certain points and sought to supplement the stories with what they thought were reasonable conjectures at other points.

Another important observation, however, was noted with verve by Albert Schweitzer in 1906. The authors just discussed, and numerous others, all managed to produce portraits of Jesus *that they personally found appealing*. For the non-Christian, the historical Jesus rather conveniently turned out to be a fraud. For the Christian, the historical Jesus seemed in every case to end up believing things that the author believed and valuing things that the author valued. The scholars, Schweitzer claimed, had modernized Jesus, dressing him in clothes of their own design. Their interest, whether conscious or not, was in discovering a figure who would be relevant for their time, and this interest prevented them from seeing Jesus as a figure in his own time, as a figure of the past, a figure *in history*. One sign of this was that the Christian studies tended to present Jesus in a fairly generic ethnic guise—there was little about him that seemed specifically Jewish.

THE WORK AND LEGACY OF SCHWEITZER

According to Albert Schweitzer (1875–1965), the so-called quest for the historical Jesus had tended to become a quest for the relevant Jesus. Historical accuracy and relevance are not, of course, necessarily mutually exclusive, but Schweitzer maintained that scholars had failed to reckon with the possibility that they might be. In the final analysis, Schweitzer concluded, the quest had yielded only negative results.[21] Did that stop Schweitzer himself from trying? No way! His survey of flawed attempts served as a prelude to his own description of the historical figure of Jesus, a portrait that did avoid the trap of modernizing Jesus and, so, came to be regarded (until recently) as the most important study of Jesus ever produced by a historian.

Schweitzer identified the missing element in most of the Lives of Jesus as eschatology. The word *eschatology* literally means "study of last things"; in theology, it usually refers to what one believes regarding the future—life after death, the final judgment, the end of the world, and so forth. Schweitzer believed that the numerous sayings of Jesus regarding the future belong to the oldest and best-preserved stratum of material in the Gospels. He maintained that this material, neglected by most previous Jesus scholars, comes as close to preserving the original, primitive setting of Jesus as we can get. It records Jesus saying things that were hardly relevant when the Gospels were written, much less today. And what does this material reveal? It reveals Jesus to be a prophet who announced the end of the world, who declared that the kingdom of God was about to arrive (Mark 1:15). Especially in the first three Gospels, Jesus talks more about the kingdom of God than he does about anything else. Drawing heavily on the work of Johannes Weiss, Schweitzer claimed that Jesus' beliefs about this coming kingdom held the key to understanding everything that he said and did.[22] This realization could be embarrassing to Christian scholars, Schweitzer realized, because in the modern world people who go about declaring, "The end is near!" tend to be regarded as crackpots. Furthermore, we are left with the unsettling possibility that Jesus might have been wrong in making such a claim since, obviously, the world did not end.

Jesus *was* wrong, Schweitzer concluded; in fact, he was wrong *twice*. In the early period of his ministry, Jesus apparently believed that God was about to send a supernatural figure whom he called "the Son of Man" to establish the kingdom. At one point, Jesus sent his disciples out on a brief preaching tour, telling them, "You will not have gone through all the towns of Israel before the Son of Man comes" (Matt. 10:23). But, of course, the disciples completed their mission and the Son of Man did not come. At this point, Jesus seems to have reconsidered the matter and come to a dark but startling conclusion. He decided that he himself was to become the Son of Man, and that he could do this only through suffering (see Mark 8:31–33). Previously, he had told his disciples that *they* would have to suffer before the Son of Man arrived (Matt. 10:17–22); now he realized that he must bear the suffering alone. He set in motion processes that would be sure to bring persecution and even death, believing this would prompt God to act, to bring in the kingdom and exalt him as the glorified Son of Man. Schweitzer's description of this plan would become famous (though he decided to omit these words from later editions of his book):

[Jesus] lays hold of the wheel of the world to set it moving on that last revolution which is to bring all ordinary history to a close. It refuses to turn, and He throws Himself upon it. Then it does turn; and crushes Him. Instead of bringing in the eschatological conditions, He has destroyed them. The wheel rolls onward, and the mangled body of the one immeasurably great Man, who was strong enough to think of Himself as the spiritual ruler of mankind and to bend history to his purpose, is hanging upon it still. That is His victory and His reign.[23]

The kingdom did not come. Jesus was wrong again. His death, as noble and inspiring as his life, did not effect the change that he believed it would.

Schweitzer's portrait of Jesus as a misguided eschatological prophet stripped him of relevance for the contemporary age. As one scholar puts it, Schweitzer "tore down sentimental portraits of Jesus and, like a revolutionary replacing the monarch's portrait on the schoolroom wall with that of the new leader, put up instead the sharp, indeed shocking, drawing of Jesus the towering prophetic genius."[24] Yet this (mistaken) genius remained a foreigner. "The historical Jesus," said Schweitzer, "will be to our time a stranger and an enigma."[25]

Schweitzer's book was a bombshell, affecting historical Jesus research for decades. Schweitzer himself went on to do many other notable things. He became one of the twentieth century's most brilliant doctors, serving as a medical missionary in West Africa, and he was eventually awarded the Nobel Peace Prize. He also earned renown as one of his century's great organists, wrote a biography of Bach, and published works on the philosophy of Goethe and on the development of Indian thought. Still, it was his book *The Quest of the Historical Jesus* for which he would be remembered in academic religious circles: at the turn of the millennium, numerous Christian magazines would include that book (published in 1906!) on their "short lists" of the most significant theological publications of the twentieth century.

SCHOLARSHIP AFTER SCHWEITZER

In the decades that followed Schweitzer's tome, historical Jesus studies continued unabated, but many of the works that were produced would not retain enduring significance for scholars working in the field today.[26] Indeed, modern scholars sometimes view the first half of the twentieth century as a time when historical Jesus research was in decline.[27] A more accurate analysis would maintain that interest in the subject waned in certain quarters, including dominant expressions of Protestant Christianity. At least two different reasons are often cited for this.

First, Schweitzer's incisive analysis of his forbears made it difficult for any scholar who followed him to avoid the stigma of bias, of modernizing Jesus in accord with their own wishful thinking or simply for the sake of contemporary relevance. Schweitzer's book had created what we might call a catch-22 in historical Jesus studies: the mark of unbiased scholarship was that it did not try to establish Jesus as relevant for today, but if the historical Jesus is *not* relevant for today, then why study him in the first place?

Second, a major movement in Protestant Christian theology drew upon twentieth-century existentialism in ways that made questions regarding the historical Jesus increasingly insignificant. Rudolf Bultmann, for instance, believed that "the Christ of faith" *alone* was significant for theology.[28] The only thing that ultimately mattered regarding the Jesus of history, Bultmann said, was that Jesus *was* a historical figure. His existence was important for theology, but what he actually did was not important.[29] Though this may at first seem outlandish, Bultmann and many others reasoned that Christian theology had developed out of the ideas put forward by people who believed Jesus had risen from the dead: the Apostle Paul, to name a prominent example, had not known the man Jesus and, in his essential Christian teaching, Paul focuses primarily on the living Christ present in Christian community rather than on reports about things that the man Jesus said or did.

This lack of interest in the historical Jesus became a hallmark of theological study in many academic settings, but it was also characteristic of Christianity at a popular level. One of the most visible exponents of Protestant Christianity in the latter half of the twentieth century was the American evangelist, Billy Graham. As a conservative Christian, Graham always insisted that all the stories about Jesus in the New Testament should be accepted as straightforward historical accounts. Still, in his preaching, Graham summoned individuals to be born again, to enter into a personal relationship with Jesus, to ask him to come into their hearts as their personal Lord and Savior. Thus, the focus of faith for Graham and his followers was the risen, spiritual Christ that the historically skeptical Bultmann also confessed. Although Graham (unlike Bultmann) would have insisted that Jesus really did do and say all the things reported of him in the Bible, the historicity of those biblical accounts seemed more important for his doctrine of scripture than for his understanding of the meaning and significance of Christ: such historicity may have been viewed as necessary to establish that the Bible was inerrant and literally true, but it would not have been necessary to establish that Christ lives in the hearts of born-again believers today.

According to one scholar's analysis, an emphasis on the benefits of Christ for modern humanity deflected interest in the specific, unrepeatable character of Jesus' historical life. For many Christians it would be "sufficient if Jesus had been born of a virgin (at any time in human history, and perhaps from any race), lived a sinless life, died a sacrificial death, and risen again three days later."[30] Granted this, the assurance of theologians that questions about the historical Jesus do not matter "formed an alliance with the fears of ordinary people as to what might happen to orthodox Christianity if history was scrutinized too closely."[31]

In any case, for half a century after Schweitzer, the quest for the historical Jesus was regarded as both methodologically impossible and theologically unnecessary in certain prominent circles.[32] Then, it took hold once again, initiated ironically enough by students of Rudolf Bultmann.

THE NEW QUEST MOVEMENT

On October 23, 1953, Ernst Käsemann gave a lecture on "The Problem of the Historical Jesus" to an alumni gathering of academics who, like him, had studied with Bultmann.[33] Rarely has a lecture been so influential. Käsemann argued that theology about Jesus must be thoroughly grounded in a historical reality or else the humanity of Jesus is lost and the Christian message becomes "docetic mythology."[34] When that happens, Jesus can be used to support anything. Most likely, Käsemann and his German colleagues were particularly concerned about what had happened recently in their homeland, as Nazi leaders had presented Jesus (who historians know was Jewish!) as a proponent of anti-Semitism. Käsemann also affirmed that it is methodologically possible to discover historically reliable and potentially relevant information about Jesus in ways that transcend theological predilections. In part, he maintained this was now possible because of advances in the discipline that had been made in the years since Schweitzer's book was published. Archaeology and related fields had greatly enhanced academic knowledge of the ancient world,[35] and refinement of methods for historical research had brought scholars closer to a consensus regarding the ground rules for such study. Käsemann, furthermore, did not project the writing of any more Lives of Jesus but simply advocated selective affirmation of what could be regarded as individual facts concerning Jesus. Historical scholars could determine whether specific sayings or deeds attributed to Jesus are likely to be authentic without engaging in speculation regarding the chronology or psychological motivations behind such matters.

James M. Robinson, another student of Bultmann who would become a prominent Jesus scholar, declared that Käsemann's lecture had inaugurated a "new quest" for the historical Jesus.[36] In reality, this so-called new quest was just a matter of mainline Protestant scholars showing renewed interest in the discipline of historical Jesus studies that had been continuing without them all along. Nevertheless, the New Quest movement would prove to be highly significant. Scholars associated with that movement (often called New Questers) produced numerous historical studies of Jesus in the 1950s and 1960s. We will note two that have been especially influential.

Günther Bornkamm (1905–1990). As Professor of New Testament at the University of Heidelberg, Bornkamm published a volume exactly fifty years after Schweitzer's tome that represented a fulfillment of what Käsemann wanted to see. It was called, simply, *Jesus of Nazareth*,[37] and for several decades it was widely used as a college textbook in both religious and secular settings. More than fifty years after its publication, Bornkamm's *Jesus of Nazareth* would still be regarded as a work of monumental importance in Jesus scholarship.[38]

Unlike his nineteenth-century predecessors, Bornkamm displayed almost no interest in chronology of events or in Jesus' motives, goals, or self-understanding. He developed a list of historically indisputable facts about Jesus, all derived from the first three Gospels: Jesus was a Jew from Nazareth, he was the son of a carpenter, he spoke Aramaic, he was baptized by John, and so forth. The real focus of Bornkamm's study, however, was on the message of Jesus, which he described in essence as "making the reality of God present."[39] The kingdom of God, Bornkamm claimed, had both a future and a present dimension for Jesus. The latter is brought out in many of his parables and in the significance of such customs as dining with outcasts. As a teacher, furthermore, Jesus challenged traditional interpretations of the law in favor of a new radical way of life that he held to be the will of God. That he could do this is an indication that he must have been a person of extraordinary authority. This is also evident from his calling of disciples and from the miracle stories that, though largely legendary, reveal the degree of authority attributed to him by his contemporaries. A historian can also affirm that Jesus was crucified and, further, may reasonably conjecture that this was because his provocative processional entrance to Jerusalem and act of overturning tables in the temple were perceived as threats to the religious and social order.

Norman Perrin (1920–1976). Perrin taught New Testament at the University of Chicago Divinity School and, along with James Robinson, was one of the first American scholars to achieve prominence in the field of historical Jesus studies (though, by the end of the twentieth century, that field would seem to be dominated by Americans). Notably, Perrin was not a student of Rudolf Bultmann, but a student of Joachim Jeremias, a scholar who also did significant work on the historical Jesus that is not usually associated with the New Quest movement.[40] But Perrin was influenced by both Bultmann and Käsemann and became the definitive apologist for what is called the criterion of dissimilarity (see pages 63–65). In 1967, he published a volume called *Rediscovering the Teaching of Jesus,* followed a decade later by *Jesus and the Language of the Kingdom.* In these books, Perrin applied the discipline of redaction criticism to sayings of Jesus recorded in the first three Gospels to determine which of them were historically authentic. The method of redaction criticism (a mainstay of Bornkamm's work also) attempts to distinguish material that would have reflected Jesus' own thinking from that which appears to reflect the aims of the Christians who compiled and edited (redacted) the Gospels. Perrin helped to define many of the criteria for historical judgments that we will review in our next chapter. His own preference was to err on the side of caution: "the nature of the synoptic tradition is such that the burden of proof will be upon the claim to authenticity."[41] This philosophy came to be expressed through the popular motto "When in doubt, discard," meaning that nothing will be affirmed as authentic unless it is absolutely certain. Thus, Perrin was able to claim that, while a great deal of the Gospel material about Jesus' teaching is *possibly* authentic, the strictest canons of historical research allow us to affirm only selected items as an "irreducible minimum" (see fig. 2).[42]

Figure 2. Norman Perrin's
"Irreducible Minimum" List of Authentic Sayings

1. Kingdom Sayings

the kingdom has come:	Luke 11:20
the kingdom is among you:	Luke 17:20–21
the kingdom suffers violence:	Matt. 11:12

2. The Lord's Prayer: Luke 11:2–4

3. Proverbial Sayings

binding the strong man:	Mark 3:27
a kingdom divided:	Mark 3:24–26
those who want to save their life:	Mark 8:35
a hand to the plow:	Luke 9:62
wealth and the kingdom:	Mark 10:23b, 25
let the dead bury the dead:	Luke 9:60a
the narrow gate:	Matt. 7:13–14
the first will be last:	Mark 10:31
what truly defiles:	Mark 7:15
receiving the kingdom as a child:	Mark 10:15 (compare 16:15)
turning the other cheek:	Matt. 5:39b–41
love your enemies:	Matt. 5:44–48

4. Parables

hidden treasure and pearl:	Matt. 13:44–46
lost sheep, coin, son:	Luke 15:3–32
great supper:	Matt. 22:1–14; Luke 14:16–24; Thomas 92:10–35
unjust steward:	Luke 16:1–9
workers in the vineyard:	Luke 15:3–32
two sons:	Matt. 21:28–32
children in the marketplace:	Matt. 11:16–19
Pharisee and tax collector:	Luke 18:9–14
good Samaritan:	Luke 10:29–37
unmerciful servant:	Matt. 18:23–35
tower builder and king going to war:	Luke 14:28–32
friend at midnight:	Luke 11:5–8
unjust judge:	Luke 18:1–8
leaven:	Luke 13:20–21; Thomas 97:2–6
mustard seed:	Mark 4:30–32; Thomas 85:15–19
seed growing by itself:	Mark 4:26–29; Thomas 85:15–19
sower:	Mark 4:3–8; Thomas 82:3–13
wicked tenants:	Mark 12:1–12; Thomas 93:1–18

Perrin claims that more material attributed to Jesus is likely to be historical, but this is a rock-bottom list of what "competent scholarly opinion would recognize as authentic."

As the examples of Bornkamm and Perrin indicate, the New Questers tended to emphasize the teaching of Jesus over his deeds. Skepticism regarding the historicity of miracles and supernatural events remained, a legacy from the Enlightenment. Most of their studies also downplayed uniquely Jewish attributes of Jesus. In addition, they tended to discount any attribution of imminent eschatology to Jesus, preferring to interpret Jesus' sayings about the kingdom of God symbolically (Bornkamm said that the "making-present of the reality of God signifies the end of the world in which it takes place"[43]). In some ways, the work of the New Quest seemed to come full circle, defying Schweitzer to affirm (with more rigorous methodology) the nonapocalyptic, generically ethnic portrait of Jesus that he had critiqued.

Contributions of the New Quest were deliberately spotty, evaluating each individual tradition on its own merits rather than considering the whole corpus of material in light of some grand hypothesis. The New Questers sought to obtain isolated insights regarding the historical figure of Jesus rather than to construct full biographies concerning him. And, regardless of whether they subscribed to Perrin's motto, most of the New Questers required even greater evidence of certainty for what they affirmed than would usually be expected for historical research in the secular academy. This scaled-back version of the quest paid off, earning a new level of academic respect for the discipline. After the initial landmark publications, however, attention to the matter quieted down. Articles and seminar papers continued to be published, but the overall sense was that, save for some fine tuning, what could be done had been accomplished. Then, suddenly, in the last decade before the turn of the millennium, a veritable explosion of Jesus scholarship revealed the topic to be hotter than ever. Those studies, and the renaissance of Jesus scholarship that continues to the present day, will be the main focus of this book.

THIRD QUEST?

The abundance of Jesus studies produced in the late twentieth century made apparent what had been true all along: the New Quest movement was not the only game in town. Accordingly, a prominent scholar named N. T. Wright coined the term *Third Quest* to refer to one particular type of historical Jesus-research that he thought should be distinguished from the New Quest studies: Third Quest studies were, by definition, ones that regarded Jesus as an eschatological prophet and that emphasized his location in first-century Palestinian Judaism.[44] Thus, in Wright's view, the Third Quest and the New Quest coexisted, as the two major streams of research in his day (though, of course, some studies would not have belonged to either the New Quest or the Third Quest movements).

The use of this term, however, would prove problematic.[45] First, many nonspecialists (and even a few Jesus scholars) applied the labels New Quest and Third Quest chronologically to describe successive phases in the history of the discipline (often with the attendant assumption that the latest phase was superior to its predecessor).[46] Thus, when Wright would claim that Crossan was not a Third Quest scholar but a New Quest scholar,[47] many would miss his nuance of definition and assume he meant Crossan was out-of-date, continuing to advance the outmoded scholarship of a previous generation—and even those who knew what Wright meant often suspected this was his "subtext."[48] Such rhetorical use of labels was nothing new: a few decades earlier Ernst Käsemann had sought to disparage the work of Joachim Jeremias by claiming it belonged to "the Old Quest" rather than to the New Quest (which he had just inaugurated).[49]

Even when the terms "New Quest" and "Third Quest" were employed as Wright intended, the lines for categorization tended to get fuzzy. Supposedly, the "Third Quest" focuses on a Jesus who is thoroughly Jewish and who functioned as an eschatological prophet. But there has never been a recognized Jesus scholar who did not think that he or she was faithfully acknowledging Jesus' identity as a first-century Jewish man—at issue is the perception of what Jewish identity entailed at that place and time. Likewise, virtually all scholars grant that Jesus used what some people would call "eschatological language" in a manner that some people might regard as "prophetic"—but much depends on definitions of those terms.

The biggest problem of all, however, may lie in the tendency for such markers (Old, New, Third Quests) to be taken as indicating that advancements in the field (or simply adoptions of new paradigms) render the work of previous generations (or of scholars using alternative paradigms) unworthy of engagement. Indeed, James Robinson once declared, "a new quest must naturally begin with the point at which the original quest was seen to be illegitimate."[50] Such a construal has inevitably led to neglect and ignorance of the history of interpretation. Even scholars working in the field of Jesus research are sometimes unaware of the legitimate contributions and enduring insights embedded in the work of previous centuries. A lesson here may be drawn from Albert Schweitzer's comments regarding the fourteen-hundred page book of David Strauss. Schweitzer ultimately found that book to be short-sighted, but he thought its chief virtue was that it completely destroyed the rationalizing explanations for miracle stories put forward by scholars like Paulus. If such ideas "continue to haunt present-day theology," said Schweitzer, "it is only as ghosts, which can be put to flight simply by pronouncing the name of David Friedrich Strauss, and which would long ago have ceased to walk if the theologians who regard Strauss' book as obsolete would only take the trouble to read it."[51] Such was the regard Schweitzer had for a very long, ultimately short-sighted book that was already eighty years old. And such is the regard that the most significant Jesus scholars today would have for Schweitzer *and* Strauss *and* Paulus . . . and countless others besides.

In terms of nomenclature, students and other novices in the field of Jesus studies should be aware that terms like *New Quest* and *Third Quest* have been used by various scholars (though not always with the same sense or meaning); these terms will be encountered in much of the literature. Still, the strong tendency in Jesus scholarship today is to regard such labels as simplistic, inaccurate, and unnecessary. There is *a* quest for the historical Jesus, and it has been going on with diverse (but not easily or helpfully categorized) expressions for more than two hundred years. In the latter half of the twentieth century, many Jesus scholars wanted to be known as part of something new (a current "cutting edge" approach to Jesus unlike supposedly failed quests of the past). The new millennium, however, would prove to be an era in which Jesus scholars were prone to *connect* their work with past research. The history of the discipline came to be viewed not as a fitful chronicle of stops and starts but as a progressive process of often insightful exploration. Most contemporary Jesus scholars embrace that history without feeling the need to define themselves over against it.[52]

HOW DID JESUS GET LOST?

The Gospel of Luke relates a rather charming story of how Jesus at age twelve was separated from his parents when his family visited Jerusalem. His parents sought diligently for him, finding him at last in the Jewish temple (Luke 2:41–51). In a corresponding fashion, some scholars aver that the Jesus of history got lost—not in the Jewish temple but in the Christian church. This claim has formed the background for much of the Jesus scholarship mentioned above and discussed below.

Even traditional Christians will sometimes complain that doctrines and dogmas developed by churches over the years can obscure the image of Jesus. They want to get back to the Jesus of the Bible, to see him as he is there, apart from religious trappings that have made him serve various interests. Some Jesus scholars have taken this a step further. The Jesus of the Bible also needs to be freed from such trappings, since by the time the Gospels were written the development of Christian doctrine and dogma was already well under way.

We will say more about what it means for Jesus to have gotten "lost in the Christian church" in a moment, but first a word is in order about the basic fallibility of human memory. Most scholars believe that the New Testament Gospels were written thirty to sixty years after the death of Jesus. Stories about him—and summaries of his teaching—would have been passed on orally during that period, but historians must question how well things would have been remembered and how accurately they would have been recounted. Dale Allison, a prominent Jesus historian, says, "Even were one to hold, as I do not, that eyewitness or companions of eyewitnesses composed the canonical Gospels, our critical work would remain. Personal reminiscence is neither innocent nor objective."[53]

The cause for Allison's concern derives from scientific studies on the nature of human memory. At the simplest level, memory seeks to impose order on the chaos of reality: the human brain facilitates memory by organizing data according to meaningful patterns. Thus, events might be remembered in a different temporal sequence than they actually occurred if such a sequence seems more sensible and makes the events easier to recall. Likewise, since stories are fairly easy to remember, the brain tends to regard history as though it were a coherent narrative: there is strong incentive for events to be remembered as having a neat beginning, a coherent middle, and a satisfactory resolution. In the same vein, historical people can be remembered as though they were stereotypical characters in a drama (e.g., as protagonists or antagonists, heroes or villains).[54] Indeed, the mental process of remembrance is closely linked to that of imagination: it is "reconstructive as well as reproductive."[55] Allison notes:

> Remembering is not like reading a book but rather like writing a book. If there are blanks, we fill them in. If the plot is thin, we fill it out. As we constantly revise our memoirs, we may well recollect what we assume was the case rather than what was in fact the case; and as we confuse thought with deed, we may suppose that we did something that we only entertained doing. In addition, we often mingle related or repeated events, so the memory of a single occurrence is often composite, a "synthesis of experiences."[56]

The point of these observations is not just that memory is fallible but that it is *selectively* fallible. Allison maintains that modern studies on memory reveal that memories are basically "a function of self-interest."[57] Humans can remember things that never happened, when it serves their interest to do so. And this is even more true for communal memories: "Groups do not rehearse competing memories that fail to shore up what they hold dear."[58] Communities that pass on more or less sacred traditions preserve approved memories only; unapproved memories are either selectively omitted or altered so as to obtain approval. Even well-intentioned people who have no conscious desire of getting anything wrong are subject to the subconscious limitations of their own mental processes. Thus, Allison concludes, even in the best-case scenario (assuming the Gospel authors intended to report what was historically accurate), we must recognize that the memories of Jesus recounted in the Gospels could often be "dim or muddled or just plain wrong."[59]

Of course, many scholars have more confidence in the Gospel materials than Allison thinks is warranted. Some would maintain that quite a bit of material was put into writing early on or that Jesus' disciples (and their followers) were trained in the art of memorization to ensure almost verbatim recollection of what their master had said.[60] At the other end of the spectrum, however, there would be many scholars who suspect the process was actually less concerned with historical accuracy than the already problematic "best-case scenario" described above would allow. We will now look briefly at the work of three scholars who think the Jesus of history was transformed somewhat radically to serve the political and theological interests of the developing Christian religion. Their studies are controversial but, whatever one makes of them, they offer a background for historical research on Jesus. If these scholars are right, then the work of historical reconstruction becomes absolutely essential for anyone who wants to know the truth about Jesus. If they are wrong, then only the work of historical reconstruction will reveal their errors.

WILLIAM WREDE

Five years before Schweitzer's book on the quest for the historical Jesus was published, a New Testament scholar at the University of Breslau in Silesia (now Poland) produced a volume on the Gospel of Mark that remains one of the twentieth century's most influential works. Called *The Messianic Secret* (1901), the volume analyzed what by any account is one of the most peculiar features in Mark's work: a propensity for Jesus to keep his identity as Messiah a secret. In Mark, Jesus silences demons because they know who he is and might make him known (1:23–25, 34; 3:11–12). He tells those who benefit from his miracles not to say anything to anyone about what he has done for them (1:43–44; 5:43; 7:36; compare 9:9). He describes his teaching about the kingdom of God as a mystery (4:11) and claims that he teaches in parables to prevent people for whom the message is not intended from understanding. When Peter identifies him as the Messiah, he rebukes his disciples, ordering them not to tell anyone about him (8:30). Scholars had long noted this theme and tried to explain it in various ways, such as that Jesus had to be circumspect about his claims to avoid being arrested too soon or to avoid being accosted by unmanageable crowds (see 1:45). But these explanations were never completely satisfying, and in 1901, William Wrede offered a solution that did seem to make sense—with disturbing implications.

Basically, Wrede proposed that the motif was a theological construction developed by Mark himself. That, in itself, was novel. And the reason Mark had developed such a theme was to promote his own Christology. What Wrede intimates (without saying in so many words) is that Mark invented the scheme of a "messianic secret" to facilitate a presentation of Jesus that was not historically accurate. Mark wanted to describe a messianic life, but memories of the actual nonmessianic life were still so fresh that he could not do this without maintaining that what he wrote about Jesus was a secret known only to a few. The problem apparently arose from the fact that Mark's Gospel was the earliest one to be written, and at the time of its writing some people who knew Jesus were probably still alive. What if they were to hear about what Mark had written and protest, "Wait a minute! I was there and I don't remember Jesus ever working all these miracles or claiming to be the Messiah"? Mark could respond, "He did say and do these things, but they were a secret. You were not among those privileged to know about them."

Wrede's thesis was actually much more profound than this description may indicate, and his arguments struck many at the time as persuasive. Even so, most

New Testament scholars today would view the secrecy motif as a literary device intended to further some theological or pastoral point rather than to facilitate deception.[61] Wrede seems to have regarded Mark as unnecessarily devious, and his assumption that Mark would be so concerned about historical credibility may be anachronistic. Most likely, Mark's readers already knew the stories that the Gospel relates and did not have to be convinced that these things happened. Still, Wrede introduced a suspicion that the earliest Gospel—the one historians regard as most reliable—might in fact be a fabrication, an account created by an author whose agenda was not simply to report the facts. Long after the specifics of Wrede's provocative thesis fell out of favor, the suspicions it engendered remained. Among historians, at least, the Gospels were never read in quite the same way again.

BURTON MACK

If we flash forward some ninety years from the work of Wrede, we discover not too dissimilar views being expounded—for different reasons—by Markan scholars of the modern era. One of the most visible of these has been Burton Mack, professor emeritus of New Testament at the School of Theology in Claremont, California. His influential but controversial book *A Myth of Innocence* lays out a process for how the historical Jesus was transformed by early Christians into a very different figure who was to be the object of faith.[62] Mack finds evidence within the New Testament for two competing strains.[63] The first is the Jesus movement, whose adherents "kept the memory of Jesus alive and thought of themselves in terms of Jewish reform,[64] and the second is the Christ cult, in which Jesus became "the Lord of a new religious society that called for abrogation of the past."[65]

The Jesus movement, composed initially of Jesus' own followers, attempted to proselytize their Jewish neighbors by spreading their master's teachings, but they were largely unsuccessful. Meanwhile, in northern Syria and across the Mediterranean basin, adherents of the Christ cult—Paul and others who had never actually known Jesus—had great success developing a religion loosely based on this same figure. In this non-Jewish, Greco-Roman environment, the notions of resurrection and ascension were first applied to Jesus. A ritual meal to facilitate social formation was introduced and invested with sacral meaning. A new notion of conversion as personal transformation emerged. The new religion had wide appeal to Gentiles, as "Jesus came to be imagined as the patron deity of a new religion on the model of the Hellenistic cults."[66] But as Jesus became a divine being, the historical image of Jesus as a simple sage was largely erased.

As a second-generation Christian, Mark drew on the traditions of both strains identified above to create a "foundation myth" that would serve the needs of his specific social situation. The Jesus movement had essentially run its course by now, bequeathing to Mark a legacy of confusion over mission, hostility toward Jewish opponents, and a desire to withdraw from the world. The Christ cult was thriving but had become almost completely divorced from any narrative of Jesus' life and ministry. Mark's accomplishment was to retell the story of Jesus in light of these developments, for the benefit of the beleaguered remnants of the Jesus movement, but also from a perspective informed by the Christ cult. The Markan Jesus is a contentious rabbi who bests his Pharisaic opponents at debate. He is an authoritative Son of God who overcomes evil spirits and works fantastic miracles. He is the apocalyptic Son of Man who announces the imminent end of the world and founds a sect composed of those privileged to know the secret of the coming kingdom. And he is the innocent redeemer whose death provides atonement for those who believe in him. All these images made sense in Mark's social setting but none of them, says Mack, has much to do with the Jesus of history.

Most of Mark's Gospel, then, is fiction. The stories of Jesus' conflicts with the Pharisees were crafted to address arguments between early Christians and their Jewish opponents. (Mack questions whether there were many Pharisees in Galilee in Jesus' day and doubts whether Jesus ever had any significant contact with them.) The miracle stories were designed to present Jesus as a semi-divine figure, on a par (at least) with other Hellenistic wonder workers. (Mack does not think that Jesus worked miracles or that he was even said to work miracles during his own lifetime.) Above all, the passion narrative was created to provide a myth to accompany the Christ cult's representation of Jesus' significance as "the innocent redeemer of the world." Of course, Mark had access to some early sources and oral traditions concerning Jesus, but he was also highly creative. Much of the time, he just made things up. With regard to the passion narrative, only the actual fact of crucifixion can be regarded as historical. Beyond this, only the account of the meal (the Last Supper) appears to have been present in pre-Markan tradition. The rest—the cleansing of the temple, the betrayal by Judas, the arrest at Gethsemane, the three denials by Peter, the trials before Caiaphas and Pilate, the mocking of Jesus, the crowning with thorns, the consignment of Simon to carry the cross, the darkness at noon, the division of Jesus' garments, the cry of dereliction ("Why have you forsaken me?"), the rending of the temple veil—all come from the creative mind of Mark:

> Mark's Gospel was not the product of divine revelation. It was not a pious transmission of revered tradition. It was composed at a desk in a scholar's study lined with texts and open to discourse with other intellectuals . . . . The story was a new myth of origins. A brilliant appearance of the man of power, destroyed by those in league against God, pointed nonetheless to a final victory when those who knew the secret of his kingdom would finally be vindicated for accepting his authority.[67]

Mark created this story for the benefit of his little apocalyptic sect, a group that had little need for a simple sage but craved the approval of a god who would shortly bring this cruel world to an end in a way that would vindicate them and them alone. Mack suggests that the Roman destruction of the Jerusalem temple in 70 CE may have been the cataclysmic event that sealed this sect's view of reality. Their Jewish enemies had been punished by God in a way that could only signal the ultimate end of all things. Thus, the message of Jesus concerning how to live in this world was exchanged for a mythology that condemns the world and defers real life to a realm beyond death. Mark "gave up on imagining a society fit for the real world."[68]

One implication of Mack's theory of Christian origins is that the New Testament offers very little that can be deemed historically authentic with regard to Jesus. Mack does not regard as historical events any number of occurrences for which the earliest witness is the Gospel of Mark: that Jesus was baptized by John, that he opposed or in some way demonstrated against practices in the temple, that he practiced or attempted to practice works of healing or exorcism. All that we have, basically, are a few scattered sayings that represent Jesus' teaching and depict him as a sort of wandering philosopher. This, Mack thinks, should be enough: "Jesus ought to be ranked among the creative minds of the Greco-Roman age. . . . His importance as a thinker and a teacher can certainly be granted, and even greatly enhanced once we allow the thought that Jesus was not a god incarnate but a real historical person."[69]

Apocalyptic sects come and go, says Mack, but this one produced a work that became the foundational document for one of the world's major religions. Mark's fictional account of Jesus' life, ministry, death, and resurrection was taken up by the other Gospel writers and came to be regarded as narrative history, indeed as sacred scripture. The myth was relatively harmless when it functioned to empower an oppressed minority struggling to hold their own on the edge of the empire. But eventually the myth became the charter for the official religion of the empire with disastrous consequences. In a broad sense, Mack thinks the crusades, the Holocaust, colonial imperialism, even the Vietnam War can be blamed on the Gospel of Mark, as societies informed by this mythology have decided their destiny is to assume the role of innocent redeemer of the world: "the Markan myth is no longer good news."[70] Mack concludes the main text of his book with these words: "The church canonized a remarkably pitiful moment of early Christian condemnation of the world. Thus the world now stands condemned. It is enough. A future for the world can hardly be imagined any longer, if its redemption rests in the hands of Mark's innocent son of God."[71]

Criticisms of Mack's daring thesis abound. His work is often regarded as speculative, lacking the kind of support from what historians would usually regard as evidence. He has been said to approach the story of Jesus the way filmmaker Oliver Stone approached such subjects as the Kennedy assassination and the Vietnam War, rejecting any authoritative or official version of events if any possible motive can be posited for the creation of such an account.[72] Specifically, his assumption that diverse social groups must stand behind the different forms of biblical material and his attempts to date accounts on the basis of their perceived relationship to the process of social formation often seem arbitrary. Critics also think he sets up false alternatives. "Casting out demons is difficult to imagine for one adept at telling parables,"[73] Mack asserts, insisting that Jesus must have either been an exorcist or a teacher who taught in parables, but not both. Likewise, Mack assumes that either the wisdom sayings or the eschatological pronouncements of doom that are attributed to Jesus must be deemed unauthentic because the same person would not have said both.[74] But, some scholars object; aren't historical figures sometimes more complex than Mack wants to allow? Further, Mack's proposal has been said to be "weakened by a rigid dichotomy between historical report and literary fiction," genres that need not be mutually exclusive.[75]

Another common critique is that Mack's thesis rests on a minimalist portrait of Jesus that simply leaves too many gaps to be credible. Perhaps the most significant of these gaps is the motivation for Jesus' crucifixion. If the controversy stories and the passion narrative are all to be regarded as fiction, if Jesus was essentially just a philosopher who talked about an alternative way of life, then why would anyone want to kill him? More to the point, why did the *government* want to kill him? Why was he crucified? The best answer Mack was able to propose was that Jesus' death might have simply been "accidental." This led to a flurry of jokes among scholars, such as one about Mack's Jesus being killed in a car crash on the Los Angeles freeway.[76] What Mack meant, of course, was that Jesus could have just been caught up in the Roman pogroms against the Jews, especially if he looked or sounded at all unconventional. In this view there is no need to suppose that his death had any particular meaning or, for that matter, that it had anything to do with his beliefs or teaching.

Mack himself admits that *A Myth of Innocence* "is an essay, not a monograph."[77] It lacks the sort of detailed argumentation and scholarly documentation that build an airtight case point by point. It seeks, rather, to propose a different way of viewing the whole matter of Christian origins by suggesting a way that makes "social sense" of the materials at hand. Mack does not prove that the church *did* come quickly (before the writing of the Gospels) to view Jesus as something very different from who he actually was historically, but for some scholars his work has described a plausible process of development that explains how the church *could* have done that. It has been enough to keep alive the sort of suspicions that Wrede introduced almost a century previous.

ELISABETH SCHÜSSLER FIORENZA

Doubt regarding the historical accuracy of the Gospels has also been brought from another quarter, namely, feminist theologians who argue that a male-dominated church shaped the story of Jesus in ways that represented its own sexist perspective. Preeminent among these scholars is Elisabeth Schüssler Fiorenza, whose book *In Memory of Her* presents a feminist reconstruction of Christian origins.[78] Schüssler Fiorenza uses models drawn from sociology of religion to reconstruct the social reality that lies behind the androcentric biblical texts. The reality that comes to the fore is a movement initiated by Jesus that defied the hierarchical structure of patriarchal society. In Schüssler Fiorenza's view, Jesus denounced the Jewish social system based on purity and holiness, which correlated well with masculine dominance, in favor of another stream of Jewish consciousness, that of the wisdom tradition evident in the deuterocanonical book of Judith. He also attacked the patriarchal family system by insisting that no one except God should be vested with the authority given to a father (see Matt. 23:9). Instead, Jesus encouraged a "discipleship of equals," creating an alternative community structure based on "a vision of inclusive wholeness." Women were especially prominent in this community, as were other frequently disenfranchised people such as the poor, the sick, and those considered to be outcasts because of their occupation or behavior. In fact, Schüssler Fiorenza theorizes, Jesus understood himself to be the representative of divine wisdom (see Luke 7:35), which is personified in the Old Testament as a woman (for example, in Prov. 1–9). Schüssler Fiorenza calls this woman "Sophia" (which means "wisdom") and suggests that Jesus encouraged people to worship God as Sophia.[79] He thought of himself as the child or prophet of Sophia and so, even though he was biologically male, Jesus came to be viewed by his earliest followers as the incarnation of the female principle of God.[80]

What is most pertinent for our concern is that Schüssler Fiorenza alleges that the egalitarian aspect of Jesus' message and ministry did not comport with the political agendas of the emerging church. For example, his idea that men and women should have equal status and roles was particularly troublesome as the church tried to establish its place in a patriarchal society. Thus, the church introduced the notion that Jesus had appointed twelve male disciples to occupy a position of leadership over the rest.

The New Testament Gospels, Schüssler Fiorenza contends, must be studied with a "hermeneutics of suspicion," that is, with a strategy that involves recognition that they were written, edited, and preserved by men. Indeed, they were produced by men in communities dedicated to the subjugation of women—that much is clear from other New Testament writings (1 Cor. 14:34–35; 1 Tim. 2:11–15). Early on, there may have been some considerable controversy in the church over such matters: the mere fact that some NT writers are adamant about restricting roles for women implies that others in the church must have favored expanding those roles. Still, church history makes clear who "the winners" were in this debate. By the second century the Christian church had become an extremely patriarchal institution, dominated by an all-male clergy. As every critical scholar knows, history is usually written from the perspective of winners, who naturally relate matters in ways that reflect their own agenda. This, Schüssler Fiorenza says, is what happened with the Gospels. They offer an androcentric description of what was in reality far more egalitarian.

Schüssler Fiorenza's view is criticized by people who think she is trying to modernize Jesus, to turn him into an exponent of contemporary thinking that may be politically correct today but would have been anachronistic for his own place and time. On the one hand, she is sometimes said to exaggerate the patriarchal character of first-century Judaism;[81] on the other, she is said to overestimate the egalitarianism of Jesus in a manner based more on wishful thinking than solid historical evidence.[82] Nevertheless, the identification of Jesus as incarnate Wisdom is also a prominent part of Ben Witherington's portrait of Jesus,[83] and the emphasis on the egalitarian aspect of the Jesus movement figures strongly in the work of John Dominic Crossan. Most of all, Schüssler Fiorenza has been extremely successful in sensitizing modern scholars to an awareness of the social and political context in which the Gospels were produced and to consideration of ways in which this might have influenced the stories they relate. We may note that her evaluation of these writings is by no means as negative as that of Wrede or Mack; she allows for far more of the Gospel material to be accepted as historical than they do. She is also careful to distinguish between the historical Jesus and what she calls "the Jesus of piety." As a Roman Catholic, she urges Catholic Christians to take historical reconstructions of Jesus seriously, but not to allow them to be the sole norm or source for Christian identity. Interpretations of Jesus in the lives of saints, in scripture, and in liturgy all contribute to the image of Jesus that she favors.[84]

CONCLUSION

As we end this chapter, let me reiterate that many historians who study Jesus have much more respect for the historical reliability of the New Testament Gospels than these whom we have just mentioned. I call attention to the works of Wrede, Mack, and Schüssler Fiorenza not because they are representative of the scholarly guild as a whole but because they exemplify the challenges that all historians must take into consideration if they want their work to be taken seriously. It will no longer do in most academic settings to summarize what the Gospels say about Jesus and present this as a historical record. The historical Jesus could have gotten lost somewhere in the theology and politics of the church before those Gospels were written. Whether he did or not is one of the questions historians hope to answer. The story in Luke's Gospel tells of Mary and Joseph seeking diligently only to discover that Jesus had never really been lost in the first place (Luke 2:41–51). That might, of course, turn out to be the case here as well. Eventually, we shall hear from several scholars who have sought diligently for the historical Jesus and who think that they have now found him. They will, of course, let us know whether the search was necessary or whether the Jesus they discovered had been right there in the Gospels and in the church all along.

Jaroslav Pelikan, longtime professor of history at Yale University, asked students to consider the following description: "There was a great teacher, and gathered around him was a small group of faithful followers. They listened to his message and were transformed by it. But the message alienated the power structure of his time, which finally put him to death but did not succeed in eradicating his message, which is stronger now than ever."

Then, Pelikan observed, "That description would apply equally to Jesus and Socrates. But nobody's ever built a cathedral in honor of Socrates."[85]

Part of the historian's task is to explain what there was about Jesus that inspired those cathedrals (and other types of churches) to be built.

Chapter 2

Sources and Criteria

[The modern historical quest for Jesus] has tried to be more sophisticated in its methodology, more self aware and self critical in dealing with a given author's preconceptions and biases, and more determined to write history rather than covert theology or christology. The quest benefits from recent archaeological discoveries, a better knowledge of the Aramaic language and the cultural context in first-century Palestine, a more differentiated view of the Judaisms developing around the turn of the era and new insights arising from sociological analysis and modern literary theory.

—John P. Meier[1]

It falls to the lot of the historian to be the person who subjects the gospels to rough handling. The historian may or may not assent to the theology of the gospels, the view that God acted through Jesus. In either case, he or she . . . has a professional obligation to subject sources to rigorous cross-examination.

—E. P. Sanders[2]

It is impossible to avoid the suspicion that historical Jesus research is a very safe place to do theology and call it history, to do autobiography and call it biography.

—John Dominic Crossan[3]

How do historians study Jesus in a way that will retain the respect of their academic peers? The most important scholars usually work out their own method and are fairly explicit in explaining how it operates. When we get to chapters

34

4 through 9, we will devote a major section of each chapter to the particular method of operation employed by each individual or group under discussion. Some matters, however, are basic and instead of repeating these six times later, it seems advisable to discuss them all in one place. We will begin with an overview of the data and sources available to historians who wish to study Jesus and then move on to a survey of key criteria that are applied to these sources in historical research.

PHYSICAL DATA

Historical scholars are interested not only in materials that teach us about Jesus himself but also in those that reveal the world in which he lived. Insights drawn from archaeology and the social sciences have become especially valuable for elucidating the context in which Jesus lived, which in turn helps us to understand his life and teaching. For example, excavations half a mile from the center of first-century Nazareth have uncovered a vineyard with walls, a winepress, and towers, features that are mentioned in a vineyard described in Jesus' Parable of the Tenants (Mark 12:1).[4] The likelihood that Jesus really did tell this parable is increased by knowledge that Jesus grew up within view of a vineyard that could be described in terms the parable employs.

Most archaeologists will agree that we have no "direct evidence" of Jesus and his first followers—we do not possess any artifacts, clothing, bones, or other physical remains that can be definitively linked to Jesus or to any follower of Jesus mentioned in the New Testament.[5] Nevertheless, archaeologists are able to make suppositions about Jesus from materials that might not be directly related to him. For instance, a few years ago, a first-century CE fishing boat was found submerged in the Sea of Galilee. Historical Jesus scholars do not suppose that this is the boat actually used by Jesus and his disciples, but they are interested in the artifact nevertheless. The 8-by-26 foot boat was rather poorly crafted—it was constructed from varied materials and had undergone numerous repairs. Thus, it may represent a vessel typical of what would have been used by ordinary fishermen of the day. It has a more narrow draft than anyone would have supposed and would have sat much lower in the water than we might have guessed would be advisable. Presumably, this lack of depth was intentional, to facilitate the hauling of nets filled with fish into the vessel—but, this also meant that the boat could be easily swamped by waves and may have been somewhat vulnerable to sinking in a storm. Of course, we have no way of knowing if the boat Jesus and his disciples used was like this one, but the possibility that it *could* have been aids historians in making sense of certain details in biblical accounts (Mark 6:37).[6]

The most useful results of archaeology, however, have not concerned individual artifacts; rather, the field assists Jesus research most poignantly through what it reveals about the social, political, and cultural climate in which Jesus lived. Jonathan Reed has studied the demographics of Galilee at the time of Jesus, estimating the population of such villages as Capernaum (between 600 and 1500) and Nazareth (about 400) as well as that of the bigger cities, Seppho-ris and Tiberias (both around 12,000).[7] Sean Freyne has analyzed the "ecology of Galilee" at the time of Jesus: the area was lush with plant and animal life in a way that might have influenced the development of a "creation theology" that viewed the blessings of the earth as a guarantee of God's continued favor (this in contrast with the harsher theology of impending wrath espoused by John the Baptist in the less fertile wilderness).[8] Marianne Sawicki has studied the ways in which Roman occupation of Galilee affected various economic and social sys-tems; for example, the building of roads increased trade, making "exotic cultural and material goods" available to those who could afford them, but also depleting local resources through the export of agricultural goods.[9]

Archaeology is often invoked with regard to one of the most significant ques-tions for historical Jesus studies, the relative hellenization of Galilee and Judea at the time of Jesus. The word *hellenization* refers to the influence of Greco-Roman culture on areas that had become a part of the Roman Empire. If the area in which Jesus lived was thoroughly hellenized, then Jesus himself may have been influenced by Greek philosophy, Roman values, and other aspects of the Gentile world—this could explain some of the tensions that he experienced with certain Jewish leaders, who perhaps identified faithfulness with resistance to helleniza-tion. But if such influences were not prominent in Jesus' world, then it might be better for historians to understand him in more exclusively Jewish categories (e.g., by placing him within the stream of apocalyptic Judaism, or by viewing him as heir to the Jewish wisdom tradition or as a politically motivated prophet of social justice).[10]

As an illustration of how archaeology influences such discussions, we may consider the excavations at Sepphoris, a Roman city that is never men-tioned in the New Testament but that was located within three miles of Nazareth, where Jesus grew up. According to the Roman historian Josephus, Sepphoris was the most pro-Roman city in Galilee (*Life* 346–48), to the extent that it refused to take part in the Jewish revolt against Rome in 66 CE (*Life* 30, 38, 124, 232, 346–48, 373–74). The ruins of Sepphoris include a magnificent Roman theater where various plays and other spectacles would have been performed. Splendid villas and homes can be found in Sepphoris as well, many featuring elaborate mosaics and other examples of Roman cul-ture and art. Such archaeological discoveries prompt historians to wonder about the Hellenistic influence of Sepphoris on Jesus. Perhaps as a young man he and his father would have found work there—the New Testament indicates they were carpenters or construction workers (Matt. 13:55; Mark 6:3), and the village of Nazareth might not have been large enough to sustain employment in such a career full time. Maybe Jesus picked up his tendency to call people "hypocrites" (e.g., Matt. 6:2; 7:5) from his exposure to the theater—the Greek work *hypokritēs* literally means "actor" (one who pretends they are someone they are not). Likewise, Jesus' alleged laxity regarding Sabbath regulations and purity codes could have been influenced by frequent contacts with Gentiles in Sepphoris.

The problem with all the above suppositions is that archaeologists admit the Hellenistic features of Sepphoris are difficult to date. Many scholars, including Jonathan Reed and Sean Freyne, now say that the city became hellenized after the Jewish war with Rome in 70 CE: excavations from the time of Jesus reveal the presence of numerous *mikvot* (Jewish baths for ritual purification) and a remarkable absence of pig bones in the city dump (but in layers of the dump corresponding to the period after 70 CE, pig bones suddenly represent thirty percent of animal remains).[11] Other scholars maintain the city was nevertheless a pet project of Herod Antipas who, according to Josephus, wanted to make it "the ornament of all Galilee" (*Antiquities* 18.27), that is, emblematic of what Romans considered to be culturally appealing: it could have been a Jewish city but one occupied by thoroughly hellenized Jews (who for the sake of tradition continued to use *mikvot* occasionally and to observe selective kosher laws). This controversy concerning the potential influence of Sepphoris on Jesus has sometimes focused specifically on the aforementioned theater: Eric Myers is adamant that the excavated theater is from a time after the ministry of Jesus, while James Strange believes an original theater was built during Jesus' childhood and only renovated at a later date (thus, he says, Myers is dating the renovations not the theater proper).[12]

In sum, archaeological data can and does get interpreted in diverse ways, but historical Jesus scholars utilize what they consider to be the best archaeological reconstructions of Jesus' context when putting together their own reconstructions of Jesus' life and ministry.

LITERARY SOURCES

In a broad sense, historians are interested in almost any writing from the ancient world that might shed light on the world in which Jesus lived and the context within which he is to be understood. For now, however, we will limit ourselves to sources in the narrow sense—ancient writings that actually mention Jesus. References to Jesus in such works are not numerous, but they are quite varied. Historical scholars are interested in anything concerning him that they can find. Sometimes even the most meager reference can become significant in surprising ways.

Roman Literature

Jesus is mentioned in a number of ancient Roman writings, including the works of the three most important Roman historians for the first-century period, Josephus, Tacitus, and Suetonius. As a general rule, however, the Roman writers were more interested in Christianity than they were in Jesus. They do not seem to know anything about Jesus except what they would have heard from Christians, and they think of him primarily as the founder of the Christian movement.[13]

Thallos (c. 55 CE). The earliest reference to Jesus by any non-Christian writer may have been in a Greek chronicle of the eastern Mediterranean area by a historian named Thallos, about whom little is known. Thallos may have said, some twenty years after Jesus' crucifixion, that the noontime darkness that accompanied the latter event was not miraculous but merely a solar eclipse. We cannot know for certain because the writings of Thallos have not survived; all that we have is a report by the Byzantine historian Georgius Syncellus (c. 800) that a third-century Christian writer named Sextus Julius Africanus (c. 220 CE) sought to refute Thallos's claim.[14] If the comments attributed to Thallos could actually be established with more certainty, historians might regard those comments as an early, extra-biblical reference to the crucifixion of Jesus (and, specifically, to the phenomenon of noontime darkness said to accompany that event in Mark 15:33). As is, most historians regard the reference as too uncertain to be taken into account: no one knows for sure whether Thallos actually said anything like this or, if he did, what he said, or when he said it.

Josephus (c. 37–100 CE). The most significant of the non-Christian writers who mention Jesus is the historian Josephus, who was both Roman and Jewish. Born just after the death of Jesus, Josephus wrote long, detailed descriptions of events in Judea, Samaria, and Galilee, the areas where Jesus lived and worked. It is impossible for any historian to predict which current events or trends will prove to be significant in the long run, and Josephus certainly missed the mark with regard to the emergence of Christianity. He actually gives more space to describing the Essenes, a community of monastic Jews who were wiped out by 70 CE, than he does to the Christians, who in a few centuries would be running the Roman Empire. But he does *mention* the Christians, as well as John the Baptist, Pontius Pilate, Herod, and other persons known to us from the Bible. He mentions Jesus twice.

One of the two references doesn't offer much. In describing the illegal execution of James, the leader of the Christian church at Jerusalem, Josephus identifies him as "the brother of Jesus, who was called Christ" *(Antiquities* 20.9.1).

The second reference is more detailed, but there is a problem with it. We have no original manuscripts of Josephus's work and the copies that we do possess have apparently been edited by later Christians who added their own remarks about Jesus to what the Jewish historian originally wrote.[15] In the quote as it appears below, I have omitted words that most scholars think are editorial additions, citing them only in the accompanying note.

> At this time there appeared Jesus a wise man.[a] For he was a doer of startling deeds, a teacher of people who receive the truth with pleasure. And he

gained a following both among Jews and among many of Greek origin.[b] And when Pilate, because of an accusation made by the leading men among us, condemned him to the cross, those who had loved him previously did not cease to do so.[c] And up until this very day the tribe of Christians (named after him) has not died out. (*Antiquities* 18.3.3)[16]

Even without the Christian interpolations, this quote is surprisingly friendly.[17] Josephus obviously thought well of Jesus, regarding him as one who taught the truth. Though not a Christian himself, he respected Jesus as "a wise man" and as a "doer of startling deeds." Both of these appellations are topics for discussion among historians. Does Josephus mean to use the adjective *wise* as a generic compliment, or by calling Jesus "a wise man" does he mean to describe Jesus' vocation, that is, indicate that he was by profession a philosopher or sage? And when Josephus says Jesus did "startling deeds" does he mean that Jesus performed what we might call "extraordinary (if unconventional) good deeds" or does he mean to say that Jesus worked miracles?

Tacitus (c. 56–117 CE). A Roman proconsul who would prove to be one of the empire's greatest historians, Tacitus records that Jesus was "executed in Tiberius's reign by the governor of Judea, Pontius Pilate" (*Annals* 15.44). The context for this remark is to introduce the Christians, who were followers of this executed man and who suffered greatly under the cruelty of Nero. Tacitus gives no indication that he knows anything about the beliefs of these Christians (whom he regards as "notoriously depraved"), much less about the life or teaching of Jesus himself.[18]

Suetonius (c. 70–140 CE). The historian Suetonius is best remembered for documenting the lives of the Roman emperors. He reports in a writing from around 120 CE that the emperor Claudius expelled Jews from Rome because of trouble arising over "Chrestus" (*Twelve Caesars* 25.4). Most scholars think this is a mangled spelling of the Latin for "Christ." The event, then, would be the same as that reported in the book of Acts, which records that Jews were expelled from Rome by Claudius (Acts 18:2). Suetonius, however, displays no knowledge of the man Jesus who lived in Palestine. He is interested only in the figure who came to be at the center of Christian religion in Rome.

Mara bar Serapion (late first century CE?). At some point in the years following the Roman destruction of Jerusalem in 70 CE, a Syriac stoic named Mara bar Serapion wrote a letter to his son in which he referred to the latter event as an illustration of how wisdom triumphs even when the wise are oppressed. Mara actually cites three examples of such attempted oppression: the Athenians murdered Socrates, the people of Samos burned Pythagoras, and the Jews killed "their wise king," whose wisdom (like that of Socrates and Pythagoras) continues "because of the new laws he laid down."[19] It is curious that Mara does not mention Jesus by name, though historians are fairly certain it is Jesus to whom he is referring. The information he offers about Jesus is, again, quite meager, but Mara seems to think of Jesus primarily as a respectable moral teacher, albeit one whose ideas were rejected by his own people only to find acceptance elsewhere. The reference to Jesus as a "king" who was killed could allude to the tradition reported in the Gospels that Jesus was crucified as "king of the Jews" (e.g., Mark 15:26).

Pliny the Younger (c. 61–113 CE). A prominent Roman administrator, Pliny the Younger writes about Christians in a letter to the emperor Trajan around 111–113 CE. He comments that they "chant verses to Christ as to a god" (*Letter to Trajan* 10.96), but he does not otherwise mention Jesus.

Lucian of Samosata (c. 115–200 CE). The renowned Greek satirist Lucian of Samosata wrote a mocking exposé of Christianity in which Christians are said to worship "a crucified sophist" and to live "under his laws." More specifically, Jesus is referred to as "the man in Palestine who was crucified because he brought this new form of initiation into the world" and as the "first lawgiver" of the Christians, who "persuaded them that they are all brothers the moment they transgress and deny the Greek gods" (*The Passing of Peregrinus* 11, 13). Lucian's reference to Jesus as "a crucified sophist" is interesting since in the second century the word *sophist* was employed derisively for phonies, e.g., traveling philosophers who spewed nonsense to the gullible in exchange for money. In any case, historians note that Lucian appears to know of Jesus only by way of his followers; the historical data that might be derived from his writings (e.g., Jesus lived in Palestine, he was crucified, he gave commandments, he taught a principle of "brotherly love," and he adhered to Jewish monotheism) are all things that Christians would have said about Jesus in the latter half of the second century CE.

Celsus (late second century CE). Sometime around 175 CE, the Neoplatonist teacher Celsus wrote a comprehensive attack on Christianity; the work itself has not survived, but a point-by-point response written seventy years later by the Christian theologian Origen quotes voluminously from it. According to Origen, Celsus related numerous tales about Jesus that provided polemical alternatives to the sacred Christian narratives: e.g., Jesus was the son of a woman who committed adultery with a soldier named Pantera, and he studied magical arts in Egypt in order to deceive people into believing he had divine powers (*Against Celsus* 28, 32). Historians place no credence in any of this material: Celsus wrote too late to have possessed independent, reliable information about Jesus, and the extravagantly tendentious character of his claims makes it unlikely that they witness to anything more than the polemical tendencies of interreligious competition.

Jewish Writings

Scholars disagree on the extent and significance of references to Jesus in ancient Jewish writings, such as the Talmuds, the Tosefta, the Targumim, and the midrashim.[20] First, many of the possible references do not refer to him by name but offer, at most, a veiled or coded reference to Jesus. Second, even the texts in which he is explicitly mentioned are difficult to date and could come from almost any time period up to and including the Middle Ages. In all cases, the references are polemical and seem to represent apologetic responses to Christian claims. Thus, one finds occasional allusions to the legend of Pantera being the real father of Jesus (*b. Shabbat* 104b; *b. Sanhedrin* 64a), a story also related by the Roman writer Celsus (see above).

The Jewish text that is most often examined in historical Jesus studies comes from the Babylonian Talmud. The materials that make up this work were collected over a long period of time, finally coming together around 500–600 CE. Thus, there is no way of knowing how early (or how reliable) the reference may be. Nevertheless, here it is:

> On the day before Passover, they hanged Jesus. A herald went before him for forty days [proclaiming], "He will be stoned, because he practiced magic and enticed Israel to go astray. Let anyone who knows anything in his favor come forward and plead for him." But nothing was found in his favor, and they hanged him on the day before Passover. (*b. Sanhedrin* 43a)

The main point of this passage could be to counter Christian charges that Jesus was given a hasty trial. In any case, scholars who regard this text as early (possibly second century) note that it seems relatively free from direct influence of the Christian Gospels but still resonates with some of the information provided in those writings. In any case, the text goes on to say, "Jesus had five disciples: Mattai, Maqai, Metser, Buni, and Todah." This, of course, is neither the traditional list of names, nor the traditional number (twelve).

New Testament Epistles

Surprisingly, the letters of Paul preserved in the New Testament tell us little more about Jesus than the non-Christian writings. The great Christian missionary did not know the earthly Jesus but says the risen Christ appeared to him (1 Cor. 15:8). Paul's thoughts are clearly guided by the belief that he and other Christians remain in a dynamic relationship with the Lord Jesus Christ who lives now in heaven with God but interacts with his followers on earth and will someday return to consummate their salvation. Most of Paul's references to Jesus are couched in present or future tenses. When he does use the past tense to refer to what we are calling the Jesus of history, he almost always refers to what he regards as the final events of that life—Jesus' death and resurrection. Once, he also describes Jesus' last meal with his followers (1 Cor. 11:23–25).

Even though Paul does not explicitly relate stories about the life or ministry of Jesus or pass on much of his teaching, he may at times allude to sayings of Jesus.[21] The command of the Lord prohibiting divorce that Paul refers to in 1 Corinthians 7:10 might be a reference to the historical teaching of Jesus (compare Mark 10:2–9). Likewise, Paul's claim that "the Lord commanded that those who proclaim the gospel should get their living by the gospel" (1 Cor. 9:14) may recall a saying of Jesus such as that reported in Matthew 10:10. Occasionally, Paul offers moral advice that may reflect the influence of words attributed elsewhere to Jesus without actually citing Jesus as his source (for example, the exhortation to love one's enemies in Rom. 12:14,17–20; compare Matt. 5:38–48). In other instances, however, Paul claims authority to give instructions "through the Lord Jesus" (1 Thess. 4:2), which may indicate that he believes he has received revelations from the risen Lord, and that people are to regard these words as similar to those spoken by Jesus when he was on earth. Whether or not this is the case, historians are cautious about taking everything Paul presents as "words of the Lord" as representative of the actual teaching of the historical Jesus.

Nevertheless, Paul's letters are regarded as an important source for what little they do reveal. This is primarily true because the letters are so early. By most estimates, Paul's letters were written some twenty to thirty years before the Gospels. Furthermore, despite the apparent lack of interest in Jesus' earthly life and ministry, details sometimes turn up almost by accident. For instance, Paul refers in 1 Corinthians 15:5 to "the twelve," confirming the (later) report in the Gospels that some of Jesus' disciples were known by this designation. Elsewhere, Paul mentions that Jesus was of Davidic descent (Rom. 1:3).

Other New Testament letters offer even less. Again, scholars note passages that may be reworked sayings of Jesus, such as the prohibition of oaths in James 5:12 (compare Matt. 5:34–37), but the epistles themselves do not attribute these sayings to Jesus. The anonymous letter to the Hebrews mentions that Jesus was of the tribe of Judah (7:14) and refers to an agonized prayer reminiscent of that which the Synoptic Gospels say he offered in Gethsemane (Heb. 5:7–8; Mark 14:32–42). These letters, however, are probably not as early as Paul's and may even be dependent on the Gospel traditions. Even the meager information they offer about Jesus is not deemed very valuable.

A few scholars have advocated for a much greater use of epistles in historical Jesus studies, albeit in a somewhat different manner. Apart from explicit references to the life or teachings of the man Jesus, the epistles bear robust witness to what people believed about Jesus. Sometimes (in the case of certain letters attributed to Paul), this testimony may be regarded as historical evidence of the early *influence* of Jesus, revealing how he was regarded by people just two or three decades after his death. Paul Barnett, starts with the historical fact (evident in Paul's letters and other early Christian literature) that the first generation of Christians worshiped Jesus and proclaimed him to be both the long-awaited Messiah and the divine Son of God. Barnett argues on logical grounds that it would be historically unlikely for Christians to have come up with these things completely on their own—even if they believed he had been raised from the dead; what would be more likely would be for Christians who believed Jesus had been raised from the dead to conclude that claims he had made about himself had now been vindicated. Thus, the early beliefs about Jesus evident in the epistles (and, for Barnett, in missionary speeches contained in the book of Acts) should be regarded as suggestive of claims the historical person made regarding his own identity and mission: the so-called "Christ of faith" is at least an indicator of the "Jesus of history."[22]

The Synoptic Gospels

The first three Gospels (Matthew, Mark, and Luke) are called the Synoptic Gospels because they have many parallel passages, that is, passages that are very similar if not identical in wording (the word *synoptic* means "seen together," and it came to be applied to these Gospels because their similar passages could be viewed together in parallel columns). Most scholars do not believe that any of these three works were written by disciples of Jesus or by eyewitnesses to the events that they report. The extent to which they rely on eyewitness testimony is greatly disputed. Luke's Gospel does indicate that some of the material it reports is based on eyewitness reports (Luke 1:2), and many scholars would probably assume that this is true for all three of the Synoptic Gospels—and, for that matter, for the Gospel of John as well (see John 19:35; 21:24). The question is how much material relies on eyewitness testimony. Richard Bauckham would say "a great deal";[23] other scholars are less optimistic.[24]

In any case, the Synoptic Gospels themselves are anonymous. Church tradition holds that the first Gospel was written by Matthew the tax collector who became a disciple of Jesus, but this is almost universally rejected by modern scholars. Traditions that the second Gospel was written by John Mark and the third by Luke the physician are also challenged, but even if these traditions are accurate, neither John Mark nor Luke was a person who had met Jesus.[25] Tradition also holds that John Mark got direct reports on the life and teaching of Jesus from the apostle Peter, and that Luke traveled with Paul, who in turn knew all Jesus' disciples and members of Jesus' family. But, again, historians are often skeptical of such traditions: they claim more for the Gospels than the Gospels claim for themselves, and are exactly the kind of thing the church would want to believe about biographies of Jesus written by people who had not known him.

From early on, Christian scholars have believed that one of these Gospels served as the prototype for the others. Augustine, for instance, believed that Matthew's Gospel was written first and that the other two copied material from Matthew, adding or subtracting information relevant to their own situations. For historians, the question of which Gospel served as the prototype is extremely important because that work would stand closest to the actual events it relates and, so, would tend to be viewed as the most reliable source for historical information. But which is it?

The matter gets complicated, but the short answer is that the great majority of scholars now believe the Gospel of Mark was the earliest of these three books. Matthew and Luke both had copies of Mark and took much of their material from him. They did not, however, just copy stories from Mark word for word but edited them, changing details in the process. For a rather extreme example, see the story of Jesus and the scribe in fig. 3. In Mark, the scribe agrees with Jesus, who then declares that he has answered wisely; in Matthew, there is no indication of agreement and the very question is posed as an attempt to test Jesus (to see what Luke does with this story, see Luke 10:25–28). If Mark's Gospel contains the original form of this story, then historians will be more likely to accept his version of the encounter as accurate. In this instance, at least, they will be inclined to believe that Jesus had a friendly encounter with a scribe who responded favorably to him rather than a potentially hostile encounter with an insincere scribe who wanted to test him.

James D. G. Dunn has recently questioned what he calls the "literary paradigm" assumed by judgments such as these.[26] According to Dunn, historians

---

Figure 3. Two Versions of a Gospel Story

Mark 12:28–34

One of the scribes came near and heard them disputing with one another, and seeing that he answered them well, he asked him, "Which commandment is the first of all?" Jesus answered, "The first is, 'Hear O Israel: the Lord our God, the Lord is one; you shall love the Lord your God with all your heart, and with all your soul, and with all your mind, and with all your strength.' The second is this, 'You shall love your neighbor as yourself.' There is no other commandment greater than these." Then the scribe said to him, "You are right, Teacher; you have truly said that 'he is one, and besides him there is no other'; and 'to love him with all the heart, and with all the understanding, and with all the strength,' and 'to love one's neighbor as oneself'—this is much more important than all whole burnt offerings and sacrifices." When Jesus saw that he answered wisely, he said to him, "You are not far from the kingdom of God."

Matthew 22:34–40

When the Pharisees heard that he had silenced the Sadducees, they gathered together, and one of them, a lawyer, asked him a question to test him. "Teacher, which commandment in the law is the greatest?" He said to him, "'You shall love the Lord your God with all your heart, and with all your soul, and with all your mind.' This is the greatest and first commandment. And a second is like it: 'You shall love your neighbor as yourself.' On these two commandments hang all the law and the prophets."

fail to give adequate attention to the role that oral tradition would have played and, especially to oral performance of stories within early Christian communities. Drawing on the work of Kenneth Bailey,[27] Dunn proposes that differences in Gospel accounts might have arisen from diverse oral presentations of the same stories rather than from literary editing of manuscripts. Thus, it is anachronistic to speak of "an original version" of a story—Mark, Matthew, and Luke may all present versions of how an event was recalled through oral tradition. Notably, Dunn accepts the thesis that Matthew and Luke did use the Gospel of Mark as a source. His point is that oral transmission of tradition would have continued alongside written transmission and may account for the differences in Gospel accounts. Thus, according to Dunn, variant accounts in the Synoptic Gospels should all be considered as evidence of how Jesus was remembered. This runs contrary to the usual tendency of historical scholars to regard redactional variations that Matthew or Luke make in the text received from Mark as revelatory of theological reflection on what Mark reported rather than as evidentiary of an alternative account of what had actually happened.[28]

In any case, things get more complex. Most scholars also believe that Matthew and Luke had copies of another early Christian document, one that has since been lost to us. For convenience, this work is called Q. This label is probably short for the German word *Quelle* (which means "source"), though nobody remembers for sure how the designation was chosen. In any case, Q was apparently an early collection of sayings attributed to Jesus. Both Matthew and Luke copied these sayings into their Gospels, sometimes altering them just as they did the material they took from Mark. The historian's dream would be for archaeologists to dig up a copy of Q somewhere, but that is not likely to happen. The next best thing from a historian's point of view is to reconstruct what Q probably said based on comparisons of what is found in Matthew and Luke.[29]

Thus, even though Mark was probably the earliest Gospel, Matthew and Luke continue to be treasured by most historians because they are thought to preserve sayings from Q, which may have been even earlier than Mark. In addition, Matthew and Luke incorporated other material into their Gospels that they may have derived from any number of sources. The extra material that is found in Matthew is called *M* and the extra material found in Luke is called *L*.

Most historical Jesus scholars follow this paradigm, but other possibilities have also been considered. One prominent alternative (sometimes called the Farrer Theory) dispenses with the idea of Q by maintaining that Mark wrote his Gospel first, Matthew expanded Mark's work, and then Luke produced his Gospel, using both Matthew and Mark as sources.[30] Another view (called the Two-Gospel Hypothesis or the Griesbach Hypothesis) questions both the existence of Q *and* the assumption that Mark's Gospel was written first: according to this hypothesis, Matthew wrote first, Luke used Matthew as a source, and Mark produced his Gospel last, as an abridgment of the other two.[31]

Nevertheless, it is quite common for historical Jesus scholars (in keeping with the dominant paradigm) to discuss material in the Synoptic Gospels not as coming from Matthew, Mark, or Luke but rather as representative of one of four major source strata: Mark, Q, M, and L. We will now offer brief commentary on each of these; a chart at the end of this section (pages 48–52) lists the material that is usually ascribed to Q, M, and L.

Gospel of Mark

As the earliest Gospel, Mark is usually thought to have been written sometime around 70 CE, either just before or just after the temple in Jerusalem was destroyed by Roman armies. A minority position places Mark about ten years earlier than this.[32] Some scholars think that the author might have had access to Peter and learned some of the stories he relates from that disciple of Jesus. This is by no means certain, however, and cannot be accepted by historians as a guarantee of authenticity. Even so, Mark is generally regarded as the most historically reliable of the four Gospels in terms of its overall description of Jesus' life and ministry. This is why theories posited by scholars such as William Wrede and Burton Mack (see pages 26–30) are potentially devastating to the historical quest for Jesus. If, as these scholars contend, the Gospel of Mark is largely fiction, then our main source for the historical reconstruction of Jesus' life is lost. As we pursue the work of historians in the next few chapters we will see that a determining factor for the outcome of their work is the value that they place on the Gospel of Mark. Some scholars, including Funk, Crossan, and others associated with the Jesus Seminar, rely little on Mark; others, such as Sanders, Meier, and Wright, make Mark foundational for their work.

Even those who do use Mark for historical research may press the further question of whether everything in Mark is of equal value. Part of this question involves the issue of whether Mark used sources for his Gospel, material that had already been memorized or put into writing before his Gospel was produced. Some scholars suggest that Mark may have had (1) a collection of controversy stories, including those found now in Mark 2:1–3:6; (2) a collection or, possibly, two collections of miracle stories, including many of those now found in chapters 4–8; (3) an apocalyptic tract containing much of what is now in chapter 13; or (4) an early version of the passion narrative, the story of Jesus' death and resurrection now found in Mark 14–16. Of course, such theories are by nature tenuous and always evoke discussion.

Q

As noted previously, some scholars doubt that the Q source ever existed. Others propose that it was a written document, perhaps a collection of notes taken by one of Jesus' own disciples. Still others think it may have been only a memorized collection of sayings that Christians passed on to one another in an age when many people were still illiterate. Or perhaps what we call Q was just a body of oral tradition upon which Matthew and Luke independently drew. Despite such uncertainties, there is broad agreement on some points. The majority of scholars do believe that the material attributed to the Q source (regardless of whether an actual document of that nature ever existed) is among the oldest and most reliable material found in the Gospels. This material is considered especially valuable in describing the teaching of Jesus though, as we will see, such highly respected scholars as E. P. Sanders and N. T. Wright manage to get by without any assumption of Q.

Beyond this near consensus lies breakdown over details. Some scholars have tried to discern a distinctive theology in the Q material and to determine the nature of the community that would have produced this material. Was there in fact an early Christian movement whose understanding of Jesus would have been defined by (if not limited to) what is found here? Furthermore, a number of scholars believe that layers of recension can be discerned within their reconstructed version of Q. In other words, they believe that some of the Q material is earlier than the rest. The best-known version of this theory is that of John Kloppenborg, who divides Q material into three recensions:[33] Q^1, Q^2, and Q^3. William Arnal builds on this thesis to propose the earliest Q material was composed by village scribes in Galilean communities who thought Jesus' sayings would encourage the sort of communal reciprocity necessary to resist Roman imperialism.[34] Burton Mack (see pages 27–30) claims that all we can really know of Jesus comes from the earliest recension of Q. Notably, the sayings of Jesus assigned to Q^1 do not deal with eschatological concerns involving the future, nor do they present Jesus as engaging what would be specifically Jewish issues (e.g., the enduring validity of Torah). We recall from the discussion in chapter 1 that the New Quest scholars tended to deemphasize precisely those two aspects of Jesus' ministry, presenting him as noneschatological in emphasis and as generic in his ethnic appeal. Scholars who continue in that tradition would maintain that this is justified because this is how the community of Christians that preserved the earliest collection of Jesus' sayings understood him.[35] Mack goes on to stress that early Q (that is, Q^1) is valuable precisely because it is pre-Christian. The Christian church had not yet come into being:

> The remarkable thing about the people of Q is that they were not Christians. They did not think about Jesus as a messiah or the Christ. They did not take his teachings as an indictment of Judaism. They did not regard his death as a divine, tragic, or saving event. And they did not imagine that he had been raised from the dead to rule over a transformed world. Instead, they thought of him as a teacher whose teaching made it possible to live with verve in troubled times. Thus they did not gather to worship in his name, honor him as a god, or cultivate his memory through hymns, prayers, and rituals.[36]

But these theories regarding Q are complex and controversial.[37] Charlotte Allen notes, "This entire edifice—building from hypothesis to document to Gospel to theology to community—is either a marvel of perceptive scholarship or a showy sandcastle."[38] But which is it? One scholar has actually proposed the opposite of what Kloppenborg suggests with regard to layers of tradition: Siegfried Schulz thinks that the Jewish tradition presenting Jesus as the eschatological Son of Man constitutes the original Q and the more generic wisdom materials are later additions.[39]

Most scholars remain cautious about describing the character of a Q community[40] or discerning layers of tradition in a source for which we have no extant manuscripts.[41] John Meier, whose work is discussed in chapter 8, says, "I doubt that we have the data and the methods sufficient to answer questions about the community, locality, tradition process, and coherent theological vision that supposedly produced Q."[42] Piqued at the confidence in Q theories evinced by some of his colleagues, he adds: "I cannot help thinking that biblical scholarship would be greatly advanced if every morning all exegetes would repeat as a mantra: 'Q is a hypothetical document whose exact extension, wording, originating community, strata, and stages of redaction cannot be known.'"[43]

M and L

Most scholars no longer believe that there was an M source or an L source as such. Thus, the sigla *M* and *L* are not used to designate specific documents that the authors of Matthew and Luke were able to draw upon but, rather, refer to whatever unique material each of those evangelists incorporated into his respective Gospel. Thus, material categorized as belonging to either M or L is usually of unknown origin and difficult to date. In most cases this material is unparalleled, that is, found nowhere else. An example would be the famous story of the Good Samaritan, which Jesus tells in Luke 10:30–37. The tale is ascribed to the L material and no reference to it is found anywhere else in the Bible. Most scholars think that the Gospels of Matthew and Luke were completed around 85 CE. A more conservative position dates them along with Mark to the sixties.[44] In either case, material designated as M or L could be from an earlier time or it could be as late as the final draft of the Gospels in which it is now found. Since it is difficult to tell, most scholars are reluctant to rely too heavily on this material when constructing their portraits of the historical Jesus. Sometimes, however, the historicity of individual passages found among the M and L material is esteemed highly on the basis of criteria to be discussed later in this chapter.

Contents of Q, M, and L[45]

    Q

    Preaching of John the Baptist (Luke 3:7–9; Matt. 3:7–10)

    Temptation of Jesus (Luke 4:1–13; Matt. 4:1–11)

    Beatitudes (Luke 6:20–23; Matt. 5:3–12)

Love for enemies (Luke 6:27–36; Matt. 5:39–48; 7:12)

On judging others (Luke 6:37–42; Matt. 7:1–5; 10:24; 15:14)

On bearing fruit (Luke 6:43–45; Matt. 7:15–20)

Parable of two builders (Luke 6:47–49; Matt. 7:24–27)

Healing of a centurion's servant (Luke 7:1–10; Matt. 8:5–10, 13)

John the Baptist questions Jesus (Luke 7:18–35; Matt. 11:2–19)

The would-be disciples (Luke 9:57–60; Matt. 8:19–22)

Jesus' missionary discourse (Luke 10:2–16; Matt. 9:37–38; 10:9–15; 11:21–23)

Thanksgiving to the Father (Luke 10:21–24; Matt. 11:25–27; 13:16–17)

The Lord's Prayer (Luke 11:2–4; Matt. 6:9–13)

Asking and receiving (Luke 11:9–13; Matt. 7:7–11)

Jesus identified with Beelzebul (Luke 11:14–23; Matt. 12:22–30)

Return of an evil spirit (Luke 11:24–26; Matt. 12:43–45)

The sign of Jonah (Luke 11:29–32; Matt. 12:38–42)

On light (Luke 11:33–36; Matt. 5:15; 6:22–23)

Woe to the Pharisees (Luke 11:37–52; Matt. 23:4–7, 13–36)

Fear of humans and God (Luke 12:2–12; Matt. 10:19, 26–33; 12:32)

Do not worry about life (Luke 12:22–34; Matt. 6:19–21, 25–33)

Be ready for the master's return (Luke 12:39–46; Matt. 24:43–51)

Divisions in the family (Luke 12:51–53; Matt. 10:34–36)

Signs of the times (Luke 12:54–56; Matt. 16:2–3)

Settle out of court (Luke 12:57–59; Matt. 5:25–26)

Parable of leaven (Luke 13:20–21; Matt. 13:33)

The narrow door (Luke 12:23–30; Matt. 7:13–14, 22–23; 8:11–12)

Lament over Jerusalem (Luke 13:34–35; Matt. 23:37–39)

Parable of the banquet (Luke 14:15–24; Matt. 22:1–14)

Carrying the cross (Luke 14:26–27; Matt. 10:37–38)

Parable of the lost sheep (Luke 15:1–7; Matt. 18:12–14)

On serving two masters (Luke 16:13; Matt. 6:24)

Role of the law and prophets (Luke 16:16–17; Matt. 5:18; 11:13)

Rebuking and forgiving sin (Luke 17:1–6; Matt. 18:6–7, 15, 20–22)

The day of the Son of Man (Luke 17:23–27, 33–37; Matt. 24:17–18, 26–28, 37–41)

Parable of the talents (Luke 19:11–27; Matt. 25:14–30)

M (all from Matthew)

Genealogy of Jesus (from Abraham)	1:2–17
Birth of Jesus (with focus on Joseph)	1:18–25
Visit of the magi	2:1–12
Flight to Egypt	2:13–21
On fulfilling the law	5:17–20
The antitheses	5:21–24, 27–28, 33–38, 43
On practicing piety	6:1–15, 16–19
Pearls before swine	7:6
Limit mission to Israel	10:5–6
Invitation to rest	11:28–30
Parables: weeds, treasure, pearl, net	13:24–30, 36–52
Peter tries to walk on water	14:28–31
Blessing of Peter	16:17–19
Peter pays the temple tax	17:24–27
Recovering the sinful sibling	18:15–20
Peter asks about forgiveness	18:21–22
Parable of unforgiving servant	18:23–35
Parable of laborers in vineyard	20:1–16
Parable of two sons	21:28–32
Prohibition of titles	23:7–12
Denunciations of Pharisees	23:15–22
Parable of bridesmaids	25:1–13
Description of last judgment	25:31–46
Death of Judas	27:3–10
Pilate washes his hands	27:24–25
Resuscitation of saints	27:52–53
Guard at the tomb	27:62–66; 28:11–15
Great Commission	28:16–20

L (all from Luke)

Dedication to Theophilus	1:1–4
Promised birth of John	1:5–25
Announcement of Jesus' birth to Mary	1:26–38
Mary's visit to Elizabeth	1:39–56

Birth of John the Baptist	1:57–80
Birth of Jesus (with shepherds, manger)	2:1–20
Presentation in the temple	2:21–38
Childhood visit to Jerusalem	2:41–52
John's reply to questions	3:10–14
Genealogy of Jesus (to Adam)	3:23–38
Good news to the poor	4:14–23, 25–30
Miraculous catch of fish	5:1–11
Raising of widow's son at Nain	7:11–17
Encounter with homeless woman	7:36–39, 44–50
Parable of two debtors	7:40–43
Ministering women	8:1–3
Rejection by Samaritan village	9:51–56
Return of the seventy	10:17–20
Parable of good Samaritan	10:29–37
Mary and Martha	10:38–42
Parable of friend at midnight	11:5–8
Parable of rich fool	12:13–21
Parable of severe and light beatings	12:47–48
Parable of barren tree	13:1–9
Healing of woman on Sabbath	13:10–17
Healing of man with dropsy	14:1–6
Lessons for table guests and hosts	14:7–14
Counting the cost (two parables)	14:28–33
Parable of lost coin	15:8–10
Parable of prodigal son	15:11–32
Parable of shrewd manager	16:1–12
Parable of rich man and Lazarus	16:19–31
Cleansing of ten lepers	17:11–19
Parable of widow and judge	18:1–8
Parable of Pharisee and tax collector	18:9–14
Story of Zacchaeus	19:1–10
Jesus weeps over Jerusalem	19:41–44
Reason for Peter's denial	22:31–32
Two swords	22:35–38

Jesus before Herod	23:6–12
Pilate declares Jesus innocent	23:13–16
Sayings associated with Jesus' death	23:28–31, 34, 43, 46
Appearance on the road to Emmaus	24:13–35
Appearance to the disciples	24:36–49
The Ascension	24:50–53

The Gospel of John

The Fourth Gospel is usually regarded as the latest of the New Testament witnesses to Jesus. Like the other Gospels, it is anonymous. Notably, however, the book claims that some of the things it records are based on the testimony of a mysterious figure called "the disciple whom Jesus loved." Indeed, it says that this disciple is the one "who is testifying to these things and has written them" (John 21:24). Some scholars doubt the legitimacy of this claim altogether, but even those who accept it face many questions: Which things reported in the Gospel go back to the testimony of this beloved disciple, and who was this person? Was he John the son of Zebedee, the fisherman who became a disciple of Jesus (as church tradition has often maintained)? Theories abound, but the questions remain unanswered.

Most scholars believe that the Gospel of John was composed in stages. As with the Synoptic Gospels, some of the material would then be earlier than the rest. One theory is that the current Gospel might include a collection of remembrances of the beloved disciple, dealing mostly with the last week of Jesus' life. Another is that material underlying the great speeches attributed to Jesus in the Gospel might derive from sermons given to the community by this beloved disciple. Even more significant, potentially, is yet another proposal, that John's Gospel has incorporated an earlier document called the "Signs Gospel." This work would have recorded seven or eight miracle stories (2:1–12; 4:46–54; 5:1–9; 6:1–13; 9:1–7; 11:1–44; 21:1–6; maybe 6:15–25) and might also have included an account of the passion and resurrection.[46] This theory of an early Signs Gospel, however, has found less acceptance among scholars than proposals concerning the existence of a Q source that was used by Matthew and Luke.

The bottom line is that historians are unsure of the date and origin of most of the material in John's Gospel, and so they do not usually rely on it as strongly as they do on Mark or on the material attributed to Q. In one sense, this means that when images of Jesus in John and the Synoptics differ, the latter is usually preferred by historians. For example, the Synoptic Gospels repeatedly present Jesus as a teller of parables, but Jesus never tells a single parable in the Gospel of John. Historians do not allow the Johannine portrait to cast doubt on the image of Jesus as a parable-teller, but assume that the Synoptic portrait is accurate and that John just missed this point (or omitted it because it did not serve his interests). Or, to look at matters the other way around, Jesus talks a great deal about himself in

John's Gospel, claiming to be "the light of the world" (8:12) and "the way, the truth, and the life" (14:6), but he does not typically make such grandiose claims about himself in the other Gospels. Historians are reluctant to admit the authenticity of such claims on the testimony of John's Gospel alone.

The twenty-first century, however, brought a new, cautious appreciation for the historical value of John's Gospel.[47] For one thing, archaeological advances revealed that John's Gospel often preserves accurate information about pre-70 Jerusalem and Judea, and Jewish studies confirmed the accuracy of John's distinctive portrayal of Second Temple festival observance and of the religious disputes between Jews and Samaritans.[48] In particular, the Johannine chronology for Jesus' ministry is now sometimes given more credence than it once was, and certain aspects of John's passion narrative are deemed preferable to their Synoptic parallels.[49] Further, a number of scholars now think that John's Gospel might have been produced within a community that did not possess any of the other Gospels; if that was the case, then John would sometimes provide independent verification of what is reported in the Synoptics.[50] Even when John differs from the Synoptics, however, his account need not be deemed necessarily inferior just because it appears to be more overtly developed theologically. Paul Anderson argues that the Markan and Johannine traditions preserve dual memories of how the ministry and intention of Jesus were perceived and experienced by his earliest followers: the divergences may actually stem from distinctive "first impressions" made on people who were among Jesus' original historical audiences.[51]

John's Gospel continues to be accorded less attention in historical Jesus studies than the three Synoptic Gospels, especially the Gospel of Mark or the material in Matthew and Luke that is often ascribed to Q. The growing trend, however, is for scholars to recognize the Fourth Gospel as a "dissonant tradition" that not only *can* be utilized but *must* be, if the Synoptic tradition is not to be accorded free reign in a manner that seems uncritical.[52] I have elsewhere attempted to tease out the implications of this point by asking scholars to imagine what might have happened if John's Gospel had been lost to history only to be discovered now:

> Imagine! A book on the life and teachings of Jesus that is almost as early as the Synoptic Gospels, that claims to be based in part on eyewitness testimony, that contains some material that is almost certainly very primitive, that may very well be independent of the other Gospels while corroborating what they say at many points, and that offers what is ultimately a rather different (though not wholly incompatible) spin on the Jesus story.[53]

Obviously, the implications of such a discovery would be phenomenal, surpassing even the discovery of the Dead Sea Scrolls or the noncanonical Gospels (see below). Of course, nothing quite like that scenario has actually occurred, but many scholars seem to be saying, "we do have such a book . . . perhaps we should not ignore it."

Apocryphal (noncanonical) Gospels

Many other Gospels besides Matthew, Mark, Luke, and John were written in the first few centuries of Christianity.[54] Those that did not ultimately become part of the New Testament are called apocryphal Gospels to distinguish them from the four canonical Gospels that Christians regard as scripture.[55] Many of these works have only recently been discovered, and some exist only in fragmentary form. A few are completely lost to us and are known only through quotations in the writings of church leaders, who often did not approve of them.

Historians, of course, are concerned not with the theological question of which books should be considered to be divinely inspired, but with the historical question of whether these books accurately reflect upon the life and teaching of Jesus. In general, however, the verdict of historians with regard to these apocryphal Gospels has been quite negative. Most of the books claim to have been authored by someone close to Jesus—one of his disciples or closest friends—but in no case is such a claim accepted by historical scholars. Rather, almost all the apocryphal Gospels appear to have been written in the second or third centuries. Their real value to historians lies not in what they reveal about Jesus but in what they disclose about the early church.[56] Many of them reflect an effort by some believers to claim the story of Jesus in support of political or theological agendas different from those that were sanctioned by the representatives of what eventually became known as "orthodox Christianity." Specifically, many of the works reflect the influence of Gnosticism, a pervasive religious philosophy that was the subject of much controversy in the developing church.[57] Other apocryphal Gospels seem to have been motivated by no more than curiosity at a popular level—they offer fanciful stories that fill in gaps left by the New Testament Gospels, relating, for instance, tales of miracles performed by Jesus when he was a small child.

Still, the apocryphal Gospels are of some interest to Jesus scholars. Scattered throughout these writings are sayings attributed to Jesus or occasional, miscellaneous comments about him that historians do take into serious consideration. For instance, a second-century work called the *Apocryphon of James* contains three otherwise unknown parables about the kingdom of God. One of them reads, "The kingdom of heaven is like an ear of grain after it had sprouted in a field. And when it had ripened, it scattered its fruit and again filled the field with ears for another year" (12:20–30). The main point of this parable (God's work spreads in a mysterious and miraculous way) is similar to that of agricultural parables that are found in the New Testament (Mark 4:3–9, 26–29, 30–32); it is possible that Jesus used a variety of slightly different images to make this point, and that this apocryphal parable recalls a variation on that theme that goes back to Jesus himself.

Furthermore, the disdain with which Jesus historians typically regard most of the apocryphal Gospels sometimes allows for two exceptions: the Gospel of Thomas and the Gospel of Peter. These two books, especially the former, are often distinguished from the other apocryphal Gospels as volumes that have the most potential for offering credible historical information about Jesus.

The Gospel of Thomas

The book popularly known as the Gospel of Thomas does not actually contain narratives about Jesus but is simply a collection of sayings attributed to Jesus. Scholars had known of this ancient book for some time, since it is referred to by certain early church leaders, but no copy of it was known to have survived. Then, in 1945, a complete manuscript was unearthed in the Egyptian city of Nag Hammadi. The text was written in Coptic and was recognized to be a translation of a Greek document, some fragments of which had been found previously. The book is thought to have been written originally in Edessa in Syria.

Often regarded as harboring a gnostic orientation, the Gospel of Thomas emphasizes wisdom motifs and the possibility of experiencing Paradise here and now. Jesus is presented as promoting radical asceticism, demanding, for instance, celibacy on the part of his followers. These themes may be reflected in the following quote, though the language is admittedly mysterious:

> Jesus said to [his disciples], "When you make the two one, and when you make the inside like the outside and the outside like the inside, and the above like the below, and when you make the male and the female one and the same, so that the male not be male nor the female be female; and when you fashion eyes in place of an eye, and a hand in place of a hand, and a foot in place of a foot, and a likeness in place of a likeness, then you will enter [the kingdom]." (Thom. 22:4–7)

The Gospel of Thomas claims to be the work of Didymus Judas Thomas who was not only one of Jesus' twelve disciples but also the twin brother of Jesus. No historian takes this claim seriously, but many do think that the book records some authentic sayings of Jesus. The group of scholars known as the Jesus Seminar identified three sayings in Thomas that they believe go back to Jesus and another forty sayings that are likely to represent authentic material. All three of the certain sayings, however, are almost exact parallels to words of Jesus found in the Synoptic Gospels (Thom. 20:2–3 = Matt. 13:31–32; Thom. 54 = Luke 6:20; Thom. 100:2 = Mark 12:17). The same is true for most of the sayings deemed "likely to be authentic." There are, however, two exceptions, brief parables found in Thomas that have no parallel in the New Testament:

> The kingdom of the father is like a woman who was carrying a jar full of meal. While she was walking on the road, still some distance from home, the handle of the jar broke and the meal emptied out behind her on the road. She did not realize it; she had noticed no accident. When she reached her house, she put the jar down and found it empty. (Thom. 97:1–4)

> The kingdom of the father is like a certain man who wanted to kill a powerful man. In his own house he drew his sword and stuck it into the wall

to find out whether his hand could carry through. Then he slew the powerful man. (Thom. 98:1–3)

In other cases, the version of a saying from Thomas is decidedly different from what is found in the New Testament. Compare the parable of the treasure from Thomas and Matthew:

The kingdom is like a man who had a hidden treasure in his field without knowing it. And after he died, he left it to his son. The son did not know about the treasure. He inherited the field and sold it. And the one who bought it went plowing and found the treasure. He began to lend money at interest to whomever he wished. (Thom. 109:1–3)	The kingdom of heaven is like a treasure hidden in a field, which someone found and hid; then, in his joy he goes and sells all that he has and buys the field. (Matt. 13:44)

As we will see in the chapters that follow, evaluation of the Gospel of Thomas is a matter of great controversy in historical Jesus research. The key issue, perhaps, is the question of when it was written. Some scholars, including many associated with the Jesus Seminar, have placed it firmly in the first century, around the same time as the four canonical writings.[58] The majority of historians, however, think that the Gospel of Thomas belongs to the second century and that it is probably dependent upon the canonical Gospels for much of its material.[59] If that is the case, its value as a historical source is greatly diminished, though, even then, the possibility that it preserves some authentic sayings of Jesus that are not found elsewhere does not have to be discarded completely.

The Gospel of Peter

Discovered in 1886, this work offers an account of Jesus' death and resurrection attributed to Jesus' premiere disciple. Only fragments of the original work remain, but these provide an account of Jesus' passion and resurrection different from the accounts found in the New Testament Gospels. In general, the account here seems to be more imaginative, describing events in nonliteral language intended to bring out their theological significance. An obvious example would be the book's most famous passage, an account of a walking, talking cross accompanying Jesus and two angels in a glorious exit from the tomb on Easter morning:

> They see three men emerge from the tomb, two of them supporting the other, with a cross following behind them. The heads of the two reached up to the sky, but the head of the one they were leading went up above the skies. And they heard a voice from the skies, "Have you preached to those who are asleep?" And a reply came from the cross, "Yes!" (Gospel of Peter 10:2–4)

Needless to say, historians are not impressed by the accuracy of such fanciful reports, but the overtly theological tone of the narrative does not necessarily mark it as later than the canonical Gospels. Indeed, John Dominic Crossan argues for the opposite: the earliest accounts of the passion and resurrection were the most obviously theological, and attempts to give the story the appearance of a historical record came later. Thus, Crossan, supported by Helmut Koester of Harvard University, argues that the Gospel of Peter drew upon a primitive version of the passion narrative (which he calls "the Cross Gospel") that also served as a source for what is found in other Gospels.[60] This view has not attracted wide support, but it has at least raised the possibility that the Gospel of Peter might have been composed in stages, with some of the material extending back to an early time.

Secret Gospel of Mark

We will make only brief mention here of another work that has sometimes been considered viable for Jesus studies but now seems to have been discredited to the extent that virtually no one appeals to it.[61] In 1958, a scholar named Morton Smith announced that while doing research at the Mar Saba monastery near Jerusalem he found an eighteenth-century copy of an otherwise unknown letter ascribed to Clement of Alexandria (d. 215) and that this letter described and quoted from an alternative version of the Gospel of Mark that the author of that Gospel had produced in Alexandria. The most extensive quotation speaks of Jesus spending the night with a naked young man and instructing the latter "in the mystery of the kingdom of God." This episode, with its homoerotic overtones, is said to be illustrative of things Mark did write in the Alexandrian version of his Gospel, though Clement assures his reader that the evangelist did not report the Lord's secret doings nor did he "divulge the things not to be uttered."

Smith photographed the manuscript of this letter but left the letter itself in the monastery—it was later photographed again in 1976 (by a library to which it had been transferred), but then it was apparently misplaced and has never been seen again. Smith and other scholars accepted the validity of this letter's claim, proposing that a Secret Gospel of Mark had in fact existed in the early church. Crossan argued that (contrary to Clement's claim) this now-lost secret version of Mark had in fact been the original edition—our current Gospel of Mark is a later, censored version.[62] Smith further interpreted the controversial text as implying that Jesus initiated the naked young man into a hallucinatory experience of heaven through which a freedom from the law was obtained; though Clement did not want to admit it, this freedom from the law "may have resulted in completion of the spiritual union by physical union."[63]

Most scholars, however, did not accept the validity of "Secret Mark," especially since the document attesting to it was not available for study. The dominant theory for years was either that Clement was referring to an aberrant second-century version of Mark produced by some heretical group of his day or that some eighteenth-century person had forged a letter in Clement's name quoting from a version of Mark's Gospel that in fact had never existed. Recent study, however, has led to a more ominous variation on the latter thesis: hand-writing analysis of the photographed manuscripts has convinced a majority of scholars that Morton Smith himself forged the document; he completely made up the idea of a variant version of Mark's Gospel and produced the copy of a letter from Clement as an academic hoax.[64] His motives for perpetrating such a hoax are unclear. An atheist, Smith was known for provoking convention-ally faithful Christians in ways that would discomfort them. It is also possible, however, that he viewed the hoax as a way of testing the establishment, to see if experts would be able to discern what he had done (or, indeed, to pick up on clues to his own authorship of the document that he is alleged to have scattered throughout its contents). There is not yet complete consensus among scholars that Secret Mark is a forgery,[65] but the possibility that it is such has been suf-ficiently established that it is now rarely appealed to by anyone engaged in his-torical Jesus studies.

Agrapha

In the first few centuries of Christianity, church leaders would often quote say-ings of Jesus that are not found in either the canonical or apocryphal Gospels. Apparently, these quotations were simply things that Jesus was remembered as having said, things that had been passed on orally without being written down. Today, they are called agrapha, from a Greek word that literally means "unwrit-ten" (though, of course, they were eventually put into writing, or else we would not have them). One example of an agraphon is found in the New Testament itself—in the book of Acts, Paul is preaching a sermon to elders in Ephesus and he tells them that throughout his ministry he has tried to remember the words of the Lord Jesus, who said, "It is more blessed to give than to receive" (Acts 20:35). Those words are not found in any Gospel, but the book of Acts portrays them as something that Jesus was known to have said.

Most of the agrapha are highly suspect in terms of historical authenticity: second-century theologians often seem to have remembered Jesus saying things that would support their particular theological position on issues that modern scholars do not actually think would have been matters of concern in first-century Judea or Galilee. In other cases, the agrapha are so similar to sayings pre-served in the Gospels that we might surmise the author was simply quoting the New Testament from memory in a way that was not quite exact. In a handful of instances, however, the agrapha do preserve sayings distinct from anything in the Gospels that nevertheless sound like something Jesus could have said. Thus, Clement of Alexandria reports that Jesus said, "Ask for the great things, and God will add to you what is small" (*Stromata* 1.24.258), and Origen likewise reports that Jesus said, "Ask for the heavenly things, and the earthly shall be added to you" (*On Prayer* 2). Tertullian quotes Jesus as saying, "No one can obtain the kingdoms of heaven who has not passed through temptation" (*On Baptism* 20). And the most widely quoted agraphon of all (with more than seventy citations) presents Jesus as saying, "Be competent [or, possibly, Be bold], money-changers!" (e.g., Origen, *Commentary on John* 19.7.12). What Jesus might have meant by this latter assertion is difficult to determine (no sure context for the remark has been discerned); still, the frequency of the attribution convinces many historians that Jesus probably did say something like this somewhere, sometime, for some reason.

CRITERIA OF AUTHENTICITY

As historical scholars review these sources, they apply a variety of criteria to determine which matters ought to be accorded the most legitimacy.[66] Obviously, the date and derivation of a source is a primary consideration. As we have indicated, there is not always unanimity on these points, but scholars will usually rely most heavily on those sources that they determine to be the earliest. Even then, however, individual points that the source recounts will be put to various tests. In the chapters that follow, we will see that some scholars rely more heavily on certain criteria than others. Some also modify the criteria that are defined here, in an attempt to apply them with more precision than their peers. For now, though, let us list nine factors that, in one way or another, come into consideration for almost all researchers studying the historical Jesus.[67]

Multiple Attestation

Matters are more likely to be accepted as historically accurate if they are attested by more than one source. For example, Jesus is portrayed as telling parables (though not the same ones) in Mark, Q, M, L, and Thomas. Thus, historians are inclined to accept as a well-attested fact the premise that Jesus taught in parables. If we ask about specific parables, however, the verdict would typically be very different: Jesus tells only the Parable of the Good Samaritan in the L material (Luke 10:30–37) and he tells only the Parable of the Ten Bridesmaids in the M material (Matt. 25:1–13). Thus, there would be no multiple attestation of sources to verify a claim that Jesus told either of these stories.

The significant point here is to find sources that are independent of each other, and, as we have seen, scholars do not always agree on which sources these would be. The story of Jesus feeding a multitude of five thousand people is found in Matthew, Mark, Luke, and John. The assumption of most scholars is that Matthew and Luke got the story from Mark and, so, these do not count as separate sources. But scholars are divided as to whether John had access to any of the Synoptic Gospels. If he did, then the feeding miracle is really only attested by one independent source (Mark, from which Matthew, Luke, and

John all copied). If he did not, then it has two sources in its favor (Mark and John).

Though all scholars make use of this important criterion, most do not think it essential for determining that an event is historical. Wright observes that the number of times that something "happens to turn up in the records is a very haphazard index of its likely historicity."[68] In other words, no matter is to be judged nonhistorical simply because it is mentioned only once. But some matters have *such* widespread support that almost no scholar would question them. The notion that Jesus had a disciple named Simon who sometimes went by the nickname "Rock" (*Peter* in Greek; *Cephas* in Aramaic) is attested by passages ascribed to Mark, John, M, and L, as well as in passages in the letters of Paul.

Memorable Content or Form

Material is more likely to be judged authentic if it is couched in terms that would have been easy to remember. The assumption here is that almost nothing concerning Jesus was written down during his lifetime. The culture in which he lived was given mainly to oral transmission, that is, to conveying information by word of mouth. Accordingly, historians think it more likely that people would have remembered short sayings, such as proverbs ("Prophets are not without honor, except in their hometown," Mark 6:4) or beatitudes ("Blessed are the meek, for they will inherit the earth," Matt. 5:5). Because stories are intrinsically memorable, parables tend to score high by this criterion also. Other factors that make material memorable include the use of humor, exaggeration, or paradox. In one instance, Jesus is said to have accused the Pharisees of straining out gnats and then swallowing camels (Matt. 23:24). In another, he bemoans hypocrites who worry about a speck in someone else's eye but don't notice the log that is in their own (Matt. 7:3–5). Sayings or deeds may also be judged memorable if their very content was shocking or unexpected, such as Jesus' call to "turn the other cheek" when anyone strikes you (Matt. 5:39) or his directive to a prospective disciple to "Let the dead bury the dead" (Luke 9:60). By contrast, long discourses such as those attributed to Jesus in John's Gospel are usually deemed too complex to have been remembered and passed on in the form that we now have them. But this criterion, like all the others, is applied differently by different scholars. Some critics insist that people who live in a primarily oral culture develop keen memories and are capable of remembering vast quantities of information word for word.

Language and Environment

Material is more likely to be deemed historical if it is compatible with the language and environment of the period it describes (the life of Jesus in Galilee/Judea) rather than the period of the source itself. The Gospels were probably written in various cities of the Roman Empire in settings different from that in which Jesus lived. If what they report of Jesus is accurate, historians say, it should be free of anachronism. Sayings of Jesus that would make more sense applied to Gentile merchants living in cities than to Jewish peasants in rural areas may be regarded with suspicion. For example, in Mark's Gospel Jesus says, "Whoever divorces his wife and marries another commits adultery against her; and if she divorces her husband and marries another, she commits adultery" (Mark 10:11–12). Under Jewish law, only husbands were normally allowed to initiate divorce. The second half of this saying, therefore, could be anachronistic. Many historians would conclude that Jesus is not likely to have warned Jewish peasant women against divorcing their husbands, since in their culture such a thing was impossible. Under Roman law, however, either the husband or the wife could initiate divorce, which could explain why the author of Mark's Gospel may have adapted Jesus' saying to address the context in which that Gospel was written.

Jesus' famous Parable of the Sower provides a good example for how many historians would apply this criterion both positively and negatively. In the Gospel of Mark, that parable is related in two parts: first, Jesus tells the story of a Sower casting seed on four different kinds of soil (Mark 4:3–9); later, he explains the story by indicating the allegorical meaning that each type of soil was intended to represent (Mark 4:14–20). Historical scholars often note that the parable itself accurately represents agricultural practices in first-century Galilee: farmers really did broadcast seed on unplowed ground. Since this method of sowing was not widely practiced elsewhere in the Roman Empire, the story fits better with the context in which Jesus lived than with the context in which Mark probably wrote. The explanation for the parable, however, likens what happens to the seed to the various ways in which people respond to proclamation of "the word" (including, in one instance, embracing the proclaimed message but then falling away when persecution comes). Now, historians are suspicious: many would say that this interpretation of the story would be more meaningful to Christians who had seen church members fail under persecution than it would have been to Jewish peasants in the world of Jesus. Of course, these points can be contested, but most Jesus historians would maintain that the Parable of the Sower itself is more easy to authenticate in accord with the criterion of language and environment than is the potentially anachronistic interpretation of the story.

Embarrassment

Material in the Gospels is sometimes judged to be historically accurate if it is likely to have caused some discomfort among the early Christians who treasured the earliest traditions about Jesus and wrote them down. The point of this criterion is simply that Christians would not have made up stories that caused problems for the church. For example, the Synoptic Gospels indicate that Jesus did not encourage his disciples to practice fasting, as did most pious Jews of the day. Indeed, this demands some kind of explanation, since the original readers of these Gospels would have probably considered fasting to be a good thing: Mark's Gospel indicates that it was only because the disciples were enjoying a brief interim when Jesus ("the bridegroom") was present with them—fasting would of course be encouraged for followers of Jesus when that was no longer the case. In such instances, the Gospel author clearly would have had no incentive for inventing the tradition about Jesus that he is reporting; rather, he must struggle to explain some piece of the tradition that he acknowledges to be ostensibly accurate.

Other examples for application of this criterion would include (1) reports that women traveled with Jesus and his disciples (Mark 15:40–41; Luke 8:2–3)—this was potentially scandalous, so the Gospels must explain the women were needed to provide for the disciples in certain nonscandalous ways; (2) accounts that indicate Jesus did not have the full support of his own family members throughout his ministry (Mark 3:21, 31–35)—this was an embarrassing acknowledgment for a church in which those family members eventually came to be highly revered.

Perhaps the most oft-cited example of the criterion of embarrassment applies to the Gospel account of Jesus being baptized by John the Baptist (Mark 1:9; compare Matt. 3:13–15). This story would have been potentially embarrassing to Christians because (1) John's baptism was for those who repented of their sins, and Christians claimed Jesus was sinless; and (2) many who were baptized by John were thought to be John's disciples, and Christians claimed that Jesus was Lord of all, not the follower of any earthly teacher. Thus, the story is told in Matthew's Gospel in a way that tries to address some of these concerns (Matt. 3:13–15). Some historians might think Matthew is doing a first-century version of "spin control," but few would doubt the basic fact that seems to need controlling: Jesus *was* baptized by John.

The criterion of embarrassment would not help to establish the historicity of things about Jesus that the church would have taken delight in reporting. The Gospels regularly claim that Jesus bested various Jewish opponents in debate (e.g., Mark 12:13–37). There would be nothing awkward or embarrassing about reporting such triumphs since at the time the Gospels were written Christians were often engaged in such debates with Jewish opponents themselves and would have been only too happy to relay stories of how their guy had always won such contests. Of course, the mere fact that a story is *not* embarrassing does not indicate it cannot also be historical—the point, simply, is that only certain material in the Gospels can be historically *authenticated* in accord with this criterion.

Indifference (or Irrelevance)

Material is more likely to be deemed historically reliable if its contents would have been a matter of relative indifference to the author of the source in which it is found. Historical scholars are by nature suspicious. They must ask whether the Gospel writers are reporting what Jesus actually said and did or whether they are attributing to Jesus things that will support their interests and promote their own agendas. Scholars are always on the lookout for reports that would not serve those interests or promote those agendas, and they tend to be dismissive of anything that would especially serve those interests or promote those agendas.

When applied in a positive sense (for inclusion of material), this criterion may simply appear to be a broader version of the criterion of embarrassment, granting historical potential to anything that does not serve the author's purpose, regardless of whether such inclusion would have caused actual embarrassment. For example, the Gospel of Mark indicates that Jesus was a carpenter (Mark 6:3): the author of Mark's Gospel probably would not have considered this embarrassing, but neither does he consider it particularly relevant for theology or anything else. It is simply reported, as a matter of indifference. Unlike the criterion of embarrassment, however, the criterion of indifference is often applied negatively to exclude material. For example, Matthew's Gospel reports that Jesus, who is usually said to be from Nazareth, was actually born in Bethlehem (Matt. 2:1); this is clearly something that Matthew would have wanted people to believe about Jesus in order that they might realize Jesus' birth fulfilled scripture and granted him messianic credentials (Matt. 2:4–6; cf. Mic. 5:2). Likewise, when Matthew 28:18–20 presents Jesus commissioning his followers to evangelize the Gentile world, it must be recognized that Matthew is claiming the historical Jesus essentially authorized the very mission in which his congregation is currently engaged—skeptical historians might be suspicious regarding the authenticity of such a claim.[69] The fact that these claims (Jesus was born in Bethlehem; Jesus authorized a Gentile mission) accord so closely with Matthew's own interests leads historians to suspect that such reports might not be historically accurate. At the very least, historians would say, these reports cannot be historically verified on the basis of the criterion of indifference (though, hypothetically, they might be established on the basis of other criteria).

At this point, we must comment on a matter of terminology that could cause confusion. Many historical Jesus scholars now use the expression "criterion of dissimilarity (or distinctiveness)" to refer to what is here described as the criterion of indifference (or irrelevance). What they mean, apparently, is that a matter of indifference is "dissimilar from the interests of the Gospel author"—but the expression "criterion of dissimilarity" has typically been used to mean something else. Consistency on this matter is not likely to be forthcoming, so readers must consider context to determine what any individual author means by the expression "criterion of dissimilarity."

Dissimilarity (or Distinctiveness)

Material is more likely to be deemed historically reliable if it is distinctive with regard to both the context of its purported origin and the context of its preservation.

With Jesus material, this means that sayings or deeds attributed to Jesus in the Gospels may be deemed historically authentic if that material presents Jesus in a way that sets him apart from both Palestinian Judaism and early Christianity. This criterion may have been first formulated by Rudolf Bultmann,[70] though it came to be associated with his students (who famously split with him over the question of whether a historical Jesus quest was theologically advisable) and with Norman Perrin.

The logic behind this criterion may be that, first, material attributed to Jesus that is *not* dissimilar from the world of Palestinian Judaism could represent material from his environment that was mistakenly attributed to him. For example, the Gospels portray Jesus as teaching the Golden Rule (Matt. 7:12), but this is something that many Jewish teachers might have espoused—it is possible that a popular proverb or saying came to be associated with Jesus as stories about him were passed on through oral tradition. Second, this criterion recognizes that material attributed to Jesus that is *not* dissimilar from early Christianity could represent thoughts and ideas that Christians retrojected back on to Jesus. For example, when Jesus says that the details of his betrayal, arrest, and impending death are unfolding in a manner that will ensure the fulfillment of scripture (Matt. 26:54, 56), many scholars would say he appears to be espousing what later Christian exegetes would say about those events.

A positive example of authentication would involve stories in the Gospels that present Jesus as eating with tax collectors and other social outcasts (e.g., Mark 1:13–17). We have no record of anyone else in Jesus' social world doing this, nor was the practice continued in the early church. Most likely, then, it was a unique and memorable facet of Jesus' ministry.

The use of this criterion has become highly controversial in Jesus studies. As indicated, the New Quest movement in the latter half of the twentieth century applied the criterion of dissimilarity vigorously in order to come up with an "irreducible minimum" of material that is reported in the Gospels but that could not have derived from either Palestinian Judaism or early Christianity and, so, had to derive from Jesus. There was a logic to this approach but, in recent years, many scholars have said that common sense dictates that much of what Jesus said and did probably accorded well with his Palestinian context. Today, some scholars say that only dissimilarity from early Christianity should be required; dissimilarity from Judaism is asking too much of a truly Jewish Jesus.[71] But others press the point even further: the early Christians probably copied Jesus in as many ways as possible, so we should expect Jesus to be similar to both Palestinian Judaism and early Christianity in key respects. The counter-response to that argument is to claim that historical science is by nature a minimalist enterprise: we will never be able to ascertain everything about Jesus but are only able to determine what was distinctive about him. Historians, so this argument goes, are most interested in discovering what was unique about Jesus, what set him apart from others. The reply to *that* point would be that historical appreciation for Jesus' accomplishments needs to recognize his influences and also needs to determine how his ideas were implemented and carried forward by his followers. If Jesus is defined only by those features of his life that were not continued in early Christianity, his significance and impact will appear necessarily slight. Indeed, if future historians were to apply the criterion of dissimilarity to Martin Luther King Jr., they would count as historical only those aspects of King's life and teaching that were dissimilar from the interests of the civil rights movement: the resulting portrait of "the historical Martin Luther King Jr." would be of a man who had nothing to say about civil rights. In a similar vein the criterion of dissimilarity, so these scholars argue, guarantees a caricatured Jesus who has little in common with anyone who might have influenced him (first-century Jews) or who might have been influenced by him (early Christians).

And so the argument continues. At this point, few scholars are adamant extremists for either position. Most recognize that this criterion can be used *positively* to establish the historical authenticity of things about Jesus that were particularly distinctive or unique. But scholars have grown increasingly reticent about using the criterion negatively, to exclude from consideration things that might be legitimately representative of Jesus' legacy or enduring influence. There is a growing sense that matters regarding Jesus that are *not* dissimilar from Palestinian Judaism or early Christianity should be further examined in terms of the criterion of plausible influence.

Plausible Influence

Material regarding Jesus is more likely to be deemed historically reliable if it strongly reflects the Jewish context in which Jesus works and also helps to explain or account for matters pertinent to early Gentile Christianity. This criterion essentially turns the criterion of dissimilarity on its head, arguing that similarity in both directions is as much a mark of reliability as similarity in neither direction. The logic runs something like this: items in the Jesus tradition that are not reflective of either Palestinian Judaism or early Christianity have no obvious alternative origin and so should be regarded as revelatory of (unique) attributes of the historical Jesus (so, the criterion of dissimilarity); but, items in the tradition that are reflective of both Palestinian Judaism and early Christianity also lack alternative origin apart from the historical Jesus who was the transitional figure between those two phenomena: the historical Jesus constitutes the primary (if not the solitary) point of convergence between those diverse social movements and, so, it is plausible that matters attributed to Jesus reflective of such convergence are revelatory of the historical person.

This criterion of plausible influence is the most recently developed of the criteria discussed in this chapter and, for the most part, has only been explicitly employed in twenty-first-century scholarship. As indicated above, it developed as a corrective on what was thought to be a narrow application of the criterion of dissimilarity. This criterion has been given its best-known expression (in slightly different forms) by two prominent scholars, Gerd Theissen (who speaks of "the criterion of historical plausibility")[72] and N. T. Wright (who speaks of "the double criterion of similarity/dissimilarity"—see page 203). Many others have followed them in an effort to recognize that the historical Jesus should be viewed as influential on early Christianity without naively assuming that *everything* in early Christianity derived from him. The criterion suggests that the elements in early Christianity that represent the most plausible influence of Jesus are those that appear to derive from the Jewish milieu of Judea and Galilee in which Jesus lived and ministered. For example, early Christianity seized on the imagery of God as a heavenly Father in a manner that surpassed anything found in Judaism or Greco-Roman religion. But in the Gospels, Jesus is not simply represented as calling God "Father" (something that could represent a retrojection of language popular in the church on to the lips of Jesus); rather, he is specifically represented as calling God *Abba* (Mark 14:36), an Aramaic Jewish term for "father" that the Gentile church did not use and would have had no reason to place on the lips of Jesus). Thus, it seems plausible that Jesus' historical use of *Abba* language for God (within a context of Palestinian Judaism) influenced the subsequent popularity of Father imagery for God in early Gentile Christianity.

To get a better grasp of how this criterion is applied, let us consider two completely different claims about Jesus offered by the New Testament Gospels: (1) the Gospels regularly report that Jesus spoke about some agent of God called "the Son of Man" (Mark 2:10, 28; 8:31, 38; 10:45); and (2) the Gospel of John indicates that Jesus spoke about the liberating effects of knowing the truth (e.g., John 8:32, "you will know the truth and the truth will set you free"). Both of these claims might be regarded as potential influences on later developments in Christianity: Christians came to believe that Jesus himself *was* the Son of Man, and they came to believe that knowing the truth about Jesus would be liberating. But such a recognition establishes similarity in only one direction—hypothetically, the Christian beliefs could have determined the reports about Jesus rather than the other way around. So, historians check for continuity in the *other* direction. As it turns out, the first of these two examples does bear continuity with Palestinian Judaism, since the term "Son of Man" derives from Hebrew scripture and was used with religious meaning by Jews (but not, outside of Christianity, by Gentiles). Such continuity cannot be established, however, for the second example: Palestinian Judaism is not known to have spoken of the liberating effects of knowledge in a manner anywhere near as prominent as was current in the Greco-Roman world in which Gentile Christianity was born. What would a historian employing the criterion of plausible influence conclude? In the first instance, the fact that Gentile Christians found the Jewish concept of "the Son of Man" to be meaningful suggests that Jesus himself probably employed that language: the historical fact that Jesus spoke about the Son of Man inspired a Gentile church that revered his teaching to adopt Jewish imagery that otherwise would have been ignored. But in the second instance, it would have been very possible for Gentile Christians (or Hellenistic Jewish ones) to have employed language from their own world to understand Jesus, recasting his claims in terminology that he did not actually use. Indeed, historians may think this *more* likely than the supposition that Jesus the Palestinian Jew stated his claims in language that would be far more meaningful, later on, to Greeks and Romans than to the Jewish peasants he was ostensibly addressing. Thus, the criterion of plausible influence would help to establish the authenticity of Jesus' use of Son of Man language but would not help to establish the authenticity of his sayings about the liberating effects of knowledge.

Coherence

Finally, material that cannot be established as historical by such criteria as those given above may nevertheless be judged authentic if it is generally consistent with the information that is so derived. In Jesus studies, historical critics test the validity of uncertain elements in the tradition by comparing them with other elements that they have previously decided to be authentic. This criterion provides something of a catch-all category for broadening the circle of what is included. For example, an agraphon attributed to Jesus by Origen that is also found in the Gospel of Thomas is often regarded as authentic: "Whoever is near me is near the fire; whoever is far from me, is far from the Father's kingdom" (Origen, *Homilies on Jeremiah* 3.3; cf. Thom. 82). Although nothing quite like this is found in the other Gospels, it sounds like the sort of thing Jesus might have said (compare Mark 9:49; 12:34).

By contrast, Jesus is sometimes quoted as sayings things in a potentially reliable source that do not cohere well with what has been established as almost certainly reliable information concerning him. A passage unique to Matthew's Gospel (ascribed to the M material) presents Jesus as telling his disciples to regard an unrepentant sinner the way they would "a tax collector" (Matt. 18:17). Attribution of this saying to Jesus does not cohere with the well-attested tradition that Jesus in fact had a welcoming attitude toward tax collectors.

In any case, what is determined to be authentic by this criterion of coherence is usually regarded as secondary, less certain than what proves reliable according to other criteria. However, at least one scholar we will discuss, N. T. Wright, has developed a method that makes "coherence with a workable hypothesis" a primary consideration for historical reconstruction. That broadens the application of the criterion considerably compared to the usual sense of "coherence with previously established data" and allows for inclusion of more material than would be recognized by other historians.

Figure 4. Criteria for Determining Historical Reliability in Jesus Research

Criterion	Passes This Criterion	Does Not Pass This Criterion
Multiple Attestation Material correlates with the witness of other, independent sources.	*Jesus told parables—* several different sources portray Jesus as telling parables.	*Jesus told the Parable of the Good Samaritan—* this particular parable is in only one source ("L").
Memorable Content or Form Material is couched in terms easy to remember (e.g., brief, humorous, paradoxical, or shocking).	*Jesus told a man, "Let the dead bury the dead" (Luke 9:60)—*the saying is provocative and would have been easy to remember.	the *"High-Priestly prayer" that Jesus is said to have prayed on the night of his arrest (John 17:1–26)—*it is long, rambling, and would have been difficult for anyone to have remembered.
Language and Environment Material is compatible with the language and culture of the period it describes (rather than reflecting the language and culture for the time and place in which the source was written).	*the Parable of the Sower (Mark 4:3–8)—*the parable accurately reflects agricultural practices in rural Galilee that would not have been widely known elsewhere in the Roman empire.	*explanation of the Parable of the Sower (Mark 4:13–20)—*it contains language that derives from the early church ("the word") and compares what happens to the seed to the effects of Christian preaching.
Embarrassment Material would have been awkward for the church to remember and report.	*Jesus was baptized by John the Baptist (Matt. 3:13–15)—*this is awkward to report and requires some explanation (since it could be taken to mean that Jesus wanted to repent and/or become John's disciple).	*stories in which Jesus bests his Jewish opponents in debate (e.g., Mark 12:13–37)—*the early church was engaged in disputes with Judaism and no doubt found these stories to be particularly appealing.
Indifference or Irrelevance Material would not serve the particular interests or agenda of the Gospel author.	*Jesus was a carpenter (Mark 6:3)—*reporting this tidbit of information does not serve Mark's theological or other purposes.	*Jesus commissioned his followers to "make disciples of all nations" (Matt. 28:16–20)—*Matthew wanted to encourage such a mission.

Criterion (cont.)	Passes This Criterion (cont.)	Does Not Pass This Criterion (cont.)
Dissimilarity or Distinctiveness Material cannot be easily attributed to influence of Palestinian Judaism or to early Christianity.	*Jesus ate with tax-collectors and sinners (e.g. Mark 2:15–17; Luke 15:1–2)*—neither Palestinian Jews nor early Christians advocated such a practice.	*Jesus said that certain things happened to him in order that scripture might be fulfilled (Matt. 26:54, 56)*—early Christians also said this about things that happened to Jesus.
Plausible Influence Material reflects the enduring influence of Jesus by explaining how a matter rooted in Palestinian Judaism would become a prominent concern in Gentile Christianity.	*Jesus spoke about the Son of Man (Mark 2:10, 28)*—early Gentile Christians made much of this term but would not have been inclined to favor such a distinctively Jewish concept on their own (i.e., unless Jesus had used it).	*Jesus told people that knowing the truth would set them free (John 8:32)*—the early Christian church was concerned with the liberating effects of knowledge but in ways that owed more to Greek philosophy than Jewish tradition.
Coherence Material that cannot be established by the above criteria is nevertheless consistent with information that is so derived.	*Jesus says in the Gospel of Thomas, "Whoever is near me is near the fire; whoever is far from me is far from the Kingdom" (Thom. 82)*—this resembles sayings of Jesus found in more reliable sources (Mark 9:49; 12:34).	*Jesus implores his followers to regard an impenitent sinner as "a tax collector" (Matt. 18:17)*—this does not cohere well with knowledge that Jesus was famously accepting of tax collectors.
Congruity with Modern View of Reality Material does not require acceptance of ideas that contradict modern views of reality.	*Jesus became a popular teacher though he lacked professional training*—such things are known to happen in our world.	*Jesus was raised from the dead*—modern science says people who are dead for three days do not come back to life.

An Unstated Criterion: Congruity with a Modern View of Reality

Some observers contend that, in addition to these criteria, most histori-ans operate with another, often-unstated criterion: the adoption of a post-Enlightenment worldview. In short, material is more likely to be regarded as historically reliable if it does not require acceptance of ideas that contradict modern views of reality. Some historians seem to operate with a view that determines some things reported in the Bible not to have happened because they could not happen. An a priori judgment about what is possible tran-scends any consideration of how many sources attest to the event, whether it was potentially embarrassing for the church to report it, or anything else. This prejudice (if we may call it that) does not apply primarily to claims regarding what may be considered "extraordinary"—historians recognize that people who are still regarded as significant two thousand years after they lived probably did some extraordinary things. The Gospels maintain that Jesus, a carpenter's son from a small village, became famous as a teacher throughout all of Galilee: that could have happened and, so, historians would be willing to examine the evidence for the claim. But when the Gospels maintain that Jesus walked on water or changed water into wine, most historians would not even bother to inquire as to whether such claims can be historically verified: history, they would claim, must respect the basic "laws of nature." Thus the case is closed before it even opens.

Such a perspective, furthermore, is not limited to non-Christian histori-ans engaged in the study of Jesus. Even historians who personally espouse the Christian faith will often impose a "methodological limitation" on what can be affirmed in accord with the rules of historical inquiry. For example, many historians who personally believe that Jesus rose from the dead would nevertheless claim that the resurrection of Jesus cannot be regarded as a his-torically verifiable event; regardless of whether resurrection accounts meet the criteria discussed above, our current understanding of the world tells us that people who have been dead for three days do not come back to life. Thus, even Christian historians would usually (but not always) claim that the resurrection of Jesus must be regarded as something that transcends his-torical analogy, necessitating consideration from a perspective of faith (his-torically informed faith, perhaps, but something more than just historical science). This is *not* the same thing as saying, "It didn't happen"; it is simply saying, "If it *did* happen, then something occurred that historical science is not able to investigate, something on which historians (when speaking *as historians*) would be wise to offer no comment." Some readers of this book will probably think that this is how history should be done, while others may think such biases are unjustified and that historians should not have to comply with them. Both types of readers will meet friends and foes before we are done.

CONCLUSION

No matter how hard they work, no matter what attention they give to sources and criteria, Jesus scholars have a hard row to hoe. The degree of personal investment alluded to in the introduction to this book (page 3) affects not only the scholars but their audience as well. Russell Shorto, a journalist who by his own admission is normally more at home in the world of *GQ* than Q, wrote a book on Jesus scholarship for general readers. As he did the usual publicity tour associated with such publications, he was amazed at the comments of average Americans:

> I'm Jewish, and we Jews have always known that Jesus received esoteric black magic . . .
>
> I think it's fascinating that these so-called scholars continue to repress the known fact that Jesus was black . . .
>
> Any astronomer will tell you that the alignment of the planets at the time of the Nativity . . .
>
> Why are these experts afraid to admit that Jesus' bloodline passed to the Knights Templar . . . ?[73]

Everyone, Shorto says, seemed to think they had the inside scoop on Jesus: he was from the future; he was an extraterrestrial; he was gay; he was married; he was actually a woman. Perhaps Shorto should not have been surprised. Jesus still gets more headlines than many rock stars or other celebrities in supermarket tabloids, which regularly scream about signs of his return or the appearance of his image on screen doors and tortillas. The Jesus of history can be a hard sell.

And then there are those who will suspect something *else* is involved, that behind all the academic platitudes and scholarly research lurks a controlling sinister force. Shorto recalls a question he received after explaining the attention Jesus scholars give to Hellenism, the influence of Greek culture on the Roman Empire during the time of Jesus. "Don't you think it's just a little bit odd," a woman inquired, "that the word *Hellenism* begins with *Hell*?"[74]

Chapter 3

Snapshots: Contemporary Images of Jesus

Who was Jesus? That disarmingly simple question is . . . asked passionately by Christians—and non-Christians—of the most widely varying theological stances. While certainly not all of that interest is in touch with the academic quest for the historical Jesus, all who seek to answer the question have a vision of who Jesus was, whether that person is a television evangelist who talks about JEE-sus with every breath or an Orthodox priest who almost shudders to say the name.

—Walter F. Taylor Jr.[1]

I asked my class, "Who was Jesus?" Most said he was a religious figure. Some said philosopher, comparing him to Socrates. Then there was Jesus as political leader, with one student comparing him to Mao and Stalin.

—Tyler Roberts[2]

Remember that playground ditty sung out by children jumping rope? "Rich man, poor man, beggar man, thief / Doctor, lawyer, merchant, chief." Scholarly theories about the historical Jesus have by now multiplied to a tangled mass every bit as disparate: "Wandering preacher, zealot, activist, magician / Cynic peasant, prophet, wisdom-logician." (The rhythm works out after about a dozen tries.)

—Robert W. Yarbrough[3]

In chapters 4 through 9, we will examine six major biographical studies of Jesus that have been produced (or are being produced) by historical scholars.

First, however, we are going to examine a few of the images for Jesus that have been suggested by modern scholars. The studies discussed in this chapter are not intended to be comprehensive; the scholars who present them do not necessarily claim that the image they describe offers a complete picture of who Jesus was. In most cases, they are calling attention to an aspect that they find especially significant or one that they may feel has been neglected. All these studies have been influential. That is, the scholars presented in the following chapters have had to wrestle with the ideas presented in this chapter. They have had to either incorporate these aspects of Jesus into their overall portraits or explain why they think particular images are not fitting.

JESUS THE SOCIAL PROPHET (RICHARD A. HORSLEY)

According to Richard Horsley, Jesus stood in the classic tradition of Israelite prophets, which is to say that he must be understood as one who was fundamentally concerned with the social and political circumstances of his day. Popular Christianity attempts to view Jesus in "religious" terms rather than "political" ones, but these categories are artificial and do not do justice to the social context or sacred tradition that informed Jesus' ministry. Horsley is professor of religion at the University of Massachusetts and is the author of *Jesus and the Spiral of Violence*, in which his main views concerning the historical Jesus were first set forth.[4] For a full appreciation of his ideas, however, this volume must be read along with *Bandits, Prophets, and Messiahs* and *Sociology and the Jesus Movement*, two works in which Horsley discusses the world with which Jesus and his followers were engaged.[5]

Horsley uses a model drawn from the social sciences to reconstruct a portrait of the political and social circumstances in Palestine at the time of Jesus.[6] Put simply, the situation was one of colonial class struggle. About 90 percent of the population consisted of rural peasants who were dominated and oppressed economically by a minority of urban elites. Horsley details multiple layers of taxation that helped those in power to maintain their status while guaranteeing that the poor would only get poorer. This situation created a "spiral of violence" as oppression led to protest, which would evoke counter-repression, which would, in turn, inspire revolt. In this context, social bandits and popular prophets arose, including Jesus.

Jesus himself was a peasant, and within his social environment, his ministry may be understood as fomenting a social revolution on behalf of peasants. He blessed the poor and condemned the rich (Luke 6:20, 24). He talked about forgiveness of debts (Matt. 18:23–33; Luke 11:4) and lending without expectation of profit (Matt. 5:42; Luke 6:34–35).[7] He spoke of abolishing hierarchical and patriarchal relationships (Matt. 10:37; 23:8–9; Mark 3:35; 10:43–44).[8] He threatened the temple, which the elite priestly establishment had turned into "an instrument of imperial legitimation and control of a subjected people."[9] It is a solid historical fact, says Horsley, "that Jesus was executed as a rebel against the Roman order."[10] The charges against him, furthermore, were valid. Jesus *was* stirring up the people. From the perspective of the political authorities, the crucifixion of Jesus was not a mistake. He was not just a religious teacher concerned with only spiritual matters; he posed a genuine threat to the social order of his day.[11]

Horsley distinguishes the *social* revolution he believes Jesus wished to foment from what is often called a *political* revolution. A political revolution, he says, is "top down," involving a replacement of leadership. Jesus had no plans to overthrow political authorities, to drive the imperial forces out of Palestine, or to effect any other change of that order. He probably believed, says Horsley, that God would do this, and do it soon, but he recognized it as something only God could do.[12] Rather, Jesus sought to change society from the "bottom up." His aim was to reorganize and renew peasant society in a way that would respect the covenantal traditions of Israel.

Jesus did not practice, organize, or advocate armed resistance, but Horsley refrains from calling him a pacifist. He maintains that Jesus did not commend or insist upon nonviolence either. The famous "turn the other cheek" passage (Matt. 5:39) referred to nonretaliation against other members of the peasant community. Likewise, the command to love one's enemies (Matt. 5:44) referred to local enemies, not to foreign military powers. Jesus counseled peasants to work out their differences peacefully and stick together, but he did not seek to dissuade resistance to Roman oppression.[13]

One of the more controversial but far-reaching aspects of Horsley's construction is that he regards the kingdom of God in Jesus' preaching as a social and political phenomenon. As a metaphor for God's transforming action, it refers always to the liberating use of power within history, and "it is important to keep in mind that the 'kingdom of God' is a political metaphor and symbol. In Jesus' preaching and action the kingdom clearly includes the social-economic-political substance of human relations as willed by God."[14] Horsley, then, does not think that Jesus spoke much, if at all, about life beyond death. He offered no vision of life other than that which is to be found in this world. Salvation for Jesus meant peace and justice, here and now.

About twenty years after the publication of *Jesus and the Spiral of Violence*, Horsley followed up with two more books called *Jesus in Context: Power, People, and Performance* and *Jesus and the Powers: Conflict, Covenant, and the Hope of the Poor*.[15] Now, he grounded his previous portrait of Jesus in an understanding of social history in a primarily oral society. Drawing on the work of political scientist James C. Scott,[16] Horsley theorized that the peasant populations of Israel were keepers of an oral "little tradition" that told their story in a manner antithetical to the "great tradition," or official version of history put into writing and propagated by the elite. As an act of defiance, peasants (including Jesus) were adept at employing "hidden transcripts" that kept their subversive rule of reality alive beneath an apparent compliance with and deference to the ruling class. Horsley interprets much of the Jesus tradition preserved in Mark and Q as illustrative of such hidden transcripts.

Horsley is usually praised by other scholars for trying to interpret Jesus in relation to his social and political environment. "More than any other North American scholar," writes Marcus Borg, "Horsley has made Jesus' engagement with his social world central to his portrait of Jesus."[17] Borg, Crossan, and Wright all make use of Horsley's insights in developing their portraits of Jesus (though of these three, Wright is the most cautious and critical).[18] Other modern scholars, however, think he overplays the this-worldly nature of Jesus' concerns, failing to account for Jewish eschatological expectations. Sanders and Meier in particular offer this critique.

Ben Witherington thinks Horsley overestimates the revolutionary climate of Galilee in Jesus' day and gives too little attention to the influence of "the literate." Furthermore, Witherington sees no reason to presume Jesus was involved in reforming village structures; the Gospels all portray his teaching as directed to the community of his own disciples, not to villagers in general or, for instance, to local village authorities.[19] Wright thinks Horsley's "frequent suggestion that the real impetus for revolution came from social rather than theological factors" poses a false antithesis that misunderstands the fundamentally religious milieu of first-century Palestine.[20]

Some of Horsley's minor points have not fared well. The notion that love for enemies is intended only as a local ethic without more general application is criticized by Walter Wink.[21] Horsley also thinks the Gospel accounts of Jesus associating with tax collectors are not historically accurate.[22] Such persons, he says, were Jewish traitors, collaborators with the Roman powers, and Jesus would not have compromised his solidarity with the oppressed by making friends with oppressors. But Horsley is probably the only historical Jesus scholar to deny the historicity of this part of the tradition, which most find well attested and established by the criterion of dissimilarity (there is little evidence that either Palestinian Judaism or early Christianity viewed association with such outcasts as commendable).

These critiques aside, the main contours of Horsley's projection of Jesus as a social prophet are widely accepted. Most historical Jesus scholars today view Jesus as one whose ministry must be understood at least on some level as a response to the political situation of his day. A major study by R. David Kaylor builds noticeably on Horsley's contributions. Kaylor attempts to interpret much of Jesus' teaching in ways that address the sort of political situation described by Horsley. Some of these interpretations are innovative, if not surprising. For example, Kaylor suggests that the story of a farmer who lets weeds and wheat grow together until the harvest (Matt. 13:24–30) is not an illustration of how God withholds judgment until the end time, but a joke depicting the poor agricultural strategies of large estate owners who buy up the land of local farmers but don't know how to care for it properly.[23] Similarly, William R. Herzog III has drawn on Horsley and Scott to interpret virtually all of Jesus' parables (and other sayings as well) as codified language that villagers could understand in ways that their oppressors might not.[24] For example, the parable of the workers in the vineyard (Matt. 20:1–15) is not about God showing mercy to all alike but, rather, is an exposé of how sadistic landowners torment their day-laborers, teasing them into thinking they will receive more than starvation wages for a day's work only to dash those hopes. In many such ways, Horsley's basic attempt to relate Jesus' ideas to concrete social situations rather than to spiritualized religious themes has been influential in historical Jesus scholarship.

JESUS THE CHARISMATIC JEW (GEZA VERMES)

When Geza Vermes published his book *Jesus the Jew* in 1973, the very title seemed to foretell a new day in historical Jesus research. No one doubted, of course, that Jesus was Jewish, but the trend in most historical studies up to that point had been to play down his connections to Judaism and emphasize the conflicts, the features that set him apart as the forebear of a new religion. Vermes's book presented Jesus as more Jewish than Christian, a shift that seemed to parallel moves the author had made in his own life. Born into a Hungarian Jewish family, Vermes's parents embraced Roman Catholicism when he was a child. Raised within that tradition he ended up entering the priesthood but, after six years, began a spiritual pilgrimage that culminated in his conversion back to the faith of his ancestors.[25] As a scholar, Vermes became professor of Jewish studies at Oxford, wrote prolifically on the Dead Sea Scrolls, and followed his groundbreaking book on Jesus with additional volumes: *The Gospel of Jesus the Jew* (1981), *Jesus and the World of Judaism* (1983), *The Religion of Jesus the Jew* (1993), *The Changing Faces of Jesus* (2000), *Jesus in His Jewish Context* (2003), and *The Real Jesus: Then and Now* (2010).

There are many aspects to Vermes's work, but the most enduring contribution has been the connections he draws between Jesus and other charismatic, pious Jews who are reputed to have been miracle workers. Vermes calls Jesus a *hasid*, a type of holy man in first-century Judaism who claimed to draw upon the power of God in ways that transcended the usual channels of religious authority. Two such persons are especially important: Honi the Circle Drawer and Hanina ben Dosa. According to the Talmud, both of these men were miracle workers who operated in Galilee. Honi was active shortly before Jesus and Hanina shortly after him. Both are said to have healed the sick and exercised power over demons. Hanina is credited with healing the son of Gamaliel from a distance *(b. Ber.* 34b; *y. Ber.* 9d; compare the story of Jesus in Luke 7:1–10). In a series of remarkable passages from the Babylonian Talmud, Hanina is referred to as "my son" by a heavenly voice *(b. Taan.* 24b; *b. Ber.* 17b; *b. Hul.* 17a; compare Mark 1:11). Both Hanina and Honi are regularly compared to Elijah, as is Jesus in the Gospels.

Vermes concludes that "a distinctive trend of charismatic Judaism existed during the last couple of centuries of the Second Temple" period and that it "is likely to have had Galilean roots."[26] The "unsophisticated religious ambiance" of Galilee and the relatively "simple spiritual demands" of the people there provided an atmosphere for men such as Honi, Jesus, and Hanina to flourish:[27] "These holy men were treated as the willing or unsophisticated heirs to an ancient prophetic tradition. Their supernatural powers were attributed to their immediate relation to God. They were venerated as a link between heaven and earth independent of any institutional mediation."[28] The logical inference is that Jesus can be understood as one in a series of such Galilean holy men, as perhaps the paramount example of *hasidim* produced by this Jewish charismatic movement.

Vermes's thesis has been criticized by scholars who think he overlooks significant differences between Jesus and these other Jewish figures and relies on inadequate sources to establish the connections he does make. The problem is that the Talmudic writings, though difficult to date, are definitely later than the Gospels and may in some cases be hundreds of years later. The accuracy of their representation of Honi or Hanina is thus even more questionable from a historical perspective than the New Testament's representation of Jesus. The earliest references to Honi and Hanina, furthermore, do not present them as miracle workers but as righteous men whose prayers were answered by God. And Josephus (writing in the first century CE) locates Honi in Jerusalem, not Galilee. The suspicion of many historians, then, is that legends about these men grew over time, possibly in response to the stories Christians told about Jesus. The late traditions regarding Honi and Hanina contain accounts similar to those in the Gospels precisely because Jewish writers wanted to create Galilean holy men of their own who would be on a par with Jesus. John Meier is one scholar who has considered Vermes's thesis carefully only to dismiss it: "Ultimately, Vermes's acritical use of sources undermines his whole argument."[29]

Others are much more friendly. John Dominic Crossan and Marcus Borg both make ample use of the parallels to Honi and Hanina in their studies of Jesus, and Borg makes Vermes's category of "charismatic holy man" a dominant model in his own portrait of Jesus.[30] Sanders also appreciates the deep connection of Jesus with Judaism emphasized by Vermes and thinks the stories of Honi and Hanina offer insightful parallels for understanding how Jesus' miracles might have been perceived.[31]

Pieter Craffert has recently contributed a study of Jesus as a Galilean shaman, a portrait that bears similarities to Vermes's construction.[32] Craffert does not refer to Jewish figures (like Hanina and Honi) who might provide parallels for understanding Jesus but draws on anthropology in general, according to which shamans are "religious entrepreneurs who enter some kind of altered state of consciousness for the benefit of the community."[33] Jesus fits into this category as someone who had visions, was believed to be possessed by a spirit, and was able to perform healings, exorcisms, and other miracles. Craffert's work has met with some of the same criticisms offered that of Vermes: he pays no attention to possible source strata in the Gospel materials and readily admits that his method "makes it difficult if not impossible to distinguish between reports about a shamanic figure and made-up stories" about the same figure.[34]

Another historical Jesus scholar, Graham Twelftree, has made observations that are sometimes thought to supplement, correct, or expand upon Vermes's view.[35] Twelftree notes first that Jesus' healings and exorcisms are not connected with prayer (as are those of Hanina and Honi) or with the use of mechanical aids as were the exorcisms of other persons of this period. Thus, "Jesus' technique of exorcism, if not innovative, would have at least been very conspicuous."[36] Jesus casts out demons and declares people healed rather than asking God to do it. Further, Twelftree notes that the Gospels link Jesus' miracles and exorcisms closely to his proclamation of the kingdom of God (a point also stressed by Vermes). Jesus is presented as claiming that his exorcisms are a demonstration that Satan's power is being restricted and God's rule is being established (Matt. 12:28; Mark 3:27). Thus, "the unique and unprecedented aspect of Jesus' exorcisms is that he gave a profound meaning to the relatively ordinary event."[37] Twelftree also maintains that Jesus' discovery that he could work miracles played a significant role in his own developing messianic consciousness: "*because* of his miracles, *Jesus appears to have been conscious that he was God's key figure or Messiah* in a situation where he thought God's expected end-time reign was taking place in and through his activities."[38] In keeping with this, Craig Keener thinks the category of shamanism is inadequate for understanding Jesus' own claim that his miracles were manifestations of the kingdom, which, for Jesus, was not simply a numinous presence but an in-breaking new reality.[39]

There is, of course, little doubt that the Gospel authors associated Jesus' miracles with his messianic identity (and with the in-breaking of God's end-time reign), but scholars like Vermes, Crossan, and Borg would be reticent about attributing those interpretations of the miracle-activities to Jesus himself. Vermes, for example, grants that Jesus' charismatic acts would have been seen as signs of the messianic age and may very well have inspired people to speculate as to whether Jesus was the Messiah, but he thinks that Jesus himself was reticent about accepting such acclamations—he told his disciple *not* to say this about him (Mark 8:29–30) and he gave evasive answers when asked directly if this was who he was (Matt. 26:64).[40]

Finally, since Vermes would become one of the best-known Jewish scholars involved in modern historical Jesus studies, this is as good a place as any to note that he is far from the only Jewish scholar associated with that field. Most Jewish historians, however, have paid little attention to Jesus as a miracle worker, focusing instead on other aspects of his ministry: Joseph Klausner viewed him as an impressive ethical teacher;[41] C. G. Montefiore saw him as a prophet who critiqued the legal institution in a manner similar to that in which prophets of old had critiqued sacrificial and political institutions;[42] Robert Eisler presented him as a nonviolent rebel who, like other Jewish revolutionaries, was ultimately killed by the Romans.[43] Hyam Maccoby maintained that he was, in fact, a Pharisee, whose teaching closely paralleled that of other Pharisaic rabbis in content and style.[44] The Jewish scholar most similar to Vermes would be David Flusser, whose biography of Jesus is regarded as sporadically insightful but flawed by idiosyncratic assumptions (e.g., Luke is the earliest of the Synoptics; all of the Gospels draw upon a written Hebrew account) and inattention to critical concerns (such as criteria for determining historical judgments).[45] Flusser ends up offering an extremely appreciative account of Jesus from a Jewish perspective, not only respecting his teaching but also allowing that the virgin birth, the miracle stories, the transfiguration, and other spectacular elements of the Jesus story might all be historical.

Other important Jewish scholars, such as Paula Fredriksen and Amy-Jill Levine, have also made a mark on historical Jesus studies. Fredriksen's work is summarized in this chapter. Levine has offered many incisive critiques of Jesus research[46] but has not authored a Jesus biography of her own.

JESUS THE MAGICIAN (MORTON SMITH)

In 1978, just five years after Vermes's study of Jesus from a modern Jewish perspective appeared, Morton Smith published a book that identified Jesus with the image assigned to him by early Jewish opponents of Christianity: *Jesus the Magician.* At the time, Smith was professor of ancient history at Columbia University. His claim that Jesus could legitimately be regarded as a magician was and still is controversial and may be offensive to many Christians. Smith had to argue against the witness of the New Testament and allege that much significant evidence had been suppressed.

Before we look at his argument, we should be clear what is meant by the term *magician.* In modern parlance, the word may refer to an entertainer, to someone who does "magic tricks," or, in other words, to someone who pretends to make things happen through magical forces, which we know do not really exist. Obviously, this was not the view of the first century. It was then widely believed that supernatural powers were at work in the world. Different cultures might attribute these to gods, angels, demons, or other types of spirits, but, in any case, magic was the art of accessing these powers. Magic in the broadest sense involved "private dealings with supernatural beings."[47]

Smith surveys the writings of ancient opponents of Christianity, which he claims almost unanimously present Jesus as a magician. Most of these writings are now known only through references and quotations found in the writings of Christians who wished to refute them. The works themselves, Smith says, "were destroyed in antiquity after Christians got control of the Roman empire."[48] There are two sides to every argument, Smith maintains, and the counterclaims of Jesus' opponents deserve to be heard.

The Gospels themselves admit that Jesus' reputed miracles were controversial even during his own lifetime. Some religious leaders believed he performed exorcisms with the aid of an evil spirit (Mark 3:22). Others may have thought he had called into himself the spirit of the murdered John the Baptist (Mark 6:14). Smith's own study of the Gospels reveals an attempt to cover up aspects of Jesus' activity that would support the charge that he was a magician.[49] For example, the earliest tradition found in the Gospel of Mark portrays Jesus as using techniques that his contemporaries would have regarded as indicative of magic: he uses spittle to effect healing of blindness (8:22–26) and speaks Aramaic words or phrases that effectively function as magic formulas ("Talitha cum" in 5:41 and "Ephphatha" in 7:34). Notably these stories are dropped or revised in the later Gospels of Matthew and Luke. Such tendencies make Smith suspicious that there was originally far more to the tradition that Jesus was a magician than we are now privileged to see.

Smith finds abundant evidence of Jesus working magic throughout the Gospels in spite of the early Christian attempts to suppress this tradition. He compares numerous Gospel passages to quotations from ancient magical papyri and compares the stories of Jesus to those of another famous miracle worker, Apollonius of Tyana. The account of a spirit entering Jesus and a bird resting upon him at his baptism describes "just the sort of thing that was thought to happen to a magician."[50] Jesus' call to hallow God's name (Matt. 6:9) has a background in magic, says Smith, for the magician would make the name of a deity famous by applying it in his craft.[51] Reliable tradition credits Jesus with the institution of the Eucharist (the Lord's Supper), which Smith calls "an unmistakably magical rite."[52] Finally, Jesus is even shown to work what is called "black magic" when he sends evil spirits into things or people. He sends demons into pigs (Mark 5:13) and, according to Smith, sends Satan into a piece of bread so that Judas will be invaded by the devil when he eats the morsel (see John 13:21–30).[53]

Lest his description of Jesus as a magician seem too polemical, Smith indicates that the distinction between a religious miracle worker and a magician is largely one of perspective. The same man may be called a divine man, or Son of God by his admirers, and a magician by his enemies: "'Jesus the magician' was the figure seen by most ancient opponents of Jesus; 'Jesus the Son of God' was the figure seen by that party of his followers which eventually triumphed; the real Jesus was the man whose words and actions gave rise to these contradictory interpretations."[54] Smith indicates that the Gospels themselves recognize that there were exorcists and miracle workers who were not accused of using magic or demonic power (see Matt. 12:27). Jesus, however, claimed to be able to do the things that he did because he was possessed of a spirit, a spirit that he and his followers called divine, but others might just as well call demonic.

Smith's study has not found wide acceptance among historical Jesus scholars: Keener observes that it is now "usually treated as eccentric."[55] Still, the project did accent the need for considering the perspective of opponents in composing a historically responsible portrait of Jesus.[56] Furthermore, John Dominic Crossan revived Smith's work and made the image of Jesus as magician a major component of his own sketch. We will look at that in more detail in chapter 5.

Elements of Smith's work also seem to resurface in Craffert's portrayal of Jesus as a shaman (see above, page 77).

One of the most informed critiques of Smith's view has come from John Meier, who offers an extensive study of magic and miracles in the ancient Near East and argues that the two phenomena must be differentiated:

> At one end of the spectrum, the ideal type of magic involves the elements of (1) automatic power possessed by a magician (2) in virtue of secret formulas and rituals, with (3) the resultant coercion of the divine powers by humans (4) in search of quick solutions to practical problems. Also, magic is usually marked by (5) a spirit of individualism or entrepreneurship as opposed to a perduring community of faith. At the other end of the spectrum, miracles belong in general to a context of (1) faith in a personal God to whose will one submits one's own will in prayer, (2) a perduring community of belief, and (3) a public manifestation of God's power (4) that is not dependent on a set ritual or formula.[57]

JESUS THE JEWISH SAGE (BEN WITHERINGTON III)

Ben Witherington III, professor of New Testament at Asbury Theological Seminary, has suggested that Jesus be thought of as a sapient figure. Witherington's first study on Jesus carried the provocative title *The Christology of Jesus* (1990) and sought to explain what Jesus thought and taught about himself. The initial proposal presented there was expanded in a later work, *Jesus the Sage* (1994). A busy author, Witherington has also written *The Jesus Quest* (1995), which relates his views to other proposals about Jesus, including many of those discussed in this book.

Witherington's understanding of Jesus is informed by the reading of numerous Jewish writings that were well known at the time of Jesus and which belong to what is called the wisdom tradition. These include the biblical books of Ecclesiastes, Job, Proverbs, and Daniel, as well as such apocryphal writings as the Wisdom of Solomon, Sirach, and the *Parables of Enoch*. A number of features in these writings have parallels with what is attributed to Jesus in the Gospels:[58]

- Jesus' use of Father language for God is not characteristic of the Old Testament, but such language is frequently found in the wisdom materials (Sir. 23:1, 4; 51:10; Wis. 14:3);
- The phrase "kingdom of God," frequently on Jesus' lips in the Synoptic Gospels, is rarely found in the Old Testament, but Wisdom 10:10 portrays Solomon being granted a vision of the kingdom of God;
- Jesus' use of Son of Man language echoes the book of Daniel as well as the *Parables of Enoch*;
- Jesus' exorcisms may be understood in light of first-century traditions that regarded Solomon (the favorite figure of the wisdom tradition) as an exorcist;

- Jesus' willingness to portray himself with female imagery (Matt. 23:37–39) may be related to personifications of Wisdom as a female figure in Proverbs 8–9 and Wisdom of Solomon 8–9;
- Jesus' parables about banquets and his practice of eating with outcasts exemplify classic wisdom themes that encourage the enjoyment of life, often with feasting as a prime symbol of such celebration.

In light of such parallels, Witherington thinks sage is a more precise description of Jesus than prophet. Most Bible readers are aware that prophets were regarded as people filled with the Spirit of God who spoke God's word to Israel. But the wisdom tradition also claimed the inspiration of God's Spirit. Isaiah describes the descendant of David who would later be called the Messiah as one whom the Spirit of God instills with wisdom, knowledge, understanding, and the fear of the Lord—characteristics most valued in wisdom literature (Isa. 11:1–3). Later Talmudic writings claimed that God took prophecy from the prophets and gave it to the sages.[59]

Jesus, Witherington notes, never uses the classic formula of prophets, "Thus says the Lord . . ."[60] He speaks on his own authority, as does the Teacher of Ecclesiastes and the author of Proverbs. The form of his speech is not oracles but riddles, parables, aphorisms, personifications, and beatitudes. The content of his message draws often on "creation theology," extolling God's providence as evidenced in nature (Matt. 6:25–33) and decrying divorce as contrary to God's original intent (Matt. 19:3–9). In all these ways, he presents himself as a sage with deep roots in the wisdom tradition of Israel.[61]

A couple of key passages fit Witherington's proposal especially well. First, Jesus contrasts himself with John the Baptist, whom he calls a prophet. He notes that whereas John is an ascetic, he has come "eating and drinking." Then he concludes, "Wisdom is vindicated by her deeds" (Matt. 11:16–19).[62] Second, Jesus claims that he is the only one who knows the Father, that all things have been handed to him by the Father, and that no one can know the Father unless he reveals the Father to them (Matt. 11:25–27). Many historical scholars would doubt the authenticity of this latter saying, since it smacks heavily of the developed theology of the early church. But Witherington argues that it not only goes back to Jesus but presents Jesus as claiming for himself the role elsewhere ascribed to the Wisdom of God (Prov. 8:14–36; Wis. 2:13, 16; 4:10–15).[63]

Witherington does not think the label *sage* captures the whole truth about the historical Jesus, but he does think it offers an important category, perhaps the dominant one, for understanding him. He thinks it may be best to describe Jesus as "a prophetic sage" or even as "a prophetic and eschatological sage." In fact, Witherington goes so far as to suggest that Jesus believed he was Wisdom made flesh, the personification of God's wisdom. Traditional writings had already personified the Wisdom of God as a heavenly figure entrusted with the secrets of God and with the task of revealing these to humans (Job 28; Prov. 1, 3, 8, 9; Sir. 1, 24). Jesus may have believed that he was this figure, descended to earth in human form. As such, he saw himself as "the revealer of the very mind of God"[64] and he believed that rejection of him constituted rejection of God's wisdom (Matt. 23:37–39).

The image of Jesus as a Jewish sage is one significant component of Marcus Borg's treatment of Jesus, presented in chapter 6 of this book. Borg emphasizes the subversive nature of Jesus' teaching, a point Witherington also develops, though in different ways.[65] Borg parts company from Witherington in that he takes the emphasis on Jesus as a teacher of wisdom (which is present-oriented) as an indication that Jesus did not speak much about the future.[66] N. T. Wright and E. P. Sanders object to any subordination of prophet to sage. They both regard the former category as the dominant model for Jesus (thus, he was not so much a prophetic sage as a prophet who sometimes drew upon wisdom traditions). Sanders complains that an emphasis on Jesus as a sage can end up presenting him primarily as a teacher whose ideas were "striking in manner but not especially in matter."[67] Most wisdom teaching, after all, deals with general advice that would apply in almost any time or place. Likewise, Wright insists that the image of a sage must not be taken to imply that Jesus "did not address the urgent state of affairs within Israel," but he praises Witherington as one who does not push the model to that extreme.[68]

JESUS THE CYNIC PHILOSOPHER (F. GERALD DOWNING)

One of the most influential of the nontraditional images associated with Jesus in recent scholarship has been that of the Cynic philosopher.[69] This, in fact, became the controlling image of Jesus for the work of Burton Mack described in chapter 1 (see pages 27–30), and it has also been a dominant concept in the work of the Jesus Seminar (chapter 4) and of John Dominic Crossan (chapter 5). Many scholars have noted similarities between traditions about Jesus and those concerning Cynic philosophers,[70] but none so persistently as F. Gerald Downing. The author of numerous books on theology and faith, Downing serves as Honorary Research Fellow for the Center for Biblical Studies at the University of Manchester.

To understand Downey's image of Jesus as a Cynic philosopher, we must first expunge negative connotations of Cynics that might derive from the English word *cynical*. Cynics were not pessimistic people who tended to expect the worst. Rather, they were radical individualists who advocated the avoidance of worldly entanglements and defiance of social convention. The Cynic movement is usually traced to Diogenes of Sinope (400–325 BCE), although it took on a variety of forms after him.[71] Diogenes embraced a simple, natural lifestyle free of hypocrisy or pretense. By living simply, he claimed to achieve self-sufficiency, which freed him from the need to impress others. So liberated, he could do as he wished—and what he wished to do was to accept whatever was "natural" without shame.

By the time of Jesus, Cynics are known to have traveled throughout many countries, practicing their eccentric lifestyle and propagating the ideas that it entailed. Stories known as *chreiai* were told about and by Cynics.[72] Typically, these are brief accounts that recall a memorable aphorism or describe a symbolic action. One *chreia* recounts how Alexander the Great visited Diogenes when he was sunbathing and asked if there was anything he could do for him. No respecter of authority, Diogenes replied, "Just now, you can get out of my light" (Cicero, *Tusculan Disputations* 5.92). Other stories record that Diogenes would defecate or engage in sexual acts in public to demonstrate the shamelessness of these natural deeds (Laertius, *Lives* 6.69).[73] This, in fact, may explain the derivation of the word *cynic;* it comes from the Greek word for dog *(kyōn),* and Aristotle commented that Diogenes behaved "like a dog" when he acted shamelessly in public.[74]

The Cynics loved being described as antisocial and deliberately sought such an identification. As John Dominic Crossan is fond of saying, "They were hippies in a world of Augustan yuppies."[75] They dressed as beggars with a cloak, bag, and staff, wore their hair long and kept their beards untrimmed. And they went barefoot. "Wearing sandals is next to being bound," wrote one Cynic, "but going barefoot gives the feet great freedom" (Musonius Rufus, Fragment 19). Another summarized his lifestyle this way: "a cloak serves as my garment, the skin of my feet as my shoes, the whole earth as my resting place" (*Pseudo-Anacharsis* 5). Seneca reports that Diogenes "on seeing a boy drink water from the hollow of his hand, forthwith took his cup from his wallet [bag] and broke it, upbraiding himself with these words: 'Fool that I am, to have been carrying superfluous baggage all this time!'" Then Seneca exhorts his readers, "If mankind were to listen to this sage, they would know that the cook is as superfluous as the soldier. . . . Follow nature, and you will need no skilled craftsmen" (Seneca, *Epistulae Morales* 90.14–16).[76]

In 1988, Downing published *Christ and the Cynics,* which was not so much a monograph as a compilation of materials from Cynic writings arranged side by side with quotations from the New Testament.[77] Here are but two of the 289 examples he adduces:

"Lots of people are praising you," Antisthenes was told. "Why?" he asked. "What have I done wrong?" (Laertius, *Lives* 6.8)	Woe to you when all speak well of you, for that is what their ancestors did to the false prophets. (Luke 6:26).
Where do the little birds go to get food to feed their young, though they're much worse off than you are—the swallows and nightingales and larks and blackbirds? Do they store food away in safekeeping? (Musonius 15)	Look at the birds of the air; they neither sow nor reap nor gather into barns, and yet your heavenly Father feeds them. Are you not of more value than they? (Matt. 6:26)

Downing admits that similarity in wording need not entail agreement in meaning, and he recognizes differences between the early Jesus tradition and Cynicism.[78] Nevertheless, on the basis of the numerous parallels, he proposes that "Christians who shared publicly the teaching and stories that go to build up our first three Gospels must have been entirely happy to sound as well as look like Cynics. . . . They focussed on the same topics, very often pressing the same conclusions, and that in very similar language."[79]

As such, Downing's study focuses more on the history of early Christianity than on the historical Jesus. We might assume that the evangelists who wrote the Gospels cast Jesus' words in ways that reflected Cynic influence in order to appeal to the Gentile world they wanted to evangelize. But in his next major work, *Cynics and Christian Origins,* Downing came to insist that Cynics exercised a direct influence on Jesus himself.[80] Though Jewish, Jesus deliberately emulated these Gentile philosophers. The implication of such a proposal is that Jesus and his Jewish audience were thoroughly hellenized, that is, acclimated to Greco-Roman culture.

Essential to this thesis is Downing's analysis of Gospel material assigned to the Q source. Here he finds the greatest abundance of parallels, such that he claims the very genre of Q may have been that of "a Cynic life," comparable to those found in a work by Diogenes Laertius (*Lives of Eminent Philosophers,* Book 6). Laertius offers brief biographical sketches of Cynic philosophers with a primary interest in collecting their more memorable sayings. Downing notes several similarities between Q and these "Lives" of Cynics, though we should note that this part of his proposal has been sharply contested by other Q scholars.[81] Still, Downing concludes that "Q would have seemed akin to Cynic teaching in its choice of topics, conclusions urged, vocabulary, and imagery used."[82] Common features in the teaching of the Cynics and that of Jesus include rejection of wealth (Mark 10:17–26; Epictetus, *Diss.* 2:14.14, 18–24), advocacy of simple living (Mark 6:8–9; Dio, *Orat.* 6:15), approval of begging (Luke 6:30; Laertius, *Lives* 6.29), and the expectation of persecution (Matt. 5:11–12; Lucian, *Demonax* 11). Furthermore, Downing says, Q presents Jesus as teaching in his own name as did the Cynics, not as the representative of a school as did rabbis or in the name of God as did the prophets (Jesus does not say, "Thus says the Lord").

The Cynics, in Downing's view, were not just cavalier vagabonds. They were "friends of freedom," outspoken and courageous protesters who stood up for individual liberty in an oppressive society.[83] Like Jesus and his followers, they mingled with the lower classes, teaching the ordinary people rather than restricting their insights to lectures at the salon. Their philosophy was termed "popular," and yet it strangely appealed to many aristocrats who sensed the emptiness of life in the higher reaches of imperial Roman society.

Some scholars have questioned whether all the parallels Downing cites for Cynicism and Christianity are legitimate. This issue is complicated by difficulty in dating Cynic materials (most extant writings are later than the New Testament) and by the spectrum and diversity of views that can be attributed to Cynics.[84]

The parallels Downing cites are, in any case, drawn from a period of over five hundred years, and many concern persons who might not technically be classed as Cynics. Both Musonius Rufus and Epictetus, cited above, are usually regarded as Stoics, though the distinction between Stoicism and Cynicism is admittedly ambiguous.[85] Downing's response is to claim that "the niceties of intellectual definition" are of little importance, but rather "how things appeared to the populace at large."[86]

Downing claims "to show not only that there are many similarities between Cynics and Christians but also that overall (and often in detail) these similarities are quite distinctive."[87] The latter part of this claim has been disputed by some who maintain that the similarities between Jesus and the Cynics can be explained in other ways (for example, by viewing Jesus' words as analogous to those of Jewish prophets or wisdom teachers). Moreover, critics of Downing's hypothesis point out key areas of contrast. In Luke 9:3, Jesus explicitly forbids his disciples from taking a staff or a bag with them when they go out as missionaries, almost as if he wanted to *avoid* any identification of his followers with Cynics.[88] But this point would actually count in Downing's favor: if Jesus (or even the author of Luke's Gospel) was worried that Jesus' disciples might be misidentified as Cynics, then there must have been a high level of similarity to prompt such concern. Furthermore, Downing indicates that even the Synoptic tradition is varied on this. In Mark 6:8–10, the disciples are allowed a staff though no bag. In Matthew 10:9–10, they are not allowed either, yet now they are required to go barefoot (like Cynics)! So if the early Christian tradition allowed variation on these minor points, why not assume that Cynic tradition did as well? The whole point, for Downing, is nonconformity with society, not imposition of a new set of regulations.[89]

Other differences seem more substantive. Cynics were Greeks and lived in the cities; Jesus was Jewish and wandered the countryside. Cynics had a strong this-worldly attitude; Jesus is represented as preaching about a coming kingdom of God, about life after death and the final judgment. Cynics were noted for embracing asceticism; Jesus, for avoiding it (Mark 2:18–19; Luke 7:33–34). Cynics advocated dependence on self; Jesus, dependence on God (Matt. 6:25–33).[90] And, notes Henry Chadwick, we hear no stories of Christian missionaries copulating in the streets.[91] On these points, Downing appeals to the diversity of themes, behaviors, and commitments that could be attributed to particular Cynics at particular times. He maintains that the "shamelessness" of Diogenes' antics had ceased to be an identifying factor for Cynics by the time of Jesus. And he claims that some Cynics did employ eschatological language; they at least took the imagery of afterlife and of judgment and applied it to life on earth.[92]

Perhaps the most sharply challenged aspect of Downing's proposal, however, has been his suggestion that Jesus was directly influenced by Cynics.[93] Some scholars wonder where Jesus would have even encountered them. There is no sure sign that Cynics were ever in Galilee, particularly in the villages that Jesus knew. Downing supposes that Jesus could have seen Cynics in the Roman city of Sepphoris, which was only three miles from Nazareth. Cynics might have been there, and Jesus might have visited there, but all this is speculation, for neither Cynics nor Sepphoris are ever mentioned in the Bible or in any of the other Jesus traditions. On surer ground, Downing points out that notable Cynics were located in Gadara both the century before and the century after Jesus' ministry. Gadara was a city of the Decapolis, a region visited by Jesus according to the New Testament Gospels.[94] And if Cynics were there, it is not unlikely that they were elsewhere too. Leif Vaage observes that this is not essential; the remarkable similarity of certain Cynics and some early Christians helps to inform our understanding of Christian origins regardless of whether the two movements are "genealogically related."[95] Given that, the question might still remain whether the Jesus tradition is distorted through comparison to material that is only superficially analogous. Witherington emphasizes that the Jesus material in question also bears close similarities to Jewish wisdom tradition and, so, should be compared with that body of material.[96]

JESUS THE ITINERANT RADICAL (GERD THEISSEN)

Gerd Theissen has been one of the most prominent and articulate voices in historical Jesus studies for over thirty-five years. Although he has never written a conventional biography of Jesus, he certainly has produced all the materials necessary for such a volume. In the 1980s he wrote a novel about Jesus that clearly encapsulated his understanding of the man, his impact, and his surroundings.[97] Ten years later, he coauthored *The Historical Jesus: A Comprehensive Guide* with his student, Annette Merz, a volume that appears to be intended for use as a classroom text: it surveys the field of historical Jesus scholarship, identifies the sources, criteria, and methods of research employed by major players, and invites the reader to join the quest by engaging in various analytical tasks for which solutions are provided in the back. In actuality, however, the volume presents a clear portrait of Jesus analogous to those provided by Crossan, Borg, Sanders, Meier, and Wright (discussed in later chapters of this book). Theissen and Merz describe Jesus as a charismatic Jew, an eschatological prophet, a healer and miracle worker, a poetic teller of parables, a teacher of radical ethics, an intentional founder of a cult, and a martyr with a messianic complex (indeed, the original messianic complex, the one that gave rise to that term).[98] Many aspects of that profile overlap with the presentations of other scholars described elsewhere in this book (sometimes because those scholars have been influenced by Theissen's earlier writings). We will focus here on particulars that are somewhat distinctive to—or especially associated with—Theissen (or Theissen and Merz).

Theissen describes Jesus as an itinerant radical preacher who took his message to the villages of Galilee in a manner that distinguished him, on the one hand, from sedentary Jewish prophets like John the Baptist (who stayed put and let people come to him) and, on the other, from Cynic philosophers who were itinerant but targeted urban areas rather than rural ones.[99] When Jesus called people to follow him, he meant that in a fairly literal sense: he invited rural people to renounce home (Matt. 8:20), family (Mark 10:29; Luke 14:26), possessions (Matt. 10:10, 17–25), and protection (Matt. 5:39) to become wandering charismatics like him, trusting in God to provide for them as they took their distinctive message of God's kingdom from place to place.[100] In each setting, Jesus would perform healings and exorcisms, which attracted considerable attention: people flocked to hear him tell how these were signs that the kingdom of God was already arriving and would soon be consummated in accord with typical apocalyptic expectations. It was the combination of such elements that was distinctive: "as an apocalyptic charismatic miracle worker, Jesus is unique in human history."[101]

As a teacher and prophet, Jesus appears to have excelled at bringing together such previously disparate strands of his tradition. He also combined elements from wisdom and prophetic traditions in his teaching and, remarkably, reinterpreted traditional militaristic understandings of "the kingdom of God" in light of equally Jewish understandings of God as Father. Thus, although Jesus taught constantly about "the kingdom of God," he did not refer to God as "king." He preferred to call God "father" and allowed this familial metaphor to transform the militaristic one: the kingdom of God became, specifically, "the kingdom of God the Father," or even "the kingdom of our Father," as is evident in the Lord's Prayer: "Our Father in heaven, your kingdom come."[102] Likewise, the genius of Jesus' ethical teaching was that he interpreted Torah in light of Jewish Wisdom tradition and in light of eschatological prophecy, two thoroughly traditional and undeniably Jewish streams that allowed him to do two things: (1) broaden the universal appeal of Torah, emphasizing the practice of love over observance of Sabbath or purity laws; and (2) sharpen the political challenge Torah offers to the rich, oppressive, and powerful.

Theissen bases much of his reconstruction on sociological analysis of Jesus' world, an area of study in which he did pioneering research and in which he possesses recognized expertise.[103] Tensions between urban aristocrats and the landless poor may be seen everywhere; for instance, Theissen takes Jesus' rude words to the Syrophoenician woman in Mark 7:24–30 as expressive of the anger Jewish peasants felt when their agricultural resources were being exported to the cities: the Jewish poor in Galilean villages should be fed first, rather than having their food sent to the rich Gentile dogs who had settled in cities like Tyre and Sidon.[104] But, generally speaking, Theissen insists that Jesus and his itinerant followers sought to practice what they preached about love for enemies: their resistance to oppression was nonviolent and illustrative. By voluntarily renouncing all worldly sources of power and security they sought to manifest "an aristocratic ethic of responsibility" that would reveal injustice and provide a living testimony to the powerful of what pleases God. Thus, Theissen believes that Jesus intended his movement of itinerant radicalism to renew Palestinian-Jewish society: the marginalized "outsiders" who composed his movement exhibited the ethic of love, reconciliation, and generosity that Jesus believed could heal the divisions within Jewish communities and enable a united, faithful response to the aristocracy of Rome.[105] Obviously, the movement failed in this objective: the society was, unfortunately, already too fractured.[106]

Criticisms of Theissen's work tend to be moderate. James D. G. Dunn thinks he reads rhetorically charged passages regarding the cost of discipleship (e.g., Luke 14:26) in an overly literal way and relies too heavily on the account of Jesus' commissioning his disciples in Mark 6:6–13, a missionary text that seems especially likely to have been worked over by the church.[107] Richard Horsley complains that Theissen "domesticates" Jesus by implying he thought his harsher demands would apply only to his inner circle of followers (an exceptional band of itinerant radicals) rather than to all people.[108] As David Gowler notes, however, "the bare fact that Jesus and many of his first followers were itinerant charismatics has stood the test of time.[109] Most of the scholars discussed in this book make some use of such a model. The focus of Jesus as a homeless, itinerant preacher looms especially large in the work of Leif Vaage, who focuses on the presentation of Jesus and his followers in Q,[110] and of Halvor Moxnes, who thinks Jesus used the language and images of family and place to redefine basic institutions of human society.[111]

JESUS THE MILLENARIAN PROPHET (DALE C. ALLISON)

Dale Allison, Professor of New Testament and Early Christianity at Pittsburgh Theological Seminary, is one of several historical scholars who continue to associate Jesus with apocalyptic eschatology in a manner reminiscent of Albert Schweitzer (see pages 15–17).[112] Sociologists and anthropologists often associate apocalypticism with what they call "millenarian movements," and Allison maintains that certain attributes of millenarianism exhibited by these groups recall aspects of the pre-Easter Jesus movement as depicted in our most reliable Gospel traditions. For example, such movements often exhibit tendencies to

- address the disaffected and less fortunate in a period of social change;
- interpret the present and near future as a time of unprecedented suffering;
- divide humanity into two camps (saved and unsaved);
- break hallowed taboos associated with religious customs;
- replace traditional familial bonds with fictive kin;
- demand intense commitment and unconditional loyalty;
- take a passive stance toward current political entities; and,
- view the teachings of their prophet as fresh revelation authenticated by that prophet's miracles or other evidence of a direct connection with God.[113]

Thus, cross-cultural comparison suggests that Jesus be understood in a manner roughly analogous to other millenarian prophets, some of whom are better known to us historically.

To be more specific, Allison proposes that Jesus promoted some version of the following story, which is prominent in postexilic Jewish literature:

> Although God created a good world, evil spirits have filled it with wickedness, so that it is in disarray and full of injustice. A day is coming, however, when God will repair the broken creation and restore scattered Israel. Before that time, the struggle between good and evil will come to a climax, and a period of great tribulation and unmatched woe will descend upon the world. After that period God will, perhaps through one or more messianic figures, reward the just and requite the unjust, and then establish divine rule forever.[114]

Allison is not unique or even distinctive in presenting the historical Jesus as a prophet of apocalyptic eschatology, but he has become one of the principle defenders of that often-beleaguered notion.[115] His principle argument derives from what he calls "the mass of relevant sayings in the extant sources"—the catalog of apocalyptic material attributed to Jesus is so vast, that this should be the quintessential example of multiple attestation.[116] Indeed, the Gospels sometimes contain explanatory comments that seem intended to tone down the radically apocalyptic sense that might otherwise be given to Jesus' reported words and deeds (e.g., Luke 19:11; John 21:20–23; cf. Acts 1:6).[117]

Beyond these considerations, the supposition that Jesus was an apocalyptic or millenarian prophet allows him to be seen as the sensible connecting link between his mentor (John the Baptist) and his followers (e.g., Paul), both of whom are known to have espoused apocalyptic ideas.[118] Further, the fact that the Gospels all interpret Jesus' death and resurrection as a specifically eschatological event (a tribulation and vindication that matches the typical apocalyptic scenario) suggests that something in the pre-Easter ministry of Jesus had conditioned his earliest followers to think in those terms.[119]

Allison is an extraordinarily cautious scholar who doubts that much of anything can be known about Jesus with certainty. He allows to a greater degree than most historians that our best sources for Jesus could be tainted by fallible and tendentious memories (see pages 24–25). Still, Allison maintains that memory's primary failings have to do with the particular. Memory tends to be more trustworthy with regard to general impressions, and, so, historians show focus on the general impressions of Jesus that we have in the literature preserved by his followers.[120] One such "general impression" is that Jesus was a prophet who expected the kingdom of God to come soon in a cataclysmic way, ushering in a new era in which the righteous would be rewarded with heavenly bliss and the wicked punished forever in hell. Another general impression would be that Jesus believed that he himself was the agent (possibly the Messiah and/or the Son of Man) God would use to execute the eschatological judgment and bring the kingdom to pass.[121] The literature is also consistent in indicating that he accepted the inevitability of his death willingly, with a certain confidence that it would benefit humanity and advance God's cause.[122] All these general impressions fit with a fundamental conception of Jesus as a millenarian or apocalyptic prophet.[123]

Allison has wrestled throughout his career with the implication of this image for Jesus that so troubled Schweitzer: if predicting the imminent end of the world was central to Jesus' message, then we must live with the realization that Jesus was wrong. Early on, Allison ended a doctoral dissertation on this topic by saying, "I am, for theological reasons, unedified by the thought that, in a matter so seemingly crucial, a lie has been walking around for two thousand years while the truth has only recently put on its shoes. But there it is."[124] Later, he mused that the realization might have some value in combating Docetism: an errant Jesus could be a "rather effective antidote to a piety that denies Jesus' humanity."[125] Thus, Allison resists what he regards as "easy ways out." For example, N. T. Wright has suggested that Jesus was talking about only the end of the "present world order," not the space-time continuum.[126] And Ben Witherington contends that Jesus only declared the end was *potentially* near not *necessarily* so.[127] No, Allison says, we must take what Jesus said at face value, admit that he meant what he said literally—and admit that it did not happen in the manner he clearly expected.[128] Still, Allison allows that "what pre-moderns took literally, we must take figuratively."[129] The best theological response (for Christians) is to regard Jesus' eschatology as mythology, to read his apocalyptic projections as though they were parables (though they were not that for him), and to focus on the vision for justice and the will of God that those projections encapsulated for him. Jesus "lived against injustice because he dreamed of its opposite," and that is a vision we all can share.[130]

Bart Ehrman has written a monograph on Jesus that parallels Allison's conception in many ways (albeit with less detailed argumentation).[131] Marius Reiser has also emphasized Jesus as a preacher of eschatological judgment, which he claimed to be imminent in a manner that demanded immediate repentance in line with acceptance of his own authority and message.[132] Reiser claims the message of judgment was an essential element of Jewish eschatology; Jesus shared the typical expectations of his people but articulated the theme in three ways that were unique: he insisted the judgment had already begun in a visible way in his own ministry; he emphasized the reign of God in a way that gave prominence to the salvational aspect of judgment; and he claimed that "the decision about salvation and destruction for the whole nation and every individual must be made in terms of an attitude toward him and his message."[133]

As we will see, these matters are greatly disputed in contemporary Jesus studies. E. P. Sanders, John Meier, and N. T. Wright would all agree with Allison that the historical Jesus was an apocalyptic/millenarian prophet who understood his role in these terms. Crossan, Borg, and the Jesus Seminar would dissent at this point, not because they question Allison's contention that the Gospels convey such general impressions but because they believe those impressions owe more to post-Easter Christianity than to the historical Jesus himself. They would apply various criteria to every one of the items in Allison's catalog of apocalyptic material attributed to Jesus and find reasons to question the authenticity of each item, one by one. Their mistake, according to Allison, lies in the focus on particulars: the parable of judgment preserved in Luke 12:42–46 may lack multiple attestation, but "sayings about a coming judgment" (considered as a general category) are found at every level of the tradition, in virtually all sources, and across all genres. If the Gospel sources are wrong on this point, Allison avers, they really should not be trusted on anything. The choice is simple: either Jesus was an apocalyptic prophetic analogous to the founders of other millenarian movements, or he was an obscure historical figure about whom we can know virtually nothing at all. Allison personally considers the first option to be the more likely one, the one that all historians should adopt if they believe authentic study of Jesus is actually possible.

JESUS THE MAMZER RABBI (BRUCE CHILTON)

An ordained Episcopalian priest, Bruce Chilton is the Bell Professor of Religion at Bard College in Annandale-on-Hudson, New York. He has published numerous works that seek to elucidate New Testament themes in light of various Jewish writings that he has researched more intensively than almost any other living Christian scholar.[134] Many of his writings are highly respected within the guild, but *Rabbi Jesus*, which he subtitles *An Intimate Biography*, did not receive high acclaim.[135] The book is written in a popular, lively style, but strikes most scholars as lacking in documentation: Chilton simply relates his version of the Jesus story, informed by knowledge of the customs and geography of the world in which Jesus lived; judgments regarding what is or is not historical appear to be based on his own intuition rather than derived from the application of any discernible methodology.[136] For example, Chilton imagines that when a preadolescent Jesus eluded his parents to remain in Jerusalem when the family visited that city (cf. Luke 2:41–51—an account most historians regard as legendary), he did not obediently return home with his parents after they found him in the temple a few days later but stayed in the city for years, scavenging for a living, only to return to Nazareth many years later in a manner that would eventually inspire his (autobiographical) parable of the "prodigal son."[137]

Nevertheless, some of Chilton's projections about Jesus have struck some scholars as plausible. One of his primary contentions is that Jesus would have been viewed throughout his life as a *mamzer*, or man of questionable parentage.[138] Chilton interprets Matthew 1:18 as implying that Joseph was living in another city at the time Mary was "found to be with child." Whatever explanation for this conception (Chilton supposes that Joseph himself had impregnated Mary on an earlier visit to Nazareth), the mere fact that Mary was not living

with Joseph at the time her pregnancy was discovered would have been problematic. The issue was not that Jesus might have been regarded as a bastard child
born out of wedlock (not a big deal, according to Chilton) but that his father
was unknown. This meant that (1) he could have been fathered by a non-Jewish
man, or (2) he might have been born of incest (as would often be assumed when
a young girl living in her father's house was found to be pregnant). A child with
such questionable lineage was called a *mamzer,* and Chilton maintains that the
mere suspicion that Jesus could be a *mamzer* would have made him an outcast
throughout his life: "Such men and women lived in a caste apart, unable to
marry within the established bloodlines of Israel, and so were often excluded
from the mainstream of religious life."[139]

Chilton believes that Jesus pursued a religious vocation but, due to his
mamzer status, it was necessarily an unconventional one. After some time as a
talmid, or apprentice-disciple of John the Baptist, he became an unofficial rabbi,
a *chasid,* who lacked institutional support or credentials. He was not identified
with (nor would he have been accepted by) any of the major parties of his day,
so his ministry had to be itinerant. Like other rabbis, Jesus was a master of oral
tradition and instructed his disciples in the Kabbalah, but his peculiar identification as a mamzer rabbi affected his teaching in key ways: he emphasized direct
communication with God (rather than mediated revelation through religious
institutions or authorities) and he found special meaning in the concept of God
as a personal Abba, or Father. Of course, he also had a heart for others who were
marginalized or regarded as outcasts for one reason or another.

Chilton's notion that Jesus was regarded as a *mamzer* has been reviewed critically by Scot McKnight in a more traditional study of the historical Jesus.[140]
McKnight dismisses several of Chilton's claims, such as the supposition that, as
a *mamzer,* Jesus would have lived in a caste apart from general society and would
have been excluded from participation in mainstream religious life.[141] Nevertheless, McKnight concludes that Chilton's basic insight is probably correct and
that *mamzer* status may explain Jesus' otherwise unusual lifelong celibacy as
well as the hostility with which family members and fellow villagers appear to
have regarded him when he began to present himself as some sort of religious
leader. McKnight thinks that several biblical texts are informed by the notion
that Jesus' birth was deemed illegitimate by his contemporaries (e.g., Mark 6:3;
John 8:41); it is also possible that Jesus' reported tendency to polemicize against
opponents with epithets that question *their* parentage (Matt. 23:15, 33; John
8:44) might be understood as a response to the sort of polemic that had been
directed against him all his life.

The theme of Jesus' illegitimacy has also informed the work of Andries
van Aarde and of Jane Schaberg, albeit in somewhat different ways.[142] James
Charlesworth, a prominent archaeologist and Jesus scholar, has also endorsed
Chilton's *mamzer* thesis and sought to strengthen it with data from the Dead
Sea Scrolls that indicate how *mamzers* would have been regarded by the Qumran
community.[143] Unlike McKnight, Charlesworth accepts the supposition that if

priests suspected Jesus of being a *mamzer*, he could have been excluded from the temple courts—or perhaps expelled from those courts after teaching in them for some time. Most scholars, however, have not been persuaded by the *mamzer* thesis. There is little evidence in the Gospel traditions that Jesus was regarded as a social or religious outcast during the time of his adult ministry; indeed, as James F. McGrath has pointed out, the fact that Jesus' fellowship with outcasts (e.g. tax collectors) was regarded as controversial presupposes that he was not regarded as an outcast himself.[144]

JESUS THE PURPORTED MESSIAH (PAULA FREDRIKSEN)

A professor at Boston University, Paul Fredriksen is a renowned scholar of ancient Christianity who, in the late 1990s, took an interest in the historical figure of Jesus himself. As a Jewish woman, she brings a distinctive perspective to a field that tends to be dominated by Christians and men.[145] In her book *Jesus of Nazareth*, Fredriksen offers numerous insights into the life and mission of Jesus that would resonate with the work of many other Jesus scholars: for example, that Jesus coupled a fairly traditional call to repentance with a prophetic announcement that God's kingdom was at hand and that he established his authority to make such a claim by performing exorcisms and healings.[146] Against many scholars, however, she argues that Jesus did not try to subvert or disregard purity laws, which were a natural (and not at all oppressive) part of the Jewish world in which he lived.[147] Likewise, Jesus' act of turning over tables in the Jerusalem temple court was not intended as a repudiation of temple sacrifices or of the commerce necessary for them to take place but, rather, was a symbolic, apocalyptic gesture indicating that the current temple would soon be destroyed by God to cede place to the eschatological temple that would mark the dawn of the new age.[148]

Fredriksen's primary contribution to Jesus studies, however, is found in her explanation for Jesus' death and, specifically, how this relates to his identification as the Messiah. First, Fredriksen notes that Herod Antipas, the Roman ruler of Galilee, took no action against Jesus or his followers during the time of his ministry in that area. It seems unlikely, then, that the title Messiah was being applied to him during that period, since he did not get into any trouble with the political authorities.[149] In Jerusalem, however, Pontius Pilate had him put to death by crucifixion, a form of execution reserved for political insurgents. The strong Christian tradition, furthermore, is that he wasn't just executed as *any* insurgent but, specifically, as a messianic pretender. The only problem with that scenario is that Pilate did *not* arrest or hunt down any of Jesus' followers: why kill Jesus by *crucifixion* (an extreme form of punishment) and yet kill *only* Jesus, when he was known to have disciples. It makes little sense to presume that Pilate would have thought Jesus was guilty of political insurgency (e.g., of being a messianic pretender) but assumed his disciples were innocent. What makes more sense, Fredriksen avers, is to presume that Pilate knew both Jesus and his disciples were innocent of any actual insurgency, but that Pilate had Jesus killed anyway because *others* were claiming he was the Messiah.[150]

According to Fredriksen's reconstruction, Pilate would have had plenty of information about Jesus, who had taught openly in the city for years. He knew that Jesus was no insurrectionist, that Jesus did not claim to be the Messiah, and that Jesus' own followers did not hail him as such. But, on one particular Passover, festive crowds of pilgrims hailed Jesus as the harbinger of the messianic kingdom in a manner that Jesus himself had not solicited. This proved his ironic undoing for, according to Fredriksen, "a straight line connects the Triumphal Entry and the Crucifixion."[151] These were not disciples or close associates of Jesus, but that did not matter. A crowd of people "noisily proclaiming the coming of the Kingdom, not to mention the coming of their King" was something that "would certainly provoke Pilate's attention and concern."[152] Jesus, then, did not claim to be the Messiah but was purported to be the Messiah by enthusiastic supporters on the fringe of his movement. Those admirers unwittingly signed his death warrant. Fredriksen speculates as to what happened next:

> Perhaps Caiaphas said something to Pilate like, "You know about the rumor spreading this week that Jesus of Nazareth is messiah. Some people actually expect him to reveal himself this Passover. The crowd seems restless." Pilate would have known what to do . . . let them wake up to their messiah already on a cross by the next morning.[153]

And so things moved quickly: Jesus was arrested at night. There would have been no need for the elaborate trials or public rituals that the Gospels report (e.g., the incredible scene in which Pilate asks the crowd of people which prisoner he should release for them; cf. Mark 15:6–15). Pilate's soldiers would have had their orders, and they would have carried them out. Then,

> day would have dawned. Gradually, sleepily, the city within the walls and the pilgrim city encamped in tents and booths in the valley below would have stirred to life. Slowly at first, then blazing rapidly, the news would have traveled. Perhaps then—astonished? shocked? bereft?—crowds of Jesus' followers together with the pilgrims would have streamed out of the city to the hill just outside, to the Place of the Skull, Golgotha. There they would have beheld the man, dying on a cross. Jesus of Nazareth. King of the Jews. As far as Pilate was concerned, that was the end of the matter.[154]

A couple of points have been raised in critique of this reconstruction.[155] First, there is some question as to whether crucifixion was *necessarily* reserved for the execution of political insurgents. The Romans appear to have crucified thousands of people: were they *all* would-be messiahs or persons who were viewed as posing serious threats to Caesar's authority? The persons crucified with Jesus are called simply "bandits" (Greek, *lēstēs*) in Mark 15:27. Second, the claim that if Jesus' closest followers had hailed him as Messiah during his lifetime the Roman authorities would have acted against them may be called into question by the fact that, later on, those followers definitely proclaimed Jesus to be the risen Messiah in Jerusalem and surrounding areas without running into apparent trouble from the Roman authorities. Crossan maintains that Pilate's decision to execute Jesus but not to bother rounding up his companions would be consistent with how Rome handled *nonviolent* revolutionaries (compare the notation in Mark 15:7 that Barabbas was in prison *with the rebels* who had committed murder during an insurrection).[156] Even more problematic may be the simple question as to why the church would have come to confess Jesus specifically as "Messiah" given the scenario Fredriksen outlines. David Gowler puts it this way: "her hypothesis assumes that the early Christians adopted the (erroneous) acclamation from an ignorant crowd about Jesus' messiahship—which they knew was incorrect—despite the fact that it was precisely this claim that led to his death."[157]

Such criticisms, however, do not completely unravel the logic of Fredriksen's proposal. Even if the Romans used crucifixion in various instances, the strong tradition preserved by all the Gospels is that the crucifixion of Jesus was connected with charges that had political implications (e.g., that he was known as "King of the Jews"). Pilate's lack of attention to Jesus' messianic followers in the years subsequent to the crucifixion might be more understandable if that movement made less of a splash than the possibly exaggerated reports in the book of Acts tend to indicate. And, if Jesus' followers believed he had been raised from the dead, they might have decided the public acclaim that led to his death had not been erroneous after all. In any case, Fredriksen knows that certainty in matters of historical reconstruction is impossible; she presents her scheme as an account of what she regards as the most probable alternative among various scenarios. A good number of Jesus scholars have followed her in this assessment and accepted her presentation as one that makes good sense of biblical tradition and historical data.

CONCLUSION

All these images of Jesus come into play for historical researchers and eventually affect perception at a popular level as well. The work of academicians has a way of trickling down to the people in the pews. "Every time we preach on a Gospel passage," seminary professor Walter Taylor tells Christian ministers, "we are stating our understanding of Jesus—is he a revolutionary, a pious teacher, a charismatic leader, or a misguided fool?"[158] Preachers are shaped by what they read, and they, in turn, shape their congregations. In recent years, furthermore, historical Jesus studies have been bypassing preachers altogether. Major news magazines run cover stories on the subject, and television networks air special documentaries (usually at religious times of the year such as Christmas and Easter), offering a curious public a glimpse of what is going on.

Still, sometimes, the scholarship does not trickle down at all. A few years ago, *Life* magazine took a different tack and published a compendium of quotes from prominent people about Jesus, informed or not.[159] Here's a sample:

- "There was no such person in the history of the world as Jesus Christ. There was no historical, living, breathing, sentient human being by that name. Ever." (Jon Murray, then president of American Atheists)
- "Jesus . . . never once yielded to sin, nor was he at any time susceptible to injury or harm or hurt from anything, mortal or otherwise. He explored creation, although he was at the same time the creator." (Jerry Falwell, then pastor of Thomas Road Baptist Church, Lynchburg, Virginia)
- "In only three years, he . . . organized Christianity, which today has branches in all the world's countries and a 32.4 percent share of the world's population, twice as big as its nearest rival. . . . Jesus was the most effective executive in history. The results he achieved are second to none." (James F. Hind, author and motivational speaker)

All three of these perceptions are snapshots of a different sort than those described in this chapter: an imaginary Jesus (Murray), a docetic Jesus (Falwell),[160] an entrepreneurial Jesus (Hind). They exemplify an almost stubborn ignorance of academia, a triumph of personal predilection over historical evidence. One would be hard-pressed to find any historical scholar who would regard any of these three statements as compatible with knowledge that the historical quest for Jesus has brought to the fore. But, of course, the scholars have their own predilections also. Let's find out what they are.

Chapter 4

Robert Funk
and the Jesus Seminar

Jesus is one of the great sages of history, and his insights should be taken seriously but tested by reference to other seers, ancient and modern, who have had glimpses of the eternal, and by reference to everything we can learn from the sciences, the poets, and the artists. Real knowledge, divine knowledge, is indiscriminate in the vessels it elects to fill.
—Robert W. Funk, founder of the Jesus Seminar[1]

Jesus taught that the last will be first and the first will be last. He admonished his followers to be servants of everyone. He urged humility as the cardinal virtue by both word and example. Given these terms, it is difficult to imagine Jesus making claims for himself—I am the Son of God, I am the expected One, the Anointed—unless, of course, he thought that nothing he said applied to himself.
—The Jesus Seminar[2]

The work of the Jesus Seminar will put both Jesus and the Bible "in the news." By so doing, it opens a window of opportunity for significant consciousness raising and education within the church, as well as more broadly in our culture. Together with biblical scholarship generally, it can provide a way for people to be both thoughtful and Christian, rather than having to choose between the two.
—Marcus Borg[3]

The most noteworthy and controversial research on Jesus in recent decades was conducted by a group of scholars who called themselves "the Jesus Seminar." Describing their work as "noteworthy" does not necessarily imply that it is valid or correct any more than describing it as "controversial" implies that it is invalid or wrong. Rather, the significance of this group's accomplishments must be measured in terms of their influence. Some of the authors described in subsequent chapters of this book were members of the Jesus Seminar and relied on that group's findings in their own descriptions of Jesus as a historical figure. Others were opposed to the Seminar's work, and their own research was motivated at least in part by an attempt to present credible alternatives. In any case, no modern student of Jesus as a figure in history can afford to ignore the Jesus Seminar.

In the last decade of the twentieth century, this group of scholars captured attention at a popular level and moved the quest for the historical Jesus out of the ivory towers of academia and into the living rooms of average Americans. Best-selling publications by and about the Jesus Seminar could be found in bookstores across America. Members appeared on televised talk shows, and such magazines as *Atlantic Monthly, Newsweek, Time,* and *U.S. News and World Report* devoted cover stories to the group's work. Hollywood producer Paul Verhoeven (known for such films as *Robocop, Basic Instinct, Total Recall,* and *Starship Troopers*) was a member of the Jesus Seminar and at one point planned to make a movie about Jesus based on the group's findings—he later wrote a book about Jesus instead.[4]

THE WORK OF THE JESUS SEMINAR

The Jesus Seminar was founded in 1985 by Robert Funk, a prominent New Testament scholar who had taught at Texas Christian, Harvard, and Emory Universities and who had served for many years as a leader of the Society of Biblical Literature. Often a figure of controversy, Funk was once described by Claremont University professor James M. Robinson as "the most brilliant, the most creative, though, understandably, the most alienated American New Testament scholar of our time."[5] The Jesus Seminar was officially launched as a research project of the Westar Institute, an organization that, at the time, was directed by Funk. Originally, the intention of this project was "to examine every fragment of the traditions attached to the name of Jesus in order to determine what he really said."[6] Eventually, their work transcended this goal to include study of deeds and actions attributed to Jesus as well. Finally, a third phase focused on developing credible profiles of Jesus as a person who would have said and done the things that the previous research had determined could be reliably attributed to him. This work was essentially completed by 2002, but the Jesus Seminar continues to operate, hosting teaching events to publicize and refine their work.

Funk assembled an impressive array of scholars to carry out the "research project" outlined above. Over two hundred persons were involved at different points in the Seminar's history, though often only thirty to forty would take part in a single meeting. The group's most widely published rosters list seventy-four to seventy-nine persons, most of whom had earned doctorates and positions at respected academic institutions (even Verhoeven—the movie producer—has an advanced degree in mathematics).[7] From the outset, furthermore, the Jesus Seminar sought to involve a wide spectrum of participants, insisting that its qualifications for membership involved academic ability, not ideological commitment. The presence or lack of religious faith was deemed irrelevant to the project. At one point or another the membership roster would include such noteworthy scholars as Andries van Aarde, Harold Attridge, William Beardslee, Marcus Borg, Bruce Chilton, Kathleen Corley, John Dominic Crossan, Joanna Dewey, Dennis Duling, Robert Fortna, Robert Funk, Stephen Harris, Charles Hedrick, Karen King, John Kloppenborg, Gerd Lüdemann, Burton Mack, Robert J. Miller, Stephen Patterson, Robert M. Price, James Robinson, Vernon Robbins, Bernard Brandon Scott, W. Barnes Tatum, Leif Vaage, Robert Webb, and Walter Wink.

Phase One

To meet the original goal of investigating the sayings of Jesus, the Seminar first compiled a numbered list of everything that Jesus is reported to have said in any document prior to 300 CE. This list included all the words attributed to Jesus in the Bible, as well as quotations found in apocryphal gospels and in other writings of early Christians. Notably, no sayings of Jesus are found in non-Christian literature; though Jewish and Roman writings occasionally mention Jesus, they contain no records of his speech or teaching.

The next task of the Seminar was to examine these sayings of Jesus to determine whether they were historically authentic or whether they had been attributed to him by Christians for one reason or another. Group members circulated papers arguing various positions and met twice a year to discuss the results of their research. Finally, they voted on whether a given saying ought to be regarded as authentic. The results of this voting were presented by classifying sayings according to a color scheme: red, pink, gray, or black. The "red" sayings were the ones deemed most likely to be authentic, and the "black" sayings were those deemed least likely to be authentic. "Pink" and "gray" represented degrees of uncertainty. When scholars voted, they would indicate what color they thought the saying should be; the weighted average of all votes cast determined the final classification.

After six years, the group completed this phase of its program and published its results in a book called *The Five Gospels*. The name of this book reflects the group's conclusion that all pink and red sayings can be found in only five books, the four New Testament Gospels plus the apocryphal Gospel of Thomas. Numerically, the results broke down as follows:[8]

	Total Number of Sayings	Red Sayings	Pink Sayings	Gray Sayings	Black Sayings
Matthew	420	11	60	115	234
Mark	177	1	18	66	92
Luke	392	14	65	128	185
John	140	0	1	5	134
Thomas	201	3	40	67	91

This color scheme was one aspect of the Jesus Seminar's project that caught the attention of the popular press. Early on, Seminar members actually voted on sayings by placing colored beads into a hopper. The practice proved cumbersome and was discontinued, but the image of scholars "blackballing Jesus" proved irresistible to journalists. Also, comparisons were drawn to red-letter Bibles popular among some Christians, in which the words of Jesus were printed in red type. Now, reporters would point out with glee, Bibles could use four colors for Jesus' words, depending on whether he really said them or not. Overall, such media reports almost always focused on the Seminar's negative conclusions.

Many of the findings *were* negative. Popular Bible verses classed as black sayings include Jesus' words regarding the salt of the earth (Matt. 5:13), bearing the cross (Mark 8:34), and being born again (John 3:3). All seven of his words from the cross were regarded as unauthentic (Mark 15:34; Luke 23:34, 43, 46; John 19:26–30), as were most of his sayings about himself, including his claim to be the Messiah (Mark 14:62) and "the way, the truth, and the life" (John 14:6). All sayings in which Jesus spoke of the end of the world or of a final judgment were included among the black material. Monologues by Jesus for which there could have been no witness were considered to be counterfeit, as were all verses in which Jesus expressed foreknowledge of events after his death.

In general, sayings recognized as red or pink tended to be ones that are not specifically Christian in tone. These include wisdom sayings that offer common-sense observations about life in a memorable way and moral aphorisms that provide what might be regarded as good ethical advice apart from any specific religious doctrine. The only pink saying in John's Gospel is Jesus' lament that prophets have no honor in their own country (John 4:44), and the only red saying in Mark's Gospel is Jesus' suggestion to "give to the emperor the things that are the emperor's, and to God the things that are God's" (Mark 12:17).

Of all the sayings examined by the Jesus Seminar, the five that garnered the most votes for authenticity were

1. "If anyone strikes you on the right cheek, turn the other also" (Matt. 5:39);
2. "If anyone wants to sue you and take your coat, give your cloak as well" (Matt. 5:40);

3. "Blessed are you who are poor, for yours is the kingdom of God" (Luke 6:20);
4. "If anyone forces you to go one mile, go also the second mile" (Matt. 5:41); and
5. "Love your enemies" (Luke 6:27).

The majority of the red and pink sayings (including all five of the examples above) were found in material attributed to the Q source. The next largest number of authentic sayings were found in the Gospel of Thomas, which is similar to Q in form, that is, a collection of sayings rather than a narrative account of Jesus' life. The significance of this point can be exaggerated, however, for only two of the Thomas sayings colored red or pink were material that has no parallel in the canonical Gospels (Thom. 97 and 98; see pages 55–56).

There was some confusion over how to interpret the Seminar's findings. Popular reports usually built on the assertion that red means "definitely yes" and black means "definitely no" to assume that pink means "probably yes" and gray means "probably no." This might seem logical, but it may not be correct. The Seminar itself struggled to define exactly what was meant by the various colors. Two different official interpretations were offered to guide members in their voting, and one member (Leif Vaage) offered a third colloquial interpretation that also became quite popular (see fig. 5).[9]

In particular, there appears to have been confusion over the meaning of a gray vote. The official introduction to *The Five Gospels* declares that gray was intended to signify "a weak form of black,"[10] but some have observed (based on the interpretations offered) that gray seems to be more of a weak form of pink. At issue is whether gray really does mean "probably no" or whether it means "maybe yes." For some, such a distinction comes down to splitting hairs; for others, the difference is considerable. In any case, Seminar member Marcus Borg alleges that *in practice*, "gray frequently functioned as an 'I'm not sure' vote." Furthermore, when the voting on a controversial saying was divided, black votes would tend to balance out pink and red ones so that the "weighted average" for a saying could end up placing it among the gray material even though very few people had actually voted to place it there. For example, the parable of the two sons in Matthew 21:28–31 ended up being printed in gray type even though only 11 percent of the voters actually cast gray votes for it (32 percent voted black and 58 percent deemed it either red or pink). Accordingly, the large number of sayings that the Jesus Seminar deemed "gray" do not necessarily represent material that they considered to be "probably unauthentic." Rather, according to Borg, the gray sayings are those on which "the verdict is not clear."[11] This caveat could lead to a less negative interpretation of the overall results than that which was popularly reported.

Given the mandates of the Seminar's research, furthermore, its results could be read in a way that is surprisingly positive. Historical scholars tend to be very skeptical, especially when dealing with literature as tendentious as the Gospels. The Jesus Seminar embraced such methodological skepticism as a working

Figure 5. What Do the Colors Mean?

Sayings and Deeds: Option 1 (Official)

Red: I would include this item (or "narrative information") unequivocally in the database for determining who Jesus was.

Pink: I would include this item (or "narrative information") with reservations (or modifications) in the database.

Gray: I would not include this item (or "narrative information") in the database, but I might make use of some of the content in determining who Jesus was.

Black: I would not include this item (or "narrative information") in the primary database.

Sayings: Option 2 (Official)

Red: Jesus undoubtedly said this or something very like it.

Pink: Jesus probably said something like this.

Gray: Jesus did not say this, but the ideas contained in it are close to his own.

Black: Jesus did not say this; it represents the perspective or content of a later or different tradition.

Deeds: Option 2 (Official)

Red: The historical reliability of this information is virtually certain. It is supported by a preponderance of evidence.

Pink: This information is probably reliable. It fits well with evidence that is verifiable.

Gray: This information is possible, but unreliable. It lacks supporting evidence.

Black: This information is improbable. It does not fit verifiable evidence, or it is largely or entirely fictive.

Third Option (Colloquial)

Red: That's Jesus!

Pink: Sure sounds like Jesus.

Gray: Well, maybe.

Black: There's been some mistake.

—based on information from Robert W. Funk et al., *The Five Gospels*, 36–37, and *The Acts of Jesus*, 36–37.

principle, adopting a new version of an old motto: "When in sufficient doubt, leave it out" (compare page 20).[12] In other words, they were encouraged to err on the side of exclusion rather than inclusion, to discover a bare minimum of material that could be regarded as almost unquestionably authentic. Some members, it is said, voted black virtually all the time.[13] Even a few black votes could pull down the weighted average of a saying's final score in a way analogous to the effect a few Fs can have on a student's overall GPA. Granted this, the proportion of sayings that were deemed pink or red is impressive. The story that, by and large, went unreported was this: two hundred historians, relying solely on the investigative techniques of secular, critical scholarship, affirmed the authenticity of some 18 percent of the sayings attributed to Jesus in books that were written a generation after his death by people who made no pretense of being objective or unbiased in what they wrote. The media, however, missed this story, reporting instead the rather bland and predictable instances in which critical scholarship was unable to affirm convictions of religious piety.

Phase Two

The second phase of the Jesus Seminar's work involved investigation of propositions concerning the life and work of Jesus. Reading through stories about Jesus in the Bible and elsewhere, the Seminar developed lists of propositions such as the following:

- Jesus was born in Bethlehem.
- Jesus was of Davidic descent.
- Jesus cured Simon's mother-in-law.
- Jesus was crucified.

After discussion, the Seminar voted on each proposition, using once again the system of four colors (the above propositions were deemed black, gray, pink, and red, respectively).[14] They now defined these color codes as reflecting a sliding scale of reliability, from "virtually certain" (red) to "improbable" (black).[15] Sometimes the Seminar would also vote on how to color code a biblical passage "as a whole." This was to facilitate publication of their next volume, *The Acts of Jesus*, which would print all the Gospel stories about Jesus in color type that reflected their reliability as historical accounts.[16]

Often the Seminar would vote on several different propositions regarding the same event. When considering the proposition "Mary conceived Jesus without sexual intercourse with a man" (black), they also voted on about a dozen related suggestions, such as "Jesus was conceived while Mary and Joseph were betrothed" (gray), "Mary conceived of Joseph" (gray), and "Mary conceived of some unnamed man by rape or seduction" (gray). The goal was to be thorough, to consider, pardon the pun, every conceivable option. They even stopped to ask whether Mary was really the name of Jesus' mother (red).[17]

The language of these propositions was often worded carefully. For instance, a proposition derived from Mark 5:1–20 reads, "Jesus exorcized a man who thought he was demon-possessed" (gray).[18] So stated, members might regard the event as historical without thereby affirming that an exorcism of an actual demon occurred. Again, rather than polling members to determine whether they believe Jesus rose from the dead, the Seminar asked them to vote on whether "Jesus' resurrection from the dead involved the resuscitation of his corpse" (black) and on whether "the resurrection of Jesus was an event open to empirical verification" (black).[19] Such careful wording was necessary because some persons might claim that Jesus did rise from the dead in a sense other than that which these propositions meant to test. Theologian Rudolf Bultmann, for instance, used to claim that Jesus rose from the dead "in the kerygma [preaching] of the church."[20]

When *The Acts of Jesus* appeared in 1998, it color coded 387 reports of 176 separate events. Of these, ten events were rated red and nineteen pink. Thus, 16 percent of the events reported in the Gospels were deemed authentic, slightly less than the 18 percent of the sayings deemed authentic in *The Five Gospels*.

Phase Three

The Jesus Seminar next decided that they would compose a sort of biography of Jesus based on the sayings and deeds that they had determined were authentic. The idea was to describe the man Jesus as Seminar members saw him. From the outset, however, such a collective witness seemed elusive. "There could be hopeless disagreement" cochair John Dominic Crossan said when the project was first announced. "Bob Funk's Jesus is quite different from mine."[21] Nevertheless, when Seminar members met in October 1997 and in March 1998, each submitted his or her own profile of who Jesus was. These accounts were compared to one another and correlations were noted, but differences were evident as well. Thus, in 2002, two books were published almost simultaneously: *A Credible Jesus* by Robert Funk offers a somewhat composite description based on the Seminar's findings (as interpreted by Funk);[22] *Profiles of Jesus* edited by Roy Hoover offers a number of portraits of Jesus from different members, along with a handful of articles about various facets of Jesus research.[23]

JESUS ACCORDING TO THE JESUS SEMINAR

Although individual members of the Jesus Seminar would differ on details, a general portrait of Jesus would come to be associated with the group as a whole.[24] According to this view, the man Jesus began his career as a disciple of John the Baptist but eventually rejected both the ascetic life that his mentor advocated and the apocalyptic message of a coming judgment that was supposed to motivate people to repent and adopt such a lifestyle. Instead, Jesus said the kingdom of God was already a reality, here and now, and he made a deliberate practice of eating and drinking in what was considered a profane style to celebrate this. An iconoclastic poet, he fraternized shamelessly with social outcasts and caricatured the empty values on which human behavior can be based. Favorite targets for his wit included reliance on wealth, uncritical respect for blood relatives, and the pomposity of religion. For Jesus, temples, priests, and all other accoutrements of religion were unnecessary, as were, ultimately, earthly possessions and family.

Jesus had a knack for telling parables and for coining paradoxical aphorisms that challenged usual ways of thinking. He also recalled and used secular proverbs. He became a traveling sage who wandered from village to village offering his eccentric brand of teaching to people in exchange for handouts. He did not call on people to repent or fast or observe the Sabbath, nor did he make any theological statements about God.[25] His message, if one can call it that, was primarily a challenge to social convention. He was a social critic, but not one who had any program or prescription for solving the world's ills. He ridiculed those who claimed to have answers and did not claim to have any answers himself. Otherwise, he was reticent and unassuming, neither enlisting followers nor initiating debate. He did not usually talk about himself, nor did he have any particular vision of the future.

He attracted attention all the same. Apparently, dozens of people began to follow him about. They (and others) would ply him with questions, to which he would never give direct answers. They also maintained that he was able to exorcize demons and cure diseases. Jesus went along with this, effecting some psychosomatic cures and accepting this as demonstrative that, indeed, life here and now can be all that it ought to be. Eventually, he made his way to Jerusalem, where he instigated some kind of incident in the temple area during a festival. He was arrested and quickly executed without a trial.

IMPLICATIONS OF THE JESUS SEMINAR'S WORK

Observer Charlotte Allen describes the figure who emerges from the Seminar's work as "a dirt-poor, illiterate peasant sage from Galilee influenced perhaps by Greek Cynic philosophers. He is also a "non-Christian Jesus"—a man who displays no interest in the end of the world, resurrection, or redemption—but who evinces great respect for cultural diversity.[26] And he is a "no-frills" Jesus—a Jesus with little supernatural baggage. All this makes the Seminar's Jesus very contemporary and potentially popular with the world at large (though, perhaps, not with the church). The Jesus of the Jesus Seminar, Allen muses, is "a Jesus for the America of the third millennium."[27] Allen is a journalist, not a historian or theologian, and some Seminar members may think her pithy comments trivialize the group's serious academic agenda. Nevertheless, the comments seem to capture the way this work has been perceived at a popular level.

Seminar members themselves have often been cited in the media as describing Jesus in unconventional terms. Leif Vaage said Jesus was "a party animal, somewhat shiftless, and disrespectful of the fifth commandment: Honor your father and mother."[28]Arthur Dewey averred, "There is more of David Letterman in the historical Jesus than Pat Robertson."[29] Funk agreed: "Jesus was perhaps the first stand-up Jewish comic."[30] Was he even religious? Not in the conventional sense. The Bible presents him as alienated from the religious institutions of his day, the temple and the synagogues. For the Jesus Seminar this was not because he wanted to start a better religion, but because he was adverse to institutional religion, period. "Starting a new religion," Funk said, "would have been the farthest thing from his mind."[31] But did Jesus believe in God? Did he, for example, pray? "I think he prayed," Hal Taussig concluded, "but I don't think he made a big deal out of it."[32]

Ultimately, different members of the Jesus Seminar may construe the implications of the group's research differently. With that in mind, we will offer here the comments of four prominent members who have published reflections on what the group's work should mean for history and theology.

Robert Funk claimed that the Jesus Seminar was laying the foundations for a new reformation. "Christianity as we have known it is anemic and wasting away," he said. "It is time to reinvent Christianity, complete with new symbols, new stories, and a new understanding of Jesus."[33] He laid out the agenda for such a reformation in his book *Honest to Jesus*. Christian faith can continue, but it must become secularized spirituality rather than institutionalized religion.

Funk contrasts the development of "creedal Christianity" with the faith that inspired Jesus:

> Popular creedalism insists on a miraculous birth, accrediting miracles, death on a cross understood as a blood sacrifice, a bodily resurrection, and Jesus' eventual return to hold cosmic court. We need only ask, Which of these doctrines derives from what we know of the historical Jesus? Which of them depends on Jesus' authorization? Or are they part of the mythological overlay invented by Jesus' early admirers?[34]

Funk contends that, indeed, Christianity as we know it was not inaugurated by Jesus, but by people like Peter and Paul. It is "a second-hand faith," not the religion *of* Jesus but a religion *about* him.[35] Jesus himself pointed people to something he called God's domain (i.e., "the kingdom of God"). Instead of looking to see what he saw, his followers tended to "stare at the pointing finger."[36]

Making Jesus the object of faith is certainly ironic, Funk says, since "the Jesus of whom we catch glimpses in the Gospels may be said to have been irreligious, irreverent, and impious."[37] The church has had to ignore this "real Jesus" in order to perpetuate its religious views regarding the mythological figure. To illustrate, Funk cites the historic Apostles Creed:

> He was conceived by the power of the Holy Spirit
> and born of the virgin Mary. He suffered under Pontius Pilate,
> was crucified, died, and was buried . . .

What's missing? The *life* of Jesus! The framers (and confessors) of such a creed, Funk fumes, apparently believe that nothing worth mentioning lies between the miraculous birth of Jesus and his death on the cross. "The creed," he says, "left a blank where Jesus should have come."[38] And the Jesus that it leaves out is one who would not have approved of its content or even of the basic idea of having authoritative creeds in the first place. With the development of Christianity into a formal religion, Funk says, "the iconoclast became an icon."[39]

Funk goes on to outline his understanding of a faith that is based on the vision of Jesus rather than on the proclamations of others concerning him.[40] Many cherished doctrines, including blood atonement, resurrection, and apocalyptic promises of reward and punishment, will have to go. In their place will be an ethical spirituality that includes and nourishes. Jesus prioritized inclusivity and reciprocal forgiveness and advocated an "unbrokered relationship with God." He condemned the public practice of piety and made it clear that all rewards and punishments are intrinsic. If Christianity can be reconstituted as the faith *of* Jesus rather than as faith *in* Jesus, Christians will also have to abandon all sense of privilege, including the notion that they can be distinguished from others as "saved" or "redeemed" people who occupy a favorable position in God's eyes.

Marcus Borg interprets the implications of the Jesus Seminar's work in a less radical way.[41] Essentially, he believes, the Jesus Seminar helped people to distinguish between "the pre-Easter Jesus and the post-Easter Jesus," that is, between the historical person who lived on this earth for a short time and the enduring figure who remains the subject of Christian tradition and experience. Borg makes this distinction with fewer value judgments than Funk does. Insights that came from early Christians are not necessarily less valuable than those that can be attributed to Jesus himself. For Borg, then, the color scheme reflects only the origin of the material, not its veracity. Some of the material in black he finds "quite wonderful." Even if the historical Jesus did not actually say, "I am the light of the world" (John 8:12), the early Christians who put these words on Jesus' lips believed he was the light of the world, and consideration of the experiences that led them to believe this may be just as important for contemporary faith as is analysis of words that the Seminar prints in red type.

Why bother with a distinction at all then? For one thing, Borg says, the pre-Easter Jesus ceases to be a credible figure if attributes properly belonging to the post-Easter Jesus are ascribed to him. He ceases to be human, which is "neither good history nor good theology."[42] The problem for Borg is not that the church has developed confessional statements about Jesus based on post-Easter experiences, but that it has allowed these to eclipse its vision of Jesus as he was before Easter. He suggests that the Seminar's work may be understood as analogous to archaeology. It sorts out the layers of tradition, so that we may see what belongs properly to each layer (Jesus himself, the later church). Each layer is important, but each ought to be understood on its own terms. Christian faith,

Borg continues, ought not be based solely on historical reconstructions of the pre-Easter Jesus any more than it should be based solely on creedal affirmations about the post-Easter Jesus. The goal should be to find "a dialogical and dialectical relationship between the two."[43]

Burton Mack is less interested in dialogue. An early member of the Jesus Seminar who dropped out before *The Five Gospels* was published, Mack embraces a radical skepticism regarding almost everything about Jesus that is not attested in the Q source (see pages 27–30). According to Mack, the effects of historical Jesus study such as that conducted by the Seminar should be devastating. It undercuts Christianity's claim to be the religion of Jesus. "It should bring to an end the myth, the history, the mentality of the Gospels," Mack avers.[44] The people behind the Q document did not view Jesus as the Messiah or Son of God, nor did they have any idea that his death offered them atonement for their sins, nor did they believe he rose from the dead. "It's over," Mack concludes, without pity. "We've had enough apocalypses. We've had enough martyrs. Christianity has had a two-thousand year run, and it's over."[45]

Robert Miller maintains that "the best way to regard the work of the Jesus Seminar is to see it as opening a door and pointing the way."[46] The research of the Jesus Seminar does point to a new way of understanding Jesus, but in making Jesus research accessible to the masses, it also "opens the door to a formerly closed room."[47] Miller claims that one of the primary attractions of the group for him was its commitment to working in public: its meetings were "open to all rather than taking place behind the closed doors of academia" and the Seminar was intentional about communicating the results of its research in ways that invited the collaboration of other scholars and, indeed, the input of any qualified commentator.[48] Ultimately, the scholars of the Seminar would be disappointed if their judgments were "taken as gospel"; the whole point of the project was to invite and enable others to join the quest for the historical Jesus.[49]

CRITIQUE OF THE JESUS SEMINAR

The Jesus Seminar had its foes. Roused by the audacity of the group's claims, by the intensity of public response, and by an awareness of what could be at stake, critics across a wide spectrum would launch an unorganized counteroffensive.[50]

Craig Blomberg, a Baptist minister and professor of New Testament at Denver Seminary, counseled Christians to believe that God's Spirit inspired the writing of the Bible, ensuring an accuracy that could not have been there otherwise.[51] Luke Timothy Johnson, a Roman Catholic layman and professor of New Testament at Candler School of Theology (Emory University), advised people to ignore questions about the historical Jesus altogether, since validation of the Christian faith is evident in the quality of life demonstrated by those who confess it.[52] N. T. Wright, an Anglican priest and historian of the classical period, said the Seminar's agenda was so shaped by opposition to fundamentalism as to foster a closed-minded caricature of scholarship that was itself ironically fundamentalistic.[53] Blomberg, Johnson, and Wright differed on their own ideas regarding Jesus as a figure in history, but they had this in common: they believed the Jesus Seminar was wrong, perhaps dangerously wrong. "Things of fundamental importance are being distorted," said Johnson.[54]

Rhetoric ran rampant. Boston University professor Howard Clark Kee called the Jesus Seminar "an academic disgrace,"[55] and Richard B. Hays of Duke University accused them of "reprehensible deception."[56] Johnson charged Funk with "grandiosity and hucksterism" and derided the Seminar as "a ten-year exercise in self-promotion."[57] Indeed, he claimed that Funk engaged in "deliberate deception."[58] Some Seminar members proved that they could give (almost) as good as they got. Funk himself was reported to have had harsh words for other historical Jesus scholars, denouncing John Meier as "a blockhead" and dismissing N. T. Wright as "eccentric."[59] Wright noted that, since the Seminar had determined Jesus' saying about turning the other cheek to be the single best attested saying in the entire database, perhaps they should heed that counsel with regard to their critics.[60]

In any case, polemic runs the risk of derailing discussion away from issues more worthy of consideration. For convenience, we will place criticisms leveled against the Jesus Seminar into seven broad categories. For what it is worth, I am presenting these according to what I personally regard as an ascending order of validity.

First, the *motives* of the Jesus Seminar were challenged. The group was often depicted in the media as comprising a goodly number of lapsed Christians. Journalist Charlotte Allen described the meetings as having "the air of a village atheists' convention," while also noting that "a favorite after-hours activity for members is to belt out the rousing evangelical hymns of their church-going childhoods."[61] When the group was in its heyday, almost every media report would mention that Funk was a *former* evangelist who once led revival meetings in rural Texas[62] and that cochair Crossan was a *former* Roman Catholic priest (he left to marry, but admits his unorthodox views would have made an eventual departure unavoidable for ideological reasons).[63] The implication of such reports may be that Funk, Crossan, and other Seminar members were simply working out frustrations born of their own crises, even getting revenge on institutionalized religion for not being more acceptable (or accepting). "Unfortunately," Wright observed slyly, "the attempt to escape from one's own past is not a good basis for the attempt to reconstruct someone else's."[64]

It seems unlikely, however, that all members of the Seminar would be so possessed or that Funk and Crossan would have been able to mold them all to their own designs. The academic credentials of the group and its founders were impeccable. No one had bothered to question Funk's motives when he produced one of the most important Greek grammars of the twentieth century, or

Crossan's when he did groundbreaking work on the literary genre of parables.[65] In any case, speculation regarding the psychological motives of scholars contributes little to evaluation of their work. Mixed or unclear motives do not invalidate research any more than pure motives (if such exist) guarantee sound results.[66]

The *tactics* of the Jesus Seminar were also disparaged, particularly the deliberate appeal to the media. Johnson says this is what provoked him to attack the group. Academic freedom allows scholars to say all kinds of outlandish things in restricted settings where the comments are open to critical scrutiny and discussion. But when statements such as "Bible Scholars Say Jesus Didn't Promise to Return" become banner headlines or sound bites on the evening news, the context does not allow for caveats or counterarguments. "There was a deliberate decision to play to the media," Crossan admits, adding that he himself had to be persuaded by Funk that "there was an ethical necessity to let the public in on what we were doing."[67] The very purpose of the Westar Institute, according to Seminar member Vernon K. Robbins, was to get public attention for "serious religious scholarship" instead of allowing "the right-wing Christian community" to dominate all talk about religious matters.[68] "What's wrong with scholarly knowledge becoming common knowledge?" Funk asked. "Heart surgeons and rocket scientists are adept at explaining their work to a general audience, at writing books and getting interviewed on television. Now it is time for the philosophers, theologians, and social scientists to do the same."[69] The debatable point, perhaps, would not be whether the public ought to be brought in on such discussions but whether, in courting the media, the Jesus Seminar opened the door for an inevitable sensationalism. Regardless of the Seminar's intentions, some observers would say that the media oversimplified complex issues, presented minority views as consensus statements, and in other respects skewed the discussion in ways that the public was not able to detect or evaluate.

The *constitution* of the Jesus Seminar was criticized and its claim to diversity rebutted. First, critics noted that almost all members were white, male, and from North America. There was no apparent attempt to exclude others. Rather, the near homogeneity of race and gender was fairly representative of the guild of historical Jesus scholars as a whole, and participation of scholars from other countries was made difficult by location of the Seminar's meetings in North America. Nevertheless, a more diverse group may very well have reached different conclusions. Even given the location in North America, the Jesus Seminar did not draw from as broad a pool of candidates as one might have hoped or expected. Hays noted that, in terms of educational background, just five schools would account for the doctorates of forty of the group's seventy-four rostered members.[70]

At the heart of this concern is a question regarding ideological diversity. Don A. Carson of Trinity Evangelical Divinity School describes the group as espousing "left-wing ideology,"[71] a charge that gains some credence when Seminar members contrast their work with that of "right-wing" Christians (see the quote by Robbins above). Likewise, Johnson's charge that the group is "hostile to any traditional understanding of Jesus as defined by the historic creeds of Christianity"[72] is hard to rebut when its founder maintained that the *goal* of the Jesus Seminar was "to set Jesus free from the scriptural and creedal prisons in which we have entombed him."[73] Still, when Johnson claims that members of the Seminar were "self-selected" according to a prior agreement that they would portray Jesus as a countercultural figure who reflects the attitudes favored by liberal academics, we enter the realm of unprovable conspiracy theory. With regard to religious affiliation, the group did try to be ecumenical. Its membership included significant numbers of Protestants, Catholics, and nonreligious persons. A few Jewish scholars took part. Even fundamentalists were invited to participate, though none accepted the offer. According to one report, "Southern Baptist scholars took part until pressure from within their denomination forced them to withdraw."[74]

The group's ideological slant, then, may have been unintentional, but the fact that certain ideological biases did govern the group's work probably does need to be acknowledged. Such an acknowledgment need not invalidate the group's work: even if the Jesus Seminar was not representative of the entire guild of New Testament scholarship, it was certainly much more than "an academic splinter group."[75] Basically, the Seminar turned out to be representative of a major voice within the guild, a voice that may have espoused minority positions on certain issues, but that was rarely, if ever, idiosyncratic. Further, that voice was a chorus. The charge "They all think alike!" was not completely accurate but, in any case, begged the question *"Why* do they think alike?" The harmony of so many usually independent voices was precisely what demanded that attention be given to this chorus of scholars.

The *content* of the Jesus Seminar's findings has been dismissed as incredible. Blomberg maintains that "the Seminar's Jesus simply is not sufficiently Jewish to be a historically credible figure."[76] Birger Pearson claims that the Jesus Seminar "performed a forcible epispasm on the historical Jesus," meaning that they turned Jesus into a non-Jew (an epispasm is a surgical operation that restores a foreskin to a penis, removing the sign of circumcision).[77]

In a similar though less colorful manner, a number of scholars complain that the Seminar has no adequate explanation for Jesus' death. If he was basically just a passive, witty spouter of aphorisms, why was he crucified? John Meier puts it this way: "Such a Jesus would threaten no one, just as the university professors who create him threaten no one."[78]

Wright echoes these concerns but focuses on another. He finds the Seminar's noneschatological portrait of Jesus remarkable, since even they grant that eschatological elements were central to the thinking of John the Baptist and to the apostolic community. Are we really to believe that Jesus was "radically different from his predecessor and mentor and was radically misunderstood by almost all his followers from the very beginning"?[79] Pearson agrees, claiming that a noneschatological Jesus "strains credulity to the breaking point."[80]

The Seminar does have answers for all of these points. They insist that they did not challenge the basic "Jewishness" of Jesus but only questioned assumptions about the extent to which Jews in first-century Galilee may have been hellenized. Crossan says, "It is not enough to insist that Jesus was Jewish. So was Josephus—or, for that matter, Caiaphas."[81] And Robert Miller explains, "The accusation that the Jesus Seminar strips Jesus of his Judaism is a powerful attention-getter, but it is an accusation without specific content. Everyone in the historical Jesus debate agrees that Jesus was Jewish. The real question is what kind of Jew he was."[82]

Likewise, some members of the Seminar suggest that Jesus' death may have been more or less incidental. Perhaps he pulled some kind of prank in the Jerusalem temple that got him labeled a subversive. Perhaps the Romans did not make fine distinctions between social critics and political revolutionaries. In any case, Jesus could have just said or done the wrong thing in the wrong place at the wrong time and been caught up in a Roman pogrom of potential insurgents.

And what about the Seminar's decision to exclude eschatological elements from its historical portrait of Jesus? On this and many other points, the Seminar would simply maintain that its conclusions, based on more than a decade of hard work by competent scholars, ought not be dismissed *solely* because they are nontraditional or surprising. Rather, those who think the findings are incredible ought to review the process through which the Seminar came to their conclusions and consider the evidence on which the controversial findings are based. This leads us to the next point.

The Jesus Seminar's *methods of research* have been subject to critique. First, the Seminar's application of criteria is criticized. It is often said that they relied quite heavily on the criterion of dissimilarity, which grants historical authenticity to elements of the Jesus tradition that differ both from what was typical of Palestinian Judaism and from what became normative within Christianity (see pages 63–65). All historical scholars make some use of this criterion, but the Jesus Seminar is said to have used it so heavily as to guarantee Jesus who bore little resemblance to either traditional Judaism or Christianity.[83] Ruling out sayings attributed to Jesus simply because they concur with later church tradition seems to assume that Jesus' followers did not learn anything from him. Other criteria were similarly challenged. The Jesus Seminar stressed "orality" as a test for the authenticity of Jesus' sayings, by which they meant that in an oral culture (where few things were written down), the sayings most likely to be remembered were short, pithy ones such as aphorisms and parables. Critics of the Seminar claim that people in oral cultures have been known to memorize epics, such that the length of a quote alone ought not eliminate it from consideration.

The group also accepted as basic operating assumptions a number of points that are debated within the field. For example, the Gospel of Thomas was understood to be a first-century work, contemporary with or earlier than the four New Testament Gospels. As indicated in chapter 2 of this book, however, many scholars date the composition of Thomas to the second century and regard it as dependent on the New Testament writings (see pages 55–56). The Seminar also relied more heavily on reconstructions of Q than many scholars would think appropriate. The Jesus that the Seminar finally presented was in large part the Jesus of Q, with eschatological elements expunged. Within the wider field of biblical studies, many scholars would be more tentative regarding reconstructions and dating of Q material, and quite a few would question any assumption that what derives from this source has more intrinsic credibility than what derives from Mark, the earliest of the four Gospels.

The charge, essentially, is that many of the Seminar's conclusions were predetermined by its methodological presuppositions. We might illustrate this with reference to one of its most prominent findings, namely that Jesus was a sage. Such a conclusion, it is said, was guaranteed by the Seminar's devotion to the criterion of orality. The process appears to critics to have gone something like this: the Seminar (1) started with the assumption that aphorisms are the type of material most likely to be authentic, (2) discovered that the material they deemed authentic on the basis of this assumption contained mainly aphorisms, and (3) concluded on the basis of this research that the authentic Jesus was a speaker of aphorisms (i.e., a sage).

A similar process of circular reasoning is sometimes said to have informed another of their findings: the conclusion that Jesus was noneschatological, that is, that he did not speak in apocalyptic language about the end of the world or a final judgment. Such a "discovery" appears to have been guaranteed by devotion to the criterion of dissimilarity. Apocalyptic language is attributed to Jesus in almost all the early material (except Thomas), including the Seminar's much-vaunted Q source. But since the early Christian church was thoroughly eschatological in its views, the Seminar eliminated such material as too compatible with Christianity to fit its image of Jesus.[84]

Within the academy of biblical studies, observers of the Jesus Seminar often recall a now-famous observation made by a promising member of the guild in the early 1970s: "Methodology is not an indifferent net—it catches what it intends to catch."[85] The scholar who offered this comment was none other than Robert W. Funk.

Thus, in 1991, Funk listed sixty-four premises that the Seminar followed in its deliberation of material.[86] Though many were noncontroversial, statements such as the following were also included:

- Premise 10: The oral tradition exhibits little interest in biographical data about Jesus.
- Premise 29: John is a less reliable source than the other Gospels for the sayings of Jesus.
- Premise 45: Only a small portion of the sayings attributed to Jesus in the Gospels was actually spoken by him.

As Wright observes, statements such as these sound not like premises but conclusions.[87] Indeed, the media has often reported such statements as *results* of the

Jesus Seminar's research. But they were not results; they were presuppositions. To be fair, the Seminar itself was usually forthright about saying this, but neither the press nor the public seem to have always appreciated the distinction.

Finally, the Jesus Seminar's *interpretation* of their own work is a matter for discussion. Two points here are especially pertinent. First, the Seminar was inclined to equate "unverifiable" with "unauthentic." Most Jesus scholars would be willing to grant that there is often insufficient evidence to establish the historicity of numerous sayings and deeds attributed to Jesus in the Gospels. For most scholars, however, lack of evidence means simply that a matter cannot be verified and that, accordingly, it should not be regarded as historical in a strict sense of the word. The Jesus Seminar consistently went further and maintained that Jesus *did not say* or *did not do* things that he is reported to have said or done. Thus, even scholars who accept the legitimacy of the Seminar's research would not necessarily accept the conclusions that the Seminar drew from that research. For example, many scholars would agree with the Seminar that there is insufficient evidence to assert with historical confidence that Jesus was born in Bethlehem or that he told people he was "the Way, the Truth, and the Life"; they would be less inclined, however, to state with historical confidence (as the Seminar did) that Jesus was *not* born in Bethlehem and that he did *not* tell people he was the Way, the Truth, and the Life. What is "unverifiable" is not usually regarded as necessarily "unauthentic."

The same principle applies to religious claims that appeal to something other than historical evidence : the Jesus Seminar was not shy about interpreting their research as having direct bearing on theology and faith (arenas in which historians typically plead "no comment"). For example, historical scholars—whether Christian or not—have typically agreed that there is no available evidence to ascertain whether or not Jesus was actually born to a virgin; the attendant conclusion to this realization, however, has usually been that this is something one would have to believe on the basis of religious faith rather than historical science. The Jesus Seminar, again, went further, maintaining that it is a historical fact that Jesus was conceived through normal sexual intercourse between a man and a woman. Thus, the Jesus Seminar may be said to have allowed a post-Enlightenment historical-scientific view of reality to determine not only what is verifiable but also what is believable. If accepted, such a stance would turn a corner in the traditional understanding of the relationship that faith and philosophy bear to science and history. In America, for instance, a public school teacher would ordinarily be regarded as violating constitutional separation of church and state for teaching that Jesus was miraculously born to a virgin. History students should be taught only what is amenable to historical verification. The Jesus Seminar's vision, however, would seem to entail public school teachers telling students that Jesus was *not* born of a virgin, that the story of the virgin birth is simply a fictive tale composed by the church, something that educated people should know did not really happen.

The Jesus Seminar's interpretation of its own work has been criticized in a second way, one that touches upon the relationship between premises and results discussed above. The Seminar is said to have presented its work in positivistic terms, claiming to offer "the assured results of historical-critical scholarship."[88] To some, this description has conveyed a false impression of "objective" scholarship, according to which evidence is impartially weighed by academics who have no vested interest in the outcome. Such was clearly not the case. Indeed, Funk reported that Seminar members found the process of voting on Jesus' sayings to be as exciting as a sporting event, occasionally cheering or moaning the outcomes.[89] No scholar is ever completely objective, and those who composed the Jesus Seminar made no pretense at being such. Before the group was even a year old, Funk was announcing that its conclusions would combat the "pious platitudes of television evangelists and the doomsday writings of modern apocalyptists."[90] How did he know, already, what the findings would be? He didn't *know,* perhaps, but he certainly had a vision of what he hoped they would be!

The essential criticism here is that the work of the Jesus Seminar was misinterpreted when its conclusions were presented as a new view of Jesus discovered by dispassionate scholars who conducted an objective and detailed study of the available data. It might be more accurate to say that the Seminar started with a particular view of Jesus and then worked through the relevant data to determine the extent to which it could be sustained.[91] This is not to say that they manipulated the evidence to support an arbitrary prejudgment, but, surely, they must have begun with some conception of Jesus that would have been recognizably distinct from that held by people whose vision of Jesus they suspected of being flawed. And then, as it turned out, they found that their view of Jesus *was* sustainable: for the most part, the image of Jesus with which they had begun held up, though, of course, the process of working through the material enabled them to refine that view of Jesus and to define it in greater detail.

The Jesus Seminar needs to be evaluated for what it was. It was not a collection of liberal apostates conspiring to undermine the Christian faith, nor was it a think tank of curious historians dispassionately following the strictures of academic research to discover what they might reveal. It was a group of relatively like-minded scholars testing a set of hypotheses regarding Jesus as a figure in history. The fact that they began with hypotheses rather than with a blank slate does not invalidate their work. All serious historians do this, including all the historians of Jesus discussed in this book.[92]

What marks the Jesus Seminar as unique—probably the *only* thing that marks them as unique—is that they were a group. Though other scholars may confer with colleagues, only the Jesus Seminar invested the time, money, and energy to meet so regularly and under such circumstances that their publications could truly be termed the work of the entire group. This is not an inconsiderable accomplishment, and this fact alone earns them the attention they have received. Some critics have said that the Jesus Seminar represented only a small minority of New Testament scholars and, statistically, that would be true. The number of persons with the academic and professional qualifications to have worked on *The Five Gospels* project would probably have been close to ten thousand in

North America alone. Only seventy-four scholars consented to place their names on that volume. Still, that is seventy-three more names than are associated with any of the other positions described in this book.

Although the group seems to have established perimeters that limited their consideration to hypotheses that fit within a particular interpretative scheme, its research was genuine in terms of fine-tuning and revising those hypotheses in the crucible of critical debate. Thus, the group may represent only one of several available positions on the historical Jesus, but it represents that position well, having presented it with intense attention to detail. As the "Introduction" to *The Five Gospels* claims:

> The Fellows of the Seminar are critical scholars. To be a *critical* scholar means to make empirical, factual evidence—evidence open to confirmation by independent, neutral observers—the controlling factor in historical judgments. . . . Critical scholars adopt the principle of methodological skepticism: accept only what passes the rigorous tests of the rules of evidence . . . Critical scholars practice their craft by submitting their work to the judgment of peers. Untested work is not highly regarded.[93]

Chapter 5

John Dominic Crossan

According to John Dominic Crossan, Jesus was a Jewish Cynic peasant with an alternative social vision.

—Marcus Borg[1]

Crossan's Jesus, whose role model seems to have been Stanley Kubrick's Spartacus, ate with outcasts and led a raggedy band of first-century hippies from village to village, preaching a message of radical egalitarianism to the oppressed denizens.

—Charlotte Allen[2]

For Crossan, the Jesus of history was the center of a Galilean Camelot, the halcyon days when Jesus and his band roamed the countryside, disregarding societal structures, defying hierarchical patterns, irritating elites and confounding the powerful, creating a grass-roots movement with nobodies while at the same time refusing to be its leader or mediator.

—Leander Keck[3]

Social revolutionary, Jewish Socrates, political troublemaker—this shocking, insightful portrait presents Jesus as a societal rebel who preached and practiced a message of radical egalitarianism.

—advertisement for John Dominic Crossan's
Jesus: A Revolutionary Biography

One thing can be said about John Dominic Crossan from the outset: no other scholar of the historical Jesus is more admired by his or her opponents. "Crossan is one of the most brilliant, engaging, learned, and quick-witted New Testament scholars alive today," opines N. T. Wright before going on to say that the Irish savant is nevertheless "almost entirely wrong" in everything he has to say about Jesus.[4] Likewise, James Charlesworth quips that "Crossan is often so attractive that one forgets to think about his methodology"—a backhanded compliment meant to imply that the man offers more in style than in substance.[5]

Crossan has earned a fair amount of praise through years of devotion to far-ranging scholarship. Archaeology, anthropology, sociology, source criticism, literary criticism—if a field has any usefulness for contemporary study of the New Testament, Crossan, it seems, has been there and left his mark. Now Professor Emeritus at DePaul University in Chicago, his knowledge of the ancient world appears to be encyclopedic. He has made seminal contributions to the study of the parables and to research on apocryphal writings.[6] His name appears in bibliographies of books that have nothing to do with the historical Jesus and yet, in retrospect, that topic would seem to have been his primary concern all along. For example, he now says that his work on parables not only helped him to decide which of the parables might be attributable to the historical Jesus, but attuned him to the necessity of metaphorical language when speaking of sacred reality: first he realized that when Jesus wanted to say something important about God, he used parable—then, he realized that when the *church* wanted to say something important about Jesus, it also used parable. Stories like the feeding of the 5,000 "scream parable," Crossan says: not history, not miracle, but parable.[7]

Crossan engages in Jesus research for what he calls ethical and theological reasons as well as historical ones. As an avowed Christian, he is able, at times, to offer his somewhat disturbing conclusions "as a challenge within the Christian faith." A Roman Catholic, Crossan served for nineteen years as a Servite monk and priest before leaving the priesthood in part because he wanted to marry and, in part, due to theological concerns. "Not even a vow of obedience could make me sing a song I did not hear," he says.[8] Still, he considers himself "a Catholic through and through."[9] For a person of faith (especially), he says the historical task need not be a "search" or a "quest," with the goal of attaining some definitive answer once and for all. His preferred term for what he does is *reconstruction:* "something that must be done over and over again in different times and different places, by different groups and different communities, and by every generation again and again and again."[10]

In 1991, Crossan published *The Historical Jesus,* followed in 1998 by *The Birth of Christianity.*[11] Together, these studies represent a magnum opus of considerable stature. We will be concerned primarily with the first work, which according to a blurb on the jacket seeks to present "the first comprehensive determination of who Jesus was, what he did, and what he said." Whether it is "first" or "comprehensive," the book is certainly thorough. It devotes some two hundred pages to laying out an approach for understanding Jesus within his own historical context and then another two hundred to describing Jesus as Crossan envisions him. Complex methodological issues are engaged, and yet the book remains informative and provocative throughout. Almost every reviewer would comment on the book's "beauty" or "elegance," words not usually associated with theological tomes. "He seems incapable," says Wright, "of thinking a boring thought or writing a dull paragraph."[12] Thus, from the moment *The Historical Jesus* appeared, Crossan evinced potential for popular success in the world beyond academia. This potential was fulfilled by a flurry of books that were essentially spin-offs from his scholarly publications but designed to reach a wider audience:

- *Jesus: A Revolutionary Biography* presents a synopsis of his more provocative ideas in a series of short vignettes tailored, it seems, for fans of *Reader's Digest*. Crossan calls this one his "baby Jesus book"—not because it is about the baby Jesus but because it is a small book about the adult Jesus;
- *The Essential Jesus* offers a compendium of ninety-three quotes, Crossan's own translations of things he believes Jesus said, arranged one per page with illustrations and lots of white space;
- *Who Killed Jesus?* provides a popular account of Crossan's views on the crucifixion story and on the unjust slander of Jewish people as responsible for a crime in which (he believes) they were not actually involved;
- *God and Empire* discusses political implications of Jesus' understanding of God's kingdom, with emphasis on peace, justice, and equality.

Crossan has also authored (or coauthored) popular books on the Lord's Prayer, Holy Week, and the Christmas narratives.[13]

These popular treatments, along with Crossan's involvement in the Jesus Seminar (which he cochaired), brought a degree of celebrity to the scholar, and this seemed to agree with him. As we will see, a similar celebrity status would eventually be accorded the scholar who is perhaps Crossan's most visible ideological opponent: N. T. Wright. For all their differences, Crossan and Wright have at least two things in common: they are both adept at communicating their (complex) ideas in simple, memorable ways; and they are famous for their dry (but surprisingly quick) senses of humor, which they often employ in ways that defuse otherwise tense situations. For example, when a student who was concerned about Crossan being too liberal told him, "My pastor says you are to the left of Borg," Crossan responded, "The really bad news is that Jesus is to the left of both of us—and, if Jesus sits at the right hand of God—that means God is to the left of Jesus!"[14]

As comfortable chatting on TV talk shows as he is engaging in academic discussions at meetings of the Society for Biblical Literature, Crossan sometimes fills a role for biblical studies that Carl Sagan once filled for astronomy. Unlike many scholars, he has not objected to "being a personality," having his work interpreted with reference to his own life journey. Indeed, he has invited this. In *The Historical Jesus,* he eschews objectivity as unobtainable and spurious, and offers in its place a more realistic credential for scholarship: honesty.[15] Instances of such honesty crop up regularly in his autobiography, *A Long Way from Tipperary*, in which he allows that some of his decisions about Jesus could be influenced by circumstances of his own life and upbringing.[16] Even more to the point, Crossan maintains that he did not endeavor to find a Jesus whom he liked or disliked, and, in fact, he ended up finding one whom he personally is unable to follow. He imagines this conversation with the historical Jesus:

> "I've read your book, Dominic, and it's quite good. So, now you're ready to live by my vision and join me in my program?"

> "I don't think I have the courage, Jesus, but I did describe it quite well, didn't I, and the method was especially good, wasn't it?"

> "Thank you, Dominic, for not falsifying the message to suit your own incapacity. That at least is something."

> "Is it enough, Jesus?"

> "No, Dominic, it is not."[17]

CROSSAN'S METHOD FOR STUDYING JESUS

Crossan's approach entails analysis at what he calls three levels of operation: the microcosmic, the mesocosmic, and the macrocosmic.

The microcosmic level involves *treatment of literary sources*. He provides a fairly comprehensive "inventory" of traditions about Jesus, assigning each element of tradition two numbers, separated by a slash. The first number indicates the age of the source in which the tradition first appears (according to his own system of dating):

1 = 30 to 60 CE

2 = 60 to 80 CE

3 = 80 to 120 CE

4 = 120 to 150 CE

A second number indicates how many independent attestations to the tradition can be found in all the sources considered. Thus, Crossan's program claims to rely heavily on the dating of sources and on what is usually called "the criterion of multiple attestation" (see pages 59–60). The value of a tradition for historical consideration is enhanced by a low first number and/or a high second number. Thus, various sayings of Jesus about "kingdom and children"[18] are given a 1/4 rating (very good), meaning that such sayings are attested in four independent sources (Thom. 22:1–2; Mark 10:13–16; Matt. 18:3; John 3:1–10), at least one of which dates from the earliest period (in his reckoning,

Thomas). The tradition that identifies Jesus as the divine Word who "in the beginning was with God and was God" (John 1:1) gets a 4/1 rating (very bad) because it is found in only one source, one that Crossan dates to the latest of the four periods.

This system appears to be more scientific than the Jesus Seminar's color coding approach, which critics claimed was unduly influenced by predilections of Seminar members and by an overreliance on the controversial criterion of dissimilarity. Still, Crossan's dating of sources has been sharply challenged.[19] He places a good deal of apocryphal material in the earliest layer, including most of the Gospel of Thomas and a "Cross Gospel" that he has reconstructed from the passion narrative of the Gospel of Peter; a majority of scholars would date these materials to the second century. The main material from the New Testament to fall into Crossan's earliest layer is the Q source and a group of miracle stories found in both Mark and John. Those assumptions might not cause much of a stir, but the mere fact that Crossan designates his third level as 80–120 CE (a forty-year period!) strikes many scholars as tendentious and arbitrary. The Gospels of Matthew and Luke are usually thought to have been completed around 85 CE. Crossan does not dispute this opinion, but his dating scheme treats the material in those canonical works (at least the material not thought to have derived from Mark or Q) on a par with second-century writings a full generation later. And almost no modern scholar would date material in the Gospel of John to the time marked by Crossan's fourth era (later than 120 CE). Thus, Wright observes that "all but a few within the world of New Testament scholarship would find his list [of sources] as extremely shaky, and all except Crossan himself would have at least some quite serious points of disagreement with it."[20]

Elsewhere, Crossan has specified six "crucial decisions about sources" that are foundational for his work: (1) the priority of Mark, (2) the existence of the Q Gospel, (3) the dependence of John on the Synoptic Gospels, (4) the independence of the Gospel of Thomas from the canonical Gospels, (5) the independence of the *Didache* (an early Christian book of community rules), and (6) the existence and independence of the "Cross Gospel." He admits that these presuppositions become increasingly controversial as the list proceeds, but he also offers fairly extensive reasons for holding to these views even when his position is a lonely one.[21]

In practice, the most significant, positive result of Crossan's source analysis is that he isolates thirty-seven units of material that are found in both the Q source and the Gospel of Thomas. He dubs this material the *Common Sayings Tradition* and treats it as the most significant material for any reconstruction of the historical Jesus. It seems such to him because it has multiple attestation in two different sources that he regards as very early and independent of each other. Most scholars do not follow him in this assessment because they do not think Thomas is that early; indeed a majority would see the overlap of material here not as an instance of multiple attestation but as a strong indication of literary dependence (e.g., that the author of Thomas had a copy of Q, or even a copy of the Gospel of Matthew, in which the Q material could be found). Be that as it may, the actual consequences of such a disagreement are minimal: almost all scholars would grant that what Crossan calls the *Common Sayings Tradition* is material that can be confidently ascribed to the historical Jesus—simply because it is in Q. They would say (with Crossan), yes, this *is* historically authentic material, though (contra Crossan) the fact that it turns up in the Gospel of Thomas has nothing to do with establishing that.

Crossan's mesocosmic (second) level of operation involves *historical reconstruction of the place and time in which Jesus lived.* Crossan is extremely knowledgeable with regard to both the Greco-Roman world and the specific Palestinian environment. He draws on a wide variety of sources, citing not only such obvious references as Josephus and Cicero but also little-known papyri, scraps of ancient manuscripts archived in various museums throughout the world. He attends, of course, to the political realities, but he does not stop there. Every detail that can be ascertained must be taken into account as potentially relevant: how business was conducted, how homes were built, how medicine was practiced, and so forth. The goal at this level of investigation is to establish a context for understanding who Jesus was and what his words and deeds would have meant.

Two parts of this context that Crossan deems especially significant are the general situation of peasant unrest and the specific phenomenon of Cynic philosophers. As for the former, Crossan describes Palestine at the time of Jesus as being in a period of *turmoil,* a technical term here for the first of three stages that would lead ultimately to a disastrous war with Rome in 66–70 CE (the next two stages are *conspiracy* and *open unrest*).[22] The principal causes of this turmoil were oppressive taxation and social policies that continued to worsen from year to year. Within this context, Crossan describes various types of peasant resistance that could be found; tales of protesters, prophets, bandits, and messiahs are all recounted by the Roman historian Josephus. All this serves as background to his presentation of Jesus as a somewhat different type of subversive, one that he thinks is best described by the term *magician.*

The phenomenon of Cynic philosophers has already been discussed in chapter 3 (see pages 83–87). The Cynics, Crossan suggests, viewed life as a struggle of "nature against culture," and their allegiance was squarely with the former. From a religious perspective, they represent what anthropologist Bryan Wilson has called "an *introversionist* response to the world"—one that assumes the world is irredeemably evil such that people must abandon it (rather than amend it or wait for God to enact some radical reform).[23] This also serves as background for Crossan's presentation of Jesus, whom he calls "a peasant Jewish Cynic" who espoused a view that Crossan calls "ethical eschatology."

Crossan's work at this descriptive level of operation is the least controversial. It involves basic research common to all historical study. Few scholars would have major disagreements with his reconstruction of the historical world at the time of Jesus, though numerous fine points are debated. Indeed, even his opponents often rely on him as a resource for information in areas on which he is an obvious expert.

What *is* sometimes debated, however, is the relevance of particular information for understanding Jesus. In other words, Crossan is sometimes thought to cast his net too far and wide, bringing into play information about Greco-Roman society that may not have had much bearing on life in the villages of Palestine.[24] At issue here is the extent of hellenization in first-century Galilee, and both historian and archaeologists remain divided on that point. What Crossan's critics sometimes miss, however, is that *commercialization* of Galilee is actually more important for his proposal than *hellenization*. He emphasizes that Herod Antipas pursued aggressive urbanization policies during the lifetime of Jesus, building up the cities of Sepphoris and Tiberias in ways that would have increased stress on rural villages (due to taxation, loss of land, diversion of agricultural resources, and so forth). The peasant unrest and the emergence of something that looked like a Jewish version of cynicism may be understood as reactions to this Roman commercialization of Galilee regardless of how hellenized individual Galilean Jews might have been.

Crossan's macrocosmic (third) level of operation involves *analysis of the Jesus movement from the perspectives of social and cultural anthropology.* Crossan attempts to reconstruct the social dynamics and structure of the world in which Jesus lived and to compose likely scenarios that relate the nuggets of tradition about Jesus to this reconstructed world. He draws upon studies regarding preindustrial peasant societies, colonial protest movements, and so forth, illuminating the value such a culture would place on honor and shame and describing the tensions that would evolve from a system of patron-client relationships. The breadth of Crossan's knowledge in this regard is again impressive. Many have noted that his work presents not simply a historical study of Jesus but a comprehensive, *multidisciplinary* study of Jesus as a historical person.

One aspect of sociocultural analysis is especially important for Crossan's work, namely, his understanding of the system of brokerage that held Mediterranean society together. Drawing on the work of anthropologist Gerhard Lenski, Crossan describes the Roman world as a society of "haves" and "have nots." About 10 percent of the population comprised aristocrats and their retainers, with the rest being artisans, peasants, or worse (beggars, bandits, and other "expendables").[25] In lieu of a middle class, society required brokers, clients of wealthy patrons who would themselves become patrons to others. The understanding of this system is so integral to Crossan's study of Jesus that it determines the very organization of his book. *The Historical Jesus* is divided into three main parts: (1) Brokered Empire, (2) Embattled Brokerage, and (3) Brokerless Kingdom. He presents Jesus' call for people to rely on God as a fundamental challenge to the fabric of his social world: people should rely *only* on God, not on socially sanctioned brokers.

In general, Crossan's work at this level has been appreciated and accepted. The criticisms that have been offered tend to indicate that his use of materials is somewhat selective, not taking into account alternative possibilities. He has been said to confuse the social categories of "peasant" and "artisan,"[26] and some think he is too quick to follow Horsley in categorizing Jesus' affront to the traditional system as a form of banditry (see pages 73–76).

Crossan's method ultimately consists of an attempt to bring these three levels of operation together. He seeks to interpret the source material that he considers most likely to be historically authentic in light of what his historical reconstruction and interdisciplinary analysis reveals about Jesus' historical and social context.

CROSSAN'S PORTRAIT OF JESUS

As an initial observation, we may note that for Crossan the life and mission of Jesus are what counts in terms of historical significance. In this respect, he may be contrasted with Paul who maintained that the three things "of first importance" were the death, burial, and resurrection of Christ (1 Cor. 15:3–4). For Crossan, the first of these is less important than the so-called apostle thinks, and the second and third did not happen (at least in the literal sense that Christians usually presume them to have happened). As usual, Crossan is honest and clear: "My thesis . . . is that Christian faith is not Easter faith."[27]

Jesus and the Brokerless Kingdom

Jesus was a member of the peasant class, not the educated, scribal class. He was probably illiterate,[28] and his message was one that would be meaningful primarily to peasants. Like the Cynics, he was concrete, not theoretical. He acted in ways that involved a shattering of convention with regard to matters that touched on the stuff of everyday life: dress, meals, family, and so forth. There were, however, differences. The Cynics were Greeks, they were usually associated with urban centers, and they were known to be individualists; Jesus was Jewish, kept to the villages and countryside, and had a social vision.

Jesus tried to inaugurate the "brokerless kingdom of God." He used the language of Israel's prophets to speak of the kingdom of God but presented this "not as an apocalyptic event in the imminent future but as a mode of life in the immediate present."[29] He tried to subvert the patron-client system of his day by encouraging everyone, especially the lowest classes, to have "unmediated physical and spiritual contact with God and unmediated physical and spiritual contact with one another."[30] He was opposed, in principle, to any form of hierarchy (including that of the traditional family system) that divides people along generational and gender lines. Drawing on such texts as Luke 11:27–28; 12:51–53; and 14:25–26, Crossan insists that Jesus would "tear the hierarchical and patriarchal family in two along the axis of domination and subordination."[31] By claiming that God's kingdom is for children (Mark 10:13–15), Jesus basically maintained that it is for anybody or—more to the point—for nobodies. He viewed himself and his companions as examples of such nobodies and told witty parables likening the group to impure leaven (Matt. 13:33) or uncontrollable weeds (13:24–30) whose influence cannot be contained.[32]

Jesus' vision of life informed by God's radical justice came to expression in his two most characteristic activities, which Crossan describes under the heading "Magic and Meal." The first term refers to what biblical scholars traditionally call miracles and the second to Jesus' practice of eating with outcasts.

First, the "magic." Crossan accepts as historically authentic a number of stories of Jesus' miracles, all ones that record him healing the sick or casting out demons. He realizes that many historians have trouble affirming that such things actually happened, but stresses that the identification of miraculous healings or exorcisms as something "supernatural" or "scientifically impossible" is anachronistic. In this regard, he appeals to a distinction some medical anthropologists make between disease and illness. Disease is the physical condition; illness is the social meaning attributed to this condition.[33] Crossan emphasizes that the historical Jesus healed people of illness, even though he did not and could not cure disease. Through Jesus' actions, for instance, lepers were deemed clean and reintegrated into society. To ask whether their lesions actually closed would impose a modern notion of healing that misses the point. The lesions may have remained, but as far as people in the first century were concerned, people who had once been "unclean" were now "clean." Thus, Jesus was able to heal the sick.[34]

Likewise, Crossan insists that Jesus did perform successful exorcisms; in such a rite, both Jesus and his observers would have believed that a literal spiritual being that had invaded a person's body had been forcibly ejected. Crossan himself does not believe such spirit-beings exist, but he maintains that through those exorcisms Jesus did heal people according to the standards of his day. Modern medical practitioners might surmise that Jesus was actually delivering people from some sort of psychosomatic trauma (e.g. multiple personality disorder).[35] Still, it is best not to impose anachronistic categories on historical occurrences: historians should simply affirm with confidence that Jesus healed the sick and exorcised demons in a manner that was considered remarkably effective.

What is most significant about Jesus' healing activity for Crossan is that he enacted these cures without official authorization and that he did so free of charge! Crossan uses the term *magic* advisedly, reserving the word *miracle* for acts of divine power that operates in accord with regular religious channels. Jesus enabled people to access divine power apart from established religion. Thus, Crossan's identification of Jesus as a magician is similar to that of Morton Smith (see pages 79–81), but Crossan goes further in exploring the social meaning of that categorization. *Magic,* says Crossan, is the term religious leaders use to denigrate miracles done by the wrong sort of people. Magic is to religion what social banditry is to politics.[36] Jesus' unsanctioned miracles had social implications. As he hints in one story, those who are healed without going through the appropriate channels may conclude that they are forgiven as well (Mark 2:1–12). What need, then, will they have for priests or scribes (religious brokers)?[37]

These stories can also be read with a political slant. Crossan views the prevalence of exorcism stories in the Gospel tradition through the lens of cultural anthropology, noting that widespread belief in demon possession is most typical for societies in which there is an occupying colonial power. The story in Mark 5:1–13 is particularly telling, for there the demons that possess the afflicted person are actually named "Legion," the term used to designate a contingency of Roman troops, such as those who had taken possession of the very territory where this tale is recounted. When the demons enter a herd of swine and rush into the sea, one can easily catch an image of Israelite hope, an image of Roman soldiers-demons-pigs running back into the sea from whence they apparently came. Building on Mary Douglas' proposal that the physical body is a microcosm of the social body, Crossan suggests that exorcisms are a form of "individuated symbolic revolution."[38]

The second element of Jesus' mission that is essential for Crossan is the practice of open table fellowship, or what he prefers to call "open commensality." In Jesus' social setting, meals were governed by rules of conduct that went well beyond modern concern for etiquette. Strict guidelines determined who was allowed to eat with whom and where the participants were expected to sit (or recline, as was the custom). Meals, even more than an individual's body, were viewed as microcosms of society, and so were fraught with symbolic meaning. Mere participation in a communal meal implied a general endorsement of the other diners, and acceptance of one's specific place at the table implied recognition of one's social standing relative to that of the others (see Luke 14:7–11). In the face of such conventions, Jesus made a point of indiscriminately eating with anyone, including those who were regarded as outcasts. He told a parable likening the kingdom of God to a person who goes into the streets to invite the poor, the crippled, the blind, and the lame to his banquet (Luke 14:21–23). He openly flaunted propriety by ignoring the boundaries between slave and free, male and female, pure and impure, patron and client, rich and poor.[39]

The conjunction of these two activities, magic and meals, is significant for Crossan. In exchange for free healing, Jesus and his followers would often be given meals. But these meals were not just a means of supporting the mission, for that could have been accomplished in other ways. The meals themselves were integral to the mission, for they became occasions for actualizing what the magic was really about. No one could be excluded because they had been categorized as sick, sinful, demon-possessed, or unclean. Jesus' generosity with spiritual aid would inspire villagers to generosity with physical sustenance. Crossan summarizes Jesus' program as follows: "*heal the sick, eat with those you heal, and announce the kingdom's presence in that mutuality.*"[40]

Together, these two activities challenged what was "normal" for Jewish religion and for Roman power. Jesus' vision of "shared egalitarianism" was an implicit attack on his social system, a system that depended on patronage and brokerage. Health care and nourishment are basic needs of earthly life. By demonstrating that people can receive these things directly from God and from each other, Jesus struck at the very heart of what made his social system work (though, of course, that system worked better for some than for others). If people were actually to begin sharing with each other, they would have little need for patrons, much less brokers. With typical literary flair, Crossan describes why the enterprise Jesus started could be called a "movement": "The mission we are talking about is not, like Paul's, a dramatic thrust along major trade routes to urban centers hundreds of miles apart. Yet it concerns the longest journey in the Greco-Roman world, maybe in any world, the step across the threshold of a peasant stranger's home."[41] In his own way, Jesus the Jewish Cynic was a social and political reformer. The open sharing of healing and food presented a political threat to Roman society. It was no less than "a strategy for building or rebuilding peasant community on radically different principles than those of honor and shame, patronage and clientage."[42]

Five more points may be noted briefly:

1. *Jesus spoke of God's kingdom in present terms only.* Crossan grants that, early on, Jesus was a disciple of John the Baptist who used apocalyptic language to speak of a future consummation of all things to be enacted by God at the impending judgment. But Crossan regards Luke 7:28 as an authentic saying of Jesus, and he interprets the latter part of this verse ("the least in the kingdom is greater than John") to mean that Jesus changed his mind about his mentor and rejected the apocalyptic message. Thus, the bottom line for Crossan is that Jesus "never spoke of himself or anyone else as the apocalyptic Son of Man" and he never spoke of God's kingdom as anything but a reality to be experienced here and now.[43]

2. *Jesus' vision of God's kingdom involved the establishment of justice through nonviolence.* In rejecting John's apocalyptic vision, Jesus came to espouse what Crossan calls "ethical eschatology," which favors nonviolent resistance to systemic evil. Indeed, Crossan suggests that it may have been John's death that prompted Jesus to change his mind about this topic: when the faithful prophet was murdered and God did nothing to avenge his death, Jesus realized that God was not going to act violently, not even against evil oppressors. "John died and still God did not come," Crossan says. "Jesus watched, learned, and changed his vision of God."[44] This vision coincided with the change mentioned above, from a theology of God's imminence to a theology of God's presence.[45] Instead of announcing that God was coming soon to put a violent end to injustice, Jesus began announcing that God was already present to establish justice through nonviolence.

3. *Jesus' vision of God's kingdom involved interactive collaboration between divine challenge and human response.* In his best-known work, Crossan labels Jesus' vision of God's kingdom "ethical eschatology," but in later writings he would often prefer the term "collaborative eschatology" to emphasize that the consummation of the kingdom depended on human action.[46] So, Jesus' insistence on the presence of God's kingdom must be modified as follows: Jesus proclaimed the kingdom "as already but only collaboratively present," that is, as present to the extent that people

accepted the challenge to live in the equality, peace, and justice that God's rule entails.[47] So, rather than telling people to wait for God to bring the kingdom, Jesus would have said that God was waiting for them to live in the kingdom that was already present. A vision of collaborative, ethical eschatology does not look for God to act violently eventually to judge the world but assumes that God wants people to act nonviolently here and now to redeem the world.

4. *Jesus' program was communal.* Eventually, Crossan decides against speaking of Jesus as having disciples at all. The better term is *companions,* and Jesus' relationship to these companions is one not of mediation but of empowerment. Thus, "Jesus announced the presence of the kingdom of God by inviting all to come and see how he *and his companions* had already accepted it."[48] Again, Jesus may have learned something from his mentor in this regard: Herod had essentially put an end to whatever challenge he believed John the Baptist posed by simply executing the man responsible for that challenge. But Jesus' strategy differed in this regard: "John had a monopoly, but Jesus had a franchise."[49]

5. *Jesus did not want to be viewed as a mediator himself.* The inherent danger in his mission was that *he* would become the new broker of God's privileges (such as healing). To prevent this from happening, Jesus remained itinerant, moving from village to village so that no one place could ever be deemed his headquarters. He insisted that any who regarded themselves as his followers be itinerant also. The last thing he ever would have wanted would have been to be viewed as a mediator between God and God's people.[50] Despite the need for human collaboration, the kingdom remains *God's* kingdom: Jesus himself "does not initiate its existence. He does not control its access."[51]

Jesus' Death and What Followed

What happened to this self-effacing proponent of justice and generosity? Crossan suggests the following scenario: he visited Jerusalem, where the act that had played so well in rural Galilee was met with swift and brutal resistance. In putting forward his message of spiritual and economic egalitarianism Jesus apparently created a disturbance at the temple ("the seat and symbol of all that was nonegalitarian"),[52] and this time soldiers were on hand who were well trained at dealing with such disturbances. Jesus was hauled outside the city and crucified. He died. The soldiers then either left his body on the cross or threw it on the ground and covered it with dirt. In either case, it was eaten by dogs.

Most of this, Crossan admits, is guesswork—but that is his main point! A disturbance in the Jerusalem temple is well attested (Mark 11:15–19), as are the attribution of anti-temple sayings to Jesus (Mark 14:58; Thom. 71). But since Jesus' followers all fled in terror when he was arrested no one knows what happened after that, except that Jesus was crucified. The fact of his crucifixion can be established by both Roman and Jewish sources in addition to Christian ones. But the elaborate passion narratives that the Gospels have constructed regarding this event are fiction. Crossan believes the stories were created years later through the conjunction of two processes. First, literate and sophisticated Christians scoured the Jewish scriptures to find texts that dealt with suffering and vindication. They created narrative incidents to correspond to such nuggets, which then came to be viewed as prophecies of what would happen. For example, the division of Jesus' garments by lot (Mark 15:24) derives from Psalm 22:18, and the noontime darkness at his crucifixion (Mark 15:33) comes from Amos 8:9.[53] The method was "hide the prophecy, tell the narrative and invent the history."[54] According to Crossan, these exegetically derived nuggets were then woven into a biographical story by women in the Jerusalem community as part of the traditional process of female lament and ritual mourning. This, of course, helps explain why much of the burial and resurrection story is told from the perspective of women. The "female lament tradition turned the male exegetical tradition into a passion-resurrection story once and for all."[55]

Thus, the passion narratives are "not *history remembered but prophecy historicized.*"[56] They reveal more about the concerns of the early church than about the fate of the historical Jesus. The now lost "Cross Gospel" (see pages 56–57) turned the story into a narrative of a type Crossan calls "Innocence Rescued." Later, the Gospel of Mark revised this account according to another typological narrative format that Crossan calls "Martyrdom Vindicated." The essential difference between the two was that the first model used a resurrection motif to present Jesus being saved from death before the eyes of his enemies. The later version made the death itself salvific and, though keeping a resurrection, postponed vindication to the Parousia. Salvation "was not from but through death, not in the here below, but in the imminent hereafter."[57]

Resurrection stories were created not only to provide closure (rescue or vindication) to an otherwise unbearable account but also to legitimate power claims in the developing church. Crossan thinks the earliest stage of tradition is represented by the Gospel of Thomas, which does not speak of resurrection at all, but of "unbroken and abiding presence."[58] In other words, Jesus' followers believed that in some sense he was still with them after he died, empowering them to continue his mission, to imitate his lifestyle, and to practice free healing and open table fellowship, what Crossan calls "open commensality." Paul represents a later stage, claiming to have experienced an apparition of the risen Jesus in some sort of a trance. Paul uses this claim, notably, to justify his position as "an apostle" (1 Cor. 15:1–11). Still later, we get the stories in Matthew, Luke, and John of Jesus walking about on earth after his death, appearing to people in a physical, tangible way. These, Crossan claims, are not "factual history" but "fictional mythology."[59] The point of the stories was not their proclamation that Jesus was raised so much as their identification of those to whom he chose to appear and commission. They are "deliberate political dramatizations of the priority of one *specific leader* over another, of this *leadership group* over that *general community.*

. . . They detail the origins of Christian leadership, not the origins of Christian faith."[60]

The bottom line, at any rate, is that the passion and resurrection narratives reveal almost nothing about what really happened to Jesus in Jerusalem. Devoid of sources, minus his microcosmic level, Crossan attempts to postulate a reasonable synopsis of what may have happened based on knowledge of the world at that time. He accepts (as do most historians) that Jesus was arrested in response to an incident at the temple. What that was, we cannot be sure; Jesus probably did something (such as upsetting a table) to demonstrate symbolically that his egalitarian movement would "destroy" the temple. It makes sense in the context of that place and time to assume he would be arrested for this. After that, what makes most sense is a tale of "casual brutality":

> I do not presume at all any high-level consultations between Caiaphas or Pilate about or with Jesus. They would no doubt have agreed before the [Passover] festival that fast and immediate action was to be taken against any disturbance and that some examples by crucifixion might be especially useful at the start. I doubt very much if Jewish police and Roman soldiery needed to go too far up the chain of command in handling a Galilean peasant like Jesus.[61]

So there is no need, historically, for a trial, much less for the series of trials (before Caiaphas, Pilate, and even Herod) reported in the Gospels.

And there is no need for a burial either. The Romans crucified thousands of Jews, Crossan points out, and yet to date only one skeleton of a crucified person has ever been found. The reason: they weren't buried. Crucifixion was an act of state terrorism, and a good part of the terror lay in its aftermath. Being devoured by beasts was a supreme Roman penalty, and historians insist that this was typically the fate of crucifixion victims. "What we often forget about crucifixion," writes Crossan, "is the carrion crow and scavenger dog who respectively croak above and growl below the dead or dying body."[62]

Crossan knows, of course, that the Gospels claim Jesus was an exception to this policy, but their stories reveal desperate hope. The account that Crossan deems earliest says Jesus was taken down from the cross by his Jewish enemies (Gospel of Peter 6:21–22). A somewhat later account has him being placed in a tomb (safe from the dogs) by a member of the Jewish Council (Mark 15:42–47). Later still, we hear that this tomb was brand new and belonged to a rich man who was actually a disciple of Jesus (Matt. 27:57–61). And then, finally, we are told that this tomb was in a garden (John 19:38–42). Thus, the tradition grew "from burial by enemies to burial by friends, from inadequate and hurried burial to full, complete, and even regal embalming."[63] Crossan no doubt recalls his Shakespeare ("The lady doth protest too much") and like Queen Gertrude in Hamlet decides such apologetics serve only to underscore the intolerable nature of the truth. That truth, cold and hard as it may be, is that, by Easter morning, no one who cared knew where the body of Jesus was. But everyone knew about the dogs.

For those who take such a "denial" of the resurrection as incompatible with Crossan's claim to be a Christian, he offers the following theological comment: "Bodily resurrection has nothing to do with a resuscitated body coming out of its tomb. . . . Bodily resurrection means that the *embodied* life and death of the historical Jesus continues to be experienced. . . . [It continues] to form communities of like lives."[64]

Crossan claims no interest in offending Christian sensibilities. His demeanor is decidedly different from those scholars who appear to delight in scandalizing the pious. He says his chapter on the passion narratives was the hardest one to write—*methodologically* hard because of the lack of sources, but also hard for another reason: "It is hard not only for those who have faith in Jesus, but also for those who have faith in humanity, to look closely at the terror of crucifixion in the ancient world. . . . But since that world did in thousands what our century has done in millions, it is necessary to look with cold, hard eyes at what exactly such a death entailed."[65]

BIRTH OF CHRISTIANITY

In his second major tome on this subject, Crossan endeavors to show what happened in the first two decades after the execution of Jesus, before the developments that become evident in the writings of Paul. He considers the best witnesses to these "lost years" between Jesus and Paul to be Q and Thomas, and to a lesser extent, his reconstructed "Cross Gospel." The social backdrop for the story he finds in these sources is one driven by Roman policies of urbanization and concomitant ruralization: the development of cities under Roman imperialism dislocated the peasant population in rural areas where indebtedness and taxation were on the rise and dispossession of the land became the rule. Against this backdrop, Crossan sketches two streams of earliest Christianity: the Life Tradition, centered in Galilee, where primarily rural Christians emphasized the sayings of Jesus, and the Death Tradition, centered in such places as Jerusalem, Damascus, and Antioch, where primarily urban Christians emphasized the death and resurrection of Jesus.[66]

As indicated above, Crossan sees the development of the Death Tradition as a conjunction of (male) scribal exegesis and (female) lament tradition. Much of *The Birth of Christianity*, however, is devoted to tracing the development of the Life Tradition, which Crossan thinks can be discerned in redactional emendations in the early collections of Jesus' sayings. He identifies, for instance, three types of eschatology in this early material: (1) Ethical eschatology, which "negates the world by actively protesting and nonviolently resisting a system judged to be evil, unjust, and violent" (this is what Crossan thinks the historical Jesus espoused); (2) apocalyptic eschatology, which "negates this world by announcing that in the future, and usually the imminent future, God will act to restore justice in an unjust world" (this is found in what Crossan thinks is later material in Q, material not representative of the historical Jesus); and (3) ascetical eschatology, which "negates this world by withdrawing from normal human life in terms of food, sex, speech, dress, or occupation" (this is found in what Crossan thinks is later material in Thomas, also not representative of the historical Jesus). In short, Crossan claims that Jesus espoused ethical eschatology, but that this was transmuted into apocalyptic or ascetical varieties within the first two decades after his execution.[67] Yet another development of the Life Tradition can be seen in an early Christian document called the *Didache,* which recounts an attempt on the part of Christian "householders" to contain the more radical elements of the itinerant movement. Jesus' call for people to abandon their possessions, for instance, is translated into an encouragement of salvific almsgiving: "having nothing" becomes "sharing everything."[68]

Crossan finds one locus in which the Life Tradition and the Death Tradition come together in earliest Christianity: the Common Meal. This principal ritual act of the early Christians was interpreted with symbolic reference to Jesus' death and resurrection but also signified the inclusive, communal sharing that was a hallmark of Jesus' ethical eschatology. In those years, we must remember, the Eucharist was a full supper, not just the token sip and morsel distributed in most Christian churches today. In a society where food was scarce and hunger constant, even those who invested this meal with symbolic and sacramental significance could not have denied its fundamental meaning:

> The Common Meal Tradition may look to a Last Supper in the past, to a communal meal in the present, or to a messianic banquet in the future—or, quite validly, to all of those at the same time. But it can never get away from this: *it is in food and drink offered equally to everyone that the presence of God and Jesus is found.* . . . So the Lord's Supper is political criticism and economic challenge as well as sacred rite and liturgical worship. . . . Christians claim that God and Jesus are peculiarly and especially present when food and drink are shared equally among all.[69]

CRITIQUE OF CROSSAN'S STUDY OF JESUS

Many of the criticisms that have been leveled against Crossan's work are similar to those made with regard to the Jesus Seminar, which he cochaired.

First, his whole method of operation is criticized as idiosyncratic, tendentious, and circular.[70] On the surface, he submits sources to a supposedly objective stratification that manifests what one critic calls "a subtle but unwitting positivism."[71] But then Crossan is also said to approach source materials with unwarranted skepticism, ignoring the basic biographical interest implied by the literary genre of the canonical Gospels, and assuming that Jesus' disciples would be quick to invent sayings for their teacher. Witherington bristles at his cute description of those disciples as "people not parrots," noting that "disciples in early Jewish settings were learners, and, yes, also reciters and memorizers."[72]

As already noted, very few (if any) scholars would accept Crossan's scheme for dating and classifying materials. Many think that Mark is just as reliable a source as Q, and most think the bulk of material in the canonical Gospels predates almost everything in the apocryphal writings.[73] A common criticism of Crossan is that he grants so much credence to the Gospel of Thomas, a source that most scholars would regard as late and unreliable—indeed, quite a few conservative voices have been prone to dismiss his work on these grounds alone. There is not, however, much substance to such a criticism: in actuality, Crossan only relies on those sections of Thomas that are closely paralleled in the Synoptic Gospels: in fact, the passages from Thomas that he deems authentic are almost all paralleled in the Q material, constituting what he calls the Common Sayings Tradition. Some scholars may be annoyed that Crossan quotes Thomas authoritatively throughout his writings but if all references to Thomas were removed, almost nothing of substance would change.[74]

A more significant matter would concern his dismissal of the passion/resurrection narratives. A majority of scholars believe that these narratives probably assumed a fairly fixed form early on rather than coming together at the tail end of the process, as Crossan has it.[75] If the majority view is correct on this matter, then we *would* have fairly reliable sources for this part of the story, sources that Crossan has not taken into account. Thus, Crossan's reconstruction of the last week of Jesus' life (which he admits is guesswork)[76] has not fared terribly well in the world of scholarly critique.

Wright argues that Crossan's dating of materials is in fact the *result* of his understanding of the historical Jesus rather than the *grounds* for it. Spurning objectivity but extolling honesty, Crossan wants us to trust him to provide us with a worthy image of Jesus and to accept his views on source materials precisely because they will lead us to the acceptance of that image. For Crossan, history itself remains a matter of brokerage, with "the historian as patron and the reader as client."[77] Other scholars have noted that Crossan does not always feel obliged to follow his own system when it does not take him where he wants to go. Sayings in which Jesus predicts his apocalyptic return are found in the first stratum and have multiple attestation but are regarded as coming from later tradition.[78] Similarly, Crossan insists that Jesus did not choose twelve disciples and that the Last Supper did not take place, despite early, multiple attestation for both traditions (i.e., references in Paul's letters in addition to widespread notice in Gospel materials). Presumably, appointment of the twelve runs counter to Crossan's image of Jesus opposing hierarchies and the story of the Supper presents a somewhat exclusive meal, marred by talk of mediation ("my body given for you").[79] We may do best to say that Crossan tries to establish interrelationships between his proposals regarding source materials and his portrait of Jesus, while recognizing that the two are not necessarily interdependent.[80]

The situation most scholars face in evaluating Crossan's work, then, is almost the opposite of what the organization of the book may seem to present. Most scholars are not going to be persuaded initially to accept his novel dating of materials and proceed from there to accept the implications of such dating for historical Jesus research. Instead, the test will be whether Crossan's hypothesis about Jesus holds up on other grounds—basically, whether it makes sense within the context of the social and historical world brought to light through his other two levels of analysis (historical reconstruction and social/cultural anthropology). If it does, then scholars might be inclined not only to accept the portrait but also to reexamine their views regarding the dating of source materials, since much of the material that has traditionally been dated late or deemed apocryphal fits Crossan's portrait of Jesus better than that which has been considered early and canonical. The essential question is whether the portrait holds up apart from any dependence on his particular source theories.

Response to this question has been mixed. Even those who are not inclined to accept Crossan's source theories sometimes do find much in his reconstruction of Jesus' life and ministry that is compelling—but, clearly, many do not. The problem is that so much of his reconstruction seems to be guesswork. Robert Price thinks this is a necessary consequence of deeming so small a fragment of the Gospel materials authentic: Crossan is left with very few bricks and, so, his edifice (impressive though it may be) is mainly "speculative cement."[81] Luke Timothy Johnson maintains that Crossan's reconstruction of Jesus' ministry owes more "to the force of his ideological framework than to historical evidence."[82] James Dunn says he falls "into the old trap of selecting the features of the Jesus tradition that he finds most amenable and adaptable" to our modern times.[83]

Leaving aside minor quibbles, at least five specific aspects of Crossan's portrait are disputed:

1. Some think that the analogy between Jesus and Cynic philosophers is strained. The same arguments are made as were discussed above with reference to the work of Downing (see pages 83–87). But Crossan's view is more tempered than Downing's, especially as it comes to expression in his later work. "We have in the final analysis, no way of knowing for sure what Jesus knew about Cynicism, or whether he knew about it at all," Crossan writes. "Maybe he had never even heard of the Cynics and was just re-inventing the Cynic wheel all by himself."[84] For Crossan, the point of invoking the Cynics is not to determine the derivation of Jesus' ideas or to identify a conscious model for his ministry and lifestyle. The point, rather, is to find a roughly contemporary historical analogy, to discuss a similar movement about which we know a good deal in order to help us form hypotheses about how Jesus' movement would have been perceived. Crossan is upfront about the differences between Jesus and the Cynics, but he finds the similarities nevertheless to be instructive.[85] When he is most clear on these points, his critics quiet down, only to raise their voices again when he persists in *calling* Jesus a Cynic, in saying he actually *was* a Cynic, albeit one of peculiar stripe ("a Jewish peasant Cynic"). Craig Keener avers, "If Jesus was a 'Jewish Cynic,' he is the only one we know about. Since the main point of placing Jesus in categories is to

help us understand him in context, this proposal therefore proves particularly unhelpful."[86]

2. Some scholars think Crossan's portrait underplays the Jewish dimension of Jesus and his world. Positively, Wright wants to ask how the social program Crossan attributes to Jesus would have related to the hopes of Israel. Negatively, he wonders why it would have offended those who saw themselves as guardians of Israel's sacred traditions. Crossan shows us how Jesus offended people in authority but, Wright says, "he never explains why there would be hostility from Jews *qua* Jews."[87] Likewise, Darrell Bock finds it odd that Crossan devotes so much material to Jesus' supposed confrontation with Roman powers (a minor theme in the Gospels) while completely ignoring all the conflicts with synagogue and Temple leaders that receive a great deal of attention in those texts: "why does Jesus challenge customs associated with the sabbath or with ritual cleanliness if Rome is his central concern?"[88] Crossan does have an answer for this: he leaves the latter accounts out of his portrait because he thinks they belong to a later stage of tradition, reflecting arguments between Christians and Jews (or, at least, between Gentile and Jewish Christians) rather than between Jesus and his historical contemporaries. Finally, and in the same vein, Witherington notes that for all the comparisons between Jesus' parables and Cynic *chreiai,* Crossan almost never compares them to the parables of Jewish sages.[89] Crossan responds by noting that Judaism at the time of Jesus was "richly creative, diverse, and variegated."[90] Furthermore, all Judaism was Hellenistic, and the most significant distinction between its various types was whether they embraced an inclusive or exclusive perspective toward Hellenism. He claims that his Jesus is thoroughly Jewish, but a representative of inclusive Hellenistic Judaism rather than of conservative exclusive Judaism. Jesus was completely Jewish but like many Jews of his day, he was more interested in adapting the customs of Israel than preserving them.[91]

3. Predictably, the specific representation of Jesus as a magician has suffered abuse. Crossan (like Morton Smith) intends this to be provocative, and his readers have not disappointed him by remaining unprovoked. The same arguments cited above in our discussion of Smith (see pages 80–81) are applied to Crossan. Notably, in his later work, Crossan would back off from using the term *magic* to describe the miracles of Jesus or his companions. In *The Birth of Christianity,* he defines a miracle as "a marvel that someone interprets as a transcendental action or manifestation."[92] The earlier distinction connecting *miracle* to official religious channels and *magic* to unofficial ones seems to have been set aside.

4. Crossan's portrayal of Jesus as the founder of an egalitarian movement is critiqued by John H. Elliott, who seems to regard such a conception as anachronistic wishful thinking. We may recall that the same complaint has been made with regard to the work of Schüssler Fiorenza, who also stresses the egalitarian nature of Jesus' movement (see pages 31–32 above). Specifically, Elliott claims that egalitarianism was a conceptual product of the Enlightenment. The mere fact that Jesus spoke about a "kingdom of God" implies that he thought in stratified

terms (a king, with subjects). Furthermore, his chief metaphor for describing relationships within that kingdom was the family, and in Jesus' day, families were not egalitarian, but highly stratified entities.[93]

5. Many scholars also challenge the likelihood of Crossan's completely non-apocalyptic portrait of Jesus. Here, again, the criticisms repeat those made of the Jesus Seminar (see pages 112–13). John Meier notes that the symbol of God's kingdom was used so prominently in eschatological contexts in the centuries immediately preceding Jesus that if Jesus wanted to use it in a different sense (to refer to a present mode of being) he would have had to make this semantic shift explicit.[94] Meier's critique of Crossan at this point is so sharp that (we may note with some irony) it amounts to a final judgment: "Future transcendent salvation was an essential part of Jesus' proclamation of the kingdom. Any reconstruction of the historical Jesus that does not do full justice to this eschatological future must be dismissed as hopelessly inadequate."[95]

Similarly, E. P. Sanders claims that if Jesus used the term *kingdom* only symbolically, then he completely deceived his disciples, who we know continued to expect a literal kingdom, giving up their time, their possessions, and ultimately their lives in the hope of receiving it. This consideration leads him to a rather pointed dismissal of Crossan's work: "The view that Jesus was entirely deceptive and misled his disciples into false hopes, while spinning parables which can be unraveled only by twentieth-century literary analysis, must be rejected."[96]

To many, the assertion that Jesus was unconcerned with the end of the world or with life beyond death seems not only unlikely, but unnecessary. Crossan apparently thinks that inclusion of such an aspect in his portrait would contradict his image of a man concerned with this-worldly affairs. Witherington thinks he sets up false alternatives: "Crossan . . . would have us choose between a Jesus who is a sage and a Jesus who is an apocalyptic seer, between a Jesus who is more like a Cynic and a Jesus who is more like John the Baptist. There are other options."[97] Paul, for example, has no trouble speaking of the kingdom of God in both future (1 Cor. 15:50) and present-day (Rom. 14:17) terms. Furthermore, a dynamic tension between "the already and the not yet" is prominent in all three of the Synoptic Gospels in a way that indicates the authors and original readers of those books did not find such emphases to be inconsistent or incompatible. Thus, if the future orientation of John and the present-day orientation of the Cynics are not mutually exclusive, why must Crossan posit Jesus rejecting the former to embrace the latter?

6. Some scholars say that the historical Jesus presented by Crossan does not offer an adequate basis for understanding Christianity's development of ideas concerning him. Wright asks, "If Jesus' work concentrated on articulating and enacting a 'brokerless kingdom,' a 'kingdom of nobodies,' then why did he die, and why did the church come to attribute to his death the significance it did?"[98] The latter part of the question is most relevant. Crossan *does* have an explanation for why Jesus was killed: he fell victim to an act of "casual brutality," all too

common in the world of his day. But why would the church come to interpret his death as an atonement for sin (Rom. 3:25; 1 John 2:2), as a ransom (Mark 10:45), or as a sacrifice (Heb. 9:11–14)? The closest Crossan comes to answering such a query is to suggest that scribal exegetes arrived at these interpretations by applying scriptural citations to Jesus (such as the "scapegoat" text in Leviticus 16:7–10, 21–22). But then the question becomes, What would motivate early Christians to interpret such texts with reference to Jesus if he had displayed no interest in the themes of atonement or ransom or sacrifice, if indeed the very concept of mediation that these terms imply ran counter to everything that he stood for?

Redemption is but one topic on which this point can be made. The presence of an apocalyptic perspective, just noted, is another. And Wright has challenged Crossan's dismissal of the empty tomb on precisely these grounds: the Christian doctrine of resurrection, according to Wright, was unique in the development of religious thought and such a view could not have developed without both resurrection appearances and an empty tomb. One might, of course, deny that doctrine (e.g., by calling the appearances "hallucinations" and by attributing the emptiness of the tomb to grave robbery), but the development of the Christian doctrine in the specific way that it was articulated demands recognition that there was a tomb and that it was empty.[99]

Such examples can be multiplied: Crossan's Jesus had no messianic consciousness, yet early Christians (even Gentiles) soon hailed him as the Jewish Messiah. Crossan's Jesus was completely self-effacing, yet Christians (even those passionately committed to monotheism) began very early to worship him. Some such gaps are no doubt to be expected in the growth of a movement, but the magnitude of the chasm in this case seems to demand an explanation. Crossan's Jesus, like that of the Jesus Seminar, is *very* dissimilar from the Jesus in whom many early Christians believed and for whom many were willing to die.

Crossan agrees with his critics that the differences between the Jesus of history and the Christ of Christianity are significant. Still, he refuses to accommodate the former to the latter. The other option, the one his critics don't want to consider, is to acknowledge that Christianity really did get it very wrong. He suggests that Christianity may have "lost its soul" in its efforts to convert the Roman Empire. This began, innocently enough, with a theological move that interpreted Christ as a mediator between God and humanity. In itself, and properly understood, such a move did not have to be devastating, but "most inappropriately and unfortunately," understanding Jesus as a broker (mediator) may have facilitated a later move away from inclusive service toward the accoutrements of power. The effects of such a move became evident by the time of Constantine, when Christianity became the official religion of the empire and the church's leaders (male bishops) now expected to be served by others:

> Christianity . . . when it attempted to define as clearly as it could the meaning of Jesus, insisted that he was "wholly God" and "wholly man," that he

was, in other words, himself the unmediated presence of the divine to the human. I find, therefore, no betrayal whatsoever in the move from Jesus to Christ. Whether there were ultimate betrayals in the move from Christ to Constantine is another question—Maybe, Christianity is an inevitable and absolutely necessary "betrayal" of Jesus, else it might have died among the hills of Lower Galilee. But did that "betrayal" have to happen so swiftly, succeed so fully, and be enjoyed so thoroughly? Might not a more even dialectic have been maintained between Jesus and Christ in Jesus Christ?[100]

Chapter 6

Marcus J. Borg

Jesus was from the peasant class. Clearly, he was brilliant. His use of language was remarkable and poetic, filled with images and stories. He had a metaphoric mind. He was not an ascetic; he was world-affirming, with a zest for life. There was a sociopolitical passion about him—like a Gandhi or a Martin Luther King, he challenged the domination system of his day. He was a religious ecstatic, a Jewish mystic, for whom God was an experiential reality. As such, Jesus was also a healer. And there seems to have been a spiritual presence around him, like that reported of St. Francis or the present Dalai Lama. And as a figure of history, Jesus was an ambiguous figure—you could experience him and conclude that he was insane, as his family did, or that he was simply eccentric, or that he was a dangerous threat—or you could conclude that he was filled with the Spirit of God.

—Marcus Borg[1]

Borg has attempted to locate Jesus within models taken from a wider history of religions context, and at the same time to integrate his findings with a positive restatement of Christian experience and theology. . . . He is clear and positive about his own Christian commitment, which by his own account has grown stronger as his work on Jesus has progressed.

—N. T. Wright[2]

Marcus Borg prefers not to talk about "the historical Jesus" as a figure of the past who can be studied apart from religious or spiritual concerns. As indicated in a previous chapter, he suggests a change in terminology; instead of talking about "the Jesus of history" and "the Christ of faith," we should speak of "the pre-Easter Jesus" and "the post-Easter Jesus" (see page 4). Both are historical realities, subject to study and critique, and both are significant for theology and faith.

A former member of the Jesus Seminar, Borg is Professor of Religion and Culture at Oregon State University. As the designation of his field implies, he is heavily invested in the relationship between matters of faith and sociopolitical realities. He has been a student of world religions, with particular interest in varieties of spirituality and mysticism. Although a confessing Christian, he admits that his own faith has been enhanced by studying Buddhism, the writings of Carlos Castenada, and the latter's Indian seer, Don Juan.

Of all the scholars whose views are described in this book, none has been so open or articulate about his personal level of engagement with these issues as Marcus Borg. His 1994 book *Meeting Jesus Again for the First Time* has become a classic of spiritual autobiography, helping numerous college students and others to maintain faith-with-integrity in a world that demands skepticism. In that volume, Borg describes his own childhood as a time marked by "precritical naivete"; he worshiped Jesus and believed whatever authority figures said to believe concerning him. His adolescence, he says, was a time of intellectual struggle and doubt. In college, he was exposed to academic study of theology in a way that did not help him to believe but, he says, "provided a framework within which I could take my perplexity seriously."[3] He went off to seminary and then to graduate school, a "closet agnostic."[4] He learned to study the Gospels as developing traditions in early Christianity rather than as divine documents or straightforward historical records. "I found all of this very exciting," Borg reports, "though it also seemed vaguely scandalous and something I shouldn't tell my mother about."[5] He also learned to identify beliefs in Christian tradition as cultural products, developed to serve psychological human needs and to expedite certain social functions. With the recognition that such beliefs could be explained naturally, without recourse to God, came an increasing suspicion "that there probably was no such reality."[6] Then, Borg says, he had a number of mystical and ecstatic experiences that fundamentally changed his understanding of God, Jesus, religion, and Christianity. "It became obvious to me," he writes, "that God—the sacred, the holy, the numinous—was 'real.' God was no longer a concept or an article of belief, but had become an element of experience."[7] Not only God, but Jesus:

> Believing in Jesus does not mean believing doctrines about him. Rather, it means to give one's heart, one's self at its deepest level, to the post-Easter Jesus who is the living Lord, the side of God turned toward us, the face of God, the Lord who is also the spirit.[8]

It was with this awareness and within the context of this understanding of faith that he now approached the study of Jesus, working still as a trained historical scholar.

BORG'S METHOD FOR STUDYING JESUS

Borg is less explicit about methodological considerations than other scholars discussed in this book. Whereas some (Crossan, Meier, Wright) have devoted hundreds of pages—even entire books—to this subject, Borg offers only a few explanatory comments. Part of the attraction of his work is that it goes right to the task at hand, presenting a vivid and persuasive description of Jesus in fewer words than some expend on prolegomena.

In general, Borg tries to "go with the flow" of mainstream historical criticism, accepting what most scholars would regard as reliable without proposing novel theories regarding sources or criteria of authenticity. There is nothing in his presentation of Jesus that depends on acceptance of the apocryphal Gospels of Peter or Thomas. In keeping with the perspective of most historical scholars, he mostly ignores the Gospel of John, relying most heavily on material in the three Synoptic Gospels. Unlike the Jesus Seminar as a whole, however, he does not noticeably elevate the Q sayings over the narrative material in Mark's Gospel.

He has described his basic method for approaching Gospel materials as involving three stages. First, he makes some basic assumptions about sources, assumptions widely held by the great majority of scholars. He accepts that the Gospel of Mark is the earliest of the Synoptic Gospels and was used by the others. This means that when material is found in both Mark and another Gospel the Markan version should be the focus of the historian's attention, and the versions in Matthew and Luke should not be viewed as providing multiple attestation for what Mark reports. Second, Borg says that he attempts to construct an initial portrait of Jesus based on what *is* multiply attested in the earliest layers of the tradition (Mark and Q). Finally, he fills out the portrait, albeit cautiously, with singly attested material that is congruent with the portrait attained through stage two.[9]

For Borg, the historical task also demands recognition that the Gospels sometimes "combine memory and testimony" and at other times "combine memory and metaphor."[10] In the first instance, he means that the Gospel authors record what was remembered about the pre-Easter Jesus in a way that provides testimony to the post-Easter Jesus: his life and teachings are recalled as the words and deeds of one who came to be known as the divine Son of God and as the Savior of the world. The Gospel authors are indeed "evangelists" and some historical work is necessary to recover the layer of pre-Easter memory that lies beneath the post-Easter testimony. Likewise, the Gospels do not simply report events as they were remembered but recount tales of Jesus and his followers with a literary flair that capitalizes on whatever metaphorical meaning the stories might be thought to possess. For example, the story of Jesus' final journey to Jerusalem (where he will be crucified) is told in the Gospel of Mark in a manner that capitalizes on a theme central to that book: following Jesus means accepting "the way of the cross," embracing service and self-denial. Similarly, stories of Jesus opening the eyes of the blind are often told in ways that highlight the need for spiritual enlightenment. Accordingly, the historian needs to recognize that the Gospels often present "memory metaphorized": the stories they tell can be "powerfully truthful, even though not literally factual."[11] Theologians may be interested in the spiritual truth conveyed in such narratives; historians, however, want to strip away the metaphorical layer to see what, if anything, can be recovered of actual events as they were first remembered.

How does one separate memory from tradition, or memory from metaphor? Again, Borg proposes nothing idiosyncratic in that regard. He relies, first, on the criterion of multiple attestation and, second, on the criterion of coherence (see pages 59–60, 67): that which is attested in independent sources (especially both Mark and Q) has a good probability of being historical, and other singly attested matters that cohere well with this material may also be accepted. But against this general backdrop, he admits that other considerations sometimes intrude. The historian's suspicion is aroused when material seems to reflect what is known to have been a developing tendency within the Christian tradition: for example, the application of christological titles to Jesus (Matt. 14:33) or the placement of a summary statement at the end of a narrative to indicate its relevance or meaning for the later Christian church (Mark 7:19). Borg also admits flat out to being suspicious about stories that report "spectacular events" (i.e., miracles): "All of us have some sense of the limits of the possible, even though we might disagree about what those limits are. . . . Does it ever happen that somebody can walk on the sea? Does it ever happen that somebody can change a large quantity of water into wine? . . . If not, then as a historian I cannot conclude that Jesus did these things."[12]

In making historical judgments, however, Borg does not obsess over the authenticity of individual sayings or deeds attributed to Jesus. He is more interested in determining what "kind of person" Jesus was than in whether he said or did specific things that are attributed to him.

> Though we cannot ever be certain that we have direct and exact quotation from Jesus, we can be relatively sure of the kinds of things he said, and of the main themes and thrusts of his teaching. We can also be relatively sure of the kinds of things he did: healings, association with outcasts, the deliberate calling of twelve disciples, a mission directed to Israel, a final purposeful journey to Jerusalem.[13]

Rather than "preoccupying ourselves with the question of whether Jesus said *exactly* the particular words attributed to him," we should notice what types of sayings and deeds are attributed to him. By doing this, "we can sketch a fairly full and historically defensible portrait of Jesus. . . . We can in fact know as much about Jesus as we can about any figure in the ancient world."[14]

Once the task is defined as determining what kind of person Jesus was, the major trajectory of Borg's method becomes clear. He uses an interdisciplinary approach to interpret the general tendencies of the Jesus tradition from a perspective informed by sociology, anthropology, and a study of the history of religions.[15] A first step in this process involves analysis of the cultural context in which Jesus lived. Borg identifies the Roman world that provided this context as "an imperial form of *a preindustrial agricultural domination system,*" and he thinks it is important to recognize the central features of such a social system: these societies were politically oppressive, economically exploitative, religiously legitimated, and marked by both armed conflict and organized violence.[16]

Borg considers the images for Jesus presented by the tradition against the backdrop of this social world and, further, compares those images to classic "religious personality types" that are known to have appeared elsewhere within the history of Israel and in other cultures.[17] Comparative study of other religious and social figures offers analogies for understanding how Jesus related to his social world. At times, Borg also draws overtly on his own experiences or observations of contemporary religion. For instance, he offers the following as one reason for the improbability of Jesus having prophesied the imminent end of the world: Most of us have heard street preachers (and others) whose message essentially is, 'The end is at hand, repent!' In my experience, people who strongly believe 'the end is near' sound very different from what I hear in the Jesus tradition considered as a whole."[18]

In short, Borg's method for studying Jesus appears to be informed by an awareness of historical-critical study of the New Testament, an appreciation for the cultural context in which Jesus lived, a consideration of analogies drawn from interdisciplinary studies of religion, and a good dose of common sense.

BORG'S PORTRAIT OF JESUS

Borg's depiction of the historical Jesus was first laid out in *Jesus: A New Vision* (1987), a groundbreaking book that was later revised and expanded to be published as *Jesus: Uncovering the Life, Teaching, and Relevance of a Religious Revolutionary* (2006).[19] His profile of Jesus incorporates five different but closely related images for Jesus: (1) a Jewish mystic, (2) a healer and exorcist, (3) a wisdom teacher, (4) a prophet, and (5) a movement initiator.[20] These images might be related to two focal points: social world and spirit. Jesus' social world was the center of his concern (not just the background for his activity) and the Spirit was the source of his sense of mission and of the perspective from which he spoke.[21] For this reason, the category of Jewish mystic (or "Spirit person")[22] becomes the umbrella designation under which the other four descriptions all fit, the glue that holds them all together. It is as a Jewish mystic that Jesus functions as healer and exorcist, wisdom teacher, prophet, and movement initiator. Or, if we take the subtitle of his 2006 book seriously we might also say that it is as a Jewish mystic that Jesus functions as a "religious revolutionary."

Jesus as a Jewish Mystic

The world in which Jesus lived was one that took for granted the existence of a world of spirit, that is, "another dimension or layer or level of reality in addition to the visible world of our ordinary experience."[23] Believing in this other reality, Borg stresses, did not take what we may call "faith." It was virtually a universal notion, accepted without question by all cultures prior to the modern period. This other world was a reality to be experienced, but since it lay beyond sensory perception it could be known only through mediation. At certain places or times, the world of spirit seemed to intersect with our ordinary world, allowing people to experience union or communion with it. In practically every culture, furthermore, certain individuals experienced such communion more frequently or vividly than most. Though they take a variety of forms, such charismatic "Spirit persons" are found in almost every culture.[24] Jesus, says Borg, was such a person.

To identify Jesus as a Jewish mystic is to place him in the "tradition of Jewish figures for whom God, the sacred, was an experiential reality."[25] Mystics, Borg says, "are people who have vivid and typically frequent experiences of the sacred and whose lives are decisively changed as a result."[26] They enjoy a relationship with God that is not dependent upon institutional or traditional mediators; they are empowered by this relationship and by what they experience as unbrokered access to God. Citing the American psychologist and philosopher William James, Borg notes that there are persons whose experiences of the sacred move them "from *secondhand religion* (what one has heard from others) to *firsthand religion*."[27] And he adds, "Whatever one makes of these kinds of experiences, and whatever one thinks their ontological implications are, we need to take seriously that they happen. Moreover, the most important figures in human religious history are spoken of as people who had them."[28]

According to Borg, the big picture of Jesus that we derive from the Gospels fits this profile well. The first episode regarding Jesus that can be regarded as a historical event is one that places him squarely in charismatic religious tradition. He is baptized by John, who was himself regarded as a Spirit person (a prophet), and at this baptism is said to have seen a vision of the heavens opening and the Spirit descending upon him like a dove (Mark 1:10). Jesus is reported to have seen other visions as well; the Q material speaks of three visions of temptation he experienced while fasting in the wilderness (Matt. 4:1–11; Luke 4:1–13), and elsewhere Jesus claims to have seen a vision of Satan falling from heaven like lightning (Luke 10:17–18).[29]

Borg also notes that Jesus is described as a man of prayer, and he calls attention to two aspects of this.[30] First, Jesus is said to have prayed for long periods of time (Luke 6:12, "all night"), suggesting that the form of prayer was not just verbal expression but deep contemplation or meditation. Second, Jesus is said to have called God, "Abba" (Mark 14:36), an Aramaic word "used by young children on the babbling edge of speech," similar to the English "Papa." Although the word was also used by adult children to address their fathers, it was a relational, familial, and intimate term,[31] and its application to God (though not completely unique to Jesus) may have seemed remarkable for a social world where a common convention was to use circumlocutions that avoided direct mention of God altogether (Mark 14:61). In short, Jesus' prayer life expressed an abiding sense of communion and intimacy with God.

Jesus' spirituality also had an external dimension, affecting how he was viewed by others and how he interacted with them.[32] Jesus is said to have evoked awe and amazement in those about him, not simply in response to things he said or did but as a general reaction to his very person. Mark 10:32 puts it vividly: "They were on the road, going up to Jerusalem, and Jesus was walking ahead of them; and they were amazed, and those who followed were [filled with awe]." The mere reports of incidents such as the transfiguration (Mark 9:2–4) testify to how Jesus was viewed by his followers as an extraordinary Spirit-filled person, regardless of whether one regards these events as actual occurrences. Somewhat ironically, reports that his opponents believed he was demon-possessed (Matt. 12:27–28; Mark 3:22) testify to this as well: Jesus' enemies did not deny that he was imbued with spiritual power; they simply questioned *which* spirit was empowering him.

Jesus as Healer and Exorcist

Borg regards the assertion that Jesus was a healer and an exorcist as "virtually indisputable" on historical grounds. He cites multiple attestation of accounts in the earliest sources and points out that "despite the difficulty which miracles pose for the modern mind," healings and exorcisms were "relatively common in the world around Jesus."[33] He cites the example of another first-century charismatic, Rabbi Hanina ben Dosa, who according to the Talmud was able not only to expel demons but also to heal people from a distance and overcome the poison of serpents—powers attributed also to Jesus (Luke 7:1–10; 10:19). The Gospels freely grant that some of Jesus' opponents—the Pharisees—were able to cast out demons (Matt. 12:27; compare Mark 9:38–39). What's more, Jewish leaders who opposed the early Christians later in the first century did not even bother to claim that his healings were the result of fakery or that they had been misreported: as indicated above, they acknowledged the healings as authentic but attributed them to power drawn from an evil spirit (see Mark 3:20–30). In short, the healing ministry of Jesus loses its uniqueness in the light of historical study, but for that very reason gains in credibility.[34] And yet, Jesus' activity in this regard must have been remarkable since far more healing and exorcism stories are told about him than about any other figure in Jewish tradition.[35]

Borg avoids trying to explain how modern medical science might perceive "what really happened" when Jesus healed people or drove demons out of them. The tendency to find "a psychosomatic explanation that stretches but does not break the limits of our modern worldview" ultimately misses the point, which is that the healings and exorcisms were experienced as an incursion of otherworldly power.[36] Historically, we must acknowledge that Jesus presented himself as a person through whom such power could and did operate, and that those around him experienced him as a channel for such power. The fact that the power was said to operate for healing is also significant, for it indicates more precisely the type of mystic or "Spirit person" that Jesus was. The world knew, for instance, of spirit-empowered warriors or of prophets who could curse their opponents in ways that would bring affliction upon them. Such stories are not found in reliable sources for Jesus.

Jesus' role as a healer and an exorcist is significant for two other reasons: (1) his identification as such brought him renown that attracted sizable crowds, generating an audience for his teaching; and (2) he connected the healings and exorcisms to a central theme of his teaching, claiming that they demonstrated the present availability of God's benevolent and transforming power (Matt. 12:28; Luke 11:20).

Jesus as a Wisdom Teacher

The image of Jesus as a sage or wisdom teacher is a popular one in modern historical study. We have already seen that this identification dominates the work of the Jesus Seminar and, in various ways, the work of Crossan, Downing, Schüssler Fiorenza, Mack, and Witherington as well. For Borg, however, the category is not dominant. It is but one expression of Jesus as a Spirit-filled Jewish mystic. Jesus taught specifically as a person who claimed to have intimate knowledge of God and the spirit world. The content of his teaching, therefore, revealed the true nature of God and reality. Borg does not appeal to the Cynics for an analogy of Jesus as sage, but to Buddha and to Lao Tzu.[37] Jesus was similar to them in that he proclaimed a way of transformation based on insight into how things truly are.

Jesus' teaching was based on a vision of reality that challenged conventional wisdom. Borg defines conventional wisdom as "what everybody knows" in a given culture, that is, the "convictions and ways of behavior so taken for granted as to be basically unquestioned."[38] One aspect of conventional wisdom for Jesus' society was the understanding that reality was organized on a basis of rewards and punishments: life goes well for those who live in a way that is wise or "right" and poorly for those who live in a way that is unwise or "wrong." Jesus challenged this perception of reality. He pointed to nature as indicative of a cosmic generosity: God feeds birds who do no labor (Matt. 6:26) and provides sun and rain for the crops of good and bad people alike (Matt. 5:45). He likened God to a father who celebrates the return of an errant son (Luke 15:11–32) or to a king who simply remits the debt of a slave who owed him an enormous amount of money (Matt. 18:23–24).[39] Borg concludes: "What distinguished [Jesus] from most of his contemporaries as well as from us, from their conventional wisdom as well as from ours, was his vivid sense that reality was ultimately gracious and compassionate."[40] In fact, Jesus' teaching about God can be summarized in terms of how he presented the character of God and the passion of God: Jesus maintained that the character of God was *compassion* and the passion of God was *justice*. These go together "for the simple reason that justice is the social form of compassion."[41]

Jesus was "neither anti-law nor anti-convention. He was a Jew who treasured his tradition."[42] The very forms of speech that he used (proverbs, parables, lessons from nature) belonged to the wisdom tradition of Israel. But "Jesus used the forms of traditional wisdom to challenge conventional wisdom."[43] Unlike the Cynics, he did not simply subvert a vision of the world; he affirmed a different vision, offering "an alternative way of being and an alternative consciousness shaped by the relationship to Spirit and not primarily by the dominant consciousness of culture."[44] Jesus' teaching did not consist primarily of doctrine or ethics, but took the form of "an *invitation to see differently.*"[45] His parables and his aphorisms tended to be "invitational rather than imperatival," intended to provoke thought and inspire discussion about assumptions that were usually taken-for-granted.[46]

Jesus contrasted the "broad way" of conventional wisdom with the "narrow way" of living in accord with his vision. Notably, the broad way that leads to destruction is not described by Jesus in terms of what most religious people consider to be gross wickedness or obvious sinfulness but rather with reference to constricting loyalties (e.g. to family rather than to God), to preoccupation with wealth, to obsession with one's own honor or status, and to devotion to standards of purity that segregate or categorize people as "insiders" and "outsiders."[47] Those who follow the broad way (most people) are simply persons who see reality as hostile or indifferent such that self-preservation becomes the first law of their being. But for those who come to see reality as supportive and nourishing, another response to life becomes possible—trust.[48] Life that is grounded in trust involves a death to self-interest (Mark 8:34) and a centering in God. Borg is clear, however, that for Jesus trust was less a matter of believing things about God than of following the way of God. Ultimately, he coins a term to describe what Jesus' subversive wisdom teaching called people to do, not simply to believe God but to *belove* God. Of course, that requires some explanation: "What does it mean to belove God? It has multiple resonances: to yearn for, to pay attention to, to commit to, to be loyal to, to value above all else . . . . And to belove God means to love what God loves."[49] According to Jesus, God loves the world (John 3:16), so a life centered in God will be focused on the world, lived in accord with God's compassionate character and passion for justice.

Jesus the Prophet

Borg's image of Jesus as a prophet is developed through analysis of conflict stories in the New Testament, which he interprets in light of the cultural dynamics of Jesus' social world. In these stories, which present Jesus in conflict with the various leaders of Israel, Jesus speaks and acts in ways similar to what we associate with the authors of the prophetic writings of the Old Testament. Like them, he identifies a threat to his social world, presents an indictment of those responsible, and summons people to repentance. Indeed, Borg claims that "of all the figures in his tradition, Jesus was most like the classical prophets of Israel."[50] There is some indication that he identified himself as a prophet (Mark 6:4; Luke 13:33) and that his contemporaries viewed him as one as well (Mark 6:15; 8:28; Luke 7:16).

As a prophet, Jesus spoke primarily against the domination system of his day. Like Crossan, Borg draws on the work of social anthropologist Gerhard Lenski regarding "pre-industrial agrarian societies."[51] According to Lenski, the single most striking characteristic of these societies was the "marked social inequality" between its two social classes: urban elites and rural peasants. The former were wealthy and owned or controlled most of the land; the latter worked the land, paid heavy taxes, and lived in poverty. As a social prophet, Jesus decried this system, pronouncing blessings on the oppressed peasants and woes on the rich (Luke 6:20, 24). In doing so, Borg claims, Jesus stood in line with the God-intoxicated prophets of the Hebrew Bible.[52]

Sometimes Jesus spoke outright against the oppressive tyrants in the world at large (Mark 10:42–43), but as a Jewish prophet he directed most of his indictments against the rulers of his own people, including Jewish authorities who collaborated with the unjust and oppressive imperial powers. He spoke against Jerusalem and its temple cult as a prime example of native collaboration with an oppressive domination system.[53] Likewise, his condemnation of scribes focused on their role as retainers who served the interests of the ruling elite, for example by foreclosing on the homes of widows and seizing their property (Mark 12:38–40) and paramount among his critique of the Pharisees was their obsession with relatively pedantic matters that failed to address the crying need of the people for justice (Luke 11:42; Matt. 23:23).[54] The wealthy in general came under indictment from Jesus because typically, in his culture, people became wealthy by belonging to a small elite class and participating in "a massively exploitative system."[55]

Positively, Jesus urged people to practice nonviolent resistance in various creative ways (Matt. 5:38–41, 43–45).[56] And he offered them a vision of what he believed life could be like: a transformed world that he liked to call "the kingdom of God." As Jesus portrayed it, this kingdom was an earthly reality; it had little or nothing to do with heaven or an afterlife. Rather, Jesus taught that God was willing to bring about a blessed state of affairs, a utopia where God alone would rule and all the domination systems of the earth would cease to be. Thus, the kingdom was very much a political reality as well as a religious one.[57] As a prophet, Jesus called upon people to participate in the establishment of this kingdom, to seek it and strive for it.

It was this role as prophet that got Jesus killed. Borg believes that Jesus brought his reform movement to Jerusalem to affect the heart of Israelite society. He performed two prophetic acts. First, he rode into the city on a donkey's colt, demonstrating that the society of which he spoke was to be a kingdom of peace, not war.[58] Then, he overturned tables of moneychangers in the temple as an act protesting "the sacred order of separation" that the temple cult with its sacrificial enterprise and ecclesiastical merchants manifested.[59] In itself this act was no big deal; it was purely symbolic, "limited in area, intent, and duration, done for the sake of the message it conveyed."[60] But it was enough. What happened next, Borg admits, is difficult to reconstruct, but he theorizes: some of the Jewish authorities in charge of the temple, who no doubt did not appreciate the message Jesus was sending, interrogated him and then handed him over to Pilate as a political claimant. He was charged with treason and summarily executed as an insurrectionist. The charge, Borg notes, was not entirely fair. As an advocate of nonviolence Jesus did not pose the sort of direct threat to the empire that such an execution could imply. But as a charismatic prophet, he did indeed pose a threat to the social order, as the Jewish leaders and, perhaps, Pilate rightly discerned.[61]

Jesus as Movement Initiator

The way of transformation that Jesus taught had social and political implications. Ultimately, says Borg, Jesus was not simply calling individuals to a new perception of reality but was offering an alternative vision for society as a whole. His "concern was the renewal of Israel" and his "purpose was the transformation of the Jewish social world."[62] To effect such a transformation, he created a sectarian revitalization movement of itinerant followers who sought to emulate what life grounded in the new vision could be. His concern that this movement represented a new way for Israel is demonstrated in his identification of twelve followers as having a special calling. Borg regards this choosing of the twelve as "one of the most certain facts of Jesus' ministry" and interprets it as a symbolic reconstitution of the twelve tribes of Israel.[63] Thus, Borg rejects the extremely Hellenistic image of Jesus offered by some historians and affirms a specific commitment to Israel.

Jesus' reform movement challenged certain aspects of Israelite society and one aspect on which Borg has focused has garnered a good deal of attention and critique: the affront that the Jesus movement would have posed to what Borg calls "the politics of holiness."[64] At the very heart of Jesus' social world was a cultural paradigm that accepted holiness as its core value and sought to define what was holy and what was not. This paradigm was expressed through a purity system that established strict boundaries. Certain times, places, and things were declared holy and had to be treated in a special way. Similar categories were established with regard to people, and distinctions were made with regard to Jews and Gentiles, men and women, oldest sons and younger siblings, and so forth. These distinctions were inevitably hierarchical, leading to a rigid mindset concerning what roles were appropriate for whom and what status should be assigned to people occupying those roles. The system was undergirded, furthermore, by a fundamental notion that holiness must be protected by *separation;* that which is holy, pure, or clean must be preserved from defilement through contact with what is unholy, impure, or unclean. Theologically, the politics of holiness was grounded in a concept of *imago Dei* (imitation of God): "You shall be holy, for I the LORD your God am holy" (Lev. 19:2).[65]

Borg maintains that the holiness system originally served to preserve Israel's cultural identity during the exile, but later it was intensified under Roman rule in ways that were unjust and instable.[66] Large numbers of the population came to be regarded as "sinners" or outcasts, similar to the lower caste of "untouchables" in India.[67] The problem, Borg says, had nothing to do with the legitimacy of the purity rules themselves (which have often been, and still are, observed by Jewish people in ways that do not foster oppressive exclusivity). The problem was the manner in which the purity system was exploited by ruling elites at the time of Jesus: there were clear correlations between purity and class structure, such that "the purity system was the ideology of the ruling elites," intended to guarantee that "their place in society was divinely sanctioned."[68] He also notes that the Pharisees as a prominent Jewish group intensified attention to purity rules in ways that had negative social consequences for many people in Jesus' world.[69] Thus, according to Borg, Jesus lived "in a world to a large extent structured by purity laws," and when he told the Pharisees that true impurity was a matter of the heart (Mark 7:21), "it was like saying in a racially segregated society that race is a matter of what people are like on the inside, not on the outside."[70] Against this backdrop, Borg understands the movement Jesus initiated as a countercultural association that deliberately defied the politics of holiness, seeking to replace it with a politics of compassion. Jesus and his followers ate openly with outcasts and associated with women in ways that violated social expectations. Jesus offered his world a new cultural paradigm, grounded as the old one was in the concept of *imatio Dei*. But Jesus sought to replace "Be holy as God is holy" with "Be compassionate as God is compassionate."[71]

Thus, violation of purity rules would not have been the defining attribute of the Jesus movement; it would simply have been one example from among many of the implications this movement drew from its understanding of the character and passion of God. Because God was compassionate and generous, Jesus and his followers strove to be also; because God wanted justice, they worked for justice. Further, this movement was decidedly charismatic; Jesus' followers performed healings and exorcisms as he did, claiming that God's Spirit was at work in and through them. They demonstrated concern for the poor that went well beyond almsgiving to suggest commitment to radical redistribution of resources. They spoke and acted in ways that counseled peaceful nonresistance to the Roman oppressors. They did all these things in a spirit of joyful celebration, claiming that God's kingdom would come. It was a movement inaugurated by Jesus' contagious vision of God and of a world loved by God, a vision of "what life would be like on earth if God were king and the rulers and systems of this world were not . . . the world the prophets dreamed of—a world of distributive justice in which everybody has enough, in which war is no more, and in which nobody need be afraid."[72]

Additional Remarks

We have sketched Borg's portrait of Jesus according to the five images for Jesus that he first offered in his book *Jesus: A New Vision*, filling in content as needed from his other, more recent writings. A few more points will now be offered regarding matters that transcend those categories.

First, Borg does not think that we possess reliable sources to determine exactly what Jesus thought about himself—his own identity or role in God's plan. He thinks it unlikely that the pre-Easter Jesus claimed to be the Messiah or Son of God; it is uncertain that he even claimed to be a prophet. In the historically authentic materials that have come down to us, he does not appear to talk about himself much at all. He certainly did not view himself as the founder of a new religion that would worship him or regard him as the Savior of the world. Recognizing this affects how a historically informed reader will understand the Gospels. For example, Jesus apparently spoke often of "something greater" that was happening (Matt. 12:41–42; Luke 11:31–32; cf. Matt. 11:4–5; Luke 10:23–24): his disciples and the people he taught were witnesses to "something greater than Jonah, the most successful of Israel's prophets, and something greater than King Solomon, fabled for his wisdom."[73] So what *was* this "something greater"? Borg does not think that it was a reference to Jesus himself or to the advent of Christianity.[74] Rather, the "something greater" of which Jesus spoke appears to have been the kingdom of God, the transformation of the world that Jesus claimed God envisioned and would bring about with human participation.

Next, Borg has usually been understood as arguing for a noneschatological Jesus,[75] though he would eventually put the matter differently: Jesus evinced a "participatory eschatology" rather than the "imminent eschatology" that often seems to be attributed to him in the Gospels.[76] In this regard, Borg's image of Jesus parallels that of the Jesus Seminar and others we have discussed.[77] He agrees with the Seminar, for instance, in assigning all the sayings attributed to Jesus regarding the coming of the Son of Man to a later development of the tradition. These sayings (for example, Mark 13:24–30; Luke 12:8–9) are unauthentic. Jesus did not speak of a supernatural figure who would come with angels at the end of the world, much less identify himself with this figure. Rather, belief in a second coming of Jesus arose in the church after Easter and came to be expressed in apocalyptic terms. Borg grants that Jesus did speak about "the kingdom of God," but he maintains that Jesus used this expression as "a tensive symbol, that is, one with a number of nuances of meaning."[78] And, as we have seen, he usually interprets this phrase as a political and religious metaphor ("the way the world would be if God were king"[79]). Borg's essential point in this regard seems to be that Jesus did not expect or predict "a dramatic supernatural intervention by God in the very near future that would establish the kingdom of God" in an unmistakable and cataclysmic way.[80] Rather, Jesus called people to respond to the vision of God's rule that he articulated and to participate in bringing it to pass—to make God's passion their passion. The point, of course, was not that human beings could bring about utopia on their own but that God expected collaboration from humans in transforming the world. According to Borg, Augustine understood this participatory eschatology of Jesus when he said, "God without us will not; and we without God can not."[81]

Finally, Borg offers some comments on the resurrection of Jesus. From a strict, historical perspective, he admits that not much can be said: "The story of the historical Jesus ends with his death on a Friday in A.D. 30." He insists, nevertheless, that the post-Easter Jesus is real: "The living, risen Christ of the New Testament has been an experiential reality (and not just an article of belief) from the days of Easter to the present."[82] The point, for Borg, is to separate the notion of resurrection from that of resuscitation of a corpse. The notion of resurrection implies that Jesus entered into another mode of being, that he is no longer limited by space and time but is able to be present—as a living, experienced reality—with his followers in a new way. This notion does not require an empty tomb. Borg admits that the empty tomb stories are relatively late and confused, but he also dismisses their significance for accepting the truth of the resurrection.[83] With regard to his own personal faith, he says, "I find [the Easter] stories to be powerfully true as parables of the resurrection. It does not matter to me as a Christian whether any of them describe events that you or I could have witnessed. It does not matter to me whether the tomb was empty."[84] Still, the historical question would be, what happened after Jesus died? In response, Borg says, "The followers of Jesus had experiences of him after his death that convinced them that he continued to be a figure of the present."[85] These experiences included visions but also nonvisionary experiences according to which they "felt the continuing presence of Jesus with them" and recognized "the power they had known in Jesus continuing to operate—the power of healing, the power to change lives, the power to create new forms of community."[86]

CRITIQUE OF BORG'S STUDY OF JESUS

Borg's view is more comprehensive than many. N. T. Wright has called him "a bridge," indicating that his description of Jesus has points in common with sketches offered by scholars whose views appear to be disparate if not irreconcilable.[87] The combined images of Jesus as healer and sage are similar to those that play heavily into Crossan's portrait (chapter 5), while the image of movement initiator parallels the work of Schüssler Fiorenza (pages 30–32) and that of social prophet echoes concerns important to Horsley (pages 73–76). Even the characterization of Jesus as a charismatic Spirit person resonates with contributions offered by Geza Vermes (pages 76–79). The upshot of all this is that practically every scholar finds things to praise in Borg's analysis, as well as points to dispute.

To put things a bit too simply, major historians of Jesus often seem to fall into two camps: those who accent the Hellenistic matrix for Jesus and downplay his eschatological teaching (the Jesus Seminar, Crossan, Downing, Mack), and those who accent a more traditional Jewish matrix for Jesus and emphasize his eschatological teaching (Meier, Sanders, Witherington, Wright). If Borg is a bridge, it is because his Jesus is traditionally Jewish (i.e., not particularly Hellenistic) but also noneschatological (i.e., not given to promoting imminent eschatology). Negatively, this means that his views may be attacked from both sides. According to Burton Mack, Galilee was such a hellenized Roman state that much of what Borg describes as conventional Jewish wisdom would not have played a significant role in Jesus' cultural environment.[88] According to E. P. Sanders, appreciation for Jewish restoration theology prominent at the time of Jesus demands that such actions as his selection of twelve disciples and symbolic destruction of the temple be interpreted as eschatological acts that anticipated God's establishment of a new age.[89] For Borg, the problem with being a "bridge" is having it both ways.

On other points, Borg is actually criticized for ruling out options that need not be mutually exclusive. Keener notes that "Jewish sources can lay side by side the alternatives of the end coming at a foreordained time or at a time contingent on Israel's repentance."[90] Thus, Jesus could have been both an eschatological prophet and a social prophet, simultaneously announcing that the end was near and challenging Israel to become the people of God they were always intended to be. Similarly, Witherington complains that Borg sets concern for compassion and holiness against each other such that Jesus can only proclaim the one at the expense of the other.[91] A large amount of material, such as sayings on divorce and adultery (Matt. 5:27–32), reveal that Jesus was concerned about maintaining purity or holiness in a moral sense. Or, to put the matter differently, Jesus' concern for social justice need not be trumpeted in a way that eclipses his frequent focus on matters of personal conduct.

As indicated, there has been a good deal of contention over Borg's construal of the Jewish concepts of purity and holiness. A number of scholars, including Paula Fredriksen, Amy-Jill Levine, and E. P. Sanders, have questioned whether purity codes were exercised in an oppressive manner. Sanders, whose views we will discuss further in the next chapter, believes that the purity codes were followed only by a select group of Jews (the *haberim)* who may have been roughly equivalent with those the New Testament designates as Pharisees. These were laity who, for theological reasons, chose to maintain themselves in the relatively high state of ritual purity expected of priests. But the decision to do this was completely voluntary. According to Sanders, the *haberim* did not consider others sinful for not following this way, nor did they exercise enough power in Galilee at the time of Jesus to have had much effect even if they had thought this. Although Sanders does not criticize Borg directly, he clearly wants to undermine the whole notion of "a politics of holiness" on which portions of Borg's presentation rest. Indeed, Sanders thinks such construals are Christian misrepresentations of Judaism that smack of anti-Semitism.[92] Levine, a Jewish scholar with strong interest in the historical Jesus, would agree with the latter assessment: presentations of Jesus as one who broke or violated purity laws in the interest of justice or inclusiveness "rest on the misunderstanding and so misrepresentation of Jewish practices."[93] Likewise, Paula Fredriksen claims that Borg thoroughly misunderstands Jewish purity laws and so presumes conflict over matters that would not have provoked Jesus or any other Jewish person of the day.[94] To be fair, in his later work, Borg seeks to connect the oppressive aspect of purity with segregationist policies of the ruling elites (and of certain Pharisees) rather than with the conventional wisdom of Jews in general, but that would not be enough to satisfy Levine or Fredriksen, who find no evidence of such oppressive or segregationist practices, period. In a 1998 second edition of his book *Conflict, Holiness, and Politics in the Teaching of Jesus*, Borg notes the criticisms (of Fredriksen and Sanders), indicates that his understanding of purity (and of the Pharisees) rests primarily on the research of the prominent Jewish scholar Jacob Neusner,[95] and emphasizes that "the critique of purity is not a critique of Judaism but a critique of a particular way of construing Judaism."[96] In this regard, Thomas Kazen indicates that there was intra-Jewish debate over these matters at the time of Jesus, such that Jesus' attitude regarding purity may have led to a clash with the ideals of Jewish leaders who did not necessarily represent the populace as a whole.[97]

Casting a wider net, Levine critiques Borg sharply for his identification of the Jerusalem Temple as a domination system. In an online commentary for preachers, Borg once explained Jesus' act of turning over tables in the Temple as an assault on "that economically exploitative and politically oppressive system that radically impoverished peasants and drove them to an existence of destitution and even desperation."[98] Similar statements are found throughout his writings, though he is careful to clarify that the problem was not intrinsic to Jewish religion or its institutions; rather, the problem was that at a particular point in time, elitist religious leaders served as pawns of the imperial authorities and collaborated with them in maintaining "an oppressive domination system."[99] But, again, Levine finds little evidence to justify castigating Jewish leaders in such a light. Indeed, "the Gospels and Acts depict Jesus, his family, and his followers as worshiping in the Temple and participating in the Temple sacrificial system." Further, "not only Jesus and his family . . . but also hundreds of thousands, if not millions, of Jewish pilgrims flocked to the Temple" at least three times a year on pilgrimage holidays. Why would they so heartily (and, apparently, voluntarily) support a "domination system"?[100]

Despite the multifaceted nature of Borg's portrait of Jesus, some critics think his view is too limited. What he leaves out is significant:

> [First], in all likelihood, the pre-Easter Jesus did not think of himself as the Messiah or in any exalted terms in which he is spoken of. Second, we can say with almost complete certainty that he did not see his own mission or purpose as dying for the sins of the world. Third and finally, again with almost complete certainty, we can say that his message was not about himself or the importance of believing in him.[101]

A number of scholars (Allison, Meier, Sanders, Witherington, Wright) do not follow the logic here: if many other Jewish categories can be applied to Jesus, they ask, why not messiah as well?[102] Josephus tells about messianic claimants, some of whom are also mentioned in the book of Acts (see 5:36–37; 21:38). Why is it unlikely that Jesus would have made such claims or at least interpreted his work in light of what was associated with messianic expectations? The notion may seem absurd to some of Borg's colleagues in the Jesus Seminar who regard Jesus as belonging to a Hellenistic milieu that did not think in such terms, but if a more traditional Jewish matrix for Jesus' ministry is allowed (as it is for Borg), the rationale for excluding this category seems to disappear. Likewise, many scholars would wonder, since Borg affirms that Jesus called God "Abba," then why deny that he would have identified himself as the Son of God in some specialized sense or that his teaching might have included reflection on the intimacy of his own (unique?) relationship with God?

The main point here seems to be that Borg (like Funk, Crossan, and many other scholars) doubts the historical veracity of sayings attributed to Jesus when they clearly anticipate post-Easter Christian identifications of his person or interpretations of his significance. In the Gospels, Jesus not only accepts identification of himself as the Messiah and the Son of God; he also speaks of his forthcoming death as having redemptive or salvific value and indicates that, as the Son of Man, he will come again (probably soon) to preside at the final judgment and inaugurate a new heaven and a new earth. Borg thinks that these Gospel passages reflect retrojections of Christian theology: post-Easter theology has been placed on the lips of the pre-Easter Jesus. Some of the scholars we will look at in the rest of this book will question that assumption, but Dale Allison offers a critique that is potentially more devastating. If Borg's assumption is correct, Allison contends, then he should not be writing about the historical Jesus at all—he should abandon the quest. Allison's point rests on a recognition that certain matters (including all those just mentioned) are exceedingly prevalent in the Gospel materials,[103] found repeatedly in virtually all sources and in many different genres of Gospel literature.[104] If such matters are not reflective of actual historical memory, Allison concludes, they should be taken as evidence that the sources were so thoroughly corrupted at so early a stage that they should be deemed worthless for historical reconstruction. According to Allison, Borg (and others) might be able to make the case that the church got to Jesus too soon and redacted all the materials concerning him to such an extent that even universally attested statements concerning the pre-Easter Jesus are inauthentic Christianized caricatures. But it does not make sense, Allison continues, to assume that this happened and then imagine that the subtraction of Christian theology will somehow yield an occasional nugget of historically preserved data. In a nutshell, Allison maintains that it goes against everything we know about memory and history to assume that the tradition got the general impressions wrong, but certain particulars right: "If the chief witnesses fail us in the larger matters, we cannot trust them in the smaller matters either."[105]

Finally, Wright says that Borg's Jesus must ultimately be considered a failure.[106] His charismatic movement to revitalize Israel by changing society's core values did not work: Israel (much less the world at large) was not transformed into a land of compassion and justice where God alone ruled. If Jesus only had noble ideas that didn't pan out in practice, we must ask historically, "Why did people continue to care about him after his death?" and theologically, "Why should people pay him any mind today?"

In response to the historical question, Borg would probably appeal to the experience of Jesus after Easter. This authenticated his movement for early and contemporary Christians in a way that success measured in social or political terms never could. And in response to the theological question, Borg insists that historical knowledge of the pre-Easter Jesus informs the vision of those who stand in relation to the post-Easter Jesus today. Put simply, it tells us something about what it means to be "a Christian":

> It means to see God as an experiential reality, not simply an article of belief. It means to live by an alternative wisdom, whose primary content is a relationship with the same Spirit Jesus knew. It means to actualize compassion in the world, both as an individual virtue and as the core value of the alternative social vision of Jesus. And it means to be a part of a community of memory that celebrates, nourishes, and embodies the new way of being that we see in Jesus.[107]

Chapter 7

E. P. Sanders

I am a liberal, modern, secularized Protestant, brought up in a church dominated by low christology and the social gospel. I am proud of the things that my religious tradition stands for. I am not bold enough, however, to suppose that Jesus came to establish it, or that he died for the sake of its principles.
—E. P. Sanders[1]

According to Sanders, Jesus was an eschatological prophet standing in the tradition of Jewish restoration theology. Jesus believed that the promises to Israel would soon be fulfilled . . . brought about by a dramatic intervention by God, involving the destruction of the Jerusalem temple and the coming of a new (or renewed) temple.
—Marcus Borg[2]

Jesus saw himself as God's last messenger before the establishment of the kingdom. He looked for a new order, created by a mighty act of God. In the new order the twelve tribes would be reassembled, there would be a new temple, force of arms would not be needed, divorce would be neither necessary nor permitted, outcasts—even the wicked—would have a place, and Jesus and his disciples— the poor, the meek, and lowly—would have the leading role.
—E. P. Sanders[3]

E. P. Sanders made a name for himself over three decades ago with a treatise titled *Paul and Palestinian Judaism*.[4] He quickly became established as a major Pauline scholar and, even more, as an expert on first-century Palestinian Judaism. After a brief stint at the University of Oxford, Sanders returned to North America, where he served until his retirement as Professor of Arts and Sciences in Religion at Duke University. His numerous writings have had a profound effect on how scholars understand the Jewish world of the New Testament.[5] Even his critics will agree: few people in the world today know as much about the life, practice, and religion of first-century Jews as E. P. Sanders.

Above all, Sanders describes Judaism as a religion of grace. This may be seen in its central doctrines of creation and election. God created the world and blessed it, then chose Israel and redeemed the people. In both instances, the fundamental view is "that God's grace preceded the requirement of obedience."[6] God's favor is not something that must be earned. Sanders realizes that many Christians do not think of first-century Judaism primarily as a religion of grace, but he credits this to caricatures produced by those who wished to promote the Christian religion at the expense of its Jewish parent. Such sentiments are found in the New Testament itself (see John 1:17) but do not stand up to critical historical scrutiny. Examination of Jewish literature that comes from this time reveals solid grounding in what Christian theologians would call a concept of "prevenient grace" (grace that comes first, that is freely offered, that precedes demand).[7]

Sanders develops this further in his explication of covenantal nomism, the understanding that God created a covenant with the Jewish people and sealed it through the divine revelation of the law:

> The "pattern" or "structure" of covenantal nomism is this: (1) God has chosen Israel and (2) given the law. The law implies both (3) God's promise to maintain the election and (4) the requirement to obey. (5) God rewards obedience and punishes transgression. (6) The law provides for means of atonement, and atonement results in (7) maintenance or re-establishment of the covenantal relationship. (8) All those who are maintained in the covenant by obedience, atonement, and God's mercy belong to the group which will be saved.[8]

Caricatures of first-century Judaism tend to focus on the fourth and fifth points above to present the faith as a legalistic religion to be contrasted with the Christian gospel of God's unmerited grace offered through Christ. But, says Sanders, the role of the law for the Jewish people must be understood in light of this whole paradigm.

The law was itself a gift of grace, offering people a guide to life, and the law provided ways for atonement that would keep people in God's grace when they failed to live as they ought. Furthermore, even though God was thought to reward or punish people based on their obedience to the law, the covenant itself did not depend on such obedience. God would be faithful to God's promises *despite* disobedience.[9] Or, to put it differently, "Obedience maintains one's position in the covenant, but it does not earn God's grace as such. It simply keeps the individual in the group which is the recipient of God's grace."[10] Sanders considers this concept of covenantal nomism to be "the common denominator which underlay all sorts and varieties of Judaism."[11] Contrary to Christian stereotypes, the Jews of the first century did not view obeying the law as something burdensome. Rather, they "understood obeying the law as the . . . appropriate response to the prior grace of God."[12]

Also pertinent to our concerns is Sanders's description of Jewish restoration eschatology, the belief that God was going to act decisively and soon to fulfill the covenantal promises to Israel.[13] This perspective was pervasive for first-century Jews who believed that they were living at the end of time. Different groups construed the restoration in different ways; for instance, some looked for political redemption, others apocalyptic salvation in another world. Still, there were recurring features. The restoration would include a new or renewed temple and a reconstitution of the twelve tribes of Israel. Those who spoke of this restoration typically described an impending judgment and issued a call for national repentance. Often, they predicted that Gentiles would finally be admitted to the full salvation enjoyed by Israel.

This restoration eschatology presupposes the covenantal nomism and its accent on grace that marked all varieties of first-century Judaism. Taking them together, Sanders lists three constitutive elements of the Jewish milieu in which Jesus lived: (1) the belief that God had graciously initiated a covenant with Israel and would be faithful to that covenant, no matter what, (2) the expectation that Israel would respond to God's grace with loyalty demonstrated through obedience to the law, and (3) the strong hope that God would act soon in history to restore the fortunes of Israel. "These three component parts," Sanders says, "are found widely in Jewish literature: chronologically from Ben Sira to the Rabbinic material" (that is, from the second century BCE until at least the second century CE).[14]

At first Sanders applied his understanding of Judaism to interpretation of Paul. Then he turned his attention to Jesus. His description of Jesus is set forth in two books: *Jesus and Judaism* (1985) and *The Historical Figure of Jesus* (1993). The first was regarded as a monumental theological contribution upon its publication, receiving several prestigious book awards. The second volume offers a more popular account of Sanders's key ideas, updated somewhat as a result of further reflection and dialogue.

SANDERS'S METHOD FOR STUDYING JESUS

Sanders displays far more confidence in the authenticity of canonical tradition than any other historical Jesus scholar discussed so far. "We should trust this information," he asserts, "unless we have good reason not to do so; that is unless the stories in the Gospels contain so many anachronisms and anomalies that we come to regard them as fraudulent."[15] This attitude would be diametrically opposed to that of the Jesus Seminar, which tended to regard Gospel tradition as guilty of fabrication unless proven innocent. At the same time, Sanders's work has shown no influence from noncanonical writings about Jesus. While admitting to the possible authenticity of a few sayings in Thomas, he also claims to "share the general scholarly view that very, very little in the apocryphal gospels could conceivably go back to the time of Jesus. They are legendary and mythological."[16] Still, Sanders does not use the biblical materials uncritically. He seems to regard traditions in John as suspect, and he often detects exaggeration or other editorial tendencies in the biblical tradition. Still, his Jesus looks quite a bit like the Jesus of the Synoptic Gospels.

Rather than beginning with an analysis of the sayings of Jesus (as the Jesus Seminar ostensibly does), Sanders begins with a list of what he calls "virtually indisputable facts about Jesus." He thinks that if we start with matters on which almost everyone would agree, these will provide a framework for discussing other points. Each of Sanders's two books about Jesus begins with such a list (as indicated in fig. 6).[17] The later list is longer than the first.[18] Still, some points that Sanders regarded as virtually indisputable facts in 1985 were no longer presented as such in 1993: that Jesus' ministry included healings, that he spoke of *twelve* disciples, that he confined his ministry to Israel, and that some Jews persecuted some parts of the movement. Sanders still believes all these points are verifiable, but in the later work he presents them more cautiously, with accompanying evidence.

For Sanders, the key to understanding Jesus as a historical figure is interpreting these facts about his life in light of what we know about his social world. By "social world" he does not mean primarily the Hellenistic world of the Roman Empire, the milieu within which the Jesus Seminar and John Dominic Crossan have interpreted Jesus' life and ministry (assuming that Galilee was hellenized at the time). He means the world of first-century Palestinian Judaism, as he understands it to have been. Christians, Sanders says, have tended to describe Jesus over against Judaism rather than within Judaism, and in so doing they have reaped the fruit of the misconceptions about Judaism described above. Having caricatured the Jewish religion that Jesus himself espoused, Christians have ended up believing in a caricature of Jesus himself.

SANDERS'S PORTRAIT OF JESUS

Sanders finds that much of Jesus' life and ministry can be related to the perspective of restoration eschatology that was so prevalent in first-century Judaism. The facts about Jesus that are most certain identify him as a figure who "fits into the general framework of Jewish restoration theology" and as "the founder of a group that adhered to the expectations of that theology."[19] Two virtually certain facts are particularly significant: the action in the temple and the selection of twelve disciples, for these correspond to key components of restoration eschatology, namely, the renewal of the temple and the reconstitution of the twelve tribes. If "magic and meal" serve as an alliterative key to Crossan's understanding

Figure 6. "Almost Indisputable Facts about Jesus" (E. P. Sanders)

Jesus and Judaism (1985)	*The Historical Figure of Jesus* (1993)
	Jesus was born c. 4 BCE, near the time of the death of Herod the Great;
	he spent his childhood and early adult years in Nazareth, a Galilean village;
Jesus was baptized by John the Baptist.	he was baptized by John the Baptist;
Jesus called disciples and spoke of there being twelve.	he called disciples;
Jesus confined his activity to Israel.	he taught in the towns, villages, and countryside of Galilee (apparently not the cities);
Jesus was a Galilean who preached and healed.	he preached "the kingdom of God";
	about the year 30 he went to Jerusalem for Passover;
Jesus engaged in a controversy about the temple.	he created a disturbance in the temple area;
	he had a final meal with the disciples;
	he was arrested and interrogated by Jewish authorities, specifically the high priest;
Jesus was crucified outside Jerusalem by the Roman authorities.	he was executed on the orders of the Roman prefect, Pontius Pilate;
	his disciples at first fled;
	they saw him (in what sense is uncertain) after his death;
	as a consequence, they believed he would return to found the kingdom;
After his death, Jesus' followers continued as an identifiable movement.	they formed a community to await his return and sought to win others to faith in him as God's Messiah.
At least some Jews persecuted at least parts of the new movement.	

of Jesus (see page 126), "temple and tribes" may exercise a similar function for that of Sanders.

The Action in the Temple

All four canonical Gospels contain accounts of Jesus creating a disturbance in the temple. Mark says, "Jesus entered the temple and began to drive out those who were selling and those who were buying in the temple, and he overturned the tables of the money changers and the seats of those who sold doves" (Mark 11:15). Most historians believe that some such incident did occur; indeed, most think it provided the immediate cause for Jesus' crucifixion.[20]

Historical knowledge sheds some light on how the incident is to be understood. When Mark says Jesus "entered the temple," he actually means that Jesus entered the temple area, not the building itself. Tables were set up in a large area surrounding the temple building called the "court of the Gentiles," where doves and other animals were sold to be used for sacrifices inside. This area was massive, and Jesus' action appears to have been limited in scope. He did not surround the temple complex with an army and order all business transactions to stop. Apparently, he just turned over a few tables in one section of the area surrounding the temple—an area specifically designed for the sort of commerce that was being conducted there. Why would he do this? If it was not a determined attempt to shut down the entire enterprise or simply a spontaneous tantrum on his part, then what did he expect to accomplish? Sanders insists, and most scholars would agree with this much, that the act was staged as a symbolic demonstration. The question is, What was it supposed to symbolize? Destruction, says Sanders. Not the need for reform, but the fact of impending doom. God was going to destroy the temple.

This suggestion flies in the face of popular interpretations that present Jesus as opposing corrupt business practices or commercialization of religion in a rather generalized sense. Sanders argues that the point could not have been a simple "cleansing of the temple." Something more radical was intended. The main function of the temple was to facilitate the offering of sacrifices to God, and the money changers and dove sellers attacked by Jesus were integral to this. Jesus is described as challenging the very essence of the temple, questioning its continued existence.

Sanders thinks the symbolism of destruction is intrinsic to the imagery of overturning things, but he also notes that many sayings in the Gospels recall a tradition that associated Jesus with threatening to destroy the temple. The authenticity of this tradition is practically guaranteed by the discomfort with which the Gospels report it—crediting it to false witnesses (Mark 14:57–59), rendering it as a prediction rather than a threat (Mark 13:1–2), investing the saying with metaphorical meaning (John 2:18–22). Whatever Jesus actually said, observes Sanders, we can be relatively certain that Jesus' contemporaries believed he had publicly indicated that the temple was going to be destroyed.

It seems natural to interpret the public act that led to his crucifixion in light of this.[21]

Christian reflection tended to interpret this tradition in ways that pitted Jesus against Judaism. The actual destruction of the temple in 70 CE was viewed by Christians as a divine punishment on the Jews for rejecting Jesus or as a divine sign that the Jewish religion was false and the Christian religion true. It followed naturally from such an interpretation that, if Jesus predicted the temple's destruction, he must have intended to give a proleptic endorsement of these later Christian views. But setting aside such post-Easter impositions, Sanders seeks to understand why Jesus—interpreted *within* Judaism—might have announced an imminent divine destruction of the temple. The most likely answer seems to be that he believed God was going to replace the old temple with a new one, an event that would attend the restoration of Israel.[22] Whether Jesus thought the new temple would be on earth or in heaven cannot be determined and is somewhat inconsequential. What is more important is that a new temple meant a new age; God was about to inaugurate the long-awaited kingdom, in which all covenant promises would be fulfilled.

The Twelve Disciples

In 1993, Sanders removed from his list of "virtually indisputable facts about Jesus" the assertion that Jesus had spoken of "the twelve" as some identifiable group among his followers (see fig. 6). This is a testimony to his integrity as a scholar, for that item is very important to his argument. He removed it simply because some historians had in fact disputed it.[23] Still, Sanders argues that the point is almost certain.[24] It is attested by Paul (1 Cor. 15:5) who wrote much earlier than the Gospels and would have had no reason to invent such a tradition since, if anything, it tended to undermine his own authority as one who did not belong to the twelve (see 1 Cor. 15:8–10). Sanders does acknowledge that some parts of the tradition regarding the twelve are shaky; the various lists provided in the Gospels and Acts do not agree on their names, for instance. What is constant, however, is the number: the "conception of the twelve was more firmly anchored than the remembrance of precisely who they were."[25] Indeed, in his later study Sanders suggests that there may never have been a definitive list, that Jesus could have described his disciples as "the twelve" without meaning to imply that there were literally only twelve of them or that twelve of them were somehow more important than the rest.[26]

The number was primarily (if not exclusively) symbolic. In speaking of his followers as "the twelve," Sanders says, "Jesus intended to show that he had in view the full restoration of the people of Israel."[27] This corresponds to a key element in Jewish restoration eschatology. First-century Jews in Palestine had a strong sense of their history as portrayed in their scriptures. These told them that they were originally a kingdom of twelve tribes but that the kingdom split after David's rule and that ten of the tribes were subsequently lost. One great sign of God's faithfulness to the covenant would be the miraculous recovery of these lost tribes. Such a restoration would indeed be a miracle. No one expected the lost tribes simply to be found somewhere on earth. They had vanished from this world, decimated by the Assyrian conquests eight centuries before. That is what made the hope for restoration eschatological. The tribes would be reconstituted when the present world came to an end and a new kingdom was inaugurated by God.[28] Jesus is quoted in Matthew's Gospel as saying that his disciples will judge or rule the twelve tribes of Israel (Matt. 19:28). The saying must be authentic, Sanders reasons, for the tradition that one of the twelve was a traitor would have prevented the church from ever inventing such a prediction.[29] Jesus probably expected that he and his followers would rule from Jerusalem over all the earth.

Jesus the Eschatological Prophet

As a result of these and similar observations, Sanders determines that the best context for understanding Jesus is that of Jewish restoration eschatology: "Jesus looked for the imminent direct intervention of God in history, the elimination of evil and evildoers, the building of the new and glorious temple, and the reassembly of Israel with himself and his disciples as leading figures in it."[30] But there is more. Jesus did not just subscribe to this theological tradition; he believed that he was called as a prophet to Israel and as a prophet he functioned within this tradition.

When Jesus called his followers "the twelve" and overturned tables in the temple he was performing prophetic acts comparable to symbolic actions associated with prophets of old: Isaiah went naked for three years (Isa. 20:3), Jeremiah wore a yoke (Jer. 27:1–7) and broke a pot (Jer. 19:1–13). Sanders further identifies other prophetic acts in the reported life of Jesus, events that are probably historically authentic. The tradition of Jesus riding into Jerusalem on a donkey (Mark 11:1–10) may have been a staged fulfillment of prophecy (Zech. 9:9) in which Jesus assumed the role of king to demonstrate that the kingdom was coming. Likewise, the tradition of Jesus gathering his disciples the night before his death to eat a meal in anticipation of the coming kingdom (Mark 14:22–25; 1 Cor. 11:24–26) probably reflects another prophetic demonstration—a symbolic act proclaiming that the kingdom was at hand and that he and his disciples would share in it.

The fundamental message portrayed in all these acts of Jesus was that the divine restoration of Israel was near. This belief affected everything he said and did, but was especially manifest in two aspects of his ministry. The first is his preaching about the kingdom.[31] A large number of sayings attributed to Jesus concern the kingdom of God. Most, in Sanders's view, describe the kingdom as a realm in heaven that people may enter after death or as a realm on earth that God will establish at the final judgment. Some, he grants, speak of the kingdom as the ruling power of God that manifests itself on earth even now (Luke

17:20–21) and that is being actualized through Jesus' own words and deeds (Matt. 11:2–6; 12:28). Sanders is willing to accept virtually all these sayings as authentic, but he strongly emphasizes the former set. Especially prominent are those sayings in which Jesus says the Son of Man will come on clouds within the lifetime of his own disciples (Mark 13:24–30; Matt. 16:27–28). The authenticity of these sayings is practically guaranteed by the simple fact that this did not happen. The church would not have attributed predictions to Jesus that were not fulfilled.[32] Sanders does not think these "Son of Man sayings" anticipate the end of the world as such, but rather "a decisive act that will put the Lord or the Son of Man in charge and gather around him the elect."[33] Neither does he think that Jesus was referring to himself as the one who would initiate this action. Originally, Jesus said that God was about to inaugurate the new age by sending the Son of Man. After Jesus' death, his disciples identified him as this Son of Man and reinterpreted sayings about the coming of the Son of Man to imply a "second coming" of Jesus. But even this did not materialize within the lifetime of the first generation, and the expectations had to be revised. It worked. Theological development allowed for an expanded understanding of eschatology (see 2 Pet. 3:3–8) and "Christianity survived this early discovery that Jesus had made a mistake."[34]

The second aspect of Jesus' ministry that Sanders believes demonstrates Jesus' commitment to restoration eschatology is his performance of miracles and healing.[35] Sanders accepts the tradition that Jesus was renowned for working miracles, especially healings and exorcisms, and he is hesitant about attempting to explain these stories in light of modern scientific knowledge.[36] More to the point for him is determining the significance that Jesus and his contemporaries ascribed to events that they considered to be miracles. "Probably most Galileans heard of a few miracles—exorcisms and other healings—and regarded Jesus as a holy man, on intimate terms with God."[37] But people do not seem to have understood the miracles the way Jesus would have wanted. Jesus himself thought of his miracles as "signs of the beginning of God's final victory over evil."[38] They were acts of an eschatological prophet, signaling or foreshadowing the dawn of the imminent kingdom, in which pain, suffering, and death would be no more (see Luke 10:17–20). Jesus seems to have believed this but also to have recognized that, of themselves, miracles would not prove to anyone that he was the end-time prophet. Other miracle workers were known. Thus, he refused to work miracles as "signs" when challenged to do so (Mark 8:11–12).

The image of Jesus as an eschatological prophet may also be secured from another angle. It not only provides a framework that makes sense of much source material but also establishes Jesus as the connecting link between two known entities. John the Baptist used apocalyptic language to speak of an imminent divine intervention in history (Matt. 3:10–12), and Paul expected the Parousia to occur soon (1 Thess. 4:15–17). On either side of Jesus—his mentor and his followers—we find lively eschatological hope that the consummation of all things and the dawn of the new age is at hand. "To pull Jesus entirely out of this framework," says Sanders, "would be an act of historical violence."[39]

For Sanders, identifying Jesus as an eschatological prophet allows for reasonable explanation both of his own self-consciousness and of the identity attributed to him by the early church. "The clearest and possibly the most important point that can be made about Jesus' view of himself," says Sanders, is that "he regarded himself as having full authority to speak and act on behalf of God."[40] Jesus rejected the title Messiah (Mark 8:27–30). He did not speak of himself as the Son of God, and even if he did refer to himself as the Son of Man, we can no longer determine in what sense he meant this.[41] He presented himself, instead, as "a charismatic and autonomous prophet" whose authority "was not mediated by any human organization, not even by scripture."[42] As an eschatological prophet, however, he viewed himself as the emissary of God's kingdom and so was able to present himself symbolically as "a king." The title most faithful to Jesus' own conception of himself, Sanders says, would be *viceroy:* "God was king, but Jesus represented him and would represent him in the coming kingdom."[43] This explains the origin of the church's later confession of him to be the Messiah. The transition after Jesus' death from king (of the messianic kingdom) to Messiah was an easy one for his followers to make.[44]

Jesus and Covenantal Nomism

We noted above (page 160) that Sanders identifies three elements as pervasive in Palestinian Judaism at the time of Jesus. So far, we have seen that he relates Jesus strongly to the last of these—the hope for divine restoration of Israel. But Sanders claims that this restoration eschatology actually assumes the other two elements, which are fundamental to what he calls covenantal nomism: the belief that God would be faithful to the covenant no matter what, and the expectation that Israel would respond to God's grace with obedience to the law. We should not be surprised, therefore, to find that Sanders relates Jesus' ministry and message to these elements as well. We might be surprised, however, when we see how he does this.

Let us take the second element first: obedience to the law.[45] Sanders argues that Jesus did not abrogate the Jewish law; in particular, he did not oppose laws governing Sabbath, food, or purity. Prime evidence for this is the fact that Christians struggled to define what their attitude should be on such issues in the generations following Easter (see, for example, Paul's discussion in Rom. 14). If Jesus had actually "declared all foods clean" (Mark 7:19), the later church would not have been embroiled in controversy over observance of dietary laws. Thus, Sanders thinks the controversy stories in the Gospels are told from the perspective of Christians who are now defining themselves over against Judaism: the different legal interpretations ascribed to Jesus and his contemporaries are either invented or, at least, greatly exaggerated. For example, Sanders doubts the authenticity of stories in which Jesus and the Pharisees debate what is proper to do on the Sabbath

(Mark 2:23–28) but notes that, in any case, "to debate details of Sabbath observance presupposes general acceptance of the law."[46] In fact, Sanders claims, modern "Jewish scholars do not find any substantial points of disagreement between Jesus and his contemporaries, and certainly not any which would lead to his death."[47]

Jesus also affirmed the unfailing nature of God's covenant with Israel. His acceptance of Israel's special covenantal status is seen in that "his mission was to Israel in the name of the God of Israel."[48] Indeed, we cannot be sure what his attitude toward Gentiles was, though Sanders is inclined to think that Jesus believed some Gentiles would participate in the coming kingdom, for no other reason than that "a good number of Jews expected this to happen" and "Jesus was a kind and generous man."[49] But with regard to Israel, Jesus appears to have proclaimed God's covenantal grace with shocking implications. He called sinners, whom Sanders takes to be not merely social outcasts but "the truly wicked." Christian interpretation sometimes "debases and falsifies Judaism" and "trivializes Jesus" by construing "the issue of 'Jesus and the sinner' as if it were 'Jesus and the common people *versus* the narrow, bigoted but dominant Pharisees.'"[50] Rather, the "sinners" are such people as dishonest tax collectors and prostitutes, people who flagrantly violate God's laws. Jesus too would have regarded such people as morally reprehensible, yet he promised them a place in the kingdom. He even told religious people (chief priests and elders) that "the tax collectors and the prostitutes are going into the kingdom of God ahead of you" (Matt. 21:31). "New ages by definition must alter the present," Sanders observes wryly. "Why offer the kingdom to those who are already running it?"[51]

Sanders finds no indication that Jesus demanded repentance on the part of the wicked. Very few of the sayings attributed to Jesus mention repentance and those that do are often either summary statements (Mark 1:15; Matt. 4:17) or edited versions of earlier material (compare Luke 5:32 to Mark 2:17). In either case, the later view of the church intrudes. Furthermore, Sanders argues, Jesus' friendship with sinners (Matt. 11:19) would not have been controversial if he had been requiring these persons to change. He would have been a national hero. But the tradition reveals that this was a major point of contention between Jesus and his contemporaries as well as a characteristic that distinguished him from John the Baptist (Luke 7:31–34): "'Change now or be destroyed' was not his message, it was John's. Jesus' was, 'God loves you.'"[52] Obviously, Jesus would not have been opposed to repentance, but he "thought that God was about to change the circumstances of the world. . . . Jesus did not want the wicked to remain wicked in the interim, but he did not devise a program that would enable tax collectors and prostitutes to make a living in less dubious ways."[53] Jesus seems to have thought (and taught) that "those who followed him belonged to God's elect, even though they did not do what the Bible itself requires."[54] This idea may provide the historical roots for the subsequent Christian doctrine of atonement. After Jesus' death, the fact that he "came to *call* the wicked was transformed into the belief that he *died to save* sinners from sin and to make them upright."[55]

Traditional Christian exegesis has held that Jesus rejected those parts of the Jewish law that have to do with purity codes but insisted on repentance and obedience with regard to moral behavior. Sanders challenges both points at once. Jesus favored the whole law, ritual and ethical prescriptions alike, but he did not demand repentance or obedience with regard to any of it. These two proposals, taken together or separately, have provoked more controversy and criticism than any other aspects of Sanders's work. Neither point, however, is really essential to his main thesis, that Jesus was a prophet of Jewish restoration eschatology. Indeed, as is often noted, these points seem to detract from that thesis, for Sanders himself says that a call to repentance was a typical feature of restoration eschatology. If he could show that Jesus (like John) called sinners to repent in face of the coming judgment, he would be able to set that element alongside his temple and tribe themes as yet another parallel with this first-century Jewish perspective. As it is, he is left to surmise that maybe Jesus omitted this because he thought that John had taken care of that part of the overall task.[56] The intriguing thing about Sanders's commitment to these controversial points, then, is that he clearly is not stretching evidence to fit his thesis. Rather, he holds to the controversial points (which are incongruous with his thesis) simply because they concur with what he believes the evidence suggests.

Jesus' Death and Resurrection

While granting that Jesus' attitude toward sinners may have been controversial, Sanders sees no reason to believe it sparked the sort of opposition that would lead to execution. Similarly, the notion presented in the Gospels that "a series of good deeds by Jesus led the Pharisees to want to kill him" is "intrinsically improbable."[57] The common view that Jesus was killed because of his position on grace has been "manufactured out of whole cloth."[58] The idea presumes that the Jews had no appreciation for God as gracious the way Christians do and then retrojects this misconception of the theological controversy back into Jesus' historical life. For those who have an accurate picture of first-century Judaism, such a scenario portrays Jesus as being executed for espousing "things about as controversial as motherhood."[59] Such a line of thinking, Sanders suggests, "is basically opposed to seeing Jesus as a first-century Jew, who thought like other Jews, spoke their language, was concerned about things that concerned them, and got into trouble over first-century issues. It is thus bad history." Then he adds, "Though I am no theologian I suspect that it is bad theology."[60]

Sanders would be likely to fault others discussed in this book (Crossan, the Jesus Seminar) for failing to understand Jesus in light of what he takes to have been Palestinian Judaism. But he agrees with them that the incident in the temple was the immediate cause of Jesus' death. This simply makes sense, for it is the one thing Jesus is reported to have done that would have been most likely to get him in trouble with the Jewish and Roman authorities. Furthermore, it is something that he did in Jerusalem (*where* he was crucified) during Passover week *(when* he was crucified). For a historian, the trick is holding together the fact that Jesus was executed as a would-be king with the fact that his disciples were not subsequently hunted down and eliminated as followers of a political claimant. Sanders does not think that either Caiaphas (the Jewish high priest) or Pilate (the Roman governor) saw Jesus and his followers as posing any serious political threat. More likely, they thought he was a religious fanatic who nevertheless might create a disturbance. Thus,

> Caiaphas had Jesus arrested because of his responsibility to put down trou-
> blemakers, especially during festivals. . . . Jesus had alarmed some people by
> his attack on the Temple and his statement about its destruction, because
> they feared that he might actually influence God. It is highly probable,
> however, that Caiaphas was primarily concerned with the possibility that
> Jesus would incite a riot. He sent armed guards to arrest Jesus, he gave
> him a hearing, and he recommended execution to Pilate, who promptly
> complied.[61]

The biblical accounts of Pilate vacillating over what to do with Jesus and then acceding to the will of the mob are probably Christian propaganda to make Jesus look more innocent in the eyes of the Roman government (at the expense of the Jewish people, who become scapegoats). Most likely, Pilate sent Jesus to the cross without a second thought, as Josephus says he was wont to do. Indeed, Pilate was eventually dismissed from office as a result of the large number of executions without trial that took place on his watch.[62]

Did Jesus intend to die? Sanders notes that all the biblical material that attributes such an intention to Jesus is heavily infected with Christian doctrine. On the surface, it doesn't make much sense. The presumption would have to be that Jesus decided that he should be killed so that his death could be understood in some particular way and then set about accomplishing this by deliberately provoking the authorities. "It is not historically impossible that Jesus was weird," says Sanders, but "other things that we know about him make him a *reasonable* first-century visionary."[63]

If Jesus did not intend to die, what did he think would happen as a result of his provocative behavior? According to Sanders, he thought the kingdom of God would come. He thought this when he entered Jerusalem, and he appears to have continued to think this even after the temple incident when he may have realized that his own days were now numbered. Sanders regards as authentic the saying attributed to Jesus at the meal with his disciples: "I will never again drink of the fruit of the vine until that day when I drink it new in the kingdom of God" (Mark 14:25). He takes this as indicating that Jesus believed God would intervene and bring the kingdom before he was arrested and executed. It is in this light, Sanders says, that we must consider the cry of Jesus from the cross, "My God, my God, why have you forsaken me?" Sanders regards these words as authentic—they represent Jesus' own reminiscence of Psalm 22, not just a motif inserted by early Christians: "It is possible that, when Jesus drank his last cup of wine and predicted that he would drink it again in the kingdom, he thought that the kingdom would arrive immediately. After he had been on the cross for a few hours, he despaired, and cried out that he had been forsaken."[64] In any case, "after a relatively short period of suffering he died, and some of his followers and sympathizers hastily buried him."[65]

Sanders considers the resurrection experiences of the early Christians in an epilogue to his study. He notes that they are varied and ambiguous, resisting the idea that the risen Jesus was a ghost but also resisting the idea that he was simply a resuscitated corpse. He dismisses rational explanations for these accounts (deliberate fraud, mass hysteria) as inadequate. The bottom line: "That Jesus' followers (and later Paul) had resurrection experiences is, in my judgement, a fact. What the reality was that gave rise to the experiences I do not know."[66] And he adds: "Without the resurrection, would [Jesus'] disciples have endured longer than did John the Baptist's? We can only guess, but I would guess not."[67]

CRITIQUE OF SANDERS'S STUDY OF JESUS

Of all the views discussed in this book, Sanders's is the most "traditional" in terms of historical scholarship (though not, of course, in terms of Christian doctrine or religion). It is similar in many respects to that of Albert Schweitzer, which held sway for over fifty years (see pages 15–17).[68] The historical representation of Jesus as a (mistaken) eschatological prophet presented problems and possibilities that occupied many of the twentieth century's biblical and theological scholars. As we have seen, however, the movement in recent studies of the historical Jesus has been away from this model. As a return toward the former consensus, Sanders's study has been extremely influential, but it has also been sharply attacked.

The first major point of contention is the degree to which Sanders locates Jesus within the world of Palestinian Judaism (as he defines it). Obviously, scholars such as Downing, Mack, Crossan, and most of those associated with the Jesus Seminar would consider this a false move, for they believe Jesus' social environment was much more influenced by the Hellenistic world of the Roman Empire. Jesus was certainly Jewish and he did live in the geographical region of Palestine, but that area was part of the Roman Empire, which offers a broader context for understanding Jesus than Sanders seems to recognize. Even scholars who do stress a more limited and traditional Jewish matrix for Jesus' life and ministry criticize Sanders for assuming too much continuity between Jesus and his Jewish contemporaries. John Meier thinks he takes "the criterion of dissimilarity and stands it on its head."[69] Sanders says that a saying of Jesus reported in Mark 7:15 cannot be authentic because it is "too revolutionary" for a first-century Jew.[70] Normally, discontinuity from the world of Judaism would count as evidence *toward* authenticity.

So, too, James D. G. Dunn applauds Sanders's concern to relate Jesus to the world of Judaism but questions whether he has "pushed the pendulum too far in the opposite direction."[71] And Borg complains that Sanders does little to indicate how Jesus differed from others. What was remarkable about him? What would have caused conflict?[72] Sanders lays himself open to such critique: "We cannot say that a single one of the things known about Jesus is unique: neither his miracles, non-violence, eschatological hope, or promise to the outcasts. He was not unique because he saw his own mission as of crucial importance, nor because he believed in the grace of God. . . . We cannot even say that Jesus was a uniquely good and great man."[73] Sanders, however, does not consider this a problem. He notes that history always has trouble with declaring anything unique and faults other New Testament scholars for exaggerating claims about Jesus in this regard.[74]

The second major point of contention with Sanders's work would concern his description of Jesus as one whose life and work was shaped by a radical eschatological expectation. Unlike Crossan, Borg, or the Jesus Seminar, Sanders thinks that Jesus announced that God was about to inaugurate a new age through some drastic disjuncture in history. This position is critiqued with many of the same arguments raised against Allison whose position actually owes quite a bit to Sanders (see pages 89–92). Borg thinks the linchpin of Sanders's position is the "connecting link" argument that Jesus must have held such a perspective because both John the Baptist and Paul did. This reasoning, Borg contends, is not as sound as it appears, for even Sanders grants that Jesus differed from these figures in other respects. Unlike John, Jesus did not speak much of judgment or repentance, and unlike Paul he did not identify the imminent eschatological event with his own return. Borg thinks it quite possible, then, that Jesus moved away from the apocalyptic perspective of John, and that the early Christians reverted to such a perspective as a result of their Easter experiences.[75] Without this "connecting link" argument, Sanders's desire to place Jesus in the context of Jewish eschatology loses its force, for such elements as the temple incident and the selection of "the twelve" can be explained in other ways. Borg also thinks that Sanders's location of Jesus within the milieu of Jewish restoration eschatology does not account for a great deal of the material concerning him, particularly the parables and aphorisms that evidence a sapiential or wisdom tradition: "I find it very difficult to reconcile the mentality that we see at work in the subversive wisdom of Jesus with a mentality that could literally expect that God would miraculously (and soon) build a new temple on Mt. Zion and establish Jesus and the twelve as the rulers of the new age. They seem like two different mentalities; it is difficult to imagine them combined."[76]

Allison, Wright, Witherington, and others rush to Sanders's defense at this point. They think the "connecting link" argument is very strong, and do not find the coexistence of wisdom and eschatological anticipation to be incredible. But even Sanders's allies—notably John Meier—have criticized him for downplaying the significance of the "present kingdom" in Jesus' message, a tendency that he showed some signs of correcting in his second volume.[77] Witherington also wants to correct Sanders on another point. He believes that Jesus proclaimed God's eschatological salvation as being *possibly* imminent, not as *necessarily* imminent.[78] This allows more easily for inclusion of other concerns and also avoids the problem of having to explain how the Christian faith remained viable after Jesus was proved wrong in his central conviction. While this could be technically correct, however, many scholars would think Witherington is trying to help the church save face by appealing to a technicality that ignores rhetorical intent. As Jonathan Goldstein says, "The authors of Israelite prophecy seldom if ever were interested in the remote future, and the audiences that preserved their works were chiefly interested in the present and in a future that included little if any more than their own lifetimes."[79] Dale Allison adds, "The rule in the ancient sources is this: if it is coming, it is close."[80]

A somewhat different tack is offered by both Scot McKnight and N. T. Wright, who believe Sanders is right in presenting Jesus as a prophet of imminent eschatology but who interpret all the end-time sayings as being fulfilled in the events of 70 CE.[81] And Nicholas Perrin argues that, while Jesus did predict the temple would be replaced he claimed the new temple was already materializing through him and his followers (as a new, alternative society)—a new, physical structure descending from the sky would not be necessary.[82]

On a related issue, many critics claim that Sanders's eschatological portrait of Jesus downplays his role as a social reformer. Sanders, they claim, relates Jesus to the world of ideas in a way that makes him an apolitical, abstract thinker. His Jesus is "so unconcerned about his social world that he is curiously otherworldly, or perhaps better, next-worldly."[83] This seems to be correct. But Sanders sees the objection as grounded in hopes and preferences rather than in solid research. Naturally, a politically correct Jesus would be more appealing to modern scholars than a mistaken prophet. Still,

> it is almost impossible to explain the historical facts on the assumption that Jesus himself did not expect the imminent end or transformation of the present world order. . . . As a desperate measure, people whom this makes uncomfortable can say that everybody misunderstood Jesus completely. He really wanted economic and social reform. The disciples dropped that part of his teaching and made up sayings about the future kingdom of God— which they then had to start retracting, since the kingdom did not arrive. . . . Such views merely show the triumph of wishful thinking.[84]

Meier appears to agree (see pages 196–97), but others claim that there is authentic material in the Jesus tradition that does point toward social and economic reform. Scholars such as William Herzog, Richard Horsley, David Kaylor, and Gerd Theissen have exposed political overtones in many of the aphorisms and parables. And Witherington wants to make his point about the distinction between necessary and possible imminence once again: "A person who believes the end *may* come soon is still likely to say and do a good deal about the interim."[85] Sanders yields little ground on this point. "It is a question of emphasis," he concludes. "Jesus doubtless had views about the social, political, and economic conditions of his people, but his mission was to prepare them to receive the coming kingdom of God."[86]

Other criticisms of Sanders's work concern arguments that are not central to his main thesis. As indicated, most scholars have disputed the notion that Jesus did not require repentance of sinners.[87] Crossan, for instance, thinks Sanders was "seduced" into reaching this "strange conclusion" by failing to identify the texts on which he draws as expressive of polemical invective: "There should never be serious historical debate on Jesus accepting unrepentant tax collectors, sinners, or prostitutes unless there is also serious historical debate on Jesus as a lunatic, a demoniac, a glutton, a drunkard, and a Samaritan."[88] Sanders himself notes a paradoxical tension within the tradition. Jesus apparently required high moral standards of his followers, for example, prohibiting divorce among them, and yet "the overall tenor of Jesus' teaching is compassion towards human frailty."[89] Jesus himself did not live a stern or strict life, and his parables reveal God to be surprisingly generous (Matt. 20:1–16) and surprisingly undiscriminating (Matt. 22:1–10).[90] Greg Carey agrees with Sanders that Jesus did not call individual sinners to repentance, but he does think that Jesus spoke of repentance in general terms—and, much more to the point, he maintains against Sanders that the unrepentant sinners with whom Jesus fellowshiped were not "truly wicked people" but social outcasts.[91] Meier is one of the only scholars who seems favorably disposed to Sanders's argument as offered, agreeing that Jesus offered a place in the kingdom to "the wicked" without requiring "the usual process of reintegration."[92] Also, in recent years, I have attempted to revive Sanders's proposal in a somewhat modified form: the sinners to whom Jesus promised the kingdom without demanding repentance may have been slaves or other individuals for whom lifestyle transformation was not an existential possibility.[93]

Sanders's argument that Jesus did not come into significant conflict with his contemporaries over matters of the law has also been disputed. Allison thinks Jesus rejected the notion of covenant nomism outright.[94] Witherington claims, more moderately, that the very acceptance of sinners that Sanders attributes to Jesus would have entailed abrogation of purity laws prescribing cultic means for readmission to the community. If Jesus would ignore these laws, why dismiss the authenticity of Gospel accounts that indicate he transgressed Sabbath rules and other purity codes?[95] Wright thinks Sanders's notion that Pharisees did not try to press their legal interpretations upon others is undercut by the personal testimony of the Pharisee Paul (1 Cor. 15:9; Gal. 1:13–14).[96] Furthermore, Wright argues that, on this point, Sanders ironically tries to interpret Jesus' relationship with the Pharisees "within the noneschatological category of 'patterns of religion'" by insisting that Jesus and the Pharisees had only minor disagreements over matters of the law.[97] If Jesus was an eschatological prophet, says Wright, it is likely that he challenged the basic tenets of "religion as usual" and this would have brought conflict:

If the synoptic scenarios are anything other than a complete fabrication, Jesus was not debating with the Pharisees on their own terms, or about the detail of their own agendas. Two musicians may discuss which key is best for a particular Schubert song. Somebody who proposes rearranging the poem for a heavy metal band is not joining in the discussion, but challenging its very premises.[98]

Meier (with less flamboyance) likewise insists on the historicity of claims that Jesus prohibited divorce for any reason whatsoever (Mark 10:9) and forbade the taking of all oaths (Matt. 5:34–37)—unprecedented positions that would have put him at odds with all other Jewish teachers known to us (see pages 193–94).[99]

A major study by Tom Holmén tries a different tack. Holmén appreciates Sanders's emphasis on covenantal nomism but suggests that Jesus' vision of the kingdom of God led him to reject what he calls "covenant path seeking": faithfulness to God no longer required attention to such matters as how much work could be done on the Sabbath, how much one should tithe, how often one should fast, or under what circumstances one could divorce a wife or swear an oath.[100] Jesus was not against such practices, but he did not regard them as "loyalty tests" for one's commitment to God. In a not-too-dissimilar vein, Joseph H. Hellerman thinks that Jesus established his followers as a surrogate kinship group who focused on doing the will of God but challenged the post-Maccabean ideology that emphasized national identity through preoccupation with Sabbath keeping, food laws, sacred space, and the like.[101]

Thomas Kazen may have shed new light on this issue through his recent study of Jesus and purity codes.[102] Kazen concludes that Jesus was essentially indifferent to certain matters, particularly contamination associated with bodily fluids, leprosy, or corpses. Kazen suggests, however, that this indifference would not have identified Jesus as unique or particularly distinctive in Galilee: there was intra-Jewish debate regarding such matters and a wide spectrum of opinions. Jesus, apparently, saw (what we call) moral evil and social injustice as more serious matters of impurity than bodily defilement, but he would have had plenty of company in thinking this way. Indeed, Jesus' position might have been more typical of the rural population, whereas Hellenistic encroachment in urban areas may have prompted an intensification of purity markers specific to ethnic identity in those locales. Further, Kazen suggests that Jesus' apparently cavalier attitude toward threats of defilement may have been fueled by his theology of the kingdom: as an exorcist who believed the power of God's coming kingdom was already residing within himself, he may have believed the force of bodily impurity was being overcome in the same manner that demons were being expelled and overthrown. Kazen's construal could open a middle way for both Sanders and his critics on this point: Jesus' indifference to impurity (rather than outright rejection of purity codes) would have brought him into conflict with *some* Jewish traditionalists, without marking him as a teacher who was noticeably out of the Jewish mainstream—and Sanders could be right that the element of conflict in those stories may have been exaggerated in a manner reflective of tensions between post-70 Jewish synagogues and the increasingly Gentile Christian church.

In terms of overall critique, Reginald Fuller accuses Sanders of applying the criterion of dissimilarity inconsistently: Sanders rejects that criterion when he suspects the authenticity of anything that marks Jesus as different from the world of Judaism but then uses it to distinguish the authentic Jesus from the antilegal tradition of the early church.[103] This comment implies that Sanders's method of operation may not be as precise as it could be—and, indeed, he has been criticized in that regard with reference to other points as well. Meier, for instance, praises Sanders for breaking out of the narrow focus on sayings, parables, and aphorisms that seems to have characterized much of Jesus scholarship, but he faults Sanders for essentially equating actions and deeds with "facts" and then interpreting sayings in light of these.[104] Meier thinks the actions and sayings must be held together. He sees Sanders trying to do this with regard to the temple incident, and he thinks his case could be strengthened elsewhere if he would demonstrate such meshing of traditions.[105] As we have seen, less friendly critics have been able to attack the very foundations of Sanders's system by taking up his lists of what are supposed to be virtually indisputable facts and then disputing them.

In his second book on Jesus, Sanders appears to be frustrated at times by what he must regard as obsessive tendencies of scholars to micromanage the tradition, by efforts to determine whether every individual saying or deed should be regarded as authentic. He prefers to note major trajectories and emphases in those parts of the tradition that are generally regarded as reliable. "We do not need to decide which of the 'antitheses' [the sayings recorded in Matt. 5:21–48] go back to Jesus," he writes at one point. "Let us say that they all do."[106] Such comments appear dismissive of the scholarly enterprise, of the painstaking deliberation on individual texts that characterizes the work of the Jesus Seminar on the one hand and (as we will see) that of Meier on the other. The criticism of Sanders has been that, in trying to paint the big picture, he has not paid enough attention to the details. To use a different metaphor, Sanders might claim that we have enough information already to describe the forest without making final decisions on the bark or root structure of every individual tree. But other scholars would respond that indiscriminate suppositions about trees lead to an unreliable depiction of the forest.

In conclusion, there are two points on which Sanders is quite certain—that Jesus must be interpreted as a representative of first-century, relatively non-hellenized Palestinian Judaism and that he expected an imminent eschatological restoration of Israel—and on these points he is resolute. In general, however, Sanders often appears to be more open to critique and revision than most scholars working in historical Jesus studies. The pages of his books are crowded with qualifiers: "maybe," "possibly," "likely," "perhaps." He frequently admits that he is guessing with regard to certain matters and that he simply does not know what to think about other ones. He acknowledges that he has been wrong about assessments in the past and yields to new interpretations. All this marks his project with a winsome humility.

As usual, we let him have the last word:

> Historical reconstruction is never absolutely certain, and in the case of Jesus it is sometimes highly uncertain. Despite this, we have a good idea of the main lines of his ministry and his message. We know who he was, what he did, what he taught, and why he died. Perhaps most important, we know how much he inspired his followers, who sometimes themselves did not understand him, but who were so loyal to him that they changed history.[107]

Chapter 8

John P. Meier

Jesus persists in veiling himself in indirect references and metaphors. . . .
It is almost as though Jesus were intent on making a riddle of himself. . . .
Whoever or whatever Jesus was, he was a complex figure, not easily subsumed
under one theological rubric or sociological model.

—John Meier[1]

Meier labels Jesus a marginal Jew because he lived at the edge of the
empire, traveled within a narrow range, identified with those on the
margins of society, and held views and performed miracles that were out of
the ordinary. . . . What made Jesus unique was a complex configuration of
factors: he was teacher, he was miracle worker, he was prophet of the last
days, and he was the gatherer of Israel. . . . Meier also sees Jesus as some sort
of messianic figure, however much Jesus eludes precise definition.

—Ben Witherington III[2]

John Meier wins the prize for length. His study of the historical Jesus is almost
three thousand pages long and not yet finished. Quantitatively, at least, he has
exceeded all other Jesus scholars, ancient and modern.

A Catholic priest educated and ordained in Rome, Meier is now professor
of New Testament at Notre Dame University in South Bend, Indiana. Though
he has been known to be critical of his church's political and theological stances,
he remains loyal. He has served as president of the Catholic Biblical Association
and as editor of the prestigious journal *Catholic Biblical Quarterly*.

When *U.S. News and World Report* sought a catchy caption to distinguish
Meier from other Jesus scholars they settled on the phrase "dogged digger."[3] And
so he is. Meticulous in his scholarship, he examines every saying and fact about

178

Jesus, rigorously applying a well-defined set of criteria for determining histori-cal authenticity. For those who are not truly committed, the presentation can become tedious, but one thing is always clear: if, at the end of a discussion, you do not agree with Meier's conclusion, you can see exactly how he reached it and identify at what juncture you parted company, and why. This, his academic peers affirm, is traditional (his critics say "old-fashioned") historical criticism at its best.

Meier's study of Jesus began as a simple prelude to a commentary on Mat-thew, but as he kept finding questions that had not been adequately researched, the project took on a life of its own. The work is being published under the grand title *A Marginal Jew: Rethinking the Historical Jesus*. When it is finished, it will be "at least" five volumes. So far, only four have been published. These are (1) *The Roots of the Problem and the Person* (on method, sources, and cri-teria); (2) *Mentor, Message, and Miracles* (on Jesus' relationship with John the Baptist and on his ministry of preaching, teaching, and healing); (3) *Compan-ions and Competitors* (on his calling of disciples and on his conflicts with Jew-ish leaders); and (4) *Law and Love* (on his ethical demands and understanding of morality).

A word may be said about the phrase "marginal Jew." Meier initially chose this phrase as a tease, a sort of riddle meant "to open up a set of questions" and to suggest "intriguing possibilities."[4] He did not mean for it to become the defining phrase for understanding his view of Jesus, though some commentators seem to take it that way. Certainly, Meier does not mean to imply that Jesus is marginal in his ultimate importance, though he does maintain that in his own day Jesus was "at most a blip on the radar screen" of the Greco-Roman world.[5] Roman historians such as Josephus, Tacitus, and Suetonius pay little attention to Jesus. But Meier may also be trying to express something else with his book's title—the paradox of seeing Jesus within his Jewish world while also recognizing what made him distinct. We have seen other scholars struggle with this: critics have said that Crossan's Jesus is so at home in the Roman Empire that he hardly seems Jewish at all; they also maintain that Sanders's Jesus is such a typical, tra-ditional Jew that there is little to set him apart from other Jews of his day. Meier wants to steer a middle course: Jewish, but not typical—at least in key respects. Jesus appears to have remained celibate. He left his home and family to pursue an itinerant ministry. He eschewed fasting and prohibited divorce. His teach-ing evinced a style and content that "did not jibe with the views and practices of the major Jewish religious groups of his day."[6] This was not unrelated to his eventual fate:

> By the time he died [Jesus] had managed to make himself appear obnox-ious, dangerous, or suspicious to everyone, from pious Pharisees through political high priests to an ever vigilant Pilate. One reason Jesus met a swift and brutal end is simple: he alienated so many individuals and groups in Palestine that, when the final clash came in Jerusalem in 30 A.D., he had very few people, especially people of influence on his side.[7]

And again,

> A poor layman from the Galilean countryside with disturbing doctrines
> and claims was marginal both in the sense of being dangerously anti-
> establishment and in the sense of lacking a power base in the capital. He
> could easily be brushed aside into the dustbin of death.[8]

MEIER'S METHOD FOR STUDYING JESUS

Meier is at the opposite end of the spectrum from John Dominic Crossan with
regard to objectivity in scholarship. Crossan dismisses objectivity as "spurious"
and "unattainable"; in its place he commends "honesty" with regard to one's own
inclinations and presuppositions.[9] Meier is all for honesty, but he insists that a
commitment to professional objectivity is fundamental to academic scholarship.
Throughout his study, he employs the image of what he calls an "unpapal con-
clave" of scholars—a Catholic, a Protestant, a Jew, and an agnostic—who have
been "locked up in the bowels of the Harvard Divinity School library, put on a
spartan diet, and not allowed to emerge until they have hammered out a consensus document on who Jesus of Nazareth was and what he intended in his own
time and place."[10] With regard to issue after issue Meier asks, What would this
committee make of the evidence? For example, in his study of miracles, Meier
concedes that one member might think that Jesus really did work miracles, while
another might claim that this is intrinsically impossible. All four, however, could
agree that Jesus did in fact do startling deeds that people in his day (friends and
foes alike) considered to be miracles. This, then, is what the historian can affirm.

As such, the historical task is necessarily reductionist. The object of historical
inquiry is not ultimately the "real Jesus" but only those aspects or facets of him
that are amenable to academic study:

> In contrast to the "real Jesus," the "historical Jesus" is that Jesus whom we
> can recover or reconstruct by using the scientific tools of modern historical
> research. The "historical Jesus" is thus a scientific construct, a theoretical
> abstraction of modern scholars that coincides only partially with the real
> Jesus of Nazareth, the Jew who actually lived and worked in Palestine.[11]

Meier has affirmed elsewhere that he personally does believe in the virgin birth,
the miracles, and the resurrection of Jesus.[12] These matters would belong to the
large portrait of what he regards as "the real Jesus," regardless of whether they
belong to the smaller portrait of what he regards as "the historical Jesus."[13]

Meier's claim to professional neutrality has been challenged more philosophically than practically. On the surface, it appears arrogant: Meier is only one
person. How can he claim that his work faithfully represents what would be
produced by a four-person committee? Meier is a Catholic. How can he claim
to represent the perspective of a scholarly Protestant, Jew, or agnostic? But, in

practice, critiques of his work have not faulted him at this point; the implications of his conclusions are sometimes as challenging to the Catholic faith as to the other three perspectives.[14] Ironically, Meier's study of Jesus has been viewed as far less tendentious than that of the Jesus Seminar, a committee that *was* in fact composed of Catholics, Protestants, Jews, and agnostics. Still, the very notion that neutrality can be symbolized adequately by a convergence of perspectives regarding *religious* ideology (rather than with regard to social, political, ethnic, gender, or class distinctions) is revealing in a way that for some undermines the claim to detachment.[15]

Given Meier's commitment to objectivity, however, clarity about methodological procedures becomes a high priority. He devotes over two hundred pages to method in the first volume of his work. To summarize, we may note that he regards five criteria as especially useful: embarrassment, discontinuity, multiple attestation, coherence, and what he calls "the criterion of Jesus' rejection and execution." The first four of these are discussed in chapter 2 of this book, but the last is not mentioned there because it is not widely used in historical Jesus studies (Meier and Wright are the two persons discussed in this book who give it the most attention). Basically, this criterion holds that words and deeds attributed to Jesus are more likely to be historically accurate if they help to explain why he was rejected by Jewish leaders, condemned by Roman authorities, and crucified: "a Jesus whose words and deeds did not threaten or alienate people, especially powerful people, is not the historical Jesus."[16] Many scholars, however, would question the legitimacy of the criterion. First, the notion that Jesus was vehemently rejected by other Jews (or their leaders) is sometimes regarded as a product of retrojection: the Gospels portray Jesus' interaction with his contemporaries in light of the Christian-Jewish hostilities of their own day. Further, the Romans are known to have crucified thousands of people, so it is at least hypothetically possible that they killed Jesus for reasons that had little to do with the details of his message or ministry. Thus, when Meier grants historical credibility to a matter that explains certain aspects of the rejection and execution of Jesus, some scholars think he is trying to authenticate material through an appeal to historical data that does not *itself* pass the tests of authentication. Scholars also question the logic behind the proposed criterion: even if it is agreed that Jesus alienated (powerful) people, he must have also done many non-alienating things, so the criterion cannot be applied negatively. Nor would the recognition that Jesus must have said and done *some* things that threatened or alienated people imply that any words or deeds attributed to him that can be construed as alienating or threatening should be deemed historical. Logically, such a recognition would only necessitate inclusion of *some* alienating/threatening material in one's final list of authentic Jesus material. In deference to the latter point, Meier agrees that the criterion of Jesus' rejection and execution is better applied to "the larger pattern of Jesus' ministry" than to consideration of individual sayings or deeds.

We should also note that Meier construes the criterion of multiple attestation in a distinctive way by indicating that the case for historicity is enhanced when there is a multiple attestation of *forms* as well as *sources*. To illustrate this point, let us consider once more the question of miracles. Most scholars note that multiple sources (Mark, Q, M, L, and John) attribute miracles to Jesus; Meier also notes that we have both *narratives* of Jesus working miracles and *sayings* about Jesus working miracles. The double attestation of "multiple sources" and "multiple forms" is a strong argument for authenticity of the tradition that Jesus did do things that were regarded as miracles.[17] This expansion of the concept of multiple attestation has been well received and is generally regarded as a strong point of Meier's work.

With regard to sources, Meier regards the four canonical Gospels as the essential documents, with "tidbits" supplied occasionally from the writings of Paul or Josephus.[18] Notably, he has been less dismissive of the Gospel of John than other historical scholars. He recognizes that the material in John has undergone more extensive development than that in the other Gospels and must be used with special care, but he does in fact find much in John that he considers to be historically authentic. One example is that he decides John's Gospel is right in portraying Jesus' ministry as lasting longer than one year and involving multiple trips to Jerusalem (the Synoptic Gospels present a shorter ministry with only one trip to Jerusalem at the end). By the same token, however, Meier is more dismissive of noncanonical Gospels than many scholars. He considers the apocryphal Gospels to be relatively late documents that are virtually worthless as sources for independent historical data about Jesus.[19] No brushstrokes from the Gospel of Thomas can be seen in his portrait of Jesus.

For Meier, historical science demands strict attention to clearly defined criteria and detailed public presentation of evidence to account for even the smallest point of each argument. This, he claims, is why his work is so long. If someone does not agree with his conclusions they can look at his record of how he reached them and try to pinpoint where they believe he went wrong. Indeed, he claims to have done this himself, imaginatively adopting the various persona of those scholars locked in the bowels of Harvard Divinity School and reviewing his work from each perspective:

> Time and time again while writing this volume, I have been constrained to reverse my views because of the weight of the data and the force of the criteria. My own experience has convinced me that, while methodology and criteria may be tiresome topics, they are vital in keeping the critic from seeing in the data whatever he or she already has decided to see. The rules of the road are never exciting, but they keep us moving in the right direction.[20]

MEIER'S PORTRAIT OF JESUS

Meier's work on Jesus is not yet complete—at least one more major volume will be released, treating "the riddle-speech of Jesus' parables, the riddle-speech of Jesus' self-designations (titles), and the ultimate riddle of Jesus' death."[21] What we present here is a synopsis of his major suppositions thus far.

Jesus' Early Years

Not much can be known with any certainty about Jesus' origins, Meier admits, though more can be affirmed about him than would be the case with most historical figures from the ancient world. We have multiple attestation that Jesus was born during the reign of Herod the Great and, therefore, before 4 BCE. The most likely time is 7–4 BCE, and the most likely place is Nazareth, since he is widely attested to have been from there. The biblical story of a birth in Bethlehem is not impossible but probably reflects later theological interests rather than historical fact. The claim that his mother was a virgin at the time of his birth has multiple attestation (M, L) but was not open to verification even in Jesus' own lifetime, much less today.

Jesus was Jewish and was raised as the firstborn son of Joseph and Mary in a family that included at least four brothers (James, Joses, Jude, and Simon) and at least two sisters (who are unnamed). The very names of these family members, as well as Jesus' own name (which is identical to the Hebrew *Joshua)*, recall significant figures from Israel's past, suggesting that the family may have nurtured the pious hopes for the restoration of Israel that were common in this environment. Joseph may even have claimed to be of the lineage of David, a fact that would later help to fuel messianic expectations with regard to Jesus.[22] Jesus' mother, brothers, and sisters apparently outlived him, but Joseph probably died before Jesus began his ministry. Reports in the New Testament that seem to be reliable indicate that there was tension between Jesus and his family during his life but that later some of his siblings were prominent leaders in the movement that continued in his name.

In the face of all this information about family members, all sources are completely silent with regard to Jesus having a wife or children. Meier notes that it would have been highly unusual for a man in Jesus' social position to choose a life of celibacy but decides that this nevertheless appears to have been the case. Thus, Jesus would have been marked among his peers as exceptional or odd at an early point.

Like his father, Jesus worked as a carpenter, a trade that involved building parts of houses in addition to the fashioning of furniture. As such, he would have been poor, but not one of the "poorest of the poor." He did not know "the grinding poverty of the dispossessed farmer, the city beggar, the rural day laborer, or the rural slave."[23] He had a trade that involved a fair level of technical skill and, Meier adds incidentally, one that marks him as healthy if not muscular.[24] As a Jew growing up in Nazareth, Jesus would have spoken Aramaic, some Greek, and perhaps some Hebrew. While there is no indication that he received education outside of his home, Meier is inclined to think that he was literate.[25]

Legends abound about the "hidden years" of Jesus' adolescence and early adulthood, but Meier has his own theory as to why the Bible is silent about this time: "nothing much happened." Apart from remaining single, Jesus appears to have been "insufferably ordinary."[26] He did nothing that would earn him religious credentials or gain him a power base.[27] Then, when he was about thirty-three years old, he left home for reasons unknown and traveled to the Judean country-side to be baptized by a man named John.

Mentor

Meier devotes over two hundred pages to a study of John the Baptist, whom he considers to be "the one person who had the single greatest influence on Jesus' ministry."[28] He thinks it possible that John was the only son of a priest who "turned his back on his filial duty of continuing the priestly line and minister-ing in the Jerusalem temple." He thinks it unlikely, however, that John had any direct connection with the antiestablishment movement at Qumran known to us through the Dead Sea Scrolls.[29]

John was, to use words attributed to Jesus, "a prophet, and more than a prophet" (Matt. 11:9). He stood in the tradition of Israel's prophets but went beyond them in significant ways. Like prophets before him, he proclaimed a message of doom, announcing an imminent fiery judgment that was going to break in upon Israel. But he also related salvation from that judgment to his own person in a way that was not typical of the prophetic tradition. Protection from the coming wrath lay in repentance, which included acceptance of baptism administered by him. This baptism was symbolic: immersion in water signified extinction of flames that would engulf the unrepentant. Yet John also declared that a mysterious "stronger one" was coming after him who would baptize with the Holy Spirit those whom John had marked with his water ritual. There is a paradox, then, in how John saw himself. On the one hand, he pointed away from himself, indicating his own insignificance in light of the coming one, whose sandals he was not worthy to carry (Matt. 3:11). On the other hand, he presented himself as the only one who was able to confer the baptism that prepares people for the salvation that this figure would bring.

John was both eschatological and charismatic, that is, he claimed "direct knowledge of God's will and plans—knowledge unmediated by the traditional channels of law, temple, priesthood, or scribal scholarship."[30] The result of his ministry was the creation of a sectarian community within Israel that was not defined by a particular approach to legal observances or temple worship. Herod noticed the extent of John's influence on people, feared (wrongly in Meier's opin-ion) that such influence would be used for seditious purposes, and—as Josephus notes—executed him as a "preemptive strike."

Jesus was baptized by John and appears to have joined his circle for a time. Since John offered his baptism for forgiveness of sins and protection against judgment, we must assume that accepting this baptism was for Jesus an act of confession and repentance. Meier warns, however, against construing such repentance in terms of "the introspective conscience of the West."[31] Rather than focusing on individual sins or personal peccadillos, Jesus' repentance would have involved humble admission that he was a member of a sinful people (the rebellious and ungrateful nation of Israel), accompanied by a resolve to be different.

Accepting John's baptism also implied recognition on Jesus' part that he was now, in some sense, a disciple of the Baptist. Thus, he must have accepted the eschatological message that John preached, including the idea that salvation was to be found only through submission to John's ritual washing. At some point, though, Jesus left John's circle and began his own ministry. The break, Meier thinks, was a moderate one. He avoids the idea of apostasy from John, which has been put forward by Paul Hollenbach and picked up in some ways by Borg, Crossan, and others.[32] He also dismisses the suggestion by Hendrikus Boers that Jesus continued throughout his ministry to see John and not himself as the final eschatological figure who would bring in the kingdom of God.[33] Rejecting these "simplistic scenarios,"[34] Meier attempts to delineate the distinctive aspects of Jesus' ministry without obscuring the enduring influence that the Baptist had on him. Jesus was no "carbon copy" of John, but "a firm substratum of the Baptist's life and message" remained with Jesus throughout his ministry.[35]

Thus, Jesus' ministry was different from John's in key respects. It was itinerant rather than localized; he toured villages and towns rather than going out into the wilderness and inviting people to come to him. His preaching also shifted in emphasis from God's imminent fiery judgment to God's offer of mercy and forgiveness. This was demonstrated dramatically in his healings and open table fellowship with sinners. And there are other differences. In contrast to Jesus, John was known to be an ascetic.[36] John is never said to have healed the sick. John is depicted as calling people to make themselves acceptable to God, to "bear fruit worthy of repentance" (Luke 3:8) rather than assuring them of their participation in the banquet God was preparing.

Still, Meier insists that Jesus never abandoned John's message of judgment. This eschatological, even apocalyptic, notion that the day of divine reckoning was at hand remained one element of Jesus' own preaching. Also, like John, Jesus chose to remain celibate, gathered disciples, and conducted a ministry to Israel. Jesus even imitated John's practice of baptizing and, in Meier's view, probably continued to baptize disciples throughout his ministry. The references to this in the Gospel of John (John 3:22, 26; 4:1) have a strong chance of authenticity due to the criterion of embarrassment, for the Christian church never would have invented this tradition and in fact tried to suppress it, as John 4:2 attests in a rather sloppy way. Meier says, "It is likely that the practice of baptizing flowed like water from John through Jesus into the early church, with the ritual taking on different meanings at each stage of the process."[37]

Thus, Meier thinks Q depicts John and Jesus as "the eschatological odd couple," divergent in accent and style but united in their effort to prepare unrepentant Israel for a coming crisis involving salvation and judgment (Matt. 11:16–19; Luke 7:31–35).[38] Meier accepts as authentic the Q tradition that John eventually wondered whether Jesus might be "the stronger one" he believed was coming (Matt. 11:2–6), while emphasizing that the tradition does not convey how or whether John resolved that question. He also accepts as authentic the tradition that Jesus declared John to be the greatest person ever born (Matt. 11:7–11), while noting that this tradition also affirms Jesus declaring that "even the most insignificant Israelite who has entered into the eschatological kingdom of God that Jesus announces enjoys a privilege and standing greater than John's."[39]

The greatest similarity of Jesus to John, however, may lie in the paradoxical construal each offered of his own person. On the one hand, Jesus made the kingdom of God, rather than himself, the main focus of his preaching. On the other hand, what he said about the kingdom involved "a monumental though implicit claim: with the start of Jesus' ministry, a definitive shift has taken place in the eschatological timetable."[40] Thus, what Jesus says about himself in relation to the kingdom echoes what John said of himself in relation to "the coming one."

Message

Meier agrees with most historical scholars in affirming that Jesus' teaching and preaching employed the phrase "kingdom of God." He seeks to establish, furthermore, that the use of this phrase was somewhat distinctive for Jesus. While not altogether absent, the words kingdom of God do not appear frequently in the Old Testament, in Jewish literature from this period, or in the writings of Paul and other early Christians. Thus, Jesus' use of the term reflects a "conscious, personal choice" and, for that reason, the study of this symbol offers a "privileged way of entering into Jesus' message."[41]

What does the phrase mean? Like Marcus Borg (see page 152), Meier maintains that it is "a tensive symbol," that is, a symbol that "evokes not one meaning but a whole range of meanings."[42] The basic sense is "the dynamic notion of God powerfully ruling over his creation, over his people, and over the history of both." In short, "kingdom of God" is a symbol for "God ruling as king." This concept, as distinct from the precise phrase that Jesus chose, is widespread, appearing in many different contexts in scripture as well as in other Jewish and Christian writings, and it acquires many facets and dimensions. Thus far, Meier and Borg would be in complete agreement. They part company when Meier insists that one meaning of the phrase (perhaps the dominant one) in the teaching of Jesus involved expectations regarding the imminent future. In the centuries immediately preceding Jesus' life (the intertestamental period), Meier claims, the most prominent use of the "kingdom of God" symbol was in eschatological and apocalyptic contexts, where it conjured up hopes of definitive salvation for Israel in the future.[43]

Meier applies his criteria of authenticity to sayings attributed to Jesus regarding the kingdom and then extrapolates the results of those that meet the test. The Lord's Prayer indicates that Jesus did expect a future, definitive coming of God to rule as king and that he taught his disciples to pray for this ("Your kingdom come," Luke 11:2). Some of the Beatitudes indicate that this kingdom will bring about a reversal of such unjust conditions as poverty, sorrow, and hunger ("Blessed are you who are hungry now, for you will be filled. . . ." Luke 6:21). Other authentic sayings affirm that the kingdom will include some Gentiles as honored guests alongside Israel's patriarchs (Matt. 8:11–12) and express Jesus' confidence in the face of death that he too will experience a saving reversal and share in the final banquet (Mark 14:25).[44]

Next Meier examines three sayings in which Jesus sets timetables for the kingdom's arrival, apparently stressing that it will come very soon (Matt. 10:23), even during the lifetime of his first followers (Mark 9:1; 13:30). Meier's results here are surprising—they surprised even him.[45] Most scholars, including Sanders (see page 166), have assumed the texts to be authentic, not least because of the embarrassment the church faced when the predictions were not fulfilled. But on further examination, Meier concludes that, in fact, they derive from the early church, composed by Christians who were disappointed that the Parousia had not come but wanted assurance that it was just around the corner. "Imminent-future eschatology has its origins in Jesus," Meier grants, but "attempts to set time limits for that eschatology have their origin in the church."[46]

Meier also studies some key sayings, which he judges to be authentic, in which Jesus speaks of the kingdom of God as a reality that is already present. The "star witness" here is the Q saying found in Luke 11:20, where Jesus declares, "If it is by the finger of God that I cast out the demons, then the kingdom of God has come to you." Here Jesus presents his exorcisms as "proof that the kingdom of God that he proclaims for the future is in some sense already present."[47] The same basic message is conveyed by the parable Jesus tells in Mark about "binding the strong man" (Mark 3:27). Jesus' response to John the Baptist's question in Matthew 11:2–6 indicates that his miracles and proclamation to the poor are signs that the time he and John have been awaiting has arrived. His rejection of voluntary fasting is grounded in the same vision (Mark 2:18–20). Other sayings that are probably authentic speak of the kingdom as already present in a generic sense, without specific reference to Jesus' ministry as the sign or vehicle of its presence (Luke 10:23; 17:21).[48]

"The precise relationship between the coming and present kingdom remains unspecified," Meier concludes.[49] He notes the tendencies in modern scholarship to resolve the dilemma one way or the other. Crossan, Borg, and the Jesus Seminar deem the "present kingdom" sayings authentic and so rule that Jesus did not speak of the kingdom as something yet to come. Sanders deems the "future kingdom" sayings authentic and tends to disregard any implication that the kingdom is already here.[50] Such concern for logical consistency, says Meier, "may be beside the point when dealing with an itinerant Jewish preacher and miracle worker of 1st-century Palestine."[51] But Meier does not find the "already/not yet" tension to be so contradictory. He (like Sanders) thinks the emphasis in Jesus' message was on the kingdom about to arrive, but he grants that Jesus saw signs that indicated the eschatological drama was already under way and he apparently thought that his own ministry constituted "a partial and preliminary realization of God's kingly rule, which would soon be displayed in full force."[52]

Miracles

Meier accepts as a historical fact that Jesus did perform extraordinary deeds that were deemed by himself, his supporters, and his enemies to be miracles. He asserts this defiantly, recognizing that "a miracle-free Jesus has been the holy grail sought by many [historical Jesus] questers from the Enlightenment onwards."[53]The attribution of miracles to Jesus is supported by widespread attestation of sources (Mark, Q, M, L, John, and even Josephus) and coheres well with other information that we know about him, including his claim to offer a preliminary experience of the future kingdom of God and his success at attracting large numbers of followers. Indeed, of all the elements in the mix of what can reliably be attributed to Jesus, Meier thinks that "miracle working probably contributed the most to his prominence and popularity on the public scene—as well as to the enmity he stirred up in high places."[54] The miracle tradition has better historical support than many facts that are commonly accepted, such as that Jesus was a carpenter or that he used the word Abba in his prayers. The rejection of this tradition can be viewed only as an imposition of a philosophical concept on objective research. If the tradition that Jesus worked miracles is to be rejected as unhistorical, says Meier, "so should every other Gospel tradition about him."[55]

This is not to say that Jesus actually did work miracles, an affirmation that would also impose a philosophical concept on the evidence. What we can affirm is the attribution of miracles to Jesus *during his own lifetime.* Contrary to the view of Burton Mack (see page 28), the early church did not simply invent this tradition and make up the miracle stories at some point after Jesus' death. At least, it did not make up all of them. Meier devotes some four hundred pages to an exhaustive historical analysis of every miracle story in the Gospels. Some, such as the exorcism of the Syrophoenician woman's daughter (Mark 7:24–30) and most of the so-called nature miracles (walking on water, changing water to wine, stilling storms, cursing the fig tree), serve theological purposes so clearly that they are likely to have developed within the church's preaching to illustrate symbolically some particular point. In such cases, it is impossible for the historian to determine the extent to which an actual event may have served as the catalyst for the story as it appears in the Bible. But some of the individual accounts of miracles do meet criteria for historical authenticity. Reports of miracles that are most likely to go back to the historical Jesus include the exorcism of an epileptic boy (Mark 9:14–29), the exorcism of Mary Magdalene (Luke 8:2), the healing of a paralytic let down through a roof (Mark 2:1–12), the healing of another paralytic by the pool of Bethesda (John 5:1–9), three healings of blind men—Bartimaeus (Mark 10:46–52), the blind man at Bethsaida (Mark 8:22–26), and the man born blind in Jerusalem (John 9)—the healing of an official's boy (Matt. 8:5–13; John 4:46–54), and the raising of Jairus's daughter from the dead (Mark 5:21–43). Meier also inclines to believe that a historical core can be found in such stories as the exorcism of the Gerasene demoniac (Mark 5:1–20), the raising of the widow's son at Nain (Luke 7:11–17), the raising of Lazarus (John 11:1–46), and the feeding of the multitudes (Mark 6:32–44).

A key text for Meier is the passage from Q in which Jesus describes his ministry in generic terms: "the blind receive their sight, the lame walk, the lepers are cleansed, the deaf hear, the dead are raised, the poor have good news brought to them" (Luke 7:22). This logion establishes the types of miracles for which Jesus claimed to be known. The specific accounts that Meier judges to be historical exemplify this general description that Jesus himself offered of his ministry. Although Meier can find no specific accounts of Jesus cleansing lepers or healing the deaf that meet his criteria of authenticity, he believes that Jesus was reputed to have done these things also.

One distinctive feature of Meier's list of authentic miracle accounts is that it contains stories found in John's Gospel, at least three of which concern miracles worked in Jerusalem (the paralytic at Bethesda, the man born blind, and the raising of Lazarus). The majority of historical scholars (following the Synoptic Gospels) do not think Jesus spent any time in Jerusalem but restricted his ministry to Galilee. The working of miracles in Jerusalem adds an element to Meier's portrait of Jesus that differs even from those of scholars such as Borg and Crossan who do assume that Jesus was reputed to work miracles in Galilee. This element derives from Meier's aversion to scholarship's prima facie rejection of the Gospel of John as unhistorical. Meier submits individual traditions in John to the same tests he uses for traditions in the other Gospels, though even he is a bit harder on the Johannine accounts. Given the recognizable tradition of theological development in the fourth Gospel, its reports start out with marks against them. It is noteworthy, then, that so many stories in John—miracle stories at that—end up receiving the Meier seal of approval.

Companions

Meier proposes that Jesus gathered or attracted followers who might be understood as forming three, somewhat-fluid concentric circles around him: crowds, disciples, and the twelve.[56]

That Jesus did in fact attract large crowds is multiply attested in the source material (texts in Mark, Q, John, M, and L)[57] and also derives support from Meier's "criterion of Jesus' rejection and execution"—indeed, it serves as a primary example of how that controversial criterion can function: "Jesus' ability to draw large, enthusiastic crowds, especially when on pilgrimage to Jerusalem for great feasts like Passover, helps explain why Caiaphas and Pilate would have increasingly considered him a dangerous figure."[58] The people who made up these crowds were drawn from the general populace and should be distinguished from the sinners with whom Jesus also associated.[59] They were Israelites (i.e., Jews, not Gentiles), and the vast majority were probably poor, though some persons of means may have been included.[60] Such people provided audiences for Jesus' public teaching and were beneficiaries of his healing ministry; they seem to have attached themselves to him with varying degrees of commitment and longevity.

Jesus' followers also included a closer circle of disciples.[61] Such persons could be differentiated from admirers and supporters among the crowds in that they not only imbibed his teaching but apparently shared his ministry of proclaiming the kingdom of God and healing the sick.[62] Three features of Jesus' relationship to his disciples are especially noteworthy. First, Jesus himself took the initiative in calling (or even commanding) a person to become his disciple—in this regard, he appears to have been unusual if not unique.[63] Second, disciples of Jesus followed him in a literal, physical sense, leaving behind their home, parents, and livelihood to accompany him on his itinerant travels.[64] Third, disciples were warned by Jesus that such a commitment not only would entail hardships but would also bring hostility and suffering.[65] In regard to the last point, Meier goes against the tide of most historical Jesus scholarship by maintaining the historical authenticity of the tradition that Jesus used graphic language to liken discipleship to "bearing one's cross" (Mark 8:34 and Matt. 10:38//Luke 14:27).[66] In addition to these disciples—but also distinct from the crowds—there appear to have been what Meier calls "sedentary supporters" of Jesus who showed Jesus hospitality when he traveled to their area and who may have also assisted him financially. People like Zacchaeus (Luke 19:1–10), Lazarus (John 12:1–2), Simon the leper (Mark 14:3), and the anonymous host of the Last Supper (Mark 14:13–15) may have been numbered among these auxiliary adherents who did not "take the plunge" of complete discipleship, perhaps because they were not summoned or allowed by Jesus to do so.[67]

The third, recognizable group of followers to which Jesus related was the inner circle known as "the twelve."[68] Like Sanders (see pages 164–65), Meier accepts the biblical tradition that Jesus used this designation for a specific entity distinct from his disciples or supporters in general. While not terribly controversial, that claim has been challenged by a few scholars who regard the hierarchical notion of a select leadership group among Jesus' followers to be a post-Easter invention that goes against Jesus' typical egalitarianism (see above on Schüssler Fiorenza, 30–31, and Crossan, 129).[69] But Meier finds three factors determinative for authentication of the tradition: (1) multiple attestation of sources and forms (independent support from Mark, Q, John, and even Paul [cf. 1 Cor. 15:5]);[70] (2) support from the criterion of embarrassment, since the tradition that Jesus was handed over by one of the twelve (e.g., John 6:71) was hardly a matter the church would invent;[71] (3) recognition that maintenance of the twelve as a recognizable entity ceased to be important soon after the time of Jesus, as individual leaders (including persons like Paul and James of Jerusalem, who were not among the twelve) came to prominence.[72] Meier also notes that the exact membership of the twelve may have varied over the course of Jesus' ministry (explaining variance in the different lists that appear in Mark 3:16–19, Matt. 10:2–4, Luke 6:14–16, Acts 1:13). Maintaining the number was important, however, even though the group was apparently called "the twelve" during brief interims when there were not literally twelve members (1 Cor. 15:5): it was the *concept* of the twelve that was important and that concept appears to have originated with Jesus, for whom the number twelve was itself significant.[73]

The function of the twelve for Jesus seems to have been diverse. Meier suggests that they probably served as exemplars of discipleship, embodying through both successes and failures a high-profile illustration of what happened when Jesus' challenging demands were undertaken.[74] Meier also thinks it is probable (but not certain) that Jesus commissioned the twelve to undertake a prophetic mission to Israel on his behalf; this is indicated by both Mark and Q (Mark 6:6–13; Luke 10:1–12) and suggested by the epithet "fishers of men" applied to certain members of the twelve (cf. Mark 1:16–20)—but, Meier admits, such texts could represent post-Easter evangelistic agendas.[75] In any case, the most important function of the twelve was probably that they served as prophetic symbols of the regathering of the twelve tribes of Israel (as recognized also by Sanders, cf. pages 164–65).[76] As an "eschatological prophet bearing the mantle of Elijah," Jesus apparently thought he had something to do with re-ordering Israel for the end times.[77] By his appointment of the twelve, Jesus stated emphatically that "God was about to fulfill his promises to Israel by recreating his chosen people as they were meant to be" (i.e., "all Israel, all twelve tribes").[78]

In conclusion, Meier notes that Jesus' conception of the people of God was both limited and expansive. On the one hand, he does not appear to have invited Gentiles to be part of renewed Israel; this may be because he thought inclusion of Gentiles would come later, at the consummation rather than the inauguration of the kingdom (cf. Matt. 8:11–12).[79] On the other hand, Jesus did address all Israelites: he did not try to create a holy remnant or establish a separatist sect (like Qumran) but called for participation from people of diverse social locations.[80] Indeed, one of the most amazing aspects of Jesus' ministry for Meier is the almost-indisputable historical fact that unchaperoned women accompanied Jesus and his male disciples as they traveled about.[81] Although these women are never explicitly identified as "disciples" (perhaps, Meier intimates, for purely philological reasons), nor were any of them among the twelve, they appear to have done what the disciples did and to have borne analogous hardships. Meier believes they were "de facto" disciples, and he accepts the tradition that indicates they ultimately proved more faithful than the male disciples in following Jesus to the cross without betraying, deserting, or denying him.[82]

Competitors

With regard to Jesus' relations vis-à-vis other Jewish groups, Meier discovers that little can be known with certainty. In part this is because our historical information about those groups is quite limited (and itself subject to dispute concerning authenticity).[83] Furthermore, stories concerning Jesus' conflicts with other Jews are prime candidates for material that might have been redacted in the early church to increase relevance for ongoing Jewish-Christian relations (hostilities).[84] The most certain conclusions can probably be drawn with regard to the Pharisees (due to the wealth of the material), but even here generalizations are more secure than specific propositions.[85] Basically, Meier thinks it is likely that the historical Jesus argued with individual Pharisees over matters of legal interpretation (e.g., divorce, fasting, tithing, purity rules, Sabbath observance, and the relative importance of external observances).[86] His position on such issues was no doubt determined by his understanding of the kingdom ("the peculiar mix of present-yet-future-eschatology"[87]) while theirs may have owed more to their reliance on an oral code they called "the tradition of the fathers (or elders)." As a prophet, Jesus may also have employed "denunciation rhetoric" against individual Pharisees, pronouncing woes against them in a manner reminiscent of Amos or Hosea (cf. Luke 11:39–44). He may have critiqued or caricatured them in some of his parables (cf. Luke 18:10–14). There does not, however, seem to be any good reason to believe that Jesus' clashes with the Pharisees were the reason he was eventually put to death—and, in fact, some Pharisees appear to have been willing to give him a serious hearing (cf. Luke 7:36–50; John 3:1–2).

Otherwise, Jesus does not appear to have had significant regular contact with Essenes, Samaritans, or Sadducees (a "mainly aristocratic and largely priestly party centered in Jerusalem"[88]). He spent most of his time addressing ordinary Jews throughout Judea and Galilee.[89] Interesting comparisons can be noted between the Jesus movement and the Essene community at Qumran: both were "Jewish eschatological groups with radical lifestyles, fervent hopes for Israel's future, and tense or hostile relations with the priestly establishment in Jerusalem."[90] Nevertheless, the two movements do not appear to have interacted.[91] Likewise, the most that can be said about Jesus and Samaritans is that Jesus apparently held a benign view of Samaritans that was considered noteworthy compared to the more hostile attitude stereotypically associated with Jews of his day. It is possible that he had fleeting encounters with individual Samaritans, but all biblical stories of such accounts (e.g., Luke 9:52–53; 17:11–19; John 4:4–42) are related with an interest in Christian mission that renders their content impossible to authenticate. Jesus did not, at any rate, initiate any programmatic mission to Samaritans during his own lifetime, which implies he did not regard them as belonging to the full complement of Israel that he was called to address (the chosen people of God who would be restored in the last days).[92]

Meier does accept the essential authenticity of one biblical account involving the Sadducees (Mark 12:18–27).[93] In what was probably an isolated incident, Jesus responded to a question the Sadducees used to ridicule the notion of general resurrection (a relatively recent idea in Jewish religion) by quoting Exodus 3:6 as a scriptural proof text. The historicity of this report can be established mainly by the criterion of discontinuity: neither the Jews of Jesus' day nor later Christians are known to have employed such an argument; likewise, there is no indication that the author of Mark's Gospel or early Christians in general "were exercised over the problem of whether or with whom a wife involved in a levirate marriage would have sex after the general resurrection."[94] Precisely because of such features (odd or even irrelevant for developing Christianity) the story remains "a unique and precious relic that allows us to appreciate more fully Jesus' own views on what the future coming of the kingdom would mean . . . past generations would rise from the dead and faithful Israelites would share in a new type of life similar to that of the angels."[95]

Law

Meier maintains that "the historical Jesus is the halakic Jesus,"[96] by which he means that Jesus was just as concerned about questions of biblical/legal interpretation as were other Jewish teachers and groups of his day. The word "halakah" (from Hebrew *halak*, meaning "to walk, go, or follow") refers to the interpretation of biblical commandments in order to determine rules and statutes that are to guide a person's life. Thus, the image of Jesus as a teacher of ethical imperatives who gave his disciples concrete directions on how to observe the Mosaic Law must be added to that of the eschatological, miracle-working prophet. But even in relation to the law, Jesus was a charismatic figure. Meier disagrees with Sanders at this point, claiming that Jesus did assume the right to rescind or change parts of the law. What's more, he located his authority to do this not in recognized or traditional channels but in "his own ability to know directly and intuitively what was God's will for his people."[97] He often prefaced his comments on the law with the phrase, "Amen, I say to you," which essentially means, "the words I speak to you are true because I speak them, and that is the end of the matter."[98]

According to Meier, Jesus' most radical stance on legal statutes came to the fore in two instances. First, he prohibited divorce for any reason whatsoever (cf. Mark 10:9; Luke 16:18; 1 Cor. 7:10–11; historicity is established through criteria of multiple attestation, discontinuity, embarrassment, and coherence—but the exception clause in Matt. 5:32 is clearly redactional).[99] Second, he forbade the taking of all oaths (cf. Matt. 5:34–37, Jas. 5:12; historicity is established through criteria of discontinuity and probable multiple attestation).[100] In both of these instances, Jesus revoked institutions of the Mosaic Law without consideration of the practical consequences of such a stance. Meier suggests that the rationale for such an unprecedented and uncompromising position may have been that, as an eschatological prophet, Jesus was declaring that his followers should live proleptically in the kingdom of God and (at least in these two matters) conduct themselves already in the manner that would prevail when Israel's total restoration by God was accomplished. Meier admits, however, that this explanation is only a guess, since Jesus himself—as a true religious charismatic—did not feel obliged to explain himself to anyone or to provide rationales for what he declared to be the will of God.[101]

On other matters, Jesus may have been less controversial than the Gospels portray him. With regard to Sabbath observance, he favored "a humane, moderate approach" over "sectarian rigorism," but this would not have distinguished him from many other Jewish leaders of the day (the Gospels caricature the Pharisees on this point to provide foils for their presentation of Jesus' views).[102] And Meier thinks the historical Jesus may have been silent on matters of ritual purity (e.g., hand washing before meals, distinctions between clean and unclean foods)—all of the Gospel passages that deal with these matters reflect later disputes between Christianity and Judaism.[103] Further, Meier rejects the historicity of occasional intimations in the Gospels that controversies over the law led Pharisees or other Jewish leaders to plot Jesus' death (e.g. Matt. 12:9–14). Meier's conclusion is that Jesus' teachings on the law did not directly lead to his execution, though of course his controversial positions "may have alienated many who might otherwise have supported or defended him."[104]

Meier also thinks that Jesus granted priority to two commands in the Mosaic Law: Deuteronomy 6:4–5 and Leviticus 19:18b. Thus, he "did not simply issue ad-hoc pronouncements on scattered topics like divorce, oaths, or the sabbath"; he also reflected on "the totality of Torah" and extracted "from that totality the love of God and the love of neighbor as the *first* and *second* commandments of the Torah, superior to all others."[105] In doing this, he did not intend to establish a hermeneutical principle in light of which all commandments should be interpreted (that would be a Christian extrapolation), but was merely engaging (quite competently) in the sort of legal debates that occupied Palestinian Jews of his day. Specifically, Jesus' combination and elevation of the two love commandments (of God in Deut. 6:4–5 and of neighbor in Lev. 19:18b) represent application of a Jewish exegetical method called the *gezera shava*. Evident in later rabbinic writings, this method allowed a rabbi to bring together two scripture texts that contained an identical key word or phrase in a manner that produced a creative or provocative interpretation of both passages. Meier takes Jesus' use of this method as evidence that he had some sort of formal training: "Anyone can declare himself a charismatic prophet. Getting the *gezera shava* right requires study."[106]

Crucifixion

Meier has not yet treated the Gospel passion narratives to intensive historical study, but he has indicated in part his response to the question of why Jesus was crucified. A variety of factors suggest why he may have been viewed as dangerous: he announced the coming of a future kingdom that would soon put an end to the present state of affairs; he claimed to be able to teach the will of God authoritatively, sometimes in ways that ran counter to scripture and tradition; he performed miracles that attracted a large following; and he evinced freewheeling personal conduct through open fellowship with recognized sinners. If one adds to this "volatile mix" the fact that some Jews took him to be the Davidic Messiah, it becomes "positively explosive," Meier says, and then we must view such events as the staged entry into Jerusalem and the demonstration in the temple as "the match set to the barrel of gasoline."[107]

Convergence

Meier understands Jesus to be "a complex figure" who does not fit easily into any known category. The historical Jesus is

> a first-century Jewish eschatological prophet who proclaims an imminent-future coming of God's kingdom, practices baptism as a ritual of preparation for that kingdom, teaches his disciples to pray to God as abba for that kingdom's arrival, prophesies the regathering of all Israel (symbolized by the inner circle of his twelve disciples) and the inclusion of the Gentiles when the kingdom comes—but who at the same time makes the kingdom already present for at least some Israelites by his exorcisms and miracles of healing. Hence in some sense he already mediates an experience of the joyful time of salvation, expressed also in his freewheeling table fellowship with toll collectors and sinners and his rejection of voluntary fasting for himself and his disciples. To all this must be added his—at times startling—interpretation of the Mosaic Law.[108]

He also thinks "at least some of Jesus' followers believed him to be descended from King David, and that they therefore took him to be the Davidic Messiah."[109]

In the final analysis, Meier thinks that "Jesus was above all an eschatological prophet in the guise of miracle-working Elijah,"[110] but he notes that such a self-conception would not preclude other roles. For example, he may have found sufficient catalyst in Malachi 4:4–6 to combine "his role as eschatological Elijah with his role as interpreter of Torah," fusing the two otherwise disparate functions in his own person.[111]

We might compare this complex understanding of Jesus with that of Borg, who also employs multiple categories for describing the historical Jesus. Borg's specific categories, however, do not figure prominently in Meier's equally diverse scheme. Meier does not present Jesus primarily as a mystical holy man who views himself as a channel for the Spirit, or as a subversive sage, movement initiator, or social reformer. Of all the historians reviewed in this book, Meier and Borg are the most eclectic in their collection of images for Jesus, but the degree of overlap in the images they employ is less than one might have supposed.

In terms of content, Meier's portrait of Jesus most closely resembles that of E. P. Sanders. He sees Jesus as an eschatological Jewish prophet who was primarily concerned with announcing and, in some sense, enacting the divine restoration of Israel. Meier, however, is less averse than Sanders to what appear to be contradictory impulses, and so, his portrait takes in qualities that Sanders rejects. Unlike Sanders, Meier thinks Jesus did engage his contemporaries in conflicts over the law, and he affirms that Jesus did regard the coming kingdom as already present in some definitive and significant way.[112] Ultimately, what sets Meier's portrait of Jesus apart from that of Sanders may be its complexity. We have seen that Sanders insists, as a historian, that no aspect of Jesus can truly be regarded as unique (see page 172). Meier contends that the "atypical configuration of Jesus' characteristics" is what marks him as unique:

At one and the same time he acted as (1) the prophet of the last days, which were soon to come and yet were somehow already present in his ministry; (2) the gatherer of the Israel of the last days, the twelve tribes of Israel being symbolized by the circle of the twelve disciples Jesus formed around himself; (3) the teacher of both general moral truths and detailed directives concerning the observance of the Mosaic Law (e.g., divorce); and last but not least (4) the exorcist and healer of illnesses who was even reputed, like Elijah and Elisha, to have raised the dead. . . . It is the explosive convergence and mutual reinforcement of all these usually distinct figures in the one Jesus of Nazareth that made him stand out.[113]

CRITIQUE OF MEIER'S STUDY OF JESUS

Meier's work has not often been subjected to the sort of detailed criticism that his method of presentation would seem to invite. This is somewhat surprising because his work would seem to undermine basic conclusions of most of the scholars we have discussed thus far (all but Sanders). The point, perhaps, is that these other scholars do not want to tangle with Meier on his own terms. We will consider what that means momentarily, but first let us note three specific matters on which many scholars have contested Meier's conclusions.

First, the suggestion that Jesus was an eschatological prophet announcing an imminent divine intervention in history meets with the same objections brought against Allison and Sanders (see pages 91–92, 172–73). We need not rehearse he arguments here but should note that many recent historians (including Funk, Crossan, and Borg) have disagreed with this emphasis on Jesus' expectation that God was about to act in history to redeem and restore Israel.

Second, Meier's specific conclusions regarding Jesus as an interpreter of Torah have been taken as overreaching what the evidence allows. William Loader maintains that there is no evidence that Jesus' teaching on divorce and oaths shocked his contemporaries or caused anyone to allege that he was revoking Torah.[114] Indeed, Loader says, his stance would *not* actually have revoked Torah but, simply, raised the standard for application of certain laws to a higher level of strictness. Further, exceptions to Jesus' generic divorce prohibition (such as that spelled out in Matt. 5:3) may have simply been assumed (cf. also 1 Cor. 7:11, 15). And the fact that many of Jesus' earliest followers, including Paul, continued using oaths without feeling any apparent need to justify doing so suggests that they did not take Jesus' teaching on that subject in the uncompromising sense that Meier supposes. Logically, one might question whether a reported saying that was apparently ignored by all of a teacher's subsequent followers ought to be taken as a primary marker of that teacher's overall position.

Third, the omission of any attribution of a political or social program to Jesus troubles many historical scholars. As we have seen, Borg, Crossan, Schüssler Fiorenza, Horsley, and others consider Jesus to have been a conscious social reformer in one respect or another. Meier's reluctance to attribute this role to Jesus is related to the previous point about eschatology. He says that "Jesus seems to have had no interest in the great political and social questions of his day. He was not interested in the reform of the world because he was prophesying its end."[115] Borg quotes this comment as evidence of why the "eschatological prophet" model does not do justice to the historical Jesus.[116] Borg would claim that many of Jesus' sayings and deeds do point to political and social reform and that (following Meier's own logic) this argues against the proposition that Jesus was expecting the world to end soon.

In general, critiques of Meier's project seem to be more sweeping, focusing either on its specific methodological premises or on its fundamental presupposition as to how one ought to do history. The best example of the former may be illustrated by comparing Meier to the Jesus Seminar. At times, Meier appears to function as a one-man Jesus Seminar, applying criteria of authenticity to individual sayings and deeds attributed to Jesus and determining whether or not they are likely to be historical. Reading his volumes, one can almost imagine him casting red, pink, gray, and black marbles in his mind as he decides that *this* bit of data is definitely authentic, *that* one might be but probably isn't, and so forth. Still, Meier's conclusions differ radically from those reached by the Jesus Seminar. Why? I discern two reasons (and there could be more).

First, Meier studies sayings and deeds attributed to Jesus together. The Jesus Seminar separated the sayings from the deeds and studied them independently, as two different types of tradition passed along separately in the church to serve different functions *(Sitze im Leben)*. Thus, when the Jesus Seminar gave black type (meaning "unauthentic") to the Q saying in Luke 7:22 where Jesus speaks of the blind seeing, the lame walking, and the dead being raised, they apparently did not consider the coherence of this saying with the stories in the Gospel tradition about those things happening. For Meier, that coherence, with an implicit multiple attestation of both sources and forms, becomes a major reason for deciding in favor of the authenticity of the Q saying as well as for the authenticity of some of the individual accounts that describe deeds illustrative of the works it mentions.

Second, Meier dismisses the apocryphal Gospels (including those attributed to Peter and Thomas) as late documents that are dependent on canonical writings, and he credits the Gospel of John with preserving independent worthwhile testimony. The Jesus Seminar decided exactly the opposite: the Gospel of Thomas, at least, is a valuable early source, while John is late and so intrinsically flawed that it hardly counts at all. Both Meier and the Jesus Seminar allowed these early decisions about the relative value of source materials to guide their decisions. Thus, the key question for evaluating their work could be, "Who has the better premises?" But some scholars think it should not come to that.

A fundamental critique of both Meier and the Jesus Seminar arises from philosophical debate as to the best way to study history. Both Meier and the Jesus Seminar pursue a time-honored approach of accumulating and evaluating data piece by piece until a reasonable interpretation of that data can be offered. They claim that they do not want to impose any conception of Jesus on these data. Instead, they want to determine first which sayings or deeds are historical and then construct a portrait of Jesus faithful to these determinations. To many people, this would seem to be the only objective or fair way to go about it. Indeed, as we have noted, one major criticism of the Jesus Seminar has been that (according to some) they did not in fact do as they claimed. They *did* start with a conception of Jesus, albeit an unstated one, and this influenced their decisions about the evidence. Not surprisingly, similar charges are whispered against Meier.[117] Skeptics find his Jesus to be conveniently amenable to Christianity, even to Catholicism.[118] Some question whether it is possible for anyone to begin with no conception of Jesus and then blandly accumulate information regarding him until they are able to construct a disinterested portrait. Others question whether it would be desirable to do so.

N. T. Wright proposes another way of doing history, a model he calls "critical realism."[119] This will be discussed in more detail in the next chapter, but for now let us note that Wright suggests the proper starting point is a hypothesis (a conception of Jesus), which one then seeks to verify by sifting through the evidence. Wright is one who thinks the Jesus Seminar's purported claim to have arrived at conclusions based on objective analysis of individual passages is only a ruse. In fact, the Seminar provides an assessment of the historicity of materials based on a particular (prior) view of Jesus that they propose to be correct. Ironically, though, Wright says this is the *proper* way to do history. He happens to think the Jesus Seminar had a bad hypothesis, which could not ultimately be sustained, but he does not fault them for trying.[120] Accordingly, he might encourage Meier to come up with a hypothesis about Jesus first, state it, and then work through the materials to see if it holds up. So, also, Dale Allison maintains that the best historical method begins with positing a paradigm: the first move of historians should not be "to discover which sayings or even what complexes are authentic"; rather, the first move should be to construct a persuasive narrative that provides context and offers "a primary frame of reference" for the consideration of such data. "As historians of the Jesus tradition," writes Allison, "we are storytellers. We can do no more than aspire to fashion a narrative that is more persuasive than competing narratives."[121]

This difference in approaches will become more evident in the next chapter when we look at Wright's work on Jesus. But, to a lesser extent, we can see a difference already by comparing Meier's approach to data with that of Sanders.[122] Sanders begins with the hypothesis that Jesus was a Jewish prophet of restoration eschatology. He works through the Jesus tradition, applying criteria of authenticity, to determine how much of the material fits his hypothesis. But he does not feel compelled to make everything fit. Some material that has reasonably good support may need to be rejected as not fitting with the overall hypothesis, or be reinterpreted so that it does fit (sayings regarding the presence of the kingdom are an example). Meier espouses a building-block approach to history, which Wright denounces as "pseudo-atomistic work on isolated fragments."[123] He wants to sift data, accumulate evidence, and see where it leads. The result, predictably, is that materials that point in diverse if not contradictory directions are judged to be authentic. With no macrohypothesis to guide him, he is committed by his method to use *all* the apparently historical blocks in his final construction. So the bottom line must be that Jesus was "a complex figure." Meier maintains that the convergence of diverse factors and images in the historical figure of Jesus marks him as unique. Sanders has said that any portrait of Jesus that presents him as historically unique is almost by definition incorrect.[124] It is not impossible that Jesus was all the things that potentially authentic materials portray him as being, but it seems more likely that he was only some of them. So, also, Crossan alleges that Meier's method does not allow him to discriminate adequately between layers of tradition with the result that "he ends up honestly unable to combine what are not only divergent but even opposing strata of the Jesus tradition."[125]

Eventually, scholars may debate individual judgments that Meier offers: Did Jesus really baptize? Does the theological tale of the raising of Lazarus go back to an actual event in Jesus' life? Did he really prohibit the taking of all oaths? Thus far, however, such discussion has not occurred to the extent that one might have supposed. Those who are potentially Meier's biggest critics seem to think that he and they have reached a methodological impasse. They do not want to quibble with the arguments he reaches in any way that respects his terms of engagement. They object to the terms themselves. Some, including members of the Jesus Seminar, accept Meier's general approach but deny foundational premises that influence his judgments as to what material should be deemed historical. Others, like Wright, challenge the approach itself as embodying a naive positivism that simply does not work in practice.

Meier is well aware of the problem of inherent subjectivity. "There is," he says, "no neutral Switzerland of the mind in Jesus research."[126] Still, "the solution to this dilemma is neither to pretend to an absolute objectivity that is not to be had nor to wallow in total relativism. The solution is to admit honestly one's own standpoint, to try to exclude its influence in making scholarly judgments by adhering to certain commonly held criteria, and to invite the correction of other scholars when one's vigilance inevitably slips."[127] Crossan, we recall, regards objectivity as "spurious" and "unattainable." Meier disagrees with the "spurious" part. He considers objectivity, even in the so-called naive positivist sense, to be an "asymptotic goal," that is "a goal we have to keep pressing toward, even though we never fully reach it."[128] But don't lessons of the past reveal the futility of this? Meier responds:

> I often remember a philosophy professor who taught me years ago asking my class why anyone should struggle with the question of whether or how we can know truth, when the greatest minds down through the centuries have come up with contradictory answers to that question. Why bother to try when the best and brightest have floundered? One thoughtful student replied that no one thinks that we should stop the quest for and practice of love, just because our forebears have made a mess of that subject.[129]

Chapter 9

N. T. Wright

Jesus was a herald, the bringer of an urgent message that could not wait, could not become the stuff of academic debate. He was issuing a public announcement, like someone driving through a town with a loudhailer. He was issuing a public warning, like a man with a red flag heading off an imminent railway disaster. He was issuing a public invitation, like someone setting up a political party and summoning all and sundry to sign up and help create a new world.

—N. T. Wright[1]

Wright makes a sustained argument that the New Testament gospels' depictions of the sayings, ministry, and crucifixion of Jesus are fundamentally reliable. . . . Jesus prophetically foresaw and symbolically enacted in his death a very specific, albeit religiously cataclysmic, first century event (and was proven quite right): the Roman destruction of the Temple in Jerusalem (A.D. 70) and its replacement by a renewed people of God. . . . Jesus also understood himself as the bearer of God's own presence in the midst of God's people.

—Mary Knutsen[2]

Wright's complex and voluminous works stem from his belief that serious study of Jesus and the gospels is best done within the context of a worshipping community. . . . His theory of interpretation, critical realism, places Jesus in the context of first-century Palestinian Judaism but builds a bridge from the first-century historical Jesus to twenty-first century "orthodoxy."

—David B. Gowler[3]

N. T. Wright burst upon the scene of historical Jesus studies in the late twentieth century and essentially took the stage by storm. A well-published scholar in Great Britain who had taught at both Cambridge and Oxford, he would become the Bishop of Durham (a high-ranking position in the Anglican church) and serve in that capacity until 2010 when he retired to become Research Professor of New Testament and Christianity at the University of St Andrews in Scotland. In addition to his major works on the historical Jesus, Wright has produced dozens of volumes aimed at explaining (or defending) biblical and theological matters in language that appeals to educated laity.[4] Wright is sometimes compared to C. S. Lewis, the Anglican author and scholar of the mid-twentieth century who also had a gift for addressing complex religious questions in simple but provocative ways. Like Lewis, Wright has earned a significant following in America among conservative Christians who describe themselves as "evangelicals," though Wright has not always courted their approval and at times has seemed to distance himself from such associations. He has indicated that he prefers to be described as "orthodox" rather than as "evangelical"—perhaps because the latter term can carry ambiguous baggage (e.g., political affiliation) in the United States. In Great Britain, however, Wright is closely associated with a movement called "open evangelicalism," a religious orientation that seeks to combine emphasis on scriptural authority and acceptance of Christianity's historic creeds with an inclusive approach toward culture that invites dialogue with a variety of theological perspectives. In recent years, Wright has also become a popular guest for interviews and panel discussions on television shows sponsored by the BBC, ABC, CNN, PBS, and even Comedy Central (*The Colbert Report*).

Other scholars have not always known what to make of him. This is evident even from comments on the back cover of his major book, *Jesus and the Victory of God*, solicited by the publisher as endorsements of the volume: "Wright is one of the most formidable of traditionalist Bible scholars," writes one critic.[5] "Wright has established himself as the leading British Jesus scholar of his generation," says another (Marcus Borg, in fact). The praise is attended by caveats: he is notable among *traditionalist* scholars or *British* scholars. Actually, as we will see, Wright is not always traditional in his views, though he is certainly formidable in his arguments. And, though he may be a notable Briton, he has established himself in the minds of many as the leading Jesus scholar, period. He has become "the force to be reckoned with" (or to use traditionalist, British grammar, "the force with which to be reckoned").

One of the more conspicuous aspects of Wright's work may sometimes attract more attention than its significance merits. Even those with only a passing acquaintance with Wright's scholarship may know him as the scholar who spells *god* with a lowercase *g*. The traditional spelling, Wright complains, "sometimes amounts to regarding 'God' as the proper name of the Deity" and "implies that all users of the word are monotheists and, within that, that all monotheists believe in the same god."[6] In any case, he does not intend any irreverence, and he does not press the point in all his writings: he uses "god" rather than "God" throughout his more scholarly tomes, but he has no problem using "God" in other writings. Further, when he quotes from writings of early Christians, he sometimes does use the capital "to indicate that the authors were making just this point, that the god they worshiped and invoked was in fact God."[7] He also sometimes refers to the god of Israel as YHWH, following a widely accepted scholarly convention: in the Hebrew Old Testament, God's name (rendered as either Yahweh or Jehovah in English Bibles) is given as a tetragrammaton, four consonants that cannot be pronounced. It was considered sacrilegious to speak the name of God aloud.

As indicated, Wright's main contribution to historical Jesus studies is *Jesus and the Victory of God,* published in 1996, but that book was actually the second volume in a projected six-volume series on the broad subject of "Christian Origins and the Question of God." The first volume in that series was *The New Testament and the People of God,* published in 1992.[8] That book dealt primarily with reconstruction of the Jewish world in which Jesus lived and in which the New Testament was produced and so laid the foundations for the study of Jesus himself. The third volume in the series, *The Resurrection of the Son of God* (published in 2003), deals with the issue of Jesus' resurrection, addressing questions of history (what actually happened?) and theology (what did it mean to Jesus' earliest followers?). The remaining volumes in this series have been announced with the following projected titles: *Paul and the Faithfulness of God; The Gospels and the Story of God;* and *The Early Christians and the Purpose of God.*

WRIGHT'S METHOD FOR STUDYING JESUS

In *The New Testament and the People of God,* Wright lays out a method for historical research that he calls "critical realism."[9] This model involves an overt process of hypothesis and verification. Rather than beginning with a supposedly objective analysis of data, Wright suggests beginning with a stated hypothesis that may or may not be substantiated through analysis of the data. The vindication of a hypothesis depends on three things: its inclusion of data without distortion, its essential simplicity of line, and its ability to shed light elsewhere.[10] These elements, especially the first two, can be in tension with each other. Historians can often find simple hypotheses that explain some of the data (for example, "Jesus was a Cynic philosopher") while ignoring the rest. Historians can also concoct elaborate, complex portraits that take everything into account but ascribe wildly diverse if not contradictory impulses to their subject. The trick is to come up with an inherently consistent picture that includes as much of the data as possible. Then if the hypothesis is sound, it should also help to explain related developments, such as (in the case of the historical Jesus) developments in the history of early Christianity. More specifically, Wright suggests that with regard to Jesus any hypothesis must provide reasonable answers to five major questions: (1) How does Jesus fit into Judaism? (2) What were Jesus' aims? (3) Why did Jesus die?

(4) How and why did the early church begin? and (5) Why are the Gospels what they are?[11]

Wright eschews the sort of microscopic study of individual sayings evident in the work of the Jesus Seminar and John Meier. He does not see the fundamental historical task as consisting of reconstructing traditions about Jesus but rather as advancing hypotheses that account for the traditions we have. In this, he claims to be suggesting "no more than that Jesus be studied like any other figure of the ancient past."[12] When historians study, say, Alexander the Great or Julius Caesar, they do not make lists of all the things the subject is reported to have said or done and then consider each of these individually, asking, "Did this really happen?" or "Did the person really say this?" Trying to "peel the historical onion back to its core," Wright says, is "the way of tears and frustration."[13]

Of course, Wright must make some judgments as to what data are most relevant. His account of Jesus' life does not incorporate as much material from John's Gospel as does that of Meier, nor does Wright's Jesus reflect the image presented in the apocryphal Gospels to the degree that Crossan's Jesus does.[14] Rather, Wright appears to draw most heavily on the traditions of the Synoptic Gospels, but he does not seem to be particular about differentiating between what might be ascribed to Mark, Q, M, or L. With regard to the Synoptic material, at least, he does manage to include more data than other scholars we have discussed.

Any solid hypothesis about Jesus, Wright continues, must make historical sense of him with reference to what we know about two contexts that can be related to him. The outside limits for understanding Jesus "are pre-Christian Judaism and the second-century church; and the puzzle involves fitting together the bits in the middle to make a clear historical sequence all the way across."[15] This leads Wright to propose a somewhat refined criterion for authenticity, which he calls the "double criterion of similarity and dissimilarity": "When something can be seen to be credible (though perhaps deeply subversive) within first-century Judaism, *and* credible as the implied starting point (though not the exact replica) of something in later Christianity, there is a strong possibility of our being in touch with the genuine history of Jesus."[16]

Wright admits that first-century Judaism and second-century Christianity are themselves difficult to describe. The task can be "like climbing from one moving boat into another" and the "history of research indicates how easy it is to fall into the water."[17] Still, the historical quest is to understand Jesus as the necessary link between these two movements. This suggestion would prove highly influential in subsequent Jesus studies such that, in the twenty-first century, a new criterion of "plausible influence" would all but displace the old criterion of "dissimilarity" to which so many scholars had appealed in previous decades (see above, pages 63–65).

Wright insists on regarding the beliefs of early Christianity not as a problem to be overcome (in order to get back to the real or historical Jesus) but as part of the phenomenon to be explained. He asks, "How do we account for the fact that, by A.D. 110, there was a large and vigorous international movement, already showing considerable diversity, whose founding myth . . . was a story about one Jesus of Nazareth, a figure of the recent past?"[18] Or, more specifically, "How did it come about that Jesus was *worshipped* . . . in very early, very Jewish, and still insistently monotheist Christianity?"[19] What was there about the person and mission of this man that, historically, would explain such developments?

We may take just one example: the meaning of Jesus' death. As we have seen, many scholars address the question of what Jesus did that led to his execution, focusing, for instance, on political implications of his ministry that might have antagonized the Romans, or on his opposition to the temple cult, which might have aroused the ire of Jewish high priests. This is all well and good, says Wright, but we also have the fact that a few years after the crucifixion, Christians such as Paul were affirming that Jesus had died for their sins. Whether we personally embrace this theological interpretation or not, Wright argues, we need to account for it. The historian should ask what there was about Jesus, and especially about his execution, that could prompt such belief.[20]

Wright's most innovative work, however, has concerned the other outside limit for understanding Jesus: first-century Judaism. He approaches this with reference to discerning what he calls "worldview" and "mindset."[21] The term *worldview* applies to the perspective of a society, and the term *mindset* applies to the perspective of a particular individual. Both imply convictions so fundamental as to be taken for granted: "If challenged, a worldview generates the answer, 'that's just the way things are,' and a mindset replies to critics with 'that's just the sort of person I am.'"[22] Both are revealed through the study of four things: characteristic stories, fundamental symbols, habitual praxis, and answers to a set of basic questions (who are we? where are we? what's wrong? what's the solution? what time is it?).

The model gets more complex. Wright goes on to suggest that worldviews and mindsets generate a set of "basic beliefs" and "aims," which in turn are expressed through "consequent beliefs" and "intentions." The detailed distinctions between these are not necessary for our survey. Basically, Wright wants to recover the mindset of Jesus, which he assumes must be set within the worldview of first-century Judaism. So he suggests that where some action or activity of Jesus is securely established, we can ask what beliefs, aims, and intentions it reveals, granted the prevailing Jewish worldview whose basic shape he may be assumed to have shared.[23] Of course, Wright realizes it is also possible to make the reverse move, to determine that some reported saying or activity is not likely to be authentic because it does not fit within the "mindset-within-worldview" that otherwise seems to hold. He is cautious about doing this, however, because "most historical characters worth studying are so because they held mindsets that formed significant variations on the parent worldview."[24]

One section of *The New Testament and the People of God* is devoted to describing the worldview of first-century Judaism. Two points are especially important for the later study of Jesus. First, Wright holds that most first-century Jews believed they were still in exile.[25] Numerous texts from the period focus on retelling the story of Israel in a way that indicates this. The Jewish people in the first century cherished the memory of how their god had delivered them from captivity in Egypt. This high point, however, was paired with the devastating memory of how the Babylonians had destroyed the temple several hundred years later. The latter event, which precipitated the exile, was a catastrophe of unspeakable proportion. Israel viewed the temple as the dwelling of their god, as the place where heaven and earth met. The destruction meant that their god had abandoned the temple, and so had abandoned them to their enemies. Of course, a new temple had been built, but the fact that the people of Israel were still in bondage to a hostile foreign power (Rome) was evidence to many Jewish people that their god had not returned to dwell in it. The hope—kept alive through retellings of the exodus story—was that Israel's god would return and the exile would finally end.[26]

A second key point Wright develops in this first book is that although eschatological expectation was widespread in first-century Judaism, the apocalyptic imagery it employed did not refer literally to the end of the world. It referred, symbolically, to the end of *a* world.[27] Jesus, then, was eschatological not in the sense that he expected the end of the space-time universe, but in the sense that he expected the end of the present world order. Thus, his "warnings about imminent judgment were intended to be taken as denoting (what we would call) sociopolitical events."[28]

WRIGHT'S PORTRAIT OF JESUS

Wright begins, as does Sanders, with "a brief list of things that few will deny about Jesus' life and public activity" (see fig. 7 on p. 206).[29] A few of the items are in fact disputed by other scholars we have discussed in this book. Sanders doubts that Jesus was a preacher of repentance. Crossan does not think Jesus accorded any special status to twelve of his disciples; he also plays down the role of any significant Jewish element in handing Jesus over to be crucified. But Wright thinks that such points are well enough established in the sources to allow them to stand. He also adds to his outline a few details about Jesus that he regards as "comparatively non-controversial," including a devotion to prayer and a relaxed stance toward family commitments.

Jesus as Prophet

Taking all these facts together, Wright proceeds to argue that the best initial model for understanding Jesus is that of a prophet, specifically, "a prophet bearing an urgent eschatological, and indeed apocalyptic, message for Israel."[30] From the above discussion, it should be clear that for Wright to call Jesus an eschatological or apocalyptic prophet does not mean to imply that Jesus was predicting the imminent end of the world. Rather, "Jesus was seen as, and saw himself as . . . a

---

Figure 7. Historical Facts about Jesus according to N. T. Wright

- born in 4 BCE
- grew up in Nazareth of Galilee
- spoke Aramaic, Hebrew, and probably some Greek
- was initially associated with John the Baptist but emerged as a public figure in his own right around 28 CE
- summoned people to repent
- used parables to announce the reign of Israel's god
- conducted itinerant ministry throughout villages of Galilee
- effected remarkable cures, including exorcisms, as enactments of his message
- shared in table fellowship with a socioculturally diverse group
- called a close group of disciples and gave twelve of them a special status
- performed a dramatic action in the temple
- incurred the wrath of some elements in Judaism, especially among the high-priestly establishment
- was handed over by this powerful Jewish element to the Romans to be crucified as an insurrectionist
- was reported by his followers to have been raised from the dead

---

prophet like the prophets of old, coming to Israel with a word from her covenant god, warning her of the imminent and fearful consequences of the direction she was travelling, urging and summoning her to a new and different way."[31]

Part of the evidence for this identification of Jesus as a prophet consists of the many sayings throughout the Gospels that refer to Jesus as a prophet.[32] Some of these, such as Mark 6:4, use the term as Jesus' own self-designation. The sayings are likely to be authentic, Wright reasons, since the early church thought this was too weak a title for Jesus and would not have invented such traditions. In fact, apart from Acts 3:22, Jesus is never referred to as a prophet in any New Testament writing other than the Gospels.

What type of prophet was Jesus? Wright notes that traditions in the Gospels model his ministry after a wide variety of Old Testament prophets: Micaiah ben Imlah (1 Kgs. 22), Ezekiel, Jeremiah, Jonah, Amos, and, above all, Elijah and Elisha. In ways reminiscent of all these figures, Jesus sought to embody the ideal of a popular "oracular prophet," delivering a message through spoken words and symbolic actions. But Jesus combined this image with that of the "leadership prophet"; he started a renewal movement consisting of a group that claimed to represent a reconstitution of Israel. Wright admits that John the Baptist had probably combined these two prophetic models before Jesus, but Jesus took the new model further and with greater effect. This was at least in part because he was itinerant while John was localized, and because his message conveyed greater urgency and was accompanied by the remarkable healings.[33]

Wright offers us "a Jesus who engaged in that characteristically Jewish activity of subversively retelling the basic Jewish story."[34] The message that Jesus proclaimed and ultimately enacted had three main components: (1) Israel's god was about to bring the exile to an end at last, (2) Israel's god was going to act decisively to defeat Israel's enemies, and (3) Israel's god was going to return to Zion to dwell with the people again. Wright says that these components were commonplace in Jewish eschatological expectation. These were the things for which the Jewish people longed. Jesus promised them but also redefined them in subversive ways; the promises would be fulfilled—indeed, *were being* fulfilled—in ways that people had not anticipated.

Return from Exile

As we have seen, Wright describes the Jewish people of the first century as a people who believed they were still in exile, held captive by foreign powers, and enamored of a hope that someday their god would return to deliver them. Jesus, says Wright, announced that this was about to happen. This is the meaning that should be attached to such statements as "Repent, for the kingdom of heaven has come near" (Matt. 4:17). It is also the central notion that informs many of Jesus' parables. Wright suggests, for instance, that the so-called parable of the prodigal son (Luke 15:11–32) retells the story of Israel (as the prodigal) being separated from god (the father) and then—after a period spent with swine—being welcomed back to the good life again. The story of the sower (Mark 4:1–9) likewise proclaims that the time of lost seed is over and the time of fruit has dawned: Israel's god "was returning to his people, to 'sow' his word in their midst, as he promised, and so restore their fortunes at last."[35]

Similarly, the mighty works that Jesus performed were prophetic acts accompanying this announcement. Wright agrees with Meier that "Jesus' contemporaries, both those who became his followers and those who were determined not to become his followers, certainly regarded him as possessed of remarkable powers."[36] The mighty works were presented as signs that prophecy was being fulfilled. Healings, in particular, worked to support the notion of a restored Israel, for now those who had been excluded as sick or unclean could be included. Exorcisms demonstrated the defeat of the true enemy—the satan—and power over nature illustrated the new harmony that Jesus said was coming into the world as Israel's god took charge. Thus, all the actions that are typically called "miracles of Jesus" may be understood as prophetic signs, announcing that Israel's god was bringing the exile to an end.

It is this announcement that marks Jesus as an eschatological prophet. So stated, Wright's view of Jesus is very similar to that of Sanders, who accentuates Jesus as a prophet of "Jewish restoration eschatology." As we continue our sketch, however, significant differences will emerge. Some of these begin to come out in what Wright presents as implications of Jesus' announcement.

First, Jesus' announcement included an *invitation* to repentance and faith (Mark 1:15). Repentance in this instance involved abandoning a way of life, a way of being Israel, and awaiting a different sort of vindication than had been expected. It did not mean primarily "moral repentance," and it did not involve the usual practices of restitution or temple sacrifices. Similarly, faith meant believing that Israel's god was acting climactically in Jesus himself. It did not mean subscribing to a particular religious system or body of doctrine.[37]

Second, Jesus' announcement included a *welcome* to sinners, evidenced dramatically by his practice of sharing meals with those who were thought to be excluded from Israel. Wright thinks that Jesus associated with both those who would have been viewed as sinners by the Pharisees (because they did not follow particular regulations) and those who would have been viewed as sinners by just about everybody (because they participated in what was widely regarded as wicked behavior). In either case, Jesus offered such people forgiveness, which is to say, inclusion in the restored people of Israel, and he did so on his own authority, outside the official structures.[38]

Third, Jesus' announcement included a *challenge* to live as a community that behaved in a distinctive way. In this sense, Jesus was announcing a "new covenant," which, like all covenants, would shape the society that adopted it. Specific expectations of this new covenant are laid out in the Sermon on the Mount (Matt. 5–7), but one fundamental principle is forgiveness. To elevate this as the central characteristic of those loyal to Jesus was to eschew the climate of the times with its emphasis on resistance to Roman tyranny. The people whom Jesus invited and welcomed as part of the new, restored Israel would be renewed in their hearts. They would love their enemies.

Fourth, Jesus' announcement included a *summons* to join him in proclaiming the kingdom. Some (but not all) of the people who believed his message were expected to follow him by taking up his task. They would assist him in his work of announcement even if it involved personal suffering and sacrifice. Thus, Jesus was in a very real sense the founder of a renewal movement and the instigator of a social revolution.

Stories of Jesus' controversies with the Pharisees are likely to be historical, but once again Wright thinks their meaning is not what has typically been assigned to them. "They were about eschatology and politics, not religion or morality."[39] At issue was Jesus' proclamation of the coming kingdom of god in a way that undermined the antipagan revolutionary zeal of certain Pharisees. The point of such Pharisaic practices as Sabbath observance and purity codes regarding meals was not (as Christian interpreters sometimes assume) to establish a means by which individuals could earn their salvation by keeping the law. The point, rather, was to guarantee a distinctive identity for the people of Israel while they were in exile. Rigorous application of the law was a defense against assimilation into the pagan Gentile world. But Jesus declared that the time of exile was ending, and "now that the moment for fulfillment had come, it was time to relativize those god-given markers of Israel's distinctiveness."[40] In fact, for Jesus, these practices had become "a symptom of the problem rather than part of the solution. The kingdom of the one true god . . . would be characterized not by defensiveness, but by Israel's being the light of the world, not by paying the Gentiles back . . . but by turning the other cheek."[41] Thus,

> the clash between Jesus and his Jewish contemporaries must be seen in terms of *alternative political agendas* generated by *alternative eschatological beliefs and expectations.* Jesus was announcing the kingdom in a way which did not reinforce, but rather called into question, the agenda of revolutionary zeal which dominated the horizon of, especially, the dominant group within Pharisaism.[42]

In some ways, Jesus' conflict within Judaism can be understood as a clash of symbols. Jesus replaced key symbols appropriate to preserving Israel's distinctiveness during exile with symbols appropriate for the new reign of god. Feasting replaced fasting; since the exile was ending, life could now be viewed as a celebration (Mark 2:18–19). Open table fellowship replaced segregating purity codes as a more appropriate symbol of life in the postexile reign of god. Likewise, healing the sick (as opposed to quarantining them) symbolized the restoration of creation that was taking place. But, above all, forgiveness replaced retribution, blessing replaced cursing, love replaced hatred. The restored Israel would seek not to conquer her enemies but to become a light to the nations.

How radical such a message would have been is difficult for us to grasp. People in living memory had died, Wright reminds us, for refusing to eat pork. Now Jesus was saying that it didn't matter or wouldn't matter in the kingdom that was dawning: "The traditions which attempted to bolster Israel's national identity were out of date and out of line."[43] Jesus "was offering the return from exile, the renewed covenant, the eschatological 'forgiveness of sins' . . . to all the wrong people, and on his own authority. This was his real offense."[44]

Jesus was announcing a message that ultimately focused on his own self. "Jesus was replacing adherence to Temple and Torah with allegiance to himself," says Wright. "He was declaring, on his own authority, that anyone who trusted in him and in his kingdom-announcement was within the kingdom."[45] Conversely, those who did not heed him and accept his message would be excluded from the kingdom, from the restored Israel. Wright therefore disagrees with Sanders and a number of others who think that Jesus was not a prophet of judgment. He cannot be contrasted with John the Baptist in this regard. The tradition simply contains too many items, a "devastating catalogue of threats and warnings"[46] attributed to Jesus and spread over a wide variety of sources (Mark, Q, M, L, and Thomas). He predicted an impending national disaster, "a coming political, military, and social nightmare"[47] that would bring about the total destruction of Jerusalem and the temple. This would come upon the Jewish people who rejected Jesus' message of peace and chose to pursue war instead. It is to such a cataclysm that the apocalyptic language in Jesus' speech points; the darkening of the sun and the falling of stars (Mark 13:24–25) are symbolic ways of indicating the transforming nature of the event, similar perhaps to what people today mean when they describe something as "earth-shattering."

Much of this judgment talk employed traditional images and language, but Jesus added his own new twist: he and his people would escape and be vindicated. The form that this vindication would take is striking. Wright accepts the authenticity of Gospel texts in which Jesus speaks of the coming of the Son of Man, but interprets these in a nontraditional way. They do not reveal Jesus speaking of a descent of some figure from heaven to earth, but the opposite: the Son of Man travels from earth to heaven, as one who has been vindicated by god and, so, is welcomed on clouds into the heavenly kingdom.[48] Jesus uses this biblical image as a symbol for how he and his followers will be vindicated by god, welcomed into the reign of god as the newly restored people of Israel. The sign that this has happened will be twofold: Jerusalem and the temple will be destroyed by the Romans, but Jesus' followers—warned of what was to come—will flee the city before this actually occurs. This, in itself, will symbolize a return from exile.[49] Furthermore, Wright suggests that Jesus predicted only the destruction of the temple, not its rebuilding. Whereas Sanders presents Jesus as claiming God is about to build a new temple of bricks and mortar, Wright thinks that "Jesus saw himself, and perhaps his followers with him, as the new Temple."[50]

There is more, but we should pause already to consider the implications of this construal. First, Wright is able, like Sanders, to present Jesus as an eschatological prophet, predicting what was to come upon his generation in the near future. Unlike Sanders, however, Wright is able to say that Jesus was right! Jesus' predictions were not subsequently shown to be mistaken, for he never said that he would return to earth in some glorified state while his followers were still alive. In fact, he never said he would return in such a fashion at all. Rather, he predicted that Jerusalem and the temple would be destroyed but that his followers would escape the conflagration, and that these events would be signs that vindicated his (and their) message about the reign of god.[51] Historically, these events did occur, pretty much as Jesus said they would, which for Wright helps to explain why the Christian movement was able to sustain itself and gain momentum in those early years.

Another implication of Wright's construal of this part of Jesus' message is that it subverts the traditional thinking about how Israel's god would deliver his people from their enemies. Jesus foresaw no holy war through which Israel's god would deliver Jerusalem from the Romans. Rather, as it turns out, Jerusalem and the temple *were* the enemies, and Israel's god would use the Romans to bring judgment upon them.[52] But actually the matter is even more complicated. In a fundamental sense, Israel's real enemy is "the satan and his hordes, who are deceiving Israel into thinking that Rome is the real enemy so that she [Israel] will not notice the reality."[53] Ultimately, the satan must be defeated, and this brings us to consideration of another aspect of Jesus' career—his crucifixion.

Defeat of Enemies

Wright accepts as entirely credible the biblical account that Jesus was crucified as the result of a convergence of Jewish and Roman interests. In the latter case, though, it was primarily a matter of self-interest on the part of one particular Roman, Pontius Pilate. As the Gospels indicate, the governor probably realized that Jesus was not an ordinary sort of revolutionary leader and that he posed no real threat to the empire. He knew the Jewish leaders wanted him dead for other reasons (what he would have regarded as "religious" concerns, not "political" ones), but he caved in to their demands for fear that failure to execute a would-be king could be interpreted as disloyalty to Caesar. Pilate "not only put cynical power-games before justice (that was normal), but also, on this occasion, put naked self-interest before both."[54]

Jewish leaders, Wright thinks, wanted Jesus put to death for the crime of leading Israel astray, a capital offense according to Deuteronomy 13. They viewed him as a false prophet. As such, Wright accepts the biblical record that hostile Pharisees would have wanted Jesus dead even before he came to Jerusalem. His actions in that city, however, particularly the temple incident, sealed his fate. The leaders conducted a hearing at which they hoped he would incriminate himself with regard to Roman law. Apparently, he did so, admitting—or at least refusing to deny—that he viewed himself as a king acting on behalf of Israel's god. Thus, the Jewish leaders could add blasphemy to their charges against Jesus[55] and, more to the point, hand him over to Pilate as a claimant to the throne: "The leaders of the Jewish people were thus able to present Jesus to Pilate as a seditious trouble-maker; to their Jewish contemporaries (and later generations of rabbinic Judaism) as a false prophet and a blasphemer, leading Israel astray; and to themselves as a dangerous political nuisance. On all counts, he had to die."[56]

Wright also considers the death of Jesus from another angle, as a symbolic action that can be understood within the context of Jesus' message and work. In contrast to most other historical scholars (with notable exceptions such as Albert Schweitzer), Wright thinks that Jesus' death might have been part of his plan. Sanders, we have seen, thinks the notion that Jesus sought to orchestrate his own death amounts to a presentation of him as "weird."[57] But Wright notes that what might seem weird to a comfortable, modern Western scholar would not be regarded as such within the worldview of first-century Judaism. Jesus is described as referring to death as his purpose or destiny numerous times and in a wide variety of ways. Aside from explicit predictions (such as Mark 8:31), there are parables (Mark 12:1–12) and riddle sayings ascribed to material from various sources (Matt. 23:37–39; Luke 23:27–31). He describes a baptism that he must undergo (Luke 12:49–50) and a cup that he must drink (Mark 10:38–40), he speaks of being anointed beforehand for his burial (Mark 14:3–9; John 12:1–8), and he eats a "last supper" with his disciples. In short, a rich theme throughout much of the tradition holds that Jesus believed death was his vocation; he was *supposed* to die and somehow his death would serve to accomplish the redemption of Israel.[58]

Wright tries to figure out how such a concept would fit with Jesus' message as described above. First, he relates it to the notion of "messianic woes." There was a widespread conviction among Jews of this period that the deliverance from exile would be accompanied by intense suffering.[59] The suffering of individual righteous persons could be interpreted within this framework; prophets would suffer for the truth that they spoke and a true king would be willing to share the suffering of his people. A number of scripture texts from Daniel, Psalms, Zechariah, Ezekiel, and especially Isaiah 40–55 could be (and were) interpreted as expressive of such suffering. Wright theorizes that, informed by such scripture, Jesus believed he was called to suffer as the representative of Israel, to take upon himself the divine wrath that must conclude the exile. The thinking seems to have been that this would somehow hasten the moment when Israel's tribulation would be complete. Based on his understanding of scripture, Jesus decided that his vocation was to assume the fate of Israel in exile and to undergo symbolically the fate that he had announced for Jerusalem as a whole. The wrath of god against Israel (appropriate for her sins) would be spent, and judgment would remain only for those who had excluded themselves from the Israel that he had constituted around himself. In other words, "Jesus intended that his death should in some sense function sacrificially."[60] Such a construal, Wright contends, meets the double criteria of similarity and dissimilarity. It derives from Jewish interpretation of Hebrew scripture *and* explains the development of Christian atonement theology, but it is not identical to either.[61]

Wright expands this proposal to include the notion of conflict and the defeat of enemies. Jesus identified the true enemy of Israel as the satan. He also taught his disciples that the victory of god will come not through armed resistance but by going the second mile and turning the other cheek. "Fighting the battle of the kingdom with the enemy's weapons meant that one had already lost it in principle, and would soon lose it, and lose it terribly, in practice."[62] Granted this, Jesus could overcome the satan only by allowing himself to be overcome. The only way to defeat evil, he had taught, was to allow it to do its worst. This he intended to do by bearing his cross, going to an unjust death without insults or threats, suffering either in silence or with words of forgiveness. This, Wright says, was "a startling innovation in the martyr tradition," one that sent echoes throughout early Christianity.[63] Normally, "followers of a Messiah who was crucified knew beyond question that they had backed the wrong horse," but somehow "the earliest Christians regarded Jesus' achievement on the cross as the decisive victory over evil."[64]

Return of the King

One more element remains. The Jewish hope was not only that the exile would end and Israel's enemies be defeated. This would count for little unless their god returned to dwell with them. Jesus, according to Wright, "was not content to announce that YHWH was returning to Zion. He intended to enact, symbolize and personify that climactic event."[65]

He spoke of it first in parables. We have already seen that Wright does not think Jesus predicted his own return to earth from heaven in clouds of glory. The texts that seem to refer to such an event he thinks describe a trip in the opposite direction—a coming of the vindicated Son of Man from earth to heaven. If this is so, then, what of the parables that Christians usually interpret with reference to Jesus' second coming? Are they all creations of the early church? Wright accepts their authenticity but thinks the subject of these parables is not Jesus' own return but the return of YHWH, Israel's god. The famous story of the talents or pounds (Matt. 25:14–30; Luke 19:11–27), for instance, speaks of a master or king returning after a time of absence to reward his faithful servants and punish the unfaithful ones. According to Wright, through this parable and others like it, Jesus was announcing that YHWH was returning to Zion while also warning that this return would bring judgment as well as blessing.[66]

Jesus also dramatized this return of God through the acted parable of his own journey to Jerusalem. He rode into the city on a donkey, an image the prophet Zechariah had used to describe the coming of Israel' s god as an offer of peace. He enacted, symbolically, a judgment upon the temple, such as Jesus had said Israel's god would do. He summoned those who represented the true Israel to participate in a banquet replete with eschatological and messianic overtones. All these elements indicate to Wright that Jesus "saw his journey to Jerusalem as the symbol and embodiment of YHWH's return to Zion."[67] The word *embodiment* is key here. Jesus, in Wright's view, did not think his actions were but one more symbolic representation of what Israel's god would someday do. Rather, through Jesus' actions, it was actually taking place: "As [Jesus] was riding over the Mount of Olives, celebrating the coming kingdom, and warning Jerusalem that it would mean judgment for those who rejected him and his way of peace, so YHWH was returning to his people, his city, and his Temple."[68]

The Mindset of Jesus

Wright goes beyond most historical studies of Jesus in an effort to reconstruct not only what Jesus said and did, but what he believed. He does not attempt to analyze Jesus from a psychologist's point of view, suggesting ulterior motives or subconscious complexes that might have driven him to be what he was. Rather, he tries to discern the historical aims and intentions of Jesus and, on the basis of these, to hypothesize what Jesus thought about his world, his god, and himself.

By way of summary, we may indicate how Wright thinks Jesus would have answered the five basic questions of worldview mentioned above (page 204):[69]

> *Who are we?* The people of Israel, chosen by god not for our own sake, but for the sake of the world.

Where are we? In exile, still, but soon to be released.

What's wrong? The satan has made its home in Israel, taken over the temple, and deceived the people into embracing an idolatrous nationalism.

What's the solution? Israel's god will at last become king through Jesus' own life and work, and, indeed, through his death—an ultimate act of obedience by which the satan will be defeated.

What time is it? Time to recognize *now* that these things are happening and to begin to live as the restored people of God.

Beyond all this, however, Wright also tries to get at what Witherington has provocatively called "the christology of Jesus." "Jesus applied to himself the three central aspects of his own prophetic kingdom announcement: the return from exile, the defeat of evil, and the return of YHWH to Zion."[70] Who, then, did Jesus think he was? Wright answers that he thought he was the Messiah. He "saw himself as the leader and focal point of the true, returning-from-exile Israel" and as the king through whose work Israel's god was bringing about this restoration.[71] In these terms, which are compatible with first-century Jewish messianic expectation, he would have accepted the designation Messiah and applied it to himself. Wright finds evidence that he did so in certain sayings (which he regards as "royal riddles") and, especially, in actions associated with the last week of Jesus' life. The entry to Jerusalem was staged with messianic overtones, the final meal with his disciples was presented as a messianic banquet, and the trial before Caiaphas focused on messianic claims. Indeed, "if Jesus did *not* want to be thought of in any way as Messiah, the Entry and the action in the Temple were extremely unwise things to undertake."[72] To assert that Jesus presented himself as the Messiah explains why he would have been charged with blasphemy by the Jews and executed as a royal pretender by the Romans. Wright grants, however, that Jesus was in some ways redefining the concept of Messiah even as he embraced it. As Messiah, he thought that he was Israel's rightful king but he defined that role in terms of his own understanding of the kingdom of god. Another way of answering this question, then, would be to affirm that Jesus thought he was "Israel-in-person, Israel's representative, the one in whom Israel's destiny was reaching its climax." For that, Wright says, is what Jesus believed it meant to be Messiah.[73]

There is still more. Jesus, as Wright depicts him, was one who spoke and acted for the god of Israel. We see this, first, in his offer of forgiveness. Such a practice had the effect, Wright says, of "a private individual approaching a prisoner in jail and offering him a royal pardon, signed by himself."[74] Jesus took upon himself to offer what only god could grant. Even more important are those scenes at the end of his life in which he appears to have maintained that his visit to Jerusalem fulfilled the hopes of Israel regarding the return of her god. In all, Jesus seems to have applied to himself numerous categories traditionally reserved for YHWH. He spoke of himself as "the bridegroom" and invoked for himself the image of a shepherd, both images that scripture used for Israel's god. He spoke of himself as the new lawgiver, giving new instructions to his followers as YHWH did to Moses. He "acted as if he thought he were the reality to which the Temple pointed . . . as if he were in some sense the replacement for Torah . . . the spokesman of the divine Wisdom."[75] In calling followers to abandon possessions and family to follow him, he indicated that "loyalty to Israel's god, astonishingly, would now take the form of loyalty to Jesus."[76]

What are we to make of this? It fits, Wright says, as the middle element between certain aspects of first-century Judaism and early Christian theology. Some texts of scripture (Ezekiel 1, Daniel 7) seem to have been interpreted as indicating that "when YHWH acted in history, the agent through whom he acted would be vindicated, exalted, and honoured in a quite unprecedented manner."[77] This figure, who might be identified with the Messiah, would in fact be allowed to share the throne of Israel's god. The fact that Jesus saw himself and was seen by his followers as assuming such a role also fits with the indisputable fact that early, monotheistic Christians worshiped him as divine. Did Jesus think he was God? Or a god? Wright does not engage that question, on those terms. But he does claim that the historical Jesus "believed he had to do and be, for Israel and the world, that which according to scripture only YHWH himself could do and be."[78] This is why Christians came to call him God. And if Jesus really did believe that he was doing what only God could do, then why should he "not also come to hold the strange and risky belief that the one true God, the God of Israel, was somehow present and active in him and even *as* him?"[79]

The Resurrection of God's Son

Wright's book on the resurrection of Jesus is over eight hundred pages long and treats a number of topics, including diverse beliefs about resurrection and life and death at the time of Jesus (among Egyptians, Romans, Greeks, Jews, and others) and the apparent beliefs of early Christians as reflected in the writings of Paul and other authors. The essential purpose of the book, however, is to address the question of what actually happened at Easter, and everything else (much of which initially seems tangential) is ultimately pressed into service to that question. The basic thesis of the book is as follows: the early Christians embraced an understanding of resurrection that was compatible with a particular Jewish view but that also modified that view in key respects. This very specific "modified Jewish view" was apparently embraced by Christians in a manner that was early and virtually unanimous. Such a development requires historical explanation, and the most likely proposal to account for the development is that these Christians had been surprised by something that they believed had happened to Jesus, something that caused them to rethink their inherited understanding of resurrection.[80] And the grand conclusion is "that the best historical explanation is the one which inevitably raises all kinds of theological questions: the tomb was indeed empty, and Jesus was indeed seen alive, because he was truly raised from the dead."[81]

We can elucidate this thesis in a bit more detail. Wright notes that, although many of the ancients believed in some form of disembodied life after death, the

Gentile world did not believe in any sort of resurrection that would involve a return to bodily existence.[82] Such a hope did develop within the Jewish world, however, where some believed that Israel's god would someday raise the bodies of the dead to new life. There was diversity of opinion regarding such a phenomenon (the Sadducees famously denying it altogether), but everyone agreed that such a resurrection would constitute, in Wright's words, "life *after* 'life after death'"; e.g., "life after death" might involve habitation in the realm of Sheol, but resurrection (understood as restoration to bodily existence) would come after that.[83] This belief seems to have developed out of, and been related to, prophetic announcements regarding the restoration of Israel: "the earlier national hope transmutes, but perfectly comprehensibly, into the hope that Israel's god will do for a human being what Israel always hoped he would do for the nation as a whole."[84] In any case, for Second Temple Judaism, resurrection (whether one believed it would happen or not) was not synonymous with "going to heaven" or with achieving immortality as some sort of disembodied soul. It was a return to bodily, earthly existence.[85]

Wright locates early Christian belief at the Pharisaic end of the Jewish spectrum. Those who have died are currently in some sort of temporary resting place ("asleep"), but they will someday be raised bodily from the dead by the power of the creator. Yet four modifications of such an understanding become immediately evident among Christians: (1) belief in resurrection becomes vastly more important, moving from the circumference of faith to its center; (2) the resurrection is suddenly understood as a two-stage event: the Messiah is to be raised bodily from the dead (indeed, this has already happened) as a proleptic guarantee of a general resurrection that will occur later; (3) resurrection is no longer understood simply as a resuscitation of dead bodies but as a dramatic transformation of those bodies into something "transphysical"; and (4) resurrection language comes to be appropriated metaphorically for such matters as baptism and holiness rather than for the national restoration of Israel.[86] In a later summary of his work, he would expand this list to "six Christian mutations with first-century Jewish resurrection belief"; the two additional elements were (1) there was no spectrum of belief in early Christianity concerning what happens after death, as there had been in Judaism; and (2) Christians made the resurrection a key element in their demonstration that Jesus was the Messiah, even though no one had previously expected the Messiah to be raised from the dead.[87]

Wright emphasizes that these modifications strike the historian as sufficiently unexpected to demand some sort of overarching explanation. Why would Christians, across the board, come to believe God's eschatological timetable involved a proleptic resurrection of the messiah, when such a view was unprecedented in Judaism and was certainly not required by any usual understanding of scripture? Wright suggests that Christians developed this view in response to what they were certain had happened to Jesus—they had been taken by surprise by his resurrection and were forced to reexamine scripture and rethink their (Jewish) understanding of God's timetable accordingly.[88] And where did Paul get his peculiar (and, again, unprecedented) notion that the dead would be raised with "spiritual bodies" as opposed to "soulish bodies" (*sōma pneumatikon* not *sōma psychikon*, 1 Cor. 15:44)? Wright suggests that Christians came to such an understanding because of the unanticipated transphysicality they were certain had characterized the risen body of Jesus.[89]

As a historian, Wright reaches conclusions both modest and daring. The modest conclusion, toward which the overall thrust of the book seems to be directed, is that the early Christians believed that Jesus had been raised from the dead in a literal and corporeal (though transphysical) sense. Thus, Wright wants to dispense with popular proposals of liberal theology that claim the New Testament authors themselves (especially Paul) merely believed that Jesus had gone to heaven to live with God or continued to be present in the kerygma of the church. The more daring conclusion comes with Wright's suggestion that a historian might conclude on the basis of historical evidence that the early Christians were correct in their belief that Jesus had been literally raised from the dead: "The proposal that Jesus was bodily raised from the dead possesses unrivaled power to explain the historical data at the heart of early Christianity."[90] Specifically, the twin facts that Jesus' tomb was empty *and* that he appeared alive to his followers on numerous occasions in a transphysical state provide the necessary and sufficient conditions for the universal emergence of distinctive elements of Christian belief that cannot otherwise be explained.[91] Of course, Wright realizes that a post-Enlightenment paradigm for reality does not allow for something like the resurrection of Jesus to occur, but he suggests that this paradigm is limited to understanding history in an ordinary sense; it is, by definition, unable to fathom the unprecedented. The problem is "not that science has disproved Easter, but that Easter challenges the social and political pretensions of modernism."[92] Further, the fact that dead people do not ordinarily rise is not a recent discovery but was universally known and strongly believed by the persons who nevertheless maintained that something unprecedented had occurred with Jesus. Thus, "the fact that Jesus' resurrection was, and remains, without analogy, is not an objection to the early Christian claim. It is part of the claim itself."[93]

CRITIQUE OF WRIGHT'S STUDY OF JESUS

Criticism of Wright's work begins with complaints about his basic methodological approach and, indeed, his construal of the historical task. As with most scholars discussed in this book, certain decisions that Wright makes cause him to lose the support of some scholars at the outset. His decision that the Gospel of Thomas belongs to a later, derivative stage of the tradition is a feature he shares with many but not all scholars. Beyond this, Wright appears to treat almost all the material in the Synoptic Gospels as though it is on an equal footing. Marcus Borg complains that "he can treat material found in only one source as equally eligible for inclusion in an overall reconstruction of Jesus."[94] In this regard, Wright is the mirror opposite of Crossan, who develops an elaborate hierarchy for weighing the relative value of different sources. But he also differs markedly from Meier, a scholar with whom he would be more theologically compatible. Meier painstakingly checks for multiple attestation of sources, and he chides Wright for employing "a summary style that avoids particular questions about particular verses," a tactic that, for example, allows him to affirm that "Jesus would have said things like" Matthew 5:17–20 without giving any apparent consideration to the fact that what is attributed to Jesus in those verses is attested only in one of the latest strata of source material (M) and is reflective of Matthean redactional tendencies.[95]

With regard to the Gospel of Thomas, Wright is in line with the majority of scholars, but with regard to the Synoptic tradition, Wright himself sometimes becomes the minority voice. Two further examples may suffice. First, Wright accepts the eschatological discourse of Mark 13 as having "a strong claim to go back, in some form or other, to Jesus himself," though he acknowledges that this material is commonly ascribed to the early church.[96] Second, Wright explains differences between common traditions in the Gospels by allowing that Jesus may have spoken on the same topic more than once:

> My guess would be that we have two versions of the great supper parable, two versions of the talents/pounds parable, and two versions of the beatitudes, not because one is adapted from the other, or both from a single common written source, but because these are two out of a dozen or more possible variations that, had one been in Galilee with a tape recorder, one might have "collected."[97]

Most Gospel scholars would not agree with this supposition. Jesus probably did say similar things in somewhat different versions, but most scholars believe the Synoptic Gospels are based on common streams of tradition that in most cases would have preserved only one version.[98] Most scholars do not think that Matthew or Luke would have had access to the numerous versions of the accounts cited above, such as might have been collected fifty years earlier. Rather, most Gospel scholars think that both of these evangelists had access to only one version of these accounts, namely, that preserved in the Q source. Accordingly, the differences in their accounts would not represent independent memories of different original versions but redactional variations on the only version that had been preserved.[99]

We noted in chapter 4 that the Jesus Seminar's emphasis on the criterion of dissimilarity seemed to guarantee a non-Christian Jesus. Wright faults them for this, but his own emphasis on including a maximum amount of data seems to guarantee a biblical Jesus (since, after all, most of the data is found in biblical materials). So, Robert Funk (founder of the Jesus Seminar) dismissed Wright as representative of "pretend questers," who are not trying to discover what is historical about Jesus but "are really conducting a search for historical evidence to support claims made on behalf of creedal Christianity and the canonical gospels."[100]

More precisely, Wright's intention to include the maximum amount of data that fits with his hypothesis of Jesus as an eschatological figure seems to guarantee an image of Jesus similar to that presented in the Synoptic Gospels, since these are the writings that attribute eschatological and apocalyptic language to Jesus (the Gospel of John and the Gospel of Thomas do not). Wright wants to present the general reliability of the Synoptic tradition as a result rather than a presupposition of his work, but to those who have challenged the reliability of that tradition (Mack, Funk, Crossan), it does not appear that way. To them, Wright's work may seem almost reactionary, a throwback to Jesus scholarship of another era before the gains of source criticism. The problem of constructing a portrait that includes a maximum amount of data, these scholars aver, is that much of the data is late and unreliable. A portrait based on the data in Q (or even, for some, an early recension of Q) yields a portrait of the historical Jesus; one that incorporates "most of the data" provides a composite portrait of Christian Christology.[101]

This criticism, of course, reflects the climate of post-Wrede skepticism described in the first chapter of this book (see pages 26–27). Wright denounces that climate as tendentious and simplistic, setting the study of Jesus into a context that would not apply for most historians working in most other fields.[102] Nevertheless, it remains part of the context in which his work gets evaluated. Wright contends that there are two basic streams in Jesus research, one harking back to the "thoroughgoing skepticism" of Wrede, and the other to the "thoroughgoing eschatology" of Schweitzer: "Do we know rather little about Jesus, with the gospels offering us a largely misleading portrait (Wrede)? Or was Jesus an apocalyptic Jewish prophet, with the gospels reflecting, within their own contexts, a good deal about his proclamation of the kingdom (Schweitzer)?"[103]

In short, if one determines to understand Jesus eschatologically, one will get a historically plausible reading of the Synoptic tradition. Wright views this as a mark of the success of the eschatological hypothesis. But those who do not view Jesus eschatologically see that hypothesis as a means of asserting the reliability of a tradition that is more representative of Christian theology than historical reporting. Indeed, that charge has even been leveled against Wright by John Meier, who would be allied with Wright in rejecting Wrede's "thoroughgoing skepticism" and in viewing Jesus as an eschatological Jewish prophet. Meier says that the "important work of N. T. Wright" represents historically informed Christology rather than historical study of Jesus per se. According to Meier, *Jesus and the Victory of God* is "not an example of the quest for the historical Jesus as such, but rather a prime example of how one goes about appropriating results of the quest for a larger theological/christological project."[104]

In response, two points can be noted. First, Wright reacts forcefully against the tendency in scholarship to attribute theological ideas to the authors of the

Gospels rather than to Jesus himself. In much scholarship, he complains, it seems that "Jesus must remain an unreflective, instinctive, simplistic person, who never thought through what he was doing."[105] This, he maintains, is intrinsically unlikely. We are on surer ground when we assume that the great ideas (including christological conceptions) that underscore the various Gospels go back to Jesus himself. The church revered Jesus, not Matthew, Mark, or Luke as the originator of its faith and, "the authors of at least the synoptic gospels . . . intended to write about Jesus, not just about their own churches and theology.[106] Second, Wright does employ a *double* criterion that demands dissimilarity as well as similarity. Hypothetically, at least, this should acquit him of sneaking in some sort of conservative confessionalism under the guise of historical scholarship. In fact, his portrait of Jesus differs significantly in some ways from that of confessional Christianity. For instance, while Wright does attribute the material in Mark 13 to the historical Jesus, he also interprets it such that Jesus is not talking about his own second coming, as the church has usually thought.

The proposal of this double criterion may well be Wright's most enduring contribution to the methodological enterprise. To many critics, it simply makes sense to say that while authentic material may be distinctive, it also ought to exhibit a logical connection to what preceded it and derived from it. It will be difficult in the future for any historian to present a portrait of Jesus that differs radically from what is in the Gospels without at least accounting for that discrepancy. Simply to say, "the church misrepresented Jesus" with regard to any and all matters congruent with Christianity will no longer do. But even as Wright's double criterion is being applauded as a hedge against those who would abuse the criterion of dissimilarity, Wright himself is being viewed as one who may have overcompensated to err on the side of similarity. Still, it may be too soon to tell whether this is actually the case. Wright's Jesus book is but volume two of a six-volume work. Subsequent volumes will address the development of Jesus' ideas in the early church, and further instances of dissimilarity may surface.

Beyond the concerns with method, a few specific points in Wright's proposal have been contested. Maurice Casey argues against the interpretation of Daniel 7 as involving an ascent rather than descent of the Son of Man.[107] The latter interpretation provides the basis for Wright's controversial claim that the Gospels present Jesus as predicting only that he will be vindicated after death, not that he will return to earth. Witherington echoes Casey's argument and notes that Paul appears to have understood both Daniel and Jesus as predicting a future descent of the Son of Man (1 Thess. 4:16–17).[108] And Allison wonders why the early church would have been troubled by the failure of prophecies to come true if those prophecies referred (sometimes metaphorically or spiritually) to events that had already taken place.[109] Nor does Allison find credible Wright's supposition that Jesus spoke words of judgment with *two* eschatological horizons in view, an imminent one involving destruction of the temple and a long-range one involving more universal judgment.[110] Indeed, Allison deems Wright's notion that Jesus meant all his end-time projections metaphorically so ridiculous that he resorts to uncharacteristic mockery: "I fancy that had Wright stood amid Noah's audience and been warned of the flood about to pour forth upon the earth, our exegete might have commended the righteous herald for his apt metaphor but would, to his own fatality, not have bothered to check the weather."[111]

Other criticisms focus on elements of Wright's representation of first-century Judaism. First, as we have seen, Wright believes the heart of Jesus' controversy with the Pharisees concerned his rejection of their policies that would increase alienation from the Gentile environment and lead ultimately to war with Rome. But were the Pharisees really revolutionaries? Wright argues that the Shammaite Pharisees were, and that this sect was dominant. On this, he has the support of a number of scholars, but the issue is debated. Both Jacob Neusner and E. P. Sanders, though differing widely on other points, would present the Pharisees as devoted almost exclusively to religious pursuits, not political ones.[112]

Second, Wright's claim that Jesus relaxed or challenged the purity regulations that were otherwise in force in pre-70 CE Palestine does not meet with universal acceptance. Both Sanders and Meier maintain (as do many scholars) that the Gospel stories portraying Jesus doing this reflect the later interests of a Christian church involved in ministry to Gentiles (see above 167–68, 193–94).[113] Some of the stories, such as the disputes over ritual hand washing (Mark 7:1–8) or Sabbath regulations (Mark 2:23–28) are strongly reflective of later Christian-Jewish controversies; others, such as the account of Jesus declaring "all foods clean" (Mark 7:19), seem incompatible with the fact that generations of Christians continued to debate what followers of Jesus should believe on these issues: if Jesus had actually commented on such a matter, why wouldn't that have settled it? Further, Paula Fredriksen and Amy-Jill Levine both argue, as Jewish scholars, that the Gospel stories portraying Jesus involved in these disputes misrepresent Jewish practices in a way that discredits their historicity: Jesus would not have argued with the Pharisees in the way these stories suggest because the Pharisees would not have actually made the arguments the stories present them as making.[114] On this question, compare the discussion of Marcus Borg's position on pages 150–51, 154–55 above (and note the suggestion of Tom Kazen).

Third, and potentially more damaging to the program, Wright's insistence that most first-century Jews thought of themselves as being still in exile is regarded as "most dubious" by James D. G. Dunn. He suggests that this might have been true for diaspora Jews (those living outside of Palestine) but thinks there is little evidence that the Essenes at Qumran or, for that matter, Paul thought in such a fashion.[115] In any case, he claims that Wright exaggerates the importance of the theme, since return from exile would be (at most) only one of several features of Jewish expectation evident in the teaching of Jesus: others features would

include removal of disabilities and defects, imagery of a great feast, an eschatological pilgrimage of the nations, the meek inheriting the land, suffering, the
defeat of Satan, and final judgment."[116] According to Dunn, Wright fails to
demonstrate that the narrative of return from exile was a "controlling factor"
in the teaching of Jesus[117] and when it is treated as such, individual passages
are misconstrued: the metanarrative of Israel in exile becomes a "hermeneutical
echo chamber" in which "various sayings and stories about Jesus resonate with
a meaning hardly evident on the face of the text."[118] The same critique may
also apply to the attention Wright plays to YHWH's return to Zion: the thesis
that this was a major factor in persuading Jesus to go up to Jerusalem—much
less that Jesus saw his journey to Jerusalem as itself enacting YHWH's return to
Zion—would "be more persuasive if the echoes were stronger, clearer, and more
persistent."[119]

Other scholars, however, have endorsed Wright's "end of exile" thesis and
sought to build upon it. In an important and carefully researched book on the
origins of Christian atonement theory, Brant Pitre argues that the historical
Jesus spoke and acted in light of a widespread expectation that a Great Tribulation would precede the final end of exile for the twelve tribes of Israel. Jesus
intended to set this Great Tribulation into motion, and he thought his own
death would end the exile and usher in the kingdom of God.[120] Even Pitre wants
to correct Wright on certain points however: he claims that first-century Jews
(whether they were living in the land or not) were awaiting the end of the *Assyrian* exile, which could only be fulfilled by the return of the ten northern tribes.
Thus, the significant factor had less to do with subjection of foreigners in the
land or return of YHWH to Zion than with the geographical displacement and
captivity outside the land.[121]

In any case, some readers of Wright's work are more troubled by his insistence that Jewish authorities were primarily responsible for the crucifixion of
Jesus. The trend in scholarship has been toward disassociation with Christian
condemnations of Jews for killing Jesus, often by placing the onus for Jesus'
death on the Romans. Wright sees his view as an alternative to two typical
ideas, that Jesus was executed either as a political figure who offended the
Romans or as a religious leader whose ideas were unpopular with Jews. Wright
envisions a *political* Jesus who offended *Jews.*[122] But, whatever the motives,
Jewish leaders were involved: according to Wright, the Romans did crucify
thousands of people in the first century but the situation of Jesus was unique
in that he was actually handed over to the Romans by Jewish authorities.
Sanders would basically agree with Wright on this point, but many contemporary scholars would not. Many would hold the Roman authorities exclusively responsible for Jesus' death, supposing that the Gospels' attribution of
responsibility for that death to the Jews is a result of post-Easter anti-Jewish
propaganda (and even Sanders would contest Wright's contention that the
Pharisees with whom Jesus sparred in Galilee would have wanted him killed).
But Wright suggests that "blaming the Romans" is an easy move to make,

since there is no antidefamation league operating on behalf of Romans today. The post-Holocaust tendency to deny any Jewish involvement in the execution of Jesus may represent a well-intentioned effort to refute claims that were tragically misused to justify centuries of violence and hostility against the Jewish people, but, Wright maintains, modern sensibilities cannot be allowed to determine the writing of history.[123] And, clearly, the significant point is not to establish who should get the blame. Rather, we need to define Jesus' relationship with Judaism—and if Jesus *was* handed over to the Romans by Jewish authorities (as Wright thinks the evidence indicates), that fact is highly significant for understanding Jesus' place within Judaism. Basically, such an unprecedented and startling action on the part of those authorities speaks volumes about just how subversive Jesus' retelling of the Jewish story must have been, how dangerous it was to those who preferred an alternative narrative.

Finally, Wright's audacious claim that the resurrection of Jesus may be regarded by historians as an actual historical event has found little support among scholars who are not ideologically disposed to favor such a view.[124] Crossan complains primarily about Wright's focus on resurrection as a "literal" event. He suggests that the innovations of Christian faith that Wright enumerates could be explained if the early believers had apparitions of Jesus following his death and also continued to experience the presence of the kingdom that he had proclaimed. They would conclude that he had been raised from the dead in some way that was both unique and "real" but not necessarily what we would call "literal" (i.e., in a manner involving a departure from the tomb that could have been photographed with a camera).[125] More generally, scholars will simply note that all the mutations in resurrection belief noted by Wright can be explained by the early Christians *believing* that Jesus' tomb was empty and that they had seen him alive after the crucifixion. The real question, then, is whether there are explanations for why early Christians might have believed these things even if Jesus had not actually been raised. Wright dismisses alternative explanations as implausible, but many historians would wonder whether proposing that a man was literally raised from the dead in an unprecedented fashion should not qualify as *more* implausible. To take just one example, Wright dismisses with a single footnote the idea that Jesus might have been placed in the tomb unconscious and then later recovered, leaving the tomb empty and subsequently appearing to his disciples in a somewhat altered condition. Such a suggestion is implausible, Wright maintains, because the Romans were very good at killing people and at making sure they were dead.[126] Without questioning that contention, many historians might still think that it is more likely that some Roman soldiers botched their job just once than that a man dead for three days was bodily raised as the first individual ever to experience "life *after* 'life after death.'"

We may conclude this chapter by noting that Wright has faced one challenge unique to scholars discussed in this book: as both a Bishop of the Anglican Church and a prominent academician, he has been expected to fulfill expectations appropriate to both intellectual and ecclesiastical leadership. Different sorts of critics have accused him of skimping on one or the other set of expectations for the benefit of the other. Noting that "we British don't like talking about ourselves in public," he nevertheless waxed autobiographical on this topic in an address to Christian students one winter day in Chicago:

> I have had a very clear vocation that has resulted in some very unclear choices. I live in a world that has done its best, since the Enlightenment, to separate the church from the academy. I believe passionately that this is deeply dehumanizing in both directions, and I have lived my adult life with a foot on both sides of the divide, often misunderstood by both. I live in a world where Christian devotion and evangelical piety have been highly suspicious and sometimes implacably opposed to serious historical work on the New Testament, and vice versa. I believe passionately that this is deeply destructive of the gospel, and I have done my best to preach and to pray as a serious historian and to do my historical work as a serious preacher and pray-er. This has resulted in some fellow historians calling me a fundamentalist and some fellow-believers calling me a compromised pseudo-liberal. The irony does not make it any less painful.[127]

Chapter 10

The Quest Continues:
Issues and Concerns

I'm not in that academic, seminary-trained world, and I think my faith is strong enough that the debate going on in that world doesn't frighten me. . . . I trust in the staying power of Christianity. Some really goofy things have happened in the past 2,000 years, but somehow, the core, the essence of the Christian religion, has survived.

—Gene Janssen[1]

I realize much of what we know about Jesus is novelistic, but I act as if it isn't.

—Peter A. Bien, professor of English at Dartmouth College[2]

You can study the scriptures till your eyes fall out, and without the gift of faith, you're not going to believe Christ was the Son of God. The miracle is faith itself.

—Archbishop John Cardinal O'Connor[3]

Here's what I imagine. If you were in Galilee, let's say in the 30s, you would have seen a person called Jesus. Let's imagine three different people responding to that same person. One says, "This guy's a bore. Let's leave him." The second one says, "This guy's dangerous. Let's kill him." The third one says, "I see God here. Let's follow this guy." Now each of these, in its own way is an act of faith.

—John Dominic Crossan[4]

The quest for the historical Jesus has been in progress for over two hundred years. At certain points, it may have seemed to run out of steam or worn out its welcome, but today the quest is alive and well, pursued with vibrancy and conviction. There are many participants, and the confusion that results from so many voices all speaking at once can disguise the common commitments these scholars share, just as their quibbles over various matters can obscure the large areas of consensus.

This book is a report on a work in progress, a quest that will continue. Many of the scholars surveyed here will continue their work, and other important scholars will also enter the fray. Nevertheless, enough has been done already to warrant this report. We conclude, therefore, with a summary of key issues on which there continues to be discussion and disagreement.

METHOD

The survey undertaken in this book has brought to the fore an ongoing debate over method. Three issues here seem to be paramount.

Sources

The value of the apocryphal Gospels, particularly the Gospel of Thomas, continues to be argued. Some scholars, such as Crossan, treat Thomas as a primary source for their research, while others, including Sanders and Meier, effectively ignore the book. In actuality, however, this disagreement does not usually have far-reaching effects. The material in Thomas that Crossan, the Jesus Seminar, and others have recognized as authentic is almost all material that is paralleled in Mark or (especially) in Q—and scholars who don't put much stock in Thomas usually accept the authenticity of the material found in those parallels anyway. The primary result of viewing Thomas as early and independent of the other Gospels is that this allows for "multiple attestation" of the material found in those parallels, which helps to establish the authenticity of Jesus sayings found in the canonical Gospels (sayings for which authenticity could probably be established on the basis of other criteria anyway). Neither Crossan, the Jesus Seminar, nor anyone else has been wont to accept material in Thomas that is not paralleled in the canonical gospels—with the exception of a couple of parables that add nothing controversial to the historical portrait of Jesus (Thom. 97:1–4; 98:1–3).[5]

The more pressing concern is not whether the Thomas material is accepted but whether it is emphasized or given priority. For example, the material in Thomas that is paralleled in Q (what Crossan calls the Common Sayings Tradition) does not present Jesus as espousing apocalyptic eschatology. There is virtually no controversy among scholars regarding the acceptance of this material, since everyone agrees that Jesus sometimes said nonapocalyptic things. The controversy concerns whether this material should be taken as the primary data base for understanding Jesus (as a nonapocalyptic sage).

Thus, the most significant question concerning sources may be the relative weight given to material found in Q and in Mark. Crossan and the Jesus Seminar regard material in Mark as generally less reliable than the sayings tradition of Q. Most other scholars put the Markan narratives more on a par with Q. Further, Crossan, Mack, and other scholars associated with the Jesus Seminar often operate with some theory regarding recensions in Q, according to which some Q material may be deemed earlier and more reliable than other Q material: the usual conclusion is that sayings that espouse apocalyptic eschatology belong to the later, less reliable layer of material. The majority of Jesus scholars, however, do not make these distinctions.

Finally, the value of material in John continues to be a topic for discussion: Fredriksen, Meier, and Wright (in his later work) are among the minority of scholars who pay ample attention to Johannine material. Most scholars use John only sparingly, if at all—though, the current trend in scholarship seems to favor increased consideration of John.

Criteria

The criterion of dissimilarity, on which all scholars rely, has proved to be controversial. At issue is whether this standard for judgment should be used to exclude data that present Jesus as similar to Palestinian Judaism or to early Christianity, or whether it should be used only to include data that present him as dissimilar. On the one hand, the Jesus Seminar is often said to have applied the criterion in both senses to produce a minimalist portrait of a Jesus who would not have fit easily into either environment. On the other hand, Wright has proposed a new "double criterion of similarity and dissimilarity" that will uncover a Jesus who bridges these two environments.

Distinctions may also be observed with regard to the degree of respect scholars show for what is sometimes called the "criterion of Jesus' rejection and execution." Meier explicitly appeals to such a criterion in that he says no historical portrait of Jesus can be convincing unless it explains why Jesus disturbed and threatened people to the point that he met with a violent and hostile death. But other scholars, such as Burton Mack, reject the logic used to support this criterion: if Jesus' death was attributable to a single incident, its occurrence would shed no light on the potential historicity of any other event that might have provoked animosity. Indeed, Mack proposes that Jesus' death could have been a historical accident.

Approach

Scholars are somewhat divided over the general question of how historical research ought to proceed at a basic level. One major issue to be decided is whether the best approach is to construct a portrait of Jesus that takes into account a maximum amount of potentially historical data concerning him (Wright, Sanders) or to construct a portrait based only on the minimum amount of data that seems to be most reliable (Crossan, Jesus Seminar).

Beyond this is the question of where to begin. One scheme, which we might call the "building block approach," is exemplified by critics as diverse as Meier and the Jesus Seminar. This strategy favors a relatively piecemeal approach to the data, considering the merits of each saying or fact on its own terms and then, finally, attempting to form a hypothesis that accounts for what has been deemed authentic. An alternative strategy, evident in the work of Sanders and Wright, might be called the "dominant paradigm approach." According to this model, scholars begin with an overall hypothesis and interpret the data to see if a reasonable accounting can be offered both for the authenticity of what fits the hypothesis and for the development of what does not fit it.[6] The former strategy appears to be biased against simplicity, and the latter against complexity. In other words, the first approach is at least hypothetically open to discovering the sort of multifaceted portraits of Jesus unveiled by Borg and Meier. The second approach is geared toward discovering a more narrowly focused image of Jesus that is internally consistent with the proposed "dominant paradigm."

Whichever approach is adopted, questions may be raised as to whether the scholars are employing that approach with integrity, whether they are actually doing what they ostensibly claim to be doing (and presumably think that they are doing). Critics of N. T. Wright have sometimes maintained that his faith convictions drive him to accept the historicity of almost everything the canonical Gospels say about Jesus such that he ends up with a far more multifaceted portrait of the historical Jesus than strict adherence to his proposed paradigm would allow. Likewise critics of the Jesus Seminar (including Wright) have maintained that they actually did operate with an unstated hypothesis about Jesus and that this influenced their decisions about the historical authenticity of individual passages: they unwittingly employed the "dominant paradigm" approach while claiming—and probably sincerely believing—that they were using the "building block" approach.

Another fundamental question of approach has been raised by James D. G. Dunn, who thinks that historical Jesus studies has missed the big picture by focusing on analysis of literary sources rather than on understanding the phenomena of memory and oral transmission.[7] Dunn contends that the quest for the "historical" Jesus must in reality be a quest for the "remembered Jesus": the only attainable goal is an understanding of how Jesus was remembered by his earliest followers. This realization means that the historical Jesus cannot be defined as something other than "the Christ of faith," since Jesus himself obviously evoked faith in people and the faith that he evoked "is the surest indication of the historical reality and effect of his mission."[8] Likewise, Anthony Le Donne says, "The historical Jesus is the memorable Jesus; he is the one who . . . set the initial parameters for how his memories were to be interpreted by his contemporaries."[9] So, Dunn encourages historians to "discern Jesus from the impression he left on/in the Jesus tradition."[10]

Furthermore, Dunn proposes that we recognize that prior to the writing of the Gospels (and yet continuing alongside and even after the production of those literary manuscripts) memories of Jesus were preserved primarily through oral tradition:

> What kind of failure in historical imagination could even suggest to us that Matthew only knew the Lord's Prayer because he read it in Q? Or that Luke only knew the words of the Last Supper because he found them in Mark? The alternative explanation positively cries out for consideration: that these were living traditions, living because they were used in regular church assemblies.[11]

Dunn extrapolates what such a recognition means for study of the Gospels. In cultures in which oral tradition functions with a communal dimension, variations do occur (which may sometimes explain divergent Gospel accounts of the same event), but a "stable core" and/or "constant elements" are discernible in all the diverse tellings (e.g., the blind man or men healed by Jesus near Jericho called him "son of David"; Jesus rode an "ass" into Jerusalem).[12] Accordingly, historical Jesus studies should not be obsessed with determining what the earliest written sources said about Jesus or with whether various dictums can be authenticated in accord with established criteria; rather, historical Jesus studies should focus on what was characteristic of Jesus, according to the constant elements in the faith he inspired and in the accounts of things for which he was remembered.[13]

The challenge Dunn poses to traditional historical Jesus studies has not prompted many scholars as yet to reconsider their basic approach to method, with reliance on literary analysis of sources and evaluation of material in light of established criteria. Robert Price says, "It will just not do to remind us in general terms that a great teacher's teaching would have been remembered, since it is equally likely that new teaching may be falsely ascribed to him"; indeed virtually all Gospel scholars, including Dunn regard the material attributed to Jesus in the apocryphal Gospels as spurious.[14] And Crossan claims that Dunn's enterprise "continues the process of historical Jesus research as synoptic theological synthesis";[15] in other words, Dunn is doing a theology of the synoptic Gospels and attributing that theology to Jesus himself. Meier thinks the "great weakness" in Dunn's otherwise important book is that he ascribes to variant storytellers differences in narratives that are clearly reflective of the individual evangelists' contexts, styles, and theologies.[16]

Dale Allison, however, has raised concerns about method that are somewhat compatible with those of Dunn. Allison is much less sanguine than Dunn with regard to the reliability of oral tradition, but he does contend that memory (for all its dysfunctions) handles major themes and characteristics better than details. Thus, historians are on the safest possible grounds when they assume that major emphases of the Jesus tradition were likely to originate with Jesus himself. For Allison, these would include the propositions that Jesus was an eschatological prophet who announced an imminent apocalypse, that Jesus understood his own life and mission as a fulfillment of messianic promises, and that Jesus believed that he was going to die and that his death would play a beneficial role in God's plan. All these points would be contested by many scholars, including Funk, Crossan, and Borg. But, in line with Dunn, Allison says that Jesus is consistently remembered in these ways, and memory tends to get general impressions right, even when it gets the particulars wrong.[17]

JESUS AND JUDAISM

Everyone agrees that Jesus was Jewish, but what sort of a Jew was he and how well did he fit into the Jewish religion of his day? Scholars try to explain both his commitment to Jewish identity and his critique or neglect of certain themes or practices that were significant to at least some Jews in his day. The former may be evident, for instance, in his respect for the Jewish scriptures; the latter, in the mere fact that within a generation his following had developed into a distinct religion. Ben Witherington describes the dilemma this way:

> The difficulty for any historian is in achieving the right balance between Jesus' continuity and discontinuity with early Judaism. Insist on too much discontinuity, and it becomes impossible to explain why Jesus had an exclusively Jewish following during his lifetime and why so many different kinds of Jews were interested in giving him a hearing. Insist on too much continuity, and differences of the church from Judaism, even in the church's earliest days, become very difficult to explain.[18]

The argument is an old one. At the beginning of the twentieth-century, Schweitzer criticized most of the historical Jesus studies that had preceded him for neglecting the Jewish matrix for understanding Jesus on his own terms, but his insistence on doing so seemed to produce a figure so foreign to modern Christians that historical interest in him waned for a time (especially among Protestants). When the New Quest movement recaptured that interest, scholars tended once more to deemphasize aspects of Jesus that were particularly Jewish.

Arguments over this issue are central to Jesus studies today. E. P. Sanders, whose understanding of Jesus is close to that of Schweitzer, insists on a traditionally Jewish Jesus, one so steeped in covenantal nomism and committed to restoration eschatology that he would appear typical for Palestinian Jews of his day. Meier steers away from the word *typical* to call Jesus "a marginal Jew," but he clearly does not mean to suggest that Jesus was "marginally Jewish." Rather, the phrase itself serves as a riddle, posing the questions: How did Jesus relate to Palestinian Judaism, and how was he different from other Palestinian Jews?

The issue is complicated by a wonderful problem that now confronts historians: the wealth of information that has come to the fore concerning first-century Palestine. Archaeological excavations, the discovery of the Dead Sea Scrolls, refinement of social-scientific methods for studying ancient cultures, and other factors have combined to broaden our view of Jesus' world. It was a more diverse world than we once thought. Indeed, most scholars are reluctant to speak of Judaism as a monolithic entity at all during this period. Rather, there were varieties of "Judaisms," developing trajectories, and competing ways of being Jewish. Crossan, for instance, maintains that Jesus was representative of an inclusive stream of Judaism that stood in contradiction to the more conservative (and exclusive) variety that ultimately became identified as rabbinic Judaism. Thus, Crossan's Jesus appears non-Jewish to some only because he differs from what later became the dominant, defining strain of Judaism.

With regard to Jesus as a Jew, at least three perspectives can be discerned among modern historical scholars.

A Hellenistic Jew

Many historians now see Jesus as a Jew who had been deeply influenced by Greco-Roman culture. We know that the influx of this culture was great for the time and place where Jesus lived. Josephus tells us, for instance, that some Jews in Roman Palestine were willing to pay for a surgical procedure that would undo their circumcision (he spares us the details of exactly what this entailed). Apparently, many Jews wanted to be like everyone else, to define their identity with primary reference to the whole human race rather than to a specific ethnic group. Some scholars think that the impact of Hellenism was especially strong in Galilee, noting that Jesus' territory is even called "Galilee of the Gentiles" at one point (Matt. 4:15). They claim, further, that Jesus' hometown of Nazareth was essentially a suburb of the great Roman city Sepphoris, which would have offered Jesus a full panoply of Greek and Roman society, a society where there could have been Cynics but probably not many Pharisees. We need to note, however, that many historical scholars and archaeologists do not accept this description of Galilee as historically accurate.[19]

Scholars who think Jesus may have been heavily influenced by Hellenism include Gerard Downing, Burton Mack, John Dominic Crossan, and the Jesus Seminar. Opponents to this view often accuse them of favoring "a non-Jewish image of Jesus," but that is not accurate. They favor a Hellenistic Jewish image. Jesus was a Jew, yes, but like many Jews in his environment, he had come to have more in common with the Greek philosophers than the Hebrew prophets. The evidence for this view comes largely from the Q source, where a generous portion of the early sayings attributed to Jesus reflect an ethnically generic outlook on life similar to that of the Cynics. As Crossan points out, those sayings are often ones that are paralleled in the Gospel of Thomas which, for scholars who believe Thomas was produced without knowledge of the other Gospels, increases the likelihood of their authenticity.

A Charismatic or Mystical Jew

Another proposal holds that Jesus may be differentiated from other Jews of his day not so much by geographical or cultural affiliations as by spiritual ones. Immersed in a stream of Jewish mysticism, he believed himself to be endowed with the divine Spirit in a way that authenticated his words and deeds apart from the usual structures of authority. This explains why he could consider himself to be faithful to the Jewish religion while other leaders of that religion might consider him hostile or dangerous. The image of Jesus as a "Spirit person" or "holy man" does not cast him in a totally unique mold. It describes him as fitting a paradigm that existed within his culture but which would have granted him a certain ambiguous status within that culture. Geza Vermes, Pieter Craffert, and Marcus Borg are all scholars who have tried to set Jesus within this charismatic or mystical strain of Judaism. Borg also stresses the dichotomy between Jewish peasants and the ruling urban elites in Jesus' society. As a Jewish mystic, Jesus related specifically to the peasant culture, on whose behalf he believed the Spirit of God was moving. The appeal to the Spirit became in essence an invocation of an alternative authority, distinct from the traditional bases of authority that preserved the hierarchy of power favoring the elite. Thus, for Borg, this category of "charismatic Jew" overlaps with that which follows.

A Jewish Prophet

A third possibility distinguishes Jesus from other Jews primarily in terms of his vocation. He believed he was called by God to be a prophet, like the biblical prophets of old. Most who hold this view do not think Jesus was overly hellenized, nor do they find it necessary to place him in a particular stream of Jewish diversity. As a peasant, he and his family remained somewhat oblivious to the allure that foreign culture might have exercised on city folk. They may also have been somewhat oblivious to the controversies that divided educated Jews into sects: Pharisees, Sadducees, Essenes, and the like. Jesus would have been a typical Jew insofar as he embraced the basic elements of that religion as it was practiced by common people: worship, ethics, and a vision of life informed by the stories in the Bible. He became atypical only in his career as a prophet, as he came to a particular understanding of what God wanted to happen and of how this would come to pass. Thus, when Meier calls Jesus "a marginal Jew," he means in part that he was marginalized in the same sense that most Jews who lived in Palestine were at this time. But he also means to suggest that Jesus marginalized himself still further by remaining celibate and adopting a vocation and lifestyle that marked him as odd and eventually aroused hostility. In one way or another, not only Meier but also Sanders, Wright, and Borg hold to this view. They think that, as a prophet, Jesus fit into an established Jewish mold and yet one that by definition would set him apart from other Jews in key respects.

JESUS AND ESCHATOLOGY

One major issue over which historical scholars currently remain divided concerns Jesus' stance toward the future.[20] This concern is closely related to the foregoing discussion because scholars who identify Jesus as a representative of traditional, non-Hellenistic Palestinian Judaism usually tend to emphasize his eschatological vision regarding some sort of imminent divine intervention. Those who construe Jesus as more influenced by Hellenism usually view him as more concerned with present-day consequences than with future judgment, more focused on this world than on the next one, and more interested in the experience of life before death than after death. Borg is an exception, the "bridge" figure who emphasizes Jesus' Jewishness in fairly traditional, non-Hellenistic terms while nevertheless describing his stance as more existentialist than apocalyptic.

Again, this argument is more than a hundred years old. In the early twentieth century, Schweitzer insisted that Jesus must be viewed as a mistaken eschatological prophet, one who went to his death maintaining that God was about to act for the deliverance of Israel in a way that God never did. The New Questers, influenced by their mentor Rudolf Bultmann, emphasized the existential component of Jesus' teaching, often interpreting sayings about the kingdom of God as applicable to life "here and now." For example, Bornkamm took Jesus' message as being about "making the reality of God present."[21] Still, Bornkamm insisted that Jesus' sayings about the kingdom of God had a range of meanings, some present in application and some future. This has been the dominant view in New Testament studies. For recent historical Jesus scholars, the question has become, which group of sayings (present or future) should receive the emphasis? And, more important, which of the sayings should be deemed authentic? Two abruptly diverse perspectives may be discerned.

Participatory or Collaborative Eschatology

A prominent view among recent Jesus scholars has been that Jesus did not expect or announce any imminent divine intervention in history. The Gospel texts that Schweitzer took to be so representative of Jesus' attitude have been understood as developments of the church prompted by such crises as the persecution of Christians and the destruction of the Jerusalem temple. Jesus' interests are taken to have been decidedly this-worldly. The Jesus Seminar, for example, deemed sayings that speak of the kingdom as a future reality to be unauthentic, as well as all sayings that speak of a coming Son of Man or future judgment. In their view, shared by Mack and Crossan, Jesus was primarily a sage, concerned with dispensing advice for making the most of life in this world. Crossan says Jesus spoke of the kingdom of God "not as an apocalyptic event in the imminent future but as a mode of life in the present."[22] Gerald Downing differs only slightly. Rather than denying the authenticity of eschatological sayings, he reinterprets them. Even the

Cynics, Downing maintains, used eschatological language, but they used it in a metaphorical sense, applying imagery of the afterlife to life on earth. Richard Horsley also thinks that Jesus spoke of the kingdom only in present terms, and he construes the phrase "kingdom of God" as a metaphor for a social-political phenomenon.

Whether they view Jesus as a sage or a political activist (or both), these scholars think Jesus' words and his deeds were directed at improving the lot of people in the present. His efforts and his counsel in this regard would have been largely pointless if the world were about to end or if things were so bad that only God could fix them. Scholars who hold to this orientation in their work on Jesus cannot imagine that he ever would have taught his followers to wait for God to put things right. "Simply translated," says Mack, "Jesus' message seems to have been, 'See how it's done? You can do it also.'"[23]

Marcus Borg allows that Jesus may have predicted political crises that would come soon upon Israel, and that he might have used end-of-the-world metaphors for this. He also grants that the phrase "kingdom of God" is a tensive symbol that may have a wide range of meaning (see page 295, n. 78), but he wants to redefine the expectations of Jesus away from imminence. In his early work, Borg maintained that Jesus was therefore " noneschatological," a term also employed for Jesus by the Jesus Seminar (of which Borg was a member). Later, however, he would shift his semantics to say that Jesus favored a "participatory eschatology": Jesus articulated a vision of what God's rule (kingdom) should look like and called people to join him in bringing it to pass. Likewise, Crossan says that Jesus espoused a "collaborative eschatology," which recognizes that the consummation of God's kingdom is dependent upon human action. Such a vision encourages an ethical stance (recognizing and opposing systemic evil in the world) rather than an ascetical or apocalyptic one. Rather than looking for God to act violently in the future to destroy the world, Jesus called God's people to act nonviolently in the present to redeem the world.

In his own survey of historical Jesus studies, Borg noted that the image for Jesus as an eschatological prophet who anticipated some sort of imminent divine intervention was on the way out. That image had dominated scholarship for much of the twentieth century, but Borg maintained (in 1988) that the old consensus to this effect was being replaced by "a growing conviction [that] the mission and message of Jesus were 'noneschatological.'"[24] But this projection proved to be premature: what Borg called "the old view" did not go quietly into the night but, instead, enjoyed a revival.

Imminent and Apocalyptic Eschatology

Many historical scholars think that Jesus had a powerful future orientation with specific ideas about what God was going to do soon. For them this does not remove the need for humans to work for God's will here and now but accentuates it.[25] The day of salvation and judgment is at hand, creating a crisis of decision:

the need to live now as God has always wanted people to live is imperative. These scholars think that the so-called apocalyptic material in the Gospels represents some of the most historically certain tradition. The church did not always know what to make of this material but preserved it because it had been so central to Jesus' message. He claimed that God was about to do something momentous through the Son of Man, something that would change the world forever. Allison, Meier, Sanders, and Wright all follow this line of thought, though they differ on particulars. Even some scholars who emphasize Jesus' role as a sage want to preserve the eschatological element in his teaching. Witherington, for instance, sees no contradiction in seeing Jesus as an eschatological prophet and as a wandering Jewish sage; he affirms the authenticity of material associated with both strains.

Sanders revives Schweitzer's notion that Jesus was mistaken in his view that God was about to establish a heavenly kingdom on earth. Wright, however, insists that Jesus predicted the end of a social world, not the space-time universe, and, further, suggests that Jesus was shown to be right. Sanders also differs from some other scholars in this camp over the authenticity of particular sayings. First, he is less inclined to accept the authenticity of present-oriented kingdom sayings than is Meier, who is more open to affirming the both/and character of present and future kingdom references. Sanders also insists that the sayings in which Jesus predicted events that would occur within the span of his own generation (for example, Mark 9:1; 13:30) must be authentic, whereas Meier attributes all date-setting references to the later church. Meier wants to affirm that Jesus spoke of an imminent divine intervention that would bring in the kingdom without setting specific times for this occurrence. Witherington takes the latter point a step further, insisting that Jesus proclaimed only that the kingdom was *possibly* imminent, not that it was *necessarily* so.

JESUS AND POLITICS

With regard to Jesus' stance toward politics, scholars seem to be moving closer to consensus, such that discussion is not as disparate as it once was. For a time, the issue seemed to be whether Jesus should be viewed as a religious figure (the traditional concept) or as the leader of a political movement. Today, such a dichotomy seems unnecessary, an anachronism imposed, perhaps, by Western scholars reared in societies that pride themselves on (supposedly) being able to separate church and state.[26] Even today, the line between politics and religion in the Mideast can be indistinct, and this was certainly true in Jesus' day as well. Nevertheless, some disparity of perspective among scholars is observable with regard to where they place the emphasis in Jesus' mission and message.

Reimarus is thought by many to have initiated the quest for the historical Jesus with his postmortem publications in the late eighteenth century. He was also the first to challenge the pious assumption that Jesus was primarily a spiritual or religious leader. As Reimarus had it, Jesus was a political claimant who thought that God was going to establish him as the new king of an earthly realm. He was, in effect, a madman, a presentation that served Reimarus's ulterior purpose of discrediting Christianity quite nicely. But even scholars who see through the tendentious aspects of Reimarus's construal often grant that he was on to something. He was able to make his case as well as he did because the Gospel narratives do indeed show Jesus speaking and acting in ways that must have had powerful political implications. Jesus entered a highly charged, politically sensitive environment (Roman-occupied Jerusalem), demonstrated against the principal political institution (the temple), and was subsequently executed by order of the governor, charged with treason or rebellion against the state.

The political dimension of Jesus' life and message would not be emphasized for two hundred years after Reimarus, but in the latter part of the twentieth century, the notion that Jesus was intensely and intentionally political would come to be regarded as the "emerging majority position."[27] Still, there are streams of Jesus scholarship that contend against such a view. First, the image of Jesus as a Jewish sage or (especially) as a Cynic philosopher moves, for some, in another direction. The Jesus Seminar appears to resolve the old question of whether Jesus was motivated by religious or political concerns in the opposite manner of most contemporary scholars; instead of affirming commitment to both spheres, they deny that Jesus had much interest in *either* religion or politics, save to denounce them. But Crossan accepts the Cynic philosopher model for Jesus and still makes considerable room for sociopolitical concerns in his description of Jesus' ideas. Similarly, both Borg and Witherington have no problem wedding the image of Jesus as a Jewish sage with that of a politically oriented prophet.

The diversity that does attend modern analyses of Jesus' relationship to politics reflects disagreement as to his primary goal or orientation. For convenience, I offer here two categories of thought, but we should recognize that these are not necessarily mutually exclusive. Even the terms I use to label them are problematic, deriving from ways of viewing the situation that, as I have indicated, are somewhat outmoded.

Social-Political Liberation

A number of scholars have suggested over the years that Jesus was primarily concerned with liberating Israel from Roman rule. He has been cast in the role of a Zealot or in some other way depicted as a political revolutionary.[28] This view has not fared well of late and, in fact, is not endorsed by any of the scholars we have discussed in this book. In its place have arisen various theories in keeping with Richard Horsley's supposition that Jesus instituted a revolution from the bottom up rather than from the top down. Jesus sought to teach the common people a better way to live, one that did not depend on the disposition of their rulers. As Borg puts it, Jesus "did not seek a position of governmental power or to reform governmental policy," yet he was political in that he "both challenged the existing social order and advocated an alternative."[29] Thus, Borg claims that Jesus challenged the politics of holiness in his day with an unconventional wisdom that gave new priority to compassion. More to the point, he challenged the mindset of the ruling urban elites in a way that offered new vision to the peasant class. Similarly, Crossan believes that Jesus facilitated the reconstitution of peasant communities by demonstrating a shared egalitarianism that defied the unjust system of brokerage. By encouraging and enacting social transformation, Jesus posed a real threat to the political system of his day, indeed, a greater threat ultimately than those who thought they would change society by overthrowing this or that particular tyrant.

Spiritual Renewal

Another view that has not fared well in recent scholarship is the understanding of Jesus as a teacher of timeless spiritual truth that had little to do with the concrete situation in which he worked. In place of this idea, however, many scholars would insist that for Jesus the concern for social justice or political liberation was specifically a religious or spiritual matter. As a preacher and a prophet, he believed that God would establish justice for those who accepted God's rule. Accordingly, he called people to live in accord with God's will and to trust in God for vindication. He sought to inspire a spiritual renewal of faith and obedience among the people of Israel. Sanders and Meier emphasize this aspect to the point that they doubt Jesus was overtly concerned with the reform of existing earthly institutions (which he expected would soon come to an end). But both Meier and Sanders are nevertheless careful to relate Jesus' message to the hopes and aspirations of Israel. They do not, for instance, present him as primarily addressing individuals with regard to how they might personally obtain peace with God. The context for Jesus' ministry concerns the eschatological hope for the kingdom of God, the divine creation of a social order in which righteousness will prevail and the fortunes of Israel will be restored. Wright likewise stresses that Jesus' vision was very political and this-worldly: a transformation of society through which Israel will at last be returned from exile and set free from her enemies. But, Wright adds, this deliverance will be accomplished by God, not Zealots, and the enemy to be defeated is Satan, not the Romans.

JESUS AND THE SUPERNATURAL

Perhaps the thorniest issue of all in historical studies of figures like Jesus is what in common parlance would be called "supernatural" forces or events. The very use of the term *supernatural* raises a host of philosophical problems[30] (some theologians prefer *supranatural*; most don't like either word). Both the term and the concept it describes are anachronistic for Jesus' context, since that world had no concept of "natural law" that could be violated or rescinded.[31] Still, at a basic level the admittedly modern term points us toward what we need to discuss: reports of what would be regarded by many as supernatural occurrences today.

In the Gospel traditions there are, first, miracles—reports of observable events that would have no reasonable explanation according to the laws of nature. The issue here is not just whether events that we would regard as supernatural may have been *perceived* as occurring by people who did not know all the laws of nature; the issue, rather, is whether the historicity of such events can ever be affirmed by modern-day, scientifically informed historians who do typically acknowledge and respect the existence of such "laws of nature." In the nineteenth century, Paulus developed elaborate rational explanations for most of the miracle stories in the Bible: raisings from the dead were actually arousals from comas or "deliverances from premature burial."[32] Renan entertained the notion that some of the miracles were hoaxes, staged events to draw attention to Jesus and his message. Then, Strauss's position became the dominant one: the miracle stories are mythological reports, poetic accounts that used symbolic imagery to convey meaning to a primitive audience that lacked categories for truth that we possess today. Such stories may convey what we would call philosophical truth rather than what we would call historical or scientific fact. The story of Jesus changing water into wine, for example, signifies the transformative impact that his word has on human lives.

This mythological understanding of miracle became best associated with the work of Rudolf Bultmann in the twentieth century. Bultmann sought to "demythologize" the New Testament stories in order to uncover the kernel of existential engagement that each story sought to convey. Such demythologizing is necessary, Bultmann maintained, because the modern worldview does not allow for miracles in a literal sense. John Meier reacts sharply to that assumption in his study of Jesus. In fact, a Gallup poll revealed that in 1989 about 82 percent of Americans surveyed believed that "even today, miracles are performed by the power of God." Thus, as far as Meier is concerned, "the academic creed of 'no modern person can believe in miracles' should be consigned to the dustbin of empirically falsified hypotheses."[33] The fact is that most people, including most well-educated people,[34] including (when he removes his historian's hat) Meier himself, do believe that what are popularly called supernatural events have occurred. Meier suggests that, if the majority of modern people do not view the world in line with what is called "the modern worldview," the accuracy of the latter label must be questioned. Craig Keener presses this point with even more urgency, insisting that this so-called modern worldview is only relevant for (portions of) Western society. What Keener calls "the majority world perspective" is quite different.[35]

Miracle stories may offer the prime example for the problem historians face in dealing with material that refers to the supernatural, but the issue for Jesus studies is actually broader than that particular concern might suggest. The Gospels also contain accounts that may be termed "mythological" because they involve interaction of humans and supernatural beings (that is, beings whose existence has not been confirmed in the world of nature as analyzed through modern science).

The story of Jesus' temptation by Satan in the wilderness (Matt. 4:1–11) provides a good example. The question of whether this is a *historical* event involves consideration of what occurred on a level that would have been empirically observable to neutral bystanders. If a camera crew from a modern television network had been on hand the day that Jesus was tempted in the wilderness, what would they have been able to document regarding his encounter with Satan? Of course, in a sense, any story that assumes the existence of God may be regarded as mythological. Eventually the question becomes whether a historian—speaking *as a historian*—can ever acknowledge the existence or activity of God. Can a historian ever say, "God did this"?

We will delineate three general stances that historical Jesus scholars seem to take with regard to this issue, allowing again for some overlap of positions.

Methodological Neutrality

Most historians adopt a position of official silence when confronted with religious claims concerning anything that might be regarded as supernatural. The principle that undergirds such silence has probably been best articulated by Robert L. Webb, founding editor of the influential *Journal for the Study of the Historical Jesus*. Webb proposes that a principle of "methodological naturalism" allows historians who are persons of faith to set a "definitional limit" for their work that prescinds from making judgments based on ontological presuppositions regarding what is or is not possible in this universe.[36] Basically, Webb says that all historians should play by what he calls "the rules of the game" for historical investigation. The field of historical inquiry should not be closed to persons who believe in divine causation, but such persons need to respect the definitional limits of historical method, which does not recognize appeals to divine causation. The limitation is a methodological one: the historian is free to believe the event was caused by God and to indicate this, but the historian should make clear that such an explanation goes beyond the definitional limits of historical method. Thus, the historian's neutrality with regard to questions involving what are sometimes called supernatural occurrences is only a self-imposed methodological neutrality that applies within a particular discipline:[37] even when the evidence for an event's occurrence is strong and the historian can find no "natural explanation" for the event, the historian must stop and "say that they have gone as far as they can go as a historian using historical method. . . . Argumentation and explanation for 'supernatural' causation, because it is of a different order by its very nature, should be understood within the sphere of theology, which has its own distinct forms of argumentation and evidence."[38]

Further, Webb encourages historians who do *not* believe in divine causation to adopt such methodological neutrality when stating their claims (as historians) as well: historical data is insufficient to sustain the conclusion that a remarkable event lacking any obvious natural explanation was *not* in fact caused by God. Webb invites all historians (but especially those studying Jesus) to adopt "epistemological humility": "neither side can 'prove' their ontological convictions to the satisfaction of the other" and "both ontological views require a form of 'faith'," the validity of which cannot be established through historical research.[39]

Of scholars discussed in this book, John Meier may be the best representative of this position. Despite his just-noted reaction against the Bultmannian description of a "modern worldview," Meier thinks it is "inherently impossible for historians working with empirical evidence within the confines of their own discipline" to attribute anything in history to God. To clarify this, he supposes that two historians, one a Christian and the other an atheist, might both conclude that an event "cannot be explained by any human ability or action, by any known force in the physical universe, or by fraud or self-delusion." Still, the atheist might maintain that "even in the absence of an explanation, I am sure that this is not a miracle." The Christian might decide that "this is a miracle worked by God." In either case, Meier maintains, the judgment is evaluative in a way that cannot be made by a person acting within "his or her capacity as a professional historian."[40] For Meier, historical investigation is a field that "stubbornly restricts itself to empirical evidence and rational deductions or inferences from such evidence."[41] Thus, even though Meier insists that Jesus did things that were considered to be miracles by his contemporaries (both supporters and opponents), he refrains from saying that Jesus did things that historians ought to regard as miracles. Invoking the supernatural is a matter of interpretation that goes beyond historical science.

Post-Enlightenment Denial

Some scholars renounce this "no comment" approach regarding supernatural occurrences as a cop-out. Historical science need not be cowed into supposedly objective silence regarding such matters but has a responsibility to speak. All modern fields of inquiry are dependent on certain presuppositions regarding what is possible and what is impossible: this is the legacy of the Enlightenment, the eighteenth-century movement in Western intellectual thought that established norms for understanding reality in a way that makes critical thinking possible. Since the Enlightenment, the legitimacy of propositions has been evaluated on the basis of logic, reason, and empirical evidence, rather than simply being posited through an appeal to political or religious authorities. No scholar would ever be taken seriously today if he or she rejected post-Enlightenment standards for critical thinking across the board (e.g., respecting the possible accuracy of authoritative statements made by all the world's religions). And, so, there is no valid reason to respect Christian scholars who make an arbitrary exception of "Jesus" or "the Bible." What such scholars regard as methodological neutrality in fact prevents them from going where the evidence would otherwise require them to go. For example, some scholars would maintain that it is a historical fact that the early church invented the story about the virgin birth of Jesus near the end of the first century: historians should investigate why such a story was invented and try to determine what purpose it was intended to serve. But a scholar who believes Jesus actually was born to a virgin will not be prompted to ask those historical questions: even if such a scholar does not claim as a historian that the virgin birth happened, the scholar will be restricted from engaging important questions that should interest any post-Enlightenment historian (who would take for granted that things that are impossible do not occur).

The leaders of the Jesus Seminar tended to endorse this stance, though the membership of that group did not always follow suit. At one meeting of the Seminar, participants were asked to vote on the statement "Mary conceived of the Holy Spirit." After some discussion, they determined to revise the statement to read "The question of whether Mary conceived of the Holy Spirit is a matter that historical science cannot determine." Robert Funk was disappointed with this move. "I think they're just a bunch of cowards," he told the press. "Jesus had a human father."[42]

The Jesus Seminar did decide by a large majority that Jesus' "resurrection" (whatever is meant by that term) did not involve "the resuscitation of a corpse."[43] Gerd Lüdemann, a member of the Seminar who delivered a paper at the meeting where that vote was taken, has written two entire books on this subject. He maintains that the resurrection appearances all have psychological explanations: for Peter, a subjective vision produced by his overwhelming guilt for having denied Jesus when he was arrested; for Paul, the resolution of an unconscious "Christ complex"; for the five hundred followers mentioned in 1 Corinthians 15:6, mass hysteria. For Lüdemann himself, the resurrection is simply "an empty formula" that must be rejected by anyone holding "a scientific world view."[44] Note how this approach is different from the neutrality advocated by Webb and Meier. In keeping with Meier's position, Marcus Borg (also a member of the Jesus Seminar) maintains that "we cannot say, on historical grounds," whether anything happened to the corpse of Jesus.[45] But Lüdemann thinks we *can* say. On historical grounds, he told *Newsweek* magazine, we may affirm that Jesus' body "rotted away" in the tomb.[46] John Dominic Crossan almost agrees, but not quite. Jesus' body, he claims, never made it to the tomb; it was left without burial and devoured by dogs.[47]

Biblical accounts of healing stories, however, are sometimes accepted by scholars who deny the historical reality of other so-called miracles: healings and exorcisms do not necessarily demand that anything supernatural or scientifically impossible occurred. Crossan thinks Jesus healed people by relieving the negative social connotations attached to their physical condition without altering the condition itself.[48] Burton Mack actually translates Jesus' command for his disciples, "Heal the sick," as "Pay attention to the sick."[49] But many of these scholars will also grant the possibility of psychosomatic healings. Exorcisms, in particular, are interpreted this way.[50] Thus, for Crossan (following Morton Smith), Jesus effected some genuine cures by working what the people of his day regarded as a form of folk magic.

We do not know for certain what actually happened, but the cures could probably now be explained from an informed understanding of the interrelationship of mental, emotional, and physiological well-being.

The so-called nature miracles are another matter: these include accounts of Jesus walking on water, controlling the weather, feeding a multitude with a paltry supply of food, and transforming water into wine. Crossan agrees with David Aune's conclusion that these are "creations out of whole cloth by the early church."[51] He also objects on ethical grounds to Meier's attempt to bracket from discussion the historicity of such supernatural events. He questions, for instance, whether Meier *as a historian* would take this stance with regard to reports of figures other than Jesus. Meier says that historians must keep silent regarding whether Jesus was actually born to a virgin. Would he say the same about Caesar Augustus, whose mother is said to have been impregnated by a serpent in the temple of Apollo? Crossan has no trouble stating his own position "as a historian trying to be ethical": "I do not accept the divine conception of *either* Jesus *or* Augustus as factual history."[52]

Scholars who deny the historicity of Jesus' miracles often point out that such miracles are not prominent in Q nor are they ever referred to by Paul. They appear to have become a prominent part of the Jesus story only after the movement initiated by Jesus had been transformed into a mostly Gentile Christian religion, when stories about Jesus were being put into writing for and by people who lived in lands far from where Jesus himself had lived. Mack is the most extreme, claiming not only that Jesus did no miracles but, further, that he was not even thought to have done miracles during his lifetime.

Postmodern Openness

A third perspective on how historians deal with this sort of material involves the allowance for (if not advocacy of) a critique of the traditional paradigm for historical research. In short, some scholars believe it is responsible, as historians, to challenge the strictures of historical-critical method when those strictures do not appear to account for reality. Even Meier agrees that this may be done philosophically, but when historians write history, he thinks they must operate with set principles of empirical research and rational deduction that are standard for those who work within the field (that is, they must accept what Webb would call "methodological" or "definitional" limits). But what Meier calls "the confines of the discipline," some regard as artificially confining. Why should scholars have to impose a particular vision of reality on the evidence when (as even Meier admits may happen) some of the data do not fit neatly into the resultant grid? If there is substantial evidence that reality is not or has not always been the way post-Enlightenment scientific analysis suggests, then that evidence should be allowed to stand in critical disjuncture with historical description rather than being arbitrarily dismissed or ignored. This perspective often draws on postmodernism, which questions all forms of absolutism, including the claim that a post-Enlightenment ("modernist") worldview is to be imposed as normative for intellectual inquiry.

N. T. Wright questions how "scientific" any method can really be if it is not open to having its own presuppositions challenged. "To insist at the beginning of an enquiry . . . that some particular contemporary worldview is the only possible one . . . is to show that all we want to do is to hear the echo of our own voices."[53] He calls for "suspension of judgment," which is not the same thing as maintaining neutrality: "It is prudent, methodologically, to hold back from too hasty a judgment on what is actually possible and what is not within the space-time universe. There are more things in heaven and earth than are dreamed of in post-Enlightenment philosophy."[54] Wright, for instance, dismisses as naive the notion that Jesus' contemporaries were prone to believe in miracles because they did not understand the laws of nature. They did not need modern science to tell them that human beings cannot walk on water. They were not stupid. They knew that five pieces of bread were not enough food to feed five thousand people. For Wright, then, the simplest and best explanation for the widespread report that Jesus worked miracles is that "it was more or less true."[55] Wright seems to think that historians as historians can and should affirm this. If the best historical reconstruction of reality and the best post-Enlightenment scientific description of reality are incongruous, that may be a problem. But why should this problem be solved by requiring the historians to fudge their discipline for the sake of the scientists?

Ben Witherington also raises this issue pointedly. He sees the suggestion that Jesus may have healed people by manipulating presently unknown natural causes as begging the question of why only explanations that are considered "natural" are to be allowed: "Are we to attribute to Jesus a scientific knowledge of cures and *natural* healing principles that have escaped other doctors in the last two thousand years? Is it not easier to believe that perhaps God does intervene in human lives in ways we would call miraculous? In view of how little we know about our universe, do we really know that nothing can happen without a 'natural' cause?"[56]

Likewise, Graham Twelftree, in his extensive study of Jesus as a miracle worker maintains that "there is good evidence and grounds for saying that the historical Jesus not only performed miracles but that he was an extraordinarily powerful healer of unparalleled ability and reputation."[57] Twelftree realizes that those who do not believe in the existence of God will not acknowledge that Jesus' miracles were acts of God but will seek other explanations for them (or simply maintain that they cannot be explained on the basis of current and available knowledge). But atheism is itself a philosophical construct and, apart from the imposition of such a construct, "it is quite reasonable to suppose that miracles are possible."[58]

A sustained critique of what is called "philosophical naturalism" or "antisupernatualism" is also mounted by evangelical Christian scholars, such as Craig Keener. The latter's two-volume book, *Miracles*, seeks to dismantle this epistemological bias, which is largely the legacy of David Hume's limitation of history to that which can be understood as occurring in accord with natural law.[59] Part of Keener's critique includes detailed documentation of miracles that have occurred throughout the world, which leads him to maintain (as indicated above) that anti-supernaturalism is not only a philosophical bias but a distinctively Western one.[60]

As we have seen, Crossan, Funk, Lüdemann, and others would want to know if scholars who accept the miracles of Jesus as historically authentic would be equally generous in admitting to the historical legitimacy of miracles attributed to individuals not associated with the Judeo-Christian tradition. Robert Miller wants scholars who argue for the historical reliability of Gospel miracle stories to explain why similar accounts in books "not about Jesus should be met with sturdy skepticism."[61] Amy-Jill Levine asks, "Why accept the purported 'eyewitness accounts' of the Gospels, but not the 'eyewitness accounts' of the authenticity of the *Book of Mormon* or the miracle of the sun at Fatima?"[62]

Marcus Borg affirms the reality of what he calls the "world of spirit." This world might correlate with what some would regard as a supernatural realm. Borg himself probably does not consider it supernatural, but an often-unrecognized or poorly understood part of nature. Still, he admits that the world of spirit is not visible or tangible, that it cannot be studied in the same way as the visible world, and that it does not necessarily follow what are traditionally called "the laws of nature." With regard to Jesus' miracles, Borg does not want to affirm absolutely that they did occur as historical events, but he is willing to bend the discipline of historical science to allow for that possibility. He says, "We simply do not know if there are limits to the powers of a charismatic mediator."[63] Borg has been a little ambiguous, however, with regard to details. In *Jesus: A New Vision*, he allowed that it remains at least hypothetically possible that power from the spirit world did enable Jesus to walk on water or to resuscitate genuinely dead people.[64] Elsewhere (and later), he said, "In common with the majority of mainline scholars, I see the nature miracles as not historical, but as symbolic narratives."[65] With regard to healings and exorcisms, he is more adamant: it is a historical fact that Jesus performed such acts, and historians should not assume that all these occurrences would have a "natural" explanation. He says, "a psyschosomatic explanation that stretches but does not break the limits of the modern worldview" works for some of the healing stories but "doesn't work as a comprehensive explanation."[66] Likewise, a "psychopathological explanation" for everything that can be documented historically regarding Jesus' exorcisms is possible but "not decisively clear."[67] The clear testimony of our sources is that Jesus' healings were acts of power, and "to attempt to explain *how* these healings happened is beyond our purpose and probably impossible."[68]

THE SELF-CONSCIOUSNESS AND INTENTION OF JESUS

What did Jesus believe about himself? What was he trying to do? What did he hope to accomplish? These questions are related to all the points discussed so far, but by way of summary, we may identify some of the answers that have been given. These answers might be arranged along a continuum that recognizes varying degrees of continuity between the views of Jesus and views that became normative for the early church.

At one end of the spectrum are those scholars who think Jesus saw himself and his mission quite differently than the Christians who later invoked his name. The most extreme viewpoint (again) would probably be that of Burton Mack, for whom the historical Jesus really had no sense of purpose or mission but was essentially aimless.[69] Without going this far, many other scholars—including Crossan, Funk, and Vermes—contrast the historical Jesus with the figure who replaced him in the creeds of Christianity. For them, Jesus was primarily a teacher, and his goal was to teach people a different way of life. In addition, Horsley (followed by Crossan) emphasizes Jesus' political interests and insists that he saw himself fundamentally as a prophet of social change. But all these scholars doubt that Jesus ever viewed himself as the Messiah or that he would have applied exalted titles such as Son of God or Son of Man to himself. Most of them would also doubt that he ever intended for his own death to serve any particular purpose, although Christians within a generation would come to view this as the primary means through which he accomplished his purpose in life (now construed as saving people from sin). Rather, Jesus' crucifixion is understood, at best, as a martyrdom that Jesus was willing to suffer for the sake of his ideas or, at worst, as an unfortunate accident that befell him when he miscalculated the social impact of his actions.

In contrast, Allison, Meier, Witherington, and Wright see far more continuity between Jesus' own perception and goals and those of his later followers. It is quite possible for them that Jesus did come to see himself as the Messiah or at least to believe that he was called to live out prophecies of scripture that were applied to that figure.[70] He saw himself as more than a teacher or social reformer; he believed himself to be an extraordinary prophet who had been sent by God to reveal God's will in a sense that was definitive and authoritative for Israel. Wright's work even suggests that Jesus believed he was called to do and be what only God could do and be, establishing a major point of continuity between Jesus' historical self-consciousness and the church's confession of him as divine.[71] His death, furthermore, was part of the plan and may have been linked in his own mind to some notion of atonement for Israel.[72] Scot McKnight likewise thinks that Jesus definitely knew he was going to die and that he understood his death as part of the eschatological tribulation that would constitute the onset of the kingdom of God.[73]

Somewhere between these perspectives are the views of most other scholars, including Borg, Sanders, and Fredriksen. Borg grants that Jesus saw himself as a Spirit-filled agent of God and that his primary mission was that of a teacher and prophet of social change. Sanders claims that Jesus saw himself as *the* end-time prophet responsible for inaugurating God's kingdom, and allows that there may have been a relatively easy transition from Jesus' own self-perception as "king of the messianic kingdom" to the church's confession of Jesus as the Messiah.[74] Fredriksen does not think that Jesus saw himself as the Messiah but proposes that the masses of people in Jerusalem may have hailed him as Messiah, such that what would become a central affirmation of Christians regarding Jesus was offered by Jews during Jesus' lifetime. But none of these scholars think that Jesus intended to die. Also, they might allow that Jesus' vision appears to have gone unfulfilled, at least in the sense that he himself intended. Borg would acknowledge that the revitalization of Israel's peasant culture Jesus hoped to effect did not occur, and both Sanders and Fredriksen (joined now by Allison) would note that the divine intervention Jesus thought would bring about an eschatological restoration of Israel did not in fact take place. Indeed, the Christian religion would never have emerged within history if reports of Jesus' subsequent resurrection had not caused some of his followers to think of him and his mission in new categories. The ultimate significance of Jesus, then, took on dimensions that transcended anything he himself had imagined.

NOW WHAT?

Some years ago, Cullen Murphy, managing editor of the popular magazine *The Atlantic*, did an article on historical Jesus studies for that publication. Murphy spent one long day in Chicago interviewing several scholars about the quest. "At times," he says of that day, "I had the distinct impression of being present at some sort of clinical procedure." This was clearly not what he had anticipated for an article about Jesus. Then, at the end of the day, Murphy departed the building to find snow lightly falling. He was met outside by a Salvation Army band, and, just as he approached, they began to play "O Little Town of Bethlehem." At that moment, Murphy would indicate, he sensed something that he felt had been missing throughout the day. "And I must say," he confessed, "it gave me quite a thrill."[75]

Murphy is not, presumably, a person given easily to sentiment. If anything, I suspect he would meet the "hardened journalist" stereotype of persons who have pretty much heard everything and are surprised by little. But he nevertheless found the specter of scholars dissecting beloved Bible stories to be somewhat daunting. Just what sort of "clinical procedure" is this? Surgical? To see if faith can be repaired, reconstituted to last another century? Or is it an autopsy? To find out why it died?

For many who have made their way this far in a survey of Jesus scholarship, the discipline may seem to lack the vibrancy, the power, and even the sentiment that a simple hymn can evoke. But it isn't that way for all. Marcus Borg affirms that "one can be a Christian without historical knowledge of Jesus,"[76] but he goes on to confess that for *himself*, the work of historians "has made it possible to be a Christian again."[77] Frederick Gaiser relates the study of the historical Jesus to the unflinching honesty that authenticates Christian faith. He finds permission to ask historical questions about Jesus and the Bible to be "magnificently liberating" and maintains that he has never "felt the need to leave the classic Christian faith in order to pursue honesty." In fact, he adds (sounding very Borgian), "it would not be putting it too strongly to say that such honesty permitted me to remain a Christian."[78] Paula Fredriksen goes so far as to say that Christianity's own claims necessitate historical study of Jesus. Specifically, the doctrine of the Incarnation (that, in Jesus, God became a human being) begs the historical question. By confessing this doctrine, the church "lays upon itself the obligation to do history." Otherwise, Christians will be docetists, believing in Jesus only as a divine figure, not as the human (historical) representation of God.[79]

Thus, many witnesses maintain that, "clinical" or not, the quest is necessary for the theological confession of the Christian church and/or for their personal faith. But historical Jesus studies may also have a usefulness to theology apart from their effect on faith. John Meier notes that these studies offer "a constant stimulus to theological renewal" in that they reveal a figure who "refuses to be held fast by any given school of thought," who evinces "strange, off-putting, embarrassing contours, equally offensive to right and left wings."[80] For others, though, all this may be beside the point. The issue, simply, is the advancement of knowledge. If we *can* learn more about Jesus—a significant figure in history—we *should*, and if what we learn troubles the believers or the unbelievers, so be it. The truth will out, if we let it.

Whether these studies feed one's faith or threaten it, whether they reveal profound insights or merely satisfy idle curiosity, they will continue. A century ago, their death knell was supposedly sounded by Schweitzer, but here we are, questing still. The secular view that Jesus is only important to religion and the theological position that the Jesus of history is not significant for faith have both eroded away. Secular and theological authorities agree: Jesus matters. Whether we are Christians or not, then, we appear to be destined to share a planet with people who think Jesus is important but who do not believe the same things about him that we do. As long as encyclopedias include articles on Jesus and public school textbooks devote space to him, someone will have to decide what counts as historical knowledge regarding him. It seems certain, then, that the quest will continue.

Something else seems certain. It may be comforting to some, frustrating to others, but it seems certain. Whatever the historical scholars decide about Jesus, Christians are not going to quit confessing creeds concerning him or offering prayers to him. Evangelists are not going to quit imploring people to call on him for salvation, and the evangelized are not going to quit asking him to come into their hearts or save their souls.

Salvation Army bands are not my personal cup of tea, but back in the 1990s (when I was finishing up the first edition of this book), I attended an outdoor concert by the rock group Jars of Clay. This group's members, young from my perspective, were openly Christian. Their audience, equally young and younger, appeared to be also. The group led some fifteen to twenty thousand of these young people in a moving hymn to Jesus, singing one line over and over:

> I want to fall in love with you. . .
>
> I want to fall in love with you . . .
>
> I want to fall in love with you . . .
>
> I want to fall in love with you.

There they were, I thought: the next generation, swaying their hands in the air, on a quest for Jesus—but a different quest than the one this book describes. Is their quest simply to know—indeed to *love*—the one whom Borg calls "the post-Easter Jesus"? Then why do they clutch in their hands those books that tell what Jesus did before Easter? Their quest, I suspect, is to encounter and embrace the Jesus of a story, a story of which history is but a part, sometimes but a shadow. Stories, unlike history, cannot always be divided neatly along a chronological axis. Good stories often involve so many anachronies—foreshadowings, predictions, flashbacks, memories—that we lose track of what was post- and what was pre-, what was then and what was now, and finally, we don't care. We just let the story take us wherever it is going.

What story are we talking about? People often refer to "the gospel story" (by which they mean something larger than any specific written account found in any particular Gospel) or even "the New Testament story." I also hear about "the church's story," but I don't want to employ such limiting descriptors: the "story of Jesus" does unfold in the New Testament and it has been preserved and proclaimed by the church, but it has also been a part of culture and history, inspiring art and music, and determining the courses of countless human lives. For many—and for me—believing in Jesus means being part of that ongoing story. It, of course, means critiquing the reception of the story, but always and only as one whose participation in and reception of the story warrants critique as well.

The quest for the Jesus of history is over two hundred years old, but the quest for the Jesus of this story is almost two thousand years old. People have been challenged by both—invigorated, frightened, angered, renewed, intrigued. I think the two quests can and should overlap, though often—unfortunately—they do not. Still, for better or worse, the story will have the last word. The hymns will make sure of that. Philip Brooks, the composer of "O Little Town of Bethlehem," was born the same year that David Friedrich Strauss published the first edition of his *Life of Jesus* (1835). Not many read Strauss anymore; far more sing the hymn. Songs by Jars of Clay will probably not have that kind of staying power, but some of my students were in that audience, and I knew they were more profoundly affected by that music than by any of my books. Actually, so am I. A bit old for this sort of thing, I can still sing and sway with the best of them, and

I do. I fell in love with *this* Jesus a long time ago, the Beautiful Savior, the Lover of my soul, the Jesus of story and song.

This has little to do with the historians' quest, but from a historical standpoint the endurance of the hymns may be appropriate, because, as most Jesus scholars will grant, the hymns came first. Before the Gospels, before the Epistles, before Josephus, even before Q, Christians were writing hymns about Jesus. A few of them even get quoted in the Bible. The hymns were there before anyone tried to write a narrative of Jesus' life or reflect systematically about his identity or message. They were inspired by a story that was beginning to emerge, a story that defied simple chronological distinctions between past and present, then and now. Jesus scholars argue over which came first: history or theology. For what it's worth, I think a story preceded them both, and that Christian worship originally consisted of hymns directed to the Jesus known and experienced through that story.

The bands aren't going to quit playing. But still, the quest continues.

> Jesus . . . asked his disciples, "Who do people say that I am?" And they answered him . . . then he asked them, "Who do you say that I am?" (Mark 8:27–29)

Appendix 1

Did Jesus Exist?

All the historians discussed in this book have one thing in common: they believe that there actually was a historical person behind all the stories and teachings attributed to Jesus of Nazareth in the Bible (and other documents). Even if they question the accuracy of some (or most) of those accounts, even if they believe the historical reality of Jesus to have been quite different from what Christian faith would make of him, they at least believe that there was a historical reality.

Not everyone believes this. Around the edges of historical Jesus scholarship there have always been a few individuals who question the basic premise that Jesus existed,[1] and that position continues to have its advocates today.[2] These people are not taken very seriously within the guild of historians; their work is usually dismissed as pseudo-scholarship that is dependent on elaborate conspiracy theories and rather obviously motivated by anti-Christian polemic.[3] Indeed, many of the people who espouse the "Jesus never existed" thesis (e.g. on various Internet websites) are not scholars in the traditional sense; they are self-taught amateurs who sometimes seem unaware of any critical, academic approach to evaluating the historicity of Jesus traditions. They often seem to assume that the only alternative to denying the historical existence of Jesus would be to accept everything the Bible reports about him as straightforward historical fact.[4] But "many" is not all—there have been scholars who have questioned the historical existence of Jesus in ways that merit some mention in a review of historical Jesus scholarship.

The first major representative of this view to gain a hearing among biblical scholars was Bruno Bauer, a respected New Testament scholar of the nineteenth century.[5] Bauer began his work with critical examination of the Gospels and became convinced that they were all written by individuals intent on promoting particular theological agendas (as opposed to simply reporting facts). Eventually, he decided that the author of Mark's Gospel had created much of the story

251

of Jesus and that the other authors had simply adapted his work (a position not too dissimilar from that of Burton Mack, discussed on pages 27–30 of this book). But, then, in his later years, he moved into a realm of conjecture that, according to Schweitzer, no longer evinced "any pretence of following a histori-cal method."[6] He decided that the religion of Christianity had been invented by Seneca, Nero's tutor, who drew on Philo of Alexandria. The letters of Paul were all forgeries, produced in the second century and backdated to give the impres-sion that the Christian faith had originated earlier and that it had connections to Palestine. In fact, the Christian religion was a purely pagan faith, created in Rome, and Jesus was simply a mythical figure to whom philosophical ideas and remarkable events were attributed in order to connect the new faith with Juda-ism and give it a semblance of ancestry.

In 1910, a German philosophy professor named Arthur Drews published an influential book that presented a different version of what has come to be called "the Jesus myth theory" (i.e., the theory that Jesus did not exist as a histori-cal person).[7] Drews suggested that the Christian religion was based on Persian mythology and that the figure of Jesus was based on an Ephraimite solar deity. Unlike most proponents of the Jesus myth theory, however, Drews did not want to attack Christianity but wanted to rehabilitate it. He claimed it was Christ as an idea, not as a historical person, that held vitality for modern humanity—a new Christian reformation would involve faith in the idea embodied by the mythical figure of Christ rather than faith dependent upon historical claims about a person who never actually existed. Some of Drews's ideas have been taken up in the modern era by Earl Doherty, who claims that Christians origi-nally envisioned Jesus as a heavenly figure who appeared to them through visions and who suffered a sacrificial death in the heavenly realm in a manner modeled on the death of Purusha in the *Rig Veda* (a Sanskrit collection of hymns sacred to Hinduism).[8]

Peter Jensen, a German Assyriologist, also sought the origin of Christianity in myth rather than history, but he espoused the distinctive thesis that the Jesus story was a retelling of the Babylonian Gilgamesh epic and that Christians, in effect, worship a Babylonian deity.[9] Notably, Jensen did not think it necessary to deny the existence of a historical Jew named Jesus entirely—he merely argued that everything we possess concerning such a person has been so thoroughly transformed that nothing can be known of the man behind the myth. Such a position exemplifies a slight variation on the dominant Jesus myth theory. The usual claim is "Jesus did not exist"; the alternative version says, "Even if Jesus did exist, nothing historical can be affirmed regarding him." Those who hold to this latter, softer version of the thesis do not feel compelled to dismiss every possible reference to Jesus in all first-century writings; they grant that there could be some vague recollection that, for some unknown reason, a man named Jesus became the catalyst for the mythological speculation and/or visionary experiences out of which Christian religion evolved. In the modern era, G. A. Wells, who promi-nently denied the existence of Jesus for many years, softened his thesis in later writings: he decided that the Q source probably did exist and that this fact alone indicates that there probably was a historical man named Jesus who said things it would have contained—but the bottom line remains that historians can know next-to-nothing about this person.[10]

The most articulate modern proponent of the Jesus myth theory is Robert M. Price, a respected biblical scholar with two doctorates from Drew University.[11] He maintains that, in his critical work as a mainstream scholar, he was surprised to discover how difficult it was to poke holes in what he had once regarded as "extreme, even crackpot, theories."[12] And, once convinced that those theories (denying the existence of Jesus) were probably correct, he felt no need to abandon his faith: "I rejoice to take the Eucharist every week and to sing the great hymns of the faith. For me, the Christ of faith has all the more importance since I think it most probable that there was never any other."[13] He bases this conclusion on a number of considerations, including (1) the absence of historical analogy for much of what is claimed regarding Jesus; (2) the lack of attention to Jesus in secular sources; (3) the lack of clear historical references to Jesus in the New Testament epistles;[14] (4) the fact that everything in the Gospels can be read as serving the interests of the developing Christian church;[15] and (5) the strong possibility that many stories of Jesus in the Gospels were developed as midrash on Old Testament passages and/or as Christianized versions of myths current in various Near Eastern religions.[16]

In sum, the Jesus myth theory has taken somewhat different forms[17] and has been expressed in various ways and in service of different ends. Most advocates, however, deny that there are any early references to Jesus outside the Gospels. The references in Roman writings (see above, pages 37–40) are dismissed as Christian interpolations. References in the writings of Paul are also viewed as later interpolations or construed in such a way that Paul is talking about Jesus only as a concept or as a mythical or literary figure rather than an historical one. Thus, the concept of Jesus as an actual historical person can be attributed to a single Gospel author (usually the author of Mark's Gospel) from whom the others copied, and various motives for the innovation of presenting Jesus as an actual historical person may be proposed: a devious motive may allege that the Gospel author had something to gain by deceiving people into believing historical falsehood; a more benign motive might suggest the author simply misunderstood an allegory or mythical tale and, so, innocently transformed fiction into biography—or that the Gospel writer/s intended his/their work to be read as allegory or myth but that it was misinterpreted as biography by later readers.

As indicated, the Jesus myth theory is not taken seriously by most historical scholars. Robert Price has gained something of a hearing because he presents his argument in a knowledgeable and nuanced manner, but historians have not found the argument persuasive.[18] Dunn notes the intrinsic "improbability of the total invention of a figure who had purportedly lived within the generation of the inventers,"[19] and Bock wonders why there would have been no challenge to Christianity from Jewish opponents if the actual existence of Jesus was a matter open to debate.[20] Crossan thinks that the earliest layers of the Jesus tradition often present a figure very different from the apocalyptic image central to Christian religion: if Christians had invented a historical figure for their faith, they would not have come up with two such divergent versions of that figure. Johnson points out that Old Testament texts offer no precedent for the New Testament's specific and nearly unanimous presentation of Jesus as a suffering and dying Messiah,[21] and Crossan indicates that pagan mythology provides no parallel for the resurrection of a hero that was not considered to be unique but the first fruit of an imminent general resurrection.[22] Further, most historical scholars (Christian or not) find the attempt to explain away all apparent references to Jesus in Roman writings, much less New Testament epistles, to be an unconvincing tour de force that lapses into special pleading.[23]

Appendix 2

Historical Jesus Studies
and Christian Apologetics

The field of historical Jesus studies is by definition a secular discipline (i.e., a science that assumes no presuppositions of faith). Still, numerous Christians have been and remain involved in the field. Accordingly, the question often arises as to how Christian scholars can contribute productively to a quest that demands respect for tenets at variance with the convictions of their faith (e.g., that the historical reliability of what is reported in biblical writings must be determined through careful analysis rather than affirmed by an appeal to the authoritative status of those writings as divinely inspired scripture).

Different Christians, of course, respond to this challenge in different ways.[1] There are many Christian scholars who have no problem discovering or even proposing that the canonical, biblical portrait of Jesus is a theological construct that may have been inspired by the historical reality but that can also be distinguished from it. Even conservative Christian scholars like John Meier have no problem admitting that the historical Jesus did not actually say or do everything attributed to him in the biblical documents. Scot McKnight, a conservative evangelical who has written extensively on the historical Jesus, allows that certain passages presented as the words of Jesus in our Bibles are actually interpretative glosses supplied by the Christian evangelists.[2] Other Christian scholars, like Ben Witherington, try to maintain a distinction between assessing "what happened" and "what is verifiable." It is then possible for a devout Christian to believe (as a matter of religious faith) that Jesus did or said what the Bible says he did or said while simultaneously admitting (as a historical scholar) that many things the Bible says about Jesus cannot be verified historically. The Christian historian may regard many things about Jesus as authentic or true on the basis of scriptural authority while maintaining that these things cannot be regarded as authentic or true from the perspective of secular, historical science.[3]

The field of Christian apologetics takes a different tack. Christian engaged in apologetics often try to establish or prove the legitimacy of what they believe to be true on grounds that do not require blatant acceptance of biblical or ecclesial authority. Frequently, the apologists themselves believe the matters to be true primarily on faith, as a result of accepting authoritative biblical or ecclesial testimony, but they seek to find non-faith-based arguments that also establish, confirm, or otherwise support the veracity of what they believe. The motivation may be simply to support faith claims in a supplementary fashion, or it may be to prompt those who are not willing to accept the matters on faith to nevertheless consider the matters more seriously than they would otherwise. Frequently, as the word *apologetics* implies, the motivation is to defend faith claims from secular challenges: if some historians are claiming Jesus did not actually do what the Bible says he did, an apologist might attempt to challenge those claims *on historical grounds* in order to ensure the faithful that their beliefs are not actually contradicted by historical evidence. In a sense, then, apologists often try to bridge the gap between faith and science or history, so that "faith" will not be reduced to stubborn insistence on the veracity of beliefs that science or history claim to be demonstrably false.

As might be expected, Christian apologetics has an uneasy relationship with historical Jesus studies. On the one hand, many apologists are brilliant, well-informed scholars who construct sensible and persuasive arguments for why biblical testimony on specific matters (as well as in a more general sense) should be accepted as reliable and historically accurate. Any honest scholar who wants to discover the historical truth about Jesus will want to give those arguments the consideration they merit. On the other hand, the involvement of apologists in historical Jesus studies always seems one-sided. Most historical scholars find it frustrating to listen with an open mind to the arguments an apologist wants to offer in favor of historicity when they know that the apologist is not willing to listen with an open mind to any arguments that can be offered against historicity.

Historical Jesus scholars usually conceive of the task to which they are committed as a *quest* rather than as a *debate*. In a quest, one searches for the truth with an open mind, marked by a willingness to follow the evidence wherever it leads, to revise one's views or even recant one's former positions when a better argument or better evidence is found. Most historical Jesus scholars would say they engage in conversation with people who disagree with them in order to discover if those people might in fact be right—or, at least, partly right. In a quest, there is always a very real possibility of having one's own thinking supplemented, altered, or even completely changed by the insights of those one initially thought were wrong. In a debate, by contrast, participants try to score points for their position and find ways to discredit the opposing position. A debate is enacted for the benefit of an audience, who will decide which side won and which side lost. No one expects either participant in the debate to be convinced by the arguments offered by their opponent.[4]

Historical Jesus studies is best construed as a quest, not a debate.[5] Apologists, almost by definition, are committed to convincing people that their position (in favor of historicity) is correct, rather than to determining whether or not their proposal (regarding a possibility of historicity) *might* be correct—faith convictions typically disqualify any potential for a negative conclusion or at least render such a conclusion remote, something the apologist would resist for reasons unrelated to the persuasiveness of evidence or argumentation. There is, of course, nothing wrong with this: apologists can and do pursue their vocation with integrity, and debates between persons who hold intractable views can be both interesting and informative.[6] But when apologists try to engage in historical Jesus studies—or when they present themselves as historical Jesus scholars—they often discover that they are not completely welcome. The reason is that they come to a quest prepared for a debate; the result is that they are politely tolerated, at best. To be frank, when apologists enter the fray of historical Jesus studies, they tend to be regarded as intruders or simply as posers—they may have *something* to contribute, but they don't seem to get what everyone else is actually trying to do (or else, many suspect, they just don't care).[7]

The situation is confused when Christian scholars are *suspected* of engaging in apologetics regardless of their actual intent.[8] Such suspicion may be furthered by the fact that some Christian scholars are willing to engage in both disciplines— apologetics *and* historical Jesus studies. They may approach the latter with a conservative bias but a general willingness to abide by "the rules of the game," recognizing a distinction between what can be verified and what cannot. Unfortunately, such scholars do not always get the attention they might otherwise deserve simply because their commitment to apologetics is well-known. They become stereotyped as intruders or posers when such labels might not actually apply.

We may note two prominent evangelical scholars who exemplify this sort of marginalization: Darrell Bock[9] and Craig Keener.[10] Both Bock and Keener have published massive works on the historical Jesus and on the field of historical Jesus studies, but they have been mentioned only occasionally in this volume. This is because, while their work has been enthusiastically received in evangelical circles, it has not had a great impact on the field of historical Jesus studies overall. Some might suppose the guild operates with a bias against evangelical or conservative Christianity in general, but the relative inattention to Bock and Keener's work could also be due to the (possibly unfounded) suspicion that these scholars are more interested in apologetics (establishing historicity) than in embarking on an open-minded quest for historical truth.[11]

Darrell Bock has sketched a portrait of the historical Jesus analogous to the major biographies of Jesus presented by other scholars discussed in this book.[12] Jesus was baptized by John and, in so doing, identified himself with John's mission of national renewal and repentance. In his own ministry, however, he announced the coming of God's kingdom, a newly dawning age of *shalom* that was already present in Jesus' own activity but would be consummated in a powerful and all-encompassing way. As he proclaimed this message, Jesus became noted for a number of things that were unique or at least distinctive: reaching out to the unclean and to others on the fringe of society; demanding that his followers exhibit intense commitment and total loyalty to the kingdom and to his own person; performing unusual works that he claimed exhibited divine power and exemplified God's benevolent care; advocating a lifestyle reflective of trust in division provision; encouraging a radical love for enemies and willingness to forgive others their sin; and promising that in the new covenant he was inaugurating, God would give people new hearts so that they could be transformed and sustained through the power of the Spirit. Jesus also claimed in some sense to be the Messiah, though he tried to refine that term away from traditional political expectations. He entered Jerusalem, enacted a symbolic prophetic action against the religious authorities in the very courts of the temple they controlled, and shared a meal with his followers that conveyed a conviction that his own suffering would inaugurate the new covenant of which he had been speaking. When he was arrested and examined by Jewish authorities, he was pressed specifically on the question of his own identity and subsequently charged with blasphemy; that is, with claiming "an equality with God that the leadership would have judged as a slander against God's unique glory."[13] He was then condemned by Pilate, who also believed he had made unwarranted claims regarding his own authority. He was crucified, and his dead body placed in a tomb; subsequent claims that he had been raised from the dead gain credibility from the fact that they were framed in ways that the church would not have invented.

Bock lays out this portrait of Jesus with careful attention to typical methods for historical inquiry.[14] He seeks to establish the probable historicity of every assertion he makes through appeals to multiple attestation, dissimilarity, and other accepted criteria, and he strives to interpret Jesus' actions within a context of Second Temple Judaism informed by knowledge of archaeology, the Dead Sea Scrolls, and other available resources. In all these ways, his work resembles that of many scholars discussed in this book. What seems distinctive is a tendency only to affirm, but never to deny, the historical reliability of biblical testimony. Thus, Luke Timothy Johnson (another conservative Christian scholar) says that Bock's work would gain credibility if "at any point he entertained the possibility of some passage of the Gospels not yielding real historical knowledge."[15] To be fair, Bock does follow convention by relying primarily on texts from Mark and Q, passages considered to have the greatest potential for historical reliability—there are texts (including most of John) that he simply doesn't consider. Still, in the passages that he *does* consider, he never decides that any material should not be regarded as historically reliable (or even verifiable). Since Bock is known to be a strong proponent of biblical inerrancy, his historical Jesus work is sometimes suspected of being an exercise in apologetics: an effort to affirm whatever he thinks can be affirmed and to ignore anything that cannot be.[16] Robert Price calls his work "opportunistic";[17] Johnson suggests that he "has not yet grasped what historical analysis requires."[18]

In one of the most dismissive critiques of Bock's work to date, Robert Miller alleges that Bock (and evangelicals like him) "use traditional historical-Jesus criteria to further their project of authenticating the Gospels" but "do not allow those same criteria to lead to negative historical conclusions."[19] Indeed, Miller says that evangelicals like Bock belong to a different "camp" than most historical Jesus scholars and that there can be no real dialogue or productive discussion between those camps (due to their very different presuppositions and understanding of the task at hand). Other scholars, however—including people as ideologically diverse as John Dominic Crossan and James D. G. Dunn—have engaged Bock's work and reflected appreciatively on portions of it.[20]

Craig Keener has written extensively on the historical reliability of the New Testament Gospels[21]—and on the credibility of the miracle stories that they report.[22] He maintains that the Gospels belong to the genre of ancient historiography and that a comprehensive survey of contemporaneous works in this genre reveals a careful concern for accuracy. Obviously, ancient biographers and historiographers had their biases, and they sometimes got things wrong, but they did not just make things up in the cavalier fashion assumed by some historical Jesus scholars (e.g., Mack, Crossan). Scholars should start with the premise that the author is reporting historical fact unless there is an obvious reason to think otherwise; this, Keener maintains, is how scholars typically use other ancient works of historiography. Furthermore, the Gospel authors relied on early written sources and oral tradition (Luke 1:1–4), both of which provide eyewitness testimony; Jesus' disciples probably took notes and committed large portions of his teaching to memory, as was typical for disciples of other rabbis and for followers of other prominent figures of the day.[23] Even the reports of miracles should be read as accurate, straightforward historical accounts since those who are not encumbered by a scientifically and philosophically indefensible antisupernaturalism are able to recognize that such occurrences have happened and continue to happen in the world today.

Keener offers his own biographical sketch of Jesus, which is not too dissimilar from that of Bock (or from that of the Synoptic Gospels).[24] Jesus was from Nazareth, and after being baptized by John he called disciples and conducted a ministry among the fishing villages of Galilee. As a teacher and prophet he told and interpreted parables (including, perhaps, all the ones found in the New Testament), preached about a kingdom of God that was both already-present and yet still-to-come, demanded that his disciples leave their families and relinquish their possessions, mingled and dined with marginalized persons considered to be sinners, quarreled with Pharisees over purity practices and Sabbath laws, and reinterpreted traditional ethics by prioritizing the necessity of love. Jesus also worked miracles and presented himself as the Messiah, albeit a messiah reinterpreted in terms of Daniel's Son of Man (Dan. 7:13–14). He claimed to be the eschatological Judge of the dawning end times, a figure who fulfilled but expanded all Jewish expectations in light of the unique relationship he had with God, his Father. He realized that he needed to die and taught his disciples that his crucifixion would function as an atonement. His tomb was subsequently found empty and, among the various explanations that can be offered for this, the most probable is that he rose bodily from the dead in a manner that aroused the otherwise incredible resurrection faith of his disciples.

The depth of Keener's erudition is remarkable, and, at some level, most scholars do take his work seriously. His knowledge of ancient literature is particularly impressive, such that almost half of his books are sometimes occupied with endnotes, hundreds of pages that offer thousands of references to parallel or analogous passages in Roman or Jewish writings suggestive of how the Gospel accounts of Jesus should be interpreted. Nevertheless, Keener has not obtained the stature within the guild that his prolific output and undeniable brilliance might suggest he would deserve. The reason is simply that he is regarded as something of an apologist, as one who is interested only in authenticating what can be authenticated rather than in determining what can and cannot be authenticated. The distinction may seem like a fine one, but scholars have not failed to notice the absence of negative verdicts. Robert Miller says, "If Keener does indeed have doubts about the historical accuracy of any Gospel material, he keeps those doubts to himself."[25] The charge goes beyond bias (all scholars have biases) to allegations that Keener engages in special pleading.[26] Amy-Jill Levine notes that he insists the accounts of Jesus working miracles be accepted without any bias of antisupernaturalism, but she questions whether he would apply that position consistently when considering accounts of people working miracles in other instances of religious historiography (the Qu'ran, the *Book of Mormon*).[27] Keener is likewise said to use ancient documents selectively, citing only the ones that help his cause. He cites numerous Roman historical writings that evince a clear attempt to get the story right, but he ignores those that do not—indeed, he does not take into account works like the *Protoevangelium of James* and other apocryphal Gospels that closely resemble the canonical Gospels in genre but obviously did invent material wholesale.[28] He also cites rabbinic documents centuries after the time of Jesus to show how disciples were like scribes who took notes and memorized teachings, but he ignores passages in the Gospels that differentiate Jesus' disciples from scribes, presenting them as infants who, unlike the wise and understanding, must rely on divine revelation (Matt. 11:25–27) and the Holy Spirit (John 14:25) to understand or even remember things about Jesus.[29] Of course, Keener would have intelligent responses to all these objections,[30] but the point is that the perception that he is engaged in apologetics rather than in an actual quest to determine what can be regarded as historical keeps his work from being engaged in the same way as work by conservative Christians like Meier who seem more open to admitting much of what the Gospels report cannot be historically authenticated. Still—not to overstate the case—Keener's main book on the historical Jesus has been endorsed by such mainstream scholars as James Charlesworth, Joseph Fitzmyer, and Gerd Theissen, and even those who regard it as an example of apologetics recognize that much of what he has to say is worthy of consideration (that is, if he *is* doing apologetics, he is at least good at it).

Appendix 3

Psychological Studies of the Historical Jesus

Psychohistory or psychobiography is a subdiscipline of the social sciences that attempts to construct psychological profiles of historical figures.[1] Both psychologists and historians tend to view such endeavors with skepticism. Psychologists claim it is a risky business to analyze someone without actually putting them "on the couch," that is, without asking them the sort of questions psychologists want to ask their patients and hearing their responses. Historians prefer to confine discussion of *motives* to what would have been apparent, to what the subject claimed his or her motives were, and to what other people might have said the subject's motives were—a rather different matter from detection of ulterior or hidden motives that neither the subject nor anyone else would have discerned at the time. Nevertheless, the practice of psychobiography has a rich history: Freud did an analysis of Leonardo da Vinci, and Erik Erikson wrote psychological biographies of Martin Luther and Gandhi, though few would now consider those works to be exemplars of the genre.[2] The field refined its methodology in the latter part of the twentieth century and became more widely respectable. That said, the possibility of doing a psychological biography of Jesus strikes many as particularly daunting, since we have nothing but third-party testimony regarding him: we have no writings from Jesus himself, only recollections of things he might have said or done, compiled by people who had never actually met him.

Albert Schweitzer wrote a dissertation on what he called "psychiatric studies of Jesus" that had been produced in the nineteenth century.[3] He regarded such studies with total disdain and offered a devastating critique of them as wildly conjectural. Nevertheless, such studies continued to be produced throughout the twentieth century, almost always by persons trained in psychology but ignorant of basic methods or procedures employed by historical Jesus scholars.[4] There was no consideration of sources or application of criteria that might allow for discernment of which material in the Gospels should actually be attributed to Jesus. For example, a psychological study of Jesus produced by Jay Haley in 1969 basically takes the Gospel of Matthew as a straightforward record of Jesus' life and teachings.[5] Many of Haley's observations regarding Jesus' psychological motivations are offered in reference to comments that Jesus makes *only* in Matthew, comments that the great majority of biblical scholars would assume Matthew himself added to the story of Jesus when he was redacting the Gospel of Mark. Thus, if Haley's observations are correct, they would apply more appropriately to the psychological motivations of Matthew (a late first-century Christian evangelist) rather than to those of Jesus (an early first-century Jewish peasant). Nevertheless, Haley's work might not need to be rejected in toto: sometimes, almost unwittingly, he does treat material that historical Jesus scholars would deem authentic and, then, his observations strike some as illuminating.[6] He regards Jesus' blistering attacks on religious leaders (found in material Gospel scholars would ascribe to Q, e.g. Matt. 23:13–36; Luke 11:37–52) as a power tactic in which one challenges the status of social superiors and so (unless successfully shamed) elevates one's own status. Likewise, Jesus' tendency to claim he is not advocating change while in fact advocating fundamental change (presenting radical deviations as "truer expressions" of tradition) displays a rhetorical strategy familiar to psychologists who study power tacticians.

The new millennium has brought a renaissance in psychohistorical studies of Jesus in that such studies are now being conducted by persons conversant with a historical-critical approach to the Bible. Three major studies produced around the turn of the millennium have attracted the most attention.

In 1997, John Miller published *Jesus at Thirty*, a brief work that sought to draw inferences regarding Jesus' likely psychological state on the basis of widely accepted facts concerning him, and to investigate the Gospel materials in light of this possible psychological portrait.[7] Miller, a theologian and a psychiatrist, starts with the presumption that at the time Jesus began his adult ministry he was unmarried and the oldest sibling in a family in which the father was no longer present (probably, though not necessarily, due to the latter's death). Miller further supposes that Jesus must have had a loving, caring relationship with his now-absent father as would be suggested by the prominent use of father-son relationships in his parables. Miller draws on insights from Erik Erikson and Daniel Levinson to describe the sort of identity crisis a person in such a situation would typically undergo. In all likelihood, a man in these circumstances would continue to seek a father figure while simultaneously developing an enhanced capacity for "generativity," becoming in effect a surrogate father to others. Miller suggests this may account for Jesus' extraordinary conceptualization of God as *Abba* (father)—he appears to have emphasized the fatherly nature of God to an unprecedented extent. It may also account for the manner in which he relates to others, evidenced for example in his habit of calling adult women "daughter" (Mark 5:34, 41).

Donald Capps, a specialist in the psychology of religion, starts with an assumption that the legitimacy of Jesus' birth was questionable: his biological father was probably unknown and Joseph did not adopt him but rather regarded James, the second boy born to Mary, as his first-born.[8] The reason Jesus did not marry, Capps suggests, was not (per Miller) because his duties as surrogate father to the family prevented it but because Joseph did not find him a wife. Jesus was a social outcast, excluded from participation in temple religion, and for this reason he was attracted to John the Baptist's alternative religious movement. Eventually, he found a fictive identity as the Son of God, believing that the heavenly Abba had adopted him when he was cleansed of his intrinsic impurity (as one illegitimately conceived) by John's baptism. He directed his repressed anger (toward his unknown biological father and toward Joseph) at demons, becoming an effective exorcist. As such, he was able to effect psychosomatic cures of people who suffered from what would now be diagnosed as "somatoform disorders," which include conditions in which paralysis, blindness, deafness, seizures, uncontrolled menstrual flow, and other actual physical disabilities are manifested without any neurological cause.[9] Jesus may be diagnosed as a utopian-melancholic personality: he looked forward to a coming kingdom of God while continuing to seek cleansing from the sexual pollution in which he had been conceived; these tendencies eventually led him to perform an impulsive act in the temple (cleansing an institution that, for him, represented his mother's body). The fact that this led to his death fits with a tendency for melancholic personalities to be suicidal.

Andries van Aarde is a biblical scholar and a member of the Jesus Seminar. His work *Fatherless in Galilee* posits a hypothetical "Ideal type" for Jesus that he believes makes sense of numerous features in the Gospel tradition.[10] Van Aarde thinks that Jesus probably grew up as the bastard son of a single mother—the very existence of Joseph is a later Christian fiction (the character being based loosely on the character of Joseph in the Pentateuch). Thus, he was an outcast and a sinner; as a *mamzer* (see above, pages 92–94) he was not allowed to marry and was excluded from Israel's primary religious institutions. Since he was fatherless, furthermore, Jesus' status as a male was not clarified in puberty, and so he grew into adulthood displaying female behavior, which in that culture included "taking the last place at table, serving others, forgiving wrongs, having compassion, and attempting to heal wounds."[11] Seeing himself as a protector of other marginalized individuals, Jesus formed an alternative religious community around himself that was largely composed of women without husbands and of children without fathers.

Despite the superficial attention to historical methodology (criteria, sources, and so on), these three studies of Jesus have not received much attention or support within the guild of historical Jesus studies as a whole. There is lingering suspicion about the field of psychohistory (dismissed by some as a pseudoscience), but even scholars willing to grant the possibility of such research note that *these* studies seem highly conjectural and speculative. Jesus' act in the temple *could* have been impulsive (rather than calculated), as Capps suggests, but most historical Jesus scholars see no reason for assuming it was.

The children whom Jesus welcomes and calls the greatest in the kingdom *could* have been orphans or bastards, as van Aarde assumes, but no document actually says that they were. Even more to the point, virtually everything these three scholars say depends upon assumptions regarding Jesus' childhood—and most historical Jesus scholars maintain that this is the one aspect of Jesus' biography about which we are least informed. It is axiomatic in historical Jesus studies to work primarily with material in Mark and Q—neither of which mentions Jesus' birth, childhood, or upbringing. So, given a paucity of data, which would be problematic in any construction, these scholars focus on points that seem especially tenuous and make those points foundational for their entire enterprises. It is possible that Jesus had a loving father who died before he reached adulthood (Miller), or that he had an estranged relationship with a potential father who refused to adopt him (Capps), or that he had no father figure in his life at all (van Aarde)—but the mere fact that all three of these scenarios are possible suggests that none of them is obviously preferable. It seems to most historical Jesus scholars that Miller, Capps, and van Aarde are working backward from the ends to the means: they are starting with the adult Jesus evident in the biblical materials and suggesting what sort of childhood traumas and father issues might have produced that person. But does psychological analysis normally proceed that way, guessing what a subject's childhood might have been like, based on the person they eventually became? And if such a procedure would be somewhat suspect with a current, living subject, should it not be regarded as even more tenuous with a historical subject for whom significant aspects of the adult portrait remain unclear? Nevertheless, some scholars (including the author of this book) have been willing to grant that any one (or possibly all three) of these studies could be on to *something*; in time, these projects may come to be viewed as pioneering efforts in a new interdisciplinary program.[12]

Another scholar, meanwhile, has taken up psychological analysis of Jesus in a somewhat different vein. Bas van Os remains critical (though respectful) of the three studies discussed above, but he still maintains that psychohistory does have a legitimate place in historical Jesus studies. Rather than attempting to write a psychological biography of Jesus, however, van Os proposes that different psychological theories may help us to understand certain well-documented aspects of Jesus' life and ministry.[13] In place of a monograph, van Os offers a series of essays. For instance, Jesus' veneration of God as Father may be understood in terms of contemporary Attachment Theory. His belief that his own death might be beneficial and in accordance with God's will can be understood as a coping mechanism, inspired first by his need to deal with the death of John the Baptist and subsequently refined in light of threats to his own life. His performance of symbolic actions predicated by scripture (entering Jerusalem on a donkey, cleansing the temple, enacting a new covenant at his final meal) can be understood in light of Role Theory, according to which people can position themselves within a cherished narrative, assuming the role of the characters, and subsequently playing out those roles in their real life. Whatever one makes of van Os's individual points, most historical Jesus scholars seem to think this modest, thematic approach to psychohistory is more promising for Jesus' studies than are the attempts to produce psychological biographies of a person for whom so much relevant data is lacking or limited.

Notes

Introduction

1. John Dominic Crossan, *The Historical Jesus: The Life of a Mediterranean Jewish Peasant* (San Francisco: HarperSanFrancisco, 1991), xi.
2. E. P. Sanders, *The Historical Figure of Jesus* (London: Penguin, 1993), 1.
3. Paul Hollenbach, "The Historical Jesus Question in North America Today," *Biblical Theology Bulletin* 19 (1989): 11–22, citation on 20.
4. Frederick J. Gaiser, "The Quest for Jesus and the Christian Faith: Introduction," in *The Quest for Jesus and the Christian Faith,* ed. Frederick J. Gaiser, Word and World Supplement Series 3 (St. Paul: Luther Seminary, 1997), 7. Gaiser is paraphrasing Hans Walter Wolff.
5. Martin Kähler, *The So-Called Historical Jesus and the Historic, Biblical Christ* (Philadelphia: Fortress, 1964; original 1892). Notably (as the title of his book implies) Kähler's point in making this distinction was to emphasize the theological significance of the Christ of faith (the biblical Jesus) over any presentation of Jesus put forward by historians. But many historians latched on to the terminology to emphasize that the Jesus of history (*not* the Christ of faith) is the object of their study and, some would say, the only appropriate focus for academic devotion.
6. Marcus J. Borg, *Jesus in Contemporary Scholarship* (Valley Forge, Penn.: Trinity Press International, 1994), 195. John Dominic Crossan gives a theological critique of this dichotomy in *The Birth of Christianity* (San Francisco: HarperSanFrancisco, 1998), xxx.
7. See the discussion on page 185 of this book.
8. Those who research my other writings would quickly discover that for over thirty years now I have consistently identified myself as "a (usually) conservative evangelical Christian" or as "a (usually) conservative evangelical Lutheran pietist."

Chapter 1: Historians Discover Jesus

1. Albert W. Schweitzer, *The Quest of the Historical Jesus,* ed. John Bowden (Minneapolis: Fortress, 2001; first German edition, 1906), 487.
2. Rudolf Bultmann, *Jesus and the Word* (New York: Charles Scribner's Sons, 1958; German original, 1926), 8.

3. Günther Bornkamm, *Jesus of Nazareth* (New York: Harper & Row, 1960), 13.
4. N. T. Wright, *Jesus and the Victory of God,* Christian Origins and the Question of God 2 (Minneapolis: Fortress, 1996), 123. The preceding three quotes from Schweitzer, Bultmann, and Bornkamm are all cited by Wright on page 3 of this same volume.
5. Cited in Schweitzer, *Quest of the Historical Jesus,* 14.
6. See, for instance, the Gospel harmony of Osiander (1498–1552) discussed in Schweitzer, *Quest of the Historical Jesus,* 14. On one occasion, Jesus cast demons out of *one* man into a herd of pigs (Mark 5:1–20) and on a different occasion he casts demons out of *two* men into a similar herd of pigs (Matt. 8:28–34). The hapless daughter of Jairus likewise ends up being raised from the dead multiple times.
7. Harold Lindsell, *The Battle for the Bible* (Grand Rapids: Zondervan Publishing House, 1976). Lindsell also reconciles apparent discrepancies in the biblical accounts of Peter's denials by having Peter deny Jesus *six* times (174–76).
8. John Calvin, *A Harmony of the Gospels of Matthew, Mark, and Luke,* trans. A. W. Morrison, 3 vols. (Grand Rapids: Eerdmans, 1972).
9. Such work continues to this day. A recent example, produced by a responsible and knowledgeable scholar, is Darrell L. Bock, *Jesus according to Scripture: Restoring the Portrait from the Gospels* (Grand Rapids: Baker Academic, 2002).
10. See Gerald R. Cragg, *The Church and the Age of Reason, 1648–1789* (New York: Penguin, 1970).
11. Hermann Samuel Reimarus, *Fragments,* ed. C. H. Talbert, Lives of Jesus Series (Philadelphia: Fortress, 1970; original 1778). This work is summarized in Schweitzer, *Quest of the Historical Jesus,* 14–26; see also the brief summary and a selection from Reimarus's book in Gregory W. Dawes, *The Historical Jesus Quest: Landmarks in the Search for the Jesus of History* (Louisville: Westminster John Knox, 1999), 54–86.
12. See Reimarus, *Fragments,* 151.
13. Schweitzer, *Quest of the Historical Jesus,* 16.
14. Heinrich Eberhard Gottlob Paulus, *Das Leben Jesu als Grundlage einer reinen Geschichte des Urchristentums,* 2 vols. (Heidelberg: C. F. Winter, 1828). For an English summary, see Schweitzer, *Quest of the Historical Jesus,* 47–55.
15. For a summary, see Schweitzer, *Quest of the Historical Jesus,* 65–109; see also the brief summary and excerpt from Strauss's book in Dawes, *Historical Jesus Quest,* 87–111. The full book has been republished many times and is available in numerous English editions.
16. For a summary, see Schweitzer, *Quest of the Historical Jesus,* 158–67.
17. Quoted in Schweitzer, *Quest of the Historical Jesus,* 161.
18. Though the concept is Renan's, this oft-cited phrase appears to have been first used by another scholar, Theodor Keim. See Schweitzer, *Quest of the Historical Jesus,* 182.
19. Schweitzer, *Quest of the Historical Jesus,* 162.
20. Schweitzer says, "There is scarcely any other work on the subject which so abounds in lapses of taste. . . . Nevertheless, there is something magical about it. It offends and yet it attracts" *(Quest of the Historical Jesus,* 159–60).
21. Schweitzer, *Quest of the Historical Jesus,* 478.
22. Johannes Weiss, *Jesus' Proclamation of the Kingdom of God* (Philadelphia: Fortress, 1972; original 1892).
23. Albert Schweitzer, *The Quest of the Historical Jesus* (New York: Macmillan, 1968), 370–71. Note that this citation comes from an English translation of Schweitzer's 1906 edition of his book; other citations are from a translation of

the 1913 edition of Schweitzer's book (published by Fortress, 2001), which does not contain this passage.

24. Wright, *Jesus and the Victory of God*, 4.

25. Schweitzer, *Quest for the Historical Jesus*, 478.

26. Fernando Bermejo Rubio provides a partial list of scholars who published during this period on page 224 of his article, "The Fiction of the 'Three Quests': An Argument for Dismantling a Dubious Historiographical Paradigm," *Journal for the Study of the Historical Jesus* 7 (2009): 211–53.

27. W. Barnes Tatum described the periods of historical Jesus study as Old Quest (1778–1906), No Quest (1906–1953), New Quest (1953–1973), Third Quest (1973–present); see Tatum, *In Quest of Jesus*, 2nd ed. (Nashville: Abingdon, 1999), 91–106; every aspect of that paradigm is problematic, but the notion that there were forty years of inactivity is especially egregious, given the amount of important (albeit often neglected) work accomplished during that period. See Dale C. Allison, *Resurrecting Jesus: The Earliest Christian Tradition and Its Interpreters*, Journal for the Study of the Pseudepigrapha: Supplement Series (New York: T&T Clark, 2005), 1–10; Rubio, "Fiction of the 'Three Quests'."

28. See especially two essays collected in Rudolf Bultmann, *Faith and Understanding*, trans. L. Smith (London: SCM, 1969): "Liberal Theology and the Latest Theological Movement" (1924), 28–52, and "The Significance of the Historical Jesus for the Theology of Paul" (1929), 220–46, esp. 238, 241.

29. Modern scholars, however, tend to exaggerate Bultmann's elevation of theology over history: Bultmann did believe that many things about Jesus could be known, and that his teaching could be fairly summarized. It was primarily details about his personal life and personality for which no information is available or necessary. On this, see John Painter, "Bultmann, Archaeology, and the Historical Jesus," in James H. Charlesworth, ed., *Jesus and Archaeology* (Grand Rapids: Eerdmans, 2006), 619–38.

30. Wright, *Jesus and the Victory of God*, 14.

31. Wright, *Jesus and the Victory of God*, 4–5.

32. W. Barnes Tatum, *In Quest of Jesus: A Guidebook* (Atlanta: John Knox, 1982), 73.

33. An English translation of the lecture was later published as "The Problem of the Historical Jesus" 15–47 in Ernst Käsemann, *Essays on New Testament Themes* (Naperville, Ill.: Alec R. Allenson, 1964). See also a follow-up piece four years later, translated and published as "Blind Alleys in the 'Jesus of History' Controversy," 23–65 in Käsemann, *New Testament Questions of Today* (Philadelphia: Fortress, 1969; original 1957). The latter piece in particular precipitated an unfortunate rift between Käsemann and his mentor (Bultmann), whose position on the historical Jesus he had criticized. For a summary of the ensuing dispute, see David B. Gowler, *What Are They Saying about the Historical Jesus?* (New York: Paulist, 2007), 18–24.

34. *Docetism* refers to the doctrine (officially rejected by most Christian groups) that Jesus only appeared to be human but was not really or actually human.

35. Sean Freyne notes that there is not a single reference to archaeology anywhere in Albert Schweitzer's 500-page review of early historical Jesus studies (i.e., his *Quest of the Historical Jesus*). See Sean Freyne, "Archaeology and the Historical Jesus," 64–83 in James H. Charlesworth, ed., *Jesus and Archaeology* (Grand Rapids: Eerdmans, 2006), 65.

36. James M. Robinson, *A New Quest of the Historical Jesus*, Studies in Biblical Theology 25 (London: SCM, 1959), 12–13.

37. Originally published in German in 1956. Numerous English editions exist.

38. James H. Charlesworth calls Bornkamm's *Jesus of Nazareth*, "the most influential book on Jesus written after World War II and before 1980." See Charlesworth, "The Historical Jesus in the Fourth Gospel: A Paradigm Shift?" *Journal for the Study of the Historical Jesus* 8 (2010): 3–46, citation on 6.

39. Bornkamm, *Jesus of Nazareth*, 62.

40. In an early work on parables, Jeremias argued memorably that the kernel of Jesus' original message could be recovered once the husks of later interpretation were removed. See Joachim Jeremias, *The Parables of Jesus*, 2nd ed. (New York: Charles Scribner's Sons, 1972; first edition 1947). Jeremias also focused on recovering the authentic Aramaic words of Jesus by uncovering distinctive elements of vocabulary and style preserved in the Gospels' Greek translations of his teaching. See his *New Testament Theology*, vol. 1, *The Proclamation of Jesus* (New York: Charles Scribner's Sons, 1971).

41. Norman Perrin, *Rediscovering the Teaching of Jesus* (New York: Harper & Row, 1967), 39.

42. Norman Perrin, *Jesus and the Language of the Kingdom: Symbol and Metaphor in New Testament Interpretation* (Philadelphia: Fortress, 1976), 41.

43. Bornkamm, *Jesus of Nazareth*, 62.

44. N. T. Wright, "Quest for the Historical Jesus," *Anchor Bible Dictionary* 3.796–802. This article, which popularized the term *Third Quest*, was published in 1992, but Wright had used the term earlier. See S. Neill and N. T. Wright, *The Interpretation of the New Testament 1861–1986*, 2nd ed. (Oxford: Oxford University Press, 1988), 363, 379.

45. Problems with such tidy categorization (and the terms used to label them) were noted in the first edition of this book and have since been exposed with greater rigor in Dale C. Allison, "The Contemporary Quest for the Historical Jesus," *Irish Biblical Studies* 18 (1996): 174–93; Stanley E. Porter, *The Criteria for Authenticity in Historical-Jesus Research*, Journal for the Study of the New Testament: Supplement Series 191 (Sheffield: Sheffield Academic Press, 2001), 29–59; Rubio, "Fiction of the 'Three Quests'."

46. Gerd Theissen and Annette Merz use the term this way in *The Historical Jesus: A Comprehensive Guide*, trans. John Bowden (Minneapolis: Augsburg Fortress, 1998), 10–11.

47. Wright, *Jesus and the Victory of God*, 28–82. Crossan, Mack, and the Jesus Seminar are, for Wright, prime representatives of "the 'New Quest' Renewed" or "the New 'New Quest'."

48. Crossan himself would say that Wright's efforts at categorization fall "somewhere between the tendentious and the hilarious." See John Dominic Crossan "Straining Gnats, Swallowing Camels: A Review of *Who Was Jesus?* by N. T. Wright," *Bible Review* 9 (August 1993): 10–11. See also Crossan, *Birth of Christianity*, 44.

49. Käsemann, "Blind Alleys," 24. The blatant (though now obviously erroneous) assumption behind this charge was that approaches associated with the "Old Quest" and the "New Quest" were the only options for studying the historical Jesus. Jeremias's work was different from that of the New Questers, but it had even less in common with the pre-Schweitzer studies usually associated with the term "Old Quest."

50. Robinson, *New Quest*, 76.

51. Schweitzer, *Quest of the Historical Jesus*, 80.

52. Problems with distinguishing disparate quests within the relatively short span of historical Jesus studies are noted by Rubio in "Fiction of the 'Three Quests.' But compare C. Marsh's attempt to outline the discipline in terms of nine distinct quests in "Quests of the Historical Jesus in New Historicist Perspective," *Biblical Interpretation* 5 (1997): 403–37.

53. Dale C. Allison, *Constructing Jesus: Memory, Imagination, and History* (Grand Rapids: Baker Academic, 2010), 1.
54. Allison, *Constructing Jesus*, 7.
55. Allison, *Constructing Jesus*, 2.
56. Allison, *Constructing Jesus*, 2–3. In Allison's book, almost every sentence of this citation contains a footnote, referencing professional studies on memory that support each of the particular claims.
57. Allison, *Constructing Jesus*, 6.
58. Allison, *Constructing Jesus*, 7.
59. Allison, *Constructing Jesus*, 8–9.
60. See Craig S. Keener, *The Historical Jesus of the Gospels* (Grand Rapids: Eerdmans, 2009), esp. 126–62.
61. See, for example, James L. Blevins, *The Messianic Secret in Markan Research, 1901–1976* (Washington: University Press of America, 1981); Christopher Tuckett, ed., *The Messianic Secret* (Philadelphia: Fortress, 1983); Jack Dean Kingsbury, *The Christology of Mark's Gospel* (Philadelphia: Fortress, 1983); and Heikki Räisänen, *The "Messianic Secret" in Mark's Gospel*, rev. ed., trans. C. Tuckett (Edinburgh: T&T Clark, 1990).
62. Burton L. Mack, *A Myth of Innocence: Mark and Christian Origins* (Philadelphia: Fortress, 1988). In another book, Mack turns his attention to the Q source to try to salvage from scripture some of the truth about Jesus that may remain hidden there. See Mack, *The Lost Gospel: The Book of Q and Christian Origins* (San Francisco: HarperSanFrancisco, 1993). For a more popular treatment, see Mack, *Who Wrote the New Testament? The Making of the Christian Myth* (San Francisco: HarperSanFrancisco, 1995).
63. Mack, *Myth of Innocence*, 78–123. I am simplifying here. Actually, Mack discusses a variety of Jesus movements and Christ cults, but these two types of development in the tradition can be distinguished from each other.
64. Mack, *Myth of Innocence*, 96.
65. Mack, *Myth of Innocence* (here describing what Jesus was *not* for the Jesus movement).
66. Mack, *Myth of Innocence*, 111.
67. Mack, *Myth of Innocence*, 322–23.
68. Mack, *Myth of Innocence*, 349.
69. Mack, *Who Wrote the New Testament?* 47.
70. Mack, *Myth of Innocence*, 368–76 (quotation on 372). He cites works by Scott Johnson and Robert Jewett.
71. Mack, *Myth of Innocence*, 376.
72. Charlotte Allen, "The Search for a No-Frills Jesus," *Atlantic Monthly* (December 1996): 51–68; citation on 57.
73. Mack, *Myth of Innocence*, 55.
74. Mack, *Myth of Innocence*, 56.
75. Adela Yarbro Collins, "Review of *A Myth of Innocence* by Burton Mack," *Journal of Biblical Literature* 108 (1989): 728.
76. Borg, *Jesus in Contemporary Scholarship*, 38. Compare Allen, "No-Frills Jesus," 55.
77. Mack, *Myth of Innocence*, 23.
78. Elisabeth Schüssler Fiorenza, *In Memory of Her: A Feminist Theological Reconstruction of Christian Origins* (New York: Crossroad, 1987).
79. James M. Robinson believes there is support for this thesis in the earliest layer of tradition found in the Gospels. See his "Very Goddess and Very Man," 81–96 in James M. Robinson, *Jesus according to the Earliest Witness* (Minneapolis: Fortress, 2007).

80. For more on this theory, see Elisabeth Schüssler Fiorenza, *Jesus—Miriam's Child, Sophia's Prophet: Critical Issues in Feminist Christology* (New York: Continuum, 1994).
81. See Kathleen E. Corley, *Women and the Historical Jesus: Feminist Myths of Christian Origins* (Santa Rosa, Calif.: Polebridge, 2002), 15–20; Judith Plaskow, "Blaming Jews for Inventing Patriarchy," *Lilith* 7 (1980): 11–12.
82. So John H. Elliott says that he wishes "with every fiber of [his] egalitarian being that the Jesus movement had been egalitarian," but the thesis that it was "lacks probative textual and historical support, is sociologically implausible, conceptually anachronistic, and appears ideologically driven." See "The Jesus Movement Was Not Egalitarian but Family Oriented," *Biblical Interpretation* 11.2 (2003): 173–210, citation on 206. See also John H. Elliott, "Jesus Was Not an Egalitarian," *Biblical Theology Bulletin* 32.2 (2002): 85–88.
83. Nevertheless, Witherington is critical of Schüssler Fiorenza's overall reconstruction. See Ben Witherington III, *The Jesus Quest: The Third Search for the Jew of Nazareth* (Downers Grove, Ill.: InterVarsity, 1995),163–85; 242–44.
84. Elisabeth Schüssler Fiorenza, "The Jesus of Piety and the Historical Jesus," *Catholic Theological Society of America Proceedings* 49 (1994): 90–99.
85. Cited in Josh Simon, "Who Was Jesus?" *Life* (December 1994): 67–82, citation on 72.

Chapter 2: Sources and Criteria

1. John P. Meier, *A Marginal Jew: Rethinking the Historical Jesus*, 5 vols. (New York: Doubleday, 1991), 2:1–2.
2. Sanders, *Historical Figure of Jesus*, 8.
3. Crossan, *Historical Jesus*, xxviii.
4. James H. Charlesworth, "Jesus Research and Archaeology: A New Perspective," 11–63 in Charlesworth, *Jesus and Archaeology*, esp. 38. Compare James H. Charlesworth, *The Millennium Guide for Pilgrims to the Holy Land* (North Richland Hills, Tex.: BIBAL, 2000).
5. There was some excitement in 2002 when some scholars believed that they had found the ossuary of James, the brother of Jesus who led the early Christian church in Jerusalem; the Israeli Antiquities authorities have since judged that ossuary to be a fake, since the inscription identifying it with James appears to have been forged at a much later time. See Ryan Byrne and Bernadette McNary-Zak, *Resurrecting the Brother of Jesus: The James Ossuary and the Quest for Religious Relics* (Chapel Hill: University of North Carolina Press, 2009). For an analysis by scholars who believe the ossuary to be authentic, see Hershel Shanks and Ben Witherington III, *The Brother of Jesus and the First Archaeological Link to Jesus and His Family*, rev. ed. (San Francisco: HarperOne, 2009).
6. Charlesworth, "Jesus Research and Archaeology," 41–42; Jonathan L. Reed, *The HarperCollins Visual Guide to the New Testament: What Archaeology Reveals about the First Christians* (New York: HarperCollins, 2007), 68–69.
7. Jonathan L. Reed, *Archaeology and the Galilean Jesus: A Re-examination of the Evidence* (Harrisburg, Penn.: Trinity Press International, 2000).
8. Sean Freyne, *Jesus, a Jewish Galilean: A New Reading of the Jesus Story* (New York: T&T Clark, 2004), 24–59.
9. Marianne Sawicki, *Crossing Galilee: Architectures of Contact in the Occupied Land of Jesus* (Harrisburg, Penn.: Trinity Press International, 2000), 126. She further notes that the system of roads led to labor displacement (migration of workers to the cities) accompanied by gender displacement (women tending fields in the

absence of men or traveling to cities themselves to find previously unavailable work as sellers of cloth or produce).

10. The classic work that first raised these issues is Martin Hengel, *Judaism and Hellenism: Studies in Their Encounter in Palestine during the Early Hellenistic Period*, 2 vols. (Minneapolis: Fortress, 1974); see also his *The "Hellenization" of Judaea in the First Century after Christ* (Philadelphia, Penn.: Trinity Press International, 1989). Louis H. Feldman argues that the extent of hellenization of Palestine during this period has been exaggerated in *Jews and Gentiles in the Ancient World: Attitudes and Interactions from Alexander to Justinian* (Princeton: Princeton University Press, 1993), esp. 3–44.

11. Reed, *Archaeology and the Galilean Jesus*, 23–62. Compare Mark A. Chancey, *The Myth of a Gentile Galilee*, Society for New Testament Studies Monograph Series 118 (Cambridge: Cambridge University Press, 2002); *Greco-Roman Culture and the Galilee of Jesus*, Society for New Testament Studies Series 134 (Cambridge: Cambridge University Press, 2005).

12. See the summary of both positions in Charlesworth, "Jesus Research and Archaeology," 51–55; compare Richard A. Batey, "Did Antipas Build the Sepphoris Theater?" 111–19 in Charlesworth, *Jesus and Archaeology*.

13. For more information on references to Jesus in Roman writings, see Robert E. Van Voorst, *Jesus outside the New Testament: An Introduction to the Ancient Evidence* (Grand Rapids: Eerdmans, 2000), 19–74, 81–104.

14. See F. Jacoby, *Die Fragmente der griechischen Historiker* (Leiden: Brill, 1962), II B, 1157.

15. For a fairly comprehensive survey of the problems with the Josephus text and the way those have been handled, regarded, or ignored throughout history, see Alice Wheatley, *Josephus on Jesus: The* Testimonium Flavianum *Controversy from Late Antiquity to Modern Times*, Studies in Biblical Literature 36 (New York: Lang, 2003).

16. The translation and reconstruction is from Meier, who gives details on the textual problems. See *Marginal Jew*, 1:56–92. Three passages are usually omitted as Christian interpolations at the spots marked by superscripted letters:

   [a] if indeed one should call him a man
   [b] He was the Messiah.
   [c] For he appeared to them on the third day, living again, just as the divine prophets had spoken of these and countless other wondrous things about him.

17. The reconstruction offered here follows a dominant theory, accepted by most contemporary Jesus scholars. Other hypotheses have been advanced including ones that suggest the original text was hostile to Jesus or, indeed, that it made no mention of him at all. For a summary, see Theissen and Merz, *The Historical Jesus: A Comprehensive Guide*, 64–74. For Christian interpolations regarding Jesus elsewhere in Josephus' writings, see the same volume, 87–89, 576–80. On all these matters, see also Van Voorst, *Jesus outside the New Testament*, 81–104.

18. Unfortunately, the portion of Tacitus' *Annals* dealing with the years 29–31 CE is missing from our manuscripts. We don't know for sure whether he described the life or death of Jesus further in the missing portion of his book.

19. For full text and translation, see W. Cuerton, *Spicilegium Syriacum* (London: Rivington, 1855). For further discussion (and bibliography), see Van Voorst, *Jesus outside the New Testament*, 53–58.

20. Meier has a good discussion of the problems involved in *Marginal Jew*, 1:93–98.

21. One study of Paul's possible use of quotations of Jesus is David L. Dungan, *The Sayings of Jesus in the Churches of Paul: The Use of the Synoptic Tradition in the Regulation of Early Church Life* (Oxford: Basil Blackwell Publisher, 1971).

22. See Paul Barnett, *Jesus and the Logic of History* (Grand Rapids: Eerdmans, 1997); *Finding the Historical Christ* (Grand Rapids: Eerdmans, 2009). Likewise (but operating with a very different methodology), Bas van Os believes he can demonstrate that certain core beliefs in the undisputed letters of Paul "cannot be easily explained on the basis of contemporary Jewish or Hellenistic thinking" and so "could conceivably go back to Jesus." See *Psychological Analyses and the Historical Jesus: New Ways to Explore Christian Origins*, Library of New Testament Studies 432 (London: T&T Clark, 2011), 187.

23. Richard Bauckham, *Jesus and the Eyewitnesses: The Gospels as Eyewitness Testimony* (Grand Rapids: Eerdmans, 2006).

24. Christopher Tuckett, "Review of Richard Bauckham's *Jesus and the Eyewitnesses*," *Review of Biblical Literature*, 12/2007. The *Journal for the Study of the Historical Jesus* devoted almost an entire issue (vol. 6, no. 2; 2008) to review and discussion of Bauckham's book and its implications for historical Jesus studies.

25. For fuller discussion on the authorship of all four Gospels, see Mark Allan Powell, *A Fortress Introduction to the Gospels* (Minneapolis: Fortress, 1998).

26. James D. G. Dunn, *Jesus Remembered*, Christianity in the Making 1 (Grand Rapids: Eerdmans, 2003). See also his *A New Perspective on Jesus: What the Quest for the Historical Jesus Missed* (Grand Rapids: Baker Academic, 2005); "Remembering Jesus: How the Quest of the Historical Jesus Lost Its Way," 199–248 in James K. Beilby and Paul Rhodes Eddy, eds., *The Historical Jesus: Five Views* (Downers Grove, Ill.: InterVarsity, 2009).

27. Kenneth E. Bailey, "Informal Controlled Oral Tradition and the Synoptic Gospels," *Asia Journal of Theology* 5 (1991): 34–54; "Middle Eastern Oral Tradition and the Synoptic Gospels," *Expository Times* 106 (1995): 363–67.

28. The problem with Dunn's thesis according to Meier is that the literary paradigm has been shown to work so well. Frequently, the differences between a Matthean and Markan account (or between a Lukan and Markan account) exhibit features attributable to Matthew's (or Luke's) particular interests within the context presumed for his Gospel. See *Marginal Jew* 4:457–58 n. 136; 523; 611 n. 159. Meier makes this point with specific reference to Matthean redaction of Mark 7:14–23 (in Matt. 15:10–20); Matthean redaction of Mark 4:35–41 (in Matt. 8:23–27); and Matthean and Lukan redaction of Mark 12:28–34 (in Matt. 22:24–40 and Luke 10:25–28). The pages from Dunn he cites as failing to take such redaction into account are *Jesus Remembered*, 173–254; 584–86.

29. Such reconstructions have, of course, been made. The "industry standard" is probably James M. Robinson, Paul Hoffmann, and John S. Kloppenborg, eds., *The Critical Edition of Q* (Minneapolis: Fortress, 2000). For discussion, see James M. Robinson, "The Critical Edition of Q and the Study of Jesus," 1–26 in Robinson, *Jesus according to the Earliest Witness*.

30. See Mark Goodacre, *The Case against Q: Studies in Markan Priority and the Synoptic Gospels* (Harrisburg, Penn.: Trinity Press International, 2002).

31. See William R. Farmer, *The Synoptic Problem: A Form-Critical Analysis* (New York: Macmillan, 1964); David Laird Dungan, *A History of the Synoptic Problem: The Canon, the Text, the Composition, and the Interpretation of the Gospels* (New Haven: Yale University Press, 1999).

32. See, for instance, Craig Blomberg, *Jesus and the Gospels: An Introduction and Survey* (Nashville: Broadman and Holman, 1997), 122–23.

33. John S. Kloppenborg, *The Formation of Q: Trajectories in Ancient Wisdom Collections*, Studies in Antiquity and Christianity (Philadelphia: Fortress, 1987); also see John S. Kloppenborg Verbin, *Excavating Q: The History and Setting of*

the Sayings Gospel (Minneapolis: Fortress, 2000). Kloppenborg himself warned against extrapolating conclusions regarding the age of individual sayings from the age of the recensions—some sayings contained in a later layer could be older than sayings contained in an earlier layer (*Formation of Q,* 244–45). This warning has seldom been heeded.

34. William E. Arnal, *Jesus and the Village Scribes: Galilean Conflicts and the Setting of Q* (Minneapolis: Fortress, 2001).

35. See, for instance, the numerous essays by James M. Robinson collected in his *Jesus according to the Earliest Witness,* especially "The Real Jesus of the Sayings Gospel Q" (65–80); "Jesus' Theology in the Sayings Gospel Q" (119–40); and "The Image of Jesus in Q" (161–78). But Helmut Koester says, "It is questionable whether the early stage of Q can really be defined as noneschatological, even more doubtful whether one can draw from such observations the conclusion that the preaching of the historical Jesus had no relation to eschatology." See Koester, "Jesus the Victim," *Journal of Biblical Literature* 111 (1992): 7.

36. Mack, *Lost Gospel,* 4.

37. Against the recension theory that would relegate eschatological sayings to a late version of Q, see Dale C. Allison Jr., *The Jesus Tradition in Q* (Harrisburg, Penn.: Trinity Press International, 1997); Brian Han Gregg, *The Historical Jesus and the Final Judgment Sayings in Q,* Wissenschaftliche Untersuchungen zum Neuen Testament 2.207 (Tübingen: Mohr-Siebeck, 2006).

38. Allen, "Search for No-Frills Jesus," 57.

39. Siegfried Schulz, *Q: Die Spruchquelle der Evangelisten* (Zurich: Theologischer Verlag, 1972).

40. Witherington says, "Arguing there was a Q community is like arguing there was a Proverbs community. . . . Besides the fact that it is wholly an argument from silence, with no data outside of Q by which to check such a view, where is there any precedent in early Judaism for such a community?" (See *Jesus the Sage,* 211–12.)

41. See Christopher M. Tuckett, "Q (Gospel Source)," *Anchor Bible Dictionary* 5:567–72.

42. Meier, *Marginal Jew,* 2:179.

43. Meier, *Marginal Jew* 2:153.18.

44. The arguments for early dates are summarized in Blomberg, *Jesus and the Gospels,* 134–35, 150–52.

45. These lists are based on ones that I developed for publication in Powell, *Fortress Introduction to the Gospels* and later revised for publication in Mark Allan Powell, *Introducing the New Testament* (Grand Rapids: Baker Academic, 2009).

46. See, for example, Robert T. Fortna, *The Gospel of Signs: A Reconstruction of the Narrative Source Underlying the Fourth Gospel* (New York: Cambridge University Press, 1970); *The Fourth Gospel and Its Predecessor: From Narrative Source to Present Gospel* (Philadelphia: Fortress, 1988); Urban C. Von Wahlde, *The Earliest Version of John's Gospel: Recovering the Gospel of Signs* (Wilmington: Michael Glazier, 1989).

47. On this trend, see Charlesworth, "Historical Jesus in the Fourth Gospel"; Mark Allan Powell, "The De-Johannification of Jesus: The Twentieth Century and Beyond," in Paul N. Anderson, Felix Just, and Tom Thatcher, eds., *John, Jesus, and History,* vol. 1, *Critical Appraisals of Critical Views,* Symposium Series 44 (Atlanta: Society of Biblical Literature, 2007), 121–32.

48. Charlesworth, "Historical Jesus in the Fourth Gospel," 31–34. In addition to the works cited here, see Freyne, *Jesus, a Jewish Galilean*; Paula Fredriksen, *Jesus of Nazareth, King of the Jews* (New York: Random House, 1999).

49. Paula Fredriksen thinks that John's information is more historically sound than what is provided by the Synoptic Gospels with regard to "the probable duration of Jesus' ministry, the Sanhedrin's concern for the political consequences of his preaching, the pitch of popular messianic excitement around Passover, the extent of the Jewish authorities' involvement on the night of Jesus' arrest, the date of his arrest relative to Passover." See *From Jesus to Christ: The Origins of the New Testament Images of Jesus*, 2nd ed. (New Haven: Yale University Press, 2000), 198–99.

50. On this controversial but highly significant point, see Dwight Moody Smith, *John among the Gospels*, 2nd ed. (Columbia: University of Carolina Press, 2001), esp. 195–241.

51. Paul N. Anderson, *The Fourth Gospel and the Quest for Jesus: Modern Foundations Reconsidered*, Library of New Testament Studies 321 (New York: T&T Clark, 2006).

52. The John, Jesus, and History Group of the Society of Biblical Literature devoted itself to studying the implications of this recognition and published three volumes of essays, edited by Paul Anderson, Felix Just, and Tom Thatcher. These works are all titled *John, Jesus, and History* and subtitled Vol. 1, *Critical Appraisals of Critical Views*, Symposium Series 44 (Atlanta: Society of Biblical Literature, 2007); Vol. 2, *Aspects of Historicity in the Fourth Gospel*, Early Christianity and Its Literature (Atlanta: Society of Biblical Literature, 2009); and Vol. 3, *Glimpses of Jesus through the Johannine Lens* (Atlanta: Society of Biblical Literature, forthcoming).

53. Mark Allan Powell, "The De-Johannification of Jesus: The Twentieth Century and Beyond," 109–20 in Anderson et al., *John, Jesus, and History*, Vol. 1; citation on 132.

54. For the texts of several significant works, see Bart D. Ehrman, *Lost Scriptures: Books That Did Not Make It into the New Testament* (Oxford: Oxford University Press, 2003); Robert J. Miller, ed., *The Complete Gospels: Annotated Scholars Version*. rev. ed. (San Francisco: HarperSanFrancisco, 1994); James M. Robinson, *The Nag Hammadi Library*, 3rd ed. (San Francisco: Harper & Row, 1990); Wilhelm Schneelmelcher, ed., *New Testament Apocrypha*, vol. 1, *Gospels and Related Writings*, rev. ed., trans. R. McL. Wilson (Louisville: Westminster/John Knox, 1990). Quotations of documents in this book are from Ehrman.

55. The process through which writings came to be regarded as canonical was complex and, at times, remains unclear. It involved the eventual coherence of both acceptance at a grassroots level (which books got used the most) and sanction by official authorities. See John Barton, *Holy Writings, Sacred Text: The Canon in Early Christianity* (Louisville: Westminster John Knox, 1997); F. F. Bruce, *The Canon of Scripture* (Downers Grove, Ill.: InterVarsity, 1988); Lee Martin McDonald, *The Biblical Canon: Its Origin, Transmission, and Authority* (Peabody: Hendrickson, 2007); H. Von Campenhausen, *The Formation of the Christian Bible* (Philadelphia: Fortress, 1972). Other Gospels were used, especially in the Eastern church, but by the beginning of the third century, collections of Matthew, Mark, Luke, and John were being widely circulated and appear to have achieved definitive scriptural standing as a group.

56. For one assessment of these works and their significance, see Helmut Koester, *Ancient Christian Gospels: Their History and Development* (Philadelphia: Trinity Press International, 1990).

57. Gnosticism evinced a radically dualistic vision of reality that contrasted the goodness of the spiritual realm with the evil of the material world. Gnostic Christians claimed that Jesus was a spirit-being who had imparted a secret

knowledge that would free people's spirits from the earthly prisons of their physical bodies. See Pheme Perkins, *Gnosticism and the New Testament* (Minneapolis: Fortress, 1993); Elaine Pagels, *The Gnostic Gospels* (New York: Random House, 1980).

58. Miller, *Complete Gospels*, 302–3.

59. Fred Lapham, *An Introduction to the New Testament Apocrypha* (London: T&T Clark, 2003), 120; Hans-Josef Klauck, *Apocryphal Gospels: An Introduction* (London: T&T Clark, 2003), 108.

60. See John Dominic Crossan, *The Cross That Spoke: The Origins of the Passion Narrative* (San Francisco: Harper & Row, 1988). The argument is updated somewhat in his *Four Other Gospels: Shadows on the Contours of Canon* (Sonoma, Calif.: Polebridge, 1992; original 1962), 85–127. See also Koester, *Ancient Christian Gospels*, 216–40.

61. For description and translation of this work (called "The Secret Gospel of Mark"), see Ehrman, *Lost Scriptures*, 87–89. The initial publication of the work, with commentary by the man who presumably discovered it, is found in Morton Smith, *Clement of Alexandria and a Secret Gospel of Mark* (Cambridge: Harvard University Press, 1973); a more popular account for nonspecialists is provided in Morton Smith, *The Secret Gospel: The Discovery and Interpretation of the Secret Gospel according to Mark* (New York: Harper & Row, 1973).

62. Crossan, *Four Other Gospels*, 107–8.

63. Smith, *Secret Gospel*, 113–14.

64. See Stephen C. Carlson, *The Gospel Hoax: Morton Smith's Invention of Secret Mark* (Waco, Tex.: Baylor University Press, 2005); Peter Jeffery, *The Secret Gospel of Mark Unveiled: Imagined Rituals of Sex, Death, and Madness in a Biblical Forgery* (New Haven: Yale University Press, 2006). Parts of Carlson's thesis are contested by Allan J. Pantuck and Scott G. Brown, "Morton Smith as M. Madiotes: Stephen Carlson's Attribution of *Secret Mark* to a Bald Swindler," *Journal for the Study of the Historical Jesus* 6.1 (2008): 106–25.

65. See Scott G. Brown, *Mark's Other Gospel: Re-thinking Morton Smith's Controversial Discovery* (Waterloo: Canadian Corporation for Studies in Religion, 2005). As of 2012, Helmut Koester of Harvard University was also still defending the authenticity of the Secret Gospel of Mark in his public teaching. Birger Pearson, who had previously accepted the work as authentic, was publicly admitting, "I was duped."

66. Stephen J. Patterson offers a summary of criteria that overlaps considerably with what is presented here. Patterson says one should eliminate from consideration material that (1) derives clearly from the redactional activity of an evangelist; (2) derives clearly from early Christian preaching about Jesus; or (3) reflects the life setting of the early church rather than any life setting plausibly imagined for Jesus himself. One should grant careful consideration, however, to material that (1) is independently attested in two or more sources; (2) appears to be unique to Jesus or unusual; (3) would have been potentially embarrassing to early Christians; (4) coheres with the ethos, attitude, or theology of material accepted by virtue of the foregoing criteria. See *The God of Jesus: The Historical Jesus and the Search for Meaning* (Harrisburg, Penn.: Trinity Press International, 1998), 265–71.

67. A possible tenth criterion, alleging that material is more likely to be historical if it helps to explain why Jesus was rejected and executed, has been proposed by John Meier and is discussed in the chapter of this book devoted to his work (see page 181).

68. Wright, *Jesus and the Victory of God*, 51.

69. Note, however, that Michael F. Bird argues that the historical Jesus *did* authorize (and initiate) a mission to the Gentiles, which he thought was an essential component of the eschatological restoration of Israel. See *Jesus and the Origins of the Gentile Mission*, Library of New Testament Studies 331(London: T&T Clark, 2007).

70. Bultmann says, "We can only count on possessing a genuine similitude of Jesus where, on the one hand, expression is given to the contrast between Jewish morality and piety and the distinctive eschatological temper which characterized the preaching of Jesus; and where on the other hand we find no specifically Christian features." See Rudolf Bultmann, *History of the Synoptic Tradition*, trans. John Marsh (New York: Harper & Row, 1963; original 1921).

71. See, for example, Tom Holmén, "Doubts about Double Dissimilarity: Restructuring the Main Criterion of Jesus-of-History Research," 47–80 in Bruce Chilton and Craig A. Evans, eds., *Authenticating the Words of Jesus*, New Testament Tools and Studies 28.2 (Leiden: Brill, 1999).

72. Theissen defines the criterion of historical plausibility as follows: "whatever helps to explain the influence of Jesus and at the same time can only have come into being in a Jewish context is historical in the sources." See Theissen and Merz, *Historical Jesus*, 116. See also Gerd Theissen and Dagmar Winter, *The Quest for the Plausible Jesus: The Question of Criteria*, trans. M. Eugene Boring (Louisville: Westminster John Knox, 2002).

73. Russell Shorto, "Who Put the *Hell* in *Hellenism?*" *The Fourth R* 10.5 (1997): 5.

74. Shorto, "Who Put the *Hell* in *Hellenism?*" 5.

Chapter 3: Snapshots: Contemporary Images of Jesus

1. Walter F. Taylor, "New Quests for the Historical Jesus," *Trinity Seminary Review* 15 (1992): 69.

2. Cited in Simon, "Who Was Jesus?" 76.

3. Robert W. Yarbrough, "Modern Wise Men Encounter Jesus," *Christianity Today* (December 12, 1994): 38–45; citation on 38.

4. Richard A. Horsley, *Jesus and the Spiral of Violence: Popular Jewish Resistance in Roman Palestine* (San Francisco: Harper & Row, 1973).

5. Richard A. Horsley, *Bandits, Prophets, and Messiahs: Popular Movements at the Time of Jesus* (Minneapolis: Winston, 1985); *Sociology and the Jesus Movement* (New York: Crossroad, 1989). See also Richard A. Horsley, *Archaeology, History, and Society in Galilee: The Social Context of Jesus and the Rabbis* (Valley Forge, Penn.: Trinity Press International, 1996); *Galilee: History, Politics, People* (Valley Forge, Penn.: Trinity Press International, 1995).

6. The particular model he uses is associated with Gerhard Lenski, *Power and Privilege: A Theory of Social Stratification* (New York: McGraw-Hill, 1966) and John H. Kautsky, *The Politics of Aristocratic Empires* (Chapel Hill: University of North Carolina Press, 1982). Marianne Sawicki notes that this is but one of several models social scientists use and suggests that Horsley's choice of the model dictates the results of his study; indeed, she accuses him of ignoring data from archaeology and texts that would challenge the model. See *Crossing Galilee*, 36, 68. Compare Freyne, "Archaeology and the Historical Jesus," 68–74.

7. Horsley, *Spiral of Violence*, 246–73.

8. Horsley, *Spiral of Violence*, 231–45.

9. Horsley, *Spiral of Violence*, 286–306, citation on 287.

10. Horsley, *Spiral of Violence*, 320.

11. Horsley, *Spiral of Violence*, 160–64.

12. Horsley, *Spiral of Violence*, 157–60, 321–22.

13. Horsley, *Spiral of Violence*, 255–73. See also Richard A. Horsley, "Ethics and Exegesis: 'Love Your Enemy' and the Doctrine of Nonviolence," in *The Love of Enemy and Nonretaliation in the New Testament*, ed. W. M. Swartley, 72–101 (Louisville: Westminster/John Knox, 1992; original, 1986).

14. Horsley, *Spiral of Violence*, 170.

15. Richard A. Horsley, *Jesus in Context: Power, People, and Performance* (Minneapolis: Fortress, 2008); *Jesus and the Powers: Conflict, Covenant, and the Hope of the Poor* (Minneapolis: Fortress, 2011).

16. James C. Scott, *The Moral Economy of the Peasant: Rebellion and Subsistence in Southeast Asia* (New Haven: Yale University Press, 1976); *Domination and the Arts of Resistance: Hidden Transcripts* (New Haven: Yale University Press, 1985). For Horsley's application of Scott's work, see also Richard A. Horsley, *Hidden Transcripts and the Arts of Resistance: Applying the Work of James C. Scott to Jesus and Paul*, Semeia Studies 48 (Atlanta: Society of Biblical Literature, 2004).

17. Borg, *Jesus in Contemporary Scholarship*, 28.

18. See, for example, the complaints offered in Wright, *Jesus and the Victory of God*, 156–59.

19. Witherington, *Jesus Quest*, 150, 153.

20. N. T. Wright, *The New Testament and the People of God*, Christian Origins and the Question of God 1 (Minneapolis: Fortress, 1992), 179–80.

21. Wink, "Neither Passivity nor Violence" and "Counter-Response to Richard Horsley," both in Willard M. Swartley, *The Love of Enemy and Nonretaliation in the New Testament* (Louisville: Westminster/John Knox, 1992), 102–25; 133–36. See also Wright, *Jesus and the Victory of God*, 290.

22. Horsley, *Spiral of Violence*, 212–17.

23. R. David Kaylor, *Jesus the Prophet: His Vision of the Kingdom on Earth.* (Louisville: Westminster John Knox, 1994), 142–43.

24. William R. Herzog II, *Parables as Subversive Speech: Jesus as Pedagogue of the Oppressed* (Louisville: Westminster John Knox, 1994); *Jesus, Justice, and the Reign of God: A Ministry of Liberation* (Louisville: Westminster John Knox, 2000); and *Prophet and Teacher: An Introduction to the Historical Jesus* (Louisville: Westminster John Knox, 2005). The same line of reasoning is followed in Luise Schottroff, *The Parables of Jesus* (Minneapolis: Fortress, 2006).

25. This intriguing story is recounted in his autobiography, *Providential Accidents* (London: SCM, 1998).

26. Geza Vermes, *Jesus the Jew: A Historian's Reading of the Gospels* (London: Collins, 1973), 79.

27. Vermes, *Jesus the Jew*, 80.

28. Vermes, *Jesus the Jew*, 79.

29. Meier, *Marginal Jew*, 2:587.

30. Crossan, *Historical Jesus*, 142–56; Marcus J. Borg, *Jesus: A New Vision* (San Francisco: Harper & Row, 1988), 25–75, esp. 30–32.

31. Sanders, *Historical Figure of Jesus*, 138–40.

32. Pieter F. Craffert, *The Life of a Galilean Shaman: Jesus of Nazareth in Anthropological-Historical Perspective* (Eugene, Ore.: Cascade, 2008).

33. Craffert, *Life of a Galilean Shaman*, 157.

34. Craffert, *Life of a Galilean Shaman*, 98.

35. Graham H. Twelftree, *Jesus the Miracle Worker: A Historical and Theological Study* (Downers Grove, Ill.: InterVarsity, 1999). See also Eric Eve, *The Healer from Nazareth: Jesus' Miracles in Historical Context* (London: SPCK, 2009).

36. Graham Twelftree, *Jesus the Exorcist: A Contribution to the Study of the Historical Jesus* (Peabody, Mass.: Hendrickson Publishers, 1993).

37. Twelftree, *Jesus the Exorcist*, 228.
38. Twelftree, *Jesus the Miracle Worker*, 275.
39. Keener, *Historical Jesus of the Gospels*, 38.
40. Geza Vermes, *The Real Jesus: Then and Now* (Minneapolis: Fortress, 2010), 23.
41. Joseph Klausner, *Jesus of Nazareth: His Life, Times, and Teaching* (London: George Allen & Unwin, 1947; original 1922).
42. C. G. Montefiore, *The Synoptic Gospels*, 2 vols. (London: Macmillan, 1909, 1927; reprint, New York: KTAV, 1968).
43. Robert Eisler, *The Messiah Jesus and John the Baptist* (London: Methuen, 1931).
44. Hyam Maccoby, *Jesus the Pharisee* (London: SCM, 2003). Maccoby died in 2004, shortly after this book was published.
45. David Flusser, with R. Steven Notley, *The Sage from Galilee: Rediscovering Jesus' Genius*, 4th ed. (Grand Rapids: Eerdmans, 2007; first German edition 1968).
46. See especially Amy-Jill Levine, *The Misunderstood Jew: The Church and the Scandal of the Jewish Jesus* (San Francisco: HarperSanFrancisco, 2006).
47. Morton Smith, *Jesus the Magician* (New York: Harper & Row, 1978), 69.
48. Smith, *Jesus the Magician*, vii.
49. Smith, *Jesus the Magician*, 94–139.
50. Smith, *Jesus the Magician*, 96.
51. Smith, *Jesus the Magician*, 132.
52. Smith, *Jesus the Magician*, 146.
53. Smith, *Jesus the Magician*, 110–11. Smith quotes an intriguing passage from Origen, who also thought Satan entered Judas through the bread.
54. Smith, *Jesus the Magician*, vii.
55. Keener, *Historical Jesus of the Gospels*, 42.
56. This premise informs all the essays in Scot McKnight and Joseph B. Modica, eds., *Who Do My Opponents Say That I Am? An Investigation of the Accusations against the Historical Jesus*, Library of New Testament Studies 327 (London: T&T Clark, 2008).
57. Meier, *Marginal Jew*, 2:12. This is a summary of the argument found on 509–75.
58. On these and other similar points, see Ben Witherington III, *Jesus the Sage: The Pilgrimage of Wisdom* (Minneapolis: Fortress, 1994), 147–208, plus Witherington's summary of his own views in *Jesus Quest*, 185–94.
59. The specific reference is *b. B. Bat.* 12a. See Witherington, *Jesus the Sage*, 158.
60. Instead, he uses the formula, "Amen, I say to you . . ." See Ben Witherington III, *The Christology of Jesus* (Minneapolis: Fortress, 1990), 186–89.
61. Witherington, *Jesus Quest*, 189–90.
62. For discussion of this text, see Witherington, *Christology of Jesus*, 45–53.
63. Witherington, *Christology of Jesus*, 221–28.
64. Witherington, *Jesus Quest*, 192–93.
65. See Borg, *Jesus: A New Vision*, 97–124; Witherington, *Jesus the Sage*, 52–74.
66. Borg, *Jesus in Contemporary Scholarship*, 47–68. Compare Witherington, *Jesus Quest*, 94–98, 101.
67. E. P. Sanders, *Jesus and Judaism* (Philadelphia: Fortress, 1985), 1.
68. Wright, *Jesus and the Victory of God*, 312, 315.
69. Articles debating the validity of the image include Hans Dieter Betz, "Jesus and the Cynics: Survey and Analysis of a Hypothesis," *Journal of Religion* 74 (1994): 453–75; Paul Rhodes Eddy, "Jesus as Diogenes? Reflections on the Cynic Jesus Thesis," *Journal of Biblical Literature* 115 (1996): 449–69; and David Seeley, "Jesus and the Cynics Revisited," *Journal of Biblical Literature* 116 (1997): 704–12.
70. See Leif Vaage, *Galilean Upstarts: Jesus' First Followers according to Q* (Valley Forge, Penn.: Trinity Press International, 1994). See also the works of Burton

Mack, and the works cited in note 11 on page 69 of Mack's *Myth of Innocence*. For parallels between Cynics and Paul, see Abraham J. Malherbe, *Paul and the Popular Philosophers* (Minneapolis: Fortress, 1989).

71. Some would trace the line back still further to Antisthenes, a pupil of Socrates. After Diogenes, famous Cynics included Crates of Thebes (c. 360–280 BCE), whose student Zeno was the founder of Stoicism.

72. On *chreiai*, see Burton L. Mack and Vernon K. Robbins, *Patterns of Persuasion in the Gospels* (Sonoma, Calif.: Polebridge, 1989) and Vernon K. Robbins, *Ancient Quotes and Anecdotes: From Crib to Crypt* (Sonoma, Calif.: Polebridge, 1989). Cynics are also said to have developed (along with their cousins, the Stoics) the rhetorical form of speech called *diatribe* (argument with an imaginary partner), which is used by Paul. See Malherbe, *Paul and the Popular Philosophers*.

73. Laertius puts it delicately: he did "everything in public, the works of Demeter and Aphrodite alike." On shamelessness, see also Diogenes Laertius, *Lives* 6.32, 46, 58, 61, and the discussion in F. Gerald Downing, *Cynics and Christian Origins* (Edinburgh: T&T Clark, 1992), 50–53.

74. Crossan, *Historical Jesus*, 74. Wright suggests a different reason for the derivation: "The Cynics barked at society, snapped at its heels" (*Jesus and the Victory of God*, 66–67).

75. Crossan, *Historical Jesus*, 421 and elsewhere.

76. Crossan notes the irony of the aristocratic, multimillionaire Seneca's attraction to the simple life (*Historical Jesus*, 75).

77. F. Gerald Downing, *Christ and the Cynics: Jesus and Other Radical Preachers in First-Century Tradition* (Sheffield: Sheffield Academic, 1988).

78. For his reckoning of Cynic themes not addressed in Christian materials, see Downing, *Christ and the Cynic*, 196–203.

79. Downing, *Christ and the Cynics*, vii.

80. See Downing, *Cynics and Christian Origins*, 154–62. Actually, this book expands the proposed range for Cynic influence in two directions. A full half of the book traces the continuation of Cynic tradition throughout church history from the second century to the dawn of the medieval period. The "Cynic strand" evident in such luminaries as Tertullian, Origen, and Eusebius forms the background for the development of Christian asceticism. Downing had begun to show this movement beyond the Gospel tradition already in *Christ and the Cynics* by presenting five pages of parallels to Pauline and Deutero-Pauline writings and *twenty-five* pages of parallels to the epistle of James.

81. See Christopher M. Tuckett, "A Cynic Q?" *Biblica* 70 (1989): 349–76.

82. Downing, *Cynics and Christian Origins*, 141.

83. See F. Gerald Downing, *Jesus and the Threat of Freedom* (London: SCM, 1987). This is a popular treatment that calls modern Christians to consider the message of Cynic radicalism.

84. In *Cynics and Christian Origins*, Downing devotes a whole chapter to the subject of dating and another chapter to the question of definition: "Who or What Counts as Cynic?"

85. Crossan says, "Cynicism was practical and radical Stoicism; Stoicism was theoretical and moderate Cynicism" (*Historical Jesus*, 74). Thus, the Stoics may have admired the Cynics and relayed stories about them without actually emulating their lifestyle.

86. Downing, *Cynics and Christian Origins*, 30.

87. Downing, *Christ and the Cynics*, 1.

88. Craig A. Evans, *Fabricating Jesus: How Modern Scholars Distort the Gospels* (Downers Grove: Ill.: InterVarsity, 2006), 107.

89. Leif Vaage has said, "The standard uniform of the Cynics was a cloak, a wallet [bag], a staff" (*Q: The Ethos and Ethics of an Itinerant Intelligence* [Ann Arbor, Mich.: University Microfilms, 1987], 374–75). Downing attempts to adduce examples of variety in dress in *Cynics and Christian Origins,* 10–11, 32–33.

90. Witherington, *Jesus Quest,* 59–63.

91. Henry Chadwick, "Review of *Cynics and Christian Origins* by F. Gerard Downing," *Journal of Theological Studies* 45 (1994): 210. Actually, there is some confusion over whether the sexual acts that Diogenes and company performed in public involved copulation or masturbation. (Yes, scholars really do debate such matters.) Chadwick's point holds either way.

92. Downing, *Cynics and Christian Origins,* 26–56, 124.

93. See Betz, "Jesus and the Cynics"; Eddy, "Jesus as Diogenes?" Evans, *Fabricating Jesus,* 100–122; Horsley, *Jesus and the Spiral of Violence,* 230–31; Keener, *Historical Jesus of the Gospels,* 14–32.

94. He may have visited the city of Gadara itself, but the manuscripts that report this story are corrupt. Some locate the story that begins in Mark 5:1 in Gadara, others in Gerasa, and still others in Gergesa.

95. Leif Vaage, "Review of *Cynics and Christian Origins* by F. Gerald Downing," *Catholic Biblical Quarterly* 56 (1994): 587–89.

96. Witherington, *Jesus the Sage,* 117–45; see also, Eddy, "Jesus as Diogenes?"

97. Gerd Theissen, *The Shadow of the Galilean: The Quest for the Historical Jesus in Narrative Form,* trans. John Bowden (Philadelphia: Fortress, 1987).

98. Theissen and Merz, *Historical Jesus.* This multifaceted profile of Jesus is primarily presented in the material contained in chapters 8–14 of the book.

99. Otherwise, Theissen does think that wandering cynic philosophers and preachers provide the nearest parallel to the radical itinerants who comprised the first followers of Jesus. See Gerd Theissen, *Sociology of Early Palestinian Christianity,* trans. John Bowden (Philadelphia: Fortress, 1978), 14–15.

100. Gerd Theissen, "The Wandering Radicals: Light Shed by the Sociology of Literature on the Early Transmission of Jesus Sayings," 33–59 in Gerd Theissen, *Social Reality and the Early Christians,* trans. Margaret Kohl (Minneapolis: Augsburg Fortress, 1992).

101. Theissen and Merz, *Historical Jesus,* 309.

102. Gerd Theissen, *A Theory of Primitive Christianity,* trans. John Bowden (London: SCM, 1999), 23–24. See also Theissen and Merz, *Historical Jesus,* 262–64. I am indebted to David B. Gowler for calling attention to how this one exegetical point illustrates Theissen's understanding of the way Jesus could creatively combine potentially disparate Jewish traditions to produce dynamic new symbols. Gowler offers an excellent summary of Theissen's contributions to Jesus studies in his *What Are They Saying about the Historical Jesus?* 121–32.

103. Theissen, *Sociology of Early Palestinian Christianity; Social Reality and the Early Christians; The Gospels in Context: Social and Political History in the Synoptic Tradition* (Minneapolis: Fortress, 1991). The later work also draws significantly on archaeology and on what Theissen calls "cultural geography."

104. Theissen, *Gospels in Context,* 65–79.

105. Theissen, *Sociology of Early Palestinian Christianity,* 97–110.

106. Theissen, *Sociology of Early Palestinian Christianity,* 118.

107. Dunn, *Jesus Remembered,* 55.

108. Horsley, *Sociology and the Jesus Movement,* 43. A different sociological critique is offered by John H. Elliott in "Social-Scientific Criticism of the New Testament and Its Social World," *Semeia* 35 (1986): 1–33.

109. Gowler, *What Are They Saying about the Historical Jesus?* 124.

110. Vaage, *Galilean Upstarts.*

111. Halvor Moxnes, *Putting Jesus in His Place: A Radical Vision of Household and Kingdom* (Louisville: Westminster John Knox, 2003).

112. See especially Dale C. Allison, *Jesus of Nazareth: Millenarian Prophet* (Minneapolis: Fortress, 1998), and Robert J. Miller, ed., *The Apocalyptic Jesus: A Debate* (Santa Rosa, Calif.: Polebridge, 2001).

113. Allison, *Jesus of Nazareth*, 61–64, 78–94. Allison actually lists nineteen features of millenarian movements, only eight of which are mentioned here.

114. Allison, *Constructing Jesus*, 32.

115. Indeed, Allison emphasized in his early work that Jesus was an *ascetic* millenarian prophet. Most Jesus scholars contrast Jesus with John the Baptist on this point: John was an ascetic (e.g., abstaining from wine and certain foods) while Jesus was known for his eating and drinking and fellowship with sinners (Luke 7:33–34). Allison thinks the contrast is overdrawn. Jesus apparently chose to live in poverty (Matt. 8:20) and called others to do so (Luke 9:58); he practiced life-long celibacy and commended that practice for others (Matt. 19:10–12). He taught a severe sexual ethic, equating lustful thoughts with adultery (Matt. 5:27–30). See Allison, *Jesus of Nazareth* 172–216. On this, see also Simon J. Joseph, "The Ascetic Jesus," *Journal for the Study of the Historical Jesus* 8.2 (2010): 146–82.

116. Allison, *Constructing Jesus*, 33–48.

117. Allison, *Constructing Jesus*, 65–67.

118. Allison, *Constructing Jesus*, 48–55.

119. Allison, *Constructing Jesus*, 55–65.

120. Allison, *Constructing Jesus*, 12–17.

121. Allison, *Constructing Jesus*, 221–304.

122. Allison, *Constructing Jesus*, 387–434.

123. Note that Allison used the term "millenarian prophet" for Jesus in his early works but shifted to "apocalyptic prophet" in later writings; the latter term is perhaps less precise but more in keeping with the terminology of other historical Jesus scholars.

124. Dale C. Allison Jr. *The End of the Ages Has Come: An Early Interpretation of the Passion and Resurrection of Jesus* (Philadelphia: Fortress, 1985), 668.

125. Allison, *Resurrecting Jesus*, 147. Compare Allison's comments in Miller, ed., *Apocalyptic Jesus*, 147–48.

126. Wright, *Jesus and the Victory of God*, 333–36, 360–65. For Allison's rebuttal, see *Jesus of Nazareth*, 160.

127. Witherington, *Jesus Quest*, 128.

128. Allison thinks there is evidence of such eschatological disappointment already in the Jesus tradition itself, for example in the woes Jesus pronounces upon cities where at least some of his expectations have not been fulfilled (Luke 10:13–15). See Allison, *Jesus of Nazareth*, 150. Allison is relying here on C. J. Cadoux, whose work he says has fallen into "underserved oblivion."

129. Allison, *Resurrecting Jesus*, 147.

130. See Allison's comments in Miller, ed. *Apocalyptic Jesus*, 147–52, citation on 150.

131. Bart D. Ehrman, *Jesus: Apocalyptic Prophet of the New Millennium* (Oxford: Oxford University Press, 1999).

132. Marius Reiser, *Jesus and Judgment: The Eschatological Proclamation in Its Jewish Context*, trans. Linda M. Maloney (Minneapolis: Fortress, 1997; original 1990).

133. Reiser, *Jesus and Judgment*, 316.

134. See especially Bruce Chilton, *The Kingdom of God in the Teaching of Jesus* (Philadelphia: Fortress, 1984), *Pure Kingdom: Jesus' Vision of God* (Grand Rapids: Eerdmans, 1996), and other works listed in the bibliography.

135. Bruce Chilton, *Rabbi Jesus: An Intimate Biography. The Life and Teachings That Inspired Christianity* (New York: Image Books, 2000).

136. A number of scholars have suggested the book (Chilton, *Rabbi Jesus*) reads like a modern version of Renan's "Life of Jesus"—discussed on pages 14–15 of this book.

137. Chilton, *Rabbi Jesus*, 32–34, 71–74.

138. On this, see also Bruce Chilton, "Recovering Jesus' *Mamzerut*," 84–110 in Charlesworth, ed., *Jesus and Archaeology*; "*Mamzerut* and Jesus," 17–33 in Tom Holmén, ed., *Jesus from Judaism to Christianity: Continuum Approaches to the Historical Jesus*, Library of New Testament Studies 352 (London: T&T Clark, 2007).

139. Chilton, *Rabbi Jesus*, 12.

140. Scot McKnight, "Calling Jesus Mamzer," *Journal for the Study of the Historical Jesus* 1.1 (2003): 73–103; "Jesus as *Mamzer* ('Illegitimate Son')," 133–63 in McKnight and Modica, eds., *Who Do My Opponents Say That I Am?*

141. The same point is made by Bas van Os, *Psychological Analyses and the Historical Jesus*, 24–25.

142. Andries van Aarde, *Fatherless in Galilee: Jesus as Child of God* (Harrisburg, Penn.: Trinity Press International, 2001); Jane Schaberg, *The Illegitimacy of Jesus: A Feminist Theological Interpretation of the Infancy Narratives*, Expanded Twentieth Anniversary Edition (Sheffield: Phoenix, 2006; original 1987).

143. Charlesworth, "Jesus Research and Archaeology," 60–63.

144. James F. McGrath, "Was Jesus Illegitimate? The Evidence of His Social Interactions," *Journal for the Study of the Historical Jesus* 5.1 (2007): 81–100.

145. Other prominent Jewish scholars include Pinchas Lapide, Amy-Jill Levine, Doron Mendels, Geza Vermes, and Alan Segal. Prominent women include Levine, Kathleen Corley, Elisabeth Schüssler Fiorenza, Karen King, Marianne Sawicki, and Jane Schaberg.

146. Fredriksen, *Jesus of Nazareth*, 194–97.

147. Fredriksen, *Jesus of Nazareth*, 197–207.

148. Fredriksen, *Jesus of Nazareth*, 207–14.

149. Fredriksen, *Jesus of Nazareth*, 215–18.

150. Fredriksen, *Jesus of Nazareth*, 236–59.

151. Fredriksen, *Jesus of Nazareth*, 242.

152. Fredriksen, *Jesus of Nazareth*, 242.

153. Fredriksen, *Jesus of Nazareth*, 254.

154. Fredriksen, *Jesus of Nazareth*, 258–59.

155. I am among the scholars who have offered these critiques. See Mark Allan Powell, "On Deal-Breakers and Disturbances: A Response to Paula Fredriksen" in *Jesus, John, and History*, ed. Anderson et al., 277–84.

156. John Dominic Crossan, "Response to James D. G. Dunn," 233–38 in Beilby and Eddy, eds., *Historical Jesus: Five Views*, 234.

157. Gowler, *What Are They Saying about the Historical Jesus?* 79. Gowler is paraphrasing a point made by Steven M. Bryan in "Review of Paula Fredriksen, *Jesus of Nazareth*," *Journal of Theological Studies* 53.1 (2002): 184.

158. Taylor, "New Quests for the Historical Jesus," 81.

159. Simon, "Who Was Jesus?" 67–82.

160. Docetism is the belief, officially rejected by most Christian churches, that while Jesus *seemed* to be human, he did not really experience the pain or hardship of being mortal.

Chapter 4: Robert Funk and the Jesus Seminar

1. Robert W. Funk, *Honest to Jesus: Jesus for a New Millenium* (San Francisco: HarperSanFrancisco, 1996), 302–3.
2. Robert W. Funk, Roy W. Hoover, and the Jesus Seminar. *The Five Gospels: The Search for the Authentic Words of Jesus* (New York: Macmillan, 1993), 33.
3. Borg, *Jesus in Contemporary Scholarship,* 178. Borg is referring specifically to publication of Funk, et al., *Five Gospels.*
4. Paul Verhoeven, *Jesus of Nazareth* (New York: Seven Stories, 2008).
5. James M. Robinson, Afterword to "The Gospel according to the Jesus Seminar" by Birger A. Pearson, Institute for Antiquity and Christianity Occasional Paper 35 (Claremont, Calif.: Institute for Antiquity and Christianity, 1996), 45.
6. Robert W. Funk, "The Issue of Jesus," *Foundations and Facets Forum* 1.1 (1985): 7–12, citation on 7.
7. See Funk et al., *Five Gospels,* 533–37; Robert W. Funk and the Jesus Seminar, *The Acts of Jesus: The Search for the Authentic Deeds of Jesus* (San Francisco: HarperSanFrancisco, 1998), 537–42.
8. These statistics are based on the official voting records of the Jesus Seminar published in *Forum* 6.1 (1990): 3–55. Slightly different numbers may be obtained by counting colored sayings as they appear in *Five Gospels.*
9. Other slightly different explanations are provided in other literature associated with the group, including Funk, *Honest to Jesus,* 8, and Robert J. Miller, *The Jesus Seminar and Its Critics* (Santa Rosa, Calif.: Polebridge, 1999), 48, 55.
10. Funk et al., *Five Gospels,* 36.
11. Borg, *Jesus in Contemporary Scholarship,* 163.
12. Funk et al, *Five Gospels,* 37.
13. Borg, *Jesus in Contemporary Scholarship,* 163.
14. See the periodic reports in the journal *The Fourth R,* some of which are cited in the notes below.
15. Even here, there appears to have been some modification of definition as the process went along. For instance, at one point the Westar Institute's journal said the black type indicated that a deed "seems to be a fabrication," but the final published report in *The Acts of Jesus* says black type indicates a deed "is largely or entirely fictive." Compare *The Fourth R* 7.1 (1994): 12; Funk et al., *Acts of Jesus,* 36–37.
16. Robert W. Funk and the Jesus Seminar. *The Acts of Jesus: The Search for the Authentic Deeds of Jesus* (San Francisco: HarperSanFrancisco, 1998).
17. "The Jesus Seminar Fall 1994 Meeting: The Birth and Family of Jesus," *The Fourth R* 7.6 (1994): 11–16.
18. "The Jesus Seminar Fall 1993 Meeting," *The Fourth R* 7.1 (1994): 15.
19. "The Jesus Seminar Spring 1995 Meeting," *The Fourth R* 8.2 (1995): 12.
20. Rudolf Bultmann, "The Primitive Christian Kerygma and the Historical Jesus," 15–42 in *The Historical Jesus and the Kerygmatic Christ: Essays on the New Quest of the Historical Jesus,* ed. Carl E. Braaten and Roy A. Harrisville (Nashville: Abingdon, 1964), citation on 42.
21. Cited in David Van Biema, "The Gospel Truth?" *Time* (April 8, 1996): 59, 55.
22. Robert W. Funk, *A Credible Jesus: Fragments of a Vision* (Santa Rosa, Calif.: Polebridge, 2002).
23. Roy W. Hoover, ed. *Profiles of Jesus* (Santa Rosa, Calif.: Polebridge, 2002).

24. The summary offered here is based on information culled from "What Do We Really Know about Jesus?" 527–34 in Funk et al., *Acts of Jesus*; Roy Hoover's introduction to *Profiles of Jesus*, 1–7; and Funk, *Credible Jesus*.

25. The key word in this last affirmation might be *theological*. Clearly, Jesus Seminar members did believe that Jesus taught often and even primarily about God, but he was not interested in questions of theological doctrine. Stephen Patterson, a member of the Seminar, devoted an entire book to Jesus' conception of God (*The God of Jesus*). Patterson emphasizes that Jesus experienced God as the source of the power to love: as a homeless wanderer who lacked status or social power in Palestine, Jesus nevertheless discovered he was able to love, and he knew that the ability to love came not from himself but from God (246).

26. Charlotte Allen, "Away with the Manger," *Lingua Franca* (Jan./Feb., 1995): 22–30, citation on 26.

27. Allen, " No-Frills Jesus," 52, 55.

28. Cited in the *Atlanta Journal-Constitution* (September 30, 1989). Vaage may have been alluding to behavior and attitudes attributed to Jesus in such biblical passages as Mark 2:15–19; Luke 7:34; 14:26.

29. Cited in Russell Watson, "A Lesser Child of God," *Newsweek* (April 4, 1994): 53.

30. Cited in Jeffery L. Sheler et al., "In Search of Jesus," *U.S. News and World Report* (April 8, 1996): 47–53, citation on 49.

31. Sheler et al., "In Search of Jesus," 49.

32. Cited in Gustav Niebuhr, "The Jesus Seminar Courts Notoriety," *Christian Century* (November 23, 1988): 1060–61, citation on 1061.

33. Cited in Sheler et al., "In Search of Jesus," 49.

34. Funk, *Honest to Jesus*, 304.

35. Funk, *Honest to Jesus*, 304.

36. Funk, *Honest to Jesus*, 305.

37. Funk, *Honest to Jesus*, 302.

38. Funk, *Honest to Jesus*, 303.

39. Funk, *Honest to Jesus*, 300.

40. Funk, *Honest to Jesus*, 305–14.

41. Borg, *Jesus in Contemporary Scholarship*, 143–200.

42. Borg, *Jesus in Contemporary Scholarship*, 172.

43. Borg, *Jesus in Contemporary Scholarship*, 195.

44. Cited in Allen, "No-Frills Jesus," 51.

45. Allen, "No-Frills Jesus," 51, 67.

46. Miller, *Jesus Seminar and Its Critics*, 60.

47. Miller, *Jesus Seminar and Its Critics*, 60.

48. Miller, *Jesus Seminar and Its Critics*, 2.

49. Miller, *Jesus Seminar and Its Critics*, 60.

50. Book-length attacks on the Jesus Seminar include Luke Timothy Johnson, *The Real Jesus: The Misguided Quest for the Historical Jesus and the Truth of the Traditional Gospels* (San Francisco: HarperSanFrancisco, 1996); Michael J. Wilkins and J. P. Moreland, eds. *Jesus under Fire: Modern Scholarship Reinvents the Historical Jesus* (Grand Rapids: Zondervan Publishing House, 1995). For a level-headed response to these and other attacks see Miller, *Jesus Seminar and Its Critics*.

51. Van Biema, "Gospel Truth?" 58. Blomberg supplements this confessional appeal to divine inspiration with academic arguments for the reliability of the Gospel tradition in his essay "Where Do We Start Studying Jesus?" in Wilkens and Morehead, *Jesus under Fire*, 17–51. See also Craig Blomberg, *The*

Historical Reliability of the Gospels, 2nd ed. (Downers Grove, Ill.: InterVarsity, 2007).

52. Johnson, *Real Jesus,* 166. See also Van Biema, "Gospel Truth?" 58.
53. N. T. Wright, "Five Gospels but No Gospel: Jesus and the Seminar," 115–58 in *Crisis in Christology: Essays in Quest of Resolution,* ed. William R. Farmer (Livonia, Mich.: Dove Booksellers, 1995), 120–21.
54. Cited in Van Biema, "Gospel Truth?" 54.
55. Letter to the editor, *Los Angeles Times,* March 30, 1991.
56. Richard B. Hays, "The Corrected Jesus," *First Things* 43 (1994): 43–48, citation on 47.
57. Johnson, *Real Jesus,* 1, 8.
58. Johnson, *Real Jesus,* 7.
59. See, for example, Allen, "Away with the Manger," 26, 30. One difference worth noting is that Funk's comments seem to have been made in informal in-house settings on occasions when reporters happen to have been present; those of his opponents cited here were all premeditated, offered in writing and intended for publication.
60. Wright, *Jesus and the Victory of God,* 84.
61. Allen, "Away with the Manger," 25.
62. An ordained Disciples of Christ minister, Funk discusses his years as "a teenage evangelist" in *Honest to Jesus* under the heading "Youthful Discretions and Indiscretions" (3–5). He would later claim to have had at that time "a string of beliefs and very little faith."
63. Crossan still considers himself "a Catholic through and through," though he does not attend mass regularly. "If you are empowered by Jesus' life," he says, "in my judgment that makes you a Christian" (Sheler et al., "In Search of Jesus," 52). The Seminar's premier critic, Luke Timothy Johnson, is also a former Roman Catholic cleric. He, too, exchanged the collar for a wedding band.
64. Wright, "Five Gospels but No Gospel," 121.
65. Robert W. Funk, *A Greek Grammar of the New Testament and Other Early Christian Literature,* 5th ed. (Chicago: University of Chicago Press, 1973); John Dominic Crossan, *In Parables; Finding Is the First Act* (Missoula, Mont.: Scholars, 1979).
66. Hardly worth mentioning is the charge that Seminar members were "in it for the money" or for status, or for some other aspect of career enhancement. Projects ought not be condemned simply because they are successful.
67. Watson, "A Lesser Child," 53–54, citation on 54; Van Biema, "Gospel Truth?" 55.
68. Cited in Niebuhr, "Jesus Seminar Courts Notoriety," 1061.
69. Niebuhr, "Jesus Seminar Courts Notoriety," 1060.
70. Fourteen from Claremont, nine from Vanderbilt, eight from Harvard, five from Chicago, and four from Union. The count is based on the 1993 roster provided in *Five Gospels.* Hays actually went on to claim that the scholars who made up the Jesus Seminar did not represent the "cream" of New Testament scholarship such as would be found at America's top universities but included a number of professors who held "relatively undistinguished academic positions." Though often cited, this remark has generally been regarded as unfair, probably untrue, and—in any case—embarrassingly elitist. See Hays, "Corrected Jesus," 47.
71. Cited in Jeffrey L. Sheler, "What Did Jesus Really Say?" *U.S. News and World Report* (July 1, 1991): 57–58, citation on 58.
72. Cited in Van Biema, "Gospel Truth?" 57.

73. Cited in Sheler et al., "In Search of Jesus," 48. Compare Funk, *Honest to Jesus,* 300.

74. Borg, *Jesus in Contemporary Scholarship,* 162. Miller also reports the following: "One Fellow [voting member of the Seminar] was fired from his teaching position at a conservative Christian college because of his participation in the Seminar. A second Fellow lost his teaching position at an evangelical Christian college, but was never told why he was terminated. A few members have been pressured by their institutions to resign from the Seminar. One ordained member of the Seminar was formally tried for heresy by his church and was acquitted" (*Jesus Seminar and Its Critics,* 19–20).

75. Hays labeled the Jesus Seminar an "academic splinter group" in "Corrected Jesus," 47. Compare the comments of Miller in *Jesus Seminar and Its Critics,* 66–69.

76. Blomberg, "Where Do We Start Studying Jesus?" 21.

77. Birger Pearson, "The Gospel according to the Jesus Seminar," *Religion* 25 (December, 1995): 317–38, esp. 334.

78. Meier, *Marginal Jew,* 1:177.

79. Wright, "Five Gospels but No Gospel," 135.

80. Pearson, "Gospel according to Jesus Seminar," 324.

81. Crossan, "Response to James D. G. Dunn," 237.

82. Miller, *Jesus Seminar and Its Critics,* 75.

83. Robert Miller maintains that, to the contrary, the Seminar employed a "soft version of dissimilarity," which Robert Funk called "distinctiveness." See "The Jesus Seminar and Its Critics: What Is Really at Stake—An Interview with Robert Miller," 79–96 in *Jesus Reconsidered: Scholarship in the Public Eye,* ed. Bernard Brandon Scott (Santa Rosa, Calif.: Polebridge, 2007), 92.

84. Actually, a number of critics have alleged that the Seminar did this in a manner that was insidious and disingenuous. Howard Clark Kee accuses the group of "manipulation of evidence" in order to rid Jesus of an apocalyptic outlook" ("A Century of Quests for the Culturally Compatible Jesus," *Theology Today* 52 [1995]: 17–28, citation on 28). I am not aware of any evidence to support such an allegation. Robert Miller maintains that as a member of the Seminar, he was not predisposed toward regarding Jesus as noneschatological. In fact, he would have tended to think the opposite but "was persuaded time and again by both the position papers and the debates to vote gray or black" on eschatological passages. See *Jesus Seminar and Its Critics,* 72.

85. Robert W. Funk, "Beyond Criticism in Quest of Literacy: The Parable of the Leaven," *Interpretation* 25 (1971): 151.

86. Jesus Seminar, *The Gospel of Mark: Red Letter Edition* (Sonoma, Calif.: Polebridge, 1991), 1–26.

87. Wright, *Jesus and the Victory of God,* 32.

88. These words were actually used in the initial flyer advertising the group. The basic idea that an unbiased application of scholarly criteria can lead to the discovery of objective "facts" or "truth" is alluded to in much of the Seminar's literature. See the discussion in Wright, "Five Gospels but No Gospel," 125–27.

89. Niebuhr, "Jesus Seminar Courts Notoriety," 1061.

90. Cited in "Scholars Vote on Sayings of Jesus," *The Lutheran* (January 15, 1986): 14.

91. Wright, *Jesus and the Victory of God,* 33.

92. Thus, Kee's oft-quoted description of the group's work as "prejudgment masquerading as scholarship" ("Century of Quests," 25) would come to be regarded as ungracious and unfair.

93. Funk et al., *Five Gospels,* 34–35.

Chapter 5: John Dominic Crossan

1. Borg, *Jesus in Contemporary Scholarship*, 34.
2. Allen, "Away with the Manger," 26.
3. Leander E. Keck, "The Second Coming of the Liberal Jesus." *Christian Century* 111 (1994): 784–87, citation on 785.
4. Wright, *Jesus and the Victory of God*, 44.
5. Charlesworth, "Historical Jesus in the Fourth Gospel," 7.
6. Major publications by Crossan on these topics include *In Parables, Finding Is the First Act, In Fragments, The Dark Interval: Toward a Theology of Story*, 2nd ed. (Sonoma, Calif.: Polebridge, 1988), and *The Cross That Spoke*.
7. Crossan, *A Long Way from Tipperary* (San Francisco: HarperSanFrancisco, 2000), 136, 167–68.
8. Crossan, *A Long Way from Tipperary*, 86.
9. Sheler et al., "In Search of Jesus," 52.
10. See *Birth of Christianity*, 17–46, citations on 30, 44.
11. In the second book, Crossan often responds to criticisms of the first.
12. Wright, *Jesus and the Victory of God*, 44.
13. See *The Greatest Prayer: Rediscovering the Revolutionary Message of the Lord's Prayer* (New York: HarperCollins, 2010). See also two volumes coauthored with Marcus Borg, *The First Christmas: What the Gospels Really Teach about the Birth of Jesus* (New York: HarperCollins, 2009) and *The Last Week: What the Gospels Really Teach about Jesus' Final Days in Jerusalem* (New York: HarperCollins, 2007).
14. Crossan related this version of the anecdote orally at a Society of Biblical Literature meeting. He has since recounted a slightly different version in *A Long Way from Tipperary*, 204.
15. Crossan, *Historical Jesus*, xxxiv. This comment has sparked response. "Unlike objectivity," writes Ben Meyer, "honesty, be it ever so flawless, will not secure the validity of historical judgments" ("Review of *The Historical Jesus* by John Dominic Crossan," *Catholic Biblical Quarterly* 55 [1993]: 575). Others note that Crossan's careful attention to methodology suggests that he is concerned with at least an attempt at or appearance of objectivity. Says Witherington, "He is not simply staring at an inkblot and stating what he thinks he sees in it" (*Jesus Quest*, 82). To clarify this, perhaps, Crossan later added to "honesty" a quality he calls "interactivism." Eventually, he would offer the following "working definition of history": "History is the past reconstructed interactively by the present through argued evidence in public discourse" (*Birth of Christianity*, 20, 42–43).
16. For example, he admits that his equation of systemic evil with the colonizing power of an unjust empire could have something to do with his Irish heritage and the way he and his forebears understand the years of British rule. See *A Long Way from Tipperary*, 50–52.
17. "The Historical Jesus: An Interview with John Dominic Crossan," *Christian Century* 108 (1991): 1200–24. Also cited in John Dominic Crossan, *Jesus: A Revolutionary Biography* (San Francisco: HarperSanFrancisco, 1994), xiv.
18. To facilitate his system of classification, Crossan groups similar sayings or stories into "complexes." The sayings about kingdom and children are not identical but probably reflect different versions of the same idea.
19. Ben Meyer calls Crossan's dating of sources "eccentric and implausible" ("Review of *The Historical Jesus*," 575). He cites Meier, *Marginal Jew*, 1:114–23, 142–52, and also Raymond Brown, "The Gospel of Peter and Canonical Gospel Priority," *New Testament Studies* 33 (1987): 321–43.

20. Wright, *Jesus and the Victory of God,* 48. Wright himself regards the Gospel of Thomas as a relatively late, secondary work, and he is far more generous than Crossan in accepting the authenticity of material found in the canonical Gospels. He has expressed the nature of this disagreement wittily for those who know that he, like Crossan, goes by his middle name (Thomas): "There will come a man called Dominic who will claim that most Jesus-material comes from Thomas; and he will be opposed by a man called Thomas who will claim that most Jesus-material is Dominical" (N. T. Wright, "Taking the Text with Her Pleasure: A Post-Modernist Response to J. Dominic Crossan's *The Historical Jesus: The Life of a Mediterranean Jewish Peasant,*" *Theology* 96 [1993]: 305).

21. Crossan, *Birth of Christianity,* 119–20.

22. Crossan, *Historical Jesus,* 218–24, drawing on the work of Robert Gurr.

23. Crossan, *Historical Jesus,* 72. He describes seven possible responses.

24. This question is raised, for instance, with regard to the system of patrons, brokers, and clients that looms large in Crossan's third level of analysis. Witherington says, "It is a mistake to ascribe the sort of Greco-Roman patronage system we find in Rome or Corinth . . . to Lower Galilee" (*Jesus Quest,* 83).

25. For a sociological description of Jesus' first-century agrarian world, see further Douglas E. Oakman, *Jesus and the Peasants,* Matrix: The Bible in Mediterranean Context (Eugene, Ore.: Cascade, 2008).

26. In *Birth of Christianity,* 346–50, Crossan adopts the term *peasant artisan,* insisting that policies of rural commercialization in the first century were forcing rural artisans (such as carpenters) into a situation only semantically different from that of the landless laborer.

27. John Dominic Crossan, "The Search for Jesus," in *The Search for Jesus: Modern Scholarship Looks at the Gospels,* ed. Hershel Shanks (Washington, D.C.: Biblical Archaeology Society, 1994), 132.

28. The most extensive study so far on the question of Jesus' literacy is Chris Keith, *Jesus' Literacy: Scribal Culture and the Teacher from Galilee,* Library of New Testament Studies 413 (London: T&T Clark, 2011). Keith concludes that, regardless of whether Jesus would have possessed some basic level of literacy, he did not possess "scribal-literacy," which would have enabled him to read and interpret the scriptures.

29. Crossan, *Historical Jesus,* 304.

30. Crossan, *Historical Jesus,* 422.

31. Crossan, *Historical Jesus,* 300.

32. Crossan, *Historical Jesus,* 266–82.

33. Crossan, *Historical Jesus,* 319–20, 336–37. He also entertains Allan Young's triadic distinction between disease, illness, and sickness as three components of "unhealth."

34. Crossan, *Jesus: A Revolutionary Biography,* 82.

35. Crossan, *Jesus: A Revolutionary Biography,* 84–88.

36. Crossan, *Historical Jesus,* 304–10.

37. Crossan, *Historical Jesus,* 323–25.

38. Crossan, *Historical Jesus,* 313–18. He cites Mark 5:1–17 only to illustrate this point, without maintaining that it records an authentic act of the historical Jesus.

39. Crossan, *Historical Jesus,* 341–44.

40. John Dominic Crossan, "Jesus and the Challenge of Collaborative Eschatology," 105–32 in Beilby and Eddy, eds., *Historical Jesus: Five Views,* 126. Crossan's emphasis.

41. Crossan, *Historical Jesus,* 341.
42. Crossan, *Historical Jesus,* 344.
43. Crossan, *Historical Jesus,* 227–60, 282–92; citations are on 259. On the concept of ethical eschatology, see *Birth of Christianity,* 273–89.
44. Crossan, "Jesus and the Challenge of Collaborative Eschatology," 123.
45. Crossan, "Jesus and the Challenge of Collaborative Eschatology," 125.
46. Crossan, "Jesus and the Challenge of Collaborative Eschatology," 125.
47. Crossan, "Jesus and the Challenge of Collaborative Eschatology," 130.
48. Crossan, "Jesus and the Challenge of Collaborative Eschatology," 126.
49. Crossan, "Jesus and the Challenge of Collaborative Eschatology," 126.
50. Crossan, *Historical Jesus,* 345–48.
51. Crossan, *Birth of Christianity,* 336.
52. Crossan, *Historical Jesus,* 360.
53. John Dominic Crossan, "The Passion Narrative," *The Fourth R* 9.5–6 (1996): 3–8, citation on 5. These examples are more precise than the complex example of the two goats in Leviticus 16 discussed in *Historical Jesus,* 376–83.
54. Crossan, *Historical Jesus,* 372.
55. Crossan, *Birth of Christianity,* 573, drawing on Kathleen Corley and Marianne Sawicki.
56. Crossan, *Jesus: A Revolutionary Biography,* 145. Crossan's emphasis.
57. Crossan, *Historical Jesus,* 383–91; citation is on 389.
58. Crossan, *Jesus: A Revolutionary Biography,* 163.
59. Crossan, *Jesus: A Revolutionary Biography,* 161.
60. Crossan, *Jesus: A Revolutionary Biography,* 155.
61. Crossan, *Jesus: A Revolutionary Biography,* 152.
62. Crossan, *Jesus: A Revolutionary Biography,* 127.
63. Crossan, *Historical Jesus,* 393.
64. Crossan, *Birth of Christianity,* xxxi.
65. Crossan, *Jesus: A Revolutionary Biography,* 124.
66. Crossan, *Birth of Christianity,* 407–17.
67. Crossan, *Birth of Christianity,* 257–89; citations on 283–84.
68. Crossan, *Birth of Christianity,* 363–406.
69. Crossan, *Birth of Christianity,* 444. Crossan's emphasis.
70. For an extended analysis and critique of Crossan's method, see Donald L. Denton, *Historiography and Hermeneutics in Jesus Studies: An Examination of the Work of John Dominic Crossan and Ben F. Meyer,* Journal for the Study of the New Testament: Supplement Series 262 (Sheffield: T&T Clark, 2004), 18–79. Denton is generally appreciative of Crossan's careful work, but he does recognize that the method is not ideologically neutral: it assumes a particular understanding of what constitutes historical truth and of how such truth is to be accessed.
71. Hal Childs, *The Myth of the Historical Jesus and the Evolution of Consciousness,* Society of Biblical Literature Dissertation Series 179 (Atlanta: Society of Biblical Literature, 2000), 55.
72. Witherington, *Jesus Quest,* 80. Crossan discusses the function of memory in oral cultures extensively in *Birth of Christianity,* 59–89.
73. Bart Ehrman says that for Crossan to give his earliest dates "to noncanonical Gospels that are, in most cases, not quoted or even mentioned by early Christian writers until many, many decades later seems overly speculative (*Jesus: Apocalyptic Prophet,* 134).
74. Robin Scroggs is one of many who questions whether Crossan's appropriation of apocryphal materials ultimately affects his final portrait of Jesus. See, "Review of *The Historical Jesus* by John Dominic Crossan," *Interpretation* 47 (1993): 301.

75. Burton Mack, as we noted in chapter 1 (see page 28), is another exception.
76. For a more extensive account of that reconstruction, with comments concerning its social, political, and spiritual implications for today, see Borg and Crossan, *Last Week*.
77. Wright, *Jesus and the Victory of God*, 55. See also Keck, "Second Coming of the Liberal Jesus": "The brokerless Jesus is himself thoroughly brokered by this biographer" (785).
78. Crossan, *Historical Jesus*, 434.
79. Witherington, *Jesus Quest*, 89–90.
80. The charge by Luke Timothy Johnson that Crossan's method is "fixed" (*Real Jesus*, 47) offers its criticism in language that has not proved helpful. Crossan responds, "It is very, very serious to charge that another scholar has 'fixed' his research methodology. . . . 'Fixing data' entails a deliberate intention to deceive" (*Birth of Christianity*, 114).
81. Robert M. Price, "Response to John Dominic Crossan," 133–37 in Beilby and Eddy, eds., *Historical Jesus: Five Views*, 135. Note that Price agrees with Crossan that very little material can be deemed authentic, but his conclusion is that no credible reconstruction of Jesus as a historical person is possible.
82. Luke Timothy Johnson, "Response to John Dominic Crossan," 138–42 in Beilby and Eddy, eds., *Historical Jesus: Five Views*, 138–39.
83. James D. G. Dunn, "Response to John Dominic Crossan," 143–47 in Beilby and Eddy, eds., *Historical Jesus: Five Views*, 146.
84. Crossan, *Jesus: A Revolutionary Biography*, 122. This is a more nuanced view than was presented in *Historical Jesus* (see, for example, page 421).
85. In his autobiography he reflects on his frustration in getting this point across: "I use the doctrine of Cynicism comparatively but do not need it constitutively. I have never considered a Cynic Jesus as some sort of replacement for a Jewish Jesus; indeed I find that idea little short of absurd" (*A Long Way from Tipperary*, 103).
86. Keener, *Historical Jesus of the Gospels*, 19.
87. Wright, *Jesus and the Victory of God*, 59.
88. Darrell L. Bock, "Response to John Dominic Crossan," 148–52 in Beilby and Eddy, eds., *Historical Jesus: Five Views*, 149.
89. Witherington, *Jesus Quest*, 84. The charge may hold for Crossan's recent works on the historical Jesus, but would not be true of his earlier studies on parables, such as *Finding Is the First Act*.
90. Crossan, *Historical Jesus*, 417.
91. Crossan, *Historical Jesus*, 417–22.
92. Crossan, *Birth of Christianity*, 303.
93. Elliott, "Jesus Was Not an Egalitarian"; "The Jesus Movement Was Not Egalitarian." See also the comments of Gowler in *What Are They Saying about the Historical Jesus?* 171–72 n. 20.
94. Meier, *Marginal Jew*, 2:269–70. Meier later evaluates Crossan's idea that Jesus proclaimed a sapiential kingdom that "imagines how one could live here and now within an already or always available divine dominion" (*Historical Jesus*, 292). Says Meier, "At this point we are indeed not far from a gnostic Jesus" (2:488 n. 164).
95. Meier, *Marginal Jew*, 2:350.
96. Sanders, *Jesus and Judaism*, 329.
97. Witherington, *Jesus Quest*, 65.
98. Wright, *Jesus and the Victory of God*, 59.
99. This point is discussed more thoroughly in this book's chapter on N. T. Wright (see pages 200–224). Wright's comprehensive argument is presented in his

book, *The Resurrection of the Son of God,* Christian Origins and the Question of God 3 (Minneapolis: Fortress, 2003). For an intriguing exchange between Crossan and Wright on this topic, see N. T. Wright and John Dominic Crossan, "The Resurrection: Historical Event or Theological Explanation? A Dialogue" 16–47 in Robert B. Stewart, ed., *The Resurrection of Jesus: John Dominic Crossan and N. T. Wright in Dialogue* (Minneapolis: Fortress, 2006).

100. Crossan, *Historical Jesus,* 424.

Chapter 6: Marcus J. Borg

1. Marcus J. Borg, *Jesus: Uncovering the Life, Teaching, and Relevance of a Religious Revolutionary* (New York: HarperOne, 2006), 164. Slightly revised (stylistically) from a summary presented nine years earlier in "From Galilean Jew to the Face of God: The Pre-Easter and Post-Easter Jesus," 7–20 in *Jesus at 2000,* ed. Marcus J. Borg (Boulder, Col.: Westview, 1997), 10.

2. Wright, *Jesus and the Victory of God,* 75.

3. Marcus J. Borg, *Meeting Jesus Again for the First Time: The Historical Jesus and the Heart of Christian Faith* (San Francisco: HarperSanFrancisco, 1994), 8.

4. Borg, *Meeting Jesus Again,* 8.

5. Borg, *Meeting Jesus Again,* 12.

6. Borg, *Meeting Jesus Again,* 13.

7. Borg, *Meeting Jesus Again,* 15.

8. Borg, *Meeting Jesus Again,* 137.

9. Marcus J. Borg, "Seeing Jesus: Sources, Lenses, and Method," 3–14 in Marcus J. Borg and N. T. Wright, *The Meaning of Jesus: Two Visions* (San Francisco: HarperSanFrancisco, 1999).

10. See the first two chapters of Borg, *Jesus: Uncovering.*

11. Borg, *Jesus: Uncovering,* 75. In a similar vein, Crossan memorably averred that the Enlightenment was actually "the Endarkenment" insofar as it obscured metaphorical truth: stories that we were "dumb enough" to take literally were simply rejected as untrue." See *A Long Way from Tipperary,* 2.

12. Borg, *Jesus: Uncovering,* 74–75.

13. Borg, *Jesus: A New Vision,* 15.

14. Borg, *Jesus: A New Vision,* 15.

15. In comparing his work with that of N. T. Wright, Borg notes that the primary strokes of his sketch of Jesus (as mystic, healer, wisdom teacher, social prophet, and movement initiator) are drawn from cross-cultural study of religion, whereas Wright's categories (Jesus as messiah and prophet of the kingdom of God) are native to the Jewish tradition. He admits that his preference for etic categories (from outside the culture) over emic ones (from within the culture) probably owes to his years of teaching university students, for whom "an emphasis upon the experience of the sacred across cultures has a credibility that a focus on a single religious tradition does not." See Borg and Wright, *Meaning of Jesus,* 230–31.

16. Borg, *Jesus: Uncovering,* 77–85, citation on 79 (emphasis Borg).

17. Borg, *Jesus: A New Vision,* 16.

18. Borg, *Jesus in Contemporary Scholarship,* 83.

19. Some of the preliminary research that would be foundational for Borg's understanding of Jesus is found in his earliest work, *Conflict, Holiness, and Politics in the Teaching of Jesus,* 2nd ed. (New York: Continuum, 1998; first edition, Edwin Mellen, 1984). See also Borg, *Jesus in Contemporary Scholarship.*

20. Borg, *Jesus: Uncovering,* 163.

21. Borg, *Jesus and Contemporary Scholarship,* 40–41 n. 59.

22. In *Jesus: A New Vision*, Borg employed the term "Spirit person" as his primary category for understanding Jesus, but in *Jesus: Uncovering* he reports, "I have begun to speak of Jesus as a Jewish mystic rather than a Jewish Spirit person. I mean the same thing" (132).
23. Borg, *Jesus: A New Vision*, 25–26.
24. Borg, *Jesus: A New Vision*, 25–27.
25. Borg, *Jesus: Uncovering*, 117.
26. Borg, *Jesus: Uncovering*, 133.
27. Borg, *Jesus Uncovering*, 115.
28. Borg, *Jesus Uncovering*, 115.
29. Borg, *Jesus: A New Vision*, 40–43; *Jesus: Uncovering*, 120–25.
30. Borg, *Jesus: A New Vision*, 43–45; *Jesus: Uncovering*, 128–30.
31. The intimate sense of "Abba" was disputed by James Barr, "Abba Isn't 'Daddy,'" *Journal of Theological Studies* 39 (1988): 28–47. Borg addresses the principle concerns Barr raised in *Jesus: Uncovering*, 129–30.
32. Borg, *Jesus: A New Vision*, 46; *Jesus: Uncovering*, 126–28.
33. Borg, *Jesus: A New Vision*, 61; compare *Jesus: Uncovering*, 146–50. In the latter work he makes clear that the Greek word that is often translated "miracle" in the New Testament literally means "mighty deeds" or "deeds of power"; what occurs is not deemed supernatural but is considered to be the result of power greater than what is typically associated with human beings.
34. Borg, *Jesus: A New Vision*, 71.
35. Borg, *Jesus: Uncovering*, 163.
36. Borg, *Jesus: A New Vision*, 66; *Jesus: Uncovering*, 148–50.
37. Borg, *Jesus: A New Vision*, 97; *Jesus: Uncovering*, 166–67, 191.
38. Borg, *Jesus: A New Vision*, 81.
39. Borg, *Jesus: Uncovering*, 168–85.
40. Borg, *Jesus: A New Vision*, 100.
41. Borg, *Jesus: Uncovering*, 185.
42. Borg, *Jesus: A New Vision*, 114.
43. Borg, *Jesus: A New Vision*, 99. Borg also notes, however, that a number of traditional forms of Jewish teaching are seldom found in the Jesus tradition: these include exposition of Torah, extended commentary on scripture, prophetic oracles. See *Jesus: Uncovering*, 151.
44. Borg, *Jesus: A New Vision*, 116.
45. Borg, *Jesus: A New Vision*. Borg's emphasis.
46. Borg, *Jesus: Uncovering*, 155, 157.
47. Borg, *Jesus: Uncovering*, 205–17.
48. Borg, *Jesus: A New Vision*, 103.
49. Borg, *Uncovering Jesus*, 222–23.
50. Borg, *Jesus: A New Vision*, 150.
51. Lenski, *Power and Privilege*. See also Kautsky, *Politics of Aristocratic Empires*. Note the critique of Sawicki regarding this choice of models (page 36 of this book).
52. Borg, *Jesus in Contemporary Scholarship*, 101–5.
53. Borg, *Jesus: Uncovering*, 243.
54. Borg, *Jesus: Uncovering*, 244–45.
55. Borg, *Jesus: Uncovering*, 244–47; citation on 244.
56. Borg, *Jesus: Uncovering*, 247–51.
57. Borg, *Jesus: Uncovering*, 186–87.
58. Borg, *Jesus: A New Vision*, 174. The symbolism of the image derives from Zechariah 9:9–10.

59. Borg, *Jesus: Uncovering*, 232–36, 241–44. Compare Crossan and Borg, *The Last Week*, 47–52.
60. Borg, *Jesus: A New Vision*, 175.
61. Borg, *Jesus: A New Vision*, 178–84.
62. Borg, *Jesus: A New Vision*, 125.
63. Borg, *Jesus: A New Vision*, 126–27.
64. Borg, *Jesus: A New Vision*, 86; the phrase is also used in his preface to the second edition of *Conflict, Holiness, and Politics*, 2, 15.
65. Borg, *Conflict, Holiness, and Politics*, 67, 73; *Jesus: A New Vision*, 86; *Jesus: Uncovering*, 213–17.
66. Borg, *Jesus: A New Vision*, 83–93. See also *Conflict, Holiness, and Politics*, 66–87.
67. Borg, *Jesus: A New Vision*, 92. See also *Conflict, Holiness, and Politics*, 98.
68. Borg, *Jesus in Contemporary Scholarship*, 110.
69. Borg, *Jesus: Uncovering*, 215–16.
70. Borg, *Jesus: Uncovering*, 216.
71. Borg, *Jesus in Contemporary Scholarship*, 26. Borg contrasts here Leviticus 19:2 with Luke 6:36.
72. Borg, *Jesus: Uncovering*, 292. When Borg's writings are arranged chronologically, resistance to purity rules receive less emphasis than in his 1984 book (*Conflict, Holiness, and Politics*); it occupies only five pages of his 2006 volume (*Jesus: Uncovering*). Nevertheless, in his preface to the 1998 second edition of *Conflict, Holiness, and Politics*, Borg reiterates his most controversial points concerning holiness (purity) and sharpens them: "the conflict was about . . . whether compassion or purity was to be the core value shaping Israel's collective life" (15).
73. Borg, *Jesus: Uncovering*, 161.
74. Borg, *Jesus: Uncovering*, 162–63.
75. Borg, *Jesus in Contemporary Scholarship*, 47–68.
76. Borg, *Jesus: Uncovering*, 253–60.
77. Borg's views on Jesus and eschatology, however, would undergo some development. In a 1994 article, he nuanced his earlier position against an eschatological Jesus, struggled with semantics, and conceded that Jesus' message could have included a peripheral eschatological component. See Marcus J. Borg, "Jesus and Eschatology: A Reassessment," 207–18 in James H. Charlesworth and W. P. Weaver, eds., *Images of Jesus Today* (Valley Forge, Penn.: Trinity Press International, 1994).
78. Borg, *Jesus in Contemporary Scholarship*, 55, drawing on Norman Perrin. Borg also suggests (on pages 87–88 of this same book) that this tensive symbol could indicate (1) the power of God; (2) the experiential presence of God; (3) covenantal life under God's rule, which is radically different from other ways of living; (4) a community within which the reality of God's presence and way of life are experienced; (5) an ideal state of affairs. Further, the phrase could refer to the world of spirit, which coexists with this material world and which will someday be united with it. In that case, we could say that Jesus did believe in a final consummation, when the worlds of matter and spirit would be related to each other at the end as they were at creation, but he gave no indication that he believed such an occurrence was imminent.
79. Borg, *Jesus: Uncovering*, 252.
80. Borg, *Jesus: Uncovering*, 254.
81. Borg, *Jesus: Uncovering*, 260.
82. Borg, *Meeting Jesus Again*, 16.
83. Borg, *Jesus: A New Vision*, 184–85, 189 n. 44.
84. Borg, *Jesus: Uncovering*, 287.

85. Borg, *Jesus: Uncovering*, 287–88.
86. Borg, *Jesus: Uncovering*, 288.
87. Wright, *Jesus and the Victory of God*, 75.
88. Mack, *Myth of Innocence*, 53–77. Mack was specifically referring to traditional concepts of holiness that Borg assumes undergirded the Jewish purity codes. In later writings, Borg would downplay themes of purity and holiness in his discussion of conventional wisdom, but a radically hellenized Galilee (à la Mack) would probably call other aspects of that discussion into question as well.
89. Sanders, *Jesus and Judaism*, 61–76. Witherington thinks that since the eschatological sayings about a coming Son of Man meet certain historical criteria (multiple attestation, dissimilarity), Borg deems them unauthentic simply because they do not fit into his overall view of the pre-Easter Jesus. He further notes that, ironically, this is because Borg misconstrues the sayings as proclaiming an end that is necessarily imminent as opposed to possibly imminent (Witherington, *Jesus Quest*, 94–95). Wright agrees with Borg's interpretation of eschatological language as referring to the end of a social order but fears he takes this so generally that he loses the sense of God "actually *doing* something climactic and unique" (*Jesus and the Victory of God*, 77). Meier says that Borg fails to grasp that "Jesus' message of future eschatology and a future kingdom does not rise or fall with Jesus' statements about a Son of Man" (*Marginal Jew*, 2:350, 396 n. 233).
90. Keener, *Historical Jesus of the Gospels*, 37.
91. Witherington, *Jesus Quest*, 103–6.
92. Sanders, *Jesus and Judaism*, 180–82, 210.
93. Levine, *Misunderstood Jew*, 146–48, 173–77, citation on 174–75. Notably, Crossan initially claimed that Jesus clashed with priestly authorities because he did not keep purity regulations (e.g., *Jesus: A Revolutionary Biography*, 83), but he later changed his mind, saying that Levine had convinced him that Jesus would have observed those codes as nonoppressive customs followed by most Jewish peasants of his time and place (*Birth of Christianity*, 580–81). Borg has toned down his emphasis on the topic, but he has not changed his position.
94. Paula Fredriksen, "Did Jesus Oppose the Purity Laws?" *Bible Review* 11 (June 1995): 18–25, 42–47. See also her "What You See Is What You Get: Context and Content in Current Research on the Historical Jesus," *Theology Today* 52 (1995): 75–97.
95. Jacob Neusner is the author of dozens of books on Jewish law and history, including a classic work on the Pharisees, *From Politics to Piety: The Emergence of Pharisaic Judaism* (Englewood Cliffs, N.J.: Prentice Hall, 1973). E. P. Sanders specifically criticized the notion of purity presented in that book in "Did the Pharisees Eat Ordinary Food in Purity?" 131–254 in his *Jewish Law from Jesus to the Mishnah: Five Studies* (Philadelphia: Trinity Press International, 1990). Neusner replied with "Mr. Sanders' Pharisees and Mine," in *Scottish Journal of Theology* 44 (1991): 73–95.
96. Borg, *Conflict, Holiness, and Politics*, 10.
97. Thomas Kazen, *Jesus and Purity Halakhah: Was Jesus Indifferent to Impurity?* Coniectanea biblica: New Testament Series 38. Stockholm: Almqvist & Wiksell, 2002. See the discussion of Kazen's thesis on pages 175–76.
98. http://www.explorefaith.org/LentenHomily03.15.01.html.
99. Borg, *Jesus: Uncovering*, 243; compare 232–36, 242–43. See also *Conflict, Holiness, and Politics*, 10 (updated remarks for the 1998 second edition): "I now see the Temple . . . as the center of a native domination system").
100. Levine, *Misunderstood Jew*, 156–57.

101. Marcus J. Borg, "Portraits of Jesus," 83–108 in Hershel Shanks, ed., *The Search for Jesus: Modern Scholarship Looks at the Gospels* (Washington, D.C.: Biblical Archaeology Society, 1994), 87.
102. Wright, *Jesus and the Victory of God*, 77.
103. Allison's foundational thesis here is that historical reconstruction must give primary attention to what has recurrent attestation; see *Constructing Jesus*, 10–17, 156–64, 459–62. Allison presses this point specifically with regard to recurrent attribution of apocalyptic eschatology to Jesus on pages 31–48, with regard to prevalent references to Jesus' self-understanding on pages 221–32, and with regard to frequent descriptions of how Jesus interpreted his impending death on pages 427–33. The implications for Borg's approach to historical study are often implicit, but see pages 44–45, 59, 141–43, 223, 253–55 for explicit remarks.
104. Borg (and others) would question the prevalence of some of the matters Allison cites. For example, many of the items included in Allison's catalogue of materials attributing apocalyptic eschatology to Jesus (*Constructing Jesus*, 33–43) would be interpreted by Borg in nonapocalyptic ways, and Borg would also maintain that there are also numerous statements attributed to Jesus that counter apocalyptic or imminent eschatology (compare *Jesus: Uncovering*, 255–58).
105. Allison, *Constructing Jesus*, 17.
106. Wright, *Jesus and the Victory of God*, 77. I say *must* instead of *might* on the assumption that Wright's series of questions (leading up to and including "Is he not . . . a failure?") is rhetorical.
107. Marcus J. Borg, "The Historian, the Christian, and Jesus," *Theology Today* 52 (1995): 6–16, citation on 16.

Chapter 7: E. P. Sanders

1. Sanders, *Jesus and Judaism*, 334.
2. Borg, *Jesus in Contemporary Scholarship*, 19–20.
3. Sanders, *Jesus and Judaism*, 319.
4. E. P. Sanders, *Paul and Palestinian Judaism: A Comparison of Patterns of Religion* (Philadelphia: Fortress, 1977).
5. See especially E. P. Sanders, *Judaism: Practice and Belief, 63 BCE–66 CE* (Philadelphia: Trinity Press International, 1992).
6. Sanders, *Judaism: Practice and Belief*, 275.
7. Sanders, *Judaism: Practice and Belief*, 275–78.
8. Sanders, *Paul and Palestinian Judaism*, 422.
9. Sanders, *Judaism: Practice and Belief*, 277. Sanders's emphasis.
10. Sanders, *Paul and Palestinian Judaism*, 420.
11. Sanders, *Jesus and Judaism*, 336.
12. Sanders, *Judaism: Practice and Belief*, 277.
13. For more on this subject, see Sanders, *Jesus and Judaism*, 77–119.
14. Sanders, *Jesus and Judaism*, 336. The wording of the three elements is my own, as is the interpretation of the chronological markers given. Rabbinic materials are notoriously difficult to date. I use the earliest estimate (second century CE) for key documents cited by Sanders.
15. Sanders, *Historical Figure of Jesus*, 54.
16. Sanders, *Historical Figure of Jesus*, 64.
17. Sanders, *Jesus and Judaism*, 11; *Historical Figure of Jesus*, 10–11.
18. This is due in part to the more popular style of *Historical Figure of Jesus*, in which Sanders does not nuance judgments as precisely as in *Jesus and Judaism*. In the latter

volume, he actually stratifies knowledge about Jesus into six categories: "virtually certain," "highly probable," "probable," "possible," "conceivable," and "incredible" (for a summary list of some key items, see 326–27). This system is similar to the Jesus Seminar's four color-coded categories, though the Seminar would not always have agreed with Sanders as to how individual items should be rated.

19. Sanders, *Jesus and Judaism*, 321.
20. Burton Mack may be the only notable exception. See page 30.
21. Sanders, *Jesus and Judaism*, 61–76.
22. Wright objects to the assumption that if Jesus expected the temple to be destroyed, he must also have expected it to be replaced. See *Jesus and the Victory of God*, 425–28. John K. Riches thinks there are "manifold problems" with assuming that the overturning of tables in the temple court would symbolize the temple's destruction, and he finds no reason at all to think such an act would also imply restoration or replacement. See Riches, *A Century of New Testament Study* (Valley Forge, Penn.: Trinity Press International, 1993), 117–19.
23. Meier lists scholars who affirm the existence of the twelve during Jesus' ministry and scholars who deny it in *Marginal Jew* 3:168–69 n. 18. Of scholars discussed in this book, Crossan is skeptical of traditions regarding "the twelve," partly because the theme is not significant for Q (*Historical Jesus*, 334). He regards the selection of twelve disciples (Mark 3:13–19) to be from the second stratum of tradition (60–80 CE) with only single attestation (444). Note also the position that Schüssler Fiorenza discussed on pages 30–32 of this book.
24. His arguments to establish the point "beyond reasonable doubt" are laid out in Sanders, *Jesus and Judaism*, 98–106. For further support of the authenticity of this point, see Scot McKnight, "Jesus and the Twelve," 181–214 in Darrell L. Bock and Robert L. Webb, eds., *Key Events in the Life of the Historical Jesus: A Collaborative Exploration of Context and Coherence* (Grand Rapids: Eerdmans, 2010).
25. Sanders, *Jesus and Judaism*, 101.
26. Sanders, *Historical Figure of Jesus*, 120. Meier disagrees with this "purely symbolic" notion of the twelve, insisting on the importance of there being exactly twelve men in the group. See *Marginal Jew*, 3:171 n. 33
27. Sanders, *Historical Figure of Jesus*, 120.
28. Sanders, *Historical Figure of Jesus*, 120, 184–88. On this point, see also Scot McKnight, "Jesus and the Twelve." McKnight suggests that the symbolism of "the twelve" simply references the whole people of Israel, not necessarily the particular or original twelve tribes.
29. Sanders, *Jesus and Judaism*, 99.
30. Sanders, *Jesus and Judaism*, 153.
31. See Sanders, *Jesus and Judaism*, 123–56, 222–41, and *Historical Figure of Jesus*, 169–88.
32. Meier rejects this reasoning. See *Marginal Jew*, 2:338–48.
33. Sanders, *Historical Figure of Jesus*, 181.
34. Sanders, *Historical Figure of Jesus*, 180.
35. See Sanders, *Jesus and Judaism*, 157–73, and *Historical Figure of Jesus*, 132–68.
36. He does think that some of the miracle stories (especially what are called nature miracles) are exaggerated, or else their impact would have been greater than that reported. See *Historical Figure of Jesus*, 154–57.
37. Sanders, *Historical Figure of Jesus*, 164.
38. Sanders, *Historical Figure of Jesus*, 168.
39. Sanders, *Jesus and Judaism*, 330.
40. Sanders, *Historical Figure of Jesus*, 238.
41. Sanders, *Historical Figure of Jesus*, 239–48.

42. Sanders, *Historical Figure of Jesus,* 238.
43. Sanders, *Historical Figure of Jesus,* 248.
44. Sanders, *Jesus and Judaism,* 307–8.
45. See Sanders, *Jesus and Judaism,* 245–69, and *Historical Figure of Jesus,* 205–24.
46. Sanders, *Jesus and Judaism,* 336.
47. Sanders, *Jesus and Judaism,* 55.
48. Sanders, *Jesus and Judaism,* 336.
49. Sanders, *Historical Figure of Jesus,* 192. Elsewhere he says that though Jesus did not institute a Gentile mission, he did start "a movement which came to see the Gentile mission as a logical extension of itself" (*Jesus and Judaism,* 220).
50. Sanders, *Jesus and Judaism,* 199.
51. Sanders, *Jesus and Judaism,* 319.
52. Sanders, *Historical Figure of Jesus,* 233.
53. Sanders, *Historical Figure of Jesus,* 234.
54. Sanders, *Historical Figure of Jesus,* 235.
55. Sanders, *Jesus and Judaism,* 322. Sanders's emphasis.
56. Sanders, *Jesus and Judaism,* 322.
57. Sanders, *Historical Figure of Jesus,* 218.
58. Sanders, *Jesus and Judaism,* 331.
59. Sanders, *Jesus and Judaism,* 333.
60. Sanders, *Jesus and Judaism,* 331.
61. Sanders, *Historical Figure of Jesus,* 269.
62. Sanders, *Historical Figure of Jesus,* 273–74.
63. Sanders, *Jesus and Judaism,* 333.
64. Sanders, *Historical Figure of Jesus,* 274–75.
65. Sanders, *Historical Figure of Jesus,* 275.
66. Sanders, *Historical Figure of Jesus,* 280.
67. Sanders, *Jesus and Judaism,* 240.
68. Sanders details some differences between his conception of Jesus and that of Schweitzer in *Jesus and Judaism,* 327–29.
69. Meier, *Marginal Jew,* 1:173.
70. Sanders, *Jewish Law from Jesus to the Mishnah,* 28.
71. James D. G. Dunn, "Review of *Jesus and Judaism* by E. P. Sanders," *Journal of Theological Studies* 37 (1986): 513.
72. Borg, *Jesus in Contemporary Scholarship,* 20–21.
73. Sanders, *Jesus and Judaism,* 319–20.
74. Sanders, *Jesus and Judaism,* 320.
75. Borg, *Jesus in Contemporary Scholarship,* 76–77; compare Borg's remarks (directed against a similar argument presented by Dale Allison) in Miller, ed., *Apocalyptic Jesus,* 38–40.
76. Borg, *Jesus in Contemporary Scholarship,* 82.
77. Meier takes him to task for this several times in *Marginal Jew,* 2:398–506. But when writing that volume (published in 1994), Meier apparently did not have access to Sanders's *Historical Figure of Jesus* (1993), where the discomfort with present eschatology is less evident.
78. Witherington, *Jesus Quest,* 128.
79. Jonathan A. Goldstein, "Biblical Promises in 1 and 2 Maccabees," in *Judaisms and Their Messiahs at the Turn of the Christian Era* (New York: Cambridge University Press, 1987), 73.
80. Allison, *Constructing Jesus,* 45.
81. Scot McKnight, *A New Vision for Israel: The Teachings of Jesus in National Context* (Grand Rapids: Eerdmans, 1999), 120–55; Wright, *Jesus and the Victory*

of God, 333–36, 360–65. Wright credits the insight for this interpretation to his mentor, George B. Caird (with whom Marcus Borg also studied). See Caird, *The Language and Imagery of the Bible* (Philadelphia: Westminster, 1980).

82. Nicholas Perrin, *Jesus the Temple* (Grand Rapids: Baker Academic, 2010).
83. Borg, *Jesus in Contemporary Scholarship,* 21.
84. Sanders, *Historical Figure of Jesus,* 183.
85. Witherington, *Jesus Quest,* 132. Witherington's emphasis.
86. Sanders, *Historical Figure of Jesus,* 188.
87. For a summary of the key arguments (and discussion of whether they succeed in completely demolishing Sanders's thesis), see Mark Allan Powell, "Was Jesus a Friend of Unrepentant Sinners? A Fresh Appraisal of Sanders's Controversial Proposal," *Journal for the Study of the Historical Jesus* 7.3 (2009): 286–310. In addition, a book-length critique is offered by J. D. Choi, *Jesus' Teaching on Repentance,* International Studies in Formative Christianity and Judaism (Binghampton, N.Y.: Global Publications, 2000).
88. Crossan, *Birth of Christianity,* 337–42, citations on 341–42. Crossan is referring to other polemical descriptions of Jesus offered by his enemies in biblical traditions.
89. Sanders, *Historical Figure of Jesus,* 202.
90. Sanders, *Historical Figure of Jesus,* 196–98, 203.
91. Greg Carey, *Sinners: Jesus and His Earliest Followers* (Waco, Tex.: Baylor University Press, 2009). According to Carey, Jesus, while remaining righteous, became one of the sinners himself.
92. Meier, *Marginal Jew,* 2:149. See also 212 n. 154 and 431, with the caveat on 485 n. 152.
93. Mark Allan Powell, "Jesus and the Pathetic Wicked: Re-Visiting Sanders's View of Jesus and the Sinners," in Robert L. Webb and Mark S. Goodacre, eds., *Standing on the Shoulders of Giants: Engaging the Historical Jesus Work of Crossan, Sanders, and Wright* [title tentative] (London: T&T Clark, forthcoming).
94. Dale C. Allison Jr., "Jesus and the Covenant: A Response to E. P. Sanders," 61–82, in *The Historical Jesus: A Sheffield Reader,* ed. Craig A. Evans and Stanley E. Porter (Sheffield: Sheffield Academic, 1995).
95. Witherington, *Jesus Quest,* 127. See also 211 for a critique of Sanders's argument regarding Mark 3:1–6 (probably Witherington's best argument against Sanders, but hidden in the chapter on Meier).
96. Wright, *Jesus and the Victory of God,* 379.
97. Wright, *Jesus and the Victory of God,* 382.
98. Wright, *Jesus and the Victory of God,* 378.
99. Meier, *Marginal Jew,* 4:74–234.
100. Tom Holmén, *Jesus and Jewish Covenant Thinking* (Leiden: Brill, 2001).
101. Joseph H. Hellerman, *Jesus and the People of God: Reconfiguring Ethnic Identity,* New Testament Monographs 21 (Sheffield: Sheffield Phoenix, 2007).
102. Kazen, *Jesus and Purity:* Halakhah.
103. Reginald H. Fuller, "Searching for the Historical Jesus," *Interpretation* 41 (1987): 301–3.
104. Meier, *Marginal Jew,* 2:464–65 n. 52.
105. Meier, *Marginal Jew,* 2:473–74 n. 97.
106. Sanders, *Historical Figure of Jesus,* 201. See similar comments on 178, 247.
107. Sanders, *Historical Figure of Jesus,* 280–81.

Chapter 8: John P. Meier

1. Meier, *Marginal Jew,* 2:453–54.
2. Witherington, *Jesus Quest,* 197, 207.

3. Sheler et al., "In Search of Jesus," 50. Crossan was "the ground shaker" and Borg "the mystic." Less cute, but accurate.

4. Meier, *Marginal Jew*, 1:6, 7. He suggests six aspects of Jesus' life and ministry that the term *marginal* may be expected to conjure.

5. Meier, *Marginal Jew*, 1:7.

6. Meier, *Marginal Jew*, 1:8

7. Meier, *Marginal Jew*, 1:9

8. Meier, *Marginal Jew*, 1:9

9. Crossan, *Historical Jesus*, xxxiv.

10. Meier, *Marginal Jew*, 1:1.

11. Meier, *Marginal Jew*, 2:4. For the full discussion, see 1:21–40.

12. Sheler et al., "In Search of Jesus," 52.

13. Witherington has complained that, so stated, this distinction is not helpful because it seems to imply that the things about Jesus that cannot be recovered through historical analysis are "real" in some sense other than being grounded in history. He suggests a distinction between "the historical Jesus" (Meier's "real Jesus") and "the Jesus that we can recover by means of the historical-critical method" (Meier's "historical Jesus"). In either case, the latter is viewed as a subset of the former. See Witherington, *Jesus Quest*, 199.

14. To cite just one example, he concludes that Jesus' commissioning of Peter in Matt. 16:18–19 represents post-Easter tradition rather than authentic words of the historical Jesus. See *Marginal Jew*, 3:229–33.

15. Feminist and third-world scholars often claim that the interpretation of data is as likely to be affected by *social location* as it is by confessional commitments. See, for example, Schüssler Fiorenza, *In Memory of Her*.

16. Meier, *Marginal Jew*, 1:177.

17. Meier, *Marginal Jew*, 2:619–22.

18. Meier's work includes a more extensive study of certain Josephus passages than has been undertaken by any other historical Jesus scholar (*Marginal Jew*, 1:66–88). He eventually decides that, like Paul, Josephus offers "little more than tidbits" (2:5), yet what he does offer is "of monumental importance" (1:68). The presentation in chapter 2 of this book concerning what may be regarded as authentic in Josephus's comments on Jesus reflects Meier's research (see pages 38–39).

19. Meier, *Marginal Jew*, 1:112–66.

20. Meier, *Marginal Jew*, 2:6.

21. Meier, *Marginal Jew*, 4:1.

22. Meier, *Marginal Jew*, 1:205–52.

23. Meier, *Marginal Jew*, 1:351.

24. Meier, *Marginal Jew*, 1:278–85.

25. Meier, *Marginal Jew*, 1:268–78; this conclusion would be challenged by Keith, *Jesus' Literacy*.

26. Meier, *Marginal Jew*, 1:352.

27. Meier, *Marginal Jew*, 1:351.

28. Meier, *Marginal Jew*, 2:7.

29. Meier, *Marginal Jew*, 2:27.

30. Meier, *Marginal Jew*, 2:40.

31. Meier, *Marginal Jew*, 2:113, quoting Krister Stendahl.

32. See Paul Hollenbach, "The Conversion of Jesus: From Jesus the Baptizer to Jesus the Healer," *Aufstieg und Niedergang der römischen Welt* 2.25.196–219.

33. Hendrikus Boers, *Who Was Jesus? The Historical Jesus and the Synoptic Gospels* (San Francisco: Harper & Row, 1989), 31–53.

34. Meier, *Marginal Jew*, 2:9.

35. Meier, *Marginal Jew*, 2:124.
36. Allison thinks the contrast between Jesus and John on this point has been overplayed: there is much in the Jesus tradition to indicate that Jesus was an ascetic also. See *Jesus of Nazareth*, 172–216. See also Joseph, "Ascetic Jesus."
37. Meier, *Marginal Jew*, 2:9.
38. Meier, *Marginal Jew*, 2:127.
39. Meier, *Marginal Jew*, 2:144.
40. Meier, *Marginal Jew*, 2:144.
41. Meier, *Marginal Jew*, 2:265.
42. Meier, *Marginal Jew*, 2:241. The language derives from Perrin, *Jesus and the Language of the Kingdom* (though Perrin, in turn, draws on literary critic Philip Wheelwright).
43. Meier, *Marginal Jew*, 2:243–70.
44. Meier, *Marginal Jew*, 2:291–337.
45. Meier, *Marginal Jew*, 2:6.
46. Meier, *Marginal Jew*, 2:348.
47. Meier, *Marginal Jew*, 2:423.
48. Meier, *Marginal Jew*, 2:398–454.
49. Meier, *Marginal Jew*, 2:451.
50. Sanders has become increasingly open to recognizing the validity of some "present kingdom" sayings. See n. 77 on page 299.
51. Meier, *Marginal Jew*, 2:452.
52. Meier, *Marginal Jew*, 2:453.
53. Meier, *Marginal Jew*, 2:617–18.
54. Meier, *Marginal Jew*, 2:4. Here he cites Craig Evans, "Life of Jesus Research and the Eclipse of Mythology," *Theological Studies* 54 (1993): 3–36, esp. 29.
55. Meier, *Marginal Jew*, 2:630.
56. Meier, *Marginal Jew*, 3:1–285.
57. Meier, *Marginal Jew*, 3:22–24.
58. Meier, *Marginal Jew*, 3:12; compare 3:24–27.
59. Meier, *Marginal Jew*, 3:28.
60. Meier, *Marginal Jew*, 3:27.
61. Meier, *Marginal Jew*, 3:40–124.
62. Meier, *Marginal Jew*, 3:48.
63. Meier, *Marginal Jew*, 3:50–54.
64. Meier, *Marginal Jew*, 3:54–55.
65. Meier, *Marginal Jew*, 3:55–73.
66. Meier, *Marginal Jew*, 3:64–67. He claims that "both the shocking imagery and the multiple attestation of sources [Mark and Q] argue for Jesus as the source of the saying" (65).
67. Meier, *Marginal Jew*, 3:80–82.
68. Meier, *Marginal Jew*, 3:125–97.
69. Meier claims that Crossan must deny the existence of the twelve during Jesus' lifetime because it would contradict his portrait of Jesus and that this leads to somewhat desperate attempts to explain away data that would otherwise be deemed historically authentic. See *Marginal Jew*, 3:145. Gowler cites this claim as an example of how Meier sometimes challenges the academic integrity or honesty of other scholars—a very serious charge that strikes me as unwarranted (see *What Are They Saying about the Historical Jesus?* 119). Meier does not here or elsewhere challenge Crossan's integrity or honesty; he simply challenges one of the assumptions of Crossan's methodology (that otherwise verifiable data can be dismissed if it does not fit with a prevailing hypothesis)—an assumption

shared by the majority of Jesus scholars. See the discussion of approach on pages 227–30 of this book.

70. Meier, *Marginal Jew*, 3:128–41.
71. Meier, *Marginal Jew*, 3:141–46.
72. Meier, *Marginal Jew*, 3:146–47.
73. Meier, *Marginal Jew*, 3:131, 140. Compare McKnight, "Jesus and the Twelve."
74. Meier, *Marginal Jew*, 3:148.
75. Meier, *Marginal Jew*, 3:154–63.
76. Meier, *Marginal Jew*, 3:148–54.
77. Meier, *Marginal Jew*, 3:250.
78. Meier, *Marginal Jew*, 3:248.
79. Meier, *Marginal Jew*, 3:251.
80. Meier, *Marginal Jew*, 3:250–51.
81. On Jesus' interaction with women (a somewhat-neglected topic in historical Jesus studies) see, Amy-Jill Levine, "The Word Becomes Flesh: Jesus, Gender, and Sexuality," 509–23 in James D. G. Dunn and Scot McKnight, eds., *The Historical Jesus in Recent Research*, Sources for Biblical and Theological Study 10 (Winona Lake, Ind.: Eisenbrauns, 2005); "Jesus, Gender, and Sexuality: A Jewish Critique," in L. J. Greenspoon, R. A. Simkins, and J. A. Cahan, eds., *Women and Judaism*, Studies in Jewish Civilization (Omaha: Creighton University Press, 2003). The most comprehensive book-length study is Corley, *Women and the Historical Jesus*.
82. Meier, *Marginal Jew*, 3:73–80.
83. Meier, *Marginal Jew*, 3:299–309, 311–13.
84. Meier says, "Clearly the struggle between Christian Jews and the Pharisaic Jews in the period of A.D. 30–100 has left a strong imprint on the four Gospels" (*Marginal Jew*, 3:336).
85. Meier, *Marginal Jew*, 3:313–40.
86. Meier, *Marginal Jew*, 3:339.
87. Meier, *Marginal Jew*, 3:338.
88. Meier, *Marginal Jew*, 3:636.
89. Meier, *Marginal Jew*, 3:637.
90. Meier, *Marginal Jew*, 3:532.
91. Meier, *Marginal Jew*, 3:488–532.
92. Meier, *Marginal Jew*, 3:532–49.
93. Meier, *Marginal Jew*, 3:431–44.
94. Meier, *Marginal Jew*, 3:435.
95. Meier, *Marginal Jew*, 3:443.
96. Meier, *Marginal Jew* 4:1. This phrase is used as the title for Meier's introduction to volume 4 of *Marginal Jew*, and it is also repeated frequently throughout that book.
97. Meier, *Marginal Jew*, 2:1046; compare 4:415.
98. Meier, *Marginal Jew*, 4:415
99. Meier, *Marginal Jew*, 4:74–181.
100. Meier, *Marginal Jew*, 4:182–234.
101. Meier, *Marginal Jew*, 4:127, 205–6.
102. Meier, *Marginal Jew*, 4:235–341, esp. 297.
103. Meier, *Marginal Jew*, 4:342–477.
104. Meier, *Marginal Jew*, 4:14.
105. Meier, *Marginal Jew*, 4:575–76. Meier's emphasis.
106. Meier, *Marginal Jew*, 4:575; compare 4:493.
107. Meier, *Marginal Jew*, 2:628.

108. Meier, *Marginal Jew*, 2:454.
109. Meier, *Marginal Jew*, 2:628; compare 1:216–19.
110. Meier, *Marginal Jew*, 3:90 n. 22, summarizing a key point that the first two volumes "have shown at length."
111. Meier, *Marginal Jew*, 4:656–57.
112. Meier also disagrees with Sanders in affirming that Jesus did call people to personal and national repentance, though Sanders's rejection of this point is based on exegetical arguments rather than a sense that it would contradict the portrait he has sketched.
113. Meier, *Marginal Jew*, 2:3.
114. William Loader, "Review of John P. Meier's *A Marginal Jew: Rethinking the Historical Jesus*, vol. 4, *Law and Love*," in *Review of Biblical Literature*, 04/2010.
115. John P. Meier, "Reflections on Jesus-of-History Research Today," 84–107 in James H. Charlesworth, ed., *Jesus' Jewishness: Exploring the Place of Jesus within Early Judaism* (New York: Crossroad, 1991), 92.
116. Borg, *Jesus in Contemporary Scholarship*, 32, 43 n. 85.
117. One significant difference between Meier and the Jesus Seminar at this point is that Meier offers detailed accounts of his reasoning, facilitating evaluation of his arguments. The Jesus Seminar published only conclusions with brief summaries indicating factors affecting each vote.
118. See, for instance, the comment in *U.S. News and World Report*: "Some criticize his work as unimaginative and too beholden to official Catholic doctrine" (Sheler et al., "In Search of Jesus," 52). I have not found any reference in which a major scholar offers such a charge in print. It is more the sort of thing that is said in hallways and elevators. Gowler does suggest that "Meier is primarily in dialogue with Christian piety in general and Roman Catholic tradition in particular" (*What Are They Saying about the Historical Jesus?* 109)—but being "in dialogue with" is not the same thing as being "beholden to."
119. See Wright, *New Testament and the People of God*, 81–120.
120. Wright, *Jesus and the Victory of God*, 33.
121. Allison, *Jesus of Nazareth*, 35–36. Allison offers these remarks as a critique of Crossan's methodology, but they would apply to Meier's as well (indeed, probably more so—since Crossan does eventually propose a framing narrative).
122. I think Meier's approach exemplifies what Wright polemically calls "chastened positivism." Somewhat ironically for my argument, Wright actually says that he detects "more than a hint of this" in Sanders (*New Testament and the People of God*, 82 n. 3). With Meier, one doesn't have to worry about detecting hints; he wears the charge with pride.
123. Wright, *Jesus and the Victory of God*, 33. Note that while Wright denounces this sort of approach, he does not specifically denounce Meier for approaching history in this way—perhaps because he usually agrees with Meier's conclusions.
124. Sanders, *Jesus and Judaism*, 320. While Sanders does not say this with reference to Meier, I am suggesting that what Sanders says in another context might apply as a critique of Meier's work.
125. Crossan, *Birth of Christianity*, 146.
126. Meier, *Marginal Jew*, 1:5.
127. Meier, *Marginal Jew*, 1:5–6.
128. Meier, *Marginal Jew*, 1:4. The word *asymptotic* derives from geometry, where it is used to refer to the tendency for a curve always to approach becoming a straight line without ever quite becoming one. It is applied as a theological metaphor in the work of Karl Rahner.
129. Meier, *Marginal Jew*, 1:3–4.

Chapter 9: N. T. Wright

1. Wright, *Jesus and the Victory of God*, 172.
2. Mary Knutsen, "Review of *Jesus and the Victory of God*," in *Augsburg Fortress Book Newsletter* 571 (1997): 1–3.
3. Gowler, *What Are They Saying about the Historical Jesus?* 51.
4. See, for example, *Simply Christian: Why Christianity Makes Sense* (New York: HarperOne, 2006) and the entire series of For Everyone commentaries that he published with Westminster John Knox covering every book of the New Testament (*Matthew for Everyone; Mark for Everyone*, etc.). Several of his writings that are intended for a more popular audience are published under the name Tom Wright.
5. Richard N. Ostling of *Time* magazine.
6. Wright, *New Testament and the People of God*, xiv. Compare his comments in *Resurrection of the Son of God*, xviii: the point is "to remind myself, as well as the reader, that in the first-century, as increasingly in the twenty-first, the question is not whether we believe in 'God' . . . but rather to wonder which god, out of many available candidates, we might be talking about." To be faithful to Wright's views on this subject, the word *god* will be spelled with a lowercase g throughout this chapter when discussing Wright's work.
7. Wright, *Resurrection of the Son of God*, xviii.
8. Like Crossan, Wright has also produced a popular version of his Jesus biography, a slim volume augmented by photos and artwork: Tom Wright, *The Original Jesus* (Grand Rapids: Eerdmans Publishing Co., 1996). See also N. T. Wright, *Who Was Jesus?* (Grand Rapids: Eerdmans, 1992); *The Challenge of Jesus: Rediscovering Who Jesus Was and Is* (Downers Grove, Ill.: InterVarsity, 1999); *Simply Jesus: A New Vision of Who He Was, What He Did, and Why He Matters* (New York: HarperOne, 2006).
9. This method is described with full detail in *New Testament and the People of God*, 81–120. It is indebted in key respects to the work of Ben F. Meyer, especially as presented in *The Aims of Jesus* (London: SCM, 1979).
10. Wright, *Jesus and the Victory of God*, 133, and *New Testament and the People of God*, 98–109.
11. Wright, *Jesus and the Victory of God*, 89–121.
12. Wright, *Jesus and the Victory of God*, 88.
13. Wright, *Jesus and the Victory of God*, 133.
14. Wright believes that the Gospel of Thomas represents a later, derivative stage of the tradition. See *New Testament and the People of God*, 442–43.
15. Wright, *Jesus and the Victory of God*, 5.
16. Wright, *Jesus and the Victory of God*, 132.
17. Wright, *Jesus and the Victory of God*, 93.
18. Wright, *Jesus and the Victory of God*, 90.
19. Wright, *Jesus and the Victory of God*, 612.
20. Wright, *Jesus and the Victory of God*, 109.
21. Wright, *New Testament and the People of God*, 109–12, 122–26. See also the summary in *Jesus and the Victory of God*, 137–44.
22. Wright, *Jesus and the Victory of God*, 138.
23. Wright, *Jesus and the Victory of God*, 139.
24. Wright, *Jesus and the Victory of God*, 139.
25. Wright, *New Testament and the People of God*, 268–72. See also *Jesus and the Victory of God*, xvii–xviii, 126–27, 203–4.
26. Wright, *Jesus and the Victory of God*, 204–6.

27. Wright, *New Testament and the People of God*, 280–338. He is dependent at this point on the views of his mentor, George B. Caird (*Language and Imagery of the Bible*). He is followed closely by McKnight, *New Vision for Israel*, 120–55.
28. Wright, *Jesus and the Victory of God*, 97.
29. Wright, *Jesus and the Victory of God*, 147–48. Wright's "list" is not a literal one. I have developed this list from the narrative paragraph in his book; the precise wording of items is sometimes my own.
30. Wright, *Jesus and the Victory of God*, 150.
31. Wright, *Jesus and the Victory of God*, 163.
32. As he notes, none of the sayings come from Q (or from Thomas), which may explain why the Jesus Seminar has not made more of this image for Jesus.
33. On all of this, see Wright, *Jesus and the Victory of God*, 162–70. The typologies of prophets are drawn from Horsley and Hanson, *Bandits, Prophets, and Messiahs* and, especially, Robert L. Webb, *John the Baptizer and Prophet: A Socio-Historical Study*, Journal for the Study of the New Testament: Supplement Series 62 (Sheffield: Sheffield Academic, 1991).
34. Wright, *Jesus and the Victory of God*, 201.
35. Wright, *Jesus and the Victory of God*, 125–31, 238–39. James D. G. Dunn calls Wright's interpretation of the Sower parable "far-fetched." See Dunn, *Jesus Remembered*, 476.
36. Wright, *Jesus and the Victory of God*, 187.
37. Wright, *Jesus and the Victory of God*, 246–64.
38. Wright, *Jesus and the Victory of God*, 268–74.
39. Wright, *Jesus and the Victory of God*, 372.
40. Wright, *Jesus and the Victory of God*, 389.
41. Wright, *Jesus and the Victory of God*, 389.
42. Wright, *Jesus and the Victory of God*, 390.
43. Wright, *Jesus and the Victory of God*, 398.
44. Wright, *Jesus and the Victory of God*, 272.
45. Wright, *Jesus and the Victory of God*, 274.
46. Wright, *Jesus and the Victory of God*, 184.
47. Wright, *Jesus and the Victory of God*, 320.
48. Wright, *Jesus and the Victory of God*, 361. See also *New Testament and the People of God*, 280–338. The argument is based in part on interpretation of Daniel 7, and on recognition that the Greek word (*erchōmenon*) often translated "coming" in Mark 13:26 can actually mean either "coming" or "going." Similarly, the Greek word *parousia* (Matt. 24:3, 27, 37, 39), which Christians often invoke when speaking of the "return" of Christ, literally means "presence."
49. Wright, *Jesus and the Victory of God*, 343–67.
50. Wright, *Jesus and the Victory of God*, 426.
51. On this, see also McKnight, *A New Vision for Israel*, 120–55.
52. Wright, *Jesus and the Victory of God*, 359. In a fundamental sense, though, the true enemy is "the satan," as indicated below.
53. Wright, *Jesus and the Victory of God*, 196.
54. Wright, *Jesus and the Victory of God*, 547.
55. On this see Darrell L. Bock, *Blasphemy and Exaltation in Judaism and the Final Examination of Jesus* (Tübingen: Mohr Siebeck, 1998).
56. Wright, *Jesus and the Victory of God*, 552.
57. Sanders, *Jesus and Judaism*, 333.
58. Wright, *Jesus and the Victory of God*, 553–76. This point is also argued in Scot McKnight, *Jesus and His Death: Historiography, the Historical Jesus, and Atonement Theory* (Waco, Tex.: Baylor University Press, 2005).

59. Wright, *New Testament and the People of God*, 277–78; *Jesus and the Victory of God*, 577–79.
60. Wright, *Jesus and the Victory of God*, 604.
61. Again, on this, see McKnight, *Jesus and His Death.*
62. Wright, *Jesus and the Victory of God*, 595.
63. Wright, *Jesus and the Victory of God*, 607.
64. Wright, *Jesus and the Victory of God*, 609, 607.
65. Wright, *Jesus and the Victory of God*, 615.
66. Wright, *Jesus and the Victory of God*, 632–39.
67. Wright, *Jesus and the Victory of God*, 639.
68. Wright, *Jesus and the Victory of God*, 639.
69. Wright, *Jesus and the Victory of God*, 443–72.
70. Wright, *Jesus and the Victory of God*, 477.
71. Wright, *Jesus and the Victory of God*, 477.
72. N. T. Wright, "Jesus, Israel, and the Cross," in *SBL 1985 Seminar Papers*, ed. K. H. Richards (Atlanta: Scholars, 1985), 87.
73. Wright, *Jesus and the Victory of God*, 538.
74. Wright, *Jesus and the Victory of God*, 435.
75. Wright, *Jesus and the Victory of God*, 647.
76. Wright, *Jesus and the Victory of God*, 646.
77. Wright, *Jesus and the Victory of God*, 624.
78. Wright, *Jesus and the Victory of God*, 653. Likewise, Sigurd Grindheim concludes that Jesus spoke and acted with an authority that only God was thought to have. He understood his relationship to God as that of a son who was both equal and subordinate to the Father." See *God's Equal: What Can We Know about Jesus' Self-Understanding in the Synoptic Gospels?* Library of New Testament Studies 446 (London: T&T Clark, 2011).
79. Wright, *Who Was Jesus?* 103. The spelling of God with a capital letter in this citation owes to its occurrence in a popular work in which Wright eschewed his tendency to spell god with a lower case "g."
80. For Wright's own summary of this central thesis as a set of seven propositions, see *Resurrection of the Son of God*, 686–87.
81. Wright, *Resurrection of the Son of God*, 10.
82. Wright, *Resurrection of the Son of God*, 32–84.
83. Wright, *Resurrection of the Son of God*, 31, 108, and elsewhere.
84. Wright, *Resurrection of the Son of God*, 123.
85. Wright, *Resurrection of the Son of God*, 85–206.
86. Wright, *Resurrection of the Son of God*, 681, summarizing the results of 207–681, Compare 477–78.
87. Wright and Crossan, "Resurrection: Historical Event or Theological Explanation?" 18–19. See also Wright's comment on page 31 of this piece to the effect that he if he were rewriting *The Resurrection of the Son of God* he would add "a seventh mutation," focusing on the emergence of what Crossan calls "collaborative eschatology."
88. Wright, *Resurrection of the Son of God*, 566–68.
89. Wright, *Resurrection of the Son of God*, 347–56, 375–98.
90. Wright, *Resurrection of the Son of God*, 718.
91. Wright, *Resurrection of the Son of God*, 686–96.
92. Wright and Crossan, "Resurrection: Historical Event or Theological Explanation?" 23.
93. Wright, *Resurrection of the Son of God*, 712.
94. Borg and Wright, *Meaning of Jesus*, 237.

95. Meier, *Marginal Jew*, 4:68 n. 67, citing Wright's comments in *Jesus and the Victory of God*, 288–89.
96. Wright, *Jesus and the Victory of God*, 339. James D. G. Dunn says Wright is "surprisingly uncritical" in his use of Mark 13 (*Jesus Remembered*, 418 n. 185).
97. Wright, *Jesus and the Victory of God*, 170.
98. James D. G. Dunn is an exception, taking Wright's point as a fair and reasonable consideration. See *Jesus Remembered*, 422 n. 210.
99. See Crossan, *Birth of Christianity*, 104.
100. Funk, *Honest to Jesus*, 65.
101. Crossan in particular has criticized Wright's approach, which he says tries to rely on hypothesis and verification "without any prior judgments about sources and traditions" (*Birth of Christianity*, 98–101, citation on 98).
102. Wright, *Jesus and the Victory of God*, 16–21, 28–32.
103. Wright, *Jesus and the Victory of God*, 21.
104. Meier, *Marginal Jew*, 4:22–23 n. 17.
105. Wright, *Jesus and the Victory of God*, 479.
106. Wright, *Jesus and the Victory of God*, 89.
107. See Maurice Casey, *Son of Man: The Interpretation and Influence of Daniel 7* (London: SPCK, 1979).
108. Witherington, *Jesus Quest*, 230–31. See also Allison, *Jesus of Nazareth*, 159–60.
109. Allison, *Jesus of Nazareth*, 165–69. On the point that (contra Wright) Jews generally took eschatological projections quite literally, see further Dale C. Allison Jr., "Jesus and the Victory of Apocalyptic," in *Jesus and the Restoration of Israel: A Critical Assessment of N. T. Wright's* Jesus and the Victory of God, ed. Carey C. Newman, 126–41 (Downers Grove, Ill.: InterVarsity, 1999); compare Edward Adams, *The Stars Will Fall from Heaven: Cosmic Catastrophe in the New Testament and Its World*, Library of New Testament Studies 347 (London: T&T Clark, 2007).
110. Allison, *Constructing Jesus*, 45. For Wright's development of that idea, see *Jesus and the Victory of God*, 320–68.
111. Allison, *Jesus of Nazareth*, 160 n. 240.
112. See Jacob Neusner, *From Politics to Piety* (Englewood Cliffs, N.J.: Prentice-Hall, 1973), and Sanders, *Paul and Palestinian Judaism*. Wright's own view is most clearly stated in *New Testament and the People of God*, 181–203.
113. Sanders, *Jesus and Judaism*, 336; Meier, *Marginal Jew*, 4:342–477.
114. Fredriksen, *Jesus of Nazareth*, 197–207; "Did Jesus Obey the Purity Laws?" "What You See Is What You Get"; Levine, *Misunderstood Jew*, 146–68; 173–77.
115. James D. G. Dunn, "Review of *The New Testament and the People of God* by N. T. Wright," *Journal of Theological Studies* 46 (1995): 242–45, citation on 244. Wright maintains that there is evidence that both the Essenes and Paul thought this way. On the Essenes, see Michael Knibb, *The Qumran Community* (Cambridge: Cambridge University Press, 1987), 20. On Paul (with reference to Gal. 3:10–14), see N. T. Wright, *The Climax of the Covenant: Christ and the Law in Pauline Theology* (Minneapolis: Fortress, 1991), 141–48. But see also M. Casey, "Where Wright Is Wrong," *Journal for the Study of the New Testament* 69 (1998): 95–103.
116. Dunn, *Jesus Remembered*, 475.
117. Dunn, *Jesus Remembered*, 475.
118. Dunn, *Jesus Remembered*, 120. Compare I. H. Jones, "Disputed Questions in Biblical Studies: 4. Exile and Eschatology," *Expository Times* 112 (2000–01): 401–5.
119. Dunn, *Jesus Remembered*, 795.
120. Brant Pitre, *Jesus, the Tribulation, and the End of Exile: Restoration Eschatology and the Origin of the Atonement* (Grand Rapids: Baker Academic, 2006). McKnight

(*Jesus and His Death*) also claims that Jesus understood his impending death and the forthcoming martyrdoms of his followers as intrinsic to the eschatological tribulation, a tribulation that would lead into the kingdom.

121. Reviewers have noted that if Pitre is right about this then the logical conclusion would be that Jesus failed: his death did not inaugurate an eschatological tribulation that resulted in an end of exile, if the latter means regathering of the twelve tribes in the promised land. See, for example, Matthew S. Harmon, "Review of Brant Pitre's *Jesus, the Tribulation, and the End of the Exile*," *Review of Biblical Literature*, 09/2007.

122. Wright, *Jesus and the Victory of God*, 370.

123. Wright, *Jesus and the Victory of God*, 542.

124. See James G. Crossley, "Against the Historical Plausibility of the Empty Tomb Story and the Bodily Resurrection of Jesus: A Response to Wright," *Journal for the Study of the Historical Jesus* 3.2 (2005): 171–86, and Michael Goulder, "Jesus' Resurrection and Christian Origins: A Response to N. T. Wright," *Journal for the Study of the Historical Jesus* 3.2 (2005): 187–95. Note that the entire issue of the journal in which these two articles are found was devoted to discussion of Wright's *Resurrection of the Son of God*, with concluding comments from Wright himself.

125. Wright and Crossan, "Resurrection: Historical Event or Theological Explanation," esp. 31–33; compare Crossan, "Bodily-Resurrection Faith," in Stewart, ed., *Resurrection of Jesus*, 171–86.

126. Wright, *Resurrection of the Son of God*, 709 n. 70.

127. Wright, *Challenge of Jesus*, 191–92.

Chapter 10: The Quest Continues

1. Cited in Van Biema, "The Gospel Truth?" 59. Janssen was reference librarian and archivist for the Publishing House of the Evangelical Lutheran Church in America.

2. Cited in Simon, "Who Was Jesus?" 68. Bien is the translator of Nikos Kazantzakis' novel *The Last Temptation of Christ*.

3. Simon, "Who Was Jesus?" 71.

4. John Dominic Crossan, "The Infancy and Youth of the Messiah," 59–82 in Hershel Shanks, ed., *The Search for Jesus: Modern Scholarship Looks at the Gospels* (Washington, D.C.: Biblical Archaeology Society, 1994), 80.

5. The fact that some scholars appeal to Thomas (a book about Jesus not found in the Bible) attracts the attention of the media and often arouses strong feelings among Christians who fear the import of heresy, but in reality this usually turns out to be much ado about very little. Scholars who think that Thomas is independent of the other Gospels often get branded as "liberals" because they think a nonbiblical book should be taken seriously in the study of Jesus. Ironically, however, the primary consequence of adopting such a position is stronger affirmation of the historical authenticity of canonical biblical material (i.e., of the canonical material understood to be multiply attested in Thomas)—and such affirmation is typically associated with "conservative" scholarship.

6. Allison was also an early advocate of this approach, claiming that one should start with "a paradigm" or explanatory matrix: this paradigm should be in place "prior to and independently of our evaluation of the historicity of individual items in the Jesus tradition." See *Jesus of Nazareth*, 39.

7. Dunn, *Jesus Remembered*; *A New Perspective on Jesus*; "Remembering Jesus." A compatible thesis is developed by Rafael Rodriguez in *Structuring Early Christian*

Memory: Jesus in Tradition, Performance, and Text, Library of New Testament Studies 407 (London: T&T Clark, 2010), and by Anthony Le Donne in *The Historiographical Jesus: Memory, Typology, and the Son of David* (Waco, Tex.: Baylor University Press, 2009).

8. Dunn, "Remembering Jesus," 203.
9. Le Donne, *Historiographical Jesus*, 268.
10. Dunn, "Remembering Jesus," 205.
11. Dunn, *New Perspective on Jesus*, 114.
12. Dunn, *Jesus Remembered*, 640–43.
13. This point is made nicely in the title to chapter 3 of Dunn's *New Perspective on Jesus*: "The Characteristic Jesus: From Atomistic Exegesis to Consistent Emphases." As early as 1971, Leander Keck had similarly argued (in a rebuff of the criterion of dissimilarity) that "we should look for the characteristic Jesus instead of the distinctive Jesus." See Keck, *A Future for the Historical Jesus: The Place of Jesus in Preaching and Theology* (Nashville: Abingdon, 1971), 33.
14. Robert M. Price, "Response to James D. G. Dunn," 226–32 in Beilby and Eddy, eds., *Historical Jesus: Five Views*, 226.
15. John Dominic Crossan, "Jesus Forgotten? The Hermeneutics of 'In Some Sense': A Review of James D. G. Dunn, *Jesus Remembered*," presented orally to the 2004 Annual Meeting of the Historical Jesus Section of the Society of Biblical Literature.
16. Meier, *Marginal Jew*, 4:457–58 n. 136, 523, 611 n. 159.
17. See Allison, *Constructing Jesus*.
18. Witherington, *Jesus Quest*, 122.
19. See especially Sean Freyne, *Galilee, Jesus, and the Gospels: Literary Approaches and Historical Investigations* (Philadelphia: Fortress, 1988); *Jesus: A Jewish Galilean*; Reed, *Archaeology and the Galilean Jesus*.
20. Wright offers a sevenfold description of how different scholars have construed the eschatological stance of Jesus. See *Jesus and the Victory of God*, 208.
21. Bornkamm, *Jesus of Nazareth*, 62.
22. Crossan, *Historical Jesus*, 304.
23. Mack, *Myth of Innocence*, 73.
24. Borg, *Jesus in Contemporary Scholarship*, 7–8.
25. Thus, those who think Jesus espoused imminent, apocalyptic eschatology do not usually set this in opposition to participatory or collaborative eschatology; they claim the two are not mutually exclusive. So, Wright, even while arguing in favor of the apocalyptic view, praised Crossan's description of collaborative eschatology and agreed that a greater emphasis on this dimension would be a legitimate corrective to his own published work. See Wright and Crossan, "Resurrection: Historical Event or Theological Explanation?" 31, 42–43.
26. Borg gives five reasons why the social location of contemporary Jesus scholars (primarily, church-related academic institutions) has discouraged recognition of the sociopolitical dimension of Jesus' activity and message. See *Jesus in Contemporary Scholarship*, 99.
27. Borg, *Jesus in Contemporary Scholarship*, 97.
28. See, for instance, S. G. F. Brandon, *Jesus and the Zealots: A Study of the Political Factor in Primitive Christianity* (New York: Charles Scribner's Sons, 1967).
29. Borg, *Jesus in Contemporary Scholarship*, 98.
30. For example, Wright notes that the biblical concept of a miracle is not the work of a force alien to nature, but an unanticipated work by a force within

the natural world, enabling nature "to be more truly itself." See *Jesus and the Victory of God*, 188.

31. Compare Borg's comments in *Jesus: Uncovering*, 146. Borg likewise objects to the term *miracle*, preferring *mighty deeds* or *deeds of power* (either of which would be more literal translations of the Greek *dynamis* (frequently translated "miracle" in English New Testaments).

32. See Schweitzer, *Quest of the Historical Jesus*, 51.

33. Meier, *Marginal Jew*, 2:520–21.

34. A nonpartisan research study in 2004 of 1,100 medical doctors in the United States found that 73 percent believe miracles sometimes occur. See "Science of Miracle? Holiday Season Survey Reveals Physicians' Views of Faith, Prayer, and Miracles," *Business Wire* (December 20, 2004). Cited in Craig S. Keener, *Miracles: The Credibility of the New Testament Accounts*, 2 vols. (Grand Rapids: Baker Academic, 2011), 427–28.

35. Keener, *Miracles*, 211–358.

36. Robert L. Webb, "The Rules of the Game: History and Historical Method in the Context of Faith: The *Via Media* of Methodological Naturalism," *Journal for the Study of the Historical Jesus* 9.1 (2011): 59–84. See also his "The Historical Enterprise and Historical Jesus Research," 9–94 in Bock and Webb, eds., *Key Events*.

37. Bernard Lonergan calls the ability to render such judgments a matter of "functional specialization" (*Method in Theology* [New York: Herder and Herder, 1972], 125–45). Meier appeals to this concept as descriptive of what distinguishes legitimate historical Jesus study from historically informed Christology (see *Marginal Jew*, 4:6).

38. Webb, "The Rules of the Game," 82.

39. Webb, "The Rules of the Game," 83–84.

40. Meier, *Marginal Jew*, 2:513–14.

41. Meier, *Marginal Jew*, 2:511.

42. Cited in Allen, "Away with the Manger," 25.

43. "The Jesus Seminar Spring 1995 Meeting," *The Fourth R* 8.2 (1995): 10, 12.

44. Cited in Kenneth L. Woodward, "Rethinking the Resurrection," *Newsweek* (April 8, 1996): 62.

45. Borg, *Jesus: A New Vision*, 185.

46. Cited in Woodward, "Rethinking the Resurrection," 62.

47. Crossan, *Jesus: A Revolutionary Biography* 123–58.

48. Crossan, *Historical Jesus*, 319–20, 336–37.

49. Cited in Allen, "No-Frills Jesus," 67.

50. See, for instance, Crossan, *Jesus: A Revolutionary Biography*, 84–88.

51. Crossan, *Historical Jesus*, 320. Compare David E. Aune, "Magic in Early Christianity," *Aufstieg und Niedergang der römischen Welt* 2.23.1507–57, citation on 1538.

52. Crossan, *Birth of Christianity*, 26–29, citation on 29. He does add that "as a Christian trying to be faithful" he *believes* that "God is incarnate in the Jewish peasant poverty of Jesus and not in the Roman imperial power of Augustus" (29).

53. Wright, *Jesus and the Victory of God*, 187.

54. Wright, *Jesus and the Victory of God*, 187.

55. Wright, *Jesus and the Victory of God*, 194. See also 186 n. 160.

56. Witherington, *Jesus Quest*, 124 (emphasis in original). He attributes the view that he is contesting to Sanders, but I do not see Sanders actually saying this on the page to which Witherington refers (*Historical Figure of Jesus*, 159); Sanders

simply notes that "some of the miracle stories cannot be explained on the basis of today's scientific knowledge."

57. Twelftree, *Jesus the Miracle Worker*, 345.
58. Twelftree, *Jesus the Miracle Worker*, 52.
59. Keener, *Miracles*, 107–208.
60. Many of the same points are made, with less detail, in Paul Rhodes Eddy and Gregory A. Boyd, *The Jesus Legend: A Case for the Historical Reliability of the Synoptic Jesus Tradition* (Grand Rapids: Baker Academic, 2007), 39–90.
61. Robert J. Miller, "When It's Futile to Argue about the Historical Jesus: A Response to Bock, Keener, and Webb," *Journal for the Study of the Historical Jesus* 9.1 (2011): 85–95, citation on 93.
62. Amy-Jill Levine, "Christian Faith and the Study of the Historical Jesus: A Response to Bock, Keener, and Webb," *Journal for the Study of the Historical Jesus* 9.1 (2011): 96–106, esp. 101.
63. Borg, *A New Vision,* 67.
64. Borg, *A New Vision,* 67.
65. Marcus J. Borg, "From Galilean Jew to the Face of God," 18. The context for this comment included a specific reference to "walking on the water."
66. Borg, *Jesus: Uncovering,* 148.
67. Borg, *Jesus: Uncovering,* 150.
68. Borg, *Jesus: Uncovering,* 148.
69. This is how Borg describes Mack's Jesus in *Jesus in Contemporary Scholarship,* 23.
70. Michael F. Bird is another strong advocate of the view that the historical Jesus did regard his vocation in messianic categories. See *Are You the One Who Is to Come? The Historical Jesus and the Messianic Question* (Grand Rapids: Baker Academic, 2009).
71. Likewise, Richard Burridge says, "The roots of the so-called 'high' Christology, seeing Jesus sharing the life of God, are there right at the earliest level within the first communities of Jewish believers, indeed perhaps in Jesus' own self-understanding." See Richard A. Burridge and Graham Gould, *Jesus Now and Then* (Grand Rapids: Eerdmans, 2004), 108.
72. Allison argues with great detail for a softer version of this thesis: "Jesus did not run from death or otherwise resist it. On the contrary, anticipating his cruel end, he submitted to it, trusting that his unhappy fate was somehow for the good." See *Constructing Jesus,* 427–33, citation on 432.
73. McKnight, *Jesus and His Death.* Further, Jesus viewed his death in a representative sense, predicting that his disciples would also suffer martyrdom and, so, share in the eschatological woes that were ultimately part of God's redemptive plan for Israel.
74. This is essentially the view of both Craig Keener and Martin Hengel: Jesus did not regard himself as one prophet among many but as *the* eschatological prophet responsible for inaugurating what had traditionally been called the messianic kingdom. But Jesus may have resisted specific applications of the term *Messiah* to himself because that term carried political baggage he did not want to assume. See Keener, *Historical Jesus of the Gospels,* 256–67; Martin Hengel, "Jesus, the Messiah of Israel: The Debate about the 'Messianic Mission' of Jesus," 323–49 in Bruce Chilton and Craig A. Evans, eds., *Authenticating the Activities of Jesus,* New Testament Tools and Studies 28.2 (Leiden: Brill, 1999).
75. Thomas G. Long, "Stand Up, Stand Up for (the Historical) Jesus," *Theology Today* 52 (1995): 4–5. The original article to which Long refers was Cullen Murphy, "Who Do Men Say That I Am?" *The Atlantic* 258 (December 1986).

76. Borg, "The Historian, the Christian, and Jesus," 7.
77. Borg, "The Historian, the Christian, and Jesus," 16.
78. Frederick J. Gaiser, "The Quest for Jesus and the Christian Faith: Introduction," in *Quest for Jesus and the Christian Faith*, 6.
79. Fredriksen, *From Jesus to Christ*, 214–15. Compare Käsemann's justification for launching a "New Quest" for the historical Jesus, cited on page 19 of this book.
80. Meier, *Marginal Jew*, 1:200.

Appendix 1: Did Jesus Exist?

1. On proponents of this thesis up to the early twentieth centuries, see Shirley Jackson Case, *The Historicity of Jesus* (Chicago: Chicago University Press, 1912); Schweitzer, *Quest for Historical Jesus*, 124–42, 355–436.
2. See Bart D. Ehrman, *Did Jesus Exist?* (San Francisco: HarperOne, 2012) and Brent Landau, "'Jesus Never Existed'": An Intellectual History of the 'Jesus Myth' Theory" (unpublished paper). Note that I did not have access to either of these items at the time I composed this appendix, though Landau summarized his research orally in a paper delivered to the Historical Jesus Section of the Society of Biblical Literature at their 2011 Annual Meeting.
3. An oft-quoted comment from Bultmann would be typical: "Of course, the doubt as to whether Jesus really existed is unfounded and not worth refutation. No sane person can doubt that Jesus stands as founder behind the historical movement" (*Jesus and the Word*, 13). Bultmann himself rejected the historicity of much (probably most) of what the Gospels report concerning Jesus, yet he thought "no sane person" could doubt the basic fact of Jesus' historical existence.
4. Robert Price, a proponent of the thesis that Jesus probably did not exist, notes that for some who hold this view, the options seem to be that there was a real superman or only a mythic superman; little consideration is given to alternative possibilities. See Robert M. Price, "Jesus at the Vanishing Point," 55–104 in Beilby and Eddy, eds., *Historical Jesus: Five Views*.
5. Bauer's books, including *Christianity Exposed* (1843) and *Christ and the Caesars: How Christianity Originated from Graeco-Roman Civilization* (1877), are rarely available in English. Summaries of his work can be found in Schweitzer, *Quest of the Historical Jesus*, 124–42 and in Case, *Historicity of Jesus*, 32–132.
6. Schweitzer, *Quest of the Historical Jesus*, 140.
7. See Arthur Drews, *The Christ Myth*, 3rd ed., trans. C. DeLisle Burns (Amherst, N.Y.: Prometheus, 1998; original German edition, 1910). Drews's book drew heavily on a 1900 work by the British rationalist J. M. Robertson called *Christianity and Mythology* (original publisher unidentified, but now available online). It has been said that Drews's book convinced Vladimir Lenin that Jesus had not actually existed as a historical figure.
8. Earl Doherty, *The Jesus Puzzle: Did Christianity Begin with a Mythical Christ?* (Ottawa: Canadian Humanist Publications, 1999); ten years later, Doherty self-published an 814-page updated version of this book titled *Jesus: Neither God nor Man* (Age of Reason Publications, 2009).
9. Peter Jensen, *Das Gilgamesh-Epos in der Welt-literatur* (Strassburg: Verlag con Karl J. Trübner, 1906; now available online at Google books). Jensen also claimed that Abraham and Moses were figures derived from this epic (such that Jews also worship a Babylonian deity). His work was representative of a now-discredited view of history called "panbabylonianism."

10. See G. A. Wells, *The Jesus Legend* (La Salle, Ill.: Open Court, 1996); *The Jesus Myth* (Chicago: Open Court, 1999).

11. See Price, "Jesus at the Vanishing Point." For a more in-depth presentation, see Robert Price, *Deconstructing Jesus* (Amherst, N.Y.: Prometheus, 2000); *The Incredible Shrinking Son of Man: How Reliable Is the Gospel Tradition?* (Amherst, N.Y.: Prometheus Books, 2003); *Jesus Is Dead* (Cranford, N.J.: American Atheist Press, 2007).

12. Price, "Jesus at the Vanishing Point," 55.

13. Price, "Jesus at the Vanishing Point," 56.

14. Price dismisses the significance of those epistolary passages that most scholars do think refer to Jesus as a historical person. For example, Paul's reference to James as "the brother of the Lord" (Gal. 1:19) could simply mean that James was part of a spiritual brotherhood who felt a close kinship with their spiritual Lord; Paul's references to Jesus instituting the Lord's Supper (1 Cor. 11:23–26) could be a later interpolation into that letter or could simply be Paul's account of something he saw in a vision (in which case, the text would evidence the beginning of the historicization of the Christ figure). See Price, "Jesus at the Vanishing Point, 63–66.

15. Price takes the "criterion of dissimilarity" (see pages 63–65 of this book) to its logical extreme: since "*every single* Gospel bit and piece must have had a home in the early church . . . *all* must be denied to Jesus by the criterion of dissimilarity" (Price, "Jesus at the Vanishing Point," 60; emphasis his).

16. For example, Mark 6:7–13 (Jesus' mission charge to his disciples) could be modeled on passages from the Elisha stories (2 Kings 4:29; 5:22) and the passion/resurrection narratives may be based on myths regarding Baal, Osiris, and other dying-and-rising gods. See further Robert M. Price, "New Testament Narrative as Old Testament Midrash," 1:534–73 in Jacob Neusner and Alan J. Avery Peck, eds., *Encyclopedia of Midrash: Biblical Interpretation in Formative Judaism* (Leiden: Brill, 2005); Tryggve N. D. Mettinger, *The Riddle of Resurrection: "Dying and Rising Gods" in the Ancient Near East*, Coniectanea biblica: Old Testament Series 50 (Stockholm: Almqvist & Wiksell International, 2001).

17. G. R. S. Mead and Alvar Ellegar suggest that Jesus did exist, but much earlier than is traditionally thought (thus, the Christian myth focuses on a man who lived around 100 BCE). See Mead, *Did Jesus Live 100 B.C.?* (London: Theosophical Society, 1903; now available online at www.gnosis.org); Ellegar, *Jesus One Hundred Years before Christ: A Study in Creative Mythology* (London: Century, 1999). G. A. Wells expressed a similar view in his early work; see Wells, *Jesus of the Early Christians: A Study in Christian Origins* (London: Pemberton, 1971); *Who Was Jesus?* (London: Pemberton, 1975); *The Historical Evidence for Jesus* (Buffalo, N.Y.: Prometheus, 1982); *Who Was Jesus? A Critique of the New Testament Record* (LaSalle, Ill.: Open Court, 1989).

18. James D. G. Dunn says that if Price's position represents "a true expression of the state of the health of the Jesus-myth thesis, I can't see much life in it." See Dunn, "Response to Robert M. Price," 94–98 in Beilby and Eddy, eds., *Historical Jesus: Five Views*. A more detailed rebuttal of Price, Wells, Doherty, and others associated with the Jesus myth theory is found in Eddy and Boyd, *Jesus Legend*.

19. Dunn, "Response to Robert M. Price," 95.

20. Darrell L. Bock, "Response to Robert M. Price," 100–103 in Beilby and Eddy, eds., *Historical Jesus: Five Views*, 102.

21. Johnson, "Response to Robert M. Price," 91.

22. Crossan, "Response to Robert M. Price," 85. Eddy and Boyd question the basic thesis that the Jesus story was influenced by pagan mythology in *Jesus Legend*, 91–164.

23. Dunn says that at this point Price displays "a readiness to offer less plausible hypotheses to explain data that inconveniences his thesis" ("Response to Robert M. Price," 96). Compare Bock, "Response to Robert M. Price," 101–2; Johnson, "Response to Robert M. Price," 92. For a more detailed rebuttal of this essential plank of the Jesus myth theory, see Eddy and Boyd, *Jesus Legend*, 165–236.

Appendix 2: Historical Jesus Studies and Christian Apologetics

1. A survey of how major theologians have addressed the problems history poses for faith can be found in Gregory W. Dawes, *The Historical Jesus Question: The Challenge of History to Religious Authority* (Louisville: Westminster John Knox, 2001).

2. Examples of such glosses would include Jesus' claim that he came "to give his life as a ransom for many" (Mark 10:45) or the clause at the Last Supper in which he says the cup is his blood "which is poured out for many" (Mark 14:24). See McKnight, *Jesus and His Death*, 356, 359.

3. Elsewhere, I have put the matter this way: an evangelical Christian historian can say, "I cannot *as a historian* say whether or not this event happened (though as a Christian who believes in the divine inspiration of scripture, I personally believe it did happen, just as the Bible says)." See Mark Allan Powell, "Evangelical Christians and Historical-Jesus Studies: Final Reflections," *Journal for the Study of the Historical Jesus* 9.1 (2011): 124–36, citation on 135. This would accurately describe my own position on numerous matters.

4. Of course, we would not want to press the *vocabulary* employed in this distinction too far—the word *debate* can be used as a synonym for an argument, a discussion, or even a dialogue. Thus, the "debate" recounted in Miller, ed., *The Apocalyptic Jesus: A Debate* is very much an open-minded discussion in which four questing scholars seek to learn from each other.

5. Somewhat to my chagrin, a European edition of the first edition of this present book was actually published under the title *The Jesus Debate* (Oxford: Lion, 1998). Suffice to say, I was not consulted concerning that title, which I would not have approved (since many of the persons described in the book [*this* book] would insist they are engaged in a quest *not* a debate).

6. See, for example, the published debate between a well-known apologist and a founder of the Jesus Seminar: Paul Copan, ed., *Will the Real Jesus Please Stand Up: A Debate between William Lane Craig and John Dominic Crossan* (Grand Rapids: Baker, 2001). In this volume, Crossan notes that the debate was fruitful precisely because the goal was understanding, not conversion: people with incompatible presuppositions can understand and respect each other's positions while recognizing there is no chance of getting the other to change their mind (149).

7. So, Crossan maintains the problem arises when someone presents themselves as belonging to one group when they are actually members of a different group "in disguise"; then theological arguments are misrepresented as historical ones. See John Dominic Crossan, "Reflections on a Debate," 147–55 in Copan, ed. *Will the Real Jesus Please Stand Up.*

8. So, Robert Funk dismissed the entire so-called Third Quest (with specific reference to N. T. Wright, Raymond Brown, and John Meier) as "an apologetic ploy." See *Honest to Jesus,* 65.

9. See Darrell L. Bock, "The Historical Jesus: An Evangelical View," 249–300 in Beilby and Eddy, eds., *Historical Jesus: Five Views*; *Jesus according to Scripture*; *Studying the Historical Jesus: A Guide to Methods and Sources* (Grand Rapids: Baker Academic, 2002).

10. See Keener, *Historical Jesus of the Gospels*; *Miracles: Credibility of New Testament Accounts*.

11. To some extent, such suspicions may also attend the reception of the book, *Key Events in the Life of the Historical Jesus*, ed. Darrell Bock and Robert Webb. The volume collects essays by biblically orthodox Christian scholars that seek to authenticate the probable historicity of twelve major events in the reported life of Jesus. The book is an undeniably significant work (ten years in the making), and the contributors all appeal to traditional criteria, employed in ways that find wide acceptance within the guild. Still, reviewers do notice that only arguments in favor of historicity are seriously entertained; there is no apparent openness to discovering that anything reported of Jesus is probably nonhistorical (or even unverifiable).

12. See especially Bock, "Historical Jesus: An Evangelical View." His book *Jesus according to Scripture* attempts to show that the Gospels present a coherent and credible portrait of Jesus, but it does not overtly attempt to determine what aspects of this portrait might or might not be authenticated historically. Indeed, the book's premise seems to be that a more adequate vision of Jesus is obtained by viewing him as he is presented in scripture rather than through tenuous historical reconstructions.

13. Bock, "Historical Jesus: An Evangelical View," 275. On the claim that a charge of blasphemy led to Jesus' execution, see Bock, *Blasphemy and Exaltation in Judaism*, and, more briefly, Darrell L. Bock, "Blasphemy and the Jewish Examination of Jesus," 589–668 in Bock and Webb, eds., *Key Events*.

14. On this see especially, Bock, *Studying the Historical Jesus*.

15. Luke Timothy Johnson, "Response to Darrell L. Bock," 293–96 in Beilby and Eddy, eds., *Historical Jesus: Five Views*.

16. For Bock's own take on this, see Darrell L. Bock, "Faith and the Historical Jesus: Does a Confessional Position and Respect for the Jesus Tradition Preclude Serious Historical Engagement?" *Journal for the Study of the Historical Jesus* 9.1 (2011): 3–25.

17. Robert M. Price, "Response to Darrell L. Bock," 282–87 in Beilby and Eddy, eds., *Historical Jesus: Five Views*, 282.

18. Johnson, "Response to Darrell L. Bock," 296.

19. Miller, "When It's Futile to Argue about the Historical Jesus."

20. John Dominic Crossan, "Response to Darrell L. Bock," 288–92 in Beilby and Eddy, eds., *Historical Jesus: Five Views*; James D. G. Dunn, "Response to Darrell L. Bock, 297–300 in Beilby and Eddy, eds., *Historical Jesus: Five Views*.

21. See especially Keener, *Historical Jesus of the Gospels*, 71–162.

22. Keener, *Miracles*.

23. On this point, see also Werner H. Kelber and Samuel Byrskog, eds., *Jesus in Memory: Traditions in Oral and Scribal Perspectives* (Waco, Tex.: Baylor University Press, 2009).

24. Keener, *Historical Jesus of the Gospels*, 163–349.

25. Robert J. Miller, "Review of *The Historical Jesus of the Gospels* by Craig Keener," *Biblical Theology Bulletin* 41.1 (2001): 50–52, citation on 51.

26. Miller says, "One gets the impression that the possibility of anything that would buttress the reliability of the Gospels is, for Keener, sufficient grounds for accepting its actuality." See "Review," 52.

27. Levine, "Christian Faith and the Study of the Historical Jesus," 101. The same point is made independently by Miller, "When It's Futile to Argue about the Historical Jesus," 90–93.
28. Levine, "Christian Faith and the Study of the Historical Jesus," 103.
29. Mark Allan Powell, "Evangelical Christians and Historical-Jesus Studies," 132–33. Compare Levine, "Christian Faith and the Study of the Historical Jesus," 101–2.
30. See, e.g., Craig S. Keener, "A Brief Reply to Robert Miller and Amy-Jill Levine," *Journal for the Study of the Historical Jesus* 9.1 (2011): 112–17. For example, he notes the *Protoevangelium of James* is a later work than the New Testament Gospels; the propensity for "free composition" is much less when the biographer treats a recent subject.

Appendix 3: Psychological Studies of the Historical Jesus

1. See James H. Charlesworth, "Psychobiography: A New and Challenging Methodology in Jesus Research," 4:21–57 in J. H. Ellens and W. G. Rollins, eds., *Psychology and the Bible: A New Way to Read the Scriptures*, 4 vols. (Westport, Conn.: Praeger, 2004); van Os, *Psychological Analyses and the Historical Jesus*; Fraser Watts, ed., *Jesus and Psychology* (Philadelphia: Templeton Foundation, 2007).
2. For bibliography of these and many other works (including studies of Ezekiel, King Herod, Ignatius of Loyola, Augustine, Joseph Smith, and Oscar Romero) see van Os, *Psychological Analyses and the Historical Jesus*, 13–14.
3. Albert Schweitzer, *The Psychiatric Study of Jesus*, trans. C. R. Joy (Boston: Beacon, 1948; original 1913).
4. For a survey, see the three chapters/essays Donald Capps contributed to Ellens and Rollins, eds. *Psychology and the Bible*, 4:89–208.
5. Jay Haley, "The Power Tactics of Jesus Christ," 19–53 in *The Power Tactics of Jesus Christ and Other Essays*, 2nd ed. (Rockville: Triangle, 1986; essay originally published in 1969).
6. Donald Capps alerted Jesus scholars to the enduring (though limited) validity of Haley's work in his article, "Jesus as Power Tactician," *Journal for the Study of the Historical Jesus* 2.2 (2004): 158–89.
7. John W. Miller, *Jesus at Thirty: A Psychological and Historical Portrait* (Minneapolis: Fortress, 1997); see also his "Jesus: A Psychological and Historical Portrait," 4:71–88 in Ellen and Rollins, eds., *Psychology and the Bible*.
8. Donald Capps, *Jesus: A Psychological Biography* (St. Louis: Chalice, 2000); see also his "A Psychobiography of Jesus," 4:59–70 in Ellen and Rollins, eds., *Psychology and the Bible*.
9. On this point, see especially Donald Capps, *Jesus the Village Psychiatrist* (Louisville: Westminster John Knox, 2008).
10. Van Aarde, *Fatherless in Galilee*; see also Andries van Aarde, "Social Identity, Status Envy, and Jesus as Fatherless Child," 4:223–46 in Ellen and Rollins, eds., *Psychology and the Bible*.
11. Van Aarde, "Social Identity," 237.
12. I shared my positive estimation of this potential in an unpublished paper at the 2006 Annual Meeting of the Society of Biblical Literature Psychology and Biblical Studies Section. Compare Charlesworth, "Pyschobiography: A New and Challenging Methodology." Charlesworth thinks that, of these three scholars (Miller, Capps, van Aarde), Miller presents the portrait that has the least congruity with historically plausible biblical data. I think the

opposite: Miller is the least conjectural of the three, sticking most closely to what many biblical scholars and Jesus historians would regard as historically plausible data.

13. See van Os, *Psychological Analyses and the Historical Jesus.* His overall project, however, is more ambitious, namely to construct a psychologically plausible theory of how Jesus could have contributed to the earliest beliefs concerning him, as discerned in key passages of the undisputed Pauline letters.

Bibliography
Selected Works in English

Allen, Charlotte. *The Human Christ: The Search for the Historical Jesus.* New York: Free Press, 1998.

Allison, Dale C., Jr. *Constructing Jesus: Memory, Imagination, and History.* Grand Rapids: Baker Academic, 2010.

———. "The Contemporary Quest for the Historical Jesus." *Irish Biblical Studies* 18 (1996): 174–93.

———. *The End of the Ages Has Come: An Early Interpretation of the Passion and Resurrection of Jesus.* Philadelphia: Fortress, 1985.

———. "The Historian's Jesus and the Church," in Beverly Roberts Gaventa and Richard B. Hays, *Seeking the Identity of Jesus: A Pilgrimage,* 79–95. Grand Rapids: Eerdmans, 2008.

———. *The Historical Christ and the Theological Jesus.* Grand Rapids: Eerdmans, 2009.

———. "Jesus and the Covenant: A Response to E. P. Sanders." In *The Historical Jesus: A Sheffield Reader,* ed. Craig A. Evans and Stanley E. Porter, 61–82. Sheffield: Sheffield Academic, 1995.

———. *Jesus of Nazareth: Millenarian Prophet.* Minneapolis: Fortress, 1998.

———. "A Plea for Thoroughgoing Eschatology." *Journal of Biblical Literature* 113 (1994): 651–58.

———. *Resurrecting Jesus: The Earliest Christian Tradition and Its Interpreters.* Journal for the Study of the Pseudepigrapha: Supplement Series. New York: T&T Clark, 2005.

Alsup, John. *The Post-Resurrection Appearances of the Gospel Tradition.* Stuttgart: Calwer Verlag, 1975.

Anderson, Hugh, ed. *Jesus.* Englewood Cliffs, N.J.: Prentice-Hall, 1967.

Anderson, Norman. *The Teaching of Jesus.* The Jesus Library. Downers Grove, Ill.: Inter-Varsity, 1983.

Anderson, Paul N. *The Fourth Gospel and the Quest for Jesus: Modern Foundations Reconsidered,* Library of New Testament Studies 321. New York: T&T Clark, 2006.

Anderson, Paul N., Felix Just, and Tom Thatcher, eds. *John, Jesus, and History.* Vol. 1, *Critical Appraisals of Critical Views.* Symposium Series 44. Atlanta: Society of Biblical Literature, 2007.

———. *John, Jesus, and History.* Vol. 2, *Aspects of Historicity in the Fourth Gospel.* Early Christianity and Its Literature 2. Atlanta: Society of Biblical Literature, 2009.

————. *John, Jesus, and History.* Vol. 3, *Glimpses of Jesus through the Johannine Lens.* Atlanta: Society of Biblical Literature, forthcoming.

Antwi, Daniel J. "Did Jesus Consider His Death to Be an Atoning Sacrifice?" *Interpretation* 45 (1991): 17–28.

Arnal, William E. *Jesus and the Village Scribes: Galilean Conflicts and the Setting of Q.* Minneapolis: Fortress, 2001.

————. *The Symbolic Jesus: Historical Scholarship, Judaism, and the Construction of Contemporary Identity.* London: Equinox, 2005.

Aulen, Gustaf. *Jesus in Contemporary Historical Research.* Philadelphia: Fortress, 1976.

Aune, David. "Magic in Early Christianity." *Aufstieg und Niedergang der römischen Welt* 2.23.1507–57.

————. *Prophecy in Early Christianity and the Ancient Mediterranean World.* Grand Rapids: Eerdmans, 1983.

Avis, Paul, ed. *The Resurrection of Jesus Christ.* London: Darton, Longman & Todd, 1993.

Badia, Leonard F. *Jesus: Introducing His Life and Teaching.* New York: Paulist, 1985.

Bammel, Ernst, and C. F. D. Moule, eds. *Jesus and the Politics of His Day.* Cambridge: Cambridge University Press, 1984.

Banks, Robert J. "Setting 'The Quest for the Historical Jesus' in a Broader Framework." In *Gospel Perspectives 2: Studies of History and Tradition in the Four Gospels,* ed. Richard J. France and David Wenham, 61–82. Sheffield: JSOT, 1981.

Barnett, Paul W. *The Birth of Christianity.* Vol. 1, *The First Twenty-Five Years after Jesus.* Grand Rapids: Eerdmans, 2005.

————. *Finding the Historical Christ.* Grand Rapids: Eerdmans, 2009.

————. *Jesus and the Logic of History.* Grand Rapids: Eerdmans, 1997.

————. *Jesus and the Rise of Early Christianity.* Downers Grove, Ill.: InterVarsity, 1999.

————. "The Jewish Sign Prophets—A.D. 40–70: Their Intentions and Origin," *New Testament Studies* 27 (1980–81): 679–97.

Barrett, C. K. *Jesus and the Gospel Tradition.* London: SPCK, 1967.

Bartsch, Hans. "The Historical Problem of the Life of Jesus." In *The Historical Jesus and the Kerygmatic Christ,* ed. Carl E. Braaten and Roy A. Harrisville, 106–43. Nashville: Abingdon, 1964.

Bauckham, Richard J. "The Brothers and Sisters of Jesus: An Epiphanian Response to John P. Meier." *Catholic Biblical Quarterly* 56 (1994): 686–700.

————. "Jesus' Demonstration in the Temple." In *Law and Religion: Essays on the Place of the Law in Israel and Early Christianity,* ed. B. Lindars, 72–89, 171–76. Cambridge: James Clarke, 1988.

————. "The Parting of the Ways: What Happened and Why." *Studia theologica* 47 (1993): 135–51.

————. "The Son of Man: 'A Man in My Position' or 'Someone'?" In *The Historical Jesus: A Sheffield Reader,* ed. Craig A. Evans and Stanley E. Porter, 245–55. Sheffield: Sheffield Academic, 1995.

————. "The Study of Gospel Traditions outside the Canonical Gospels: Problems and Prospects." In *Gospel Perspectives 5: The Jesus Tradition outside the Gospels,* ed. David Wenham, 369–404. Sheffield: JSOT, 1985.

Beasley-Murray, George R. *Jesus and the Kingdom of God.* Grand Rapids: Eerdmans, 1986.

Becker, Jürgen. *Jesus of Nazareth.* Hawthorne, N.Y.: Walter de Gruyter, 1998.

Beilby, James K., and Paul Rhodes Eddy, ed. *The Historical Jesus: Five Views.* Downers Grove, Ill.: InterVarsity, 2009.

Betz, Hans Dieter. "Jesus and the Cynics: Survey and Analysis of a Hypothesis." *Journal of Religion* 74 (1994): 453–75.

Betz, Otto. *What Do We Know about Jesus?* Philadelphia: Westminster, 1968.

Bird, Michael. *Are You the One Who Is to Come? The Historical Jesus and the Messianic Question*. Grand Rapids: Baker Academic, 2009.

———. *Jesus and the Origins of the Gentile Mission*. Library of New Testament Studies 331. London: T&T Clark, 2007.

Blackburn, Barry L. "The Miracles of Jesus." In *Studying the Historical Jesus: Evaluations of the State of Current Research*, ed. Bruce Chilton and Craig A. Evans, 353–94. Leiden: Brill, 1994.

Blomberg, Craig. *The Historical Reliability of the Gospels*. 2nd ed. Downers Grove, Ill.: InterVarsity, 2007.

———. "The Parables of Jesus: Current Trends and Needs in Research." In *Studying the Historical Jesus: Evaluations of the State of Current Research*, ed. Bruce Chilton and Craig A. Evans, 231–54. Leiden: Brill, 1994.

———. "Where Do We Start Studying Jesus?" In *Jesus under Fire: Modern Scholarship Reinvents the Historical Jesus*, ed. Michael J. Wilkins and J. P. Moreland, 17–51. Grand Rapids: Zondervan Publishing House, 1995.

Bock, Darrell L. *Blasphemy and Exaltation in Judaism and the Final Examination of Jesus*. Tübingen: Mohr Siebeck, 1998.

———. "Faith and the Historical Jesus: Does a Confessional Position and Respect for the Jesus Tradition Preclude Serious Historical Engagement?" *Journal for the Study of the Historical Jesus* 9.1 (2011): 3–25.

———. *Jesus according to Scripture: Restoring the Portrait from the Gospels*. Grand Rapids: Baker Academic, 2002.

———. *Studying the Historical Jesus: A Guide to Methods and Sources*. Grand Rapids: Baker Academic, 2002.

———. "The Words of Jesus in the Gospels: Live, Jive, or Memorex?" In *Jesus under Fire: Modern Scholarship Reinvents the Historical Jesus*, ed. Michael J. Wilkins and J. P. Moreland, 73–100. Grand Rapids: Zondervan Publishing House, 1995.

Bock, Darrell L., and Robert L. Webb, eds. *Key Events in the Life of the Historical Jesus: A Collaborative Exploration of Context and Coherence*. Grand Rapids: Eerdmans, 2010.

Bockmuehl, Markus. *This Jesus: Martyr, Lord, Messiah*. Edinburgh: T&T Clark, 1994.

Bockmuehl, Markus, ed. *The Cambridge Companion to Jesus*. Cambridge: Cambridge University Press, 2001.

Boers, Hendrikus. *Who Was Jesus? The Historical Jesus and the Synoptic Gospels*. San Francisco: Harper & Row, 1989.

Bokser, Baruch M. "Wonder-Working and the Rabbinic Tradition: The Case of Hanina ben Dosa." *Journal for the Study of Judaism* 16 (1985): 42–92.

Borg, Marcus J. *Conflict, Holiness, and Politics in the Teaching of Jesus*. 2nd ed. New York: Continuum, 1998.

———. "From Galilean Jew to the Face of God: The Pre-Easter and Post-Easter Jesus." In *Jesus at 2000*, ed. Marcus J. Borg, 7–20. Boulder, Col.: Westview, 1997.

———. *The God We Never Knew: Beyond Religion to a More Authentic Contemporary Faith*. San Francisco: HarperSanFrancisco, 1997.

———. "The Historian, the Christian, and Jesus." *Theology Today* 52 (1995): 6–16.

———. "The Historical Study of Jesus and Christian Origins." In *Jesus at 2000*, ed. Marcus J. Borg, 121–47. Boulder, Col.: Westview, 1997.

———. "Jesus and Eschatology: A Reassessment." In *Images of Jesus Today*, ed. James H. Charlesworth and W. P. Weaver, 207–18. Valley Forge, Penn.: Trinity Press International, 1994.

————. "Jesus and the Buddha." *The Fourth R* 10.6 (1997): 11–13, 15–17.

————. *Jesus: A New Vision.* San Francisco: Harper & Row, 1988.

————. *Jesus in Contemporary Scholarship.* Valley Forge, Penn.: Trinity Press International, 1994.

————. "The Jesus Seminar and the Passion Sayings." *Foundations and Facets Forum* 3.2 (1987): 81–95.

————. *Jesus: Uncovering the Life, Teaching, and Relevance of a Religious Revolutionary.* New York: HarperOne, 2006.

————. *Meeting Jesus Again for the First Time: The Historical Jesus and the Heart of Contemporary Faith.* San Francisco: HarperSanFrancisco, 1994.

————. "An Orthodoxy Reconsidered: The End-of-the-World Jesus." In *The Glory of Christ in the New Testament,* ed. L. D. Hurst and N. T. Wright. Oxford: Clarendon, 1987.

————. "The Palestinian Background for a Life of Jesus." In *The Search for Jesus: Modern Scholarship Looks at the Gospels,* ed. Hershel Shanks, 37–58. Washington, D. C.: Biblical Archaeology Society, 1994.

————. "Portraits of Jesus." In *The Search for Jesus: Modern Scholarship Looks at the Gospels,* ed. Hershel Shanks, 83–108. Washington, D. C.: Biblical Archaeology Society, 1994.

————. "Reflections on a Discipline: A North American Perspective." In *Studying the Historical Jesus,* ed. Bruce Chilton and Craig A. Evans, 9–32. Leiden: Brill, 1994.

Borg, Marcus J., ed. *Jesus at 2000.* Boulder, Col.: Westview, 1997.

Borg, Marcus J., and John Dominic Crossan. *The First Christmas: What the Gospels Really Teach about the Birth of Jesus.* New York: HarperCollins, 2009.

————. *The First Paul: Reclaiming the Radical Visionary behind the Church's Conservative Icon.* New York: HarperCollins, 2010.

————. *The Last Week: What the Gospels Really Teach about Jesus' Final Days in Jerusalem.* New York: HarperCollins, 2007.

Borg, Marcus J., and Ray Riegert, eds. *Jesus and the Buddha: The Parallel Sayings.* Berkeley, Calif.: Ulysses, 1997.

Borg, Marcus J., and N. T. Wright. *The Meaning of Jesus: Two Views.* San Francisco: HarperSanFrancisco, 1999.

Boring, M. Eugene. "Criteria of Authenticity: The Lucan Beatitudes as a Test Case." *Foundations and Facets Forum* 1.4 (1985): 3–38.

————. *The Continuing Voice of Jesus: Christian Prophecy and the Gospel Tradition.* Louisville: Westminster/John Knox, 1991.

————. "The 'Third Quest' and the Apostolic Faith." *Interpretation* 50 (1996): 341–54.

Bornkamm, Günther. *Jesus of Nazareth.* New York: Harper & Row, 1960.

Bowden, John. *Jesus: The Unanswered Questions.* London: SCM, 1988.

Bowker, John. *Jesus and the Pharisees.* Cambridge: Cambridge University Press, 1993.

Boyce, James. "The Quest for Jesus and the Church's Proclamation." In *The Quest for Jesus and the Christian Faith,* ed. Frederick J. Gaiser, 175–90. St. Paul: Luther Seminary, 1997.

Boyd, Gregory A. *Cynic Sage or Son of God? Recovering the Real Jesus in an Age of Revisionist Replies.* Wheaton, Ill.: Bridgepoint, 1995.

Braaten, Carl E. "Martin Kähler on the Historic Biblical Christ." In *The Historical Jesus and the Kerygmatic Christ: Essays on the New Quest of the Historical Jesus,* ed. Carl E. Braaten and Roy A. Harrisville, 79–105. Nashville: Abingdon, 1964.

Braaten, Carl E., and Roy A. Harrisville, eds. *The Historical Jesus and the Kerygmatic Christ: Essays on the New Quest of the Historical Jesus.* Nashville: Abingdon, 1964.

Brandon, S. G. F. *Jesus and the Zealots: A Study of the Political Factor in Primitive Christianity.* New York: Charles Scribner's Sons, 1967.

Braun, Herbert. "The Significance of Qumran for the Problem of the Historical Jesus." In *The Historical Jesus and the Kerygmatic Christ: Essays on the New Quest of the Historical Jesus,* ed. Carl E. Braaten and Roy A. Harrisville, 69–78. Nashville: Abingdon, 1964.

Breech, James. *The Silence of Jesus: The Authentic Voices of the Historical Man.* Philadelphia: Fortress, 1983.

Brown, Colin. *Jesus in European Protestant Thought, 1778–1860.* Grand Rapids: Baker Book House 1988.

———. *Miracles and the Critical Mind.* Grand Rapids: Eerdmans, 1984.

Brown, Raymond E., *The Death of the Messiah: From Gethsemane to the Grave: A Commentary on the Passion Narratives in the Four Gospels.* Anchor Bible Reference Library. New York: Doubleday, 1994.

———. "The Gospel of Peter and Canonical Gospel Priority." *New Testament Studies* 33 (1987): 321–43.

Bruce, F. F. "The Background to the Son of Man Sayings." In *Christ the Lord: Studies in Christology Presented to Donald Guthrie,* ed. Harold Rowdon, 50–70. Downers Grove, Ill.: InterVarsity, 1982.

Bryan, Christopher. "Discerning Our Origins: The Words and Works of the Jesus Seminar." *Sewanee Theological Review* 39 (1996): 339–48.

Buchanan, George W. *Jesus: The King and His Kingdom.* Macon, Ga.: Mercer University, 1984.

Büchler, A. *Types of Jewish-Palestinian Piety from 709 BCE –70 CE: The Ancient Pious Man.* New York: Ktav, 1968 (originally published in 1922).

Bultmann, Rudolf. *Faith and Understanding.* Trans. L. Smith. London: SCM, 1969.

———. *History and Eschatology: The Presence of Eternity.* New York: Harper and Brothers, 1957.

———. *The History of the Synoptic Tradition.* Trans. John Marsh. New York: Harper & Row, 1963 (originally published in 1921).

———. *Jesus and the Word.* New York: Charles Scribner's Sons, 1958 (originally published in 1926).

———. *Jesus Christ and Mythology.* New York: Charles Scribner's Sons, 1958.

———. "The Primitive Christian Kerygma and the Historical Jesus." In *The Historical Jesus and the Kerygmatic Christ: Essays on the New Quest of the Historical Jesus,* ed. Carl E. Braaten and Roy A. Harrisville, 15–42. Nashville: Abingdon, 1964.

Burridge, Richard A. *What Are the Gospels? A Comparison with Graeco-Roman Biography.* Cambridge: Cambridge University Press, 1992.

Burridge, Richard A., and Graham Gould. *Jesus Now and Then.* Grand Rapids: Eerdmans, 2004.

Butts, James R. "Probing the Polling: Jesus Seminar Results on the Kingdom Sayings." *Foundations and Facets Forum* 3.1 (1987): 98–128.

Cadbury, Henry A. *The Peril of Modernizing Jesus.* New York: Charles Scribner's Sons, 1962 (originally published in 1937).

Caird, George B. *Jesus and the Jewish Nation.* London: Athlone, 1965.

———. *The Language and Imagery of the Bible.* Philadelphia: Westminster, 1980.

Calvert, David G. A. "An Examination of the Criteria for Distinguishing the Authentic Words of Jesus." *New Testament Studies* 18 (1971–72): 209–19.

Cameron, Ronald D. *The Other Gospels: Non-Canonical Gospel Texts.* Philadelphia: Westminster, 1982.

Capps, Donald. *Jesus: A Psychological Biography.* St. Louis: Chalice, 2000.

———. "Jesus as Power Tactician," *Journal for the Study of the Historical Jesus* 2.2 (2004): 158–89.

————. *Jesus the Village Psychiatrist*. Louisville: Westminster John Knox, 2008.

Carey, Greg. *Sinners: Jesus and His Earliest Followers*. Waco, Tex.: Baylor University Press, 2009.

Carlson, Jeffrey. "Crossan's Jesus and Christian Identity." In *Jesus and Faith: A Conversation on the Work of John Dominic Crossan*, ed. Jeffrey Carlson and Robert A. Ludwig, 31–43. Maryknoll, N.Y.: Orbis Books, 1994.

Carlson, Jeffrey, and Robert A. Ludwig, eds. *Jesus and Faith: A Conversation on the Work of John Dominic Crossan*. Maryknoll, N.Y.: Orbis Books, 1994.

Carver, Stephen. *The UnGospel: The Life and Teachings of the Historical Jesus*. Eugene, Ore.: Wipf and Stock, 2004.

Case, Shirley Jackson. *The Historicity of Jesus*. Chicago: Chicago University Press, 1912.

Casey, Maurice. *From Jewish Prophet to Gentile God: The Origins and Development of New Testament Christology*. Louisville: Westminster/John Knox, 1991.

————. *Son of Man: The Interpretation and Influence of Daniel 7*. London: SPCK, 1979.

————. "Where Wright Is Wrong," *Journal for the Study of the New Testament* 69 (1998): 95–103.

Cassels, Louis. *The Real Jesus: How He Lived and What He Taught*. New York: Doubleday, 1968.

Catchpole, David R. *Jesus People: The Historical Jesus and the Beginnings of Community*. Grand Rapids: Baker, 2006.

————. *The Quest for Q*. Edinburgh: T&T Clark, 1993.

Charlesworth, James H. "The Dead Sea Scrolls and the Historical Jesus." In *Jesus and the Dead Sea Scrolls*, ed. James H. Charlesworth, 1–74. New York: Doubleday, 1992.

————. "The Foreground of Christian Origins and the Commencement of Jesus Research." In *Jesus' Jewishness: Exploring the Place of Jesus within Early Judaism*, ed. James H. Charlesworth, 63–83. New York: Crossroad, 1991.

————. "From Messianology to Christology: Problems and Prospects." In *The Messiah: Developments in Earliest Judaism and Christianity*, ed. James H. Charlesworth, 3–35. Minneapolis: Fortress, 1992.

————. *The Historical Jesus: An Essential Guide*. Nashville: Abingdon, 2008.

————. "Jesus, Early Jewish Literature, and Archaeology." In *Jesus' Jewishness: Exploring the Place of Jesus within Early Judaism*, ed. James H. Charlesworth, 177–98. New York: Crossroad, 1991.

————. "Jesus Research and the Appearance of Psychobiography," in *Revelation, Reason, and Faith: Essays in Honor of Truman G. Madsen*, ed. D. W. Parry et al, 55–84. E Provo, Utah: FARMS, 2002.

————. "Jesus Research Expands with Chaotic Creativity." In *Images of Jesus Today*, ed. James H. Charlesworth and W. P. Weaver, 1–41. Valley Forge, Penn.: Trinity Press International, 1994.

————. *Jesus within Judaism: New Light from Exciting Archaeological Discoveries*. Garden City, N.Y.: Doubleday, 1988.

————. "Psychobiography: A New and Challenging Methodology in Jesus Research," in *Psychology and the Bible: A New Way to Read the Scriptures*, 4 vols., ed. J. H. Ellens and W. G. Rollins, 4:21–57. Westport, Conn.: Praeger, 2004.

Charlesworth, James H., ed. *Jesus and Archaeology*. Grand Rapids: Eerdmans, 2006.

————. *Jesus and the Dead Sea Scrolls*. Anchor Bible Reference Library. New York: Doubleday, 1992.

————. *Jesus' Jewishness: Exploring the Place of Jesus within Early Judaism*. New York: Crossroad, 1991.

————. *The Messiah: Developments in Earliest Judaism and Christianity*. Minneapolis: Fortress, 1992.

Charlesworth, James H., and Craig A. Evans. "Jesus in the Agrapha and Apocryphal Gospels." In *Studying the Historical Jesus: Evaluations of the State of Current Research*, ed. Bruce Chilton and Craig A. Evans, 479–534. Leiden: Brill, 1994.

Charlesworth, James H., and Petr Pokorný. *Jesus Research: An International Perspective. The First Princeton-Prague Symposium on Jesus Research*. Grand Rapids: Eerdmans, 2009.

Charlesworth, James H., and W. P. Weaver, eds. *Images of Jesus Today*. Valley Forge, Penn.: Trinity Press International, 1994.

Childs, Hal. *The Myth of the Historical Jesus and the Evolution of Consciousness*. Society of Biblical Literature Dissertation Series 179. Atlanta: Society of Biblical Literature, 2000.

Chilton, Bruce. *A Galilean Rabbi and His Bible*. Wilmington, Del.: Michael Glazier, 1984.

———. *God in Strength: Jesus' Announcement of the Kingdom*. Sheffield: JSOT, 1987.

———. "The Gospel according to Thomas as a Source for Jesus' Teaching." In *Gospel Perspectives 5: The Jesus Tradition outside the Gospels*, ed. David Wenham, 155–76. Sheffield: JSOT, 1985.

———. "Jesus and the Repentance of E. P. Sanders." *Tyndale Bulletin* 39 (1998): 1–18.

———. "The Kingdom of God in Recent Discussion." In *Studying the Historical Jesus: Evaluations of the State of Current Research*, ed. Bruce Chilton and Craig A. Evans, 255–80. Leiden: Brill, 1994.

———. *The Kingdom of God in the Teaching of Jesus*. Philadelphia: Fortress, 1984.

———. *Pure Kingdom: Jesus' Vision of God*. Grand Rapids: Eerdmans, 1996.

———. *Rabbi Jesus: An Intimate Biography. The Life and Teachings That Inspired Christianity*. New York: Image Books, 2000.

———. *The Temple of Jesus: His Sacrificial Program within a Cultural History of Sacrifice*. University Park, Penn.: Pennsylvania State University Press, 1992.

Chilton, Bruce, and Craig A. Evans. "Jesus and Israel's Scriptures." In *Studying the Historical Jesus: Evaluations of the State of Current Research*, ed. Bruce Chilton and Craig A. Evans, 281–336. Leiden: Brill, 1994.

———. *Jesus in Context: Temple, Purity, and Restoration*. Leiden: Brill, 1997.

Chilton, Bruce, and Craig A. Evans, eds. *Authenticating the Activities of Jesus*. New Testament Tools and Studies 28.2 Leiden: Brill, 1999.

———.*Studying the Historical Jesus: Evaluations of the State of Current Research*. New Testament Tools and Studies 19. Leiden: Brill, 1994.

Chilton, Bruce, and J. I. H. MacDonald. *Jesus and the Ethics of the Kingdom*. London: SPCK, 1987.

Choi, J. D. *Jesus' Teaching on Repentance*. International Studies in Formative Christianity and Judaism. Binghampton, N.Y.: Global Publications, 2000.

Cohen, Shaye J. D. *From the Maccabees to the Mishnah*. 2nd ed. Louisville: Westminster John Knox, 2006.

———. *Josephus in Galilee and Rome: His Vita and Development as a Historian*. Columbia Studies in the Classic Traditions 8. Leiden: Brill, 1979.

Conzelmann, Hans. *Jesus*. Philadelphia: Fortress, 1973.

———. "The Method of the Life-of-Jesus Research." In *The Historical Jesus and the Kerygmatic Christ: Essays on the New Quest of the Historical Jesus*, ed. Carl E. Braaten and Roy A. Harrisville, 54–68. Nashville: Abingdon, 1964.

Copan, Paul, ed., *Will the Real Jesus Please Stand Up: A Debate between William Lane Craig and John Dominic Crossan*. Grand Rapids: Baker, 2001.

Copan, Paul, and Craig A. Evans, eds. *Who Was Jesus? A Jewish–Christian Dialogue*. Louisville: Westminster John Knox, 2002.

Corley, Kathleen E. *Maranatha: Women's Funerary Rites and Christian Origins*. Minneapolis: Fortress, 2010.

————. *Women and the Historical Jesus: Feminist Myths of Christian Origins.* Santa Rosa, Calif.: Polebridge, 2002.

Cornfeld, Gaalyahu. *The Historical Jesus: A Scholarly View of the Man and His World.* New York: Macmillan Publishing Co., 1982.

Craffert, Pieter F. *The Life of a Galilean Shaman: Jesus of Nazareth in Anthropological-Historical Perspective.* Eugene, Ore.: Cascade, 2008.

Craig, William Lane. *Assessing the New Testament Evidence for the Historicity of the Resurrection.* Lewiston, N.Y.: Edwin Mellen, 1989.

————. "The Bodily Resurrection of Jesus." In *Gospel Perspectives 1: Studies of History and Tradition in the Four Gospels,* ed. Richard T. Prance and David Wenham, 47–74. Sheffield: JSOT, 1980.

————. "Did Jesus Rise from the Dead?" In *Jesus under Fire: Modern Scholarship Reinvents the Historical Jesus,* ed. Michael J. Wilkins and J. P. Moreland, 141–76. Grand Rapids: Zondervan Publishing Co., 1995.

————. *The Historical Argument for the Resurrection of Jesus.* Lewiston, N.Y.: Edwin Mellen, 1985.

————. "The Problem of Miracles: A Historical and Philosophical Perspective." In *Gospel Perspectives 6: The Miracles of Jesus,* ed. David Wenham and Craig Blomberg, 9–48. Sheffield: JSOT, 1986.

Crossan, John Dominic. "Aphorism in Discourse and Narrative." *Semeia* 43 (1988): 121–40.

————. *The Birth of Christianity.* San Francisco: HarperSanFrancisco, 1998.

————. *The Cross That Spoke: The Origins of the Passion Narrative.* San Francisco: Harper & Row, 1988.

————. *The Essential Jesus: Original Sayings and Earliest Images.* San Francisco: HarperSanFrancisco, 1994.

————. "Exile: Stealth and Cunning." *Foundations and Facets Forum* 1.1 (1985): 59–61.

————. *Four Other Gospels: Shadows on the Contours of Canon.* Sonoma, Calif.: Polebridge, 1992 (originally published in 1962).

————. *God and Empire: Jesus against Rome, Then and Now.* New York: HarperCollins, 2007.

————. *The Greatest Prayer: Rediscovering the Revolutionary Message of the Lord's Prayer.* New York: HarperCollins, 2010.

————. "The Historical Jesus in Earliest Christianity." In *Jesus and Faith: A Conversation on the Work of John Dominic Crossan,* ed. Jeffrey Carlson and Robert A. Ludwig, 1–21. Maryknoll, N.Y.: Orbis Books, 1994.

————. *The Historical Jesus: The Life of a Mediterranean Jewish Peasant.* San Francisco: HarperSanFrancisco, 1991.

————. "The Infancy and Youth of the Messiah." In *The Search for Jesus: Modern Scholarship Looks at the Gospels,* ed. Hershel Shanks, 59–82. Washington, D. C.: Biblical Archaeology Society, 1994.

————. *In Fragments: The Aphorisms of Jesus.* San Francisco: Harper & Row, 1983.

————. *In Parables: The Challenge of the Historical Jesus.* New York: Harper & Row, 1973.

————. "Jesus and the Kingdom: Itinerants and Householders in Earliest Christianity." In *Jesus at 2000,* ed. Marcus J. Borg, 21–54. Boulder, Col.: Westview, 1997.

————. *Jesus Parallels: A Workbook for the Jesus Tradition.* 2nd ed. Philadelphia: Fortress, 1991.

————. *Jesus: A Revolutionary Biography.* San Francisco: HarperSanFrancisco, 1994.

————. "The Passion, Crucifixion, and Resurrection." In *The Search for Jesus: Modern Scholarship Looks at the Gospels,* ed. Hershel Shanks, 109–34. Washington, D. C.: Biblical Archaeology Society, 1994.

———. "The Passion Narrative." *The Fourth R* 9.5–6 (1996): 3–8.

———. "Thoughts on Two Extracanonical Gospels." *Semeia* 49 (1990): 155–68.

———. *Who Killed Jesus? Exposing the Roots of Anti-Semitism in the Gospel Story of the Death of Jesus.* San Francisco: HarperSanFrancisco, 1995.

———. "Why Christians Must Search for the Historical Jesus." *Bible Review* 12.2 (1996): 34–39, 42–45.

Crossan, John Dominic, Luke Timothy Johnson, and Werner H. Kelber. *The Jesus Controversy: Perspectives in Conflict.* Harrisburg, Penn.: Trinity Press International, 1999.

Crossan, John Dominic, with Jonathan L. Reed. *Excavating Jesus: Beneath the Stones, Behind the Texts.* New York: HarperCollins, 2001.

———. *In Search of Paul: How Jesus' Apostle Opposed Rome's Empire and God's Kingdom.* New York: HarperCollins, 2004.

Crossan, John Dominic, with Richard G. Watts. *Who Is Jesus? Answers to Your Questions about the Historical Jesus.* San Francisco: HarperSanFrancisco, 1996.

Dalman, Gustav H. *The Words of Jesus Considered in the Light of Post-Biblical Jewish Writings and the Aramaic Language.* Edinburgh: T&T Clark, 1903.

Dapaah, Daniel S. *The Relationship between John the Baptist and Jesus of Nazareth: A Critical Study.* Lanham, Md.: University Press of America, 2005.

Davaney, Sheila Greeve. "A Historicist Model for Theology." In *Jesus and Faith: A Conversation on the Work of John Dominic Crossan,* ed. Jeffrey Carlson and Robert A. Ludwig, 44–56. Maryknoll, N.Y.: Orbis Books, 1994.

Davids, Peter H. "The Gospels and Jewish Tradition: Twenty Years after Gerhardsson." In *Gospel Perspectives 1: Studies of History and Tradition in the Four Gospels,* ed. Richard T. France and David Wenham, 75–100. Sheffield: JSOT, 1980.

Davies, Stevan L. *The Gospel of Thomas and Christian Wisdom.* New York: Seabury, 1983.

———. "Whom Jesus Healed and How." *The Fourth R* 6.2 (1993): 1–11.

Davis, Stephen T. *Risen Indeed: Making Sense of the Resurrection.* London: SPCK, 1993.

Dawes, Gregory W. *The Historical Jesus Question: The Challenge of History to Religious Authority.* Louisville: Westminster John Knox, 2001.

———. *The Historical Jesus Quest: Landmarks in the Search for the Jesus of History.* Louisville: Westminster John Knox, 1999.

deHaven-Smith, L. *The Hidden Teachings of Jesus: The Political Meaning of the Kingdom of God.* Grand Rapids: Phanes, 1994.

de Jonge, Marinus. *Jesus, the Servant Messiah.* New Haven: Yale University Press, 1991.

———. *Jewish Eschatology, Early Christian Christology and the Testaments of the Twelve Patriarchs: Collected Essays of Marinus de Jonge.* Leiden: Brill, 1991.

den Heyer, C. J. *Jesus Matters: 150 Years of Research.* Valley Forge, Penn.: Trinity Press International, 1997.

Denton, Donald L. *Historiography and Hermeneutics in Jesus Studies: An Examination of the Work of John Dominic Crossan and Ben F. Meyer.* Journal for the Study of the New Testament: Supplement Series 262. Sheffield: T&T Clark, 2004.

DeRosa, Peter. *Jesus Who Became Christ.* London: Collins, 1974.

Derrett, J. D. M. *Jesus's Audience: The Social and Psychological Environment in Which He Worked.* New York: Seabury, 1973.

———. *Law in the New Testament.* London: Darton, Longman & Todd, 1970.

Dimont, M. I. *Appointment in Jerusalem: A Search for the Historical Jesus.* New York: St. Martin's, 1991.

Doherty, Earl. *The Jesus Puzzle: Did Christianity Begin with a Mythical Christ?* Ottawa: Canadian Humanist Publications, 1999.

Downing, F. Gerald. *Christ and the Cynics: Jesus and Other Radical Preachers in First-Century Tradition.* Sheffield: Sheffield Academic, 1988.

————. *Cynics and Christian Origins*. Edinburgh: T&T Clark, 1992.

————. "Cynics and Christians." *New Testament Studies* 30 (1984): 584–93.

————. "Deeper Reflections on the Jewish Cynic Jesus." *Journal of Biblical Literature* 117 (1998): 97–104.

————. *Jesus and the Threat of Freedom*. London: SCM, 1987.

————. "Words as Deeds and Deeds as Words." *Biblical Interpretation* 3.2 (1995): 129–43.

Duling, Dennis C. *Jesus Christ through History*. New York: Harcourt Brace Jovanovich, 1979.

Dungan, David L. *The Parting of the Ways between Christianity and Judaism and Their Significance for the Character of Christianity*. Philadelphia: Trinity Press International, 1991.

————. "Pharisees, Sinners, and Jesus." In *The Social World of Formative Christianity and Judaism: Essays in Tribute to Howard Clark Kee*, ed. J. Neusner et al., 264–89. Philadelphia: Fortress, 1988.

————. *The Sayings of Jesus in the Churches of Paul: The Use of the Synoptic Tradition in the Regulation of Early Church Life*. Oxford: Basil Blackwell Publisher, 1971.

Dunn, James D. G. *Christology in the Making*. Philadelphia: Westminster, 1980.

————. *The Evidence for Jesus*. Philadelphia: Westminster, 1985.

————. "The Historicity of the Synoptic Gospels." In *Crisis in Christology: Essays In Quest of Resolution*, ed. William R. Farmer, 199–216. Livonia, Mich.: Dove Booksellers, 1995.

————. *Jesus and the Spirit: A Study of the Religious and Charismatic Experience of Jesus and the First Christians as Reflected in the New Testament*. Philadelphia: Westminster, 1975.

————. *Jesus Remembered*, Christianity in the Making 1. Grand Rapids: Eerdmans, 2003.

————. "Jesus Tradition in Paul." In *Studying the Historical Jesus: Evaluations of the State of Current Research*, ed. Bruce Chilton and Craig A. Evans, 155–78. Leiden: Brill, 1994.

————. "The Making of Christology—Evolution or Unfolding?" In *Jesus of Nazareth: Lord and Christ*, ed. Joel B. Green and Max Turner, 437–52. Grand Rapids: Eerdmans, 1994.

————. *A New Perspective on Jesus: What the Quest for the Historical Jesus Missed*. Grand Rapids: Baker Academic, 2005.

Dunn, James D. G., and Scot McKnight, eds. *The Historical Jesus in Recent Research*. Sources for Biblical and Theological Study 10. Winona Lake, Ind.: Eisenbrauns, 2005.

Eckardt, A. Roy. *Reclaiming the Jesus of History*. Minneapolis: Fortress, 1992.

Eddy, Paul Rhodes, "Jesus as Diogenes? Reflections on the Cynic Jesus Thesis." *Journal of Biblical Literature* 115 (1996): 449–69.

Eddy, Paul Rhodes, and Gregory A. Boyd. *The Jesus Legend: A Case for the Historical Reliability of the Synoptic Jesus Tradition*. Grand Rapids: Baker Academic, 2007.

Edersheim, Alfred. *The Life and Times of Jesus the Messiah*. Peabody, Mass.: Hendrickson Publishers, 1993 (originally published in 1883).

Edwards, David L. *The Real Jesus*. London: HarperCollins, 1992.

Ehrman, Bart D. *Did Jesus Exist?* San Francisco: HarperOne, 2012.

————. *Jesus: Apocalyptic Prophet of the New Millennium*. Oxford: Oxford University Press, 1999.

Ellegar, Alvar. *Jesus One Hundred Years before Christ: A Study in Creative Mythology*. London: Century, 1999.

Ellens, J. Harold, and Wayne G. Rollins. *Psychology and the Bible: A New Way to Read Scripture.* Vol. 4, *From Christ to Jesus.* Praeger Perspectives. Westport, Conn.: Praeger, 2004.

Ellis, E. Earle. "Gospels Criticism." In *The Gospel and the Gospels,* ed. Peter Stuhlmacher, 237–53. Grand Rapids: Eerdmans, 1991.

———. "The Synoptic Gospels and History." In *Crisis in Christology: Essays in Quest of Resolution,* ed. William R. Farmer, 83–92. Livonia, Mich.: Dove Booksellers, 1995.

Ellis, Marc H. "The Brokerless Kingdom and the Other Kingdom: Reflections on Auschwitz, Jesus, and the Jewish-Christian Establishment." In *Jesus and Faith: A Conversation on the Work of John Dominic Crossan,* ed. Jeffrey Carlson and Robert A. Ludwig, 100–114. Maryknoll, N.Y.: Orbis Books, 1994.

Evans, Craig A. *Fabricating Jesus: How Modern Scholars Distort the Gospels.* Downers Grove: Ill.: InterVarsity, 2006.

———. *Jesus.* Grand Rapids: Baker Book House, 1992.

———. "Jesus' Action in the Temple: Cleansing or Portent of Destruction?" *Catholic Biblical Quarterly* 51 (1989): 237–70.

———. *Jesus and His Contemporaries: Comparative Studies.* Leiden: Brill, 1995.

———. "Jesus and the 'Cave of Robbers': Toward a Jewish Context for the Temple Action." *Bulletin of Biblical Research* 3 (1993): 93–110.

———. *Jesus and the Ossuaries: What Jewish Burial Practices Reveal about the Beginning of Christianity.* Waco, Tex.: Baylor University Press, 2003.

———. "Jesus in Non-Christian Sources." In *Studying the Historical Jesus: Evaluations of the State of Current Research,* ed. Bruce Chilton and Craig A. Evans, 443–78. Leiden: Brill, 1994.

———. "Life of Jesus Research and the Eclipse of Mythology." *Theological Studies* 54 (1993): 3–36.

———. *Life of Jesus Research: An Annotated Bibliography.* 2nd ed. Leiden: Brill, 1996.

———. *Non-canonical Writings and New Testament Interpretation.* Peabody, Mass.: Hendrickson Publishers, 1992.

———. "Opposition to the Temple: Jesus and the Dead Sea Scrolls." In *Jesus and the Dead Sea Scrolls,* ed. James H. Charlesworth, 235–53. New York: Doubleday, 1992.

———. "The Recently Published Dead Sea Scrolls and the Historical Jesus." In *Studying the Historical Jesus: Evaluations of the State of Current Research,* ed. Bruce Chilton and Craig A. Evans, 547–65. Leiden: Brill, 1994.

———. "What Did Jesus Do?" In *Jesus under Fire: Modern Scholarship Reinvents the Historical Jesus,* ed. Michael J. Wilkins and J. P. Moreland, 101–16. Grand Rapids: Zondervan Publishing House, 1995.

Evans, Craig A., ed. *Encyclopedia of the Historical Jesus.* London: Routledge, 2008.

Evans, Craig A., and Stanley E. Porter, eds. *The Historical Jesus: A Sheffield Reader.* Sheffield: Sheffield Academic, 1995.

Evans, C. Stephen. *The Historical Christ and the Jesus of Faith: The Incarnational Narrative as History.* Oxford: Clarendon, 1996.

Eve, Eric. *The Healer from Nazareth: Jesus' Miracles in Historical Context.* London: SPCK, 2009.

———. *The Jewish Context of Jesus' Miracles.* Journal for the Study of the New Testament: Supplement Series 231. Sheffield: Sheffield Academic Press, 2002.

———. "Meier, Miracles, and Multiple Attestation," in *Journal for the Study of the Historical Jesus* 3.1 (2005): 23–45.

Falk, Harvey. *Jesus the Pharisee: A New Look at the Jewishness of Jesus.* Mahwah, N.J.: Paulist, 1985.

Farmer, William R. "The Historical Perimeters for Understanding the Aims of Jesus." In *Crisis in Christology: Essays in Quest of Resolution,* ed. William R. Farmer, 175–98. Livonia, Mich.: Dove Booksellers, 1995.

———. *Jesus and the Gospel: Tradition, Scripture, and Canon.* Philadelphia: Fortress, 1982.

Farmer, William R., ed. *Crisis in Christology: Essays in Quest of Resolution.* Livonia, Mich.: Dove Booksellers, 1995.

Fletcher, Crispin H. T. "Jesus as High Priestly Messiah, Part 1," *Journal for the Study of the Historical Jesus* 4.2 (2006): 155–75.

———. "Jesus as High Priestly Messiah, Part 2," *Journal for the Study of the Historical Jesus* 5.1 (2007): 81–100.

Flusser, David. "Jesus, His Ancestry, and the Commandment of Love." In *Jesus' Jewishness: Exploring the Place of Jesus within Early Judaism,* "ed. James H. Charlesworth, 153–76. New York: Crossroad, 1991.

Fortna, Robert T. "The Gospel of John and the Historical Jesus." *The Fourth R* 8.5–6 (1995): 12–16.

France, Richard T. *The Evidence for Jesus.* Downers Grove, Ill.: InterVarsity, 1986.

———. *Jesus and the Old Testament.* London: Tyndale, 1971.

———. "Jewish Historiography, Midrash, and the Gospels." In *Gospel Perspectives 3: Studies in Midrash and Historiography,* ed. Richard T. France and David Wenham, 99–128. Sheffield: JSOT, 1983.

France, Richard T., and David Wenham, eds. *Gospel Perspectives 1: Studies of History and Tradition in the Four Gospels.* Sheffield: JSOT, 1980.

———. *Gospel Perspectives 2: Studies of History and Tradition in the Four Gospels.* Sheffield: JSOT, 1981.

———. *Gospel Perspectives 3: Studies in Midrash and Historiography.* Sheffield: JSOT,1983.

Francis, L. J., and J. Astley, "The Quest for the Psychological Jesus," *Journal of Psychology and Christianity* 16 (1997): 247–59.

Fredriksen, Paula. "Did Jesus Oppose the Purity Laws?" *Bible Review* 11 (June 1995): 18–25, 42–47.

———. *From Jesus to Christ: The Origins of the New Testament Images of Jesus.* 2nd ed. New Haven, Conn.: Yale University Press, 2000.

———. *Jesus of Nazareth: King of the Jews.* New York: Random House, 1999.

———. "What You See Is What You Get: Context and Content in Current Research on the Historical Jesus." *Theology Today* 52 (1995): 75–97.

Freyne, Sean. "Archaeology and the Historical Jesus." In *Jesus and Archaeology,* ed. James H. Charlesworth, 64–83. Grand Rapids: Eerdmans, 2006.

———. *Galilee from Alexander the Great to Hadrian: A Study of Second Temple Judaism.* Wilmington, Del.: Michael Glazier, 1980.

———. *Galilee, Jesus, and the Gospels: Literary Approaches and Historical Investigations.* Philadelphia: Fortress, 1988.

———. "The Geography, Politics, and Economics of Galilee and the Quest for the Historical Jesus." In *Studying the Historical Jesus: Evaluations of the State of Current Research,* ed. Bruce Chilton and Craig A. Evans, 75–122. Leiden: Brill, 1994.

———. *Jesus, a Jewish Galilean: A New Reading of the Jesus Story.* New York: T&T Clark, 2004.

———. "The Quest for the Historical Jesus: Some Theological Reflections." *Concilium* (1997): 37–51.

Fuller, Reginald. *The Formation of the Resurrection Narratives.* Philadelphia: Fortress, 1980 (originally published in 1971).

———. *The Foundations of New Testament Christology.* London: Lutterworth, 1965.

Funk, Robert W. *A Credible Jesus: Fragments of a Vision.* Santa Rosa, Calif.: Polebridge, 2002.

————. *Honest to Jesus: Jesus for a New Millennium.* San Francisco: HarperSanFrancisco, 1996.

————. "The Issue of Jesus." *Foundations and Facets Forum* 1.1 (1985): 7–12.

————. *Jesus as Precursor.* Rev. ed. Ed. E. Beutner. Sonoma, Calif.: Polebridge, 1993.

————. "Jesus of Nazareth: A Glimpse." *The Fourth R* 9.1, 2 (1996): 17–20.

————. "On Distinguishing Historical from Fictive Narrative." *Foundations and Facets Forum* 9.3–4 (1993): 179–216.

————. "Unraveling the Jesus Tradition: Criteria and Criticism." *Foundations and Facets Forum* 5.2 (1989): 31–62.

Funk, Robert W., Roy W. Hoover, and the Jesus Seminar. *The Five Gospels: The Search for the Authentic Words of Jesus.* New York: Macmillan, 1993.

Funk, Robert W., and the Jesus Seminar. *The Acts of Jesus: The Search for the Authentic Deeds of Jesus.* San Francisco: HarperSanFrancisco, 1998.

Gager, John G. "The Gospels and Jesus: Some Doubts about Method." *Journal of Religion* 54 (1974): 244–72.

Gaiser, Frederick J., ed. *The Quest for Jesus and the Christian Faith.* Word and World Supplement Series 3. St. Paul: Luther Seminary, 1997.

Gallagher, Eugene V. *Divine Man or Magician? Celsus and Origen on Jesus.* Society of Biblical Literature Dissertation Series 64. Chico, Calif.: Scholars, 1982.

Galvin, John P. "'I Believe . . . in Jesus Christ, His Only Son, Our Lord': The Earthly Jesus and the Christ of Faith," *Interpretation* 50 (1996): 373–82.

Gammie, John G., and Leo G. Purdue. *The Sage in Israel and the Ancient Near East.* Winona Lake, Ind.: Eisenbrauns, 1990.

Gaventa, Beverly Roberts, and Richard B. Hays. *Seeking the Identity of Jesus: A Pilgrimage.* Grand Rapids: Eerdmans, 2008.

Geisler, Norman L. "In Defense of the Resurrection: A Reply to Criticisms." *Journal of the Evangelical Theological Society* 34 (1991): 243–61.

Geivett, R. Douglas. "Is Jesus the Only Way?" in *Jesus under Fire: Modern Scholarship Reinvents the Historical Jesus,* ed. Michael J. Wilkins and J. P. Moreland, 177–206. Grand Rapids: Zondervan Publishing House, 1995.

Georgen, Donald. *A Theology of Jesus.* Vol. 1, *The Mission and Ministry of Jesus.* Wilmington, Del.: Michael Glazier, 1986.

————. *A Theology of Jesus.* Vol. 2, *The Death and Resurrection of Jesus.* Wilmington, Del: Michael Glazier, 1986.

Gerhardsson, Birger. *The Gospel Tradition.* Lund: Gleerup, 1986.

————. *Memory and Manuscript: Oral Tradition and Written Transmission in Rabbinic Judaism and Early Christianity.* Uppsala: Gleerup, 1961.

————. *The Origins of the Gospel Tradition.* London: SCM, 1979.

————. *Tradition and Transmission in Early Christianity.* Uppsala: Gleerup, 1964.

Gnilka, Joachim. *Jesus of Nazareth: Message and History.* Peabody, Mass.: Hendrickson, 1997 (originally published in 1977).

Goetz, S. C., and Craig Blomberg. "The Burden of Proof." *Journal for the Study of the New Testament* 11 (1981): 39–83.

Goodman, Martin. *The Ruling Class of Judea.* Cambridge: Cambridge University Press, 1987.

Goppelt, Leonhard. *Theology of the New Testament.* Vol. 1, *The Ministry of Jesus in Its Theological Significance.* Grand Rapids: Eerdmans, 1981 (originally published in 1975).

Gowler, David B. *What Are They Saying about the Historical Jesus?* New York: Paulist, 2007.

Grant, Frederick C. "The Authenticity of Jesus' Sayings." In *Neutestamentliche Studien für Rudolf Bultmann,* Beihefte zur Zeitschrift für die neutestamentliche Wissenschaft, 137–43. Berlin: Topelmann, 1954.

Grant, Michael. *Jesus: A Historian's Review of the Gospels.* New York: Macmillan, 1992 (originally published in 1977).

Grant, Robert. *Gnosticism and Early Christianity.* 2nd ed. New York: Columbia University Press, 1966.

Gray, Rebecca. *Prophetic Figures in Late Second Temple Jewish Palestine.* Oxford: Oxford University Press, 1993.

Green, Joel B., and Max Turner, eds. *Jesus of Nazareth, Lord and Christ: Essays on the Historical Jesus and New Testament Christology.* Grand Rapids: Eerdmans, 1994.

Gregg, Brian Han. *The Historical Jesus and the Final Judgment Sayings in Q.* Wissenschaftliche Untersuchungen zum Neuen Testament 2.207. Tübingen: Mohr-Siebeck, 2006.

Grindheim, Sigurd. *God's Equal: What Can We Know about Jesus' Self-Understanding in the Synoptic Gospels?* Library of New Testament Studies 446. London: T&T Clark, 2011.

Guillet, Jacques. *The Consciousness of Jesus.* New York: Newman, 1971.

Habermas, Gary R. *Ancient Evidence for the Life of Jesus: Historical Records of His Death and Resurrection.* Nashville: Thomas Nelson, 1984.

———. "Did Jesus Perform Miracles?" In *Jesus under Fire: Modern Scholarship Reinvents the Historical Jesus,* ed. Michael J. Wilkins and J. P. Moreland, 117–41. Grand Rapids: Zondervan Publishing House, 1995.

———. "Resurrection Claims in Non-Christian Religions." *Religious Studies* 25 (1989): 167–77.

Hagner, Donald A. *The Jewish Reclamation of Jesus: An Analysis and Critique of Modern Jewish Study of Jesus.* Grand Rapids: Zondervan Publishing House, 1984.

Hahn, Ferdinand. "Methodological Reflections on the Historical Investigation of Jesus." In *Historical Investigation and New Testament Faith: Two Essays,* 35–105. Philadelphia: Fortress, 1983.

Haight, Roger. "The Impact of Jesus Research on Christology." *Louvain Studies* 21 (1996): 216–28.

Harrington, Daniel J. *Historical Dictionary of Jesus.* Lanham: Scarecrow, 2010.

———. "The Jewishness of Jesus: Facing Some Problems." *Catholic Biblical Quarterly* 49 (1987): 1–13.

Harrisville, Roy A. "Representative American Lives of Jesus." In *The Historical Jesus and the Kerygmatic Christ: Essays on the New Quest of the Historical Jesus,* ed. Carl E. Braaten and Roy A. Harrisville, 172–96. Nashville: Abingdon, 1964.

Harvey, Anthony B. *Jesus and the Constraints of History: The Bampton Lectures, 1980.* London: Duckworth, 1982.

———. *Strenuous Commands: The Ethic of Jesus.* Philadelphia: Trinity Press International, 1990.

Harvey, Van A., and Schubert M. Ogden. "How New Is the 'New Quest of the Historical Jesus'?" In *The Historical Jesus and the Kerygmatic Christ: Essays on the New Quest of the Historical Jesus,* ed. Carl E. Braaten and Roy A. Harrisville, 197–242. Nashville: Abingdon, 1964.

Hays, Richard B. "The Corrected Jesus." *First Things* 43 (1994): 43–48.

Head, Peter. "The Nazi Quest for an Aryan Jesus," *Journal for the Study of the Historical Jesus* 2.1 (2004): 55–89.

Hebblethwaite, Brian. "Jesus Christ—God and Man: The Myth and Truth Debate." In *Crisis in Christology: Essays in Quest of Resolution,* ed. William R. Farmer, 1–12. Livonia, Mich.: Dove Booksellers, 1995.

Hedrick, Charles W. *When History and Faith Collide: Studying Jesus.* Peabody, Mass.: Hendrickson, 1999.

Hellerman, Joseph H. *Jesus and the People of God: Reconfiguring Ethnic Identity.* New Testament Monographs 21. Sheffield: Sheffield Phoenix, 2007.

Hengel, Martin. *The Atonement: The Origins of the Doctrine in the New Testament.* Philadelphia: Fortress, 1981.

———. *The Charismatic Leader and His Followers.* Edinburgh: T&T Clark, 1996 (originally published in 1968).

———. *Crucifixion in the Ancient World and the Folly of the Message of the Cross.* Philadelphia: Fortress, 1977.

———. *The Hellenization of Judea in the First Century after Christ.* Philadelphia: Trinity Press International, 1989.

———. "Jesus, the Messiah of Israel." In *Crisis in Christology: Essays in Quest of Resolution,* ed. William R. Farmer, 217–40. Livonia, Mich.: Dove Booksellers, 1995.

———. *Judaism and Hellenism: Studies in Their Encounter in Palestine during the Early Hellenistic Period.* 2 vols. Philadelphia: Fortress, 1974.

———. *Victory over Violence: Jesus and the Revolutionists.* Philadelphia: Fortress, 1973.

———. *Was Jesus a Revolutionist?* Philadelphia: Fortress, 1971.

———. *The Zealots: Investigations into the Jewish Freedom Movement in the Period from Herod I until 70 A.D.* Edinburgh: T&T Clark, 1995.

Hennecke, Edgar, and Wilhelm Schneemelcher, eds. *New Testament Apocrypha.* 2 vols. Philadelphia: Fortress, 1963, 1965.

Herzog, William R., II *Parables as Subversive Speech: Jesus as Pedagogue of the Oppressed.* Louisville: Westminster John Knox, 1994.

———. *Prophet and Teacher: An Introduction to the Historical Jesus.* Louisville: Westminster John Knox, 2005.

Hobsbawm, Eric J. *Bandits.* London: Penguin Books, 1985 (originally published in 1969).

———. "The Passion Narratives and Historical Criticism." *Theology* 75 (1972): 58–71.

———. *Primitive Rebels: Studies in Archaic Forms of Social Movement in the Nineteenth and Twentieth Centuries.* New York: W. W. Norton and Co., 1965.

Hoehner, Harold W. *Chronological Aspects of the Life of Christ.* Grand Rapids: Zondervan Publishing House, 1977.

Hofius, Otfried. "Unknown Sayings of Jesus." In *The Gospel and the Gospels,* ed. Peter Stuhlmacher, 336–60. Grand Rapids: Eerdmans, 1991.

Hoistad, Ragnar. *Cynic Hero and Cynic King.* Uppsala: Bloms, 1948.

Hollenbach, Paul. "The Conversion of Jesus: From Jesus the Baptizer to Jesus the Healer." *Aufstieg und Niedergang der römischen Welt* 2.25. 196–219.

———. "The Historical Jesus Question in North America Today." *Biblical Theology Bulletin* 19 (1989): 11–22.

Holmén, Tom. *Jesus and Jewish Covenant Thinking.* Leiden: Brill, 2001.

Holmén, Tom, ed. *Jesus from Judaism to Christianity: Continuum Approaches to the Historical Jesus.* Library of New Testament Studies 352. London: T&T Clark, 2007.

Hooker, Morna D. "On Using the Wrong Tool." *Theology* 75 (1972): 570–81.

Hoover, Roy W. "Answering the Critics: A Scholar Responds to *Jesus under Fire.*" *The Fourth R* 8.5–6 (1995): 17–20.

———. "The Work of the Jesus Seminar." *The Fourth R* 9.5–6 (1996): 9–15.

Hoover, Roy W., ed. *Profiles of Jesus.* Santa Rosa, Calif.: Polebridge, 2002.

Horbury, William. "The Messianic Associations of 'the Son of Man.'" *Journal of Theological Studies* 36 (1985): 34–53.

———. "The Passion Narratives and Historical Criticism." *Theology* 75 (1972): 58–71.

Horsley, Richard A. *Archaeology, History and Society in Galilee: The Social Context of Jesus and the Rabbis.* Valley Forge, Penn.: Trinity Press International, 1996.

———. "Archaeology of Galilee and the Historical Context of Jesus." *Neotestamentica* 29 (1995): 211–29.

———. "The Death of Jesus." In *Studying the Historical Jesus: Evaluations of the State of Current Research,* ed. Bruce Chilton and Craig A. Evans, 395–423. Leiden: Brill, 1994.

————. "Ethics and Exegesis: 'Love Your Enemy' and the Doctrine of Nonviolence." In *The Love of Enemy and Nonretaliation in the New Testament,* ed. W. M. Swartley, 72–101. Louisville: Westminster/John Knox, 1992 (originally published in 1986).

————. *Galilee: History, Politics, People.* Valley Forge, Penn.: Trinity Press International, 1995.

————. *Hidden Transcripts and the Arts of Resistance: Applying the Work of James C. Scott to Jesus and Paul.* Semeia Studies 48. Atlanta: Society of Biblical Literature, 2004.

————. *Jesus and Empire: The Kingdom of God and the New World Disorder.* Minneapolis: Fortress, 2003.

————. *Jesus and the Powers: Conflict, Covenant, and the Hope of the Poor.* Minneapolis: Fortress, 2011.

————. *Jesus and the Spiral of Violence: Popular Jewish Resistance in Roman Palestine.* San Francisco: Harper & Row, 1973.

————. *Jesus in Context: Power, People, and Performance.* Minneapolis: Fortress, 2008.

————. "Jesus, Itinerant Cynic or Israelite Prophet?" In *Images of Jesus Today,* ed. James H. Charlesworth and W. P. Weaver, 68–97. Valley Forge, Penn.: Trinity Press International, 1994.

————. "Messianic Figures and Movements in First-Century Palestine." In *The Messiah: Developments in Earliest Judaism and Christianity,* ed. James H. Charlesworth, 276–95. Minneapolis: Fortress, 1992.

————. *Sociology and the Jesus Movement.* New York: Crossroad, 1989.

————. "What Has Galilee to Do with Jerusalem? Political Aspects of the Jesus Movement." *Hervormde Teologiese Studies* 52 (1996): 88–104.

Horsley, Richard A., and John S. Hanson. *Bandits, Prophets, and Messiahs: Popular Movements at the Time of Jesus.* Minneapolis: Winston, 1985.

Houlden, J. Leslie. *Jesus: A Question of Identity.* London: SPCK, 1992.

Hull, John M. *Hellenistic Magic and the Synoptic Tradition.* Studies in Biblical Theology 2.28. Naperville, Ill: Alec R. Allenson, 1974.

Hultgren, Arland. "Jesus of Nazareth: Prophet, Visionary, Sage, or What?" *Dialog* 33 (1994): 263–73.

————. "The Use of Sources in the Quest for Jesus: What You Use Is What You Get." In *The Quest for Jesus and the Christian Faith,* ed. Frederick J. Gaiser, 33–48. St. Paul: Luther Seminary, 1997.

Hurst, L. D. "The Neglected Role of Semantics in the Search for the Aramaic Words of Jesus." In *The Historical Jesus: A Sheffield Reader,* ed. Craig A. Evans and Stanley E. Porter, 219–36. Sheffield: Sheffield Academic, 1995.

Hurtado, Larry W. *How on Earth Did Jesus Become a God? Historical Questions about Earliest Devotion to Jesus.* Grand Rapids: Eerdmans, 2006.

————. *One God, One Lord: Early Christian Devotion and Ancient Jewish Monotheism.* Grand Rapids: Eerdmans, 1988.

Hurtado, Larry W., and Paul L. Owen, eds. *"Who Is This Son of Man?" The Latest Scholarship on a Puzzling Expression of the Historical Jesus.* Library of New Testament Studies, 390. London: T&T Clark, 2011.

Jacobson, Arland. *The First Gospel: An Introduction to Q.* Sonoma, Calif.: Polebridge, 1992.

Jacobson, Diane. "Jesus as Wisdom in the New Testament." In *The Quest for Jesus and the Christian Faith,* ed. Frederick J. Gaiser, 72–93. St. Paul: Luther Seminary, 1997.

Jeremias, Joachim. *Jesus and the Message of the New Testament.* Minneapolis: Fortress, 2002 (originally published 1963–1965).

————. *Jesus' Promise to the Nations.* Studies in Biblical Theology 24. London: SCM, 1958.

————. *New Testament Theology.* Vol. 1, *The Proclamation of Jesus.* New York: Charles Scribner's Sons, 1971.

Johnson, Elizabeth A. *Consider Jesus: Waves of Renewal in Christology.* New York: Crossroad, 1992.

Johnson, Luke Timothy. *The Real Jesus: The Misguided Quest for the Historical Jesus and the Truth of the Traditional Gospels.* San Francisco: HarperSanFransisco, 1996.

Johnson, Paul. "An Historian Looks at Jesus." In *Crisis in Christology: Essays in Quest of Resolution,* ed. William R. Farmer, 25–38. Livonia, Mich.: Dove Booksellers, 1995.

Jones, I. H. "Disputed Questions in Biblical Studies: 4. Exile and Eschatology," *Expository Times* 112 (2000–2001): 401–5.

Joseph, Simon J. "The Ascetic Jesus," *Journal for the Study of the Historical Jesus* 8.2 (2010): 146–82.

Juel, Donald H. *Messianic Exegesis: Christological Interpretation of the Old Testament in Early Christianity.* Philadelphia: Fortress, 1988.

———. "The Trial and Death of the Historical Jesus." In *The Quest for Jesus and the Christian Faith,* ed. Frederick J. Gaiser, 33–48. St. Paul: Luther Seminary, 1997.

Kähler, Martin. *The So-Called Historical Jesus and the Historic, Biblical Christ.* Philadelphia: Fortress, 1964 (originally published in 1892).

Käsemann, Ernst. "Blind Alleys in the 'Jesus of History' Controversy." In *New Testament Questions of Today,* 23–65. Philadelphia: Fortress, 1969 (originally published in 1957).

———. "The Problem of the Historical Jesus." In *Essays on New Testament Themes,* 15–47. Naperville, Ill.: Alec R. Allenson, 1964.

Kasper, Walter. *Jesus the Christ.* New York: Paulist, 1977.

Kaylor, R. David. *Jesus the Prophet: His Vision of the Kingdom on Earth.* Louisville: Westminster John Knox, 1994.

Kazen, Thomas. "The Coming of the Son of Man Revisited." *Journal for the Study of the Historical Jesus* 5.2 (2007): 155–74.

———. *Jesus and Purity: Halakhah: Was Jesus Indifferent to Impurity?* Coniectanea biblica: New Testament Series 38. Stockholm: Almqvist & Wiksell, 2002.

Kealy, Sean P. *Jesus and Politics.* Zacchaeus Studies. Collegeville, Minn.: Liturgical, 1990.

Keck, Leander E. *A Future for the Historical Jesus: The Place of Jesus in Preaching and Theology.* Nashville: Abingdon, 1971.

———. "The Second Coming of the Liberal Jesus." *Christian Century* 111 (1994): 784–87.

———. *Who Is Jesus? History in Perfect Tense.* Minneapolis: Fortress, 2001.

Kee, Howard Clark. "A Century of Quests for the Culturally Compatible Jesus." *Theology Today* 52 (1995): 17–28.

———. *Jesus in History.* 2nd ed. New York: Harcourt Brace Jovanovich, 1977.

———. *Medicine, Miracle, and Magic in New Testament Times.* Society for New Testament Studies Monograph Series 55. Cambridge: Cambridge University Press, 1986.

———. *Miracle in the Early Christian World.* New Haven, Conn.: Yale University Press, 1983.

———. *What Can We Know about Jesus?* Cambridge: Cambridge University Press, 1990.

Keeley, Robin, ed. *Jesus 2000.* Oxford: Lion, 1989.

Keener, Craig S. *The Historical Jesus of the Gospels.* Grand Rapids: Eerdmans, 2009.

———. *Miracles: The Credibility of New Testament Accounts,* 2 vols. Grand Rapids: Baker Academic, 2011.

Keith, Chris. *Jesus' Literacy: Scribal Culture and the Teacher from Galilee.* Library of New Testament Studies 413. London: T&T Clark, 2011.

Kelber, Werner H., and Samuel Byrskog, eds. *Jesus in Memory: Traditions in Oral and Scribal Perspectives.* Waco, Tex.: Baylor University Press, 2009.

Keller, Catherine. "The Jesus of History and the Feminism of Theology." In *Jesus and Faith: A Conversation on the Work of John Dominic Crossan,* ed. Jeffrey Carlson and Robert A. Ludwig, 71–82. Maryknoll, N.Y.: Orbis Books, 1994.

Kelly, J. Landrum. *Conscientious Objections: Towards a Reconstruction of the Social and Political Philosophy of Jesus of Nazareth.* Toronto Studies in Theology 68. Lewiston, N.Y.: Edwin Mellen, 1994.

Kilpatrick, G. D. "Jesus, His Family, and His Disciples." In *The Historical Jesus: A Sheffield Reader,* ed. Craig A. Evans and Stanley E. Porter, 13–28. Sheffield: Sheffield Academic, 1995.

Kim, Seyoon. *The Son of Man as the Son of God.* Tübingen: Mohr, 1983.

King, Karen L. "Kingdom in the Gospel of Thomas." *Foundations and Facets Forum* 3.1 (1987): 48–97.

Kissinger, W. S. *The Lives of Jesus: A History and Bibliography.* New York: Garland, 1985.

Klausner, Joseph. *Jesus of Nazareth: His Life, Times, and Teaching.* London: George Allen & Unwin, 1947 (originally published in 1922).

Kloppenborg, John S. "Alms, Debt, and Divorce: Jesus' Ethics in Their Mediterranean Context." *Toronto Journal of Theology* 6 (1990): 182–200.

———. *The Formation of Q: Trajectories in Ancient Wisdom Collections.* Studies in Antiquity and Christianity. Philadelphia: Fortress, 1987.

———. *Q Parallels: Synopsis, Critical Notes, and Concordance.* Sonoma, Calif.: Polebridge, 1988.

Kloppenborg, John S., ed. *The Shape of Q: Signal Essays on the Sayings Gospel.* Minneapolis: Fortress, 1994.

Kloppenborg, John, Marvin Meyer, Stephen Patterson, and Michael Steinhauser. *The Q-Thomas Reader.* Sonoma, Calif.: Polebridge, 1990.

Kloppenborg, John S., with John W. Marshall, eds. *Apocalypticism, Anti-Semitism, and the Historical Jesus: Subtexts in Criticism.* Journal for the Study of the New Testament: Supplement Series 275. London: T&T Clark, 2005.

Knibb, Michael. "The Exile in the Literature of the Intertestamental Period." *Heythrop Journal* 17 (1976): 253–72.

———. *The Qumran Community.* Cambridge: Cambridge University Press, 1987.

Knutsen, Mary M. "The Third Quest for the Historical Jesus: Introduction and Bibliography." In *The Quest for Jesus and the Christian Faith,* ed. Frederick J. Gaiser, 13–32. St. Paul: Luther Seminary, 1997.

Koch, Klaus. *The Rediscovery of Apocalyptic: A Polemical Work on a Neglected Area of Biblical Studies and Its Damaging Effects on Theology and Philosophy.* Studies in Biblical Theology 2.22. London: SCM, 1972.

Koester, Helmut. *Ancient Christian Gospels: Their History and Development.* Philadelphia: Trinity Press International, 1990.

———. "The Historical Jesus and the Cult of the *Kyrios Christos.*" *Harvard Divinity Bulletin* 24 (1995): 13–18.

———. "The Historical Jesus and the Historical Situation of the Quest: An Epilogue." In *Studying the Historical Jesus: Evaluations of the State of Current Research,* ed. Bruce Chilton and Craig A. Evans, 535–46. Leiden: Brill, 1994.

———. "Jesus the Victim." *Journal of Biblical Literature* 111 (1992): 3–15.

Landau, Brent. "'Jesus Never Existed': An Intellectual History of the 'Jesus Myth' Theory" (title tentative). *Journal for the Study of the Historical Jesus,* forthcoming.

Le Donne, Anthony. *The Historiographical Jesus: Memory, Typology, and the Son of David.* Waco, Tex.: Baylor University Press, 2009.

Leivestad, Ragnar. *Jesus in His Own Perspective: An Examination of His Sayings, Actions, and Eschatological Titles.* Minneapolis: Fortress, 1987.

Lenski, Gerhard. *Power and Privilege: A Theory of Social Stratification.* New York: McGraw-Hill, 1966.

Levine, Amy-Jill. "Christian Faith and the Study of the Historical Jesus: A Response to Bock, Keener, and Webb," *Journal for the Study of the Historical Jesus* 9.1 (2011): 96–106.

————. *The Misunderstood Jew: The Church and the Scandal of the Jewish Jesus.* San Francisco: HarperSanFrancisco, 2006.

————. "Who's Catering the Q Affair? Feminist Observations on Q Paraenesis." *Semeia* 50 (1990): 145–61.

Levine, Amy-Jill, Dale C. Allison, and John Dominic Crossan, eds. *The Historical Jesus in Context.* Princeton Readings in Religions. Princeton: Princeton University Press, 2006.

Levine, Lee I., ed. *The Galilee in Late Antiquity.* New York: Jewish Theological Seminary, 1992.

Lieu, Judith. "'The Parting of the Ways': Theological Construct or Historical Reality?" *Journal for the Study of the New Testament* 56 (1994): 101–19.

Loader, William. *Jesus and the Fundamentalism of His Day.* Grand Rapids: Eerdmans, 2001.

————. *Jesus' Attitude toward the Law: A Study of the Gospels.* Grand Rapids: Eerdmans, 2002 (originally published, 1997).

————. *Sexuality and the Jesus Tradition.* Grand Rapids: Eerdmans, 2005.

Lohfink, Gerhard. *Jesus and Community.* Philadelphia: Fortress, 1984.

Luck, Georg. *Arcana Mundi: Magic and the Occult in the Greek and Roman Worlds.* Baltimore: Johns Hopkins, 1985.

Lüdemann, Gerd. *Jesus after 2000 Years.* Trans. John Bowden. London: SCM, 2000.

————. *The Resurrection of Jesus: History, Experience, Theology.* Minneapolis: Fortress, 1994.

————. *What Really Happened to Jesus? A Historical Approach to the Resurrection.* Louisville: Westminster John Knox, 1996.

Ludwig, Robert A. "Reconstructing Jesus for a Dysfunctional Church: Crossan's Christology and Contemporary Spirituality." In *Jesus and Faith: A Conversation on the Work of John Dominic Crossan,* ed. Jeffrey Carlson and Robert A. Ludwig, 57–70. Maryknoll, N.Y.: Orbis Books, 1994.

Lunny, William J. *The Jesus Option.* Mahwah, N.J.: Paulist, 1994.

Maccoby, Hyam. *Jesus the Pharisee.* London: SCM, 2003.

————. *The Mythmaker: Paul and the Invention of Christianity.* London: Weidenfeld & Nicolson, 1980 (originally published in 1973).

Mack, Burton L. *The Lost Gospel: The Book of Q and Christian Origins.* San Francisco: HarperSanFrancisco, 1993.

————. *A Myth of Innocence: Mark and Christian Origins.* Philadelphia: Fortress, 1988.

————. *Who Wrote the New Testament? The Making of the Christian Myth.* San Francisco: HarperSanFrancisco, 1995.

Maier, Paul L. *In the Fullness of Time: A Historian Looks at Christmas, Easter, and the Early Church.* San Francisco: HarperSanFrancisco, 1991.

Malina, Bruce J. *The Social Gospel of Jesus: The Kingdom of God in Mediterranean Perspective.* Minneapolis: Fortress, 2001.

————. *The Social World of Jesus and the Gospels.* New York: Routledge & Kegan Paul, 1996.

Manson, T. W. *The Servant-Messiah: A Study of the Public Ministry of Jesus.* Cambridge: Cambridge University Press, 1953.

————. *The Teaching of Jesus: Studies of Its Form and Content.* Cambridge: Cambridge University Press, 1931.

Marsh, C. "Quests of the Historical Jesus in New Historicist Perspective," *Biblical Interpretation* 5 (1997): 403–37.

Marsh, John T. *Jesus in His Lifetime.* London: Sidgwick & Jackson, 1981.

Marshall, I. H. *The Origins of New Testament Christology.* Downers Grove, Ill.: InterVarsity, 1990.

Marshall, Mary J. "Jesus: Glutton and Drunkard?" in *Journal for the Study of the Historical Jesus* 3.1 (2005): 47–60.

Martin, David. "Jesus Christ and Modern Sociology." In *Crisis in Christology: Essays in Quest of Resolution,* ed. William R. Farmer, 29–46. Livonia, Mich.: Dove Booksellers, 1995.

Martin, Raymond A. *Studies in the Life and Ministry of the Historical Jesus.* New York: University Press of America, 1995.

McArthur, Harvey K. *The Quest through the Centuries: The Search for the Historical Jesus.* Philadelphia: Fortress, 1966.

McArthur, Harvey K., ed. *In Search of the Historical Jesus: A Source Book.* New York: Charles Scribner's Sons, 1969.

McAteer, Michael R., and Michael G. Steinhauser. *The Man in the Scarlet Robe: Two Thousand Years of Searching for Jesus.* Etobicoke, Ont.: United Church Publishing House, 1996.

McCann, Dennis P. "Doing Business with the Historical Jesus." In *Jesus and Faith: A Conversation on the Work of John Dominic Crossan,* ed. Jeffrey Carlson and Robert A. Ludwig, 132–41. Maryknoll, N.Y.: Orbis Books, 1994.

McCown, C. C. *The Search for the Real Jesus: A Century of Historical Study.* New York: Charles Scribner's Sons, 1940.

McGaughy, Lane C. "The Search for the Historical Jesus: Why Start with the Sayings?" *The Fourth R* 9.5–6 (1996): 17–26.

McGrath, James F. *The Burial of Jesus: History and Faith.* BookSurge (published online at Booksurge.com).

———. "Was Jesus Illegitimate? The Evidence of His Social Interactions," *Journal for the Study of the Historical Jesus* 5.1 (2007): 81–100.

McKnight, Edgar V. *Jesus Christ in History and Scripture: A Poetic and Sectarian Perspective.* Macon, Ga.: Mercer University Press, 1999.

———. *Jesus Christ Today: The Historical Shaping of Jesus for the Twenty-First Century.* Macon, Ga.: Mercer University Press, 2009.

McKnight, Scot. *Jesus and His Death: Historiography, the Historical Jesus, and Atonement Theory.* Waco, Tex.: Baylor University Press, 2005.

———. *A New Vision for Israel: The Teachings of Jesus in National Context.* Grand Rapids: Eerdmans, 1999.

———. "Who Is Jesus? An Introduction to Jesus Studies." In *Jesus under Fire: Modern Scholarship Reinvents the Historical Jesus,* ed. Michael J. Wilkins and J. P. Moreland, 51–72. Grand Rapids: Zondervan Publishing House, 1995.

McKnight, Scot, and Joseph B. Modica, eds. *Who Do My Opponents Say That I Am? An Investigation of the Accusations against the Historical Jesus.* Library of New Testament Studies 327. London: T&T Clark, 2008.

McRay, J. *Archaeology and the New Testament.* Grand Rapids: Baker Academic, 2008.

Meier, John P. "The Circle of the Twelve: Did It Exist during Jesus' Public Ministry?" *Journal of Biblical Literature* 116 (1997): 635–72.

———. "Dividing Lines in Jesus Research Today: Through Dialectical Negation to a Positive Sketch." *Interpretation* 50 (1996): 355–72.

———. *A Marginal Jew: Rethinking the Historical Jesus.* Vol. 1, *The Roots of the Problem and the Person.* New York: Doubleday, 1991.

———. *A Marginal Jew: Rethinking the Historical Jesus.* Vol. 2, *Mentor, Message, and Miracles.* New York: Doubleday, 1994.

———. *A Marginal Jew: Rethinking the Historical Jesus.* Vol. 3, *Companions and Competitors.* New York: Doubleday, 2001.

———. *A Marginal Jew: Rethinking the Historical Jesus.* Vol. 4, *Law and Love.* New York: Doubleday, 2009.

———. "On Retrojecting Later Questions from Later Texts: A Reply to Richard Bauckham." *Catholic Biblical Quarterly* 59 (1997): 511–27.

———. "Reflections on Jesus-of-History Research Today." In *Jesus' Jewishness: Exploring the Place of Jesus within Early Judaism,* ed. James H. Charlesworth, 84–107. New York: Crossroad, 1991.

Mendels, Doron. "Jesus and the Politics of His Day." In *Images of Jesus Today,* ed. James H. Charlesworth and W. P. Weaver, 98–112. Valley Forge, Penn.: Trinity Press International, 1994.

———. *The Rise and Fall of Jewish Nationalism: Jewish and Christian Ethnicity in Ancient Palestine.* Grand Rapids: Eerdmans, 1997

Meyer, Ben. *The Aims of Jesus.* London: SCM, 1979.

———. "Appointed Deed, Appointed Doer: Jesus and the Scriptures." In *Crisis in Christology: Essays in Quest of Resolution,* ed. William R. Farmer, 271–310. Livonia, Mich.: Dove Booksellers, 1995.

———. *Christus Faber: The Master Builder and the House of God.* Princeton Theological Monograph Series 29. Allison Park, Penn.: Pickwick Publications, 1992.

———. *Critical Realism and the New Testament.* Princeton Theological Monograph Series 17. Allison Park, Penn.: Pickwick Publications, 1989.

———. "Jesus' Ministry and Self-Understanding." In *Studying the Historical Jesus: Evaluations of the State of Current Research,* ed. Bruce Chilton and Craig A. Evans, 337–52. Leiden: Brill, 1994.

———. "'Phases' in Jesus' Mission." *Gregorianum* 73 (1992): 5–17.

Meyer, Marvin, and Charles Hughes, eds. *Jesus Then and Now: Images of Jesus in History and Christology.* Harrisburg, Penn.: Trinity Press International, 2001.

Michaels, J. Ramsey. "The Kingdom of God and the Historical Jesus." In *The Kingdom of God in Twentieth Century Interpretation,* ed. Wendell Willis, 109–18. Peabody, Mass.: Hendrickson Publishers, 1987.

Miller, John. *Jesus at Thirty: A Psychological and Historical Portrait.* Minneapolis: Fortress, 1997.

Miller, Robert J. "Historical Method and the Deeds of Jesus: The Test Case of the Temple Demonstration." *Foundations and Facets Forum* 8.1–2 (1992): 5–30.

———. *The Jesus Seminar and Its Critics.* Santa Rosa, Calif.: Polebridge, 1999.

———. "The Jesus Seminar and Its Critics: What Is Really at Stake?" *The Fourth R* 10.1–2 (1997): 17–21.

———. "When It's Futile to Argue about the Historical Jesus: A Response to Bock, Keener, and Webb," *Journal for the Study of the Historical Jesus* 9.1 (2011): 85–95.

Miller, Robert J., ed. *The Apocalyptic Jesus: A Debate.* Santa Rosa, Calif.: Polebridge, 2001.

———. *The Complete Gospels: Annotated Scholars Version.* Rev. ed. San Francisco: Harper SanFrancisco, 1994.

Miller, Robert J., and Ben Witherington III. "Battling over the Jesus Seminar." *Bible Review* 13 (April 1997): 18–26.

Mitchell, Stephen. *The Gospel according to Jesus: A New Translation and Guide to His Essential Teachings for Believers and Unbelievers.* New York: HarperCollins, 1990.

Moltmann, Jürgen. *The Way of Jesus Christ: Christology in Messianic Dimensions.* San Francisco: HarperSanFrancisco, 1990.

Moo, Douglas J. "Jesus and the Authority of the Mosaic Law." In *The Historical Jesus: A Sheffield Reader,* ed. Craig A. Evans and Stanley E. Porter, 83–130. Sheffield: Sheffield Academic, 1995.

Moule, C. F. D. "The Gravamen against Jesus." In *Jesus, the Gospels, and the Church,* ed. E. P. Sanders, 177–95. Macon, Ga.: Mercer University Press, 1987.

———. *The Origin of Christology.* Cambridge: Cambridge University Press, 1977.

Moxnes, Halvor. *Putting Jesus in His Place: A Radical Vision of Household and Kingdom*. Louisville: Westminster John Knox, 2003.

Neil, John C. *Messiah: Six Lectures on the Ministry of Jesus*. Cambridge: Cochrane, 1980.

———. *Who Did Jesus Think He Was?* Leiden: Brill, 1995.

Neirynck, Frans. "The Historical Jesus: Reflections on an Inventory." *Ephemerides theologicae lovanienses* 70 (1994): 221–34.

Neusner, Jacob, William S. Green, and Ernst Frerichs, eds. *Judaisms and Their Messiahs at the Turn of the Era*. Cambridge: Cambridge University Press, 1987.

Newman, Carey C., ed. *Jesus and the Restoration of Israel: A Critical Assessment of N. T. Wright's Jesus and the Victory of God*. Downers Grove, Ill: InterVarsity, 1999.

Nolan, Albert, *Jesus before Christianity*. Rev. ed. Maryknoll, N.Y.: Orbis Books, 1992.

Oakman, Douglas E. *Jesus and the Economic Questions of His Day*. Studies in the Bible and Early Christianity 8. Lewiston, N.Y.: Edwin Mellen, 1986.

———. *Jesus and the Peasants*. Matrix: The Bible in Mediterranean Context. Eugene, Ore.: Cascade, 2008.

O'Collins, Gerald. *Christology: A Biblical, Historical, and Systematic Study of Jesus*. Oxford: Oxford University Press, 1995.

———. *The Resurrection of Jesus Christ: Some Contemporary Issues*. Milwaukee: Marquette University Press, 1993.

O'Neill, John C. *Who Did Jesus Think He Was?* Leiden: Brill, 1995.

Osiek, Caroline. "Jesus and Galilee." *Bible Today* 34 (1996): 153–59.

Ott, Heinrich. "The Historical Jesus and the Ontology of History." In *The Historical Jesus and the Kerygmatic Christ: Essays on the New Quest of the Historical Jesus*, ed. Carl E. Braaten and Roy A. Harrisville, 142–71. Nashville: Abingdon, 1964.

Pagels, Elaine. *The Gnostic Gospels*. New York: Random House, 1980.

Pals, D. L. *The Victorian "Lives" of Jesus*. Trinity University Monograph Series. San Antonio: Trinity University Press, 1982.

Parrinder, E. Geoffrey. *Son of Joseph: The Parentage of Jesus*. Edinburgh: T&T Clark, 1992.

Patterson, Stephen J. "The End of the Apocalypse: Rethinking the Eschatological Jesus." *Theology Today* 52 (1995): 29–48.

———. *The God of Jesus: The Historical Jesus and the Search for Meaning*. Harrisburg, Penn.: Trinity Press International, 1998.

———. *The Gospel of Thomas and Jesus*. Sonoma, Calif.: Polebridge, 1993.

———. "Sources for a Life of Jesus." In *The Search for Jesus: Modern Scholarship Looks at the Gospel*, ed. Hershel Shanks, 9–36. Washington, D. C.: Biblical Archaeology Society, 1994.

Pearson, Birger. "The Gospel according to the Jesus Seminar." *Religion* 25 (December, 1995): 317–38.

Perelmuter, H. Goren. "Jesus the Jew: A Jewish Perspective." *New Theology Review* 1 (1994): 27–36.

Perkins, Pheme. *Jesus as Teacher*. Cambridge: Cambridge University Press, 1990.

———. "The Resurrection of Jesus of Nazareth." In *Studying the Historical Jesus: Evaluations of the State of Current Research*, ed. Bruce Chilton and Craig A. Evans, 423–42. Leiden: Brill, 1994.

Perrin, Nicholas. *Jesus and the Temple*. Grand Rapids: Baker Academic, 2010.

Perrin, Norman. *Jesus and the Language of the Kingdom: Symbol and Metaphor in New Testament Interpretation*. Philadelphia: Fortress, 1976.

———. *The Kingdom of God in the Teaching of Jesus*. Philadelphia: Fortress, 1963.

———. *Rediscovering the Teaching of Jesus*. New York: Harper & Row, 1967.

Petersen, W. L. *Tatian's Diatessaron: Its Creation, Dissemination, Significance, and History in Scholarship.* Supplements to Vigilae Christianae 25. Leiden: Brill, 1994.

Piper, Ronald A., ed. *The Gospel behind the Gospels: Current Studies on Q.* Novum Testamentum Supplements 75. Leiden: Brill, 1995.

Pitre, Brant. *Jesus and the Jewish Roots of the Eucharist: Unlocking the Secrets of the Last Supper.* New York: Doubleday, 2011.

————. *Jesus, the Tribulation, and the End of Exile: Restoration Eschatology and the Origin of the Atonement.* Grand Rapids: Baker Academic, 2006.

Pokorný, Petr. *The Genesis of Christology.* Edinburgh: T&T Clark, 1987.

Porter, Stanley E. "Jesus and the Use of Greek in Galilee." In *Studying the Historical Jesus: Evaluations of the State of Current Research,* ed. Bruce Chilton and Craig A. Evans, 123–54. Leiden: Brill, 1994.

Powell, Evan. *The Unfinished Gospel: Notes on the Quest for the Historical Jesus.* Westlake Village, Calif.: Symposium Books, 1994.

Powell, Mark Allan. "Authorial Intent and Historical Reporting: Putting Spong's Literalization Theory to the Test," *Journal for the Study of the Historical Jesus* 1.2 (2003): 225–49.

————. "The De-Johannification of Jesus: The Twentieth Century and Beyond." In *John, Jesus, and History.* Vol. 1, *Critical Appraisals of Critical Views.* Symposium Series 44. Ed. Paul N. Anderson, Felix Just, and Tom Thatcher, 121–32. Atlanta: Society of Biblical Literature, 2007.

————. "Evangelical Christians and Historical-Jesus Studies: Final Reflections," *Journal for the Study of the Historical Jesus* 9.1 (2011): 124–36

————. "Jesus and the Pathetic Wicked: Re-Visiting Sanders's View of Jesus and the Sinners," in Robert L. Webb and Mark S. Goodacre, eds., *Standing on the Shoulders of Giants: Engaging the Historical Jesus Work of Crossan, Sanders, and Wright* [title tentative] (London: T&T Clark, forthcoming).

————. "Was Jesus a Friend of Unrepentant Sinners? A Fresh Appraisal of Sanders's Controversial Proposal," *Journal for the Study of the Historical Jesus* 7.3 (2009): 286–310.

Powelson, M., and R. Riegert, eds. *The Lost Gospel Q: The Original Sayings of Jesus.* Berkeley: Ulysses, 1996.

Price, Robert. *Deconstructing Jesus.* Amherst, N.Y.: Prometheus, 2000.

————. *The Incredible Shrinking Son of Man: How Reliable Is the Gospel Tradition?* Amherst, N.Y.: Prometheus Books, 2003.

————. *Jesus Is Dead.* Cranford, N.J.: American Atheist Press, 2007.

Quarles, Charles L. "Jesus as *Merkabah* Mystic." *Journal for the Study of the Historical Jesus* 3.1 (2005): 5–22.

Rajak, Tessa. *Josephus: The Historian and His Society.* London: Duckworth, 1983.

Reimarus, Hermann Samuel. *Fragments.* Ed. C. H. Talbert. Lives of Jesus Series. Philadelphia: Fortress, 1970 (originally published in 1778).

Reiser, Marius. *Jesus and Judgment: The Eschatological Proclamation in Its Jewish Context.* Trans. Linda M. Maloney. Minneapolis: Fortress, 1997 (originally published in 1990).

Remus, Harold E. *Pagan-Christian Conflict over Miracle in the Second Century.* Patristic Monograph Series 10. Cambridge, Mass.: Philadelphia Patristic Foundation, 1983.

Renan, Ernst. *The Life of Jesus.* New York: Random House, 1972 (originally published in 1863).

Reumann, John. *Jesus in the Church's Gospels: Modern Scholarship and the Earliest Sources.* Philadelphia: Fortress, 1968.

Riches, John K. *Jesus and the Transformation of Judaism.* London: Darton, Longman & Todd, 1980.

————. "The Social World of Jesus." *Interpretation* 50 (1996): 383–93.
Riesner, Rainer. "Jesus as Preacher and Teacher." In *Jesus and the Oral Gospel Tradition.* Journal for the Study of the New Testament Monograph Series 64, ed. Henry Wansbrough, 185–210. Sheffield: Sheffield Academic, 1991.
Rivkin, Ellis. *What Crucified Jesus? The Political Execution of a Charismatic.* Nashville: Abingdon, 1984.
Robinson, James M. *Jesus according to the Earliest Witnesses.* Minneapolis: Fortress, 2007.
————. "Jesus from Easter to Valentinus (or to the Apostles' Creed)." *Journal of Biblical Literature* 101 (1982): 5–37.
————. *The Nag Hammadi Library.* 3rd ed. San Francisco: Harper & Row, 1990.
————. *A New Quest of the Historical Jesus.* Studies in Biblical Theology 25. London: SCM, 1959.
Robinson, James M., and Helmut Koester. *Trajectories through Early Christianity.* Philadelphia: Fortress, 1971.
Robinson, John A. T. *Jesus and His Coming: The Emergence of a Doctrine.* Philadelphia: Westminster, 1979.
Rodriguez, Rafael. *Structuring Early Christian Memory: Jesus in Tradition, Performance, and Text.* Library of New Testament Studies 407. London: T&T Clark, 2010.
Rowdon, Harold, ed. *Christ the Lord: Studies in Christology Presented to Donald Guthrie.* Downers Grove, Ill.: InterVarsity, 1982.
Rubio, Fernando Bermejo. "The Fiction of the 'Three Quests': An Argument for Dismantling a Dubious Historiographical Paradigm," *Journal for the Study of the Historical Jesus* 7 (2009): 211–53.
Sacchi, Paolo. "Recovering Jesus' Formative Background." In *Jesus and the Dead Sea Scrolls,* ed. James H. Charlesworth, 123–39. New York: Doubleday, 1992.
Sanders, E. P. "Defending the Indefensible." *Journal of Biblical Literature* 110 (1991): 463–77.
————. *The Historical Figure of Jesus.* London: Penguin, 1993.
————. *Jesus and Judaism.* Philadelphia: Fortress, 1985.
————. "Jesus and the First Table of the Jewish Law." In *Jews and Christians Speak of Jesus,* ed. Arthur E. Zannoni, 55–76. Minneapolis: Fortress, 1994.
————. "Jesus and the Sinners." In *The Historical Jesus: A Sheffield Reader,* ed. Craig A. Evans and Stanley E. Porter, 29–60. Sheffield: Sheffield Academic, 1995.
————. "Jesus in Historical Context." *Theology Today* 50 (1993): 429–48.
————. *Jesus' Jewishness.* New York: Crossroad, 1991.
————. *Jewish Law from Jesus to the Mishnah: Five Studies.* Philadelphia: Trinity Press International, 1990.
————. *Judaism: Practice and Belief, 63 BCE–66 CE.* Philadelphia: Trinity Press International, 1992.
Sawicki, Marianne. *Crossing Galilee: Architectures of Contact in the Occupied Land of Jesus.* Harrisburg, Penn.: Trinity Press International, 2000.
Schaberg, Jane. "A Feminist Experience of Historical Jesus Scholarship." *Continuum* 3 (1994): 266–85.
————. *The Illegitimacy of Jesus: A Feminist Theological Interpretation of the Infancy Narratives.* Expanded Twentieth Anniversary Edition. Sheffield: Phoenix, 2006 (originally published in 1987).
Schiffman, Lawrence. "The Jewishness of Jesus: Commandments concerning Interpersonal Relations." In *Jews and Christians Speak of Jesus,* ed. Arthur E. Zannoni, 37–54. Minneapolis: Fortress, 1994.
Schillebeeckx, Edward. *Jesus: An Experiment in Christology.* New York: Seabury, 1979.
Schmidt, Daryl D. "The Witness of Gospel Fragments." *The Fourth R* 9.1–2 (1996): 3–8, 21.

Schnabel, Eckhard J. "Jesus and the Beginnings of the Mission to the Gentiles." In *Jesus of Nazareth, Lord and Christ: Essays on the Historical Jesus and New Testament Christology*, ed. Joel B. Green and Max Turner, 37–58. Grand Rapids: Eerdmans, 1994.

Schnackenburg, Rudolf. *Jesus in the Gospels: A Biblical Christology*. Louisville: Westminster John Knox, 1995.

Schüssler Fiorenza, Elisabeth. *In Memory of Her: A Feminist Theological Reconstruction of Christian Origins*. New York: Crossroad, 1987.

———. *Jesus—Miriam's Child, Sophia's Prophet: Critical Issues in Feminist Christology*. New York: Continuum, 1994.

———. "The Jesus of Piety and the Historical Jesus." *Catholic Theological Society of America Proceedings* 49 (1994): 90–99.

Schweitzer, Albert. *The Kingdom of God and Primitive Christianity*. Ed. U. Neuenschwander. London: A & C Black, 1968.

———. *The Mystery of the Kingdom of God*. London: A & C Black, 1925 (originally published in 1901).

———. *The Psychiatric Study of Jesus*. Trans. C. R. Joy. Boston: Beacon, 1948 (originally published in 1913).

———. *The Quest of the Historical Jesus*. First Complete Edition. Ed. John Bowden. Minneapolis: Fortress, 2001 (originally published in 1906).

Schweizer, Eduard. *Jesus Christ: The Man from Nazareth and the Exalted Lord*. Macon, Ga.: Mercer University Press, 1987.

———. *Jesus the Parable of God: What Do We Really Know about Jesus?* Allison Park, Penn.: Pickwick Publications, 1994.

Scott, Bernard Brandon. "From Reimarus to Crossan: Stages in a Quest." *Currents in Research: Biblical Studies* 2 (1994): 253–80.

———. "The Reappearance of Parables." *The Fourth R* 10.1–2 (1997): 3–14

———. "to impose is not/To Discover: Methodology in John Dominic Crossan's *The Historical Jesus*." In *Jesus and Faith: A Conversation on the Work of John Dominic Crossan*. Ed. Jeffrey Carlson and Robert A. Ludwig, 22–30. Maryknoll, N.Y.: Orbis Books, 1994.

Scott, Bernard Brandon, ed. *Jesus Reconsidered: Scholarship in the Public Eye*. Santa Rosa, Calif.: Polebridge, 2007.

Seeley, David. "Jesus and the Cynics Revisited. "*Journal of Biblical Literature* 116 (1997): 704–12.

———. "Jesus' Death in Q." *New Testament Studies* 38 (1992): 222–34.

Segal, Alan F. "Jesus and First-Century Judaism." in *Jesus at 2000*, ed. Marcus J. Borg, 55–73. Boulder, Col.: Westview, 1997.

———. "Jesus the Revolutionary." In *Jesus Jewishness: Exploring the Place of Jesus within Early Judaism*, ed. James H. Charlesworth, 199–225. New York: Crossroad, 1991.

Segundo, Juan Luis. *The Historical Jesus of the Synoptics*. Maryknoll, N.Y.: Orbis Books, 1985.

Senior, Donald. "The Never Ending Quest for Jesus." *Bible Today* 34 (1996): 141–47.

Shanks, Hershel, ed. *The Search for Jesus: Modern Scholarship Looks at the Gospels*. Washington, D. C.: Biblical Archaeology Society, 1994.

Sheehan, Thomas. *The First Coming: How the Kingdom of God Became Christianity*. New York: Random House, 1988.

———. "The Resurrection: An Obstacle to Faith?" *The Fourth R* 8.2 (1995): 3–9.

Shorto, Russell. *Gospel Truth: The New Image of Jesus Emerging from Science and History, and Why It Matters*. New York: Riverhead Books, 1997.

Sloyan, Gerard S. *The Crucifixion of Jesus: History, Myth, Faith*. Minneapolis: Fortress, 1995.

————. *Jesus on Trial: A Study of the Gospels.* 2nd ed. Minneapolis: Fortress, 2006.

Smith, Huston. "Jesus and the World's Religions." In *Jesus at 2000,* ed. Marcus J. Borg, 107–20. Boulder, Col.: Westview, 1997.

Smith, Morton. *Jesus the Magician.* New York: Harper & Row, 1978.

Sobrino, Jon. *Jesus the Liberator: A Historical-Theological Reading of Jesus of Nazareth.* Maryknoll, N.Y.: Orbis Books, 1993.

Spencer, F. Scott. *What Did Jesus Do? Gospel Profiles of Jesus' Personal Conduct.* Harrisburg, Penn.: Trinity Press International, 2009.

Spong, John Shelby. *Born of a Woman: A Bishop Rethinks the Birth of Jesus.* San Francisco: HarperSanFrancisco, 1992.

————. *Resurrection: Myth or Reality? A Bishop's Search for the Origins of Christianity.* San Francisco: HarperSanFrancisco, 1994.

————. *This Hebrew Lord: A Bishop's Search for the Authentic Jesus,* 2nd ed. San Francisco: HarperSanFrancisco, 1993.

Stanton, Graham N. *Gospel Truth? New Light on Jesus and the Gospels.* Valley Forge, Penn.: Trinity Press International, 1995.

————. "Jesus of Nazareth: A Magician and a False Prophet Who Deceived God's People?" In *Jesus of Nazareth: Lord and Christ: Essays on the Historical Jesus and New Testament Christology,* ed. Joel B. Green and Max Turner, 164–80. Grand Rapids: Eerdmans, 1994.

Stauffer, Ethelbert. *Jesus and His Story.* London: SCM, 1960.

————. "The Relevance of the Historical Jesus." In *The Historical Jesus and the Kerygmatic Christ: Essays on the New Quest of the Historical Jesus,* ed. Carl E. Braaten and Roy A. Harrisville, 43–53. Nashville: Abingdon, 1964.

Stein, Robert H. "The 'Criteria' for Authenticity." In *Gospel Perspectives 1: Studies of History and Tradition in the Four Gospels,* ed. Richard T. France and David Wenham, 253–63. Sheffield: JSOT, 1980.

————. *Jesus the Messiah: A Survey of the Life of Christ.* Downers Grove, Ill.: InterVarsity, 1996.

————. *The Method and Message of Jesus' Teachings.* Rev. ed. Louisville: Westminster John Knox, 1994.

Stern, Frank. *A Rabbi Looks at Jesus' Parables.* Lanham, Md.: Rowman & Littlefiled, 2006.

Stewart, Robert B, ed. *The Resurrection of Jesus: John Dominic Crossan and N. T. Wright in Dialogue.* Minneapolis: Fortress, 2006.

Strain, Charles R. "Sapiential Eschatology and Social Transformation: Crossan's Jesus, Socially Engaged Buddhism, and Liberation Theology." In *Jesus and Faith: A Conversation on the Work of John Dominic Crossan,* ed. Jeffrey Carlson and Robert A. Ludwig, 115–31. Maryknoll, N.Y.: Orbis Books, 1994.

Strauss, David Friedrich. *The Life of Jesus Critically Examined.* Philadelphia: Fortress, 1972 (originally published in 1835–1836).

Strecker, Georg. "The Historical and Theological Problem of the Jesus Question." *Toronto Journal of Theology* 6 (1990): 201–23.

Stroker, William D., ed. *Extracanonical Sayings of Jesus.* Atlanta: Scholars, 1989.

Strudum, J. M. "The 'Unconventionality' of Jesus from the Perspective of a Diverse Audience: Evaluating Crossan's Historical Jesus." *Neotestamentica* 29 (1995): 313–23.

Stuhlmacher, Peter. *Jesus of Nazareth—Christ of Faith.* Peabody, Mass.: Hendrickson Publishers, 1993.

————. "Jesus of Nazareth—the Christ of Our Faith." In *Crisis in Christology: Essays in Quest of Resolution,* ed. William R. Farmer, 1–12. Livonia, Mich.: Dove Booksellers, 1995.

Stuhlmacher, Peter, ed. *The Gospel and the Gospels.* Grand Rapids: Eerdmans, 1991 (originally published in 1983).

Swidler, Leonard J. *Jesus Was a Feminist: What the Gospels Reveal about His Revolutionary Perspective*. Lanham, Md.: Sheed & Ward, 2007.

Talbert, Charles H. "Political Correctness Invades Jesus Research." *Perspectives in Religious Studies* 21 (1994): 245–52.

Tàrrech, Puig i Armand. *Jesus: A Biography*. Waco: Baylor University Press, 2011.

Tatum, W. Barnes. *In Quest of Jesus: A Guidebook*. Atlanta: John Knox, 1982.

——. *John the Baptist and Jesus: A Report of the Jesus Seminar*. Sonoma, Calif.: Polebridge, 1993.

Taussig, Hal. "The Jesus Seminar and Its Public." *Foundations and Facets Forum* 2.2 (1986): 69–78.

Taylor, Walter F. "Jesus within His Social World: Insights from Archaeology, Sociology, and Cultural Anthropology." In *The Quest for Jesus and the Christian Faith*, ed. Frederick J. Gaiser, 49–71. St. Paul: Luther Seminary, 1997.

——. "New Quests for the Historical Jesus." *Trinity Seminary Review* 15 (1992): 69–83.

Telford, William R. "Major Trends and Interpretive Issues in the Study of Jesus." In *Studying the Historical Jesus: Evaluations of the State of Current Research*, ed. Bruce Chilton and Craig A. Evans, 33–75. Leiden: Brill, 1994.

Thatcher, Adrian. "Resurrection and Rationality." In *The Resurrection of Jesus Christ*, ed. Paul Avis, 171–86. London: Darton, Longman & Todd, 1993.

Thatcher, Tom. *Jesus the Riddler: The Power of Ambiguity in the Gospels*. Louisville: Westminster John Knox, 2006.

Theissen, Gerd. *The Gospels in Context: Social and Political History in the Synoptic Tradition*. Minneapolis: Fortress, 1991.

——. *The Shadow of the Galilean: The Quest of the Historical Jesus in Narrative Form*. Trans. John Bowden. Philadelphia: Fortress, 1987.

——. *Social Reality and the Early Christians*. Trans. Margaret Kohl. Minneapolis: Augsburg Fortress, 1992.

——. *Sociology of Early Palestinian Christianity*. Trans. John Bowden. Philadelphia: Fortress, 1978.

——. *A Theory of Primitive Christianity*. Trans. John Bowden. London: SCM, 1999.

Theissen, Gerd, and Annette Metz. *The Historical Jesus: A Comprehensive Guide*. Trans. John Bowden. Minneapolis: Augsburg Fortress, 1998.

Theissen, Gerd, and Dagmar Winter. *The Quest for the Plausible Jesus: The Question of Criteria*. Trans. M. Eugene Boring. Louisville: Westminster John Knox, 2002.

Torjeson, Karen Jo. "'You Are the Christ': Five Portraits of Jesus from the Early Church." In *Jesus at 2000*, ed. Marcus J. Borg, 73–88. Boulder, Col.: Westview, 1997.

Tuckett, Christopher M. "A Cynic Q?" *Biblica* 70 (1989): 349–76.

——. *Q and the History of Earliest Christianity: Studies on Q*. Edinburgh: T&T Clark, 1996.

Twelftree, Graham H. "Jesus in Jewish Traditions." In *Gospel Perspectives 5: The Jesus Tradition outside the Gospels*, ed. David Wenham, 289–343. Sheffield: JSOT, 1985.

——. *Jesus the Exorcist: A Contribution to the Study of the Historical Jesus*. Peabody, Mass.: Hendrickson Publishers, 1993.

——. *Jesus the Miracle Worker: A Historical and Theological Study*. Downers Grove, Ill: InterVarsity, 1999.

Vaage, Leif. *Galilean Upstarts: Jesus' First Followers according to Q*. Valley Forge, Penn.: Trinity Press International, 1994.

——. "Q¹ and the Historical Jesus: Some Peculiar Sayings (7:33–34; 9:57–58, 59–60; 14:26–27)." *Foundations and Facets Forum* 5.2 (1989): 159–76.

——. *Q: The Ethos and Ethics of an Itinerant Intelligence*. Ann Arbor, Mich.: University Microfilms, 1987.

van Aarde, Andries. *Fatherless in Galilee: Jesus as Child of God.* Harrisburg, Penn.: Trinity Press International, 2001.

van Beeck, Frans Jozef. "The Quest of the Historical Jesus: Origins, Achievements, and the Specter of Diminishing Returns." In *Jesus and Faith: A Conversation on the Work of John Dominic Crossan,* ed. Jeffrey Carlson and Robert A. Ludwig, 83–99. Maryknoll, N.Y.: Orbis Books, 1994.

van Os, Bas. *Psychological Analyses and the Historical Jesus: New Ways to Explore Christian Origins.* Library of New Testament Studies 432. London: T&T Clark, 2011.

Van Voorst, Robert E. *Jesus outside the New Testament: An Introduction to the Ancient Evidence.* Grand Rapids: Eerdmans, 2000.

Verhoeven, Paul. *Jesus of Nazareth.* New York: Seven Stories, 2008.

Vermes, Geza. *The Gospel of Jesus the Jew.* Newcastle: University of Newcastle upon Tyne, 1981.

———. *Jesus and the World of Judaism.* London: SCM, 1983.

———. *Jesus in His Jewish Context.* Minneapolis: Fortress, 2003.

———. *Jesus the Jew: A Historian's Reading of the Gospels.* London: Collins, 1973.

———. *Providential Accidents.* London: SCM, 1998.

———. *The Real Jesus: Then and Now.* Minneapolis: Fortress, 2010.

———. *The Religion of Jesus the Jew.* Minneapolis: Fortress, 1993.

———. *The Resurrection: History and Myth.* New York: Doubleday, 2008.

Viviano, Benedict T. "The Historical Jesus in the Doubly Attested Sayings: An Experiment." *Revue Biblique* 103 (1996): 367–410.

Wallis, Ian G. *The Faith of Jesus Christ in Early Christian Traditions.* Society for New Testament Studies Monograph Series 84. Cambridge: Cambridge University Press, 1995.

Wansbrough, Henry, ed. *Jesus and the Oral Gospel Tradition.* Journal for the Study of the New Testament: Supplement Series 64. Sheffield: Sheffield Academic, 1991.

Watson, Alan. *The Trial of Jesus.* Athens: University of Georgia Press, 1995.

Watts, Fraser, ed., *Jesus and Psychology.* Philadelphia: Templeton Foundation, 2007.

Weaver, William P. *The Historical Jesus in the Twentieth Century (1900–1950).* Harrisburg, Penn.: Trinity Press International, 1999.

Webb, Robert L. "John the Baptist and His Relationship with Jesus." In *Studying the Historical Jesus: Evaluations of the State of Current Research,* ed. Bruce Chilton and Craig A. Evans, 179–230. Leiden: Brill, 1994.

———. *John the Baptizer and Prophet: A Socio-Historical Study.* Journal for the Study of the New Testament: Supplement Series 62. Sheffield: Sheffield Academic, 1991.

———. "The Rules of the Game: History and Historical Method in the Context of Faith: The *Via Media* of Methodological Naturalism." *Journal for the Study of the Historical Jesus* 9.1 (2011): 59–84.

Weiss, Johannes. *Jesus' Proclamation of the Kingdom of God.* Philadelphia: Fortress, 1972 (originally published in 1892).

Wells, G. A. *The Historical Evidence for Jesus.* Buffalo, N.Y.: Prometheus Books, 1982.

———. *The Jesus Legend.* La Salle, Ill.: Open Court, 1996.

———. *The Jesus Myth.* Chicago: Open Court, 1999.

———. *Who Was Jesus? A Critique of the New Testament Record.* La Salle: Open Court, 1989.

Wengst, Klaus. *Pax Romana and the Peace of Jesus Christ.* Philadelphia: Fortress, 1987.

Wenham, David. "Paul's Use of the Jesus Tradition: Three Samples." In *Gospel Perspectives 5: The Jesus Tradition outside the Gospels,* ed. David Wenham, 7–38. Sheffield: JSOT, 1985.

Wenham, David, ed. *Gospel Perspectives 5: The Jesus Tradition outside the Gospels.* Sheffield: JSOT, 1985.

Wenham, David, and Craig Blomberg, eds. *Gospel Perspectives 6: The Miracles of Jesus.* Sheffield: JSOT, 1986.

Wenell, Karen J. *Jesus and Land: Sacred and Social Space in Second Temple Judaism.* Library of New Testament Studies 334. New York: T&T Clark, 2007.

Wheatley, Alice. *Josephus on Jesus: The* Testimonium Flavianum *Controversy from Late Antiquity to Modern Times.* Studies in Biblical Literature 36. New York: Lang, 2003.

Wiebe, B. *Messianic Ethics: Jesus' Proclamation of the Kingdom of God and the Church in Response.* Waterloo, Ont.: Herald, 1992.

Wilkins, Michael J., and J. P. Moreland, eds. *Jesus under Fire: Modern Scholarship Reinvents the Historical Jesus.* Grand Rapids: Zondervan Publishing House, 1995.

Willis, Wendell, ed. *The Kingdom of God in Twentieth Century Interpretation.* Peabody, Mass.: Hendrickson Publishers, 1987.

Willits, Joel. "Presuppositions and Procedures in the Study of the 'Historical Jesus': Or, Why I Decided Not to Be a 'Historical Jesus' Scholar." *Journal for the Study of the Historical Jesus* 3.1 (2005): 61–108.

Wilson, Ian. *Jesus: The Evidence—The Latest Research and Discoveries.* 2nd ed. San Francisco: HarperSanFrancisco, 1997.

Wink, Walter. *John the Baptist in the Gospel Tradition.* Society for New Testament Monograph Series 7. Cambridge: Cambridge University Press, 1968.

———. "Neither Passivity nor Violence: Jesus' Third Way Out (Matt. 5:38–42 par.)." In *The Love of Enemy and Nonretaliation in the New Testament,* ed. Willard M. Swartley, 102–25. Louisville: Westminster/John Knox, 1992.

Winter, Paul. *On the Trial of Jesus.* Berlin: Walter de Gruyter, 1974 (originally published in 1961).

Winton, Alan P. *The Proverbs of Jesus.* Journal for the Study of the New Testament Supplement Series 35. Sheffield: Sheffield Academic, 1990.

Witherington III, Ben. *The Christology of Jesus.* Minneapolis: Fortress, 1990.

———. *Jesus, Paul, and the End of the World: A Comparative Study in New Testament Eschatology.* Downers Grove, Ill.: InterVarsity, 1992.

———. *The Jesus Quest: The Third Search for the Jew of Nazareth.* Downers Grove, Ill.: InterVarsity, 1995.

———. *Jesus the Sage: The Pilgrimage of Wisdom.* Minneapolis: Fortress, 1994.

Wrede, William. *The Messianic Secret.* London: James Clarke, 1971 (originally published in 1901).

Wright, N. T. *The Challenge of Jesus: Rediscovering Who Jesus Was and Is.* Downers Grove, Ill.: InterVarsity, 1999.

———. "Five Gospels but No Gospel: Jesus and the Seminar." In *Crisis in Christology: Essays in Quest of Resolution,* ed. William R. Farmer, 115–58. Livonia, Mich.: Dove Booksellers, 1995.

———. "How Jesus Saw Himself." *Bible Review* 12 (June 1996): 22–29.

———. "Jesus." In *Early Christian Thought in Its Jewish Context,* ed. J. P. M. Sweet and J. M. G. Barclay, 43–58. Cambridge: Cambridge University Press, 1996.

———. *Jesus and the Victory of God.* Christian Origins and the Question of God 2. Minneapolis: Fortress, 1996.

———. *The New Testament and the People of God.* Christian Origins and the Question of God 1. Minneapolis: Fortress, 1992.

———. *The Resurrection of the Son of God.* Christian Origins and the Question of God 3. Minneapolis: Fortress, 2003.

———. *Simply Jesus: A New Vision of Who He Was, What He Did, and Why He Matters.* New York: HarperOne, 2006.

———. *Who Was Jesus?* Grand Rapids: Eerdmans, 1992.

Wright, Tom. *The Original Jesus.* Grand Rapids: Eerdmans Publishing Co., 1996.

Yamauchi, Edwin M. "Jesus outside the New Testament: What Is the Evidence?" In *Jesus under Fire: Modern Scholarship Reinvents the Historical Jesus,* ed. Michael J. Wilkins and J. P. Moreland, 207–30. Grand Rapids: Zondervan Publishing House, 1995.

———. "Magic or Miracle? Disease, Demons, and Exorcisms." In *Gospel Perspectives 6: The Miracles of Jesus,* ed. David Wenham and Craig Blomberg, 89–184. Sheffield: JSOT, 1986.

Yoder, John H. *The Politics of Jesus:* Vicit Agnus Noster. 2nd ed. Grand Rapids: Eerdmans, 1994.

Yoder Neufeld, Thomas R. *Recovering Jesus: The Witness of the New Testament.* Grand Rapids: Brazos, 2007.

Young, Brad H. *Jesus and His Jewish Parables: Rediscovering the Roots of Jesus' Teaching.* Mahwah, N.J.: Paulist, 1989.

———. *Jesus the Jewish Theologian.* Peabody, Mass.: Hendrickson Publishers, 1995.

———. *Meet the Rabbis: Rabbinic Thought and the Teachings of Jesus.* Peabody, Mass.: Hendrickson, 2007.

Young, Norman H. "Jesus and the Sinners: Some Queries." *Journal for the Study of the New Testament* 24 (1985): 73–75.

Zahl, Paul F. M. *The First Christian: Universal Truth in the Teachings of Jesus.* Grand Rapids: Eerdmans, 2003.

Zannoni, Arthur E., ed. *Jews and Christians Speak of Jesus.* Minneapolis: Fortress, 1994.

Zeitlin, Irving M. *Jesus and the Judaism of His Time.* Oxford: Basil Blackwell Publisher, 1988.

Scripture and Ancient
Sources Index

This index does not include the biblical references cited in the list "Contents of Q, M, and L" on pages 48–52.

Author Index

CPSIA information can be obtained at www.ICGtesting.com
Printed in the USA
BVOW01s2135300916

463865BV00001B/14/P